JOHN KEAY was educated at Ampleforth College, York and Magdalen College, Oxford. As an author and broadcaster specialising in Asian history and current affairs, he has been treading the trail of the East India Company since the 1960s. His other books include *Into India*, *When Men and Mountains Meet*, *Eccentric Travellers*, *Explorers Extraordinary*, *India Discovered*, *India: A History* and *The Great Arc*.

Married with four children, he lives in the Scottish Highlands with his wife Julia. They are the joint editors of the *Collins Encyclopaedia of Scotland*.

From the reviews of *The Honourable Company*:

'What a marvellous story is that of the East India Company! . . . And John Keay tells it well, humanely and spicily, as well as all we need about organisation, background, etc . . . Mr Keay gives us the spectrum, the trade with China and Japan, the Arabian Gulf, the East Indies, India, the lot.'
A. L. ROWSE, *Contemporary Review*

'Splendid, tumultuous narrative history . . . The sotry is so colourful, at least in its early stages, that it can be read as a bumper book of Indian adventure.'
ANTHONY QUINTON, *The Times*

'A tale worth retelling in detail, when it is done with as much as flair and imagination as this.'
GEOFFREY MOORHOUSE, *Guardian*

'A gem of a book on a vast and complex adventure of British trading, maritime and colonial history . . . highly recommended not only for scholars but to all those interested in an important segment of British and human history.'
Catholic Herald

'Full of delicious anecdotes . . . fascinating reading.'
WILLIAM DALRYMPLE, *The Spectator*

By the same author

INTO INDIA

WHEN MEN AND MOUNTAINS MEET

THE GILGIT GAME

ECCENTRIC TRAVELLERS

EXPLORERS EXTRAORDINARY

HIGHLAND DROVE

THE ROYAL GEOGRAPHICAL SOCIETY'S
HISTORY OF WORLD EXPLORATION

INDIA DISCOVERED

THE ENCYCLOPAEDIA OF SCOTLAND
(WITH JULIA KEAY)

INDONESIA: FROM SABANG TO MERAUKE

LAST POST: EMPIRE'S END

INDIA: A HISTORY

THE GREAT ARC

The HONOURABLE COMPANY

A History of the English East India Company

JOHN KEAY

HarperCollins*Publishers*

For Alexander and Anna

HarperCollins*Publishers*
77–85 Fulham Palace Road,
Hammersmith, London W6 8JB

www.harpercollins.co.uk

This paperback edition 1993

2 4 6 8 1 0 9 7 5 3 1

First published in Great Britain by
HarperCollins*Publishers* 1991

A catalogue record for this book
is available from the British Library

ISBN 978-0-00-743155-7

Set in Itek Garamond by Ace Filmsetting Ltd,
Frome, Somerset

Printed and bound in India by Thomson Press (India) Ltd.

Contents

Illustrations

IOL = India Office Library; NPG = National Portrait Gallery;
NMM = National Maritime Museum; RGS = Royal Geographical Society

Maps

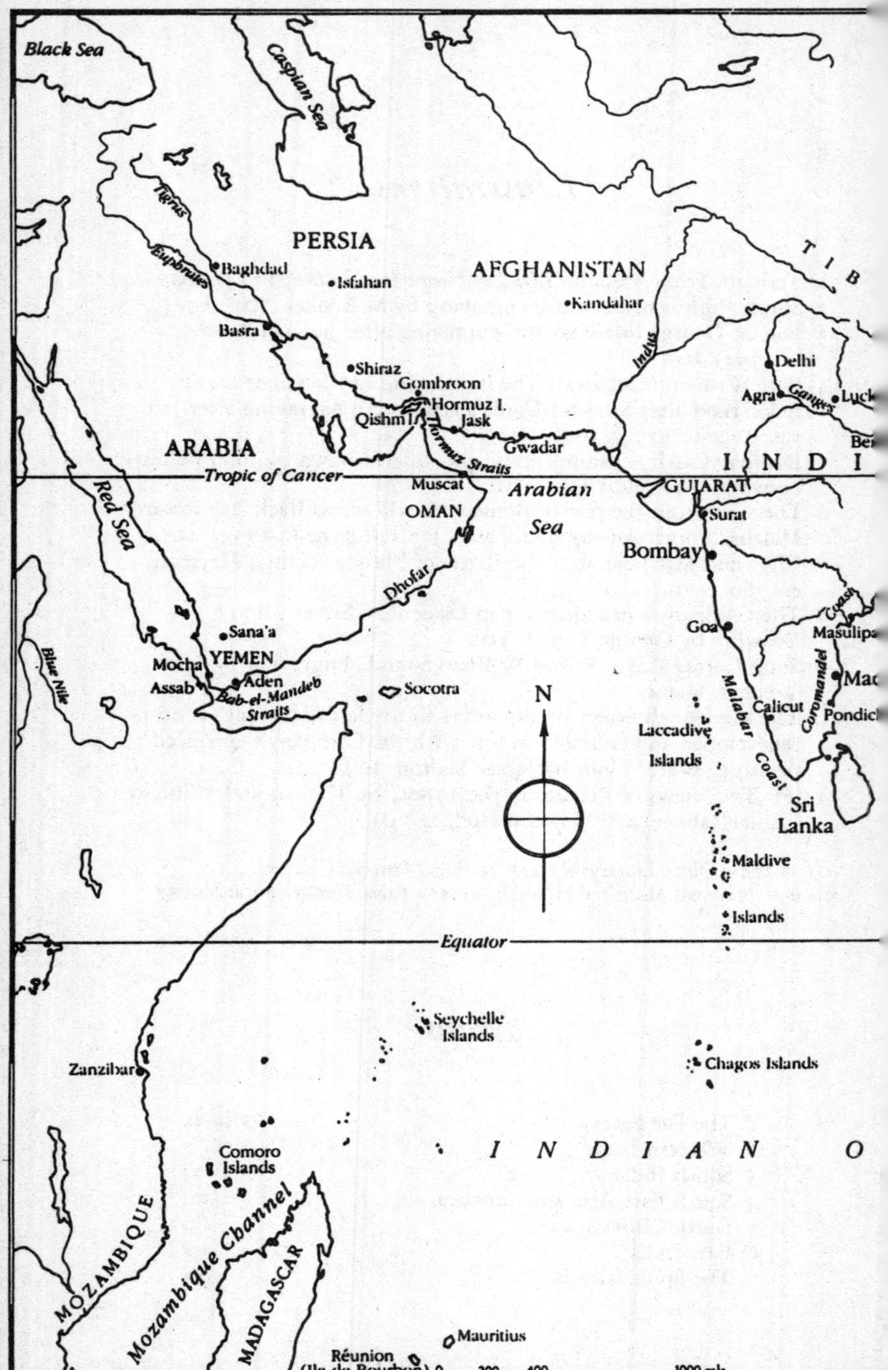

Black Sea
Caspian Sea
Tigris
Euphrates
PERSIA
Baghdad
Isfahan
AFGHANISTAN
Kandahar
Basra
Shiraz
Gombroon
Hormuz I.
Qishm I.
Jask
Hormuz Straits
Gwadar
Indus
Delhi
Agra
Ganges
ARABIA
Tropic of Cancer
Muscat
OMAN
Arabian Sea
GUJARAT
Surat
Bombay
Red Sea
Dhofar
Sana'a
YEMEN
Mocha
Assab
Aden
Bab-el-Mandeb Straits
Socotra
Blue Nile
Goa
Malabar Coast
Calicut
Coromandel Coast
Laccadive Islands
Sri Lanka
Maldive Islands
N
Equator
Seychelle Islands
Zanzibar
Chagos Islands
Comoro Islands
INDIAN O
MOZAMBIQUE
Mozambique Channel
MADAGASCAR
Mauritius
Réunion (Ile de Bourbon)
0 200 400 1000 mls.
100 300 500

100 300 500
0 200 400
1000 mls.
Hokkaido
JAPAN
Honshu
Tokyo
Osaka
Peking
Tientsin
KOREA
CHINA
Yellow River
Fukuoka
Hirado
Nagasaki
Kyushu
Yangtze Kiang
Lhasa
Salween
hmaputra
Pearl River
Okinawa
NGAL
Canton
Formosa
(Taiwan)
Tropic of Cancer
Mandalay
alcutta
BURMA
TONGKING
Hong
Kong
Hainan
Chieng Mai
Rangoon
Luzon
PHILIPPINES
ANNAM
Mekong
SIAM
(THAILAND)
Manila
Ayuthia
CAMBODIA
Mergui
COCHIN
CHINA
Marianas
Islands
Nicobar Is.
South
China
Sea
Balambangan
Island
Pelew Is.
(Palau)
Aceh
Mindanao
Malacca
Singapore
SUMATRA
BORNEO
Equator
Sulawesi
Molucca Is.
(Spice Islands)
New
Guinea
Ambon
Banda Is.
Benkulen
Makassar
INDONESIA
Bantam
Krakatoa
Batavia
JAVA
Timor
A N
Cocos Islands
NEW HOLLAND
(AUSTRALIA)

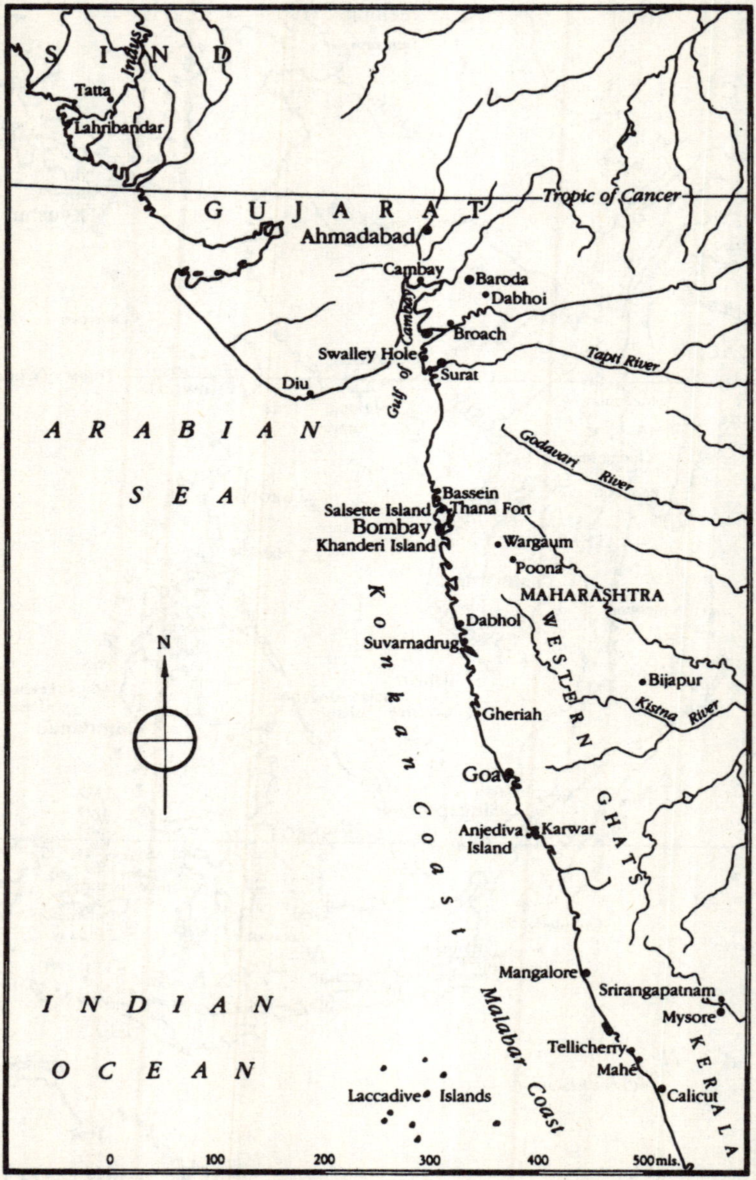

S I N D
Indus
Tatta
Lahribandar
Tropic of Cancer
G U J A R A T
Ahmadabad
Cambay
Baroda
Dabhoi
Gulf of Cambay
Broach
Swalley Hole
Surat
Tapti River
Diu
A R A B I A N
S E A
Godavari River
Bassein
Salsette Island
Thana Fort
Bombay
Khanderi Island
Wargaum
Poona
MAHARASHTRA
Konkan Coast
Dabhol
Suvarnadrug
WESTERN GHATS
N
Bijapur
Kistna River
Gheriah
Goa
Anjediva Island
Karwar
Mangalore
Srirangapatnam
Mysore
KERALA
Malabar Coast
I N D I A N
O C E A N
Tellicherry
Mahé
Calicut
Laccadive Islands
0
100
200
300
400
500 mls.

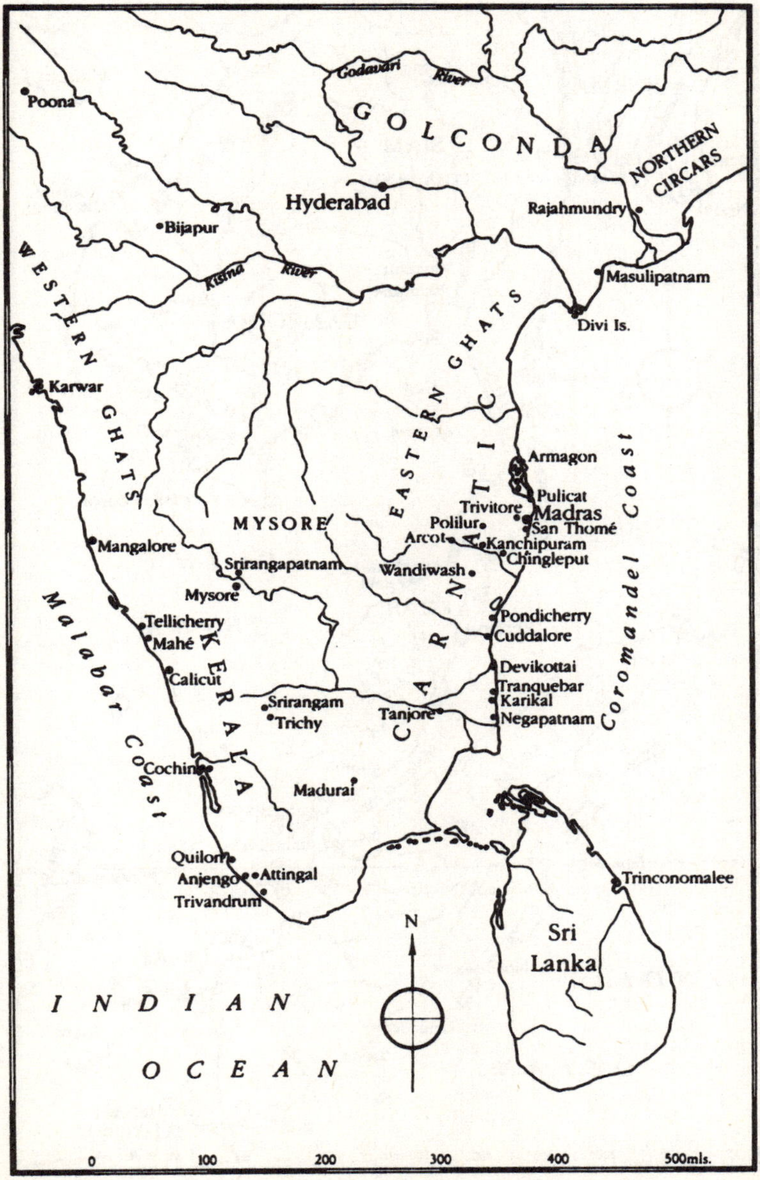

Godavari River
GOLCONDA
NORTHERN CIRCARS
Poona
Hyderabad
Rajahmundry
Bijapur
Kistna River
Masulipatnam
WESTERN GHATS
EASTERN GHATS
Divi Is.
Karwar
Armagon
Pulicat
Trivitore
Madras
MYSORE
Polilur
San Thomé
Arcot
Kanchipuram
Chingleput
Mangalore
Srirangapatnam
Wandiwash
Mysore
CARNATIC
Coromandel Coast
Pondicherry
Tellicherry
Mahé
Cuddalore
Devikottai
Calicut
KERALA
Tranquebar
Karikal
Srirangam
Trichy
Tanjore
Negapatnam
Malabar Coast
Cochin
Madurai
Quilon
Anjengo
Attingal
Trivandrum
Trinconomalee
N
Sri Lanka
INDIAN OCEAN
0
100
200
300
400
500mls.

BURMA
Irrawaddy
Salween
Pegu
Bassein
Rangoon
Syriam
Negrais
Chieng Mai
SIAM
(THAILAND)
Menam
Ayuthia
Bangkok
Mekong
ANNAM
Hainan
Hué
Tourane
(Da Nang)
CAMBODIA
COCHIN CHINA
(SOUTH VIETNAM)
Pulo Condore
N
Mergui
KRA ISTHMUS
Gulf
of Siam
SOUTH
CHINA
SEA
Singhora
Patani
KEDAH
Penang
MALAY
PENINSULA
Aceh
SUMATRA
Malacca Straits
Malacca
Johore
Singapore
Rhio (Riau) Is.
Equator
BORNEO
Pontianak
Lingga
Islands
Priaman
Bangka
Moco-Moco
INDIAN
OCEAN
Benkulen
Tecu
Java
Sea
Krakatoa
Sunda Straits
Bantam
Batavia
(Jakarta)
JAVA
0 100 200 300 400 500 mls.

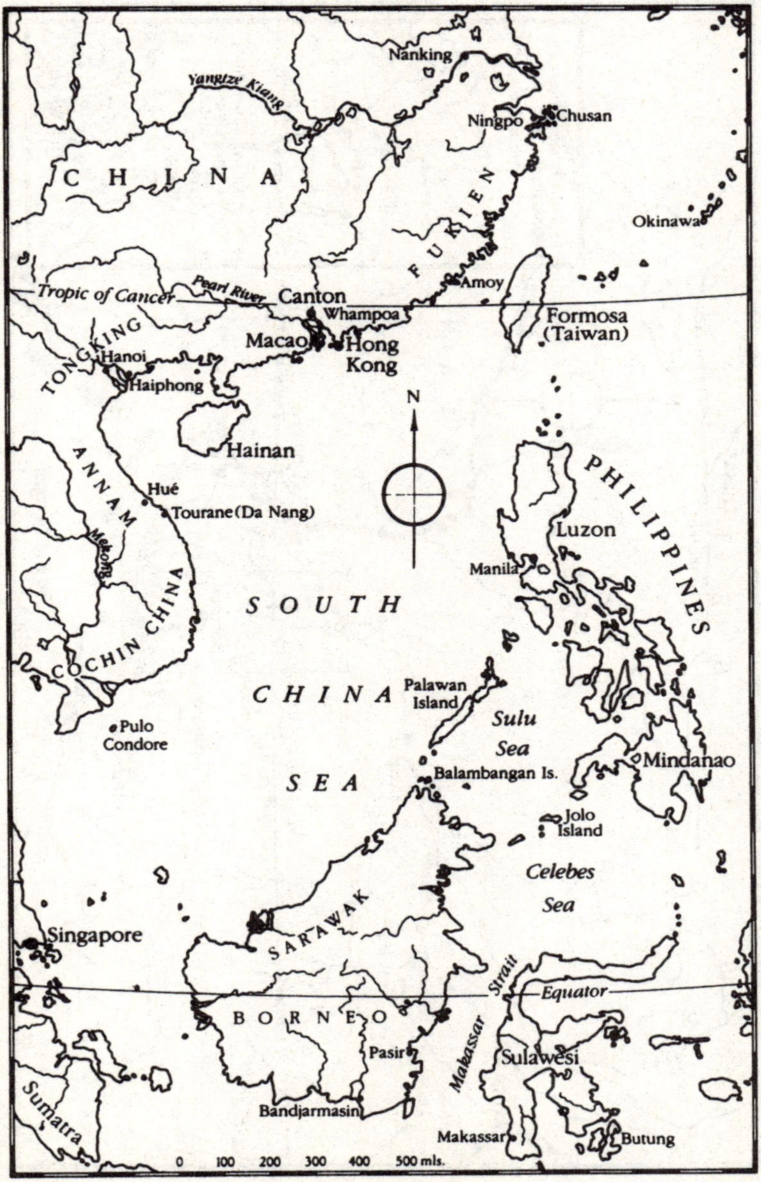

Nanking
Yangtze Kiang
Ningpo
Chusan
C H I N A
F U K I E N
Okinawa
Tropic of Cancer
Pearl River
Canton
Amoy
Whampoa
Formosa (Taiwan)
Macao
Hong Kong
TONGKING
Hanoi
Haiphong
N
Hainan
ANNAM
PHILIPPINES
Hué
Tourane (Da Nang)
Luzon
Mekong
Manila
COCHIN CHINA
S O U T H
C H I N A
S E A
Palawan Island
Sulu Sea
Pulo Condore
Mindanao
Balambangan Is.
Jolo Island
Celebes Sea
Singapore
SARAWAK
Strait
Equator
B O R N E O
Makassar
Pasir
Sulawesi
Sumatra
Bandjarmasin
Makassar
Butung
0 100 200 300 400 500 mls.

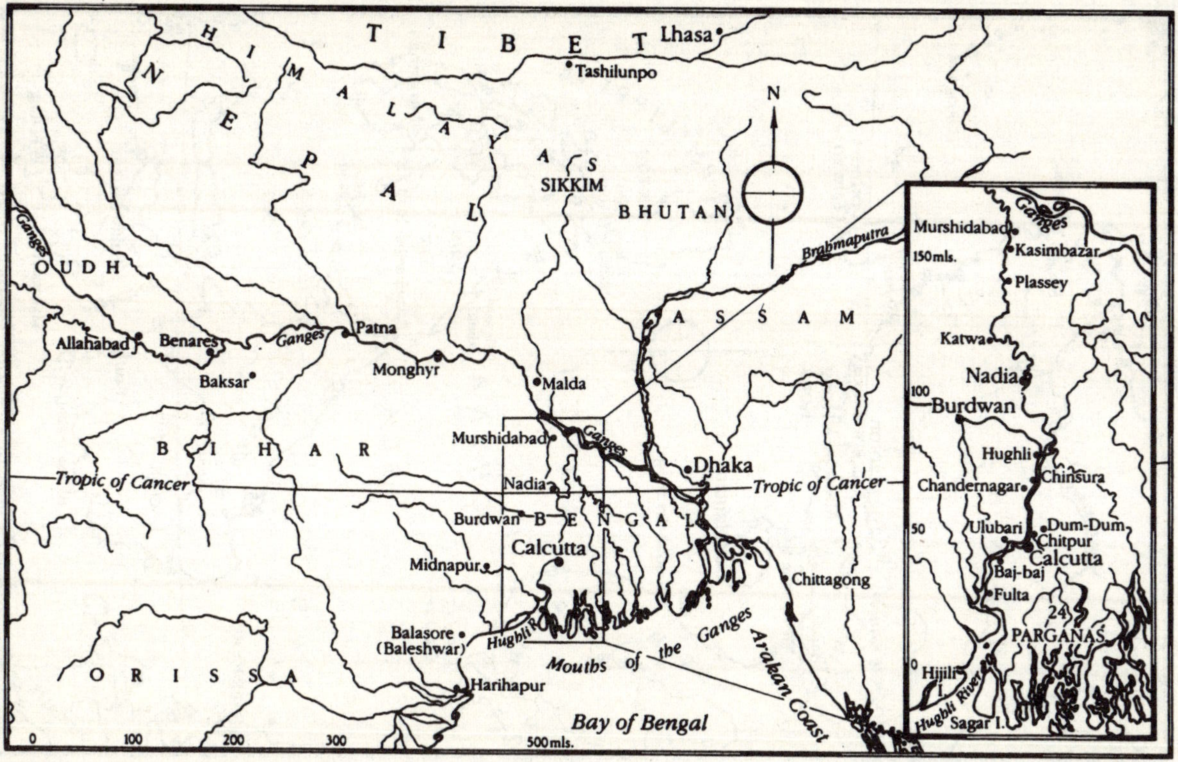
TIBET
Lhasa
Tashilunpo
HIMALAYAS
NEPAL
SIKKIM
BHUTAN
N
OUDH
Ganges
Allahabad
Benares
Baksar
Patna
Monghyr
Malda
ASSAM
Brahmaputra
BIHAR
Murshidabad
Nadia
Burdwan
BENGAL
Calcutta
Dhaka
Tropic of Cancer
Tropic of Cancer
Midnapur
Chittagong
Balasore
(Baleshwar)
Hugbli R.
Mouths of the Ganges
Arakan Coast
ORISSA
Harihapur
Bay of Bengal
0
100
200
300
500 mls.
Murshidabad
Kasimbazar
150 mls.
Plassey
Katwa
Nadia
100
Burdwan
Hughli
Chinsura
Chandernagar
50
Ulubari
Dum-Dum
Chitpur
Calcutta
Baj-baj
Fulta
24
PARGANAS
0
Hijili
I.
Hugbli River
Sagar I.

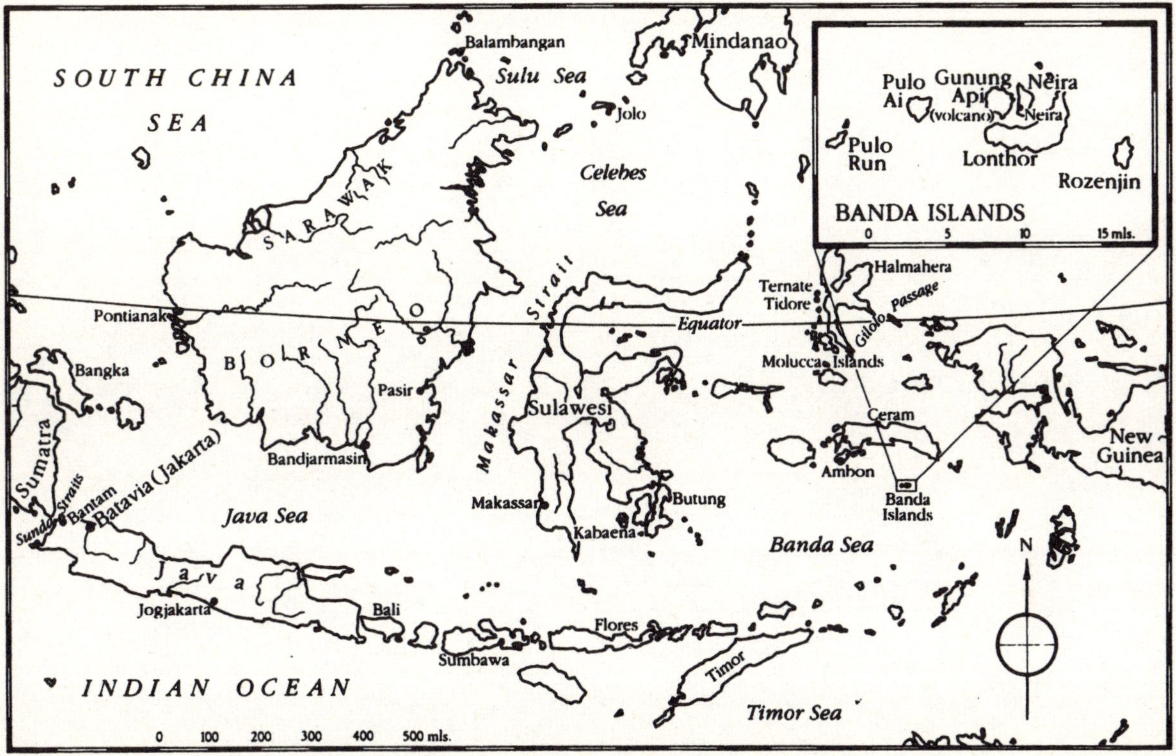
SOUTH CHINA SEA
Balambangan
Sulu Sea
Mindanao
Jolo
Celebes Sea
SARAWAK
BORNEO
Pontianak
Bangka
Pasir
Bandjarmasin
Sumatra
Sunda Straits
Bantam
Batavia (Jakarta)
Java Sea
Java
Jogjakarta
Bali
Sumbawa
Flores
Timor
Timor Sea
INDIAN OCEAN
0 100 200 300 400 500 mls.
Makassar Strait
Makassar
Sulawesi
Kabaena
Butung
Equator
Ternate
Tidore
Halmahera
Gilolo Passage
Molucca Islands
Ceram
Ambon
Banda Islands
Banda Sea
New Guinea
N
Pulo Ai
Gunung Api (volcano)
Neira
Neira
Pulo Run
Lonthor
Rozenjin
BANDA ISLANDS
0 5 10 15 mls.

Acknowledgement and Author's Note

It would take more than one lifetime to compile a history of the East India Company from its voluminous records. I have referred to them only occasionally. Books like this necessarily depend on other books. But wherever possible I have based the narrative on reprints, selections, extracts and calendars of the original records. Happily the Company has been well served in this respect. My main debt is therefore to those scholars and archivists, mostly long deceased, who laboured to elucidate different aspects of the Company's history by reproducing, abbreviating, or summarizing original materials. Their names will be found amongst the authors listed in the bibliography. I should, however, like to single out the works of Sir William Foster, Sir George Forrest, Sir Henry Yule, Sir William Hunter, Dr J. Long, Dr C. R. Wilson, Professor H. H. Dodwell, Colonel H. D. Love, and Dr S. C. Hill.

It is customary to offer some explanation for adopting a particular system of rendering foreign words into English. Since no system informs my choice of spellings I must pass on this. Familiarity and common usage have prevailed over consistency. The same goes for proper names. In the case of place names I have tried to use those designations or spellings in use now, giving the contemporary version in brackets. But this does not always work. Sometimes the current names seem less appropriate than those of 200 years ago. Thus I have stuck with Gombroon rather than have to choose between Bandar Abbas and Bandar Khomeini; with Macassar, which looks like making a comeback, rather than Ujung Pandang; and with Trichy and Tanjore because their currency seems to have survived the polysyllabic reformation of south Indian names. There are many other such inconsistencies for which I accept full responsibility.

The five years spent on this book have been a gross indulgence. I thank Carol O'Brien at HarperCollins for raising no objection to its being twice the proposed length and taking twice the allotted time. Being so long busy about the Company could also have placed a strain on personal relationships. Yet Julia has never baulked at having a hardback rodent for a husband and has in fact encouraged his ferreting with insight, good cheer, and love. My debt to her defies acknowledgement.

Preface

A hundred years ago the high-minded rulers of British India regarded merchants as a lesser breed in the hierarchy of imperial pedigree. To 'gentlemen in trade', as to servants, ladies, natives, dogs, the brass-studded doors of Bombay's and Calcutta's more exclusive clubs were closed. Like social climbers raising the ladder behind them, the paragons of the Raj preferred to forget that but for the 'gentlemen in trade' of the East India Company there would have been no British India.

The Honourable Company was remembered, if at all, only as an anomalous administrative service; and that was indeed what it had become in the early nineteenth century. But before that, for all of 200 years, its endeavours were seen as having been primarily commercial, often inglorious, and almost never 'honourable'. Venal and disreputable, its servants were believed to have betrayed their race by begetting a half-caste tribe of Anglo-Indians, and their nation by corrupt government and extortionate trade.

From those 200 years just a few carefully selected incidents and personalities sufficed by way of introduction to the subsequent 150 years of glorious British dominion. Occasionally greater attention might be paid to the Company's last decades as an all-conquering force in Indian politics, but still the perspective remained the same: the Company was seen purely as the forerunner to the Raj.

Closer acquaintance reveals a different story. The career of 'the Grandest Society of Merchants in the Universe' spans as much geography as it does history. To follow its multifarious activities involves imposing a chronology extending from the reign of Elizabeth to that of Victoria upon a map extending from southern Africa to north-west America. Heavy are the demands this makes on both writer and reader. (And hence perhaps the dearth of narrative histories of the Company in this post-imperial age.) But the conclusion is inescapable. The East India Company was as much about the East as about India. Its Pacific legacies would be as lasting as those in the Indian Ocean; its most successful commercial venture was in China, not India.

Freed of its subservient function as the unworthy stock on which the mighty Raj would be grafted, the Company stands forth as a robust association of adventurers engaged in hazarding all in a series of preposterous gambles. Some paid off; many did not but are no less memorable for it. Bizarre locations, exotic produce, and recalcitrant personalities combine to induce a sense of romance which, however repugnant to the scholar, is in no way contrived. It was thanks to the incorrigible pioneering of the Company's servants that the British Empire acquired its peculiarly diffuse character. But for the Company there would have been not only no British India but also no global British Empire.

PART ONE

A QUIET TRADE

1600–1640

CHAPTER ONE

Islands of Spicerie

THE VOYAGES OF JAMES LANCASTER

Every overseas empire had to begin somewhere. A flag had to be raised, territory claimed, and settlement attempted. In the dimly perceived conduct of a small band of bedraggled pioneers, stiff with scurvy and with sand in their hose, it may be difficult to determine to what extent these various criteria were met. There might, for instance, be a case for locating the genesis of the British Empire in the West Indies, Virginia, or New England. But there is a less obvious and much stronger candidate. The seed from which grew the most extensive empire the world has ever seen was sown on Pulo Run in the Banda Islands at the eastern end of the Indonesian archipelago. As the island of Runnymede is to British constitutional history, so the island of Run is to British imperial history.

How in 1603 Run's first English visitors ever lit upon such an absurdly remote destination is cause for wonder. To locate the island a map of no ordinary dimensions is needed. For to show Pulo Run at anything like scale and also include, say, Darwin and Jakarta means pasting together a sheet of room size – and still Run is just an elongated speck. On the ground it measures two miles by half a mile, takes an hour to walk round and a day for a really exhaustive exploration. This reveals a modest population, no buildings of note, and no source of fresh water. There are, though, a lot of trees amongst which the botanist will recognize *Myristica fragrans*. Dark of foliage, willow-size, and carefully tended, it is more commonly known as the nutmeg tree.

For the nutmegs (i.e. the kernels inside the stones of the tree's peach-like fruit) and for the mace (the membrane which surrounds the stone) those first visitors in 1603 would willingly have sailed round the world several times. Nowhere else on the globe did the trees flourish and so nowhere else was their fruit so cheap. In the minuscule Banda Islands of Run, Ai, Lonthor and Neira ten pounds of nutmeg cost less than half a penny and ten pounds of mace less than five pence. Yet in Europe the same quantities could be sold for respectively £1.60 and £16, a tidy appreciation of approximately 32,000 per cent. Not without pride would James I come to be styled 'King of England, Scotland, Ireland, France, Puloway [Pulo Ai] and Puloroon [Pulo Run]'. The last named, thought one of its visitors, could be as valuable to His Majesty as Scotland.

True, the island never quite lived up to expectations. Indeed it would become a fraught and expensive liability. But as it happened, the importance of Run for the East India Company and so for the British Empire lay not in its scented groves of nutmeg but in one particular nutmeg seedling.

A peculiarity of the Banda islands at the beginning of the seventeenth century was that thanks to their isolation they owed allegiance to no one. Moreover, the Bandanese recognized no supreme sultan of their own. Instead authority rested with village councils presided over by *orang kaya* or headmen. In the best tradition of south-east Asian *adat* (consensus), each village or island was in fact a self-governing and fairly democratic republic. They could withhold or dispose of their sovereignty as they saw fit; and whereas the inhabitants of neighbouring Neira and Lonthor had already been bullied into accepting a large measure of Dutch control, those of outlying Ai and Run had managed to preserve their independence intact.

By 1616 Run and Ai valued their contacts with the English and, when menaced by the Dutch, voted to pledge their allegiance to the men who flew the cross of St George. They did this by swearing an oath and by presenting their new suzerains with a nutmeg seedling rooted in a ball of Run's yellowish soil. As well as the symbolism, it was an act of profound trust. Seedlings were closely guarded, and destroyed rather than surrendered. Who knew what effect the naturalization elsewhere of a misappropriated seedling might have on the Bandanese monopoly?

The recipients of this gratifying presentation were, like all the other doubleted Englishmen who had so far reached Run, employees of the East India Company. But therein lay a problem. For in this, its infancy, the Company was not empowered to hold overseas territories. Its royal charter made no mention of them, only of trading rights and maritime conduct. It was therefore on behalf of the Crown that Run's allegiance had to be accepted. And when, after an epic blockade of the island lasting four years, the Company would eventually decide that it had had enough of Run, it was in fact the British sovereign who stood out in favour of his exotic windfall and of his Bandanese subjects.

Even Oliver Cromwell was to have a soft spot for Run, and at his instigation arrangements would be made for re-establishing a permanent colony there. Solid Presbyterian settlers were recruited; goats, hens, hoes, and psalters were piled aboard the good ship *London*; and it was only at the very last minute that renewed hostilities with the Dutch led to the ship being redirected to St Helena in the south Atlantic. More important, though, it was with Run in mind that the Protector issued the Company with a new charter which included the authority to hold, fortify and settle overseas territories. Thanks to the *orang kaya* of Run, first St Helena, soon after Bombay, then Calcutta, Bengal, India, and the East would come under British sway.

But there Run's celebrity would end. Ironically it was in the same year that the East India Company took over Bombay that Charles II relinquished his rights to Run. Sixty years of Dutch pressure had finally paid off. By the treaty of Breda the British Crown would cede all rights in the Bandas, receiving by way of compensation a place on the north American seaboard called New Amsterdam together with its own spiceless island of Manhattan. It may have seemed like a good swop but the little nutmeg of Run had arguably more relevance to future empire than did the Big Apple.

ii

Of those first Elizabethan Englishmen who in 1603 trooped, sea weary and surf soaked, on to Run's scorching sands we know only from the protest registered by a Dutch admiral who happened to be on the Banda island of Neira at the time. The Dutch had reached the Bandas two years earlier and, but for their sensational success there and elsewhere in the East Indies, it must be doubtful whether London's merchants would ever have entered the 'spice race' or subscribed to an East India Company. But then the Dutch were only emulating the Portuguese who had been trading with the Indies for nearly a century; and although it was the Portuguese who had discovered the sea route round the Cape of Good Hope, even they had not invented the spice trade.

Since at least Roman times the traffic in exotic condiments from east to west had sustained the most extensive and profitable trading network the world had yet seen. The buds of the dainty clove tree, the berries of the ivy-like pepper vine, and of course the kernel and membrane of the nutmeg had been ideal cargoes. Dried, husked and bagged, they were light in weight, high in value, and easily broken into loads. Shipped to the Asian mainland in junks, *prahus* and dhows, they were repacked as camel and donkey loads for the long overland journey to the Levant, and then reshipped across the Mediterranean to the European markets.

In the process their value appreciated phenomenally. What were basic culinary ingredients in south Asia had become exotic luxuries by the time they reached the Mediterranean and the Atlantic. They were the precious metals of the vegetable kingdom and their pungency seemed to enhance their rarity by conferring a whiff of distinction on every household that could afford them. In brines and marinades nutmeg proved a vital preservative; in stews and ragouts pepper masked the smell of ill-cured meat and improved its flavour; and the clove, as well as its culinary uses, was credited with amazing medicinal properties. Like later tea, coffee, and even tobacco, it was as expensive health foods that spices gradually entered everyday diet. As the supply increased, the merchants' profit margins would fall, but in the sixteenth century it was still calculated that if only one sixth of a cargo reached its destination its owner would still be in profit.

Control of this lucrative trade rested traditionally with the Chinese and Malays in the East, with the Indians and Arabs in its middle reaches, and with the Levantines and Venetians in the West. But around the year 1500 other interested parties had appeared on the scene. It was to reroute the spice trade to the greater advantage of Christendom and their own considerable profit that European seafarers from Spain and Portugal first ventured on to the world's oceans. Improvements in marine design, in navigational instruments, cartography and gunnery soon gave the newcomers an edge over their Asian rivals. They could sail further, faster, and for longer. They had less need to hug the coastline and, since the spice-producing islands lay on the opposite side of the world, they had a choice of sailing east or west.

But what their charts failed to show was that other lands lay in the way. Hence the search for the Spice Islands threw up the discovery of America, of the Pacific archipelagos, of sub-Saharan Africa, and of the Indian and south-east Asian coastlines. Knowledge of, and eventually dominion over these 'new worlds' would follow. Yet such incidental discoveries could not immediately deflect the European parvenus from their main objective. Trade, not conquest or colonization, was the priority. In 1511, only twenty-three years after first rounding the Cape of Good Hope, the Portuguese had reached Java; and in 1543, twenty-three years after discovering the Magellan strait near Cape Horn, a Spanish fleet from Mexico had laid claim to the islands soon christened the Philippines. Somewhere in the gap remaining between these two global pincer movements lay the Spice Islands.

The perversity of nature in lavishing her most valued products on islands so small and impossibly remote prompted wonder and fable. To what Milton called the 'islands of spicerie' an air of mystery clung. When Christopher Columbus had cast about for a sponsor for his projected voyage over the western horizon, he made much of the idea that if he did not find the spice-rich Indies he had a good chance of finding the lost continent of Atlantis. Neither was a geographical certainty; both owed much to the imagination.

Even today, with better and more comprehensive maps, it is hard to put a finger on the exact spot. 'Spice Islands' was as much a description as a proper name, and mostly it was reserved for islands which had no other claim on the map-maker's attention. Thus somewhere as important as Sri Lanka, although always the main producer of cinnamon bark, did not qualify and neither did the main pepper-producing areas of Sumatra and of India's Malabar coast.

The real spice islands were less obvious and more mysterious, and lay much further to the east between Sulawesi (Celebes), New Guinea, and the Philippines. This, the Moluccan triangle, is also the epicentre of Indonesia's volcanic 'Ring of Fire'. On average there is an eruption every five years and deposits of volcanic soil are as crucial to the location of spice groves as the humid sea-breezes. In seventeenth-century drawings Tidore and Ternate, the main clove-producing islands, figure as smoking volcanoes rising sheer from the ocean, the only vegetation being a fringe of coconut palms at their base. Horticulturally they look most unpromising. Yet this is in fact a fairly accurate depiction. The cones rise a mile into the sky and only the narrowest of margins between the encircling ocean and the funnel of fire is available for clove gardens. Likewise the Banda Islands are dominated by the great central volcano of Gunung Api which periodically showers the nutmeg groves with rich volcanic dust. If the production of spices required such an elemental setting, it was no wonder they were a rarity.

The first spice race, won by the Portuguese, was confirmed by the terms of a Papal bull which drew a sort of international date-line between the advancing fleets of Spain and Portugal. With a chain of heavily fortified bases stretching from Hormuz in the Persian Gulf to Goa in India, then Malacca near the modern Singapore, and finally Ambon in the central Moluccas, the Portuguese made good their claim to control of the entire spice route. Barring occasional interference from the Spanish in the Philippines, they enjoyed as near a monopoly of the oceanic spice trade as they cared to enforce for most of the sixteenth century.

Other European rivals simply failed to materialize. As yet the Dutch were still enduring the birth pangs of nationhood; and the English, who with the loss of Calais and the break with Rome were at last looking away from Europe, were nevertheless looking in the wrong direction. Observing how, although the Portuguese sailed into the sunrise and the Spanish into the sunset, both had successfully found a path to the Spice Islands, Englishmen had concluded that they too could expect to discover their own corridor to the East. The fact that that same Papal bull gave the Iberian powers a monopoly over their respective routes which might be enforced by any available means was also good reason for Tudor seafarers to find their own route. Like their Spanish and Portuguese rivals, the English were familiar with the latest advances in marine technology and were dimly aware that being located on the European periphery should no longer be a disadvantage. In what was to be the age of the Atlantic powers, the English were not behindhand; only five years after Columbus, John Cabot in an English vessel had been the first to reach the American mainland. But they were unlucky. Portuguese endeavour had been handsomely rewarded by the discovery of a 'south-east passage' round the Cape of Good Hope; thereafter the Indies had been plain sailing. Similarly a 'south-west passage' round the Horn had awaited the Spanish. But where were their northern equivalents?

Throughout the second half of the sixteenth century English ships determinedly pushed up into the Arctic Circle. In the north-west Frobisher and Davis probed the sounds and channels of Canada's frozen north; none turned out to be a Magellan strait. Earlier Willoughby and Chancellor, in search of a north-east passage, had rounded Norway's North Cape and entered the Barents Sea. Novaya Zemlya was no place of balmy refreshment like Madagascar but in an age when men still welcomed some medieval symmetry in their maps, the Norwegian cape showed a happy longitudinal correspondence to that of southern Africa.

'Good hope' sprang eternal. Forcing its way through the pack ice, an English ship at last entered the Kara Sea which may fairly be considered as Asiatic water. The fogs and the ice floes drove it back. Instead of rich and civilized Cathay, all that had been discovered was the rough and ready Russia of Ivan the Terrible.

The story did not end there. Well into the seventeenth century London's Muscovy Company would continue to trade with the Tsar's territories via Murmansk and to encourage Arctic exploration. In 1602 the East India Company would itself despatch an expedition to the north-west and in 1606, in conjunction with the Muscovy Company, it tried again. Four years later Henry Hudson, cast away by his mutinous crew in the bay that bears his name, probably died believing that he had cleared the north-west passage. It fell to Bylot and Baffin to show that he had done no such thing. The search went on.

The idea that to the English it would be given to open their own sea route to the East proved mighty persistent. It needs to be emphasized that when the East India Company was founded it was by no means a foregone conclusion that its ships would always be sailing east nor, for that matter, that they would ever be going to India. Indeed the Company which received its royal charter on 31 December 1600 was not the 'English East India Company' at all but 'The Company of Merchants of London trading into the East Indies'. The 'London' was important and so were the 'East Indies' which then as now were not synonymous with India.

How the Company's ships were to get to the Indies was up to them. But if the northern corridor proved elusive, disappointment served only to strengthen an even more fundamental conviction – that somehow or other a share of world trade would nonetheless fall to the English. To the Tudor merchant-adventurer freedom of trade was much like freedom of conscience; he could invoke scripture to justify it and would not have been surprised to see it enshrined in the Thirty-Nine Articles. Just as Rome's presumptuous claims to a monopoly of Christian truth and authority were no longer acceptable, so Madrid's claim to the treasures of the Americas and Lisbon's to the trade of the Indies, for each of which Papal authority was again invoked, were seen as 'insolencyes'.

Wherever English shipping called, the argument for free trade would be vigorously rehearsed. It was quite simple. In His 'infinite and unsearchable wisdom', according to the text of Queen Elizabeth's standard letter of introduction to eastern princes, God had so ordained matters that no nation was self-sufficient and that 'out of the abundance of ffruit which some region[s] enjoyeth, the necessitie or wante of others should be supplied'. Thus 'severall and ffar remote countries' should have 'traffique' with one another and 'by their interchange of commodities' should become friends. 'The Spaniard and the Portingal', on the other hand, prohibited multilateral exchange and insisted on exclusive trading rights. Such rights, if granted, would be interpreted as tantamount to a surrender of sovereignty. Any prince, warned the Queen's letter – she could not be more precise because these letters were unaddressed and it was up to whoever delivered them to fill in the name of the local potentate – any prince who traded with only one European nation must expect a degree of political subordination to that nation.

The first prince to receive one of these unconventional and unsolicited royal circulars was most impressed; the sentiments could have been his own. Ala-uddin Shah was Sultan of Aceh, an important city-state on the north-western tip of Sumatra; the date was June 1602; and the bearer of the letter was James Lancaster, commander of the East India Company's first fleet.

iii

Lancaster's career well illustrates the momentous events which immediately preceded the foundation of the Company. Born at Basingstoke in the mid-1550s, he had somehow found his way to Portugal where he quickly amassed both wealth and experience, as a merchant and soldier. Then in 1580 the Portuguese crown passed to Philip II of Spain. As a result of this dynastic union Spain's enemies, notably England and Holland, became those of Portugal too. Lisbon was soon closed to English shipping and Lancaster, like other Englishmen, left in a hurry; it seems that he may well have lost property and rank by this unexpected turn of events. The union also cut off the supply of Portuguese spices to Spain's enemies, thus giving the Dutch and English an incentive to go seek them at source; and it also freed English adventurers from the constraints of the traditional Anglo-Portuguese alliance. Portuguese ships and Portuguese trade routes were now fair game.

Coincidentally it was also in 1580 that Francis Drake returned from his voyage round the world. *En route* he had called at the clove-rich island of Ternate, one of the Moluccas, and at Java, and had had no difficulty in procuring a cargo. This was thought most encouraging; evidently the Portuguese in the East were neither as well established nor as vigilant as expected. In 1582 an English fleet was sent to renew contacts. It failed to find the Cape of Good Hope, let alone cross the Indian Ocean; this was less encouraging. But in 1587 Drake's raids in the eastern Atlantic resulted in the capture of a Portuguese carrack, or galleon. The ease with which the giant vessel was overpowered showed, according to the contemporary chronicler Richard Hakluyt, that 'carracks were no such bugs that they might be taken'; when its cargo was valued at over £100,000 Elizabethan seafarers took up bug hunting in earnest.

Lancaster may well have been serving under Drake at this time. Alternatively he may have been involved in the Levant Company, which, like the Muscovy Company, was another new London syndicate trading, in this case, with the Middle East; from its ranks would come many of the prime movers in the East India Company. At all events, by 1588 Lancaster had learnt something of navigation and had command of a Levant Company ship, the *Edward Bonaventure*.

In her, he like many others who would sail to the East put to sea to oppose the Invincible Armada. For a generation of English seamen the defeat of the Armada was a turning point. To them, and to all who cared to line the cliffs along the English Channel during the last week of July 1588, it demonstrated that the earlier successes of Drake and Raleigh were not just isolated flashes of brilliance-cum-effrontery; and that well armed, well manned, and cleverly sailed, the smaller English ships were more than a match for the great galleons and carracks. With national self-esteem fluttering at the masthead, the English were now ready to carry their challenge for maritime supremacy down the Atlantic and beyond. Often news of the Armada's defeat would precede them. Sultan Ala-uddin of Aceh's gracious reception of his unknown visitors would owe a good deal to rumours that these were the selfsame people who had repelled the most formidable navy either east or west had ever seen. And when the Sultan actually congratulated Lancaster on the affair, the Englishman visibly blushed with delight.

Three years after the Armada, Lancaster again commanded the *Edward Bonaventure*. She was one of three 'tall ships' and she was sailing south from Plymouth, heading at last for the Cape and the East Indies. This voyage, which lasted from 1591 to 1594, is generally regarded as a reconnaissance for those of the East India Company. A Dutch fleet sailed in its wake and the second spice race had begun. But whereas the Dutch voyage would prove a resounding success, that of the English proved the grimmest of odysseys and the most disastrous of investments; if anything it ought finally to have discredited the whole idea of pursuing eastern trade.

Even on the first leg down the African coast things had gone badly wrong. While the ships drifted from one Atlantic doldrum to another, so many of those aboard succumbed to scurvy that from the Cape one of the ships had to be sent home with fifty sick men aboard. In the event they were the lucky ones. The two remaining ships pushed on around the coast of Africa. Somewhere off Mozambique the flagship was lost with all hands in a storm which also killed some of the *Bonaventure*'s men. Lancaster repaired to the Comoro Islands where a further thirty of his followers were massacred by the natives. He continued on to Zanzibar and, by-passing India, eventually reached Penang and the Malay peninsula.

Neither here nor anywhere else was any attempt made to open honest trade; it was easier to plunder Portuguese ships and easier still to waylay Burmese and Indian vessels which paid for, but rarely enjoyed, Portuguese protection. No doubt Lancaster was under pressure from his decimated and prize-hungry crew. Ever a considerate commander, he openly discussed his plans with his officers and showed unusual solicitude for his men. Thus it was their representations which eventually forced him to head for home, and which, when provisions ran low in the Atlantic, persuaded him to visit the West Indies. There the *Bonaventure* plus her ill-gotten cargo was finally lost, and the remnant of her crew shipwrecked. Out of 198 men who had rounded the Cape only twenty-five would ever make it back to England; two out of three ships had been lost; and the only cargo to reach home was that boatload of scurvy victims.

Lancaster was among the survivors. Within a few months of his return he was sailing to Brazil in command of a much more successful expedition which managed to storm Pernambuco (Recife) and to get away with so much loot, including the contents of another carrack laden with spices, that additional ships had to be chartered to carry it all home. Undoubtedly no Englishman had more experience of outwitting the Portuguese or of navigation in the Indian Ocean. Lancaster was the obvious choice as commander of the first East India Company fleet.

He had, however, done nothing to persuade merchants and investors that expeditions in search of eastern trade were worthwhile. It was the Dutch with a succession of rewarding voyages to the East Indies in the late 1590s who showed what could be achieved. They too had first hoped to find a north-eastern passage to the Indies, had been duly disappointed, and in 1595 had tried their luck with a small fleet sent round the Cape of Good Hope. A Dutch agency, or 'factory', had been established at

Bantam in western Java, and the fleet returned home laden with spices. In rapid succession new Dutch syndicates were formed; by 1598 several fleets totalling some eleven vessels were sailing for the Indies. It was one of these which established the Dutch presence at Neira, the nutmeg capital of the Banda Islands. By the end of the century the Dutch had opened further factories in the Moluccas and on the Indian peninsula and had begun trading with Sumatra, Sri Lanka, and the coast of China.

Here was an object lesson in what could be achieved by concerted endeavour and it was not lost on London's merchants. In particular the members of the Muscovy and Levant Companies, men already accustomed to take a world view of trade, organized into powerful and exclusive syndicates with access to capital and influence, yet independent of both court and government, rose to the challenge. The Levant Company's hopes of tapping into the overland trade in spices and other eastern commodities through agencies in Persian and Turkish territory were clearly doomed now that the Dutch had shown that they could drive a highly profitable trade direct with the Spice Islands. Imitation remained the only sincere form of competition and it is a measure of the English success that within a decade the Levant Company, instead of importing spices from the Middle East, would be exporting them from London to the Middle East.

The final straw came with the news that the Dutch were now seeking to augment their eastern fleets by purchasing English shipping. Arguing that the national interest was at stake, in July 1599 – just two months after ships of the second Dutch fleet began returning with packed holds – a petition was ready for Queen Elizabeth's perusal.

For a critical year Her Majesty stalled. Peace negotiations with Spain were at a sensitive stage and it was rightly thought that they would be prejudiced by any English commitment to contest the spice trade. The petitioners responded by producing a list of all the 'islands, cities, townes, places, castels and fortresses' occupied by the Portuguese plus another list, even longer, of all those they did not occupy. Their argument, which would later become all too familiar as the interloper's apologia, was simply that if the Portuguese had no interest in these other 'places' – which included such significant markets as Siam, Bengal, Japan, Cambodia and 'the most mighty and wealthy empire of China' – then there could be no harm in 'other princes or people of the world repairing unto them'. There was no need for a direct confrontation with the Portuguese and, as will be seen, the English would go out of their way to develop and explore all of them. On the other hand Her Majesty knew her swashbuckling subjects well enough not to suppose that they would ever willingly forgo a laden carrack. It was not therefore until negotiations with Spain faltered that a new petition was invited and the Royal Charter at last granted.

Amongst the names of the 218 petitioners who celebrated New Year's Eve 1600 as 'The Company of Merchants of London trading into the East Indies' was that of James Lancaster. He probably helped to draft the original petition and he was certainly one of the Company's first 'committees' (directors). He also had a hand in drafting that standard royal letter, a copy of which he would present at Aceh. But already there were those at Court, like the Lord Treasurer and the Earl of Essex, who saw the new company as a rich mine of patronage and who were all for working it, notably by leaning on the directors to appoint Sir Edward Michelborne as commander of the first fleet. The directors stood firm; their choice was Master James Lancaster and by way of explanation they insisted on being allowed 'to sort out theire business with men of their own qualitye'. Indeed, lest suspicions of jobbery scare off any of their investors, they resolved 'not to employ any gentleman in any place of charge'. They approved of Lancaster's democratic style of leadership and, more to the point, they vigorously resented any Court interference. But as the Company's annalist would gloomily note, here was evidence that even before the Company had been fully constituted 'that influence which in the sequel will be found to be equally adverse to the prosperity of their trade and the probity of their directors had its commencement'. Michelborne, incidentally, instead of being the Company's first commander, would become its rival as the first interloper.

iv

After frantic preparations Lancaster sailed from Woolwich with four ships in February 1601. The *Red Dragon*, his flagship, had been bought from the Earl of Cumberland who was at this time the only titled member of the Company. The vessel partook of his Lordship's 'quality'. She was of 600 tons, had been built for privateering in the West Indies, and like most subsequent 'East Indiamen' was as much warship as cargo carrier with thirty-eight guns plus space, if not accommodation, for 200 men. To maintain her complement at 200 Lancaster, mindful of past disasters, prescribed lemon juice for all ranks. Three spoonfuls per man were administered every morning as they sailed into the scurvy latitudes of the south Atlantic. The dosage seemed to work. During the six months that it took to reach the Cape the men of the *Red Dragon* remained in rude health.

It was not so in the rest of the fleet. The *Hector*, the *Susan* and the *Ascension* were somewhat smaller ships and had all been active in the Levant trade. Each carried about 100 men, the total for the whole fleet being 480. Of these, 105 were dead by the time they reached the Cape. So weak were those that remained that men from the *Red Dragon* had to be sent to assist in bringing the other ships into Table Bay.

Then known as Saldania, Table Bay proved a good spot to recuperate. Sails were taken ashore and a tented rest camp prepared. Good water, fresh fruit and the mellow winter climate saw the sickly men quickly recover and provided 'a royal refreshing' for all. Meanwhile Lancaster renewed his acquaintance – he had stopped here in 1591 – with the 'Saldanians'. 'Of a tawny colour, of reasonable stature, swift of foot, and much given to pick and steal', the Africans were as yet shy of European visitors and were easily kept at a distance. Additionally there was a problem of communication. The natives 'spoke through the throat' and 'clocked with their tongues in such sort that in . . . seven weeks . . . the sharpest wit amongst us could not learn one word of their language'. Lancaster, rising to the occasion in a way that no gentleman would have contemplated, spoke to them 'in cattel's language'. Thus, wishing to buy sheep, he said 'baah' and 'for oxen and kine "moath", which language the people understood very well without any interpreter'. Soon droves of livestock were converging on the camp and changing hands at rates which the English found frankly laughable. A piece of old iron, rowlock-size, bought a sheep, and two pieces bought an ox 'full as bigge as ours and very fat'. With 1000 sheep and 42 oxen – plus wine, olive oil and meal removed from a small Portuguese supply ship which had fallen into English hands – the fleet left Table Bay as well provisioned as it had Woolwich.

As an alternative to Saldania future voyages would often make for one of Madagascar's sheltered bays. Lancaster's fleet passed along the east coast of the island and on Christmas Day 1601 put into the bay of Antongil to load water, rice and fruit and to replenish stocks of lemon juice. Here they also assembled a small pinnace of about eighteen tons which they had brought from London in kit form. Of lesser draught, it would be used for sounding in coastal waters and as a tender for bringing cargoes out to the main fleet.

While the 'pinis' was being 'sheathed', as the anonymous chronicler charmingly puts it – he means the pinnace was being clad with an outer shell of local timber – men again began dying. From the *Red Dragon* were lost the master's mate, the preacher, the surgeon and 'tenne other common men'. Similar losses were reported from the rest of the fleet. 'Those that died here died most of the flux [dysentery] which, in our opinion, came with the waters which we drancke.' This was not, however, the case with Captain Brand of the *Ascension*, who had the unusual misfortune of being shot by the guns of his own ship. In sombre mood he was being rowed ashore to attend the funeral of the *Red Dragon*'s mate when the *Ascension*'s gunner let fly with the usual three-gun salute for a deceased officer. Unfortunately the gunner, 'being not so careful as he should have beene', had forgotten that his guns were loaded and that the Captain was within range. One ball scored a direct hit and 'slew the Captain and the boatswain's mate starke dead; so that they that went to see the funeral of another were both buried themselves'.

This indiscriminate firing of a few 'pieces', often on the flimsiest of pretexts, would account for a good many lives. So much so that in London the directors would be moved to protest that it was quite unnecessary to salute every port, every passing vessel, every visitor, every imaginable anniversary. Yet if anything the practice grew and there was probably more powder expended in ceremonial than in battle. To Lancaster and subsequent commanders it was self-evident that the morale and efficiency of their crews demanded the firing of frequent practice salvoes.

Leaving Madagascar in early March the fleet stood out into the Indian Ocean. Its next landfall was at the Nicobar Islands off Sumatra. Here the decks were cleared for action, Lancaster again anticipating prize-taking as much as trade. On 5 June, sixteen months after leaving the Thames, they finally anchored off Aceh.

> Here we found sixteen or eighteen sail of shippes of diverse nations – Gujeratis, some of Bengal, some of Calicut [south India] called Malibaris, some of Pegu [Burma] and some of Patani [Thailand] which came to trade here.

To the Muslims of Indonesia Aceh is still 'The Gateway to Mecca'. Here pilgrims embark for the *haj* to Arabia and here Arab and Indian traders first brought the teachings of Islam to the Archipelago. Like Venice in the eastern Mediterranean, Aceh traditionally controlled the western approaches to the busy trading world of south-east Asia. It was a cosmopolitan sea power and much of its population was of Arab and Indian descent. By 1602 its concourse of shipping could probably not compare with that at the rival Portuguese establishment of Malacca on the other side of the Straits. It must, nevertheless, have seemed to Lancaster and his men that they had at last, and in every sense, arrived. Ala-uddin Shah was reportedly anxious to meet them and in due course sent 'sixe greate ellifants with many trumpets, drums and streamers' to convey the English to his court. The Queen's letter, suitably addressed by the fleet's calligrapher, travelled in front, wrapped in silk and reposing in a ewer of gold which was housed in a sumptuous howdah on the biggest elephant of all.

Like most of his contemporaries, Lancaster was easily impressed by oriental magnificence and willingly prostrated himself before Ala-uddin Shah 'after the manner of the country'. Newcomers in need of a patron and trading partner could do worse than cultivate the Acehnese. They controlled much of Sumatra's pepper output and had repeatedly contested command of the Malacca straits with the Portuguese. They had also, two years previously, felt no compunction about murdering an objectionable Dutch commander and imprisoning his colleagues.

But that reputation for Islamic fanaticism which would lead a later writer to describe Acehnese hospitality as 'equivalent to an abduction' was not yet in evidence. Lancaster found himself confronted with nothing more daunting than an enormous Sumatran banquet which was served on platters of gold while the Sultan sat apart toasting his guests in arrack so fiery that 'a little will serve to bringe one asleepe'. Belying the myth of the hard-drinking sea-dog, Lancaster diluted his drink and was thus still awake to witness the arrival of a bespangled all-female gamelan orchestra complete with willowy dancers. 'The king's damosels', explained the fleet's chronicler with obvious pride, 'are not usually seene of any but such as the king will greatly honour.'

And greatly honoured the English were. Cockfights and other gruesome royal entertainments – buffalo fights, tiger fights, elephant fights – followed. Doubtless there was also a chance to sample the Acehnese speciality of a sub-aqua cocktail party. This usually took place in a nearby river, the guests being seated on submerged stools with water up to their armpits while servants paddled between them with an assortment of spicy delicacies and quantities of that fiery arrack. In 1613 one such party attended by British visitors lasted four hours. Next day two of the party-goers died; their condition was diagnosed as 'a surfeit taken by immeasurable drunkenness'.

In between these social diversions the Sultan, with the help of Lancaster's translator, studied Queen Elizabeth's standard letter. After assurances that Her Majesty's sentiments on free trade 'came from the heart' he graciously acceded to most of its requests. The English were granted a house in Aceh, royal protection, full trading rights, and exemption from customs duties. All that remained was to load the fleet with Sumatra's famous black pepper and head for home.

But here a problem arose. The previous year's crop, it was said, had failed – either that or it had just failed to reach Aceh. As would become apparent in future years, Aceh's importance was political and strategic but not commercial. The main pepper-growing areas and the main pepper ports were hundreds of miles down the Sumatran coast in the Minangkabau forests. To Priaman, one of the Minangkabau ports on the south coast of the island, Lancaster now despatched the *Susan* while with the remainder of the fleet plus a Dutch vessel he sallied forth into the Malacca straits to take by force what he had so far failed to secure by trade.

In return for the promise of 'a faire Portugal maiden' Ala-uddin Shah connived at this move to the extent of detaining a Portuguese emissary who might have alerted his fellow countrymen. With surprise on their side Lancaster's ships fanned out across the straits. Almost immediately they trapped and overpowered an enormous Portuguese carrack. She was so laden with Indian piece goods, mostly white calicoes and the famous batiks or 'pintadoes' of southern India, that it took six days to unload her.

As yet Indian cottons could not be expected to command much sale amongst fustian-clad Englishmen but they were extremely popular in south-east Asia and were more acceptable as barter for spices than any other commodity. Lancaster carried £20,000 of bullion, mostly in Spanish rials or 'pieces of eight', plus some £6000 worth of English exports. But, as he readily appreciated, these Indian cottons more than doubled the value of his stock. Somewhat clumsily he had set a precedent, which would soon become an imperative, of exploiting the existing carrying trade of Asia. He was under no illusions as to its importance. Thanks to an action that had lasted perhaps two hours the success of the Company's first voyage was assured. Mightily relieved, he confided to his diarist 'that he was much bound to God that hath eased me of a very heavy care and that he could not be thankful enough to Him for this blessing'.

> For He [God] hath not only supplied my necessity to lade these ships I have, but hath given me as much as will lade as many more ships if I had them to lade. So that now my care is not for money but rather where I shall leave these goods . . . in safety till the returne of ships out of England.

Here was one good reason to establish a 'factory' or trading establishment though not, in view of the pepper shortage, in Aceh. Instead he would proceed to Bantam in Java where pepper was supposedly plentiful and the Dutch were already well established.

First, though, he returned to pay his respects to Ala-uddin Shah. Some choice items from the prize had already been set aside for the Sultan. They did not include 'a faire Portugal maiden' because Lancaster had seen fit to release all his captives and because Ala-uddin Shah already had wives aplenty. In respect of their own subjects the Sultans of Aceh brooked no refusals in their exercise of the *droit de seigneur*. 'If the husband be unwilling to part with her', noted an English visitor, 'then he [the Sultan] presently commands her husband's pricke to be cut off.'

Yet for harem exotics there was always a steady demand. Ala-uddin's successor would go one better by lodging a request with the Company for two English maidens. By way of incentive he added that, if either bore him a son, the child would be designated his heir. Rather surprisingly the directors of the Company would take him seriously. There could, of course, be no question of condoning bigamy by sending *two* girls; but one was a possibility and it so happened that 'a gentleman of honourable parentage' had a daughter with just the right qualifications, she being 'of excellent parts for musicke, her needle, and good discourse, also very beautiful and personable'. So keen was the gentleman of honourable parentage to part with this paragon that when theological counsel raised certain objections to marriage with a Muslim, he was ready with a long and closely argued paper rich in scriptural citations which the directors adjudged 'very pregnant and good'. Happily it was not quite good enough; for the matter was then referred to King James who, as with other contentious issues, determinedly ignored it.

Lancaster was no less diplomatic in the matter of the missing Portuguese maiden. He told Ala-uddin 'that there was none so worthy that merited to be so presented', at which, we are told, the Sultan smiled. A fulsome reply to the Queen's letter plus suitable gifts were now handed over and, having at last got the measure of his guests, Ala-uddin bade them farewell by singing a hymn for their prosperity. Lancaster and his followers replied with a lusty rendering of the psalm of David and on 9 November 1602 the fleet sailed out of Aceh. Two days later the *Ascension*, being near enough laden with all that Aceh had been able to provide in the way of pepper and spices, was despatched for home. She reached London to a joyous welcome in June 1603 after a voyage remarkable only for the fact that she called at St Helena, thus inaugurating the Company's long association with that island, and that she fell in with a pair of 'marmaides'. They were definitely mermaids because 'their hinde parts were divided into two legges' and according to the ship's naturalist they were probably husband and wife 'because the moste of one of their heads was longer than the other'. 'They say they are signes of bad weather', he added, 'and so we found it.'

Meanwhile the *Red Dragon* and the *Hector* had met up with the *Susan* at Priaman and found her lading almost completed. She sailed for home a few days later and arrived soon after the *Ascension*. Continuing to coast along the forest-fringed beaches of Sumatra, the main fleet passed the then dormant Krakatoa, entered the Sunda straits between Sumatra and Java, and 'with a great peale of ordnance such as had never been rung there before' anchored off Bantam in time for Christmas.

The Portuguese had never really troubled themselves with Java and Sumatra. Their preoccupation had been with the Spice Islands and their pepper requirements had been more than met by the tangled vines of Kerala's forests. It was thus unsurprising that first the Dutch and now the English would choose Java as their main base in the East Indies. With its enormous population, its rich soil, and its wealthy courts, Java represented a domestic market second only to India and China. Additionally the twin north-coast ports of Bantam and Jakarta attracted maritime trade from all over the archipelago. They were also visited by an annual fleet of magnificent junks, laden with silks and porcelain, from China, and they were home for thriving communities of Chinese financiers and middlemen. Once again Lancaster was reminded that commercial activity in the East had long since spawned a vast and sophisticated network in which the export of spices to Europe was still a marginal sideline.

The Sultan of Bantam turned out to be a mere child of ten years. Government was exercised by a council of nobles headed by a Regent, a state of affairs destined to last long after the Sultan came of age. Lancaster, having sorted out the protocol, applied for trading rights, protection, and permission to establish a factory, all of which were granted. 'We traded there peacably', wrote the diarist, 'although the Javians are reckoned amongst the greatest pickers and theeves in the world.' So it would prove; but after a few marauders were cut down in the act of breaking into the Company's premises, business proceeded briskly. 'Within five weekes much more was sold in goods [mostly Indian cottons] than would have laden our two ships.' The surplus stock was entrusted to senior factors, or merchants, who were to be left at Bantam to buy and sell in readiness for the next fleet from England. Thus was established the first English factory in the East. In no sense, of course, did this modest agency represent a colonial nucleus or a political toehold. It was simply an expedient which by spreading the Company's trading activities throughout the year eliminated those market factors which would otherwise inflate the price of spices and deflate the price of piece goods every time an English ship entered port. In theory it also reduced the turn-round time for shipping by ensuring that a cargo was always ready for loading.

As well as the factors left at Bantam, another small group was dispatched to establish a similar factory in the Moluccas. The latter sailed from Bantam in a forty-ton pinnace (which must have been commandeered or chartered since it was considerably larger than that assembled in Madagascar) in early 1603. Such satellite voyages were a necessary feature of European trade throughout the East and especially in the archipelago. The fleets of 'tall ships' plying between Europe and India represented only the main trunk of the spice trade. Its twigs and branches were an infinitely complex web of subsidiary voyages in small pinnaces and galleys, in Malay *prahus* and Chinese junks, often commanded but rarely crewed by Europeans, by which the produce and intelligence of remote parts and shallow waters were delivered to the factories and the fleets. The factory system necessitated this involvement in what was really another aspect of the carrying trade. But to the Company's directors in London this branch of their servants' activities, with all its bizarre and colourful ramifications, would ever be a subject for misunderstanding and suspicion. The 'country trade', as it was called, invariably confounded the auditors but enriched the adventurers.

In the event the pinnace assigned to the Moluccas was back in Bantam after two months, supposedly defeated by adverse winds. But if it had failed to reach the clove-producing islands of Ternate and Tidore, it is clear from the report of the Dutch admiral at Banda Neira that in March 1603 it had somehow found its way to Pulo Run in the nutmeg-scented Bandas. The English had lost the spice race – but only just and not irrevocably. John Middleton, Lancaster's second in command, would have been the obvious man to have taken up the challenge of finding more places like Pulo Run where neither the Dutch nor the Portuguese had established monopolies. But he now died, the first of many to succumb to Bantam's lethal combination of enteric amoebae and malarial mosquitoes. Instead it would be his two brothers, Henry and David, who would open up the Moluccas. Both were now serving under Lancaster; and both would eventually join brother John in an eastern grave.

On 20 February 1603, with another 'great peale of ordnance', the fleet at last 'set sayle to the sea toward England'. Steering straight across the Indian Ocean they crossed the Tropic of Capricorn in mid-March and were off the coast of southern Africa by the end of April. There a storm whipped up such seas 'that in the reason of man no ship was able to live in them'. Somehow they survived, but on 3 May came 'another very sore storme' which so buffeted the *Red Dragon* that it caused its rudder to shear off. The rudder sank without trace and there was no replacement.

> This struck a present fear into the hearts of all men so that the best of us and most experienced knew not what to do. And specially, seeing ourselves in such a tempestuous sea and so stormy a place so that I think there be few worse in all the world. Now our ship drove up and down in the sea like a wreck so that sometimes we were within three or four leagues of the Cape Buena Esperanza [Good Hope], then cometh a contrary wind and drove us almost to forty degrees to the southwards into the hail and snow and sleetie cold weather. And this was another great misery to us that pinched exceeding sore so that our case was miserable and very desperate.

All this time the *Hector* kept company with the *Red Dragon*, standing by to take off survivors when it became necessary. A lull in the storms prompted an attempt to improvise a new rudder by using the mizzen mast as a sweep. It failed and the weather again worsened. This time the men were all for abandoning ship. But their commander stood firm and to quell any further ideas of desertion, sent orders to the *Hector* to leave them immediately and head for England. He also enclosed a note to his employers advising them of his situation and prospects. He would try, he said, to save his ship. He thought there was a good chance and that was why he was risking his life and the lives of his crew. 'But I cannot tell where you should look for me if you send out any pinnace to meete me.' Rudderless and undermanned, he might end up anywhere. 'I live', he explained, 'at the devotion of the wind and seas.'

Next day the *Hector* was seen to be still keeping her station a couple of miles away and carrying little sail. Observing this flagrant disregard of orders Lancaster was clearly moved. 'These men regard no commission', he muttered in a celebrated aside which, like his 'devotion to the wind and seas', would be remembered long after names and dates and places were forgotten. Of such sentiments myths are made and to an enterprise as ambitious and enduring as the East India Company myths would matter.

With the help of the *Hector*'s crew a second attempt was made to rig a makeshift rudder. This time it held; so did the weather. On 16 June, after nearly four months out of sight of land, the two ships approached St Helena 'at the sight whereof there was no small rejoicing among us'. Three weeks of resting, refitting, and replenishing their provisions with the island's then plentiful stocks of wild goat were followed by an uneventful voyage back to England. They anchored in the Downs on 11 September 1603 'for which thanked be Almightie God who hath delivered us from infinite perils and dangers in this long and tedious navigation'.

CHAPTER TWO

This Frothy Nation

THE SPICE RACE

So Lancaster's fleet had reached the East Indies and returned without losing a single ship. It was no small achievement. Valuable experience of the eastern seas had been acquired and something had been learnt of the complexities and potential of the eastern carrying trade. More tangibly a factory with adequate trading capital had been left at Bantam while in London nearly 500 tons of peppercorns were soon being laboriously transferred from the *Red Dragon* to the Company's warehouse. A handsome profit was expected and the Company's future looked promising. Lancaster had earned the nation's gratitude. James I, who had succeeded Elizabeth earlier in the year, rose to the occasion by rewarding him with a knighthood.

But though a success, the Company's first voyage had been no sensation. For one thing it had failed to make direct contact with the clove islands, thus giving the Dutch two more crucial years in which to make good their claim to succeed to the Portuguese monopoly. Then there was the question of economics. Already there were those who failed to see how exchanging precious bullion for an inessential condiment like pepper could possibly be in the national interest; they likened the Company to the gullible native of Central America who supposedly congratulated himself on acquiring pretty beads and funny toys in exchange for boring old gold and silver; their numbers would swell with every voyage. But to a benign commander like Lancaster it was the loss of 182 men, two-fifths of his entire following, that rankled. Here was a less equivocal drain on the nation's resources and one which even lemon juice had failed to staunch.

In the hard-nosed estimation of his fellow directors an even greater source of anxiety was the unfortunate effect that discharging a million pounds of pepper was having on the London market. A dip in prices was anticipated, but it so happened that in late 1603 the King too had come by a large stock of pepper, probably the contents of a captured carrack. His Majesty, as always, had a pressing need for cash and consequently placed an embargo on the Company's sales until his own stocks had been sold. Naturally the directors protested. A dividend was immediately declared in kind – that is, pepper – and the London market was soon awash with the stuff. Prices halved. Some underwriters would complain that they were still burdened with stocks from the first voyage 'six or seven years after'.

Had the Company been the brave new venture in joint-stock ownership which it later became, this would not greatly have mattered. After all, the whole point of a company operating on a stock jointly subscribed by its members is that this working capital should be long term, transcending individual ventures and so less vulnerable to the hiccups of the market. But in fact the 218 petitioners who in 1600 had become the Company of Merchants of London trading into the East Indies had subscribed for only one voyage. The majority now wanted their money back; they were not amused when instead they were told that for every £250 they had subscribed, £200 must be reinvested in a second voyage.

From the start the Company's stock had appealed to two very different types of investor. On the one hand there was the shareholder interested primarily in a quick and substantial return on his investment. He might be anything from a tradesman to a courtier and, as the Company grew, he might entertain ulterior expectations of influence and patronage within it; but he had no obvious interest in the specifics of its trade. On the other hand there were those who perceived some collateral advantage in the trade itself. This group consisted of wealthy and influential City merchants with extensive commercial and financial interests outside the Company. Such interests might coincide with the Company's upstream requirements, like the supply of bullion and broadcloth for export, of ships and provisions, of sources of finance, or with its downstream requirements like the sale, re-export and distribution of eastern produce.

At the risk of further over-simplification, these two types of investor may be roughly identified with the Company's two institutional bodies, the General Court (later the Court of Proprietors) and the Court of

Committees. The General Court comprised all those with voting rights, the qualification for which in the early seventeenth century was a minimum holding of, usually, £200. It therefore represented the generality of investors amongst whom those interested primarily in profits and dividends predominated. It was also, of course, the supreme authority within the Company. But, several hundred strong, it necessarily met infrequently and had little to do with the day-to-day running of the business.

Under the terms of the original charter this was left to the Court of Committees consisting of the Governor, Deputy-Governor and twenty-four 'committees', or directors, all of whom were elected by the General Court. The Court of Committees was the Company's executive, making policy decisions which had to be ratified by the General Court as well as directing all operations. For specific and recurrent functions like purchasing bullion, timber, provisions, etc., handling correspondence with overseas factors, and managing the Company's sales it divided into a host of influential sub-committees. Both these and the Court of Committees met frequently. Naturally their work demanded managerial and commercial experience, and so naturally the 'committees' were predominantly City merchants.

Such men were usually senior members of one of the City's livery companies and leading figures in some line of business that was relevant to the Company's. Thus Alderman Sir Thomas Smythe, the Company's first governor, was also involved in the Levant Company, previously the main importer of Eastern produce, in the Muscovy Company and in settlement projects in North America. On and off he held the governorship until 1621. Three years later Sir Morris Abbot, also of the Levant Company and also a founder member of the East India Company, succeeded. Abbot, originally of the Mercers' Company, operated a large export business in cloth, indigo and spices. Retiring in 1638 to become Lord Mayor of London, he was succeeded first by Sir Christopher Clitherow and then by Sir Henry Garraway, both leading City merchants and both themselves ex-Lord Mayors. Other directors had financial interests in Europe's capitals whence the supply of rials for export must be obtained and whither the Company was now looking to re-export its Eastern imports. In other words these City interests saw English participation in Eastern trade in an international context and attached more importance to its ramifications in terms of borrowing, shipping and commercial requirements than they did to the profit or loss on a single cargo. They took a longer view of the Company's prospects and a broader view of its role in the national economy.

The potential for conflict between the Company's management and the majority of its shareholders stemmed also from a flaw in its structure. The organization of the Company is usually characterized as a half way stage in the evolution of the medieval guild into today's public limited company. It is also regarded as the most sophisticated example of an Elizabethan chartered company; and certainly it was significantly different from most of its Tudor predecessors. An organization such as the Levant Company was more like a regulatory body, licensing and governing the commercial activities of its members who formed individual syndicates to raise capital and trade on their own account. The Levant Company was not itself an operational concern and in this respect resembled the guilds of old.

In contrast the East India Company was both regulatory body and sole operator. In recognition of the national importance that attached to its activities and of their long term, high risk nature which must involve considerable overheads – shipping, factories – it was accepted that the Company, and the Company alone, must itself conduct all business. From this it followed that raising capital must also be on a corporate basis. And thus, as the directors put it, 'the trade of the Indias being so far remote from hence [it] cannot be traded but in a joint and united stock.' Theoretically this opened the Company's membership to any who were willing to subscribe and indeed, initially, subscription was the commonest avenue of induction into the Company. This remained the case during the boom years of 1610–20 and the bust years of mid century. But later it would work the other way. Come the Restoration, when profits became more dependable and stock less terminable, the privilege of subscribing to new stock was effectively restricted to existing shareholders.

Perhaps the most significant point about the Company's organization is not where it stood in the evolutionary chain of commercial institutions but the extent to which this organization itself evolved. For though indeed a self-declared joint stock company, it began operations more like a regulated company. One third of those who first petitioned for a charter were, like Sir Thomas Smythe, members of the regulated Levant Company. They included its treasurer, its governor, and two of its founders. Initially the two organizations shared the same secretary and even used the same correspondence book. The Court of Committees and its numerous sub-groups met in Sir Thomas Smythe's house, which doubled as the Company's headquarters until Smythe's retirement in 1621. Even by then the Company's permanent London staff consisted only of the secretary, a beadle, a book-keeper-cum-accountant, a cashier, a solicitor and a 'ship's husband' (who organized the provisioning, loading and unloading of fleets). Almost an offshoot of the Levant Company then, the East India Company was expected to operate with the minimal staff and informal arrangements typical of a regulatory body.

Consistent with such traditional thinking the Company had begun life with no fixed capital, the idea being simply to raise a separate stock for each voyage; hence the expectation by investors in the First Voyage of a speedy pay-out. Since a willingness to invest in further voyages depended on the success of previous ones, this *ad hoc* system bred uncertainty and delay; and because in uncertain times new subscriptions were often hard to realize, it also put an additional strain on relations between the directors and the majority of shareholders.

The normal procedure for raising a new subscription began with the Court of Committees recommending a new voyage to the General Court. If the idea was approved, a target figure was set and a subscription book was opened. It was first taken round by the Company's beadle; then, assuming the target figure was not already reached, it was taken up by the Committees who privately urged its merits on those susceptible to pressure. Such arm-twisting usually proved effective, but there was still the problem of actually collecting the subscribed sums. They were called in by instalments as and when expenditure was required. But late payment frequently necessitated heavy borrowing, and non-payment obliged the Committees to petition the Privy Council for injunctions against the defaulters.

Prosperous times would, of course, make for more amicable relations; from 1609–16 the subscription books would fill readily enough. But in 1601–3, while the fate of the First Voyage was still unknown, the General Court had refused to hear of a new venture round the Cape. Even when Lancaster returned and a second voyage was at last approved, the new subscription brought in only £11,000 against the £60,000 subscribed for the First Voyage. It was in this crisis that the Court of Committees insisted that investors in the First Voyage support the Second to the tune of £200 for every £250 previously subscribed. It was not a popular move and it would appear that it was strongly resisted. For whereas the First Voyage had exported freight, mostly silver, to the value of over

£28,000, the Second carried only £12,000. Assuming that, as with subsequent stocks, up to two thirds of the total subscription went on fixed costs and shipping (including provisioning, manning, armaments, etc) and little more than one third on exports, the sum actually realized cannot have exceeded £40,000.

In this fraught climate Henry Middleton, brother of Lancaster's second in command and captain of the *Susan* on her return voyage, received his orders as commander of the Second Voyage. Not surprisingly he was instructed to make the Spice Islands his priority and to bring back cloves, nutmegs, mace, cinnamon, raw silk – anything rather than pepper. He was also to avoid 'refreshing' at Table Bay, presumably because of Lancaster's near-disaster off the stormy Cape, and to forgo taking any Portuguese prizes, peace negotiations with Spain–Portugal being near a happy conclusion. Far from capitalizing on the successes of Lancaster's voyage, Middleton was in effect to make good Lancaster's failures. With the same four ships, a similar complement and a similar mix of cargo and bullion, he sailed from Gravesend on 25 March 1604.

Four months later the long bluff of Table Mountain hove above the horizon. Already sixty of the *Red Dragon*'s men were down with scurvy including Middleton. 'Perusing their pitiful complaint and looking out his cabin door where did attend a swarme of lame and weake diseased cripples' he decided to ignore orders and succumb to the temptation of fresh fruit and red meat. They spent nearly five weeks in Table Bay. The sick recovered and Middleton began to exhibit that spirited conduct which would characterize his later career. He organized a rather amateurish ambush of the Saldanian herdsmen and very nearly came to grief in an epic struggle with a mother whale. Thence, without stopping at Madagascar, the fleet made straight for Bantam, arriving, once again crewed by 'diseased cripples', on 22 December 1604.

'They had hardlie fiftie sound men in theire foure ships' noted Edmund Scot who came aboard from the Bantam factory. His 'extraordinarie great joye' at the prospect of relief after nearly two years marooned in Java quickly evaporated. Middleton was again on the sick list and, as Scot knew only too well, Bantam was no place for convalescence. Here, unlike at the Cape, the sick died and the healthy sickened. An equatorial haze hung over the mud flats and marshes which passed for a coastline and across which the tide oozed its way towards the city's brimming sewers. During the four hot months men longed for the drenching rains and during the eight wet months they longed for the unbearable heat. Neither was remotely agreeable and even the nights brought no relief. Sweat seeped from ever-open pores, soaking bedding and clothing alike and blistering the skin with prickly heat. This did not deter the mosquitoes which rose in clouds from the marshes and sought out the palest flesh on offer. Malaria was unavoidable; so was dysentery. Typhoid came and went – only to be replaced by cholera. Within a matter of decades Bantam would be abandoned to the undergrowth and insects which to this day smother its unhappy ruins.

To men who had already spent nine months at sea it can have been little comfort to be told that their only hope of survival lay in again putting to sea as quickly as their business permitted. Yet Scot's account of life at Bantam left them no choice. He had been one of eight factors left behind by Lancaster. Now he was one of two. (The other survivor, Gabriel Towerson, must have been blessed with a constitution of concrete for he would outlast all his contemporaries only to succumb, twenty years later, to the cruellest cut of all.) Times had been hard in Bantam. The factory, a compound consisting of a timber warehouse with adjoining living quarters surrounded by a high palisade of stakes, had been in a state of siege for most of the two years, Scot's visit to the *Red Dragon* being only his second outing since the previous summer. 'My feare was so great', he explained, 'because I thought all would be burnt before I could come back againe.' Indeed there had been so many attempts to set the place on fire that he had become quite paranoid on the subject.

> Oh this worde fire! Had it been spoken in English, Malay, Javan or Chinese, although I had been sound asleep, yet I should have leapt out of my bedde, the which I had done sometimes when our men on watch had but whispered to one another of fire; insomuch that I was forced to warn them not to talke of fire in the night except they had great occasion.

Sometimes it was just the danger of those general conflagrations that raged in all the wood-built cities of the tropics whenever a dry wind blew. At other times it was more personal. In the dead of night a shower of flaming arrows would come arcing over the stockade or a gang of Javanese arsonists would rush the gate. Once some Chinese managed to tunnel under the fence, across the compound, and up under the floor of the warehouse. Here their attempt to burn a hole through the floorboards went disastrously wrong. There was an almighty blaze and although the thieves got away with nothing, precious bundles of calicoes were destroyed. The stench of burnt pepper hung about for days.

Hearing their story Middleton must have found it hard not to sympathize with the beleaguered Bantam factors. In the suffocating heat of their West Javan hell-hole they fought their fires and buried their dead, filled their ledgers and said their prayers, all with a clear conscience and three cheers for the Company. Yet they were no innocents abroad and, if one may judge by their penal code, their ideas of civilized conduct fell short of those of their Javanese hosts. In an otherwise beguiling narrative Scot cheerily announces the capture of the Chinese tunnellers. Instantly the Honourable Factors of the Worshipful Company turn demon torturers. Out come the pincers and the bone screws. The smell of burnt pepper gives way to that of burnt flesh. They collect white ants to tip over open wounds and at last despatch their victims with a brutality worthy of Tyburn. 'Now a worde or two concerning the Dutch shipping,' continues Scot's breezy narrative, 'and shortly after into fyre and troubles againe.'

At the root of these troubles lay the failure of the Javanese to distinguish between Dutchmen and Englishmen. The former, now organized into the United East Indian Company (V.O.C.) with Bantam as its eastern headquarters, were a formidable presence. Their fleets shuttling between the Moluccas and Europe regularly disgorged into the city unruly mobs of red-faced sex-starved sailors while their merchants became increasingly high-handed in their dealings with the local authorities. The Dutch were deservedly unpopular and this unpopularity rubbed off on to the English. Hence, thought Scot, the endless fires and raids.

But at this stage there could be no question of denouncing the Dutch. Their presence was actually some comfort to the English. 'Though we were mortal enemies in our trade', wrote Scot, 'yet in other matters we were friends and would have lived and died for one another.' In Europe the English had championed the cause of Dutch independence; there was no shame in Englishmen now accepting a measure of Dutch protection in the East. All that was needed was some way of showing the Javanese that there was a difference. A solution of dazzling simplicity was proposed by Gabriel Towerson. They would mount a parade. Mastering his 'fear of being counted fantasticall' Scot agreed and, as 17 November approached, 'the which we held to be our coronation day', the factors and their servants 'suited ourselves in new apparel of silk and made us all scarves of red and white taffeta (being our country's colours) and a flag with the redde cross through the middle'.

> Our day being come, we set up our banner of St George upon the top of our house and with drum and shot we marched up and down within our grounde; being but fourteen in number, we could march but single one after another, plying our shot and casting ourselves in rings and S's.

The commotion duly attracted a goodly audience to whom it was explained that they were celebrating their Queen's coronation ('for at that time we knew no other but that Queen Elizabeth was still lyving'). In the afternoon Scot took a calculated risk and dismissed his whole company with instructions to roam the town. 'Their redde and white scarves and hatbands made such a shew that the inhabitants of these parts had never seen the like.' And to every enquiry as to why 'the Englishmen at the other factory' were not also celebrating, it was emphatically pointed out that 'they were no Englishmen but Hollanders and that they had no king but the land was ruled by governors'.

> Ever after that day we were known from the Hollanders; and manie times the children in the streets would runne after us crying 'Oran Engrees bayck, Oran Hollanda jahad' which is 'The English are good, the Hollanders are nought'.

Vigilance was necessary but Scot and Towerson were no longer held responsible for the riotous conduct of every drunken Dutchman. They were free to sell their calicoes and, blissfully unaware of trends in the London market, to amass substantial stocks of pepper.

These stocks, and the need to withdraw from Bantam as quickly as possible, soon persuaded Middleton to ignore the Company's instructions once again. Within two months the *Hector* and the *Susan* were loaded with pepper and sent to England. Even this speedy turnaround proved too slow for most of the sick, the *Hector* losing its captain, its master and its master's mate not to mention 'common men'. Matters stood no better on the *Susan* and after recruiting local seamen both ships were still woefully undermanned. They left Bantam on 4 March 1605. What happened thereafter is unrecorded. We know only that the *Susan* with a crew of forty-seven was never seen again; and that of the *Hector*'s crew of fifty-three only fourteen reached the Cape, where they were discovered ineffectually trying to beach their ship to save her cargo.

Meanwhile Middleton, with the *Red Dragon* and the *Ascension*, was at last exploring the Moluccas. His first port of call was Ambon (Amboina), a well populated island off the coast of Ceram with some clove plantations and much to recommend it as the key to the Spice Islands. On the south shore of a deep inlet which nearly severs the island, the Portuguese had erected an impressive fortress whence troops could be dispatched north to the clove kingdoms of Ternate and Tidore or south to the nutmeg isles of Banda. But the Dutch were also aware of its importance and were already planning the replacement of this Portuguese garrison with one of their own. A large fleet had assembled at Bantam for precisely this purpose. To win time for Middleton, the breezy Scot arranged a send-off party at which the Dutch consumed so much 'likker' that they were sick for a week. Middleton therefore got there first. On 10 February he concluded an agreement with the Portuguese to load his ships with cloves but on 11 February five Dutch ships entered port and proceeded to pound the Portuguese into surrender. Not wishing to get involved, the English withdrew from Ambon. Thus, inauspiciously, the Company's direct involvement with the Spice Islands began at the very fort where – within a couple of decades – it was to end so catastrophically.

Anxious to stay ahead of the Dutch fleet the *Ascension* was now sent post-haste to the Bandas. There Captain Colthurst renewed contacts with the remote outposts of Run and Ai, and secured a good cargo of nutmegs. When the Dutch ships eventually anchored beneath the smoking mass of Gunung Api, relations were strained but not openly hostile. Indeed the two commanders dined amicably together; if they could share the same chicken pie they could surely share the nutmeg harvest.

Middleton in the *Red Dragon* was also successful up to a point. Sailing north for the twin volcanoes of Ternate and Tidore he unwittingly entered another war zone in which the Dutch were allied with the Sultan of Ternate against the Portuguese and the Sultan of Tidore. To Middleton, a choleric commander with no head for niceties, it was all Tweedledum and Tweedledee. Even supposing it had been self-evident which party it was politic to support he had neither the authority nor the ships to engage in hostilities. For what it was worth he did exploit the situation, accepting a load of cloves at Tidore and the promise of permission to settle a factory at Ternate. But once it was clear that he had no intention of lending either side his active support, he was no longer welcome.

With the English looking on, the Dutch at last stormed Tidore.

Middleton was permitted to negotiate the Portuguese surrender and then, on the suspicion that he had supplied the Portuguese with arms, was peremptorily ordered away. It was Dutch policy, he was informed, to allow no other nation to trade with their island subjects. Middleton left in a black rage. 'If this frothy nation [he meant the Dutch] may have the trade of the Indies to themselves (which is the thing they hope for) their pride and insolencie will be intollerable.' He headed back to Bantam, was there joined by the *Ascension*, and reached the Cape in time to save the *Hector* from being beached by her depleted crew. Together the three ships returned to England in May 1606.

To Middleton, who would prove anything but battle-shy, and to most of those Englishmen who followed him to the Moluccas, the Company's insistence on 'a quiet trafficke' would seem dangerously naive. The Portuguese had boasted of their *Estado da India*. From strongly fortified havens they had policed the sea lanes and overawed the coastlines. Now the Dutch, although less bothered with the sea lanes, were pursuing a no less ruthless policy of acquisition in respect of the spice-producing islands. As befitted an emergent nation sensitive about foreign rule, they gave their eastern adventures a gloss of international respectability by signing treaties of protection with the islanders. But the treaties were often exacted under duress and enforced by brutal reprisals against any dissenters. The forts supposedly built to protect the islands against the 'Portingall' were as often used to subdue the islanders. And any trade that the islanders held with other than the Dutch was regarded as treason.

By contrast the English Company would build no forts east of Sumatra and would rarely land any guns. It deployed no troops in the East Indies and its objectives there would remain purely commercial. Unlike the Portuguese, the English were not as yet conscious of fulfilling some Christian destiny and unlike the Dutch they were not proudly investing in their nation's future. However patriotically inclined, they served the Company not the King, and put profits – their own as well as the Company's – before power.

Every man in the Company's employ, whether factor or deckhand, expected a financial reward commensurate with the risks he faced; and since salaries were notoriously miserly, he devoted most of his energies to realizing it through private speculation. The Court of Committees took every possible precaution against this infringement by exacting a bond, often for as much as £500, from their factors and by taking great care in their initial selection. Applicants, besides being of blameless character, were expected to have some particular aptitude 'in navigation and calicoes' like Nathaniel Courthope, or 'in Merchant account and arithmetic' like John Clark. Others spoke Turkish, Portuguese, Arabic or some other relevant language. Many, and nearly all the more senior factors, had some previous experience of working overseas either with the Levant Company or the Merchant Adventurers. In such regulated companies individual merchants were often involved in the syndicate they served or at least received some form of commission from it. They expected to share in any corporate profits and the East India Company at first acknowledged this fact by remunerating their appointees with a small amount of stock in the voyage to which they were attached.

In 1609 this was replaced with a system of fixed salaries ranging from £5 to £200 per year. There were also allowances for outfit and for a small quantity of private trade goods. But neither the stick of censure nor the carrot of concessions made much difference. Entrusted with vast stocks, surrounded by tempting opportunities, and a world away from the day of reckoning, the Company's overseas factors followed their entrepreneurial instincts to the full. At the top of the scale a Bantam factor might become a very rich man indeed. Judging from the Company's records the squabbling in Bantam over the personal estates of those who succumbed to the climate was almost as bitter as the actions brought against those who returned home to enjoy their fortunes. Even the conscientious Scot would be involved in lengthy recriminations with his employers.

Yet the majority of the Company's shareholders subscribed to no loftier principles. Their expectations of a quick and handsome profit were tempered only by their acute anxiety to keep the expenses of eastern trade to a minimum. With each voyage representing a separate investment on which the profits were of interest only to its subscribers, there was little incentive for ensuring long-term profitability. And it was the same overseas where factors from different voyages would soon be openly competing for trade. Under these circumstances, to secure a loading of, say, cloves, while the Hollanders' back was turned was thought wonderfully clever. It was as good as Drake singeing the King of Spain's beard. The English positively relished their role of underdogs.

ii

'They had privie trade with the island people by night and by day were jovial and frolicke with the Spaniards', wrote the Reverend Samuel

Purchas, not without relish, of the next English vessel to visit the Moluccas. The ship, the *Consent*, at 150 tons little more than a pinnace, was even less capable of asserting an English presence than the *Red Dragon*. David Middleton, the third of the brothers and now commander of the *Consent*, was aware of the problem. In an unofficial capacity he had accompanied his brother Henry aboard the *Red Dragon* and had been back in England a mere nine months before being assigned to the Company's Third Voyage (1607). Nothing if not impatient he left ahead of the rest of the fleet and never in fact joined it. With a healthy crew and favourable winds he saw no reason to delay – which was just as well, the Third Voyage proving the slowest on record. By the time it reached the Moluccas the *Consent* would be back in England.

Putting into Table Bay and St Augustine's Bay (Madagascar) the youngest Middleton took just eight months from Tilbury to Bantam. There the indestructible Towerson had taken over as chief factor, Scot having returned with Henry Middleton. 'We found the merchants in verie good health and all things in order', noted David Middleton. Unlike his brother, he would invariably find things in order and he would make a point of leaving them so.

Continuing east he reached Tidore in early January 1608 and again found a pleasant surprise. The Portuguese had received assistance from their Spanish allies in the Philippines and had thus managed to evict the Dutch and their Ternate friends. Not that this made the English any more welcome. Again they were expected 'to do, or seeme to doe, some piece of service' – like sailing against the Dutch – 'which our Captain absolutely refused, being against his commission'. Trading rights were therefore withdrawn and hence that necessity for 'privie trade by night'. By the time they were ordered to sea the *Consent* had obtained perhaps half a loading of cloves.

She sailed south-west for one of Sulawesi's (Celebes) many tentacles and there established excellent relations with the rulers of Butung and Kabaena. These two islands, though densely forested, produced no spices. However, like Macassar on Sulawesi's next tentacle, they were of considerable importance as free ports and safe harbours in the native trade of the Archipelago. At Butung, or 'Button', where the king threw a series of memorable parties, Middleton found a Javanese vessel laden with cloves which her skipper readily sold to the English. Evidently such local craft stood a much better chance of sneaking spices past the Dutch than did an English vessel. Moreover, with Sulawesi dominated by

Malays and Bugis, the most formidable seafarers and warriors in the whole archipelago, there was no danger of the Dutch coming in hot pursuit. Here then was a weak spot at which the Dutch monopoly might be dented without inviting hostilities. Middleton resolved to return to Butung, and the Company would soon be posting a factor to Macassar.

On 2 May 1608, with a three-gun salute to the jolly king of 'Button', the *Consent*, now fully laden, sailed for Bantam and home. She reached England in six months, another notably fast voyage, and her cargo of cloves, purchased for less than £3000, sold for £36,000. Three months later, in command of the much larger *Expedition*, David Middleton was again sailing for Butung.

Off Bantam he narrowly missed making the acquaintance of Captain Keeling, commander of the Third Voyage. This was the dilatory fleet, now at last homeward bound, with which David Middleton was supposed to have sailed on the previous voyage. 'He passed us in the night,' reported Keeling who must by now have been having serious doubts about the chimerical Middleton, 'else we should surely have seene him.'

As usual Middleton was crowding on the sail. He spent just ten days at Bantam and by the New Year of 1610 was again bearing down on Butung. Its king had promised to lay in stocks of cloves, nutmegs and mace, and he had been as good as his word. But as he now explained amidst convulsions of grief, the whole lot had just been burnt along with his palace and 'sundry of his wives and women'. The jolly king was anything but jolly and was now committed to a war with one of his neighbours. There could be no guarantee of a cargo here; Middleton therefore determined to try his luck elsewhere.

From the Bandas the news was not good. Keeling had been there and had left word of his reception with the factors at Bantam who had duly informed Middleton. Evidently the Dutch were losing patience with both the Bandanese and the English. One of their fleets numbering no less than thirteen ships had anchored off Neira and proceeded to land troops, erect forts, and cajole the bemused Bandanese into signing away the bulk of their produce exclusively to the V.O.C. Keeling in high dudgeon had been forced to withdraw to the outermost islands of Ai and Run. 'Sixtie-two men against a thousand or more could not perform much', he explained. He had defiantly left representatives on Ai and Run, but basically the English were relegated to their usual role of spectators as the Dutch doggedly pursued their monopolistic ambitions.

On the whole Middleton preferred not to try the Bandas. But in the event he had no choice; the usual alternative of a foray to Tidore for cloves was precluded by adverse winds. He therefore resolved on one last bid to establish the Company's right to a share of the nutmeg market. Feigning that sublime confidence that was his hallmark, he approached the Dutch shipping at Neira 'with flagge and ensigne [flying] and at each yard arm a pennant in as comely a manner as we could devise'. The Dutch were unmoved. There was no trade here but for ships of the V.O.C. They rejected his argument that 'it were not good' for nations that were friends in Europe to be 'enemies among the heathen people', they refused his offer of a bribe, and they were unimpressed by a sight of his royal commission. More words were exchanged, 'some sharpe, some sweete' according to Middleton, yet all to no avail. He was ordered back to sea. Complying in all but spirit, he gave the fortress at Ambon a wide berth and set up base a day's sailing from the Bandas on the little-frequented island of Ceram.

For if the Dutch were anxious to see him off, the Bandanese were no less anxious to have him trade with them. In particular the outlying islands of Run and Ai were still resisting the 'frothy' Hollanders and saw the English as their natural allies. Middleton, 'knowing well that in troubled waters it is good fishing', set about frustrating the Dutch blockade by improvising a bizarre fleet to ply back and forth between the Bandas and the *Expedition* in her safe haven on Ceram. There was the *Hopewell*, his pinnace, which alone made nine trips, and the *Middleton*, a chartered junk which jauntily sailed amongst the Dutchmen. Then there was the *Diligence*, a resurrected barque which did her best, and finally a six-oared skiff which came to grief in a typhoon off the coast of Ceram.

Amongst the skiff's castaways was Middleton himself. Washed ashore, he managed to evade Ceram's supposed cannibals as he made his way back to base. He must have been almost there when, attempting to swim an alligator-infested river, he was swept out to sea and battered on the rocks 'till neere hand drowned'; for 'every suffe washed mee into the sea againe'. He was eventually hauled to safety clinging to a long pole. 'After resting a reasonable space', he declared himself fit 'to the amazement of all my company.'

Six months of such scrapes, and as many near disasters at the hands of the Dutch, found the *Expedition* crammed with spices and a sufficient surplus to fill the *Middleton* and another still larger junk. Leaving men on Ai to complete the lading of the latter, Middleton sailed for Bantam and home, reaching London in the summer of 1611. His two voyages, the Company's Third (which included Keeling's ships) and Fifth, were financed by the same subscribers. In effect, as with the First and Second Voyages, investors in the Third had been obliged to reinvest in the Fifth. But confidence in the trade, which had reached such a low ebb at the end of the Second Voyage that 'most of the members were inclined to wind up their affairs and drop the business', was now reviving. For whereas the combined profit on the first two voyages had come to 95 per cent, that on the Third and Fifth was put at 234 per cent.

What these figures represented in terms of an annual rate of return on investment is difficult to calculate. Each stock took many years to sort out, dividends – like subscriptions – being paid in instalments. Thus 95 per cent over as much as eight years represented no great improvement on standard rates of interest then prevailing. But 234 per cent over a similar period was a much more exciting prospect. The Third and Fifth voyages represent a turning point in the infant Company's fortunes. David Middleton had demonstrated that the high-value trade in nutmegs, mace and cloves was not yet lost to the Company; Keeling's fleet, as will be seen, had located a source of calicoes in India with which to pay for them; and thanks to better arrangements for re-export to European markets, even pepper was looking a more attractive prospect.

In the light of these encouraging developments, the Company secured in 1609 a new and more favourable charter from the King. Elizabeth's original grant had given the Company a guaranteed monopoly of Eastern trade for only fifteen years. The new grant made it indefinite. It also redefined the monopoly to exclude interlopers like Sir Edward Michelborne (who with Royal encouragement had ravaged Dutch trade while supposedly endeavouring to open markets in China) and even any shipping that should chance to reach the East 'indirectly', that is via the Pacific or one of the polar 'passages'. No less significantly, the new charter was seen as evidence of clear and unequivocal backing of the Company by His Majesty. His lead was followed by his government and court. Heading the list of subscribers under the new charter were the Lord Treasurer, the Lord High Admiral, and the Master of the King's Horse. Henceforth the Company's General Court would invariably include a large and influential group of courtiers and peers. Their interests might not always coincide with those of the committees (directors) but they endowed the Company's stock with greater respectability and they provided access and insight into the corridors of power.

iii

To secure some concession in the way of access to the spice-producing islands, and to win redress for past wrongs, the government now took up the Company's cause and entered into protracted negotiations with the Dutch States General. These negotiations would have some bearing on events in the East; but word of any agreement could take a year to reach the Moluccas and even then amity between the two governments was no guarantee of amity between the two Companies. All too often a dispatch from London would add only poignancy to the disasters that now unfolded.

In the Bandas Keeling and David Middleton had occasionally cleared their decks for action and had supposedly unmasked several Dutch plots to assassinate them. Whether or not their fears were justified there can be no doubting Middleton's assertion that the Hollanders, seeing his cockleshell fleet beating round the islands, 'grew starke madde'. 'The Dutch envy is so great towards us,' noted one of the Company's Bantam factors, 'that to take out one of our eyes they will lose both theire own.' While the English stood by, pretending neutrality but in fact encouraging local resistance, the V.O.C. was incurring enormous costs and losing good men – in 1610 their garrison in Neira had been almost annihilated in a Bandanese ambush. Methodical and determined, the Dutch bitterly resented both Michelborne's piracy and the Company's opportunism. They saw no reason why, because of services rendered in Europe under a previous sovereign and in the previous century, the English – 'a pernicious, haughty and incompatible nation' – should now presume on preferential treatment from a Dutch trading company on the other side of the world.

'The Hollanders say we go aboute to reape the fruits of their labours', wrote John Jourdain as he renewed the arguments of his English predecessors during a visit to Ambon and Ceram in 1613. 'It is rather the contrarye for that they seem to barre us of our libertie to trade in a free countrye, having manie times traded in these places, and nowe they seeke to defraud us of that we have so long sought for.' The young Dutch commander who had just intercepted him was unimpressed. With vastly superior forces at his command, Jan Pieterson Coen forbade Jourdain any trade and declared that every bag of cloves that found its way into an English hold was a bag stolen from the Dutch nation. Jourdain, 'a clever fellow' according to Coen, stood his ground and unexpectedly invoked the principle of self-determination. He summoned an assembly of the local headmen and, knowing full well their answer, asked them in the presence of the Dutch whether they would trade with him.

> To which wordes all the country people made a great shoute saying 'we are willing to deal with the English' [and] demanding the Hollanders what say they to itt. Whereunto they [the Dutch] were silent, answering neither yea nor naye.

Needless to say this impromptu referendum, conducted to the accompaniment of a pounding 'suffe' on some Ceramese promontory, did nothing to improve Jourdain's chance of securing a cargo. He was ordered to sea and could retaliate only with a muttered threat to settle matters 'when next we meete twixt Dover and Calais'. It also did nothing to endear him to Jan Pieterson Coen. As Governor-General of the Dutch East Indies, Coen was destined to become his lifelong adversary. They would meet again, but not 'twixt Dover and Calais'.

Calling at Butung, where Middleton had left a lone British factor who was now happily married to an island siren and reluctant ever to move (although truly grateful for a new supply of linen), and then at Macassar where he established a factory among 'the kindest people in all the Indies', Jourdain repaired to Bantam and the unenviable job of Chief Factor for the next four years. Towerson was gone (he was now commanding the *Hector* on her fifth and last voyage to the East) and there were more Englishmen in Bantam. But not much else was changed.

As he entered the oily waters of Bantam's sheltered anchorage Jourdain looked for a resounding welcome from the *Trades Increase* of the Sixth Voyage. At 1200 tons far and away the biggest ship in the Company's fleet, she had been launched with great ceremony by James I and was now on her maiden voyage with Sir Henry Middleton in command. It had not been a happy voyage. As will appear, the choleric Sir Henry had spent part of it in an Arab dog-kennel and, far from increasing trade, his flagship had seemingly hastened the demise of British commerce in India.

Spying her enormous bulk now lying off Bantam, Jourdain fired a salvo. There came no reply. Then 'we hailed them but could have no answer, neither could we perceive any man stirring'. The Company's flagship had in fact become a grounded and gutted hulk; her commander was dead, her crew decimated, and her hull was now serving as a hospice for the terminally sick. Instead of a rumbustious homecoming Jourdain was received by four factors, 'all of them like ghosts of men fraighted', who came aboard from a native *prahu*.

> I demanded for the General [Middleton] and all the rest of our friends in particular; but I could not name any man of note but was dead, to the number of 140 persons; and the rest remaining were all sick, these four being the strongest of them and they scarce able to go on their legges.

To malaria and dysentery were now added the perils of 'our people dangerously disordering themselves with drinke and whores ashoare'. But a worse disorder stemmed from the system of separate voyages, which meant that there were now three separate English factories in Bantam, each with its residue of competing, quarrelling and dying factors and each a prime target for the town's busy 'pickers, thievers and fire raisers'. In search of a peaceful solution Jourdain visited each establishment. At one he was greeted by a fevered factor 'who came running forth like a madman asking for the bilboes [shackles]' and at the next by another tottering invalid who tried to run him through with a sword. 'If he had been strong he might have slaine me.'

Just preserving some order among his own people taxed Jourdain's considerable abilities, never mind the Dutch threat. In 1614 no shipping at all could be spared for the Moluccas but in 1615 a vessel was sent to Ceram and a pinnace to the Bandas. Both fared badly, their crews being captured and briefly imprisoned by the Dutch. A factor was again left on the Banda island of Ai and he was still there a year later when a much larger British fleet meekly withdrew at the first threat of a Dutch attack.

By now there had been regular visits to Run and Ai for ten years, and for at least six years there had been a permanent British representative on the islands. It could be argued that two isolated spice gardens, together totalling little more than three square miles, were scarcely worth an armed confrontation between two of the world's strongest maritime nations. But that, according to Jourdain, was not the point. Principle was at stake. The Dutch based their claims on prior occupation and on the dubious treaties they had signed with the islanders. But in the case of Ai and Run the English could claim to have been first on the scene; and if documentary evidence were needed, it would be found.

In 1616 the Dutch prepared for another attack on Ai. On behalf of the Company, Captain Castleton agreed not to interfere so long as an English factor was allowed to continue on the island and so long as Run was recognized as being outside the Dutch sphere of monopoly. The Dutch commander agreed to these terms in writing. All that remained was to secure the consent of the Run islanders. It was not hard to come by. When the Dutch duly overran Ai, the headmen of both islands voluntarily and indeed eagerly pressed their little nutmeg seedling on Richard Hunt, the English factor. It was a token, he understood, that they formally made over their 'cattel and countrie for the use of the English nation'. In due course it was ratified in an impressive document declaring King James I 'by the grace of God, King of England, Scotland, Ireland, France, Puloway and Puloroon'. Henceforth the status of Run and Ai would involve more than commercial concessions and the rights of a trading company. The issue of national sovereignty was involved and the rights of the English Crown would have to be taken into account.

Escaping from Ai in the company of its loyal chiefs, Hunt made his way back to Bantam. There the outwitted Dutch showed what they thought of his treaty and his wilting nutmeg tree. Hunt was immediately waylaid in the street by a mob of Hollanders, beaten up, 'halled through the durte by the haire of the head', and clamped in irons 'in the hotte sun without hatt'. Jourdain retaliated by seizing a Dutch merchant and giving him the same treatment. Although the prisoners were eventually exchanged, English and Dutch now fought openly in the city's lanes and Jourdain determined to strike back in the Bandas.

iv

In October 1616 Nathaniel Courthope, who had previously served in one of the Company's speculative agencies on the Borneo coast, was despatched to the Bandas with the *Swan* and the *Defence*, both of 400 tons. His instructions were simple: occupy the island of Run and hold it – indefinitely. After purchasing such provisions as Macassar had to offer, he arrived on 23 December. The islanders again proclaimed their loyalty to King James while Courthope's men 'spread St. George upon the island and shot off most of our ordnance'. Christmas Day brought the first snooping Dutch vessel. Courthope hastily landed guns to command the only anchorage and thus began his long, anxious and soon forgotten resistance.

A variety of exotic fruits grew on Run but most of its 700 acres were down to nutmeg trees. Rice had to be imported, and to drink there was only such rain water as could be collected. The ships were therefore essential for any long-term defence; yet the ships were the first to go. In

January the master of the *Swan*, 'obstinately contrarying' Courthope's orders, took his vessel over to the largest of the Banda islands in search of fresh water. He was promptly captured. Five of his men were killed and the rest were clamped in irons and stowed aboard Dutch vessels. Two months later the *Defence* broke – or was cut – from her moorings and also came into Dutch possession. Using these ships and their crews as bargaining counters the Dutch commander opened negotiations; if Courthope would relinquish Run he would return both prizes and prisoners. Many of the prisoners also wrote urging compliance. They were being wretchedly treated and, worse still for men on the make, they had been robbed of all they possessed. 'If I lose any more by your [Courthope's] arrogance', wrote the master of the *Swan* from his captivity, 'our lives and blouds shall rest upon your head.'

Courthope refused to budge. He would not withdraw because to do so would be an act of treason to his king and a betrayal of the good people of Run. Instead he dispatched a *prahu* to Bantam urgently requesting assistance. It would be the first of many such pleas to go unanswered. Though Dutch ships repeatedly tested his defences, the year 1617 wore away with no sign of relief.

On 12 March 1618 the islands were shaken by a major earthquake. This triggered the volcano of Gunung Api, which for some years had been ominously grumbling as if to protest at the European presence. It erupted with unprecedented fury, showering the Dutch forts on neighbouring Neira with scorching debris. Two weeks later Courthope spied 'two of our ships coming from the westwards with the last of the westerly winds'. Excitement mounted. The guns were primed for a mighty welcome and the English lined the rocks. But the first shot came not from the approaching ships but from the east. Four Dutch vessels, beating into the wind, were manoeuvring to cut off the English fleet. Their range was greater, the English ships lying low in the water under the weight of their provisions for the besieged. As the sun went down the issue was still unresolved. But then the wind changed. The Dutchmen's sails filled and they bore down on the English. By eight o'clock it was all over; next day saw the Dutch ships trailing the English colours from their sterns as they escorted their prizes to the fort of Neira.

Courthope believed that had the relief force arrived even a day earlier all would have been well. The winds were seasonal, blowing hard from the west from December till March and from the east from March onwards. The master of one of the captured vessels agreed. 'For what cannot now be' he blamed the factors in Bantam where Jourdain's departure for England had heralded more quarrelling and indecision. They had 'so carelessly kept these ships there so long, unto the 8th of Januarie last, before they sent them away from thence which hath brought upon us all this miserie'.

Shackled and incarcerated in the Dutch fort the new prisoners were indeed in some misery. According to the deposition of one of them 'they kept twelve of us in a dungeon where they pisst and shatt upon our heads and in this manner we lay until we were broken out from top to toe like lepers, having nothing to eate but durtie rice and stinking raine water'. 'But God will provide for his servants', declared Kellum Throgmorton, another prisoner, 'though He give these Horse-turds leave to domineere a while.'

To Courthope it now seemed certain that the Horse-turds must descend on Run any minute.

> I have but thirtie-eight men to withstand their force and tyranny, our wants extreame: Neither have we victuals nor drinke but only rice and water. They have at present here eight ships and two gallies, and to my knowledge all fitted to come against us. I look daily and howerly for them.

In fact a Dutch attack would be positively welcome. 'I wish it', he wrote, 'being not so much able to stand out as willing to make them pay deare.' In eighteen months he had received not a word from his superiors in Bantam. He could only assume his original orders still stood and in April 1618 sent two more desperate appeals, advising of the capture of the relief fleet and begging for provisions and reinforcements.

Forwarded via Butung and Macassar these letters reached Bantam in the late summer. Soon after, Jourdain returned to Bantam for a second term as Chief Factor and found himself in the happy position of having more ships in the Java Sea than the Dutch. It was a God-given opportunity to hit back once again. In December the richly-laden *Zwaarte Leeuw* was captured off Bantam. Coen retaliated by setting fire to a new English factory in Jakarta. Provocation had at last become war. In a full-blooded battle off Jakarta both fleets proclaimed victory but neither followed it up. Coen retired – or 'fled' – to refit at Ambon and, after an inconclusive siege of Jakarta, the British, instead of heading for the Bandas, repaired – or 'retreated' – to the east coast of India.

With the easterly winds of April Coen returned to the fray. Off the

Malay peninsula his ships surprised two English vessels. Both were worsted and in the course of the surrender negotiations the English commander was killed by a single shot from a Dutch marksman. Such a flagrant disregard of a flag of truce was a serious matter, but in this case the culprit, far from being punished, would be rewarded. For the man he had shot was John Jourdain.

Jourdain died in July 1619. From then on the English position rapidly worsened. In August the *Star* was captured in the Straits of Sunda and in October the *Red Dragon*, the *Bear*, the *Expedition* and the *Rose* were surprised while loading pepper at the Sumatran port of Tecu. When finally the main fleet arrived back from India in March 1620 it was intercepted by the news that in Europe the Anglo-Dutch negotiations had at last been concluded and that far from being enemies the two Companies were now allies. In fact the agreement had been signed in July 1619. The English losses had all occurred after the hostilities were officially over. This was neither consolation nor compensation; the agreement would soon prove to be unworkable and the losses irreparable.

And what of Courthope and his hard-pressed band on Run? They had not been entirely forgotten. In June 1618 they had repulsed a Dutch attack and in January 1619 they had welcomed a small pinnace sent from Bantam with instructions to 'proceed in your resolution' and a promise that the whole English fleet would soon be coming to their rescue. In the event, of course, the fleet withdrew to India. Another year, Courthope's third on Run, slipped slowly by. The activities of Jourdain and the English fleet did have the effect of diverting Dutch attention and for once he was able to raise his head above Run's makeshift parapets. Encouragement was sent – and support promised – to pockets of Bandanese resistance on the other islands and in return came provisions and protestations of loyalty to the English crown. 'Had the English ships come as promised I verilie thinke there would not at the end of this monsoon have beene left one Hollander enemie to us.' But the ships did not come and although basic provisions were now reaching him, he had no money to pay for them. Even the islanders 'had spent their gold and estates, beggaring themselves . . . in expectation of the English forces'. 'We have rubbed off the skinne alreadie', reported Courthope, 'and if we rub any longer, we shall rub to the bone. I pray you looke to it etc.'

By now he must have known every nutmeg tree on the island. In June, three and a half years after he had begun his heroic resistance, he wrote again to Bantam demanding, in the name of all that Englishmen held dear, some means of redeeming his pledges to the Bandanese. 'Except some such course be taken', he advised, 'you shall see me before you heare any further from me.' Needless to say, no word of the peace, signed eighteen months before, had yet reached him. No word ever would.

On 20 October 1620, for reasons that remain obscure, he broke cover for the first time and rowed over to the neighbouring island of Lonthor. On the way back his *prahu* with twenty-one men aboard was surprised by two Dutch vessels. 'Not so much able to stand out as willing to make them pay deare', the English fought back and Courthope was shot in the chest. He had always maintained that English commanders were too faint-hearted and had criticized the manner in which ships were surrendered while yet afloat and amply crewed. War was war, declared or not, and three and a half years had done nothing to alter his views. True to form, he therefore refused to surrender, preferring to roll overboard and swim for it. 'What became of him I know not', wrote Robert Hayes, his second in command. In fact the Dutch recovered his body and 'buried him so stately and honestly as ever we could'; it was, they said, 'only fitting for such a man'.

Thus ended the protracted defiance of Nathaniel Courthope. Here surely was another episode to savour, another saga of truly heroic proportions. Yet Courthope's is not a name to conjure with; Run features on no roll of honour; and the English affair with the Banda Islands was speedily forgotten. For, conducted with spirit, it ended with ignominy. Two months after Courthope's death Hayes intercepted letters to the Dutch containing news of the peace treaty. He could hardly bring himself to tell the islanders and when he did so they rightly saw it as a betrayal. By the summer of 1621 Dutch troops were swarming all over Run and the Bandanese were either fleeing for their lives or being systematically deported. Later critics would call it genocide. The Dutch claimed they were acting in the interests of both Companies. This did not prevent them from treating their English allies with hostility and even brutality. The latter complained, protested, denounced, but could do nothing. As so often before, they had neither the authority nor the ships to interfere.

v

On the face of it the Anglo-Dutch agreement of 1619 had given the English all they wanted. With at last a guaranteed share of the spice trade they quickly established factories at Ambon, Ternate, and Banda Neira, and they removed their headquarters from Bantam to Batavia (Jakarta). Officially, though, the agreement was a 'Treaty of Defence' which bound both signatories to contributing ships, men and money to the defence of the Indies. Military expenditure had never appealed to the London Company and it was highly suspicious of this clause. It had in fact only signed the treaty under pressure from the government. To the Dutch, however, this commitment on defence was the treaty's saving grace. As they cheerfully mounted a series of expensive campaigns, like that against the Bandanese, they put the English in the embarrassing position of being party to objectionable policies which they could neither moderate nor afford. And when English ships and cash failed to materialize, the Dutch had every reason to make life and business for the English factors more difficult than ever.

Surveying the position at the end of 1622 the Chief Factor – or President as he then was – at Batavia decided that enough was enough. In January he discussed the dissolution of all the new factories with Coen and by 9 February the order had evidently gone out. Sadly it was once again too late to avert a tragic postscript to the English involvement in the spice trade.

On that same night, while pacing the low parapets of the gloomy Dutch fort at Ambon, a Japanese mercenary in Dutch employ fell into conversation with a Hollander on guard duty. 'Amongst other talke', the Japanese asked the Dutchman some pertinent questions about the disposition of the fort's defences. He was promptly arrested and under torture confessed that he and several other Japanese had been planning a mutiny. Tortured again he implicated the English.

In charge of the English factory on Ambon was none other than Gabriel Towerson who twenty-two years earlier had sailed with Lancaster and been left at Bantam with Scot. Under him were about fourteen other Englishmen – factors, servants, a tailor and a surgeon-cum-barber. On 15 February all were invited to the fort and, suspecting nothing, all attended. They were immediately arrested and imprisoned, some being held in the fort's dungeons, others aboard ships riding nearby. Next day, and for the whole of the following week, each in turn was tortured.

Remembering how Towerson himself had treated the arsonists at Bantam, the ordeals that he and his men now underwent at the hands of the Dutch fiscal (judge) were not perhaps exceptional. It was indeed a brutal age. On the other hand the subsequent outrage in England, and the embarrassment in Holland, belie the idea that what happened at Ambon was acceptable. Typically the prisoner was spread-eagled on a vertical rack that was in fact a door frame. A cylindrical sleeve of material was then slipped over his head and tightly secured at the neck with a tourniquet.

> That done, they poured the water softly upon his head untill the cloth was full up to the mouth and nostrils and somewhat higher; so that he could not draw breath but must withal suck in the water; which still being poured in softly, forced all his inward partes [and] came out of his nose, eares and eyes; and often as it were stifling him, at length took his breath away and brought him to a swoone or fainting.

The prisoner was then freed and encouraged to vomit. Then the treatment began again. After thus being topped up three or four times 'his body was swollen twice or thrice as big as before, his cheeks like great bladders, and his eyes staring and strutting out beyond his forehead'.

Some got off lightly. As soon as they confessed to whatever role in the plot they were supposed to have played, and as soon as they had implicated Towerson and the other factors, they were returned to their cells. Others proved extremely hard to break. Clark, one of the factors, survived four water sessions and then was subjected to lighted candles being played on the soles of his feet 'untill the fat dropt and put out the candles'. He still refused to co-operate. The candles were relit and applied to his armpits 'until his innards might evidently be seene'. 'Thus wearied and overcome by torment', he confessed.

So eventually did they all with the possible exception of Towerson whose fate was unknown. He was, however, alive for at the end of the week he was brought forth to hear his men denounce him. Confronted by their commander, 'that honest and godly man', according to one of them, 'who harboured no ill will to anyone, much lesse attempt any such business as this', most retracted. 'They fell upon their knees before him praying for God's sake to forgive them.'

On 25 February they were sentenced; ten were to die; so were nine Japanese and one Portuguese. They were returned to their cells to settle their affairs and say their prayers. In signing (or 'firming') a payment release for some small consignment of piece goods, Towerson wrote his last words.

Firmed by the firme of mee, Gabriel Towerson, now appointed to dye, guiltless of anything that can be laid to my charge. God forgive them their guilt and receive me to his mercy, Amen.

Others scribbled on the fly-leaves of their prayer books. 'Having no better meanes to make my innocence knowne, I have writ this in this book, hoping some good Englishman will see it.' 'As I mean, and hope, to have pardon for my sins, I knowe no more than the child unborn of this business.' 'I was born in Newcastle-upon-Tyne, where I desire this book may come that my friends may knowe of my innocency.' With the merchant's instinct to turn every situation to some profit, one of the factors shouted as they were led off to execution, 'If I be guilty, let me never partake of thye heavenly joyes, O Lord'. 'Amen for me', cried each in turn, 'amen for me, good Lord.' Assuredly no crime had been committed by the condemned. They died like martyrs and indeed the account of their sufferings reads much like a piece of Tudor martyrology. It was another massacre of innocents, and hence, ever after, it would be remembered and glorified as 'The Amboina Massacre'.

The job of winding up the factory's affairs fell to Richard Welden who for more than a decade had been the lone factor left on Butung by David Middleton. Transferred to the Bandas, where he had also had to pick up the pieces, he now shrugged off Dutch attempts to implicate him and sailed over to Ambon to collect the survivors and enquire into the circumstances. Thence he proceeded to Batavia, where complaints were duly lodged and duly rejected, and then on to England.

He arrived in the summer of 1624. Word of the massacre had preceded him via Holland but now 'this crying business of Amboina' provoked a major furore. Some wanted to take the next Dutch ship that entered the English Channel and see the culprits 'hung up upon the cliffs of Dover'. Protests were lodged in Holland. Reluctantly James I agreed to reprisals. But nothing was actually done and in 1625 a Dutch fleet from the East was allowed to sail quietly past Dover in full view of the Royal Navy. This was too much for the East India Company. Suspecting the then Governor, Sir Morris Abbot, of being too easily duped by royal promises, subscribers withheld their payments and pressured the directors into announcing that due to Government inaction they must finally 'give over the trade of the Indies'.

In reality they had already done so. Closure of the factories in the Spice Islands and a withdrawal from Batavia – temporary but soon to be permanent – signalled a long hiatus in English ambitions to participate in the spice trade. At Macassar a small English establishment buying cloves from native *prahus* would survive until 1667; and Bantam would linger on until the 1680s as a source of pepper. But perhaps the disillusionment of the English is best seen in the unlikely outcome of diplomatic wrangles over the status of Run. For, frequently revived, English claims to the islet were actually recognized after Cromwell's Dutch War and in 1665 the place was officially handed over. Vindication at last. A fort and colony were planned and several ships revisited the island. Yet never, it would appear, was it actually reoccupied. Depopulated and denuded of its nutmeg trees, it may well have been worthless.

To the likes of Nathaniel Courthope, turning in his sandy grave on a neighbouring atoll, the neglect of Pulo Run must have seemed like a terrible betrayal. Yet, after a lapse of forty years, his refusal to concede to the Dutch yielded that substantial dividend on the other side of the world at the mouth of the Hudson river. Just as improbably, more than 150 years later, servants of the same Honourable Company that Courthope had served so devotedly would revive his hopes of the spice trade and again load nutmegs at the Bandas and pace the parapets of Ambon's unhappy fort.

CHAPTER THREE

Pleasant and Fruitfull Lands

JAPAN, SIAM, AND THE COAST

History is not short of reasons why the East India Company was founded. Some have already been noticed: the expected profits from the spice trade, the growth of English sea power in the Armada period, the about-turn in Anglo-Portuguese relations following the dynastic union of Spain and Portugal, and the encouragement afforded by the first Dutch voyages to the East. Another and an older reason of which much was made in contemporary debate was the need to find new markets for England's staple export of woollen cloth. Ever since the 1570s and the sack of Antwerp, the traditional entrepôt for English cloth, the search for new markets and new distributive systems had been a national priority. The Muscovy (Russia), Eastland (Baltic), and Levant Companies were all export-orientated and the various attempts to find a north-west passage were partly inspired by expectations of discovering potential buyers for English woollens shivering somewhere in the northern hemisphere.

The East India Company, it is true, was different. Right from the start its directors insisted on their ships carrying more bullion than broadcloth. They had no illusions about clothing the spice islanders in tweed; the Company was determinedly import-orientated and much criticized for it. But to counter this criticism, to assuage national expectations about woollen exports, and to find some alternative to bullion as a purchasing agent, the directors urged early diversification of the Company's trading activities. Factors were encouraged to report on the patterns of existing trade in the East and, in the case of Bantam, they quickly discovered the south-east Asian archipelago's insatiable demand for both Indian cottons and Chinese silks. In a perfect world, of course, the Indians and the Chinese would have been crying out for tweeds and thus a triangular trade, boosting English exports and involving no transfer of bullion, would have been established.

Unfortunately no such simple solution would emerge; but between 1607 and 1611 departing fleets were instructed to conduct commercial reconnaissances in the Indian Ocean *en route* to Bantam and indeed in the South China Sea beyond Bantam. These remarkable voyages would have far-reaching consequences. They gave the Company a multi-national complexion which would never fade. And they provided an alternative direction for the Company's activities once expectations of the spice trade dimmed.

Given the desirability of starting any trade cycle with an outgoing fleet laden with broadcloth, those countries with a cooler climate were of particular interest. Judging by Dutch experience, China was exceedingly difficult to penetrate but in 1608 John Saris (or sometimes 'Sayers'), serving as a factor under Towerson at Bantam, submitted a report on all those eastern lands with which the Dutch were trading and singled out as especially promising the islands of Japan. There and there alone he foresaw substantial sales for 'broad-cloathes' and he put them at the top of his list of 'requestable commodities'.

This information was soon after confirmed from a most unlikely source, namely an Englishman who was already resident in Japan; indeed he had been there since 1600. William Adams had apparently sailed through the Straits of Magellan as pilot of a Dutch fleet and had eventually come ashore, one of only six men on his ship still able to walk, on the island of Kyushu. The ship had been confiscated but Adams had since done extremely well for himself. He was now in high favour with the Shogun as a marine architect and had been handsomely rewarded with a salary and an estate. He had also acquired a Japanese wife and family. But he had not forgotten his home in Rochester in Kent, nor his English wife to whom he somehow managed to write, nor his countrymen. He was at their service, and his story seemed to confirm that in Japan not only was woollen cloth in demand but also that 'there is here much silver and gold [which would] serve their turnes in other places where need requireth in the East Indies'. The Dutch, he said, already recognized Japan as 'an Indies of money', so much so that 'they need not now bring silver out of Holland'.

Such news was music to English ears. Broadcloth to Japan, Japanese silver to Java and the Spice Islands, and pepper and spices back to England – it was the perfect trading cycle. In 1611 John Saris, just back from his first five years in the East, was given command of a new fleet (the Company's Eighth Voyage) and instructed, after numerous other commissions, to take the *Clove* and proceed from Bantam 'with all possible speede for Japan'. There he was to consult with Adams, assess the commercial climate and, if favourable, establish an English factory.

The first part of his voyage, a veritable Odyssey if ever there was one, will be noticed later. By the time he left Bantam for Japan in January 1613 he had sailed right round the Indian Ocean and had been at sea for most of the past twenty-one months. He had also earned for himself the reputation of an able but harsh commander whose men had more than once been on the point of mutiny. Specifically they had complained of their rations, which were more inadequate and monotonous than usual and which Saris refused to supplement with those local delicacies that more considerate commanders made a point of procuring. Aware that such complaints would reach the ears of his employers, he now adopted the unusual practice of filling his journal with catering details. 'Two meales rice and honey, sack and biskett', '1 meale beefe and dumplings, 1 meale wheate'; it was hardly mouth-watering. But as the *Clove* sailed east for the Moluccas and then north into unknown seas, only the weather and the menu afforded his diary any variety at all.

For a chart he used the book of maps and sailing directions prepared by the Dutch cartographer, Jan Huyghen van Linschoten. During five years as secretary to the Archbishop of Goa (the Portuguese headquarters in India) van Linschoten had quietly compiled a dossier on the eastern sea routes which he then smuggled back to Europe, an achievement which may constitute the most momentous piece of commercial and maritime espionage ever. Published in Holland in 1595–6, Linschoten's works were the inspiration for the first Dutch voyages to the East and, translated into English in 1598, they played no small part in the East India Company's designs on the spice trade. The book of maps was required reading for every Dutch and English navigator, and Saris for one found it invaluable and 'verie true'.

On 3 June, seven long weeks after leaving the Moluccas, the *Clove* came within sight of an island which Saris identified as part of Linschoten's 'Dos Reys Magos'. It may well have been Okinawa and to men who had now spent over two years sailing half way round the world in a ship not much bigger than a railway carriage this first glimpse of Japanese soil and journey's end was not without excitement. 'It seemed', as well it might, 'a most pleasant and fruitfull lande as anye we have seene since we came out of England', wrote Saris. A sudden squall prevented their landing but other islands took its place and a week later they learned from a fishing fleet that they were off Nagasaki. The Portugese had trading rights at Nagasaki and had long since converted many of its people to Catholicism. As yet the English preferred the company of co-religionists, so the *Clove* made for Hirado, an island just off the west coast of Kyushu where the Dutch had established themselves four years earlier.

Unlike in the Spice Islands, in Japan there was of course no question of Europeans dictating their own terms. Here foreigners prospered or languished at the Shogun's pleasure; they came as petitioners and they stayed on sufferance. A martial and self-sufficient state, Japan was ruled by warlords who tolerated Europeans only so long as they were an irrelevance. Hirado buzzed with rumours of distant campaigns and sacked cities while the Europeans doled out presents and paraded their wares in an atmosphere of friendship tinged with menace. Saris and his seventy-odd followers were in for a number of surprises.

As the *Clove* dropped anchor some forty boats 'some with tenne, some with fifteen oars a side' raced forth to meet them. From one the 'king' (governor) of Hirado and his grandson came aboard. They were dressed in silk with long swords by their sides and 'the forepartes of their heads were shaven to the crowne, and the rest of their hair, which was very long, was gathered together and bound up in a knot behind'. The 'king' was about seventy. Both seemed friendly and saluted Saris 'after their manner which is this':

> First . . . they put off their shoes (stockings they weare none), and then clapping their right hand with their left, they put them downe towards their knees, and so wagging or moving of their hands a little to and fro, they stooping steppe with small steps sidcling from the party saluted, and crie 'Augh, Augh'.

Sadly Saris fails to mention whether he returned this salute. 'I led them into my cabbin where I had prepared a banquet for them and a good consorte of musicke.' Saris was fond of music and had managed to purloin a viol, flute and tabor from the *Trades Increase*, Henry Middleton's ill-starred flagship that was now rotting at Bantam. Being 'much delighted' with the madrigals, the 'king' next day returned the compliment, coming aboard with four female musicians. Although 'somewhat bashfull' they soon recognized Saris as a connoisseur and 'became frolicke'. 'They were well faced, headed and footed, clear skinned and white but wanting colour which they amended by arte.' Their hair was long and tied up 'in a comely fashion' and he could not but notice that beneath gowns of silk their legs were bare.

Between these official exchanges the ship became overrun with such a multitude of visitors that it was impossible to move on deck. All, 'boath men and women', had produce to sell and services to offer. It was the sort of landfall sailors dreamt of and soon the entire crew would be absconding ashore. Not that Saris himself was setting much of an example. Singling out 'divers of the better sort of women' he enticed them into his cabin 'where a picture of Venus hung, most lasciviously sett out'. Pin-ups and pornography were destined to cause him some embarrassment, but in this instance they were simply misunderstood. For 'with showes of great devotion' the ladies 'fell down and worshipped the picture [mistaking it] for Our Ladye . . . whereby we perceaved them to be of the Portingall-made papists'.

Tainting pleasure with business, Saris wrote to summon Adams, rented a house and store-room, and began to unload his cargo. Trade was far from brisk. His journal for the period, while less exercised over the catering, is taken up with a succession of disciplinary actions. The gunner's mate, one Christopher Evans, was the worst offender, habitually staying ashore without leave and refusing to come even when summoned. 'In most lewd fashion' he persisted in 'spending his time in most base bawdy places.'

> For which cause I gave order to sett him in the bilbowes [stocks] where, before the boatswain and most of the company, he did most deepelye swear to be the destruction of Jack Saris, for so it pleased him to call me.

Fearing Evans quite capable of breaking loose and making good his threat, Saris ordered a double guard. He still broke loose and when, a month later, he was dragged reluctantly from a Hirado whorehouse, he had to be chained to the masthead, 'the bilbowes by one of his crew having been throwne overboard'. Other commanders might have sentenced him to the lash or the near fatal ordeal of being dragged underneath the ship's keel. Perhaps Saris, usually far from lenient, had a sneaking admiration for the incorrigible Evans whose best defence had been 'to stand boldly in it that he was a man and would have a woman if he could get her'.

On 29 July the long-awaited Adams at last made his appearance. Saris ordered a nine-gun salute and 'received him in the best manner I could for his better grace'. But Adams seemed not to notice. He was more inscrutable than the Japanese. He evinced no discernible pleasure at meeting some of his long lost countrymen, and when quizzed about trading prospects, became infuriatingly vague. 'He said it [trade] was not always alike, but sometimes better and sometimes worse, yet doubted not that we should doe as well as others and saying he would doe his best.' He then talked, with some enthusiasm, about the delights of Japan and prepared to take his leave. This was not at all what Saris had in mind. Rooms in the house were ready for him and Mr Cocks, Saris's senior merchant, was looking forward to showing him round the town. 'Praying him to remember that I was alone and that I should be glad to enjoy his most acceptable company which I had long expected', Saris prevailed on him to stay for dinner. But there was no moving him in the matter of accommodation. He had hoisted his colours – 'a St George made of coarse cloth' – over a run-down house on the other side of town and there he would stay, refusing entry to his fellow countrymen and not even permitting them to walk home with him, 'which unto us was very strange'. The men of the *Clove*, 'thinking that he thought them not good enoffe to walk with him', concluded that Adams was already 'a naturalised Japanner'.

Dealing with such a man was never going to be easy; but in fairness to Adams it may be noted that he had far more to lose than Saris and could ill afford to identify himself too closely with the truculent crew of the *Clove*. As an intermediary and patron he would prove as good as his word and, two weeks later, he was ready to accompany Saris on the long journey to Yedo (Tokyo) where presents and a letter from King James must be delivered as a preliminary to any grant of trading privileges.

The first leg of this journey was from Hirado off the island of Kyushu to Osaka on that of Honshu. They passed a mammoth junk, 'much like Noah's ark', of 1000 tons (the *Clove* was a mere 500) and found both Fukuoka and Osaka 'as bigge as London is within the walls'. The latter boasted 'a marvellous large and strong castle' with walls seven yards thick and bristling with drawbridges. Thence they continued overland, riding in palanquins with a pike-bearer jogging in front to clear the way. Shizuoka (Sampu) was even larger than Osaka, 'as bigge as London with all the suburbs', and Yedo larger still and of dazzling magnificence with its gilded roofs and lintels. The whole country was an eye-opener and

Saris marvelled unreservedly at the roads, the people, the towns and the temples. (James I would not be impressed; on reading one of Saris's letters he pronounced its observations 'the loudest lies I have ever seene'.)

By contrast the audiences with Iyeyasu and his son, the latter the Shogun but the former still the power in the land, were somewhat disappointing. The gilt basin and ewer, standard centrepieces in any Company presentation to an Eastern potentate, were received without comment; so were the assorted lengths of finest cambric, lawn, and kersey, and the ornate looking-glass. Evidently the Japanese regarded such things as nothing wonderful; they accepted them out of a sense of obligation. But trading rights were granted and Saris returned towards Hirado well pleased. He even signified his gratitude to Adams by sending presents to Mrs Adams and the children.

It was November (1613) by the time the Yedo party put into Hirado and right glad was Richard Cocks, Saris's second in command, to see them. 'The honest Mr Cocks', as Saris always called him, was an elderly and endearing figure already much attached to his vegetable garden and his pigeons. He was not cut out for authority and had made heavy weather of his stewardship. A Hirado brothel owner had threatened to kill him if he came calling for his men again, and Cocks had twice had to make official apologies for their drunken assaults on the townsfolk. Finally indiscipline had become mutiny when seven men, the womanizing Evans amongst them, had made off with one of the *Clove*'s boats; they were now said to be living it up with the 'Portingalls' in Nagasaki. Additionally a typhoon had demolished part of the English factory, several fires had almost consumed it, and trade was at a standstill. Even news of the privileges granted by the Shogun was making little difference. The Dutch had evidently resolved to dispose of their new rivals by undercutting them, and in effect, dumping on to the Japanese market all the woollens they could obtain.

That, at least, was the official reason. Saris, though, thought there might be another.

> The natives were now more backward to buy than before because they saw that we ourselves were no forwarder in wearing the thing which we recommended to them. 'For', said they, 'you commend your cloth unto us but you yourselves wear least thereof, the better sort of you wearing silken garments, the meaner fustians'. Wherefore I wish our nation would be more forward to use and spend this

> natural commoditye of our own countrey; so shal we better encourage and allure others to the entertainment and expence thereof.

It would seem that this advice was ignored. The market for broadcloth remained sluggish and of that famous Japanese silver little found its way into the *Clove*'s coffers. There were, however, other reasons for the factory which Saris devoted his last few weeks to setting up. Adams still maintained that cloth would sell, if not in Kyushu and Honshu then certainly in Hokkaido, the northernmost of the islands. He also urged that from there there was a real prospect of discovering the western end of the north-west passage (i.e. in the vicinity of the Bering Strait). In this view he no doubt received some encouragement from the youngest of the Hirado factors, Richard Hudson, whose father, Henry, had perished in the search for the eastern end. To assist in this and other projected ventures, Adams was taken into the employ of the Company as second in command to 'the honest Mr Cocks' as Chief Factor.

For their part, Cocks and Saris pinned their hopes on the China trade. Disappointingly the Shogun had specifically refused their request to land any goods taken from Chinese junks by force. But Chinese silks and satins were in great demand and there were other ways of obtaining them. Hirado, facing the Chinese mainland, was ideally sited for contacts with China and Cocks would soon be engaged in delicate and protracted negotiations for direct access to this forbidden market. Yet another possibility was that of trading with the fleets of Chinese junks which annually coasted the South China Sea to Siam (Thailand) via Cochin China (south Vietnam) and Cambodia. In 1614 Adams was dispatched to Siam to intercept this Chinese trade and buy local dyes and leathers; and in the same year two other Hirado factors would be sent to Cochin China. What made the first of these ventures especially attractive was the news that two English factories had just been established in Siam.

But the future of Far Eastern trade would be of no concern to Saris himself. To take advantage of the winds the *Clove* sailed from Hirado on 5 December (1613) leaving Cocks and Adams to handle affairs in Japan. After some bitterness with Jourdain at Bantam over a loading of pepper, Saris continued homewards and reached Plymouth in September 1614. There, for several weeks, the *Clove* stayed, much to the fury of the Company's directors who assumed that any ship which put into a Channel port must be up to no good. The interception of a letter from Saris to his brother bidding him to meet him off Gravesend with a barge added substance to these suspicions; for 'they gave the Company great cause to suspect that Capn Saris had used very great trade for himself and proposed to convey away his goods out of the ship'. To the inevitable hue and cry that followed over Saris's private trade were added the wrath of his crew's womenfolk for that meanness over the rations and the indignation of all right-minded shareholders when tipped off about his 'lascivious bookes and pictures'. Soon after his arrival in London a bonfire was lit in the courtyard of Sir Thomas Smythe's house and, with a crowd of indignant shareholders acting as official witnesses, Saris's entire collection of pictures and books was dumped in the flames 'where they continewed till they burnt and turned to ashes'. The row over his personal trade lasted longer; he was never again employed by the Company.

ii

Like other commanders, Saris would attempt to justify his personal trade on the grounds that it was common practice. So it was and so, in spite of repeated proscriptions, it would remain. There were a few exceptions, a few men of extraordinary probity like 'the honest Mr Cocks' who never ventured a penny on their own account; but, as will be seen, they rarely made effective factors. It stood to reason that any man willing to gamble his life on a voyage to the Indies would think nothing of gambling his wages on a few diamonds or a sack of cloves.

Even the Dutch Company was finding it impossible to suppress the entrepreneurial spirit of its merchants. In 1609 two Dutchmen, lately returned from the East with a handsome profit of £600, offered to invest their nest egg in the London Company. From the uncertainty over their real identities it may be assumed that the V.O.C. had refused to re-employ them and that they were keen to cover their tracks. To the directors of the London Company they were 'Peter Floris' and 'Lucas Antheuniss' and their offer was in the nature of a rather intriguing proposal.

Evidently both men had served at Dutch establishments on the east, or Coromandel, coast of India. This was an area of considerable interest to the London Company as a principal source of those Indian cottons so beloved of the Javanese. Keeling had been instructed to call there on the Company's Third Voyage (1607) but had failed to do so. Now Floris and Antheuniss were proposing to take up the challenge on the Company's behalf and open trade not only on the Coromandel coast but also in the

Gulf of Siam. They asked no wages, they would venture their own £600 towards the capital, and they would be happy with a share of the returns which they confidently predicted at 300 per cent.

After due consideration and some careful vetting of the Dutchmen's characters, their proposal was accepted by the Court of Committees. A subscription book was opened and a single ship, the *Globe* of about 300 tons, was made ready. She sailed, the Company's Seventh Voyage, in January 1611 (so three months ahead of Saris).

Apart from its casual inception the voyage of the *Globe* was unusual in that it afforded clear evidence of the Company's interest in Asia's internal carrying trade. The original proposal envisaged an absence of four years during which the ship would ply back and forth between the Coromandel coast, Bantam and Siam. In the event some of this shuttling had to be curtailed; but the *Globe* would still be away some four and a half years and for most of that time would be carrying, or awaiting, cargoes that were never intended for European consumption. The two Dutchmen knew the eastern markets and the trading seasons and they had done their sums carefully. While English commanders like Saris or the Middletons were making speculative calls and optimistic assessments at any port that would entertain them, Floris and Antheuniss had a definite plan of investment.

The total subscription for the voyage came to some £15,000 of which perhaps £7,000 was available as trading capital (after equipping and provisioning the ship). Most of this sum was in pieces of eight. By repeatedly investing them in Indian cottons and then reinvesting them in Thai and Chinese products, and eventually buying pepper and Chinese silks for the homeward voyage, they aimed to raise the value of their trading stock to over £45,000, thus giving the desired return of 300 per cent on the original £15,000. Other voyages of the period operated on a similar cumulative principle; but in this case because there was only one ship, because its commanders had a high stake in its success, and because they were in no position to engage in any political posturing, the bare commercial realities are more pronounced. It is significant that the Court of Committees when faced with such a juicy proposal allowed no reservations about the proposers' nationality to cloud their judgement.

With all possible speed the *Globe* made straight for the Bay of Bengal. By late August 1611 its factors were ashore at Petapoli and Masulipatnam, ports within the independent kingdom of Golconda (later Hyderabad, now Andhra Pradesh) at which the Dutch were already established. Cottons suitable for the eastern market were ordered and monies advanced to the weavers and dyers. There was the usual wrangling over customs dues but by February they had acquired a good loading 'without having made any penny in bad dettes or leaving any remnants behind us on shoare'. Profits on the sale of their few English exports had more than covered all duties and gifts, and 'having yett a good monsoon to performe our voyage' Floris was pleased to report that 'our estate is att this present in verye good being'.

In April 1612 they called at Bantam and landed part of their Indian cargo plus a factor who was to sell the cottons and buy pepper whenever the markets were favourable. The *Globe* then sailed north and thereafter matters went less smoothly. The plan had been for a quick turn-round in Siam so that the ship could catch the south-east monsoon back to India at the end of the year. This proved over-optimistic, and the *Globe* was to remain in the Gulf of Siam until the autumn of the following year, 1613.

Floris and Antheuniss had miscalculated on three counts. The first was the attitude of their countrymen. At both Patani and Ayuthia, the two Siamese cities at which the *Globe* attempted to trade, Dutch factories were already in existence. Not without reason would Coen complain that the English fed off Dutch enterprise. Relations between the two nations were rapidly deteriorating and, as in Japan, the Dutch did their utmost to flood the local markets. They also agreed to exorbitant customs dues and other restrictions that might discourage their would-be competitors. Floris was frankly nonplussed. Four years earlier he had seen 'such a vente [sale]' at Patani that 'it seemed the whole world had not clothings enough to provyde this place as was needful'. Now it was so 'overcloyed' that instead of a 400 per cent profit 'I cannot at this present make 5 per cento'. He would happily have abandoned the Siamese trade altogether were it not for the fact that his remaining stock of Indian cottons had been specially ordered for the Siamese market and would not sell elsewhere.

But if disposing of his cargo presented difficulties so did the purchase of a new lading. Siam turned out to be in a state of turmoil, with war threatening on several fronts and internal trade at a standstill. When a factor was sent north to Chieng Mai in search of those forest products – skins, dyes and resins – for which the country was famous, he was captured by the Burmese and not heard of for four years. Yet somehow Floris must employ his capital during the long sojourn in Siam. He therefore dispatched another factor with a cargo for Japan (he knew of Adams's existence but not yet of Saris's arrival) and yet another for Macassar. Neither of these ventures brought a speedy return so that when in the spring Chinese junks began to appear at Patani and Ayuthia he had no cash with which to buy their silks and porcelains.

To make matters still worse he was having acute problems with his men. The captain of the *Globe*, Anthony Hippon, had died as soon as the ship reached Patani. Of the three men who in turn took his place, two proved to be dangerous drunkards, the third turned mutineer, and all were professionally incompetent. To the crime of fisticuffs on deck they added that of private trade ashore. Floris and Antheuniss, if anyone, might have been disposed to overlook this matter were it not that the crew's trade was competing directly with that of the Company. The men were habitually underselling their chief factors by 'up to 50 per cento'.

With his estate now far from 'in verie good being', the methodical Floris dreamt up contingency plans and reworked his figures. The case looked nigh on hopeless when in January 1613 help came from an unexpected quarter. In Ayuthia, the capital, the king of Siam, anxious to encourage English competition with the Dutch, bought a substantial part of the *Globe*'s cargo. Then, following suit, in Patani the local Sultana advanced Floris the cash he needed to buy Chinese goods. Suddenly they were in business again.

The Sultana, or 'queen', of Patani made a deep impression on Floris. 'A comely oulde woman nowe about three score yeares . . . she was tall of person and full of majestie.' She was also 'a good sport', thought nothing of hunting wild buffalo in the forest, and was a great patron of the arts. Her dance troupe was the best Floris had ever seen; and when by request the Dutch and English obliged her with a few steps in their national idioms 'the oulde Queen was much rejoyced'. With perhaps a republican's sneaking respect for monarchy, Floris was moved to uncharacteristic adulation 'having in all the Indies not seene any lyke her'.

Leaving Antheuniss in charge of the factory at Ayuthia, Floris sailed back to India at the end of 1613. By now the *Globe* was leaking badly and with the prospect of the long voyage to England ahead of her, he resolved to beach and repair her in an estuary near Masulipatnam. In the meantime the factors were busy selling their Thai and Chinese goods to Golconda's merchants and buying more Indian cottons. When another Company vessel arrived to continue the Coromandel–Siam trade, Floris finally abandoned the idea of a return visit to Patani and Ayuthia. With the cottons he was now ordering at Masulipatnam, plus the Bantam pepper he had still to collect, he reckoned that he already had a cargo that would sell in London for the desired £45,000.

In the event it did rather better. Thanks to a growing expertise in the re-exporting of pepper to Europe, London prices had started to climb. Pepper was still being offered to subscribers to each voyage as a dividend in kind; but what in 1603 had been an unwelcome expedient to offset a market glut had now become a prized privilege. The Company itself took no part in the re-export trade; on the advice of the directors the General Court, i.e. the shareholders, set a price and then the same shareholders could bid to the value of their shareholding for stocks. This practice continued until the 1620s; for shareholders with the right commercial connections in Europe it could mean a profit comparable with that on the original voyage.

There is some confusion about the exact profit of the Seventh Voyage but it certainly showed a return of 318 per cent and possibly 400 per cent. The *Globe* had eventually reached London in August 1615. Sadly Floris never lived to enjoy the fortune that awaited him. He was taken ashore on a stretcher and died in London three weeks later.

Antheuniss continued the good work alone. At about the time of his partner's death he was transferring from Ayuthia to Masulipatnam. The Siamese trade was scarcely buoyant but this was mainly due to the infrequency of English shipping. Indeed more news and more ships were reaching Siam from Japan than from Bantam. Most years 'the honest Mr Cocks' managed to send Adams or one of his other factors in a variety of junks either to Ayuthia, Patani or Cambodia (where Antheuniss had posted a small agency).

In 1617 even this lifeline slackened. The Dutch negotiated new and more favourable terms with the Siamese and began to show those monopolistic tendencies that were making life impossible for the English in the Spice Islands. Then in 1618 came news of the capture of the *Zwaarte Leeuw* at Bantam. The Companies were now at war and the English in Siam isolated. It was while trying to redress this situation that Jourdain, in 1619, was surprised off Patani and killed by that marksman's bullet.

iii

In Japan Cocks was also complaining bitterly about the dearth of English shipping. The *Hosiander* in 1614 and the *Thomas* and *Advice* in 1615 called at Hirado but thereafter 'by the indirect dealinges and unlooked for proceadings of the Hollander' four years passed without sight of an English sail. Cocks withdrew his factors from Osaka and Yedo as trade ground from a crawl to a halt. The Dutch had put a price upon his greying head, '50 Rials to any man that could kill me and 30 Rials for each other Englishman they could kill'. Pitched battles took place at the gates of the English factory and only Japanese protection saved them.

By March 1620 Cocks was at his wits' end. He could now see no hope of ever interesting the Japanese in broadcloth and even Siamese hides were not selling. The Dutch were waylaying his men at every opportunity. The Shogun had curtailed the original trading privileges. And what support was he getting? Two of his factors were permanently sick and Adams was now behaving like a naturalized Hollander. 'I cannot chuse but note it down', whispered Cocks to his diary, 'that both I myself and all the rest of our nation doe see that he (I mean Will Adams) is much more frend to the Dutch than to the Englishmen which are his own countreymen, God forgeve hym.' An English ship had at last entered Hirado but it turned out that her crew was Dutch; she had been taken in the Spice Islands. More disgrace.

The last straw was that the President at Bantam was querying his accounts. 'He never gave me roast beef but beat me with the spit', moaned Cocks in a letter to the Company in London. 'I beseeke Your Worships to pardon me if I be too forward of tongue herein', he rambled on, 'but my griefe is that I lie in a place of much losse and expence to Your Worships and no benefit to myself but loss of tyme in my ould age, although God knoweth my care and paines is as much as if benefite did come thereby.'

Of course, even Japanese clouds had silver linings. His sweet potatoes were doing well and he had acquired some much prized goldfish. They came from China and of the China trade in general he still had high hopes. Yet even these were destined for a setback. Late in 1620 there reached Hirado an English ship bearing news of the Anglo-Dutch agreement. To the amazement of their Japanese hosts, Dutch and English buried the hatchet and immediately took it up again against the Portuguese. Well placed to savage Portuguese shipping carrying China goods from Macao to the Philippines, both the Dutch and English companies were soon doing a brisk trade in Chinese silks without the expense of a Chinese factory. For perhaps the first time in its history the English house at Hirado was busily and profitably engaged.

It was not to last. As elsewhere the Anglo-Dutch alliance was resented by both parties. The Dutch complained of English indifference and the English of Dutch extravagance. When in 1622 it was officially terminated, Cocks felt that he was again on the verge of a breakthrough in his China negotiations. He therefore ignored orders from Bantam to withdraw from Japan, much to the fury of his superiors. In April 1623 Bantam tried again to winkle him out. This time a ship was sent with orders to remove the whole Hirado factory and to bid its inmates 'to fulfil our said order as you will answer the contrary at your perils'. The same letter accused Cocks of having squandered vast sums on his China contacts 'who hath too long deluded you through your own stupidity' and of having 'made what construction you pleased of our previous commission for coming from thence'. 'We do now reiterate our commission [to depart]', ended the letter, 'lest, having read it in the former part hereof, you should forget it before you come to the end.'

Poor 'honest Mr Cocks', this was not the gratitude he had looked for. Reluctantly he gathered in his debts, sold off his stock, and found homes for his pigeons and his goldfish. 'On December 22 many of the townsfolk came with their wives and families to take leave of the Factors, some weeping at their departure.' Adams had died in 1620 but there were now other Englishmen who were leaving behind much loved wives and mystified children. Even the Dutch seemed to regret the passing of their old sparring partners. To save face, Cocks claimed that it was just a temporary withdrawal. But he knew otherwise. Disgraced and disgruntled, he died on the voyage home.

As part of the same retrenching policy the factories at Ayuthia and Patani were also closed. As in the Spice Islands, the English bid for a commercial role in the Far East had proved to be an historical cul-de-sac. Yet the experience was not forgotten. The Company would never abandon its interest in either the Far East or the archipelago. In ten years' time English ships would again be trying to force open the China trade; and plans to reopen the Hirado factory were resurrected at least once a decade throughout the seventeenth century. In 1673 an English vessel would actually call at Nagasaki but be refused trading rights. It was said that the house at Hirado was still being kept vacant pending an English return and the same was found to be true of the Ayuthia factory to which, in 1659, a party of Company factors would repair after being driven out of Cambodia. As a result of their favourable reception, Ayuthia would reopen for another fraught but colourful interlude.

In what may seem like a catalogue of defeats and retreats, of commercial bravado undermined by political reticence, there was, though, one outstanding exception: the factory established at Masulipatnam survived and continued to supply the eastern market and to look for new maritime outlets. Antheuniss had arrived back there in 1616. He did not send any factors inland, not even apparently to the court of Golconda (Hyderabad); but he did try to trade with Burma. From native merchants he learnt that Thomas Samuel, the man he had sent from Ayuthia to Chieng Mai in 1613 only to be captured by the Burmese, had been taken to Pegu (north-east of Rangoon). There he had died but it was reliably reported that the king was holding his merchandise pending the arrival of a claimant.

In 1617 claimants in the shape of two Masulipatnam factors duly landed on Burmese soil. They had come in an Indian ship and with only sufficient goods 'to make tryall of the trade' This was a disappointment to the Burmese king who had high expectations of English shipping. His visitors, though well received, soon found themselves in the altogether novel position of being so welcome that they were detained. 'We beseech you,' they wrote to Masulipatnam, 'to pitie our poor distressed estate and not to let us be left in a heathen country slaves to a tyrannous king.' For, they went on, 'we are like lost sheepe and still in feare of being brought to the slaughter'. It sounded much like a cry of 'Wolf' and indeed it was. A year later news reached Masulipatnam that the two men had in fact sold all their stock and were now borrowing heavily on the expectation of a well-laden English ship coming to relieve them. When, in 1620, no such vessel materialized, the king had 'to enforce them to depart'. Very sensibly he withheld Samuel's stock until they were already afloat 'lest their ryot should consume all'. When eventually brought to book by their superiors 'they could give no other account [for their expenditure] but that most was lost at play and the rest profusely spent'.

The man who had the job of enquiring into these irregularities was William Methwold, who had succeeded to the charge of the Masulipatnam factory in 1618. Destined for a long and distinguished career in the Company, he remained on the Coromandel coast till 1622 and thus piloted it through the crisis years in Anglo-Dutch relations. Under the terms of the 1619 agreement, or Treaty of Defence, the English company obtained the right to establish a factory at the Dutch base of Pulicat. This accorded well with Methwold's wishes. Masulipatnam he found 'unwalled, ill-built and worse situated'; the exactions of its governor siphoned off the profits; and the local chintzes were not those in greatest demand in Java. Better by far were the 'pintadoes' (batiks produced by applying the wax with a pen), which were a speciality of the Tamil country for which Pulicat was the principal outlet. The place was also well walled, having been fortified against the Portuguese, and it was beyond the reach of Golconda's venal officials in a pocket of south India still ruled by a Hindu dynasty.

But once established at Pulicat the English found that, as at Ambon, they were at a serious disadvantage. For they were expected to contribute to the expense of the Dutch fortress yet not permitted to settle within the security of its walls. Far from being any protection, the place was a distinct menace and trade suffered accordingly. In 1626 the English finally withdrew to the village of Armagon and there, for the first time on Indian soil, landed guns and constructed some basic fortifications. The disturbed state of the country, where there was no strong authority as in Golconda, plus the hostility of the Dutch, seemed to justify this departure from usual practice. In London the Company was unconvinced and repeatedly refused authorization for improving these defences.

During the course of the 1630s the headquarters of the Coromandel factors shifted from Masulipatnam to Armagon and back again to Masulipatnam. Famine, the Dutch, and wars between Golconda and its neighbours all contributed to the uncertain climate. But in 1633–4 the first English factors were sent north to Bengal and obtained permission from the Moghul Governor of Orissa to establish agencies at Harihapur and Balasore (Baleshwar) to the west of the mouth of the Hughli river. Thenceforth Bengal supplied the Coromandel factories with rice, sugar and a few items of trade, especially raw silk and muslins.

Of greater significance at the time was a short voyage made by Francis Day, the agent at Armagon. In 1639 he sailed down the Coromandel coast calling at San Thomé, the Portuguese fort, and then at a fishing village three miles north of San Thomé where he successfully negotiated with the local *naik*, or ruler, for a building plot. The plot was of about one square mile and on it he proposed to build a fort to which the Armagon agency should remove. The name of the village, he was told, was Madraspatnam. Precisely why these few acres of surf-swept beach, dune and lagoon should so have attracted Mr Day is hard to explain. To all appearances they were as exposed, featureless and uninviting to shipping as the rest of India's east coast but with the added disadvantage of being only a few minutes' march from the Portuguese establishment.

Day, though, had his reasons of which the most convincing must be that he had a 'mistris' at San Thomé. According to common report he was 'so enamoured of her' and so anxious that their 'interviews' might be 'more frequent and uninterrupted' that his selection of Madras (the 'patnam' was soon dropped) was a foregone conclusion. Certainly he had been to call at San Thomé on previous occasions and certainly his passionate advocacy of the new site now went rather beyond the call of duty. He wagered his salary for the whole of his period of service in the Company that cottons would there prove fifteen per cent cheaper than at Armagon; he threatened to resign if his plan was not accepted; and he volunteered to meet all interest charges on money raised to build the fort out of his own pocket. This latter undertaking only became necessary when it transpired that the wording of the *naik*'s grant was misleading. It seemed to say that the *naik* himself would pay for the new fort and under this happy impression the Coromandel factors voted to remove there. In fact it could be read as meaning that the English would pay for the fort, a more reasonable construction but one which came to light only when the English had already deserted Armagon and were encamped on the new site. Probably Day was not alone in wanting to force the Company's hand. When he eventually reneged on his offer to defray the interest charges, he again met with no opposition from his colleagues.

It was in February 1640 that the English landed at their new base. Soon the first of the fort's bastions was rising above the flat sandscape. Fort St George, as it was to be called, was an elementary castle, square, with four corner bastions and curtain walls of about 100 yards long. It took fourteen years to complete and the Court of Directors in London baulked at every penny of the £3000 it cost. But if not immediately realized, 'the growing hopes of a new, nimble and most cheape plantation' continued to grow. By the end of the first year some 300–400 cloth weavers and finishers had set up home outside the fort, a motley collection of merchants, servants, publicans, money-lenders, gardeners, soldiers and prostitutes had decamped there from San Thomé, and the English factors were busy turning beach into real estate.

But Madras was to prosper against the odds. 'The most incommodious place I ever saw' was how Alexander Hamilton would describe it towards the end of the century. He was a sea-captain and to seamen it would ever remain a place of hideous danger. In 1640, while Day and his men were encamped round their first bastion, the ships which had transported them from Armagon were overtaken by a typhoon. In so exposed an anchorage they stood little chance. One ran aground and 'sodainly spleet to peeces' while the other, after an epic struggle, was also beached and then found to be past repair. Hair-raising stories of crossing the 'bar' – that continuous reef of sand running parallel to the beach and near which no large vessel dared venture – became part of the Madras experience. Men and merchandise, pets, wives and furniture, had all to be transhipped over it in lighters and catamarans of minimal draft while a pounding surf tossed them like a salad. Thrills and spills were commonplace, disasters fairly regular. Scarcely a decade would pass without at least one fleet being pounded to 'peeces' in Madras roads.

In 1656 'a common country boate' carrying the captains of three departing East India ships, plus most of the local factors who had come to see them off, grounded on the bar and immediately capsized. It was an open boat but with a decked poop on which most of the Englishmen were reclining 'verie merrie in discourse' as they 'solemnised the day in valedictory ceremonies'. As the ship struck they were all washed overboard; three were drowned. The whole thing happened so suddenly that others in the bottom of the boat simply rolled over with her. 'Suddenly we found ourselves tumbled together in the water among chests, cases of liquor and other such lumber and with a score of sheep that we were carrying aboard.' The writer, three other Englishmen, and some twenty native seamen were still in the boat although now under it 'as within a dish swimming with the bottome upwards and the keele in the zenith'.

'It was thare as dark as in the earth's centre.' But amazingly a pocket of air had been trapped with them. By sitting on the thwarts in water up to their necks, twenty-four men and several sheep, gulping like goldfish, survived. 'And in this condition we lived two hours.' They prayed of course, they debated their chances of survival, and they thought much about Jonah in the whale. They also stripped off their clothes in case they should have to swim for it.

> In fine [or to cut a long story short], the boate running ashore upon the sand, and whyles the water was still as high as our necks, with our feet we digged a pitt in the sand near the boate's side, in doing whereof the current helped us; and then sinking down into the water and diveing, krept out under the side of the boate one by one.

They emerged to find themselves 180 paces from the shore. The water, though only waist deep, was running with such a ferocious undertow that sixteen of the survivors were immediately sucked out of their depths and drowned.

> Captaine Lucas and I held each other by the armes and (naked) waded through the current, suckering each other in perilous stips; for if either had but lost his footing, the violent torrent was so great that we should neaver have rise more in this world.
>
> At last being gott out of the water as naked as Adam, we had a mile and a halfe to run to the towne, with the hot sand scalding our feet, and the sun scorching over our heads, which caused all the skin of our bodies to peel off although we ran a pace; and the first Christian whom we met was a good Dutchman who lent me his hatt and his slippers.

CHAPTER FOUR

Jarres and Brabbles

THE ARABIAN SEA

In the seventeenth century the words 'India' and 'Indies' had no precise geographical connotation. They were used indiscriminately to describe anywhere east of the Cape and west of the Azores. Thus the Spice Islands might be regarded as part of 'India', and Goa as somewhere in the 'Indies'. As seen from the crow's nest of a European merchantman the south Asian subcontinent, like the Far East, comprised several distinct trading areas – the Coromandel coast, the Malabar coast, Bengal, Gujarat, etc. Each belonged to a different and independent state with its distinctive language and its particular productions; each was historically and commercially linked to various trading areas in east and west Asia; and each was separated from the others by weeks, even months, of sailing. For the Jacobean navigator, as for his employers in England, India as a political entity simply did not exist.

The case of the Coromandel coast was typical. Its commercial and historical links were with Burma, Bengal, Persia (the kings of Golconda were of Persian extraction) and above all with the south-east Asian archipelago. The English retained Masulipatnam and founded Madras because on the supply of cottons from 'The Coast' depended the purchase of pepper in Java and Sumatra. 'The Coast' served Bantam and was administered from Bantam. In the same way the Portuguese had their Coromandel base at San Thomé which served Malacca, and the Dutch their Coromandel base at Pulicat which served Jakarta (Batavia). At none of the Coromandel ports did Europeans glance further inland than they need for their own trade and security. Rather did they face resolutely out to sea, scanning the eastern horizon for a sail and sniffing the breeze for new overseas markets.

It was the same on the coast of Gujarat where at Surat the London East India Company would establish its main factory in what we now call India. Gujarati ships had always sailed to Java and Sumatra to exchange cottons for spices and pepper, but no less important were their annual sailings to the ports of the Red Sea and the Persian Gulf. It was to exploit these trade links, not to open up India's internal trade and certainly not to gain a political toehold on the subcontinent, that the Company first directed its ships to western India.

Of course, from a nineteenth-century perspective things would look very different. British imperialism craved as long and proud a pedigree as possible; it was a kind of legitimization. Hence Surat, whence its 'founders' were known to have treated with 'The Great Mogoll', was represented as the seed of the Raj. Into all the earliest English contacts with the subcontinent a special significance had to be read. Factories in India were different; they were 'settlements'. Their disposition round the perimeter of the peninsula was seen as a pincer movement which would lead inexorably to the acquisition of the whole country. If there was no master plan, there was surely a destiny at work; and the factors at Surat, Masulipatnam and Madras were seen as living and labouring with a rugged spirit born of the conviction that one day their Clive would come.

The effects of such chronological rewinding are still evident in twentieth-century studies. It may, for instance, be unhelpful to bill the first visit by a Company factor to the Moghul court as 'the opening scene in the history of British India'; or to applaud his successor as 'the first of the many great Englishmen who have served their country in India'; or to describe the commander of a fleet that called at Surat in 1615 as 'a most undoubted worker on the foundations of Empire in India'. The imperial perspective wildly distorts the endeavours of the young Company in India just as it marginalizes the activities of the Company elsewhere.

In 1607, as part of that policy to diversify its activities, exploit the existing carrying trade, and find a market for English woollens, the Company instructed the ships of its Third Voyage to proceed to Bantam by way of the Arabian Sea. Specifically they were to call at Socotra, Aden 'or some other place thereaboute', and Surat. Lancaster, whose advice is evident in the detailed instructions for the voyage, had identified the Arabian Sea as a distinct trading basin with the Gujarat–Red Sea axis as its main trade route. This was the last leg of the sea journey by which spices, cottons, silks and other luxury items reached the Middle East. The London Company's numerous ex-Levant directors were familiar with the desert caravans which conveyed these goods onward to Cairo and Damascus; and they knew that most Red Sea purchases of such goods were made for cash.

The Company's factors were therefore to inquire into all aspects of this trade with three objectives in mind. One was the possibility of selling broadcloth for cash; another the possibility of obviating the Company's existing and much troubled trade with the Spice Islands by buying spices at Aden or Surat; and the third and ideal solution was that of improving their purchasing position at Bantam by obtaining, in return for English exports, the Indian cottons so sought after in the East. This could be done either at source in Gujarat (Surat) or where the Gujaratis finally disposed of their cottons (Aden and Mocha).

Whichever scheme proved more viable it was hoped, as usual, that English woollens would find a better market in the ports of the Asian mainland than they were ever likely to in Java and the archipelago. The Third Voyage carried an unusually large stock of broadcloth samples and included a factor 'brought up in the trade of woollen commodities'. There was also William Hawkins, who spoke Turkish, a useful medium throughout the Islamic world, and who, as second in command, would be entrusted with all diplomatic negotiations.

The commander was William Keeling, although there was some doubt about his appointment until the fleet was actually under way. Keeling, a family man, had submitted an unprecedented request to the effect that Anne, his wife, might accompany him. She was willing; the Company was not. Undeterred, Mrs Keeling smuggled herself aboard the *Red Dragon*. As was surely inevitable in a ship of 600 tons crammed with nearly 200 men, her presence was quickly detected and Keeling was ordered to land the stowaway or hand over command. She was put ashore at the Downs. Three years later when Keeling returned, it is pleasant to record that she was again at the Downs. Having been the last to leave the ship, she would be the first to board it.

Perhaps it was the delay caused by this domestic affair which led the *Consent* of David Middleton to leave ahead of the other two ships. As already noted, Keeling never caught up with her. Minus a wife and minus a ship, he left the Downs in the *Red Dragon* accompanied by the *Hector* on April Fool's Day 1607. Experience showed that April was rather late for seeking the trade winds of the South Atlantic and so it proved. By June they were on the coast of Brazil and by August they were back at Sierra Leone in West Africa. Here they spent a whole month reprovisioning and awaiting a change of wind. The crew of the *Red Dragon* staged a performance of *Hamlet* and Keeling fought the pangs of separation with net and gun. 'I tooke within one houre and a halfe six thousand small and good fish', he reports. Looking for sterner stuff, he then tried tracking an elephant – or, according to a colleague, 'a behemoth'. 'He hath a body like a house but a tayle like a ratte, erecting it like a cedar, little eyes but great sight, very melanchollу but wise (they say) and full of understanding for a beaste.' This succinct description applied to an Indian elephant. Keeling's quarry was African and distinctly less melancholic – until, that is, 'I shot seven or eight bullets into him and made him bleed exceadingly'. The behemoth made off and so did the hunters; 'being neare night, we were constrayned aboord without effecting our purposes on him'.

In September the ships again weighed anchor, crossed the Equator for the third time, and reached Table Bay for Christmas. A message scratched on a rock informed them that the *Consent* was already six months ahead of them. With no hope of effecting a rendezvous, the Third Voyage continued its leisurely progress calling at Madagascar, where one of the *Hector*'s men had the misfortune of 'being shrewdly bitten with an aligarta', and then attempting a landing at Zanzibar. It was late April, more than a year since leaving England, when they finally sighted Socotra off the horn of Africa.

Here, in an island setting of date palms and desert that might have been designed for *The Tempest*, the *Red Dragon*'s Shakespearian enthusiasts perversely rehearsed for *Richard II*. Meanwhile Keeling quizzed the skipper of a Gujarati vessel for navigational tips. His informant spoke highly of Aden's trade but, as the English ships discovered on an abortive excursion to the west, the winds were now unfavourable.

Socotra itself, apart from its strategic position as a safe haven at the mouth of the Red Sea, was popular with shipping because it produced large quantities of the 'nauseous, bitter purgative' known as aloes. According to the dictionary this substance is produced 'from the inspissated juice of the agalloch plant'. Socotra was covered with the prickly agalloch and annually inspissated 'more than Christianity can spende'. But aloes enjoyed a good demand throughout the constipated East and Keeling bought nearly a ton of the stuff. Subsequent visitors to the island would not fail to follow his example although the Socotrans, marooned on their burning rocks amidst a boiling sea, would never discover a use for English woollens.

With plans for Aden aborted, Keeling now wrote off the Arabian Sea and shaped his course direct for Bantam, leaving Hawkins in the *Hector* to investigate Surat's potential. On 28 August 1608, the latter became the first commander of an East India Company vessel to set foot on Indian soil. Muddy tidal creeks and low-lying mangrove make Gujarat's coast one of India's less inviting. Surat owed its considerable importance simply to its being the principal port of the as yet mainly land-locked Moghul empire. From the account of Will Finch, Hawkins's companion, it appears that the city lined the banks of the Tapti river some twenty miles upstream from its mouth and the inevitable 'bar' beyond which lay the *Hector*. (Because of estuarine silting it is now rather less accessible from the sea.) 'Many faire merchants houses' fronted the river and flanked the castle and *maidan* 'which is a pleasant greene in the midst wherof is a maypole'. Beside it stood the custom-house, scene of many all too taxing encounters. Here Hawkins's trunks were 'searched and tumbled to our great dislike'. Doubtless their owners, like later factors, were also frisked. 'They very familiarlye searched all of us to the bottome of our pocketts and nearer too (in modestie to speak of yt [i.e. to put it modestly]).'

Hawkins's journal is silent on these details. He fails even to marvel at the city's busy streets 'humming like bees in swarmes with multitudes of people in white coates'. In truth he was far too worried for such trivial observations. For within days of landing he had crossed swords with the two parties who for the next ten years would make it their business to frustrate English endeavours. On the one hand there was the man whom Hawkins usually called 'that dogge Mocreb-chan', otherwise Mukarrab Khan, the Moghul official in charge of the Gujarat ports; his would be the happy task of impounding the Company's goods, extracting what he pleased, and referring all complaints and requests to his emperor seven hundred miles away at Agra. And on the other hand there were Mukarrab Khan's accomplices and *agents provocateurs*, the Portuguese.

For over a century the Portuguese had policed the maritime trade of the Arabian Sea and, although their power might be declining further east, they still had formidable influence at the Moghul court and at every port between Goa and their Persian base at Hormuz. England and Spain (and hence Portugal) were now at peace, a point which Hawkins ingenuously pressed as reason enough for the Portuguese in India not to molest Englishmen. Empowered by the usual royal commission to deliver James I's letter of introduction to the Emperor Akbar (now, incidentally, dead)

Hawkins made no bones about calling himself 'the King of England's Embassadour'. And in this capacity he protested vigorously when two of the *Hector*'s boats were taken by 'Portingalls' in the Tapti river.

But the Portuguese had no intention of surrendering any part of the lucrative Moghul trade to newcomers, friend or foe. Their commander at Surat, 'a proud rascall' and 'base villain' according to Hawkins, rejected the latter's complaint in language distinctly combative. England he called 'an island of no import', King James was 'a king of fishermen' and subject to Portugal, and the English were really Hollanders and so traitors; as for Hawkins, 'a fart for his commission'. It was too much. Exploding with rage, Hawkins challenged the man to a duel. 'Perceaving I was moved' the Portuguese commander withdrew and promptly sent his English prisoners off to Goa. Soon after the *Hector* too left for Bantam. Trade at Surat was obviously going to be long term. Only Hawkins and Finch remained behind. They would seek redress, sell their merchandise, and petition the Emperor for a factory.

Posterity, and especially the chroniclers of British India, have been hard on Hawkins. They criticize his willingness to play the oriental courtier, condemn his moral laxity, and complain that during three years in India he achieved nothing. Whether or not he was the William Hawkins, from the third generation of the Tudors' most distinguished naval family, who had sailed round the world with Drake is uncertain. But he was undoubtedly a colourful and rumbustious figure. With or without a ship, Finch always calls him 'The Captain'. He was no stripling and in both conduct and character he seems to belong among the adventurers of Elizabeth's reign.

Combining vigilance with a ready resort to the sword, he survived two Portuguese attempts on his life before, in February 1609, departing from Surat on the long overland journey to the Moghul court at Agra. (Finch, who had been suffering from dysentery, was left behind at Surat 'with all things touching the trade of merchandise in his power'.) The journey took ten weeks. Hawkins had a guard of faithful Pathans and was mostly well received. But unlike Saris on his way to Yedo, he scarcely noticed the countryside and was not easily impressed even by Agra, 'one of the biggest cities in the world'. Although he was an employee of the Company his circumstances were really more analogous to those of Will Adams than of Saris. He too was alone, without a ship, with little to sell, and utterly dependent on an emperor's favour. Like Adams he would quickly attain a position of considerable influence at an oriental court.

And like Adams, there would be some uncertainty as to where his real loyalties lay.

Initially Jehangir, who had succeeded the illustrious Akbar on the Moghul throne in 1603, probably saw the 'embassadour' from King James as an acceptable adornment to his circle of courtiers. But this relationship seems to have developed into something much closer. Hawkins was elevated to a pride of place in the imperial entourage which none of his successors would achieve. He was bidden to remain indefinitely at the Emperor's side and by way of inducement was offered a salary equivalent to £3200 per annum, the rank of 'khan' ('in Persia it is the title for a Duke', he explains) and permission for a factory at Surat. His reasons for accepting he gave in a convoluted but revealing passage addressed to his employers.

> I trusting upon his [Jehangir's] promise and seeing it was beneficial both to my nation and myself, being dispossessed of that benefite I should have reaped if I had gone to Bantam, and [seeing] that after halfe a dozen yeeres Your Worships would send another man of sort to my place, in the meane time I should feather my neast and doe you service; and further perceaving great injuries offered us by reason the king is so farre from the ports, I did not think it amiss to yeeld unto this request.

Nor, a few weeks later, did he think it amiss to yield to another imperial request. Jehangir, ever considerate, was insistent that he 'take a whyte mayden out of his palace'. It was simply a precaution, of course; the girl could oversee the preparation of his victuals and thus frustrate attempts to poison him. Jehangir would supply her dowry and her servants and, if the 'Inglis Khan' so wished, she might turn Christian. Hawkins, feigning strong religious scruples, claims to have refused unless the white maiden were already baptized. 'I little thought', he writes, 'that a Christian's daughter could be found.' But lo, Jehangir knew just the person. She was the daughter of an Armenian Christian who had been high in Akbar's favour but had since died leaving her 'only a few jewels'. To the Emperor's solicitude were now added the dictates of compassion. 'I, seeing she was of so honest descent and having passed [i.e. given] my worde to the king, could not withstand my fortune.' They were duly married by his English servant and 'for ever after I lived content and without feare, she being willing to go where I went and live as I lived'.

When Hawkins prevaricates he is at his most transparent. Subtlety was never his strongest suit but for six months he had successfully consolidated his position and was now one of the Emperor's closest companions. Matters began to change as soon as news reached Agra that another Company vessel was approaching the 'bar' at Surat. At first the change was in Hawkins' favour. In expectation of at last receiving worthy tokens of English esteem, Jehangir issued the desired trading rights. When word came that the ship had in fact been wrecked on the Gujarat coast he even issued orders for the reception of the castaways and their cargo.

But such favours aroused the jealousy of Jehangir's ministers 'for it went against their hearts that a Christian should be so great and neere the king'. Additionally the threat of more English shipping activated the Portuguese at court. And, to cap it all, 'that dogge' Mukarrab Khan put in another appearance. Officially he was in disgrace for having appropriated Hawkins's cargo but, with an ingenuity one can only admire, he managed to turn an imperial order to reimburse Hawkins into the means of disgracing him. He did this by undervaluing the goods in question and then representing Hawkins's refusal to accept payment at this questionable valuation as an act of disobedience to the Emperor. It was a complex dispute but with so many anxious to discredit the Englishman, and with Hawkins himself exhibiting a pugnacious stubbornness, his reputation plummeted.

The arrival of 'unrulie' English hordes from the wrecked *Ascension* contributed to his discomfiture. In Surat they had already disgraced themselves 'with palmita drinke (toddy) and raisin wine'. According to Finch they 'made themselves beasts and soe fell to lewd women that in shorte time manie fell sicke'. Worse still, one Thomas Tucker, perhaps tired of singing for his supper, butchered a calf which Finch rightly described as 'a slaughter more than murther in India'. Local Brahmins organized a lynch mob and Tucker was saved only when the English themselves were seen to whip him into insensibility. To Finch's immense relief the officers and men of the *Ascension* at last set off for Agra. Many never arrived but amongst those who did was the factor, John Jourdain, who was to figure so prominently at Bantam.

Hawkins, Jourdain reported, was 'in some disgrace with the kinge'. The factor had taken an instant dislike to the Captain and, not without gloating, he proceeded to list the reasons for Hawkins's disgrace. Amongst them occurs the oft-quoted reference to Hawkins's drunkenness. According to Jourdain he had been publicly reprimanded for appearing at court after 'filling his head with stronge drinke'. Perhaps he had. But Jehangir was not noted for his abstinence and Hawkins mentions having passed many paralytic hours in the Emperor's company. Even if the Emperor had undergone some conscience-stricken reformation it seems unlikely that he would have objected to Hawkins drinking in his own home. More probably this was simply another instance of the Captain's many enemies trying to engineer his disgrace.

After five wasted months Jourdain and most of his followers returned towards Surat in the hopes of being rescued by another English vessel. Hawkins remained at Agra and briefly his fortunes revived. 'Againe I was afloat', he writes. Jehangir seemed disposed to make Mukarrab Khan settle with him and to grant the cherished *farman* for an English factory. Hawkins also had high hopes of receiving back payment of his promised salary. Then once again his enemies rallied and the Portuguese outbid him for the Emperor's favour. He applied for leave to depart from Agra and, instead of being detained with fair promises as expected, he found himself dismissed. With Mrs Hawkins, her few jewels and her many relatives, he left Agra in November 1611. His plan was to head for Goa and with the help of the Portuguese, only too pleased to hasten his retreat, to sail from there to Europe. In the event he changed his plans and headed for Surat. An English vessel, indeed a most impressive fleet, was off the 'bar' and its commander was adopting a radically different approach to both Moghul officialdom and the Portuguese.

ii

While English attempts to establish themselves at Surat were getting nowhere very slowly, events on the other side of the Arabian Sea had overtaken them. Although Keeling and Hawkins had failed to reach the Red Sea ports the *Ascension*, before running aground on the coast of Gujarat, had made good this omission. By chance she had also discovered the Seychelle Islands. 'They seemed to us', opined the ship's boatswain, 'an earthly paradise.' But they were as yet uninhabited save for giant turtles and even the most pie-eyed of factors could see no commercial potential for turtle flesh 'because they did look so uglie before they were boyled'.

Aden, 'that famous and stronge place', could hardly compare with the Seychelles. 'A most uncomfortable place', thought Jourdain, 'for within the walls there is not any green thing growing, onlie your delight must be in the cragged rocks and decayed houses.' The city was still in ruins following its conquest by the Turks in 1538. Small quantities of gum arabic, frankincense and myrrh were obtainable but the main terminus for oceanic shipping was now round the coast at Mocha in the Red Sea itself.

While the *Ascension* made for Mocha through the straits of Bab-el-Mandeb, Jourdain, with the usual royal letter of introduction, journeyed inland to Sana'a, the capital. Yemen was a land of picturesque surprises; high passes gave way to fertile valleys in one of which he identified extensive plantations of what he called 'cohoo. 'The seeds of this cohoo is a great marchandise for it is carried to Grand Cairo and all other places of Turkey and the Indias.' 'Kahwa' was the word used by the Arabs; in English it was sometimes rendered as 'coughe' and eventually 'coffee'. Nowhere else in the world was it to be found and as yet there was no market for it in Europe. But by the 1660s coffee would become the staple export of the Red Sea ports.

At Sana'a Jourdain obtained permission to trade from the Turkish Pasha, or governor, and then proceeded on to Mocha. Thence a letter was sent via Cairo to London representing the potential of Mocha in highly favourable but misleading terms. In fact the town proved 'unreasonable hott'; the Pasha's permission was for the *Ascension*'s trade only, not for the establishment of a factory; and a profitable sale for the ship's ballast, mostly iron, was lost through her commander 'bursting out in anger saying that the merchants of Mocha mocked him to offer so little'.

But the Company knew nothing of this and in 1609, believing Hawkins favourably established in India and the Red Sea trade already wide open to them, the directors instructed the ships of their Sixth Voyage to concentrate on the Arabian Sea. After much deliberation James I had just granted the Company that new and enlarged charter; thanks largely to David Middleton's success in the Spice Islands, confidence in the profitability of Eastern trade was growing; peers of the realm and ministers of state were willing to invest. To discredit the arguments of its critics and to capitalize on this spirit of optimism, it was vital that the Company be seen to be making the most of its eastern monopoly and to be doing its utmost for English exports. At £82,000 the subscription raised for this voyage was the highest yet. Two of its three ships – the wishfully named *Trades Increase* and the *Peppercorn* were brand new and the total tonnage for the voyage was second only to that of Lancaster's fleet. English manufactures, mostly woollens, made up half the value of its trading stock. And Henry Middleton, now Sir Henry, was appointed commander. It was the sort of fleet of which a man of quality need not feel ashamed.

Having taken seven months over a voyage which took Keeling eighteen, all three ships were off the coast of Socotra by 18 October 1609. They 'sheathed their pinis' and learnt from the sultan of the island that the *Ascension* 'had sold all her goods' at Mocha. 'This newes gave mee good content,' noted Middleton. In expectation of doing as well if not better he headed for the Red Sea. The *Peppercorn* was left at Aden and on 13 November the other two ships came to rest off Mocha. In the case of the *Trades Increase* anchors were unnecessary. The enormous ship was in fact aground and had to be almost entirely unloaded before she could be refloated. This was contrary to the Company's instructions which insisted that, where there was no factory, goods should never be landed until sold. Under the circumstances Middleton had little choice; but the landing of his cargo undoubtedly weakened his bargaining position and aroused the cupidity – and suspicions – of Mocha's officials.

The Turkish official in charge of the port had the title of Aga and for two weeks the English could find no fault with the warmth of his welcome. They were given an extensive property, Middleton was honoured with a robe of crimson silk embroidered with silver thread, and every day presents arrived from the castle. On the evening of 28 November, records Middleton, 'according to my wonted custom I caused stooles to be sett at the doore where myself, Master Femmel and Master Pemberton [the principal factors] sat to take the fresh aire'. The red sun slid, orb-like, into the Red Sea; the *muezzin* sounded from the city's mosques; contentment reigned. An emissary from the Aga dropped by and Middleton sent his servant to fetch the interpreter. The man burbled on in Arabic. 'As he was aboute to say somewhat else, my man returned in great feare telling us wee were all betrayed, for that the Turkes and my people were by the eares at the backe of the house.'

> I myself ranne after them, calling upon them as loud as I could to return backe and make good our house. But whiles I was thus speaking I was strooke upon the head downe to the grounde by one that came behinde mee.

Consciousness returned with the 'extreame paine' of having his hands tightly bound. He was immediately jerked to his feet and dragged off to prison. On the way he was robbed of all his money and of his three gold rings. 'Then beganne they to put us in irons, myself with seven men being chained by the neckes all together.' Eight of his men had been killed in the fighting, fourteen were badly wounded, and the remaining forty-eight were in chains. The only ray of hope was that a simultaneous assault on the ships had failed. But there too blood had been spilt and three Englishmen killed.

Why the Aga had so abruptly changed his tune was something of a mystery. In the interrogations that followed he accused the English of having broken a long-standing embargo against any Christian shipping calling at the pilgrim ports of the Red Sea. This was nonsense, although Islamic sensibilities could easily be aroused so near the sacred cities of Medina and Mecca and particularly so when, as now, fanaticism was heightened by the pangs of Ramadan. The Aga claimed to be acting on the orders of the Pasha at Sana'a; but the sight of Middleton and his men brazenly quaffing their madeira outside their house would have constituted a powerful provocation.

There was also, of course, the incentive of loot. To persuade Middleton to order the surrender of his shipping was now the Aga's top priority. He tried bargaining – life and liberty for his captives in return for their ships' cargoes – and he tried intimidation.

> They stowed me all that day in a dirty dogge's kennell under a paire of stairs . . . my lodging was upon the hard grounde, my pillow a stone, and my companions to keep me waking were griefe of heart and multitude of rats which, if I chanced to sleepe, would awake me with running over me.

For three weeks Sir Henry languished in his kennel daily expecting to be led away for execution. Instead he and all the rest were ordered up to Sana'a. 'Our irons were knockt off our legges' and a string of donkeys was provided for their conveyance. So was a guard of soldiers.

At Ta'iz, four days from Mocha, they were 'marshalled into the citie two by two in a ranke as they doe at Stamboul with captives taken in the warres'. The townsfolk stood, stared and jeered and a sickly youth in Master Pemberton's employ fell by the wayside. It was Christmas Day.

> I kept no journal from this time forward [writes Middleton] but this I remember: we found it very colde all the way from Ta'iz to Sana'a, our lodging being the colde grounde covered with horie frost. In Sana'a we had ice a finger thicke in one night, which I could hardly have beleeved had I not seene it. I bought most of our men furred gowns to keep them from the colde; otherwise I think they would have starved.

They were fifteen days on the road and at Sana'a, 'a citie somewhat bigger than Bristoll', they were again paraded ignominiously through the streets. Then they were 'clapt in waightie irons' and consigned to prison.

The Pasha, like the Aga, claimed that he was only following orders. But it now emerged that the orders came from Istanbul and were in fact based on sound commercial considerations. In outbidding local merchants for the cargoes of Indian vessels reaching Mocha, the *Ascension*'s factors had unwittingly stirred up a hornets' nest of resentment. From Mecca, Cairo and Damascus had come complaints about the consequent dearth of Indian goods; additionally Mocha had been deprived of its customary import duties. Not so long ago the Arabs and the Turks had seen the bulk of their transit trade in spices diverted round the Cape by the Portuguese; now the remaining trickle of spices plus the valuable trade in Indian cottons and indigo were being threatened on their own doorstep by the English. English trade in the Red Sea was clearly detrimental to that of Arabia and Egypt; the English must therefore be discouraged from ever again entering the region.

Middleton took the point. While still fuming over the treacherous manner in which he had been treated, he had no answer to the Pasha's logic and agreed that English ships would in future steer clear of the area. The way was now open for negotiations over the release of the hostages. In these Middleton relied heavily on the intercession of other merchants, especially the powerful Indian community. The Gujaratis had welcomed the English as trading partners and were not without blame in dislocating Arabian trade. They were also fearful of English retribution – and with good reason.

For by the time Middleton and his men had been authorized to trail back to Mocha, it was March and the season for the arrival of shipping from India. April saw the port fill with dhows from Cambay, Surat and Dabhol, from the Malabar coast, Socotra, Sri Lanka and the Maldives. They were met by enormous camel caravans from Damascus, Suez and Mecca. This was the ancient exchange on which the prosperity of Arabia had subsisted and which the advent of English shipping threatened. There was no chance of Middleton being allowed to open shop but there was every chance that if the bullish Englishman were to regain his ships he would come amongst the dhows to wreak vengeance. The Aga therefore prevaricated over actually dismissing the English and saw to it that their commander was closely guarded.

On 11 May Middleton smuggled a note out to his fleet. The Turks were feasting their Indian guests, his guards were drunk, and 'God had put into my head a devise.' The 'devise' was a plan of escape. He instructed his men to saunter, ever so casually, to two pre-arranged embarkation points and await a boat. He himself climbed into an empty water butt; the butt was then sealed and floated out to sea. After what, even by seventeenth-century standards, must have been a cramped voyage, he was taken in tow by a tender from the English fleet, 'which being done, I forced out the heade of the caske and came aboord'. His men fared less well, half of them being taken before they could be embarked'. But Middleton was free and once back on the heavily armed *Trades Increase* he gave his anger full rein. 'I sent the Aga word that if he did not send me all my people with those provisions of the ships which he detained . . . I would fire the [Indian] ships in the road and do my best to batter the towne about his eares.' To show he meant business he blockaded the port, interposing his own ships between the dhows and the shore.

The Aga 'began to sing a new song' – but at the same tempo; he was still playing for time. It was 28 May before all the English were released and 2 July before a final settlement was reached about the cargo. Middleton still hankered after revenge and for a whole month more he lay in wait for a richly laden vessel that was expected from Suez. Both the Pasha and the Aga supposedly had shares in her. 'Yett she escaped us in the night.' On 9 August, to catch the last of the westerly monsoon, Middleton ordered his ships to sail for Surat. The Aga must have breathed a long Turkish sigh of relief. It seemed reasonable to suppose that he had seen the last of the English and the last of Sir Henry Middleton.

iii

In India Middleton's appraisal of the English position was inevitably coloured by his recent experiences at Mocha. He had hoped to find a factory at Surat, Hawkins in high favour at Agra, and the *Ascension*'s factors manfully extending English trade. In the event he found no factory and no factors. His letters ashore were answered by a ship's carpenter (the well named Nicholas Bangham who had absconded from the *Hector* in 1607) who reported that Jourdain and his followers were even now straggling back from Agra and that a disgraced Hawkins with his family were not far behind. Worse still, Middleton could not even get ashore to ascertain matters. A small armada of Portuguese frigates was blocking the mouth of the Tapti and both on land and sea Portuguese patrols lay in wait for his men. Under the circumstances trade seemed out of the question. Another rescue mission was the most he could hope to achieve. Accordingly he positioned his fleet alongside three Gujarati vessels that were anchored off the 'bar' and announced in a now familiar ultimatum that they 'should not depart till I had all the Englishmen aboord of me'.

The first of his would-be passengers to arrive at Surat was Jourdain. With help from Mukarrab Khan, of whom he had a better opinion than did Hawkins, he donned disguise and slipped past the Portuguese land patrols. Then he hid in the fields for three days, swam across a muddy creek, and eventually gained the attention of one of the English fleet's boats by scaling a sand dune and waving his unravelled turban. 'The skiffe came near the shore and I waded into her.' He had arrived in India as a castaway (from the *Ascension*); now he left in the same bedraggled state.

His news, however, was not all depressing. Mukarrab Khan was evidently keen to obtain whatever the new fleet carried in the way of novelties suitable for Jehangir and was therefore making tempting offers about trade. So was the governor of Surat and from him Jourdain had learnt of a safe inshore anchorage just north of the mouth of the Tapti. It was called, rather uninvitingly, Swalley Hole. On the second attempt Middleton found the spot and safely eased two of his ships over its mud 'bar'. It was not exactly a port, just an unremarkable piece of Gujarati shoreline. But amidst the lush fields and marsh grasses there soon sprang up an instant bazaar. The English fleet badly needed fresh water, meat, vegetables, whatever the land could offer; the men hankered after exercise and alcohol, and the merchants revived their expectations of trade. Swalley became the first purely English addition to the map of India.

From November 1611 till February 1612 the fleet remained there. Portuguese troops continued to molest any who trod the twelve cross-country miles to Surat but at Swalley itself the English were safe. So much so that goods were landed and some calicoes and indigo bought. When Mukarrab Khan himself came aboard and was visibly impressed by the ships' strength and contents, it looked as if Middleton's gloomy forebodings had been misplaced. A factory at Surat was again being mentioned, although it was unclear to what extent this depended on further gratifying Mukarrab Khan's curiosity. Already he had been through Middleton's lockers and successfully wheedled out of him his 'perfumed jerkin', a beaver hat and a 'spaniell dogge'. 'Whatsoever he sawe there of mine that he tooke liking to, I gave him for nothing.'

There were a few tense exchanges about the price of Indian goods and the accuracy of Indian scales but well into January trade was still proceeding and Mukarrab Khan still smiling. Then the Hawkins *ménage* reached Surat and matters abruptly changed. Without so much as an explanation Mukarrab Khan denied ever having mentioned a factory and peremptorily ordered the English fleet to depart. Jourdain, for one, made the obvious connection; Hawkins 'was the chiefest cause Mukarrab Khan made such haste for us to be gone' and was 'the cause that Sir Henrie had not settled a factory'. But this was surely just another attempt to discredit 'the Captain'. It was Jehangir, under pressure from the Portuguese, who had dismissed Hawkins and it was almost certainly Jehangir who ordered Mukarrab Khan to get rid of the English fleet.

With Hawkins, Mrs Hawkins, Jourdain, most of the *Ascension*'s factors and officers, and any other Englishmen keen to see their homes again, the fleet finally sailed on 9 February. After four years the first English attempt to trade with the Moghul empire had come to nothing; and during four months Middleton had not so much as seen Surat. Ironically, just as he was leaving he received a letter 'from one Peter Floris' recently arrived at somewhere called Masulipatnam. His 'estate', Floris reported, was 'in good being'. There at least trade had been established.

Middleton proceeded on down the west coast of India to Dabhol, the main port of the kingdom of Bijapur and a place of considerably more importance than the nearby Portuguese settlement at Bon Bahia (later Bombay). At Dabhol some broadcloth was sold while on board the *Trades Increase* an important conference took place. The question was whether the fleet should continue to Bantam or whether it should first return to the Red Sea. The monsoon winds favoured the Red Sea and so did Middleton. The others concurred 'though for divers reasons'.

One was that the letter from Floris had spoken of another Company fleet already on its way there; they must be warned off. Another was the juicy prospect of interfering with that great spring concourse of Indian shipping at Mocha. Jourdain saw this simply as a means of 'recompense of the wrong done us at Suratt'; and in conformity with this Indo-centric view, Middleton's conduct has often been represented as a vengeful and unscrupulous act of piracy against the Moghul shipping.

But this was not how Middleton saw it. He had no quarrel with the commanders of India's Arabian Sea fleets and had in fact received much kindness from them during his earlier tribulations in the Yemen. As he explained, by staying their ships 'I thought we should do ourselves some right and them no wrong to cause them to barter with us, we to take their goods as they were worth and they ours in lieu thereof'. It would be trade under duress certainly, but not pillage; and the party to suffer most by it would not be the ships of the Moghul, but the officials of Mocha. For in Sir Henry's opinion the decisive reason for sailing back to the Red Sea was 'to take some revenge for the great and insufferable wrongs and injuries done me by the Turkes there'. He was thinking of his dead comrades, of those 'waightie irons' and of the 'dirty dogge's kennell'.

By April the fleet was in position across the straits of Bab-el-Mandeb and the Indian dhows were being corralled into a holding area in the Bay of Assab. Here, on the Ethiopian coast, each vessel was 'rommaged'. A selection was made of its most desirable commodities, and broadcloth put in their place. Middleton meanwhile wrote to the Aga of Mocha explaining his behaviour and inviting compensation if not capitulation. Dearly would he have loved to witness the Aga's reaction. But his old adversary had, it transpired, been replaced; and the new incumbent claimed an unexpected ally in John Saris, commander of the Company's Eighth Voyage amongst whose ships was the Japan-bound *Clove*.

Armed with a magnificent specimen of Arabic calligraphy that was in fact a safe-conduct from the Sultan in Istanbul, Saris had seen fit to ignore a letter of caution left by Middleton at Socotra and had duly sailed into Mocha. A sumptuous reception from the new Aga and his entourage – Saris called them 'his buggering boyes' – left the newcomers in no doubt that their trade was welcome. Already the first bargains had been struck and an English deputation was about to pay a courtesy call on the Pasha at Sana'a.

Not surprisingly word of Middleton's interference went down badly with the Aga and badly with Saris. The former abruptly broke off trade and accused Saris of abusing the Sultan's protection. Saris himself saw what he called 'Sir Henrie's brabbles and jarres with the Turkes and the Cambayans [i.e. the people of Surat]' as threatening the success of his own voyage throughout the Arabian Sea. On 15 April he went aboard the *Trades Increase* and demanded an explanation. Middleton stuck to his guns; he would take from the Indian ships 'what he thought fitting and then', according to Saris, 'if I would, I might take the rest'. Saris replied that in that case he would sail away to windward and forestall him. 'Whereat Sir Henrie swore most deeply that if I did take that course he would sinke me and sett fire of all such ships as traded with me.'

The preoccupation with personal trade plus the system of separate accounting for each voyage meant that the common good of the Company received little consideration. It was every fleet for itself, and although Middleton and Saris eventually reached an agreement on the division of spoils, the bickering continued; mutineers on 'Jack' Saris's ships looked to Middleton for redress; Middleton tried to deprive Saris of any cottons that might compete with his own cargo when they eventually reached Bantam. Jourdain and Hawkins looked on in disgust. The two commanders 'used very grosse speeches not fitting to men of their ranke' thought Jourdain, 'and were so crosse the one to the other as if they had beene enymies'.

In all some fifteen Indian vessels were 'rommaged' including one of over 1000 tons. Their goods were generally valued at above cost price but then so was the English broadcloth given in exchange. In a letter to Jehangir Middleton described his proceedings and, by way of explanation, catalogued the English grievances, especially Hawkins's losses on Mukarrab Khan's account. Jehangir, it seems, was not much bothered. Whilst not exactly approving, he refused to take up the cause of his skippers and thought that they had been reasonably treated.

In August 1612, having effectively ended all hopes of trade both in the Red Sea and in Gujarat for the foreseeable future, the last English vessels departed. They sailed for the pepper ports of Sumatra and Java and were soon locked in further quarrels with one another. Most of Middleton's men succumbed to that Bantam epidemic which Jourdain so graphically described. As the *Trades Increase* burnt and then rotted, Middleton's own demise was credited simply to a broken heart. In the meantime Saris went on to Japan, Jourdain to the Moluccas, and Hawkins to England. 'The Captain' sailed on the *Hector*, the ship which five years before had deposited him at Surat; but he died before he reached home. That left Mrs Hawkins, the Armenian 'mayden', an English widow before she saw England. She was not, however, friendless. Gabriel Towerson, the indestructible Bantam factor, was the commander of the *Hector* and by the time he sailed back to the Indies Mrs Hawkins had become Mrs Towerson. She sailed with him, regained her numerous family in India, and, courtesy of the Amboina Massacre, would be a widow once again within the decade.

CHAPTER FIVE

The Keye of All India

THE CAPE, SURAT AND PERSIA

In 1613, as well as Mrs Hawkins, his future bride, Gabriel Towerson brought home another curiosity – the first South African to set foot in England. 'Coree', as the man was called, was a reluctant immigrant. With a fellow 'Saldanian' of Table Bay he had made the mistake of accepting an invitation to board the *Hector*. Acting on previous instructions from the Company, Towerson detained both men. The ship put back to sea, 'the poor wretches' grieved pitifully, and the companion died; it was 'merely out of extreme sullenness', complained his captors, 'for he was very well used'. Coree, although equally unappreciative of his good fortune, had at least the grace to survive and was duly landed in London. There Sir Thomas Smythe himself, still Governor of the Company, accommodated him and nobly assumed the responsibility of equipping him for civilized society.

By common consent – and not a little conceit – the natives of Table Bay were reckoned the most primitive creatures Europe had yet encountered. Indeed 'I think the world could not yield a more heathenish people and more beastlie', declared Jourdain as he witnessed a horde of them devouring a mound of putrid fish guts 'that noe Christian could abyde to come within a myle of'. Their meat too, especially entrails, they preferred well hung; and for convenience as well as appearance, where they hung it was round their necks. 'They would pull off and eate these greasy tripes half raw, the blood loathsomely slavering.' To English eyes it was not a pretty sight and because the Saldanians also anointed their bodies with decomposing animal fats, to English noses they gave off a most offensive smell. Additionally they stole, cringed and lied. They tilled no fields (they were, as their visitors knew to their advantage, pastoralists), they said no prayers, and they wore very few clothes, 'onlie a short cloake of sheepe or seale skinnes to their middle, a cap of the same, and a kind of ratte skinne about their privities'.

> The women's habit is as the men's. They were shamefac'd at first; but on our returne homewards they would lift up their ratte skinnes and shew their privities. Their breasts hang to the middle; their hair curled.

This was the Reverend Patrick Copland, chaplain of the Tenth Voyage. The nicest thing that he could find to say of them was that they danced 'in true measure' and that, once they had overcome a fear born of too many Dutchmen rustling their cattle, they were 'loving'.

If Coree was anything to go by, they were also obstinate. 'He had good diet, good cloaths, good lodging and all other fitting accommodations . . . yet all this contented him not.' With perverse determination he pined for his heathenish homeland and 'would daily lie upon the ground and cry very often thus in broken English "Coree home go, Saldania go, home go"'. His only consolation was a suit of chain mail complete with armoured breastplate, helmet and backplate and all forged out of brass, 'his beloved metal'. This conspicuous outfit he cherished greatly and wore whenever occasion offered. In it, in March 1614, he at last stumbled aboard the *New Year's Gift* and, still wearing it, clanked off into Africa when the ship called at Table Bay. It was his only memento of civilization for 'he had no sooner sett foot on his own shore but did presently throw away his cloaths, his linen and other covering and got his sheepskin upon his back and guts aboute his neck'.

Whether, as hoped, he repaid his patrons by disposing his people towards the English remains a moot point. One seafarer complained that he simply acquainted the Saldanians with the going rates for fatstock and ironmongery in London. As a result 'we had never after such a free exchange of our brass and iron for their cattle'. But in 1615 the commander of the *Expedition* was royally entertained by Coree's family and found the people 'nothing as fearful as at other times nor so thievish'. Cattle were both plentiful and cheap and in Coree's 'towne' even the youngest inhabitants could say 'Sir Thomas Smythe' and 'English ships' which 'they often with great glorie repeat'. Some actually begged a passage to England 'seeing Coree had sped so well and returned so rich with his brass suit which he yet keepeth in his house very charily'.

While the Company's fleets plied back and forth grimly bent on momentous matters of war and trade, southern Africa – whose undreamt of reserves in gold and diamonds could have bought more cottons and spices than all Europe could consume – provided mere light relief. Here outgoing crews took a last bracing breath before plunging into Asia's malarial miasma and here returning wanderers dared to dream again of cool green pastures and dank ale houses. The Cape was deliciously temperate and many a passing factor marvelled at its agricultural potential. A dedicated band of horticulturalists and hoteliers could turn it into a veritable paradise 'healthfull and commodious for all who trade the East Indyes'. Jourdain even suspected that it might afford some saleable commodities. For it was 'in the midst of two rich countries, Ginnee [Guinea] and Mozambique'. He was thinking particularly of 'elephaunt's teeth', for that we saw the footinge of manie'. Much in demand throughout the East, ivory sometimes made up a substantial percentage of outgoing investments. But it could only be purchased in Europe which it reached by way of north Africa, and was therefore never cheap.

Responding to such promptings, in 1615 the Company agreed to an experiment. Ten condemned men who had lately been awaiting execution in Newgate prison were shipped aboard the *Expedition*. They proved troublesome shipmates and reluctant pioneers. But in due course they were dumped at one end of Table Bay and thus became the first English convicts to be deported to the southern hemisphere. They were also the Company's first colonists and south Africa's first white settlers. With such dubious claims to fame it was hardly surprising that they fared badly.

Tools and provisions were also landed and one Captain Cross, a yeoman of the royal guard who had been convicted of several duelling deaths, assumed command. Expectations of 'a plantation or at leaste a discoverye further into that countrye' were quickly disappointed. When the homeward-bound *Hope* sent Cross in search of beef cattle he was ambushed by Coree's Saldanians and one of his followers killed. A peace of sorts was patched up and Coree obligingly sent cattle 'and as an extraordinarie favour one of his wifes'. 'The cattell we bought', wrote the *Hope*'s commander, pointedly. In return for the promise of a house 'built after the mannor in England' Coree also agreed to help the settlers. Captain Cross, however, was taking no chances. He successfully pleaded for muskets and a boat and was understood to be planning the removal of his camp to an island in the bay. Already densely populated with creatures described as part beast, part bird and part fish 'which hath a strange and proude kind of going and finny wings', the island was duly called Penguin Island. Its name has since been changed to Robben Island. Captain Cross and his men must have been the only convicts ever voluntarily to have removed to a penal settlement more notorious than Alcatraz.

Like later exiles, Cross soon discovered that penguins were poor company and rank eating, and that escaping from Robben Island could be difficult. Their boat was 'split in pieces' and a raft constructed in its stead proved far from satisfactory. While paddling out to rendezvous with the *New Year's Gift* in February 1616 it was upset by two whales. 'Terrified with the whales and benummed with water' Cross somehow regained the island and 'having shifted a shirt and refreshed himself' tried again. He seemed to be making fair progress, then suddenly disappeared 'which is the last newes of him'.

With Cross gone, his followers made it known that they would rather return to Newgate than continue the unequal struggle. The *New Year's Gift* gave passage to three of them and the rest seem to have got aboard a passing Portuguese ship. When news of their failure reached a second consignment of deportees they begged that rather than be abandoned in Africa they be hanged from the yard-arm. Instead they were landed at Bantam, which was much the same thing. Meanwhile Coree and his people enjoyed a few more precious years in undisputed possession of their homeland.

In 1620, with James I taking a lively interest in East India Company affairs as a result of the Anglo-Dutch Treaty of Defence, Saldania was unofficially annexed by the Company on behalf of the Crown. Andrew Shilling, commander of the *London*, performed the honours by issuing to the empty veldt 'a solemn publication of His Majesty's title' and causing the erection of 'King James his mount' at Table Bay. But no fort was built and no English were settled. It was purely a tactical move designed to pre-empt the Dutch 'since no European power had at this time claimed a right to that part of the coast of Africa'. Coree was eventually superseded by Hadah who after picking up some English at Bantam was deposited on Robben Island, there to act as the Company's 'postman'. Whenever a ship anchored in the Bay he quickly donned jacket and hose and pushed past the penguins with whatever messages had been left in his care. Not till 1652 and Cromwell's Anglo-Dutch war was a permanent station established. Five years later the first colonists began erecting their homesteads. They were Dutch. A century and a half would elapse before the Company's claims, based on the adventures of Coree and Cross and the opportunism of Andrew Shilling, would be revived.

ii

Although for much of the seventeenth century the Dutch and English were bitter rivals throughout the East, on the long voyage to and from Europe hostilities were usually suspended. At the Cape and at St Helena ships of the London Company amicably exchanged news and provisions with those of the V.O.C. Hadah was postman for both Companies; and occasionally Dutch and English ships actually sailed together.

This was not the case with the Portuguese. Anywhere outside European waters Spain/Portugal continued to regard the ships of the Protestant powers as little better than pirates and, peace treaties notwithstanding, they jealously maintained the exclusive character of their eastern bases. In the Arabian Sea further English endeavours at Surat and Swalley between 1612 and 1620 were seen as a direct challenge to Portugal's maritime supremacy on the very threshold of its eastern metropolis at Goa. The Portuguese would respond vigorously. But once again a purely Indo-centric reading of these engagements is misleading. At stake was a dominant role not just in India's external trade but in that of all the trading coasts of the Arabian Sea including the Red Sea and the Persian Gulf. Naval battles in the Gulf of Cambay would have counted for little had not the Portuguese also been challenged at Hormuz, Goa, and a host of lesser ports from the coast of Mozambique to that of Malabar. Hostilities would last for twenty years; and they would embrace the whole trading world between Africa and India.

In 1612, blissfully ignorant of Sir Henry Middleton's débâcles at Mocha and Surat, the Company had despatched two more ships for Surat, the Twelfth Voyage, under the command of Thomas Best, a highly experienced master mariner. The commander, or 'General', of an East India Company fleet controlled two distinct establishments, the one nautical and headed by his subordinate captains and masters and the other commercial and headed by one or more chief merchants. Almost invariably commanders were appointed on the strength of their performances during a previous voyage; and usually they were merchants who had thus acquired some knowledge of navigation. Hence the ideal commander should be part sailor, part merchant and, if possible, part 'man of fashion and good respect'. But Thomas Best was just a sailor. Presumably the loss of the *Ascension* had convinced the directors that amongst Gujarat's treacherous mud banks navigational skills were more important than social graces. The difference is evident in Best's journal which triumphantly belies the idea that seventeenth-century travelogues were necessarily discursive and entertaining. True to his calling, Best merely kept a log.

Terse and laconic as it is, it is nevertheless odd that this document contains no mention of the fleet's first contact with the Portuguese which occurred in the Mozambique channel north of Madagascar. In what may be a reference to it, Best elsewhere refers to 'the goodliest ship thatt ever I sawe' as being a Portuguese carrack 'with a tower of ordnance beseeming a castell'. From the journal of one of his subordinates it appears that there were in fact two such ships off Madagascar, each of over 1500 tons and each intent on putting its tower of ordnance to good use. Broadsides were exchanged and at least three Portuguese killed before Best 'steered away his course'. 'For yt was contrarie to commission to meddle with them in respecte of peace we have with their king.' But the English crews were 'prepared to feight' and if they felt somewhat cheated by Best's delicacy, their rancour would be short-lived.

Best reached the mouth of the Tapti river in September 1612, only six months after Middleton had been ordered to sea by Mukarrab Khan. The news that all the English factors had been withdrawn was depressing enough but when word arrived of Middleton's retaliatory activities in the Red Sea, Best despaired. The news affected him 'like a drinke of cold water to a man on a cold and frostie morning'. Already two of his factors had been captured by the Portuguese. As soon as he could secure their release he was all for beating a hasty retreat towards Bantam.

But his remaining factors were more sanguine and Best, reckoning they knew their own business best, sensibly deferred to them. It seemed that for once the Moghul officials were being positively obliging. Perhaps they were worried that Best might follow Middleton's example and blockade their shipping in the Red Sea. Perhaps they had simply re-evaluated the advantages of a new trading partner and a new source of largesse. At all events a *farman* granting interim trading rights was immediately forthcoming, a promise was made that within forty days it would be ratified by Jehangir, and the English were invited to send another representative to Agra to negotiate a permanent agreement. It was as if the dismissals of Hawkins and Middleton had all been a terrible mistake. Within days of the fleet's arrival new emissaries and a new letter from King James were on their way to Court. So were some of the presents known to please the dilettante emperor. There were paintings 'espetially such as discover Venus' and Cupid's actes' and there were various musical instruments in the care of Lancelot Canning, a virtuoso on the virginals, and Robert Trully, a cornettist. The latter found high favour with Jehangir. He converted to Islam and eventually blew his cornet in half the courts of India. Not so Lancelot Canning. The virginals proved too insipid for Moghul tastes and the mortified Canning, a distant kinsman of India's future Viceroy, is described as having 'dyed of conceitt'.

Best meanwhile repaired to Swalley to await Jehangir's confirmation of the *farman*. As usual during any period in port the crews took to drinking and gambling. Even at ill-appointed Swalley Hole two men were ducked from the yard-arm for swimming ashore on the Sabbath and getting 'drinking drunke with whores ashore'. Instructions issued to the commanders of all Company fleets proscribed such conduct in the most vigorous terms. But as with the injunctions against private trade, those against blasphemy, gaming and drunkenness were habitually ignored. They may be seen as implying not that the English seafarer of the seventeenth century was a God-fearing paragon of Puritan virtues but exactly the opposite.

It took the arrival of an impressive Portuguese fleet to bring the Swalley revellers to their senses. There were four galleons (warships, smaller than the cargo-carrying carracks but larger than any of the English vessels) and twenty-five inshore frigates. They had been dispatched from Goa and their instructions were to disperse the new English challenge by force of arms.

In the engagements that followed – and in those fought by ships of Richard Downton's fleet two years later – the Portuguese were apparently the stronger. They had more ships and their ships had more men. They were also larger and, under full sail, faster. But they were of deeper draught, less manoeuvrable, poorly crewed, and under-gunned. Portuguese tactics still relied heavily on grappling-irons and fire-ships, the idea being to panic the enemy and then get alongside him for a full-blooded boarding in which higher superstructures and numerical superiority must prove decisive.

But all this assumed that men-of-war were just floating castles and that their defenders would always heave to and fight it out. This was not how the English had frustrated the Armada and, according to a disgruntled Portuguese account, it was not how Best chose to conduct his battles in the Gulf of Cambay.

> The reason [for the Portuguese failure] was that the enemy's [i.e. the English] vessels drew less water and thus could retreat or attack

> when they pleased, not making it a point of honour never to show their backs as did our men; for being ships of war we should feel it a great disgrace to avoid an encounter, while they, relying only on artillery fire from a distance, withdrew or came on as they pleased thanks to the hardiness of their vessels which were well-fitted and better sailers than ours.

Although the Portuguese galleons never got within grappling-iron distance of Best's ships they did manage to surprise the *Merchant's Hope* of Downton's fleet. Swordsmen swarmed aboard her and a desperate struggle ensued. Three times the English appeared to be done for, and it was only thanks to the timely arrival of their whole fleet that the boarders were finally repelled. The ship had been dismasted and would require an elaborate refit. 'I never sawe menn fight with greater resolution than the Portingales', declared Downton; in no way could they be 'taxed with cowardice as some have done.'

But this close encounter was the exception. For the most part the English persisted with their gun-boat tactics, keeping at a safe distance and exploiting wind and tide to manoeuvre over the mud banks and swoop in open water. All the aggression came from the gunners. 'We began to play upon their Vice-Admiral with great and small shott', writes Best of his first engagement. In the second the *Red Dragon* (Lancaster's old flagship) 'steered from one to another and gave them such banges as maid their verie sides crack'. Her sister ship, the *Hosiander*, is described as 'dancing the hay' amongst the enemy or, better still since her master was a certain Nathaniel Salmon, as 'swimming, frisking lightly (but not without effect), and leaping about these huge whale carkasses'. Among the English, losses were negligible, typically three or four dead and as many injured. The Portuguese fared worse but since no large ships were either sunk or captured, estimates of several hundred dead were probably exaggerated. There would be sterner battles between the English and the Portuguese but they were not fought in the waters off Surat and are therefore often ignored in histories of the Company's doings in India.

Best outsmarted the Portuguese in two two-day encounters and Downton in a series of protracted skirmishes. The factors naturally took great delight in these victories. Besides confounding their commercial rivals, they had made a most salutary impression on the Moghul authorities. Best's second assault was watched by a whole Moghul army which lined the shore and later 'divulged the same farre and near to our nation's great fame'. Yet at the time both Best and Downton, mindful of the Company's instruction to avoid hostilities, were reluctant warriors. Best could see no prospect of either loot or lasting commercial advantage and to provide his men with some token of appreciation for their bravery he was obliged to waylay a number of innocent Malabar dhows. The moment the Portuguese backed off he too was all for withdrawing and hastening to Bantam to proceed with the main business of his voyage. Only the urgent protestations of Thomas Aldworth, one of his factors, persuaded him to wait on for Jehangir's confirmation of the *farman* and then to leave behind goods and factors at Surat.

Aldworth was immensely optimistic about prospects for trade at Surat. It was, he told the Company in a letter of January 1613, 'the fountainhead from which we may draw all the trade of the East Indies, for we find here merchandise we can take and sell in nearly all parts of the Indies and in England'. Moreover he hazarded that it could all be paid for with exports of English broadcloth. Best was too 'incredulous'; in other words he was unconvinced. Profits – his own as well as the Company's – lay in pepper and spices. He proved his point by eventually showing a handsome return on the investment for his voyage and a colossal profit on his own investment. On his private stock of pepper the freight charges alone would be estimated at £300 and in the wake of his returning fleet the Channel ports were said to be awash with contraband spices. He was saved from prosecution only by the celebrity that attached to his victories over the Portuguese.

Aldworth's expectations of driving a brisk trade in broadcloth soon proved mistaken. Some was sold as horse blankets – or as their elephant equivalents – but in India as in Japan English tweed never caught on as human apparel. Nevertheless the Indian trade prospered. Indigo, the blue dye obtained from a species of vetch, and of course the usual cornucopia of Indian cottons were readily available and sold well both in the Indonesian archipelago and, increasingly, in England. The *Merchant's Hope*, refitted after the Portuguese attack, was the first vessel to sail straight from Surat to England where her cargo of mainly cotton goods was quickly disbursed. Instead of English tweeds revolutionizing Eastern fashions, Indian cottons were about to invade English domestic life. Napkins and table-cloths, bed sheets and soft furnishings, not to mention underwear and dress fabrics, quite suddenly became indispensable to every respectable household. A new vocabulary of chintzes and calicoes, taffetas, muslins, ginghams and cashmeres entered everyday use. Having first invaded the larder, Eastern produce was about to take over the linen cupboard.

iii

In 1614 the Indian trade was particularly profitable thanks to a temporary falling out between the Emperor and his Portuguese allies which led to an embargo on Portuguese shipping. Cottons became cheaper, indigo plentiful.

At about the same time the Company in London voted to end the system of a separate subscription for each voyage and to replace it with what is usually called the First Joint Stock (1613–16). The joint-stock principle of corporate investment had of course applied to the separate voyages; and in that some of these subscriptions had been extended to include a second voyage while others had been subject to long delays before they could be finally wound up, subscribers had seldom received the quick return which they had anticipated. The First Joint Stock, which was to finance a fleet every year for four years, did not therefore represent a very significant change from the shareholders' point of view. As with subsequent issues – the Second Joint Stock (1617–22), etc – subscriptions were called in by yearly instalments and dividends paid out in the same way. But it did ensure greater continuity of investment; it enabled the Court of Committees to plan operations over a longer period; and, above all, it promised to end that spectacle, so prevalent at Bantam and to a lesser extent in India, of voyages undercutting one another and of rival factors squabbling over cargoes.

With a view to reorganizing and integrating its various overseas establishments in the light of this development, the Company dispatched William Keeling in 1614 with a supervisory authority to appoint regional Agents, later known as Presidents or Governors. A year later, with encouraging news of Best's activities at Surat, the Company judged the time right to step up its investment in India; and to match Portuguese influence there, the directors hit on the idea of appealing to King James to appoint an ambassador to the court of Jehangir. This was a novel departure, especially in the context of oriental diplomacy which scarcely recognized commerce as a legitimate reason for accreditation. It seemed sensible enough, though, to King James, especially when the Company volunteered to meet all the ambassadorial expenses.

Accordingly, armed with suitable presents and a long list of demands, in 1615 Sir Thomas Roe sailed for Surat. It was, according to most accounts, 'the turning point in the history of the British in Western India' and 'a landmark in the relations between England and India'.

For once the directors had broken their resolution to consort only with 'men of their own quality'. Roe, a courtier, diplomat and sometime Member of Parliament, described himself as 'a man of quality' which, as he proceeded to demonstrate, was a very different thing. When the Governor of Surat received him sitting down and advised him of the usual customs inspection and body search, Roe simply gathered up his entourage and returned to the fleet. Clearly the Indians did 'not sufficiently understand the rights belonging to my qualitye'; for 'my king's honour was engaged more deeply than I did expect and I was resolved to rectifye all or lay my life and fortune both in the ground'. Too many money-grubbing factors – like Hawkins – had been posing as ambassadors. Roe had to make the difference in 'quality' plain. He saw his job as 'repayring a ruined house and making streight that which was crooked' by, in both speech and conduct, conveying an altogether more exalted and dignified impression of English society and sovereignty. He would make no secret of his contempt for India; it was 'the dullest, basest place that ever I saw and maketh me weary of speaking of it'. Nor would he brook any nonsense from Moghul officials who 'triumph over such as yield but are humble enough when they are held up'.

In such utterances there is more than a hint of that distasteful conviction of moral superiority which would one day characterize imperialistic jingo. And perhaps some sense of affinity with Roe explains the enormous importance attached to his mission in later accounts of British beginnings in India. But Roe's posturing was based on 'quality' and class consciousness, not colour and race consciousness. If he was scathing about Jehangir's subordinates he was no less disdainful of the English factors. In Gujarat, as at Bantam, representatives of the different Company voyages had been quarrelling. Roe was expected to act as peacemaker. In the event it was the universal distrust of his motives and conduct, plus the death of Aldworth (after two years of dysentery he was described as 'more like an anatomy than a man'), which did most to unite the factors.

With matters of protocol at Surat still unresolved, Roe proceeded inland with a growing list of complaints to lay before the Emperor plus the terms of a rather one-sided treaty of trade and friendship which he hoped to persuade the Emperor to sign. His sobriety and high principles created a favourable impression. Jehangir 'had never used any ambassadour with so much respect', he reported. Aloof to the point of priggishness he shunned any imperial *camaraderie* that might prejudice his own dignity and proved more than a match for the Portuguese representatives. But during three long and weary years at court he failed to secure the desired treaty, he further alienated most of the Company's factors, and he very nearly sabotaged the one encouraging development of the period. When his term of office ended he was generously applauded by both King and Company but it is significant that a successor was never sought and indeed Roe himself advised against it. 'My qualitye either begets you enemies or suffers unworthily', he told the directors; a consul on 1000 rupees a year 'will serve you better than ten ambassadours'. Jehangir opposed any treaty that would impose limitations on his autocratic behaviour, and his court was no place for a selfless public servant; 'no conversation,' moaned Roe, '. . . no such entertainment as my qualitye requireth'.

In matters of trade the Ambassador's commission forbade him to interfere with the English factors. Although he eventually prevailed on the Company to change this, and although he frequently expressed his commercial opinons with much cogency, they were neither consistent not convincing. The man who is often credited with having established the Company's affairs in India on a sound commercial basis in fact condemned what he called 'the errour of factories', advised against opening trade with Bengal and Sind (although he had at first favoured both and, from Masulipatnam, Antheuniss was strongly urging the case of Bengal) and took the gloomiest possible view of future prospects. Because English exports, other than bullion, were not in great demand in India, the trade 'must fall to the ground by the weakness of its own legs'. 'I hope not in success but I would not the failing were on my part'. At one point he was all for abandoning Surat as the main English port, at another he was asking for permission to build a fort there. Yet, in an oft quoted and supposedly prophetic passage, he strongly advised against fortified settlements. 'If he [Prince Kurram , the future Shah Jehan] would offer me ten I would not accept one . . . for without controversy it is an errour to affect garrisons and land warrs in India'. He was thinking of the Portuguese whose 'many rich residences and territoryes' were the 'beggering' of their trade. 'Lett this be received as a rule, that if you will profitt, seek it at sea and in quiett trade.'

This quiet maritime trade was, however, to include gratuitous assaults on both Moghul and Portuguese shipping 'for the offensive is both the nobler and safer part'. 'We must chasten these people. . . .' Goa should be blockaded and 'if the Mogul's shipps be taken but once in four years there shall come more clear gayne without loss of honour than will advance in seven years by trade'.

Roe was aware that his own influence at Court had as much to do with English naval prowess as with his supposed 'qualitye'. In 1616 a fleet from England had again fallen in with a Portuguese carrack off the east African coast. 'She was a ship of exceeding great bulk and burthen, our *Charles* though a ship of 1000 tons looking like a pinnace when she was beside her.' Within an hour of the cannonade beginning Benjamin Joseph, commander of the English fleet, was slain. Again the Portuguese fought gallantly, hanging out a lantern at night so that the English could not accuse them of flight. Next day Captain Pepwell of the *Globe*, Floris's old ship, was struck by 'a great shot in his halfe deck'. His master lost an arm and 'another had his head shot away'. But the carrack was dismasted and rather than surrender, was run aground on one of the Comoro islands. There she was set on fire to prevent the English extracting her cargo. 'This is the greatest disaster and disgrace that has ever befallen them', gloated Roe when he heard the news, 'for they never lost . . . any such vessel as this which was esteemed invincible; and without supplies they [i.e. the Portuguese at Goa] perish utterly.'

In the same year William Keeling, while making his supervisory tour of the East, violated another Portuguese preserve by entering the Malabar ports. At Calicut he signed a treaty with the ruler, at Cranganore he left a small factory, and at Quilon he captured a Portuguese vessel. But the Dutch also had an eye on the Malabar trade and it would be some time before it figured prominently in English ambitions. The real trial of strength with the Portuguese was to take place a thousand miles away off the coast of Persia.

iv

Under the great Shah Abbas, Persia had achieved the distinction of being the one Eastern country to reverse the west–east tide of commercial endeavour by actively canvassing its exports, particularly raw silk, in Europe. As the sequel would show, the value of this trade was not inconsiderable. Yet Persia was slow to figure in the reckonings of the London Company.

Interest was first kindled when in 1611 a Persian ambassador presented himself to King James at Hampton Court. Oddly the Shah's emissary turned out to be an Englishman. Sir Robert Sherley, one of two Catholic brothers who had entered the Shah's service during the reign of Elizabeth, was also extremely plausible. To end Persia's dependence on the good will of her Turkish neighbour he sought a contract for the export of raw silk direct from a Persian port to Europe. There was, though, a catch. Payment must be made in bullion and, as well as Turkish resentment, the successful contractor would have to cope with the Portuguese who from their fortress at Hormuz controlled the Persian coast. On the whole the Company, scarcely able to finance its existing trade, felt obliged to decline. But the directors did undertake to provide a passage home for the ambassador, his glamorous Circassian wife and their considerable entourage, plus King James's ambassador to the Shah, his wife and their entourage. Thus, in 1613, the first Company vessel to sail for Persia was carrying mainly passengers.

After calling at Dhofar in Oman the *Expedition* somehow managed to overshoot Persia and first attempted to land its distinguished company at Gwadar in 'the rugged and mouldy land' of Baluchistan. This was almost a disaster. Far from being loyal Persian subjects as the Sherleys imagined, the Baluchis were in fact at war with the Shah and had every intention of massacring both ambassadors. Fortunately the mistake was discovered in time and the *Expedition* put back to sea. The next port was Lahribandar in Sind, near the modern Karachi. Here the party was put ashore amid considerable protest. Sir Thomas Powell, the English ambassador, died immediately and was soon followed by his wife, who died in childbirth. Their infant son (probably the first entirely English child to be born in India) survived his parents by only a few days. But the Sherleys fared better; after a visit to Jehangir at Agra, they eventually regained Isfahan, the Persian capital.

It was word of Sherley's influence there, plus the encouraging reports of an overland traveller called Steel, which alerted the English factors at Surat to the possibilities of the Persian trade. With large stocks of unsaleable broadcloth on their hands they first sent Steel back to Persia to assess the tweed market. Then, in 1616, they dispatched the first vessel to the Persian port of Jask. Sherley had secured from the Shah the necessary *farman* and the factors were thus willing to take up an initiative that had been scorned by the Company in London.

It was also being scorned by Sir Thomas Roe. In 1615 he had declared

Jask the ideal place for selling cloth and buying silk; and in 1618 he would rightly see the Persian silk trade as 'the best of all India'. But in 1616, because the initiative was coming from the factors, he told them the venture was 'against all reason' and 'at extreme peril and chardge'. Far from deterring the factors this only encouraged them. The *James* landed her cargo at Jask, the chief factor was well received by Shah Abbas, and factories were opened at Shiraz and Isfahan. Roe continued to try and discredit the venture but in 1618 the first consignment of raw silk reached Surat and eventually London. It sold for three times its cost price. The factors were vindicated.

In the following year the whole Surat fleet went on to Jask and in 1620 Andrew Shilling, he who had just annexed the Cape, also took his four ships into Persian waters. But by now the Portuguese had bestirred themselves. Ruy Freire de Andrade, 'the Pride of Portugal', had been dispatched from Lisbon and was awaiting the English fleet off Jask with four ships and numerous frigates. 'In a word', recalled one of Shilling's men, 'the drums and trumpets summoned us and we went chearfully to the business.'

Persia's rugged and uncompromising coastline was little suited to wily English tactics. For two days the opposing fleets slogged it out with a murderous exchange of shot and ball, fireworks and bullets. On the second day, 'while we were wrapt in smoake and sweating in blood' Shilling was hit. He died in what the English chose to regard as the hour of victory; for 'not to receive a supper as hot as their dinner' the Portuguese ships 'cut their cables and drove with the tide'. The English, who were practically out of ammunition, did not give chase.

Next year John Weddell in command of five ships and as many pinnaces came well prepared. Ruy Freire was known to have received reinforcements and Weddell confidently expected another trial of strength. He was not however expecting to end Portugal's 100 years of domination in Persian waters and was neither prepared nor authorized for any such offensive.

Just as in south-east Asia Portuguese power hinged on command of the Malacca Straits so in south-west Asia it hinged on command of the Straits of Hormuz at the mouth of the Gulf. On the island of Hormuz their main fortress was seen as the western bastion of their empire. If the world were an egg, Hormuz, according to the proverb, was its yolk. The fortress was thought to be impregnable and likely to outlast even Malacca. But this had not deterred the Shah. Stung into action by a series of Portuguese raids designed to induce him to dismiss the English, he had dispatched to the Straits in 1621 a formidable army. Given that Hormuz was an island, a navy might have been more effective but the Persians possessed no such force. Thus when Weddell sailed into sight at the end of the year, stalemate had been reached. The Persians were besieging a fort on the nearby island of Qishm (Kishm) whence the Hormuz garrison usually obtained its water and provisions. But Portuguese ships still controlled the seaways and Hormuz itself looked as impregnable as ever.

Naturally Weddell was never so welcome. The Persians hailed his timely arrival as evidence of divine intervention and quickly explained what was expected of him. Though often dubbed 'the stormy petrel' of the Company's commanders, Weddell hesitated. There was some doubt about whether morally the English should side with a heathen prince against fellow Christians, albeit of the most detested persuasion; there was good reason to suppose that a skipper's right to defend himself on the high seas did not extend to taking the offensive against a land base belonging to a nation with whom England was supposedly on good terms; and there was the absolute certainty that what the Surat President (or Chief Factor) chose to call 'this airye enterprise' would be censured by their employers on the grounds of cost, risk and delay.

Yet this was all by the by. The Persians were offering attractive incentives – like a contribution to costs, a share of the plunder, increased trading rights, customs exemption, and half the proceeds from the customs of the nearby port of Gombroon (Bandar Abbas, Bandar Khomeini) – and they were backing them with some unthinkable threats. Unless the English co-operated they could expect to leave without a cargo and without a trading future in Persia.

Under the circumstances and after much heart searching and persuasion, Weddell declared that he had no choice. Accordingly on 23 January 1622 'it was resolved to invite our enymies to a banquet of fire flying bullits'. The Portuguese refused to relinquish the safety of Hormuz's batteries so the English went into Qishm. Guns were landed and on 1 February 'the Pertian general and wee hand in hand' took possession of Qishm fort. It was probably the first time that the cross of St George had flown beside the Shah's ensign. Ruy Freire was among the prisoners and was duly sent to Surat. But the English too had lost a valued Captain. 'The man who we shall find the greatest miss of', wrote Weddell, 'is Mr Baffin who was killed outright with a muskit on shoare.' Apparently he 'gave three leaps and died immediately.' In a grave of Persian sand the Arctic explorer was laid to rest.

The Persian troops were now ferried across to Hormuz and on 9 February the main siege began. Mining and tunnelling to great effect the Persians breached the walls; but more Portuguese poured out than Persians in. For two months, while the English concentrated on battering the enemy's ships to extinction, the issue remained in doubt. Without hope of relief the Portuguese yet defended valiantly. In the end it was disease as much as destruction that gradually undermined their position. A second breach was repaired but, knowing a third must prove fatal, on 23 April the garrison surrendered and Albuquerque's fortress fell to the allies. It was indeed St George's Day.

Subsequent squabbles somewhat obscured the achievement. Weddell and his men would be held responsible for the general pillage that took place and would be suspected of having made off with much of the booty. Moreover, the Company's complaints about the cost of the operation would be doubly compounded, first by the Lord High Admiral demanding a £10,000 share of the supposed proceeds and then by the King demanding a similar sum for ignoring the inevitable diplomatic protests from Lisbon. But on the credit side, English prestige throughout the East now soared. 'If you may have possession of Ormuz', wrote President Fursland from Bantam, 'Your Worships may reckon that you have gotten the keye of all India.' He had just presided over the English withdrawal from the Spice Islands, Japan and Siam. Success at Hormuz and the vitality of the Persian trade was a greater compensation than anything that had been achieved within the realm of the Moghul; it would be 'a bridle to our faithless neighbours the Dutch and keepe all Moores in awe of us'. Without doubt the capture of Hormuz was the most sensational proof yet afforded of the Company's naval might in Asia.

The Portuguese took their loss to heart. In Lisbon the commander of the Hormuz garrison was tried in his absence and hanged in effigy. Fleets from Goa attempted to blockade Gombroon, the port to which the English had removed from Jask, and in 1625 they precipitated another titanic engagement. It was 'thought to be one of the greatest that ever was fought' according to Weddell who again commanded the English contingent and who was not given to exaggeration. But this time he had a new ally. The Dutch had duly noted English successes in the Arabian Sea and had opened their own factory at Surat. They still regarded the Portuguese as their natural foe and, by that Treaty of Defence which proved so disastrous for the English in the Archipelago, they were officially in alliance with the Company. Thus Weddell's four ships were now joined by a Dutch fleet of similar size.

In all sixteen vessels plus a host of frigates and pinnaces were involved. The battle raged for three days and a final reckoning seemed to give victory to the allies; to their sixty dead it was claimed that the Portuguese had lost nearly 500. But this must have been an exaggeration for six months later the same Portuguese fleet was back in Persian waters and taking its revenge. It fell on the ill-starred *Lion*, a ship of about 400 tons crewed, if John Taylor, 'the water-poet', is to be believed, entirely by heroes. At their first attempt the Portuguese detached the *Lion* from her fleet, partially fired her, then boarded her and took her in tow. The English prepared to blow her up, but 'God in his wisdome stayed us by putting it into the mind of some of our men to let fall an anchor'.

> Which being done (the tide running very strong) brought our ship to so strong a bitter [i.e. halt] that the fast which the Portugals had upon us brake, whose unexpected suddaine departure from us left 50 or 60 of their men upon our poope, who still maintained their fire in such sort that we were forced to blow them up, which blast tore all the sterne of our ship to peeces from the middle decke upwards.

Miraculously the *Lion*, charred, battered and half demolished, was still afloat. She limped into Gombroon, discharged her cargo, and was promptly assailed by another Portuguese squadron. This time there was no escape. Forty-two men died as they finally blew up the ship, twenty-six were captured and beheaded, and of the rest all except ten had fallen in battle. 'Thus was this good ship and men unfortunately and lamentably lost', writes Taylor with admirable restraint, 'yet as much courage and manly resolution as possibly could bee was performed by the English, nor can it bee imagined how more industry and truer valour could have been shewed.'

Nothing fuelled English resolve like a magnificent disaster. When word reached Surat that the Portuguese had 'got into a hole called Bombay' to refit, Weddell's Anglo-Dutch fleet stormed down the coast. They were too late; the enemy had fled leaving only the town for the English to avenge themselves on. Thus, in October 1626, the first English to visit Bombay came as raiders. Warehouse, friary, fort and mansions were put to the torch along with two new frigates 'not yett from the stocks'. A wild notion that this 'excellent harbour' with its 'pleasant fruitfull soil' might be worth occupying was scouted but firmly rejected as far too provocative.

Hostilities with the Portuguese rumbled on. The eventual peace which was signed at Goa in 1635 by William Methwold, now President at Surat, should have changed the whole balance of maritime power in the East. That was how the Dutch and the Moghul emperor saw it and they bitterly opposed it. It opened to the English Goa itself, the Portuguese settlements on the Malabar coast, and numerous other ports from Basra in Iraq to Tatta in Sind and Macao off the Chinese mainland. It would also last indefinitely, thus ironically enabling the Portuguese settlements in India to survive even the British Raj. But at the time its possible advantages were not paramount. The main point was that neither the Portuguese nor the English could afford to go on quarrelling. Thanks mainly to the Dutch in the East and the Spanish at home, the Portuguese empire was in an advanced state of decline. (In 1641 Malacca itself would fall to the Dutch.) And as for the English, the London Company was now approaching what may be regarded as the nadir of its eastern commerce.

PART TWO

FLUCTUATING FORTUNES

1640–1710

CHAPTER SIX

These Frowning Times

RECESSION, FAMINE AND WAR

Overseas the growth of the East India Company during the first two decades of its existence had been decidedly impressive. By 1620 the Presidencies of Bantam and Surat – 'Presidencies' because from about that time their Chief Factors were designated 'Presidents' – controlled nearly 200 factors scattered over more than a dozen trading centres. In the case of Bantam these stretched from Macassar to Masulipatnam and in the case of Surat from the Malabar Coast to the Red Sea.

But to the stay-at-home Englishman, dodging the sewers of his timbered metropolis and worrying about the next outbreak of plague, these exotic claims meant little. Masulipatnam could have been Mars – and to the lazy-tongued it probably was. For a peck of pepper and a bolt of brocade why, he might have asked, so much fuss? Or to so much fuss, why so little substance?

To remedy such unenlightened comment the loyal Company servant would have recommended a trip down the Thames. As yet the Company boasted no prestigious offices and until 1621 it still operated from the home of Sir Thomas Smythe, its governor. Built by his father, 'Customer Smythe' (because he had belonged to a syndicate which farmed the realm's customs), this establishment was in Philpot Lane off Fenchurch Street. It was evidently of some size for it included a hall large enough for meetings of the General Court and could sleep 120 people. But with a permanent staff of half a dozen, the Company occupied only two or three rooms. For a warehouse it leased a disused section of Cosby House, a much grander edifice in Bishopsgate. In 1617, with subscriptions for the Second Joint Stock pouring in, the optimistic directors rented the whole of Cosby House. Here Sir Morris Abbot presided over the Court of Committees as they fulminated over the Amboina affair or greeted the news of Methwold's Anglo-Portuguese truce. But in 1638 the Cosby House lease expired and once again the Company became a live-in tenant, this time in the Lime Street home of its new governor, Sir Christopher Clitherow. Although destined to remain on this site, colonizing abutting buildings and eventually acquiring a frontage on adjacent Leadenhall Street, the Company's initial occupancy extended only to a few small and badly lit apartments.

But downriver from the City's cramped thoroughfares, anytime during the winter months, the launch-pad of Eastern enterprise provided a sight to savour. Here, attended by a host of lighters, seven or eight of the tall ships later known as Indiamen might be viewed riding at anchor while final preparations were made for their dispatch. From every masthead and yard-arm there flapped flags and pennants of disproportionate size; all bore the red on white cross of St George. Seamen swarmed through the rigging; crates of livestock cluttered the decks. It was a sight, according to one traveller, rivalled only by that of 'St Paul's great church'.

Larger than most merchantmen of their day and as heavily armed as warships, the Indiamen were a source of national pride. Maritime artists generally preferred a low-angle half-profile from astern which would reveal the architectural character of a high blunt poop. Here arabesques in red and gold framed a deep veranda with, stacked above it, a row of leaded Tudor casements and perhaps a bow window. Lace curtains hinted at luxury within, for this was the roundhouse, the most sought-after accommodation on board; the captain's apartments were on the next timbered storey. But amidships the 'tea-shoppe' aspect disappeared. From a row of square ports cannon and culverin of brass gleamed brightly between the scuppers and the waterline.

By 1620 the Company operated thirty to forty 'tall ships'. Most belonged to the Company and many had been built in its own dockyards at Deptford and Blackwall. The latter, commissioned in 1614, was the first yard to be constructed on the left bank of the Thames and was the genesis of the later East India Dock. To anyone curious about technological advance, it was another of the capital's sights 'daily visited and viewed by strangers as well [as] Embassadours'. Here, besides wet and dry docks, there were timber yards, a foundry and cordage works for supplying the ships' hardware and a bakery and saltings for their provisioning. More than 200 craftsmen were directly employed in the yard.

Added to the ships' crewing requirements they made the Company one of London's largest employers.

An industrial as well as a mercantile enterprise, the Company had also become a financial giant. The First Joint Stock (1613–16) raised £418,000 and the Second (1617–22) a colossal £1.6 million. Part of these sums had somehow to be converted into Spanish silver rials, the most acceptable currency in the East. Thus the procurement of rials – like that of ships, ships' supplies, armaments, provisions, and export cargoes – became a major preoccupation which absorbed the attentions of an important sub-committee drawn from the members of the Court of Committees. It also spawned a network of financiers and overseas agents. In conjunction with the Company's other financial requirements, particularly borrowing facilities, it is no exaggeration to say that East India business generated the London money market just as it did the London docks.

But expansion so fast and so furious had not gone unnoticed. Abroad it had attracted enemies, notably the Dutch in the East Indies and the Portuguese in the Arabian Sea; at home it stimulated outspoken critics both outside the Company and within it plus, eventually, determined rivals. Extraneous factors – like famine in India and civil war in England – would prove catastrophic. Yet so dramatic had been the rise in the Company's fixed charges for ships, dockyards, factories, and office staff (whose number had risen to eighteen in the spacious surroundings of Cosby House) that even in ideal trading conditions the pace of expansion must have faltered.

In the event it was dramatically reversed. If histories of the Company in the seventeenth century tend to dwell at length on its first few decades this is simply because so much of its business was concentrated in that period.

Statistics tell one side of the story. Whereas between 1611 and 1620 the Company despatched fifty-five ships to the east, during the 1620s the total fell to forty-six, during the 1630s to thirty-five, and during the 1640s and 1650s to around twenty. On the twelve separate voyages prior to 1613 profits had often been sensational; an average figure of 155 per cent has been suggested. And on the First Joint Stock a respectable 87 per cent was recorded. But on the Second Joint Stock the figure was down to 12 per cent and the period of investment was the longest yet; on an annual basis it appreciated less than 1 per cent. Not surprisingly a Third Joint Stock, launched in 1631, raised only a comparatively modest

£420,000 much of which proved difficult to call in. And four successive stocks between 1636 and 1656 raised just £600,000 in aggregate.

As in 1602–6, the crisis of confidence provoked bitter disagreements between the directors, or Committees, and the shareholders, or General Court. The latter, primarily interested in a quick return on their investment and now including factions representing both court and government, saw their declining dividends as evidence of mismanagement. They vigorously attacked the conduct of the directors and of Sir Morris Abbot in particular, demanding greater access to the Company's accounts, a secret ballot for the election of directors, and regular quarterly meetings of the General Court. The directors, most of whom were still wealthy city merchants and aldermen, fought back. They conceded the ballot and conciliated their more influential opponents; but Abbot, supported by the King, insisted that the Company's constitution could only be changed by altering its charter. In 1628 Abbot also managed to push through a resolution that in future only those with holdings worth £2000 or more could stand for election as directors. Far from undermining the directors' authority, these early quarrels therefore tended to entrench it. Between them just three men (Smythe, Abbot and William Cockayne, governor from 1643 till 1657) monopolized the governorship for forty-seven of the Company's first fifty-seven years; and it was much the same story with the deputy-governorship. Continuity of management made up for the discontinuity inevitable with a system of short-term stocks. Boardroom dissent was not therefore the cause of the financial crisis, merely a symptom of it.

Until the middle of the century, and in spite of Persian silk and Indian cottons, pepper continued to provide the bulk of the Company's trade in terms of volume and of value. Both were now hard hit and this undoubtedly did contribute to the crisis. First the 1618–19 hostilities with the Dutch – in which John Jourdain lost his life – saw a decline in shipments which was almost as serious as the loss of shipping from which it resulted. Then, when shipments recovered in the early 1620s with the Anglo-Dutch Treaty of Defence, it was prices that began to decline. By 1627 pepper was down to seventeen pence a pound (from twenty-six pence at the beginning of the First Joint Stock) and was no longer acceptable to shareholders as a dividend. Instead it was sold in bulk, like the Company's other imports, at one of its periodic sales.

These sales took place in the Exchange. One inch of candle was lit for each lot and bids closed when the flame finally guttered out. Cautious bidding no less than the spluttering candle seemed to sum up the Company's plight. For just as returns seemed to be adjusting to the loss of the spice trade and the steady decline in the pepper trade, disaster struck in Gujarat, now regarded as the Company's one saving grace. It came courtesy of India's capricious climate in that the monsoon of 1630 failed to materialize. Shah Jehan, who had now succeeded his father on the Moghul throne, chose to see this meteorological hiccup as the inevitable portent of his wife's death. His subjects, more concerned for their own survival, would happily have foregone the Taj Mahal, which he raised in her memory, for a good downpour. In fact, in Agra it did rain; but in the Deccan, on the Coromandel Coast, and above all in Gujarat, not a drop. The drought 'burnt up all the vegetables, dried up all the rivers, and rent the ground'. Livestock died, trade ceased, and by October of 1630 the panic of famine gripped the whole province.

At Surat President Rastell sought grain and dates from Persia, rice from as far away as Macassar and the Comoro Islands. Ships arriving at Swalley were told to eke out their biscuit; there was no hope of the usual provisioning. In November one of the factors, Peter Mundy, set off for Agra. Each village presented a sight more harrowing than the last. One place was 'allmost voyde of inhabitants, the most part fledd, the rest dedd'. At the next, mothers were selling their children. Open graves overflowed with corpses and 'the hie waies were so full of dead bodyes that we could hardlie pass them without treading on or going over some'.

> Noe less lamentable was it to see the poor people scrapeing the dunghills for food, yea in the very excrement of beastes . . . This was their estate in every streete and corner. And from Suratt to this place our noses were never free of the stinck of corpses, especially about the towns; for they dragg them out by the heels stark naked, of all ages and sexes, till they are out of the gates, and there they are left so that the way is half barred up.

Mundy had set out with a caravan of 150 people. By the time he reached Burhanpur the number had increased to 1700 as more and more fled their homes. Prices for carriage were astronomical but it scarcely mattered; as weavers, dyers and indigo growers joined in the general exodus, there was precious little in the way of produce to carry. 'It puts us allmost into despaire of a competent lading,' wrote Rastell in November; 'and yet,' he added, 'these are but the beginnings of greater woe to come.'

He was right. The 1630 monsoon did eventually arrive – but at the same time as that of 1631. Whereas one year's crop had been lost to drought, the next was lost to flood. And with the floods came typhoid. A Dutch factor arriving back at Swalley in December 1631 could scarcely believe it was the same place. 'Whereas heretofore there were in that town 260 families, there was not remaining alive above ten or twelve families ... and when we came to Surat we hardly could see any living persons where heretofore was thousands.' He put the death toll in the city alone at 30,000. Flood water still filled the streets 'so that we could pass from one house to another but by boat'. And the English factory reminded him of a hospital. More than half the factors were already dead, the latest victim being Rastell himself. It would take at least three years, he reckoned, for trade to recover.

Peter Mundy, on his return from Agra in 1633, took an even gloomier view. 'In my opinion it will hardlie recover its former estate in 15, nay 20 yeares; I meane Gujarat.' The extent of the disaster was now more apparent. 'Women were seen to roast their children, men travelling in the waie were laid hold of to be eaten.' Over a million had died and several times that number had fled. When he had left Surat there had been twenty-one English factors at work there. Now all but seven were dead and, of those, three more would be laid to rest immediately after his arrival. Seventeen out of twenty-one – it was probably about the average mortality throughout what had once been 'in a manner [of speaking] the garden of the world'. Now, according to the captain of the *Mary*, it was 'turned into a wilderness, having fewe or noe men left to manure their ground nor to labour in any profession.'

> Soe that places here that have yielded 15 bayles of cloth in a day hardly now yield three in a month. Ahmadabad that likewise yielded 3,000 bayles of indigo yearly or more now hardly yields 300.

Quite suddenly the Surat trade, which was about to supersede that of Bantam in value, was at a standstill. Frantically the Company redirected ships and money to Masulipatnam and Gombroon. There too the famine had been felt but less severely. 'The Coast' profited at Surat's expense and its factors were emboldened to attempt their first experiment in Bengal. But in Persia the death of Shah Abbas had introduced new uncertainties about the silk trade. Increasingly ships sailing between Surat and Gombroon carried only the freight of Indian merchants. The Surat factory slid into debt and when Methwold returned to India as its

President, outlying establishments at Broach, Baroda, Cambay and Ahmadabad were all withdrawn. Such then was the situation in 1633 when peace negotiations were opened with the Portuguese.

By 1635, when the Convention of Goa was actually signed, conditions had much improved and Methwold was quietly confident. 'You shall find such a certain benefitt to result unto you', he wrote to the directors of his peace negotiations, 'that you shall now begin to valew your trade.' A new factory had been opened at Lahribandar in Sind and another was planned at Basra, both former Portuguese preserves. For the first time an English ship had sailed to Macao on the coast of China 'to experience the trade in those partes which hath ever beene desired'. And after thirty years of Portuguese molestation in the Tapti river, the factors at Surat could at last sail safely down to the anchorage at Swalley.

On 6 April 1636 Methwold preferred to drive along the well-trodden road to the north of the river. He had been to Swalley to supervise the lading of the 500-ton *Discovery* which for five years had been shuttling to Persia, Sind and Masulipatnam. At last he had accumulated a cargo of indigo and cottons with which she was to sail for England. Better still, he had just paid off the factory's debts to various Indian brokers. His carriage, drawn by two white oxen, their horns tipped with gold, lurched through a landscape of verdant abundance. Buffalo wallowed in mulligatawny mud-pools, harvesters bent beneath haystack bundles. Beaming on this evidence of Gujarat's revival, Methwold felt at one with the world, a sensation no doubt heightened by the goodly number of toasts customary on the departure of a homeward bound ship. It remained only for him to complete his London postbag and with this in mind he drove straight to the spacious English premises in the heart of the city.

Scarcely had he climbed from the coach when a whispered confidence shattered his *bonhomie*. Unthinkable stories had reached the bazaar: an English ship had supposedly been raiding Indian vessels near the Red Sea. To scotch such a dangerous rumour, Methwold sped to the house of Surat's Governor. Admittance was granted; a welcome was not. 'I found a sad assembly of dejected merchants, some looking through me with eyes sparkling with indignation, others half dead at the sense of their losses; and soe I satt a time with the generall silence until the Governor brake it.' Where, the governor wanted to know, were the English ships and in particular what vessels were in the vicinity of Aden. For these were no rumours; he had voluminous depositions to prove them. Two ships, the *Taufiqui* of Surat and the *Mahmudi* of Diu, had been taken by an English vessel, their officers had been brutally tortured, and their cargoes valued at £10,000 appropriated.

This bald statement of the tragedy roused Methwold's 'sad assembly' from their silent dejection. They 'mouthed at once a general invective at me and the whole English nation which continewed some time with such a confusion as I knew not to whom to addresse myself until they had runne themselves out of breath.' He then begged for 'suspension of soe much choller' until the complainants' ships should arrive. He was quite sure there had been a mistake. It must have been a Dutch ship or perhaps a French privateer masquerading under English colours. He was so sure of it that he willingly agreed to deposit a sum equivalent to the supposed loss until such time as the matter was cleared up.

This did not satisfy the Governor. There were, after all, precedents for English assaults on Indian shipping to the Red Sea. Middleton had tried it and in 1618 Sir Thomas Roe had prevailed on the reluctant factors to reopen trade with Mocha so that, amongst other things, 'the Mogul's shippes' might again be 'taken once in every four yeares'. In 1623 Rastell had actually put this plan into practice; to win redress for various grievances, eight Indian vessels were waylaid and held hostage until the Surat authorities capitulated. Rastell and his colleagues had got away with it but not before a few chastening days in irons where, in Rastell's copious words, they had become 'the shameful subjects of daily threats, revilings, scorns, and disdainful derisions of whole rabbles of people whose vengeful eyes never glutted themselves to behold the spectacle of our miseries'.

Something similar now awaited Methwold. For two days he was closely guarded at the English factory then, along with his principal assistants, transferred to an airless dungeon where 'we found ourselves almost eaten up with chinches, a vermine well-known to swarme about nasty rooms'. At last the unhappy *Taufiqui* sailed into port. Her skipper was absolutely positive his attackers were English; one of them 'wore a gold ring in his ear' – and no doubt a red bandana round his head – and was called Simon. Methwold was still unconvinced. But this Simon had thoughtfully issued the *Taufiqui* with a certificate of having been robbed (presumably to be shown to any other would-be pirates). It was this document, written in English, which finally convinced Methwold that he had been mistaken and that there was indeed an English ship in the area carrying the royal commission and yet engaging in piracy. He was almost too embarrassed to spell out the enormity of it.

Admittedly it was not the first such scare. A trickle of ships, some with a royal commission, some without, had ventured to infringe the Company's monopoly ever since Michelborne's voyage in 1602. But it was much the most serious. For it transpired that the *Roebuck*, the offender in question, was financed by a man in the employ of Sir William Courteen, one of the richest merchant adventurers of the age. And even as Methwold lay mouldering in his Surat dungeon, Courteen was dispatching another and a far more formidable fleet to challenge and embarrass the Company.

ii

Over the years the Governor and Company of London Merchants trading to the East Indies had stirred up a good deal of controversy. A recurrent criticism, already noticed, was that the Company must be impoverishing the nation since it exported treasures and imported only luxury consumer items. In the case of Indian cottons these were manufactured goods which must be killing off English manufactures. Sir Thomas Roe was one of many who sympathized with this point of view which was why he took such a gloomy view of the Surat trade. It was also one of his reasons for the reopening of the Mocha trade, Mocha being the one place in Asia where spices and cottons could be sold for specie.

But in 1620 Thomas Mun, a director of the Company, met these and other objections in his *Discourse of Trade unto the East Indies*. Mun argued convincingly that there was nothing inherently wrong with exporting precious metals provided that the value of such exports was less than the value of the imported goods. 'For let noe man doubt that money doth attend merchandise, for money is the price of wares and wares are the proper use of money, so that coherence is inseparable.'

This in itself was a considerable advance on the economic theories of the day. But, more important, he drew attention to the idea that the nation's wealth could never be assessed purely in terms of one particular exchange. The trade of specie for spices and cottons, he argued, was but a small segment in a much larger and more complex trading cycle. It began with the importation of silver rials from Europe (originally, of course, from Mexico). The rials were invested in eastern trade and eventually came back in the form of cottons and pepper, most of which was then re-exported to Europe (and America and Africa). The re-export trade, although not handled by the Company itself, was particularly important since it was this which completed the trading cycle by financing the purchase of more rials. Hence, declared Mun, 'the East India Company alone is the meanes to bring more treasure unto this realme than all the other trades of this kingdome being put together'. Home consumption accounted for only a small percentage of the Company's imports. Moreover, without the Company's pepper it would be necessary to import expensive Dutch pepper and without India's cottons it would be necessary to import expensive continental linens.

Mun evaded the vexed question of English woollens and he said nothing about another common objection: that if the trade was so valuable and extensive how could it be in the national interest to make it the exclusive monopoly of one commercial organization? After all, those whose criticisms of the Company's trade derived from viewing it as an isolated and distinct activity could hardly have done so had the Company not enjoyed a monopoly of it. Both the monopoly and their line of criticism were in fact based on traditional commercial logic.

But the Company could of course advance other and excellent reasons for its monopoly. It was how both the Dutch and the Portuguese operated; without it, investors would shy away, the concerted and continuous activity necessary for such a long term and expensive adventure would be impossible, and the management of factories, of purchasing, and of local relations would be chaotic. Furthermore, it appeared that a monopoly was the arrangement favoured by the Crown. In a good year the Company's imports were yielding some £20,000 per annum in customs duties. Together with other exactions (like the £10,000 demanded by James I for ignoring diplomatic protests over the capture of Hormuz) they made the Company an important source of revenue to the embattled monarchy.

But if the Crown looked to the Company, so did the Company look to the Crown. The periodical need for a revision or confirmation of its charter, plus diplomatic and political support in its differences with the Dutch and the Portuguese, rendered it dependent on royal support. So did the need for various financial concessions like the authority to import Spanish rials. Although not a state venture like the V.O.C., the Company never enjoyed all the freedoms usually associated with a private sector enterprise. It could, and often did, threaten to cease operations when, as in the aftermath of Amboina, royal support seemed in doubt. But such a threat would have been difficult to put into practice and neither Crown nor Company relished the idea of seeing hard-won markets abandoned to continental rivals.

So the monopoly had advantages for both parties and James I seemed generally to have accepted its logic; after remonstrations and *douceurs*, he had usually discountenanced those who infringed it. And perhaps Charles I intended to follow his example. The commission he had granted to the adventurers in the *Roebuck* made no mention of trade, their licence being only to 'range the seas all the world over . . . [and] to make prize of all such treasures, merchandise, goods and commodities which they shall be able to take of infidels or anye other prince, potentate or state not in league or amitie with us beyond the line equinoctiall'. In other words it was purely an invitation to piracy and, however scandalous and provocative, was not intended to test the Company's trading monopoly. When, after ships of the Company had eventually run the *Roebuck* to ground, protests were lodged in London, Charles I was persuaded to disown the miscreants and to write a letter of apology to Shah Jehan.

And there the matter might have ended had the sudden news of Methwold's treaty with the Portuguese not appeared to throw a whole new light on Eastern trade. Methwold, a cautious man, had spoken of 'certaine benefitt'. But Charles I was easily persuaded that it was in fact a sensational breakthrough. With no further danger of Portuguese attack and with entry to all of Portugal's cherished markets, the English had the chance of doubling their trading empire. What more natural than that the king should accede to the suggestion of a second, separate, trading empire? And that a second trading empire justified a second chartered company? Behind the idea was once again the ambitious Courteen; but this time Courteen's influence and cash were nicely matched by the reputation and experience of others in his consortium. For the new association's first fleet was to be commanded by Captain Weddell, the victor of Hormuz, and staffed by a bunch of the ablest factors of whom nearly all had lately served the London Company.

Dissatisfaction amongst the Company's employees was nothing new. It had been well expressed by George Ball while President at Bantam in 1618.

> At home men are famous for doing nothing [wrote Ball]; here they are infamous for their honest endeavours. At home is respect and reward; abroad disrespect and heart-breaking. At home is augmentation of wages; abroad nothing so much as grief, cares and displeasure. At home is safety; abroad the best is bondage. And in a word at home all things are as a man might wish, and here nothing answerable to merit.

Such home thoughts from abroad were prompted not by homesickness but by the ever suspicious and badgering tone of the Company's correspondence. For the Company, in the persons of its directors, was not yet an impersonal business entity; in its attitudes even more than in its constitution it harked back to the age of the guilds. In the sub-committee which handled correspondence with overseas factories the emphasis was ever on collegiate discipline, like that of the universities, which presumed a high degree of subordination in its representatives. Hence the respectful modes of address – 'Your Worships', 'the Most Honourable and Worshipful company', etc. – and hence the presumed right to regulate the personal conduct of its factors. But at such an impossible remove London's exhortations commonly became paranoid suspicions. It was assumed that every factor once clear of the Thames would, like Hawkins, live as an oriental courtier and set about feathering his 'neast'.

In the case of Ball this assumption proved well founded. He was eventually recalled in disgrace, arraigned for embezzlement, and fined £2000; all things were not always 'as a man might wish'. But better men than Ball – 'the honest Mr Cocks', for example – would also take umbrage at the relentless barrage of criticism from London. Even in an age of strong language it was no encouragement to be constantly lambasted for incompetence. Goods, it seemed, were always badly packed, of inferior quality, or too expensive; accounts were either faulty or late; living expenses were far too lavish. Rarely indeed was honest endeavour acknowledged or rewarded. And just as an energetic factor was presumed to be expending as much energy on his personal trade as on the Company's, so a successful commander was presumed to be recompensing himself from whatever booty came his way.

Such was certainly the attitude to Weddell whose services against the Portuguese had won him nothing but complaints about the cost of the operation plus 'fines, and undeserved public reproaches'. When therefore it fell to the same Weddell to convey to London the good tidings of Methwold's Goa Convention, his thoughts and those of most of the factors in his fleet turned to revenge. The scheme to apply for a charter to open trade at all the Portugese ports in the East seems to have been hatched during this voyage. In London Courteen immediately lent his support and through Endymion Porter, one of the King's favourites, secured the necessary charter. £120,000 were quickly raised and in 1636 Weddell put back to sea at the head of an impressive fleet of four vessels.

The directors of the Company protested in the most vigorous

language at this blatant infringement of their own charter; and they would continue to do so for the next twenty years. It was to no avail. For, according to the preamble to Courteen's charter, the Company had forfeited its exclusive monopoly by having 'neglected to establish fortified factories or seats of trade to which the King's servants could resort with safety . . . [having] consulted their own interests only without any regard to the King's revenue . . . and in general [having] broken the conditions on which their charter and exclusive privileges had been granted to them'. It was further argued that the new association need not constitute a rival since it would be trading only at places within the Portuguese sphere of influence – places whose trade the London Company had signally failed to exploit and whose potential in such difficult times it could not be expected to realize. The Company retaliated by ordering its factors to have nothing to do with those of the new association and to report any prejudicial activity immediately. But thereafter, and for the next twenty years, it would have to reckon with rivals who competed for finance and favour at home and for trade and concessions abroad and whose activities were a constant source of embarrassment and conflict.

And all this in spite of the fact that Courteen's Association scarcely prospered. Weddell's fleet spent three months at Goa but received no cargo and little encouragement, 'just delaies, faire wordes, and breach of promisses' according to Peter Mundy who had also gone over to the competition. They sailed on for Aceh, Malacca, Macao and Canton where Weddell was the first Englishman to have direct dealings with the Chinese – if, that is, an exchange of fire, several skirmishes and a blunt refusal by the Chinese to countenance any future trade may be termed 'dealings'. After six frustrating months the fleet put back to sea and, disavowing the original plan of sailing home by way of the still elusive north-west passage, headed back to Aceh. A quantity of pepper was obtained and a profitable outcome seemed at last possible. But of the four original ships, two had already departed for London. That left only the *Sun*, which called at Mauritius (where Peter Mundy duly noted the still extant dodo) and was then wrecked on the coast of Madagascar, and the *Dragon*, Weddell's flagship, which joined the growing list of ships that simply disappeared without trace somewhere in the Indian Ocean. Weddell, 'the stormy petrel', had paid the price of what Lancaster had called a 'devotion to the wind and seas'.

The Association never really recovered from this crushing blow. With its finances in a desperate plight its greatest asset proved to be its charter, under which a variety of adventurers would continue to make speculative voyages throughout the 1640s and 1650s. An attempt promoted by the Association to form a settlement in Madagascar proved a dismal failure, as did a second attempt along the same lines. The latter was promoted by an association headed by Lord Fairfax but largely consisting of Courteen's former associates. The same group also planned a settlement on Pulo Run, the half-forgotten legacy of earlier English endeavours in the Banda Islands. Like most English attempts to reach the place it never materialized.

But Courteen's Association and its successors did leave their mark on two of India's trading coasts, Malabar and Bengal. Weddell settled factors at three of the Malabar ports who, though soon reduced to pleading for assistance from the Company's factory at Surat, inaugurated the export of Malabar pepper to London. Access to this new source of pepper and to the area's production of cinnamon and cardamom would soon occasion a further downgrading of the Company's investment at Bantam. Similarly, future trends were anticipated by the establishment of an English factory at Hughli just a few miles from the marshes that would one day become Calcutta. This was settled in 1650 under the auspices of the 'United Joint Stock' so called because it was supposed to finance both the original Company and the remnants of the Association. In fact it was a temporary expedient of inadequate means and unsatisfactory duration designed simply to keep the eastern trade alive in what the directors now tactfully called 'these frowning times'.

iii

The English Civil War was not physically contested in the Company's far flung establishments. To the belated news of military manoeuvres by Royalists and Parliamentarians and of theological squabbles between Presbyterians and Independents, distance lent a certain unreality. If the Company's factors felt any urge to take up arms it was more likely to be against competitors, like the Dutch or Courteen's men, than against one another. Only one ship was actually lost – seized by mutineers of Royalist sympathies in the Comoro Islands. For the most part anxiety over the constitutional crisis at home centred on its likely effect on the English reputation abroad. Thus the Company's factors at Isfahan saw 'this tragicall storie of our King's beheading' simply as dangerous propaganda which could be 'deemed so haynos a matter' by the Shah that he might see fit to deprive them of that share of the Gombroon customs granted as a result of the capture of Hormuz. To reassure his Majesty that not all Englishmen were regicides, presents of plate and then a couple of mastiffs were forwarded to the Court. When the Shah let it be known that some rosy-cheeked additions to his harem would be more acceptable, the Isfahan factors lamely responded with a consignment of beaver hats. Their trade was already declining and Dutch ships now outnumbered those of the Company in Persian waters by four to one.

It was this dearth of shipping and of investment capital, the result of the political and commercial instability at home, which really crippled the Company. Hoping to secure a restitution of their monopoly, the directors were willing to treat with whoever held the reins of power. In 1641 they 'sold' £60,000 worth of pepper to the king; in effect it was a loan and was never repaid. Similarly, after the conclusion of Cromwell's Dutch War, £50,000 was advanced to the Protector from the Dutch indemnity (for Amboina and other losses in the archipelago). This too was never repaid. Acceptance of such gifts was seen as constituting an important acknowledgement by the sovereign power of the Company's role in the country's financial welfare and therefore as the basis for reinstating its charter. In both instances the Company further regarded the financial risk as acceptable since the debts could theoretically be recouped by withholding future customs duties.

But these were vast sums in the depressed circumstances of the day and, needless to say, Cromwell would no more assume the financial obligations incurred by Charles I than would Charles II those incurred by Cromwell. The Company lost out right along the line. As the size and frequency of its Eastern sailings declined, and as the Dutch stepped up their commercial rivalry in the Arabian Sea, the English factors found themselves left to their own devices. For three or four years at a time Bantam received no shipping at all and no investment capital. Matters were only slightly better at Masulipatnam and Madras where further famines, plus a power struggle between Golconda and its neighbours, precipitated the search for new markets in Bengal and the renewal of trade with Burma.

In order to show a modest profit the Company's factors turned increasingly to the 'country trade'. From this period dates the freighting and even building of small local vessels suited to the inter-port trade of the Arabian Sea and the Bay of Bengal. Thanks to the failure of Courteen's Malabar factories and of his Madagascan settlements, there was now in the ports of the East a fair number of footloose Englishmen willing to accept employment wherever it offered. The garrison of Fort St George (Madras) was recruited from such people and so were the officers of this new class of shipping. Circumstance necessitated a spirit of improvization and although the despatch of homeward cargoes was still the priority, consideration was now given to the preservation of an English presence in the East that could withstand the fluctuations of both European politics and oriental patronage. On 'the Coast' the fortified settlement at Madras seemed to be paying off. With the idea of finding a similar base in the west of India to which Englishmen could 'resort with safety' the factors at Surat began to float the idea of obtaining from the Portuguese a secure and fortifiable harbour. Diu or Bassein, where most of the Company's local vessels were built, were suggested; alternatively there was Bombay.

The Anglo-Dutch war of 1652 lent weight to this idea. Although the Company still nursed grievances against the Dutch dating back to the days of Amboina and Pulo Run, the war was essentially Cromwell's. He employed the Company's grievances to justify it and he exploited the Company's willingness to have the Protectorate espouse its cause. But the defence of Eastern trade did not figure in his strategy. He refused a request to send warships to Persian waters and thus abandoned the Company to its fate. With enormous damage to English prestige the Dutch defeated two English fleets off Persia and one off the coast of Sind. It was little consolation to the bealeaguered factors at Surat and Gombroon that in the English Channel Cromwell's navy had triumphed, or that by the Peace of Westminster compensation was granted to the descendants of Towerson and his fellow Amboina 'martyrs'. Even the restitution of Pulo Run, an achievement particularly dear to Cromwell's heart, seemed of little consequence. Far preferable in the Company's estimation would have been the acquisition of a base like Bombay. They urged the Protector to pursue the matter but without success.

Throughout 'these frowning times' instructions from London as to the actual conduct of trade were often contradictory and unhelpful. Their general drift was to the effect that long-term investments should be avoided, expenses reduced, and that the limited hold space available be filled only with cargoes of high value and certain sale. This was not exactly news. Up-country factories in India were again being closed and at Surat the number of factors had been cut to eight. Left to make their own selection, they and their colleagues at Madras invested heavily in saltpetre, the essential ingredient in gunpowder. In Ireland and the Low

Countries as well as in England Cromwell had good reason to be grateful to the Company for its foresight; henceforth saltpetre would remain an important item in the Indian trade. Silk, on the other hand, did not command a ready sale amongst dour republicans. Their 'rigid and austere manners', combined with fierce rivalry from the Dutch, saw the gradual decline of English interest in the Persian silk trade; when demand eventually revived it would be met increasingly from the silk farms of Bengal.

That the Persian trade survived at all was largely thanks to hostilities between the Moghul Empire and the Shah. Their fluctuating campaigns to secure the Afghan city of Kandahar interruped the overland trade and obliged Moghul shipping to avoid Persian ports. The Dutch and the English exploited this situation, becoming deeply involved in the freighting of Persian goods on behalf of Indian merchants. It was the busiest arm of the 'country trade' and one greatly facilitated by the customs exemption granted to the English by Shah Abbas. At Mocha and Basra no such privileges pertained, but there too English ships continued their sporadic calls. Again they carried mainly freighted cargoes although a notable exception was a small consignment of 'coho seedes' bought at Mocha in 1658 and forwarded to London. The capital's first coffee house had just opened.

iv

Declining fortunes abroad were faithfully reflected in drastic economies at home. In 1635 the Company's eighteen London employees had to take a cut in salaries; a further cut followed in 1639. In the same year the Company was obliged to suspend its shipbuilding programme and revert to the chartering practices of its earliest voyages. Four years later the Deptford yard was sold and Blackwall used only for refitting purposes. In 1650 even this, the Company's most valuable and impressive asset, was put up for sale. Since most of its overseas establishments, including the Surat factory, were rented, that left just Fort St George and the still elusive atoll of Pulo Run; otherwise the Company was just people and paper. It continued to trade on both the Fourth Joint Stock and the United Joint Stock but it was unclear exactly which of these was supposed to be the legitimate Company, and by 1655 both had anyway expired.

Ships still sailed but most were privately financed and even when their subscribers were members of the Company they were no more bound to acknowledge the directors' authority than were those of other private adventurers. Indeed there was now a strong current of opinion both within the Company and without which favoured this looser arrangement. As Cromwell procrastinated over the future of Eastern trade, it seemed that these 'free adventurers' might well have their way. The debate on the subject, which lasted from 1654–1657, was not over a renewal of the Company's charter but over whether the trade should be conducted on a monopolistic joint stock principle at all. With a host of adventurers already competing for cargoes abroad and sales at home, the chaos that must result from a free-for-all was plain enough. As Mun had foreseen, prices rose, customs receipts fell, and even the adventurers began to have second thoughts. Yet still Cromwell hesitated, referring the matter to his Council of State who in turn referred it to yet more select committees.

Eventually, on 14 January 1657, the directors took a deep breath and declared for liquidation. Bills were printed and posted at the Exchange; on this day month would be sold by public auction 'to any natives of this Commonwealth to and for their owne proper use' the Company's 'island [Pulo Run], customs [Gombroon], houses and other rights in the Indies'. An asking price of £14,000 was mentioned – not much to show for nearly sixty years of trade. All that stood between the Company and extinction was an inch of candle. It was, however, generally understood that the object of the exercise was simply to force the Goverment's hand. And so it did. On 6 February the Council declared in favour of the joint stock principle. The sale was postponed and both the Company and the free adventurers joined forces for a new flotation. In March a draft charter was approved and on 19 October 1657 the new charter passed the Great Seal. A new subscription, known as the New General Stock, was immediately opened and raised £786,000. Evidently both cash and confidence were not lacking if the trade could be properly regulated. Within six months no less than thirteen vessels were on their way to the East well provided with treasure and bursting with the good tidings.

Although Cromwell was dead within the year, his charter would be quickly replaced with an almost identical grant from Charles II which became the foundation of the Company's future prosperity. It differed from those of Elizabeth and James I in three important respects. The New General Stock, unlike all previous stocks, was to be permanent; thus ensuring a continuity of capital which had hitherto been lacking. In Sir William Hunter's words the Company at last 'cast its medieval skin, shook off the traditions of the regulated system and grew into one united, continuous and permanent joint stock corporation'.

A stipulation that in future the Governor, Deputy-Governor and directors must all stand down every two years had less dramatic results. Designed to prevent that monopoly of office which had been a feature of the pre-Restoration Company, it failed to anticipate the even greater danger of a monopoly of stock. Amongst the names listed as subscribers to the new stock were those of Thomas Papillon, who would devote most of his career to combating this danger, and of Josiah Child, who would ruthlessly exploit it.

Finally the new charter included a grant authorizing the Company to fortify and colonize any of its establishments and to transport to them settlers, stores and ammunition. The Protector was again thinking of Pulo Run; doubtless an autopsy would have revealed the name of the island engraved on his stony heart. But the Company's thoughts were elsewhere. They were thinking of Bombay, still in Portuguese hands, of the Cape, recently occupied by the Dutch, and of St Helena, supposedly the next place on the Dutch agenda. In December 1658, to gratify Cromwell's concern, John Dutton at the head of a determined band of settlers, prepared to depart for Pulo Run. The *London* was actually ready to sail when, on the pretext of impending Dutch hostilities, she was redirected to St Helena. Thus in May of the following year Dutton officially took possession 'with trumpet and drum' of the Company's first settlement. Near a clapboard chapel built by the Portuguese and to which passing fleets had habitually nailed the news of their movements, a fort was built, then a town – Jamestown. By a curious train of circumstance Nathaniel Courthope's epic resistance on the nutmeg isle of Pulo Run had, forty years on and half a world away, presented the Company with an island of comparable size plus a golden nutmeg in the form of a colonizing concession of quite incomparable portent.

CHAPTER SEVEN

A Seat of Power and Trade

BOMBAY AND SURAT

Of the three great cities which the East India Company would bequeath to its successors in India, Bombay was always the odd one out. Both Madras and Calcutta owed their existence to the predilections of eccentric individuals acting on their own initiative. On a strand of still virgin Coromandel sand Francis Day had traced out the walls of Fort St George (Madras); and, fifty years later, Job Charnock would light upon a wooded embankment, girt by swamps and the Hughli river, as the site for Fort William (Calcutta). But Bombay was different. The trickle of off-shore islands which would become the capital of western India changed hands in London; the acquisition was handled by the Company's directors themselves; and the man usually described as the founder of Bombay, Gerald Aungier, is revealed as a most upright and unexciting administrator. A swashbuckling pioneer was not needed. Comparatively speaking, the place came as a going concern.

The Governor's mansion, a relic of Bombay's long Portuguese period, already loomed above the coconut palms. 'A pretty well-seated but ill-fortified house', thought Dr John Fryer, Surgeon to the Company, who first saw it in 1673; it would require the addition of 'war-like walls', 'bold rampires', and 'hardy cannon' to become a modest fort and eventually 'Bombay Castle'. Scattered through the palm-roofed hamlets round about, there already lived some 10,000 souls, both Indian and European and including many of part-Portuguese descent. There were Catholic churches and Hindu shrines and attached to the Governor's house there was 'a delicate garden, voiced to be the pleasantest in India'.

But most important of all, when acquired by the Company in 1668, Bombay would already be a Crown colony. The Union Jack fluttered from the Governor's flagpole and British troops with tall hats and crossed breast-straps paced the parapets. In Bombay the Company would succeed to a bit of Indian soil, albeit small, pestilential and problematic, which was already British. So much so that in the letters patent under which it would be leased to the Company, it was described as pertaining to 'the Manor of East Greenwich in the County of Kent'; and the rent of £10 per annum was to be paid 'in gold, on the 30th day of September, yearly, for ever'. Done. One can almost hear the rap of the auctioneer's gavel. Surplus to Charles II's requirements, Bombay would be knocked down to the only serious bidder, and the directors of the East India Company would thereby find themselves custodians 'in free and common soccage' of all British India. Admittedly it was only some twenty square miles, mostly water; but it made the Company a sovereign power, of sorts, in Asia.

Charles II, as everyone knew, was heartily glad to be rid of the place. During six years it had brought him only an expense which he could not afford and an obligation which he could not discharge. By the 1661 Treaty of Whitehall Bombay had been gifted to him as part of the dowry of Catherine of Braganza, his Portuguese bride. But a secret clause attached to the Treaty specified that it was to be employed by the British in the defence of Portugal's other Indian settlements. Like Methwold's Goa Convention it implied a mutual defence pact against the ever encroaching might of the Dutch V.O.C. but with the onus on the English Crown rather than the Company.

This had suited the territory-shy Company. In 1660 the directors had greeted the restoration of their old Stuart patrons with genuine enthusiasm, voting £3000 of silver plate to His Majesty and £1000 to his brother, James Duke of York. In 1661 Cromwell's charter was duly replaced with one in the King's name and in 1662 a further £10,000 was loaned to the sovereign; the two events were not unconnected. More loans, totalling £150,000, would be voted and more charters, each conferring additional privileges, would be awarded. King and Company understood one another well and their alliance was cemented by a like-minded approach to foreign affairs, both favouring an alliance with the Catholic powers rather than one with the Dutch.

Hence the King's initial willingness to accept the obligation, attached to Bombay, of supporting the Portuguese in the East and hence the Company's congratulations. The directors had regretted that they could not see their way to shouldering the burden of actually occupying the place for His Majesty but, when Charles nobly dispatched a squadron complete with garrison, they had agreed to supply all necessary victuals. Commanded by the Earl of Marlborough (no relation to the John Churchill on whom the same title would be conferred thirty years later) and accompanied by a Portuguese Viceroy who was to oversee the transfer of power, the squadron of five ships and 400 troops reached its destination in late 1662. There its problems began.

Without sanction from Goa the Portuguese Governor refused to hand over his charge, while the Portuguese Viceroy began to query what exactly they were supposed to be handing over anyway. Was it just Bombay island itself as he contended or was it, as the British insisted, the whole minuscule archipelago (since, through infilling and reclamation, become Greater Bombay)? Apparently there had been a map but no one had seen fit to bring it. 'Whereupon Marlborough [or 'Marlberry' as Fryer calls him] examining his commission, was vexed.' 'He was pinched and knew not how to ease himself.' Inevitably his men were suffering from scurvy and could ill withstand further delays cooped up on board. The squadron therefore sailed away to Surat and anchored beside the Company's moorings in Swalley Hole. Again they were unwelcome. Sir George Oxenden, the new President at Surat, surmised that the city's Moghul governor would not rest easy at the sight of 400 regular soldiers drilling on his doorstep. He was right. Unless the British troops were immediately re-embarked he could expect, he was told, to see his factory and his investment confiscated.

Obligingly, Marlborough 'bid adieu to Swalley' and sailed south. Decidedly a cargo of soldiery bent on anything but war was uncommonly hard to offload. In despair he finally selected a desert island not far from Goa. 'Barren, unhealthy and uninhabited' it might be, but there he landed his men, left them one of his ships, and sailed for home. Anjediva measured 'a mile long and 300 paces broad'. It had water and soon the 400 Robinson Crusoes had thrown up temporary shelters. Then, for most of a year, they paced the 300 paces, drank the water, and died miserably. Over 200 perished according to Alexander Hamilton, 'near 300' according to Fryer, 'chiefly by their own intemperance'. One must assume that this harsh verdict sprang from some inside knowledge that water was not the only refreshment to which they had access.

Meanwhile, negotiations with Goa and Lisbon dragged on. In 1664 Sir Abraham Shipman, commander of what remained of the would-be garrison and Governor-designate of Bombay, himself died. He was succeeded by his secretary, a one-time grocer named Humphrey Cooke, and it was Cooke who in 1665 eventually negotiated landing rights at Bombay. Out of Marlborough's force of 400 just 97 emaciated castaways finally sailed north and at last scrambled ashore at Bombay.

Mortality was not the only price exacted by Portuguese prevarication. To secure a haven for his men Cooke had been obliged to make heavy concessions in the matter of Bombay's territorial extent which, when relayed to London, were promptly repudiated by Charles II. 'The Portugalls have choused [i.e. cheated] us,' wrote Samuel Pepys in his *Diary*. Another detachment was soon on its way from England together with a new governor, Sir Gervase Lucas, to supersede Cooke. In fact Lucas went one better and established something of a Bombay tradition by denouncing his predecessor and clapping him in gaol. The charge, originally of extortion and peculation, was upgraded to treason when Cooke made good his escape and began intriguing with the Portuguese for his reinstatement.

Lucas took a firmer line and no doubt 'would have made the Portugalls perform their compact' had he not died within the year. Whereupon he too was succeeded by his secretary, 'a person of mercuriall brain' – and no less mercurial origins – called Captain Henry Gary. His name, like his rank, was open to doubt since Hamilton calls him a Greek and Fryer a Venetian. With a house in Goa and plantations in Bombay he flitted between the opposing camps and, according to most accounts, was cordially detested by the Portuguese as 'an awfull heretick' and by the British on account of 'his vainglorious boastings'. He was, we are told, 'forever seeking to magnifye himself by debasing us (soe much as in him laye)'. Yet evidently he was a most plausible companion and a good businessman. He was also one of Bombay's true survivors and, however rare this quality, he seems to have expected others to share it. Either that or he was extraordinarily forgetful. For having condemned a miscreant to be hanged on a Tuesday, on the following Friday he recalled the man for further testimony. When 'the poor dead fellow' failed to comply, Gary is supposed to have flown into a rage and ordered his arrest for contempt.

The story is told with some relish by Captain Alexander Hamilton and has been embellished by later writers. 'We may picture him with wig awry and face inflamed with the overnight's debauch, laying down the law in the rude language of the military camp.' Happily for history, if sadly for its popularizers, it has since been proved that if any such incident did occur it was not in a court presided over by Gary who, on closer scrutiny, emerges as a sober and trusted figure. Appointed a factor back in 1643, he had served on the Council at Surat before serving his king and then the Company again until well into his seventies. Indeed his cosmopolitan origins, his ambiguity in matters of religion, his acumen as an accountant and his impartiality during many years as Chief Justice, mark him out as one of the colony's most influential founders. Although none of this could save him from the disgrace which eventually overtook almost every one of Bombay's functionaries, it is further testimony to his integrity and ability that his principal detractor would be the vindictive and hot-headed Sir John Child.

Child it would be who, during the first twenty years of the Company's tenure of Bombay, would contrive almost to lose it twice. In 1668, when Charles II made the place over to the Company's directors, its loss would not perhaps have greatly troubled them. Their reluctance to ease His Majesty 'of that great burthen and expense which the keeping of it hath hitherto beene' was probably genuine. It seemed that Bombay's negligible trade and limited access to the mainland, plus its unhealthy climate, could never repay the cost of fortifying and garrisoning it against the marauding fleets of the Dutch and of Indian pirates. But by 1688 it was a very different story. Bombay had become a thriving colony with a population of 60,000. Briefly eclipsing even Madras, it was 'the seat of power and trade of the English in the East Indies'. Far from being dispensable, on it seemed to hang the fate of the Company in India.

This remarkable transformation came about thanks to a combination of vigorous moves by the Company's servants and a dramatic change in the Indian political scene. Bombay might have had little trade but, as men like Oxenden and Aungier came from Surat to assess its potential, they soon perceived other possibilities well worth exploiting. In Surat the Company had only its factory. It was 'the best accommodation of any in the city' and the factors were proud of its busy courtyard, which served as a stock exchange, of the crowded warehouses, of its grand dining hall where gargantuan meals were taken at long polished tables, and of the spacious roof gardens where whatever breeze there was buffeted the cobwebs of over-indulgence. Occasionally there were picnics in the city's formal gardens and rides down river to view the shipping at Swalley. But it was still a constricted and collegiate existence dependent alike on the indulgence of the Moghul authorities and the forbearance of the Court in London. There was no security. The factory was rented, fortunes could be made and lost but rarely enjoyed, and family life was almost unknown.

At Bombay, on the other hand, a man could build his own house on British soil and acquire his own few acres of coconut grove. To encourage settlement the Company now permitted its employees to stay on after their term of service and even outsiders, provided their business did not compete with that of the Company, were welcome to take up residence. Administering a colony involved a host of unfamiliar responsibilities of which populating the place was by no means the least. For mortality in Bombay was probably higher than anywhere in India. 'Three years was the average duration of European life', declared Chaplain Anderson; 'two mussouns [i.e. monsoons] are the age of a man', contradicted Chaplain Ovington, adding that of English children born on the island 'not one in twenty live beyond their infant days'. Dr Fryer, whose diagnoses invariably bear more on the man than the malady, blamed the Portuguese arrack (made apparently from jelly-fish) and 'foul women'.

'To prevent the latter of which, and to propagate their colony, the Company have sent out *English* women.' They came in two varieties, 'gentlewomen' for the factors and officers, 'other women' for the troops. One 'suit of raiment' was allowed to each girl – and one can imagine how carefully the Company's directors scrutinized that issue – and they were supposed to receive free board and lodging for a year and a day. This, however, was not always forthcoming. The directors preferred a quick turnover and were generally satisfied. 'They goe pretty fast, some married, some sure, some in a fair way,' reported one Governor. But in the mad rush to nuptials, that matching of pedigrees went by the board. 'Be they what they will, at their arrival all pretend to be gentlewomen, high born, great parentage and relations, and scorn to marry under a factor or commissioned officer, though ready to starve.' In vain did the Governor indent for a supply of 'country girls' or even 'Hospital girls'. With the next consignment came a note that such were simply not available. And although the utmost care had been taken to select only the truly 'civil', they too proved highly troublesome 'not only daily dishonouring the nation and their own sex but declaring their utmost endeavour to make their impudence more notorious'.

The presence of a growing and, all too often, impudent population demanded all manner of judicial, fiscal and administrative institutions. Gerald Aungier, Governor from 1669–77, was not only Bombay's 'true founder' but also the first of the Company's servants to try his hand at civilian government. During the 1670s he regulated the existing magistrates' courts and set up a Supreme Court of Judicature. For the first time in India juries were employed and, with the appointment to the bench of Henry Gary, long since superseded as Governor, was introduced the idea of separating judicial and executive authority. Orders from Surat enjoined Gary to uphold the integrity of his office and not bring the court into disrepute by showing partiality or by 'countenancing common barristers in which sort of vermin they say Bombay is very unhappy'.

When the Company had taken over Bombay, a plan of London as it was to be rebuilt after the Great Fire of 1666 was thoughtfully sent to the new colony. Aungier took this seriously and was soon planning what he called 'the city which, by God's assistance, is intended to be built'. The tidal swamps must be drained, the islands linked by causeways, and there must of course be a hospital and an Anglican church. A mint, the first operated by the British in India, was established to turn the Company's bullion exports into rupees, xeraphins, shahis and all the other exotic denominations then in use in India. Meanwhile fortifications consisting of a chain of Martello towers were erected. By 1673 they looked formidable enough to discourage a Dutch fleet from attempting to land.

It all cost money, of course, and the directors in London were soon groaning at Aungier's extravagance. 'Our business is to advantage ourselves by trade', they reminded him in 1675, 'and what government we have is but the better to carry on and support that [trade].' But, as Aungier might have replied, trade at Bombay had first to be created. To attract the weavers, planters, merchants and money-lenders on whom it depended, Bombay had to establish a reputation for security, religious harmony, and impartial justice. And thanks to his reforms it was doing just that. Additionally it offered a new source of income in the form of revenue. Under Portuguese rule Bombay's residents had remitted a fourth of their crop to the government. Aungier, after meeting with the principal residents, remitted this in favour of a land tax which yielded some £1666 per annum and was based on his famous Convention, 'a sort of Doomesday Book in which the properties of the island were registered'. It was a significant precedent. For the first time the Company was enjoying the easy pickings of land revenue. Within a decade the Governor of the Company was urging something similar on the Madras authorities. 'People protected ought in all parts of the universe, in some way or other, to defray the charge of their protection and preservation from wrong or violence.' If commercial activity in the East depended on the fortifying of land bases, then all who enjoyed their security must pay for it. Trade preceded the flag; taxes followed it.

But in Bombay financial stringency remained the order of the day and, as with the women so with the cash, scarcity bore most heavily on the troops. In the 1670s Fryer put the garrison at 300 English, 400 Topazes (Indo-Portuguese), 500 native militia and 300 Bhandaris (club-wielding toddy tappers 'that lookt after the woods of cocoes'). The nucleus of the English contingent had originally served the Crown, having come out with Marlborough and Lucas, and although they had since transferred their loyalty to the Company they continued Royalist in their sympathies. But the high mortality meant that new recruits from England were required almost yearly and it was one such consignment which in 1674 staged the first Bombay mutiny. Absconding with their weapons, they barricaded themselves in a fort on Mazagaon (then a separate island), and listed their grievances. Aungier, to prevent the mutiny spreading, quickly conceded. The demands were not excessive – the men claimed that they were losing on the exchange rate by not being paid in rupees, that they were owed a month's pay, that they could not afford to buy their own scarlet coats, and that inflation had pushed the price of some foodstuffs beyond their means. Aungier, a scrupulously fair governor, may even have sympathized. But mutiny was mutiny and there was even a suggestion that their commanding officer was implicated. Courts martial resulted in the execution of the ringleader, by name Forke (or sometimes Fake), and the cashiering of Captain Shaxton. The whole affair was over in a matter of weeks; but not forgotten.

For in 1682 what Fryer called 'the not yet extinguished feud between the merchants and the soldiers' flared again. Representing the military, Captain Richard Kegwin, formerly governor of St Helena, had come to Bombay as a freelance planter in 1676. He was soon inducted by the Company, given the job of raising a small contingent of cavalry, and then appointed to the command of the whole garrison and a seat on the governing Council. This was in 1681. In 1682 John Child, representing the merchant interest, succeeded to the Presidency of Surat which carried the additional responsibility of Governor of Bombay. Child had been factoring on the west coast for some twenty years and knew its trade as well as anyone. He had the confidence of the directors in London and a wide circle of cronies and relations in India. He would soon receive a baronetcy, a fairly normal distinction for any President in times of good Company–Crown relations; and posterity has thought well of him.

But this favourable press seems to have resulted from an understandable but quite mistaken assumption that he was a brother of Sir Josiah Child, the Company's thrusting chairman in the 1680s. The two men had indeed more than a name in common. To secure allies 'I know,' wrote a discontented Surat factor, 'that Child at home scatters the guineas there, as the other Child does the rupees here, and both to one purpose.' They were equally unscrupulous, equally possessive of the Company's monopoly, and equally premature in their idea of the Company's strength in India. But they were not related and had probably never met; and whereas Josiah's broad entrepreneurial genius lent a degree of credibility to his proto-imperialist ambitions, the narrow horizons and factional obsessions of John boded ill for their execution.

In 1683 John Child, obeying instructions from London where there was 'a general and unparalleled run or demand for money upon all the public funds in this city and especially on this Company', launched a cost-cutting policy in India and appointed his brother-in-law to see it through in Bombay as Deputy-Governor. Kegwin had his own quarrel with Child but Child stayed put in Surat. It was another rising by the Bombay garrison which precipitated Kegwin's rebellion. Threatened with a cut in numbers, a cut in privileges, and a cut in pay, the troops turned as one on their civilian overlords, imprisoned the Deputy-Governor, and elected Kegwin their leader. There were two ships in the harbour, one of which conveniently contained £50,000 in gold. Kegwin seized it and then issued a proclamation in the King's name terminating the Company's rule and giving as his reasons its 'intollerable extortions, oppressions and unjust impositions' plus its 'not maintaining the honour due to His Majesty's crown'. In long letters to the King and the Duke of York he protested his loyalty and undertook to abide by their decision. Meanwhile, for nearly a year, he governed Bombay with restraint, pursued friendly relations with his Indian neighbours, and made the city a sort of free port open to all those traders whom the Company regarded as interlopers. His only act of incitement was an abortive attempt to convince the Surat factors to follow his example and arrest John Child.

News of the revolt reached London in the summer of 1684. The King, heavily in the Company's debt and with no fond memories of Bombay, promptly disowned the zealous Kegwin and commanded him to restore the colony to the Company. John Child must have been delighted. But the terms to be offered to Kegwin and his followers included a full pardon; and the enforcement of the order was entrusted to Sir Thomas Grantham, a royal protégé who happened to be cruising the East as a one-ship enforcement agency. At the time he was in Java hoping to avenge the Bantam factors who had just been expelled by the Dutch. Next he had an assignement in Persia – the customs dues owed to the Company at Gombroon were heavily in arrears – but by October he had cleared his backlog and, after reporting to Child at Surat, sailed on to Bombay.

Kegwin, it seemed, was expecting him. He was permitted to land and was received courteously. 'The monster' whom Grantham had earlier wanted to hang showed a genuine respect for his royal commission and now became 'a stout rebel'. By 10 November the terms of surrender were agreed; Kegwin handed over the still intact £50,000 of gold; and Grantham wrote to Child reassuring him that in spite of the rebellion having lasted nearly a year, 'Your Honours are not much embezzled'. In two days' time the garrison would lay down their arms and 'march out by agreement'. But next day, when Grantham attempted to explain the terms of the surrender to a mass meeting of the men, he was shouted down. 'They shut the gates on me, hissed, and broke out with "No Governor but Kegwin" '. Suddenly a pistol was pressed into the small of his back and, 'but for the Providence of God Almighty' (plus the timely action of 'one Henry Fletcher, a Captain'), 'I had been basely and cowardly murdered'. The assailant was disarmed, Grantham was bundled away, and under cover of darkness smuggled back aboard his ship. For the next week he stayed there.

Clearly not all of Kegwin's men shared their commander's touching regard for the royal command. A few days later Kegwin wrote to Grantham that he fully anticipated 'being put in irons [by them] or having my throat cut'. Nevertheless he patiently set about winning them over, a task in which old Henry Gary, still a local resident, assisted. 'They begin to grow colder,' reported Kegwin on the 15th. On the 16th he was even more optimistic and by the 18th he could announce 'there is not now a dissenting person'; Grantham might come ashore again. On the 18th he did so and a further agreement was signed by both parties. This document, supposed to be one of surrender, in fact contains nothing in the way of condemnation or recrimination and is totally taken up with pledges of pardon and indemnity. All the rebels were to go scot free, none of their transactions could be held against them, and no monies or goods could be reclaimed from them. Kegwin was even confirmed in the salary he had paid himself, congratulated on his 'dutiful compliance', and guaranteed a passage home at the Company's expense.

He sailed with Grantham but, before leaving India, the ship called again at Surat to ensure that Child 'do ratify, sign and confirm' the agreement 'in as large and ample a manner and form as is usual in law'. Child obliged – he had little choice – but not without registering his disapproval. Spluttering with rage he addressed the Company.

> Kegwin, the notorious naughty rascal, is on board the *Charles II*, as impudent as hell, glorying in his roguery, being secure under Sir Thomas' [Grantham's] protection . . . We cannot but see that he will get out of our hands, but indeed it's ten thousand pities he should escape the halter, being the very false rascal without whom the revolt on Bombay would not have been.

Curiously, aboard the *Charles II* there was also a real 'monster'. Purchased by Grantham in India, this poor creature must have been suffering from some extreme form of goitre for, we are told, 'he had the perfect shape of a child [no pun intended, I think] growing out of his chest as an excrescency, all but the head'. Perhaps this curiosity was intended for the King. His Majesty was keen on exotic species and was endlessly badgering the Company for birds and deer for his Birdcage Walk menagerie. In the previous year he had written off for 'one Male and two Female Blacks'. They were for purposes of pageantry rather than experimental genetics 'but they must be Dwarfs and of the least size that you can procure'. The King, however, was not amused by Grantham's 'monster' who, although baptized, passed the rest of his days being 'exposed to the sight of the people for profit'.

In Child's book, such a fate would have been too good for Kegwin; that 'naughty rascal' had escaped his clutches, but there remained the grey-bearded Gary whom Child considered 'a great encourager of the rebels' and therefore another 'very naughty man'. In spite of the general pardon and a personal commendation from Grantham, Gary became a marked man. At last, in 1689, a trumped up charge of treason was brought against him. At the time Bombay was being besieged by the Moghul fleet; Gary's plantation had been ravaged and his house gutted. Not surprisingly the 'mercurial' old man decided it was time to move on. He retired, probably to Goa, reflecting surely that the colony he had handed over to the Company twenty-five years before was this time done for.

ii

In 1687, two years after Kegwin's rebellion, orders had come from the Company in London that Bombay was to supersede Surat as their headquarters on the west coast of India. Accordingly John Child, now a baronet and with authority over all the Company's establishments in India, was to move to Bombay Castle. Bombay would become the Presidency, Surat a mere Agency. 'Though our business is only trade and security, not conquest,' explained the directors, 'yet we dare not trade boldly or leave great stocks where we have not the security of a fort'. This harder line was echoed in instructions to Madras 'of which we claim the sovereignty, and will maintain and defend against all persons, and govern by our laws without any appeal to any prince or potentate whatsoever'. And it was also at this juncture that the need for a fortified settlement in Bengal was being urged.

The Portuguese had always accepted that trade depended on an assertion of sovereignty and the military expenditure to support it. Now new rivals, the French, were fortifying Pondicherry and in 1672 had stormed and occupied San Thomé just down the beach from Madras. But it was still the Dutch whom the English feared most and, just as imitation of their endeavours had proved the sincerest form of competition in Lancaster's day, so now it was the Dutch example which the directors urged. Their new Chairman (or Governor), Sir Josiah Child, ordered Madras to form a municipal corporation on the Dutch model and adopted many Dutch terms; thus apprentice factors were now called 'writers' after the Dutch 'shcruyvers'. When in 1682 the British were driven out of Bantam Child suggested that, if the lesson of Dutch supremacy was thereby learnt, it would be ample compensation. And that lesson was that to trade simply as merchants was a recipe for disaster. Prosperity and permanence depended on the Company operating in the East as a sovereign power with secure bases, adequate firepower, and efficient government.

This was, of course, a complete reversal of those axioms propounded, after much wavering, by Sir Thomas Roe in the 1620s ('. . . if you will profitt, seek it at sea and in a quiett trade; for without controversy it is an errour to effect garrisons and land warrs in India'). One explanation for this abrupt change to a more assertive stance is that it simply reflected the spirit of the age and the reality of the Company's power. Since Cromwell's charter trade had grown prodigiously; the Company was now the largest and wealthiest corporation in the English-speaking world; and while so closely allied with the Crown through those hefty donations to the royal exchequer it was inevitable that it would espouse the maritime and commercial 'imperialism' of its royal patrons. Sir Thomas Grantham, before he sailed east to deal with Kegwin, had put down a revolt in Virginia; and Sir Josiah Child was himself involved in a plantation in Jamaica. The success of settlements in the New World was suggesting a pattern of expansion and a form of overseas authority which might, with modifications, be applied in the Old.

But of more direct bearing on the Company's thinking was the unpredictable trading climate that now prevailed at the Moghul ports of Surat and Hughli (Bengal) as a result of political insecurity and the competition posed by interlopers. Under Aurangzeb (1658–1707) the Moghul Empire passed slowly through its zenith. Even as it achieved its greatest geographical extent it was assailed by enemies from within, foremost of whom were the Marathas, a warrior caste from the mountains just east of Bombay. Under the leadership of the great Sivaji, Maratha cavalry raided deep into the Deccan and Maratha fleets ranged along the west coast. In 1664 these 'Seevagees', as the English called them, swooped on the rich province of Gujarat and made for the great port of Surat. Panic gripped the city and business came to a standstill. Encountering little resistance Sivaji's men overran the metropolis and 'plundered it for forty days together'. Only the Governor's castle and the English factory held out. Indeed so successful was the resistance offered by President Oxenden and so staunch his loyalty to the Moghuls that Aurangzeb conferred on him a robe of honour and partially remitted the year's customs dues. Equally grateful, the Company awarded him a gold medal and £200 in gold.

Six years later Sivaji gave a repeat performance. Once again the citizens of Surat fled, again the city was plundered and burnt, and again the English staged a stout defence. More expressions of imperial gratitude followed. But they scarcely made up for the loss of trade and Aungier was soon seeking a non-interference pact with the Marathas. The wars raged on. Surat, haunted by rumours of further raids, was itself fortified. But the Emperor evidently had no more faith in the new walls than did the Company. He removed his treasure; the Company diverted more shipping to Bombay. Yet even in Bombay the Company was commercially disadvantaged, for what trade there was remained a hostage to events on the mainland. While trying to keep on good terms with Sivaji, the Company was obliged to permit the Moghul fleet to ride out the monsoon at anchor off Bombay. In 1679 the Moghul and Maratha fleets clashed in the harbour itself. The punctilious neutrality observed by the English endeared them to no one.

Meanwhile in distant Bengal relations between the Company's abrasive factors and the Moghul's most powerful Governor reached breaking point. In 1686 a fleet was despatched from England with, as will be seen, the absurd intention of 'entering into a war with the Mogull'. This extraordinary turn of events also influenced the decision to downgrade the Company's presence at Surat. Sir John Child supported the resort to arms and as Admiral and Captain-General of the Company's forces was nominally in charge of operations. But Surat was a long way from Bengal and he seems to have imagined that the west coast trade would be allowed to continue regardless of events in the Bay of Bengal. No doubt he reasoned that any move against the Company at Surat could, as in the days of Sir Henry Middleton, be countered by blockading the port or raiding Moghul shipping on the vital Red Sea route.

This deterrent, however, failed simply because no one could believe that Child could be quite so naive. In November 1686, six months before he finally withdrew to Bombay, the Bengal factors were under the impression that he was already safely ensconced in Bombay castle and 'possessed of a good store of their (the Moghuls') rich shipps . . . news of which will mightily delight us'. Similarly the Moghul Governor of Surat assumed that Child was taking the offensive. He therefore went out of his way to molest the English and embarrass their trade. For, as Hamilton asked, 'by what rule of policy could Sir Josiah [Child] or Sir John Child think to rob, murder and destroy the Mogul's subjects in one part of his dominions, and the Company to enforce a free trade in the other parts? Or how could they expect that he [the Moghul] would stand neuter?' Finally even the merchants of Surat, normally well disposed towards the Company, assumed that Child was engaged in hostilities. Thus, when in 1686 one of their ships was indeed waylaid coming from the Red Sea, they held the English responsible. In reality the culprits were 'two Danish pirates'; but that only emerged later. At the time it was not unreasonable for Surat's Governor to freeze the Company's assets nor for Surat's merchants to shun further dealings with the English.

It was also not unreasonable under the circumstances that the Moghul authorities should accommodate anyone with a grievance against the Company. Captain Hamilton, who was evidently on the scene at the time, makes much of the role played by two senior ex-factors, Messrs Petit and Boucher (or Bourchier), who, like him, were regarded by the Company as interlopers. Both had been dismissed by John Child when they refused to pay him a commission on their private trade. (Coming from Hamilton the accusation is suspect but even the impartial Reverend Ovington put Child's personal fortune at a staggering £100,000.) Subsequently the two men had frustrated Child's attempts to arrest them and, while Petit 'bought a ship to go a trading in Persia', Boucher repaired to the Moghul court and secured a trading licence.

The Company's anxiety about interlopers and pirates was now little short of paranoid. Suppressing Kegwin's rebellion had been as much about suppressing the interlopers he welcomed to Bombay as about the rights and wrongs of Company rule. And in Bengal the decision to take on the Moghul empire had as much to do with its Governor entertaining interlopers as with its exactions on the Company's trade. Thus the defiance of Petit and Boucher may, as Hamilton suggests, have preyed more upon the vindictive John Child than did the political crisis. Certainly they figured prominently, along with the Danish pirates, in the list of grievances which he drew up soon after reaching Bombay in 1687. The list was sent to the Governor of Surat. Receiving no satisfaction, Child at last took the offensive. Moghul shipping was boarded wherever it was encountered and in mid 1688 Hamilton counted fourteen prizes lying in Bombay harbour.

Wholly predictably, the Moghul governor in Surat retaliated by imprisoning those factors left behind by Child. In the hope of freeing them Child returned to Surat towards the end of 1688 and was soon announcing that the city's governor had agreed to his terms. Overjoyed, the Company voted him an unusually generous 1000 guineas by way of thanks. But it was premature. The governor promptly rearrested the factors and paraded them through the streets in irons. With a price on his head Child scuttled back to Bombay.

On the way he fell in with a fleet of barges carrying corn to Sidi Yakub, commander of a formidable fleet that was operating against the Marathas as the Moghul's navy. This was enough for Child. He ordered that the barges be taken. His senior captain protested that taking these provisions would practically oblige the Sidi to attack Bombay. Child scoffed at the very idea and accused the captain of cowardice. If Sidi Yakub came anywhere near Bombay he would 'blow him off with the wind of his bum'.

On the night of 14 February 1689 the Sidi's force of 20,000 men entered Bombay harbour and landed unopposed. The only gun to be fired was that which gave the alarm; and since most of the English lived outside the Castle, the only response was a frantic stampede as 'the poor ladies, both black and white, ran half naked to the fort and only carried their children with them'. The garrison was unprepared, the fortifications neglected; Child had failed to take even the most elementary precautions. 'Better skilled at his pen than his sword,' writes the Reverend Ovington, 'the merchant was unfit for that great post [of General] and grown unwieldy with too much honour.'

Next day the enemy took the lesser Bombay forts of Mazagaon and Mahim, still without a shot being fired. Advancing on Bombay Castle, the Sidi erected batteries which 'bombarded our fort with massy stones' that 'disturbed the garrison very much'. Forays by the English proved ineffectual. 'Buoyed up with a strong opinion of their own valour and of the Indians' pusillanimity . . . they promised themselves victory in the most dubious engagements.' But 'our men being good runners', the casualties were outnumbered by desertions. Even detested interlopers like Hamilton had to be pressed into service. And so 'we passed the months from April till September very ill'. An appeal to the Marathas produced 3000 'Seevagees'. They fought well and probably saved the Castle; but feeding them put a terrible strain on the provisions.

By August only the Castle itself and about half a mile to the south of it remained in the Company's hands. Their warehouse had been ransacked and burnt and they were running low on both powder and ammunition. But the end of the monsoon gave Hamilton and others a chance to put to sea in the few small ships that remained to them. They had 'pretty good success' taking several prizes and so relieving the food shortage. As always the Company was more formidable afloat than ashore. But given the Sidi's superior numbers and Child's now obvious incompetence, a military solution looked more unlikely than ever. In December, cap in hand, a delegation of two Bombay factors was sent to the Moghul court to seek what terms they could. As in Bengal, so on the west coast, the war with the Moghul had proved an unmitigated disaster.

Yet, even as the siege was at its height, Sir Josiah Child in London remained confident that it was the mighty Aurangzeb who would have to capitulate. 'The subjects of the Mogull', he opined, 'cannot bear a war with the English for twelve months together without starving and dying by thousands for want of our trade.' To the merchants and officials of the port cities, and to the producers in the hinterland, overseas trade *was* important. But it scarcely impinged on the Court or on the bulk of the population. As one historian puts it, 'to Aurangzeb the Company was still a mere flea on the back of his imperial elephant'.

When the Emperor deigned to receive the two peace envoys from Bombay he treated them not as representatives of a sovereign power but as errant subjects. With their hands bound they 'were obliged to prostrate' ('after a new mode for ambassadors', sneers Hamilton) while the Emperor delivered a severe reprimand. They then 'made a confession of their faults and desired pardon' adding a plea for the withdrawal of the Sidi's forces and the restitution of their cancelled trading rights. Graciously Aurangzeb obliged but only on the most humiliating terms. The Company must pay an indemnity of 150,000 rupees, must restore all plundered goods and ships, and must 'behave themselves for the future no more in such a shameful manner'. Their case against the interloper Boucher (Petit had died) must be proved in court, Sir John Child 'who did the disgrace' must be 'turned out and expelled', and henceforth the Company 'must proceed according to my will and pleasure, and be not forgetful of the same'. They were surely the hardest terms the Company would ever have to swallow.

John Child evidently felt so. He died, 'a shrewd career move', during the course of the negotiations. Either he was terrified that any terms that 'would suit with the honour of his Masters' would be unacceptable to the Emperor, or he was heartbroken by 'their grating articles'. His successor would be obliged to make Surat once again his headquarters. Although the Company's credit there had taken a severe blow, the Moghul authorities insisted that the Company's senior representative remain amongst them as a guarantee of good behaviour. Meanwhile Bombay was left to moulder. Of 'seven or eight hundred English' before the war 'not above 60 were left by the sword and the [subsequent] plague'. The plantations were devastated and houses destroyed. 'Bombay', writes Hamilton, 'that was one of the pleasantest places in India was brought to be one of the most dismal deserts.'

In the many histories of Britain's involvement with India the Moghul War of 1688–90 receives little attention. Ill advised and worse prosecuted, it spawned no heroes yet fell short of sublime tragedy. Indecision induced adversity; adversity ended in ignominy. Its only saving grace, it would seem, was its irrelevance. Such inglorious and eminently forgettable incidents doubtless account for that typically dismissive attitude towards the Company which presents its history as opening in a blaze of exploratory endeavour in the early 1600s after which nothing happens until Clive's exploits in the 1750s.

Only one generalist historian, admittedly writing solely about the Company, perceives some significance in this precedent for an armed assault on India's sovereign power. 'If only', he writes, 'Sir Josiah could have had his way and his brother [*sic*] Sir John had lived!' Then, we are told, 'they might easily have made themselves masters [of India?]'. The book in which this surprising statement appears was written in the twentieth century. Moreover its author fashionably disclaims any 'intermediary perversion due to national prejudice or to an avowed admiration for the Old Company.'

CHAPTER EIGHT

Fierce Engageings

CALCUTTA AND BENGAL

The temptation to discern in the history of the Honourable Company events and personalities which presage the Raj is understandable but not necessarily helpful. It may even be misleading. For instance, in or about the year 1690 it fell to Job Charnock, an old and respected servant of the East India Company, to found the future city of Calcutta. That much is certain. But since Calcutta would soon come to epitomize British power in India, around both Charnock and the circumstances of his foundation myths and legends accrued as around no other event in the Company's history in India in the seventeenth century.

These fabrications took predictable forms. Thus native accounts of the affair emphasize the liberality of native rulers. One has it that the site was magnanimously granted to the Company by the emperor Aurangzeb in gratitude for provisions furnished from Madras to his troops in the south of India; another that Charnock himself won 'the King's favour by routing some rebellious subjects and pledging undying loyalty to the Emperor's (or Nawab's) person.

But, flatly contradicting all this, the version favoured by British historians has Charnock at loggerheads with the Moghul and courageously defying imperial power. Hounded down the Ganges by vast native armies, the desperate little band of English merchants discover their destined haven at Calcutta only to be driven from it and forced back on to the river. They continue downstream with Charnock wielding his sword like a Sir Galahad to slice through steel chains strung across the current to prevent his escape. Eventually a desperate last stand is made on a pestilential island in the mouth of the river. Suffering appalling losses the English gallantly stand their ground and finally cow the enemy into retreat by a ruse which greatly exaggerates their numbers. Peace negotiations thus find Charnock in a position of some strength. He is rewarded with the lease of Calcutta to which he triumphantly leads back his little band of heroes to start building the future metropolis.

In all these accounts there are nuggets of truth, each badly flawed by retrospective sentiment. For in reality the Calcutta episode reflects credit neither on Charnock's ability nor his companions' prowess, and neither on the Moghul's liberality nor on the Company's good sense. Calcutta, as one might surmise from the city of today, was born not out of courage or design but out of commercial greed and political mayhem. There are few highlights in the Calcutta saga and no heroes. It is not a pretty story.

First contacts with Bengal had been made from Masulipatnam by the Dutchman, Lucas Antheuniss, and his successor, William Methwold, in the 1620s. But it was during the English Civil War and the commercial chaos of the 1640s and 1650s (when Methwold, one of the first Company servants to hold office, was deputy-governor in London) that trade with 'The Bay' as opposed to 'The Coast' (Madras and Masulipatnam) began to prosper. Factories were established at Balasore and then inland at Hughli, Kasimbazar, Malda, Patna and Dhaka (Dacca). With the Restoration of the British monarchy the demand for Bengal's saltpetre was supplemented by a growing appreciation of the area's cheap raw silks and molasses. Ships were sent direct to the mouth of the Ganges and in 1681 the Company's Bengal establishment was for the first time constituted as a separate Agency (or Presidency) independent of Madras and Bombay/Surat. To direct its operations, discipline its factors and secure its trade, William Hedges, a director of the Company, sailed from London with a small escort and extensive powers. He arrived at the town of Hughli, where the Company had its main headquarters about twenty miles north of what was to be Calcutta, in 1682.

By virtue of an imperial grant dating back thirty years, the Company's establishments in Bengal claimed exemption from customs duties in return for a lump sum paid direct to the Nawab, who was the Moghul's regent, kinsman, and governor for what was the richest province in the whole empire. Negotiations as to the amount and frequency of such payments had to be reopened with each new Nawab; but the beauty of this system was that in principle it eliminated the far worse wrangles and delays that would result from dealing with the numerous and none too scrupulous officials to whom customs and excise collection was farmed.

In practice, of course, the Company was never free of local exactions; and as trade increased so did the need to lubricate all moving parts in what was necessarily a most cumbersome commercial machine. But in about 1680 the situation had been rendered intolerable by the imposition of a five per cent duty on imported bullion and a three and a half per cent duty on exports – in addition to the lump sum payment. The Nawab responsible was the recently reappointed and very able Shaista Khan and it was to demand redress that Hedges soon presented himself at Dhaka, the Nawab's capital (and now that of Bangladesh).

Whatever the Company might think, though, and whatever Hedges might demand, the fact was that the Moghul emperor, through his provincial governors, was entitled to tax foreign traders as he saw fit. They had come as uninvited guests and they continued at his pleasure. Except in Bombay and Madras the Company had no territorial rights and even its commercial privileges had no validity beyond the reign of whoever had granted them.

But this is not to say that the English were merely tolerated. When Hedges duly played his last card and threatened to withdraw all the Company's factors from Bengal, Shaista Khan was deeply and genuinely concerned. The days of Elizabeth and Akbar when European trade to India had been valued principally for its limited stock of novelties, trinkets and sporting dogs had long since passed. In the period 1681–5 the Company would export, mainly to Moghul India, a grand total of 240,000 kg of silver and nearly 7000 kg of gold. With Aurangzeb's armies permanently locked in combat with either Afghans or Marathas, the demand for coin throughout the empire was unprecedented and to an important extent it was being met by the European trading companies. Additionally the manufacturing industries of Gujarat, the Tamil country and Bengal had come to depend on Europe's insatiable demand for cottons and silks. And although on land the trading companies were militarily insignificant, at sea they retained that potential for nuisance which Henry Middleton had discovered and which John Child was to essay with a blast of 'air from my bum'.

All in all then an uneasy and unwritten reciprocity underlay relations between the Company and the Moghul authorities. Instead of fleas on the back of Aurangzeb's imperial elephant, the European companies were more like egrets busily delousing the Moghul water-buffalo. They pecked and flapped about the imperial person knowing full well that their humble services, although mildly irritating, were both appreciated and necessary. And of this symbiotic relationship neither party quite lost sight, either in the protracted negotiations undertaken by Hedges or in the hostilities which rapidly succeeded them.

In the event Hedges came away from the Nawab's court at Dhaka well satisfied. In return for various sureties, Shaista Khan had agreed to petition the emperor for a renewal of the Company's customs exemption and in the meantime to give the Company a period of grace. 'I bless God,' wrote Hedges in his diary, 'for the great success I have had, beyond all men's expectations.' He reckoned to have saved his honourable masters £20,000 per annum and, once the imperial *farman* should arrive, he confidently predicted that its preferential terms would give the Company such a commercial edge over its competitors that it 'shall never more be much troubled with interlopers'.

Supplementing Hedges's diary with the visual cameos afforded by Moghul paintings of the period, there emerges a vivid impression of what was probably – with the Emperor himself forever in the field – the most refined court in India at the time. Hard bargaining was left to intercessors and intermediaries operating behind the latticed scenes. Meanwhile Hedges and the old Nawab observed the niceties of civilized intercourse, exchanging mutual flatteries and waiving minor points of etiquette (which the Englishman construed as a 'greater kindness than he has ever shewn before to any Christian'). Hedges, as a one-time director of the Levant Company, had spent some years in Constantinople. He spoke Turkish and Arabic and he relished the courtly values of the Islamic world; brocade diplomacy was his speciality.

How very different was the coarse, vituperative and money-grubbing atmosphere which awaited him at the Company's Kasimbazar establishment in west Bengal. Here merchants bickered over who should have the raw silk sweepings from the factory floor; with a commission on this and a backhander for that, scarce a man was not busily lining his own pocket. But the level of corruption was a direct reflection of the level of trade; the more silk passing through the warehouses, the more sweepings for feathering factors' nests. Thus the man who presided over this turbulent mob, the indestructible Job Charnock, was both the most abrasive and yet the most effective of all the Company's Indian factors.

Whereas Hedges's considerable vanity was flattered by the company of Moghul courtiers, Charnock was at home with their Hindu agents and subjects. Smitten rather than outraged, he had once snatched a young Hindu girl from her husband's funeral pyre and now lived contentedly with the sari-ed maiden and her extended Indian family. His Christianity was suspect and he was certainly every bit as venal and cantankerous as the worst of his subordinates. But he had been in Bengal long enough to know its trade backwards. From the money-lending Seths or the tax-gathering Chands, as from the weavers and growers, he stood no nonsense. In his warehouses substantial cargoes were always ready for the next ship to call at 'The Bay' and over the years he had won the confidence of the directors back in London. In their book 'good honest Job' could do no wrong. True he perhaps lacked those finer points of breeding desirable in a President – and he had in fact been passed over in the promotion race, most recently by the appointment of Hedges – but that in no way prejudiced his standing with the directors and in particular with Sir Josiah Child whose long and influential career as a director of the Company had begun in 1677.

That Hedges would clash with Charnock and his companions was thus understandable. In fact by appointing outsiders to investigate and adjudicate in the affairs of its regular factors – while at the same time encouraging those same regular factors to report direct and in secret to London – the Company seemed positively to encourage an atmosphere of distrust and rancour. Within weeks of Hedges's return from Dhaka, accusations and counter-accusations were passing up and down the river between Hedges at Hughli town and Charnock at Kasimbazar with the regularity of the dreaded tidal bore. Each in turn accused the other of peculation, nepotism, atheism, entertaining interlopers, fornicating with heathens and any other crime considered heinous enough to win censure from the Court of Committees in London. Tough-skinned and frankly contemptuous, Charnock had seen off Hedges's predecessor and did not doubt that the new Agent would soon follow. But to the refined and unhappy Hedges these base insinuations were 'insufferable'. 'I can no more bear them than an honest virtuous woman can be questioned for her chastity', he moaned. 'It's absolutely necessary that one of us two be replaced.'

Hedges could not have known that even as he penned this *cri de coeur* the directors in London were reaching precisely the same conclusion. Six months later, in July 1684, word duly reached Bengal that Agent Hedges had been dismissed the service and that their establishments in Bengal were again to come under the governorship of Madras. The reason given for terminating so abruptly the services of one in whom they had supposedly placed their confidence was that Hedges, or one of his over-zealous supporters, had intercepted private letters from one of

Charnock's henchmen to Sir Josiah Child. Significantly, more heinous in Child's eyes than adultery or malpractice was the crime of having interfered with his system of informers.

This pernicious system would last as long as the Company, and although the charge of subverting it would ever be of the most serious, it was not Child's invention. He merely exploited it for his own often devious purposes. Never, in more than 150 years from the time of William Hawkins till that of Warren Hastings, did the Company in London master its profound distrust of its overseas employees or encourage among them the development of a responsible command structure. In Bantam, Surat, Bombay and Madras the same spectacle of bickering and bitterly divided factors would be witnessed year in and year out. Occasionally, and thanks mainly to the high mortality in the East, outstanding talents rose to the fore and commanded widespread respect. But this was in spite of the Company's direction, rarely because of it; and invariably such luminaries were eventually disowned or discredited. The pleas repeatedly voiced by Hedges that he be accorded the confidence and authority to carry out the task for which he had been appointed would be repeated almost word for word by Warren Hastings a century later. By then Calcutta was 'the city of palaces' and Hastings Governor-General of a sizeable chunk of the Indian subcontinent; but in this one crucial respect nothing had changed.

Observing the unseemly Hedges–Charnock affair from the scented halls of his seraglio in Dhaka, Shaista Khan drew the obvious conclusion. 'The English are a company of base, quarrelling people, and foul dealers', he muttered as he ordered one of Charnock's henchmen to be removed from court. Any intention he had had of interceding for such men in the matter of their customs exemption was now far from his mind. On the contrary, he pressed them for the duties which had accrued in the intervening months and showed more favour to the Dutch and to the detested interlopers than to the Honourable Company. Compared to the well-regulated Dutch company, which also had a chain of factories stretching up the Hughli river, the English seemed as keen to sell their brethren as their bullion. In short, they were fair game and their divisions played into the Nawab's hands.

Hedges had advised that if the English were ever to be masters of their destiny in Bengal they must seek a fortified settlement there equivalent to Bombay or Madras. He understood the Dutch were contemplating something similar and he strongly recommended the island of Sagar at the mouth of the Hughli. As the Nawab leant ever harder on the Company's upriver factories, Charnock at Kasimbazar and Child in London also came to accept the need for drastic action. But instead of quietly occupying Sagar, a move which would probably have entailed an immediate interruption of trade plus the long-term expense of fortifications, they resolved on a show of strength with the Nawab to make him 'sensible of our power as we have of our truth and justice'. The idea seems to have been that they would continue to trade – but at the point of a gun – while at the same time prospecting for a permanent base and ideally one that was already fortified.

Such was the muddled thinking that lay behind the Moghul War, or sometimes 'Child's War', the results of which in so far as they affected Bombay and Surat have already been noticed. Interrupting the movement of Indian shipping in the Arabian Sea was all part of the plan but the main thrust of the attack was to be made where the main provocation was perceived – in Bengal. And to this end two ships carrying three companies of infantry arrived at the mouth of the Hughli river in the autumn of 1686.

'308 soldiers to make war on an empire which had at that moment an army of at least 100,000 men in the field', writes Sir William Hunter in his *History of British India*. With a fine sense of the absurdity of it all Hunter reckons that the Nawab alone had 40,000 troops at his command. 'Conceived in ludicrous ignorance of the geographical distances and with astounding disregard of the opposing forces' here was a contest with all the ingredients for sublime tragedy plus limitless scope for personal heroics; a foretaste perhaps of Clive at Arcot, or more likely a repeat of the Run blockade and the Amboina Massacre.

Yet not so. With extraordinary perversity the war insisted on taking a course of its own which bore no more relationship to the show of force that was intended than it did to the sound drubbing that was invited. For a start, it was never actually declared. Somehow the Company's ultimatum which was to have signalled the outbreak of hostilities never reached the Nawab. He must, however, have had some inkling of trouble for long before the invasion force reached Bengali soil he took the precaution of surrounding the Company's headquarters in Hughli with a few thousand troops. They were well behaved and, having no clear idea why 308 infantrymen from the other side of the world should choose to land in their midst, they duly permitted the newcomers to join their fellow-countrymen in the English factory.

Oddly, as it must have seemed to the Nawab's troops, these alien soldiers included no officers above the rank of lieutenant. In their wisdom the Company's directors had decreed that the conduct of their 'warr with the Moghul' would best be left to their much mistrusted factors and their passing ships' captains, overall command being reserved for the head of the Hughli factory. There was no way that the directors could have known that this worthy had in fact succumbed during the previous monsoon, leaving the indestructible Job Charnock of Kasimbazar as the senior factor. Thus to 'good, honest Job', still wheeling and dealing to his heart's content and a man with no military experience whatsoever, it fell to command the assault on the most powerful empire in Asia.

According to his instructions, this assault was not to be made from Hughli. The object of landing troops there seems to have been simply that of protecting the factory while its considerable stocks of saltpetre ('soe necessary and valewable at this time') were transferred to river craft. The English were then to take to their ships, waylay Moghul vessels in the river, and eventually stage an invasion by taking Chittagong, a place which figured largely in Sir Josiah Child's calculations as the Achilles heel of the Moghul empire. The war thus began with the contradictory spectacle of the invaders endeavouring to withdraw, while the invaded, ever mindful of the value of European trade, sought to persuade them to stay.

As recorded by Charnock, hostilities actually commenced on 28 October 1686 when three of his soldiers, going peaceably about their shopping in the Hughli bazaar, were (reportedly) 'beate, cut, and carried prisoner' to the town's governor. Without waiting to establish the circumstances, 'Colonel' Charnock responded with a series of ferocious reprisals during which the town's guns were spiked, a Moghul ship was taken, and several houses set on fire. Only one English soldier was killed to the sixty fatalities of the enemy. 'We had an absolute conquest and might have made the towne our own', crowed the jubilant 'Colonel', oblivious of the fact that the Nawab might well have settled for just such an outcome. But Charnock had his orders and they 'would not beare us out'; he was not to occupy Hughli but evacuate it.

To allow time for the loading of the saltpetre, a ceasefire was agreed and desultory negotiations were opened. They were still going on when, the warehouse at last empty, Charnock duly embarked his whole contingent and sailed downriver. No attempt was made either to hasten his departure or to prevent it. 'Our coming off was very peaceable.' If anything the evidence suggests that Charnock was as reluctant to leave as his hosts were to see him go. But he was not going far. Having followed to the word the Company's orders to evacuate Hughli, he now flatly contradicted their spirit by landing his entire force just twenty miles downstream.

The spot chosen was a long deep-water basin where the river curled to the west leaving a high mud ridge on its eastern flank. Although technically accessible to ocean-going ships at high tide, it was still seventy miles from the sea up a river which English skippers were as yet reluctant to navigate in any vessel over 300 tons. It was not much better than Hughli in this respect and, according to Charnock, it was even more vulnerable to attack by land. But at least it commanded the river and was well removed from the Moghul centres of power. Here negotiations could continue on more neutral ground while he cast about for alternative sites for a fortified base. He called the place 'Chuttanutteea' after the neighbouring village of Sutanati; others called it 'Kalikata' and eventually Calcutta after another nearby village, Kalighat.

During the winter months of 1686–7 negotiations with the nawab's representatives seemed to be going well. In his mud and timber huts beside the river Charnock drew up his terms – a site for a fort, all the usual customs exemptions, and the payment of an outrageous indemnity of 6.6 million rupees (including one item of 2 million rupees for '1000 men and 20 ships for the warr'). Amazingly an agreement in principle seemed to be forthcoming. But in reality both sides were playing for time.

As per the Company's orders, Charnock was now supposed to have taken the offensive by attacking the Moghul marine and storming the town of Chittagong. But he lacked the men and ships for such an extensive programme, only a third of those originally intended for Bengal having materialized. It may be, therefore, that he was waiting for reinforcements. More plausibly he was also hoping that his instructions would be cancelled. For he realized that if carried out to the letter they would antagonize the Emperor as well as the Nawab and so 'forfeit all our trade in the Bay'. Similarly the Nawab banked on the English in time coming to their senses. He understood their reluctance to jeopardize such a valuable trade and, seeing no reason for generous concessions, sought to prolong the negotiations. He therefore adopted his usual ploy of repudiating the agreement already reached in principle.

At this point Charnock once again panicked. Claiming that 'the country about us was up in arms' and the Nawab raising an army 'to thrust us out of the kingdom' he went on the rampage, burning down 'the King's salt houses', storming one of his riverside forts, ordering the destruction of Balasore, and sailing on downriver to Hijili, the last island before the Bay of Bengal, which he duly commandeered. There appears to have been no direct provocation for any of these attacks. Once again English losses were minimal – 'one man's leg' – whilst at Balasore the whole town was sacked, some thirteen Moghul ships destroyed and much coin and merchandise plundered. So much for the English being 'harried out of Bengal'.

For the Nawab this second assault was too much. Troops were ordered down to the delta – Charnock says 12,000 – and guns were landed on the shore opposite Hijili island. But Hijili was not an easy place to blockade. Although separated from the mainland by only a narrow waterway, to the east it was open to the main river, here some ten miles wide and navigable by the largest vessels. On the other hand it was not a healthy spot. There was a village, a fort that was rapidly improved, and a few fields; the rest was dense undergrowth, swamp and marsh with its full complement of tigers, insects and amoebae. It was now May and in the hottest month of the Bengali year the air scarcely stirred save when shots whistled across the narrows. Far more deadly than lead, though, were the fevers, the ague and the distemper which quickly 'became epidemicall'. By the end of the month more than half of the Colonel's men had been laid to rest in sandy graves and of the survivors less than a hundred were fit for duty. They included just four of the twenty-six NCOs and one of the fourteen junior officers. 'Most desperate and deplorable' was the position, then, when the enemy mounted their main attack.

Taking the fever-ridden defenders by surprise, on 28 May 700 cavalry splashed on to the island, took the village and were among the trenches round the fort before the English rallied. 'Fierce engageings' continued all that night and most of the next day. But 'the Mogull's courage, as their nature is, going out of them with their Bang [*bhang*, a marijuana decoction]', some ground was regained and contact re-established with the Company's shipping. More provisions and powder were landed as more enemy troops crossed on to the island. The first rains arrived, increasing the misery and exhaustion of the defenders and claiming yet more fever victims. Meanwhile the ships stood by. It was not now a question of victory or defeat, merely of evacuation or surrender.

'Thus we held out for 4 daies', wrote Charnock who seems to have remained in robust health throughout. On the fifth day tall ships appeared to seaward. For once the Company's annual fleet from London to Bengal had made good speed. Amid joyful scenes seventy sailors marched ashore and 'chearfully sallied out and beate the enemy from their gunns'. The same men 'by 1 and 2 at a time' were then spirited through the undergrowth back to their ships and, with much beating of drums and blowing of trumpets, ceremoniously relanded. The ploy worked. Convinced that the fleet contained unlimited stocks of fresh fighting men, the Moghul commander 'grew dull upon it . . . and held forth a flag of truce'. The tables had turned once again.

Although 'we would have accepted of any terms to have our Selves, Shipps and Goods conveighed off the island', Charnock was not about to let his good fortune go to his head. It was the enemy who had sued for peace and, more to the point, he now had – and they knew that he had – bullion to spend and holds to be filled. There was nothing like a reminder of that mutual commercial advantage to bring all sides to their senses. Charnock therefore dug out the highly favourable terms negotiated at Sutanati and awaited events.

Whether or not a treaty was actually signed with the Nawab is uncertain. But evidently trading rights were restored and it was agreed that Charnock might select a site for a factory. With colours flying he led his much reduced band away from Hijili and moved back upriver to a place called Ulubari. It was ideal as an anchorage and perfect for ship repairs, but had little else to recommend it. Three months later he decided against Ulubari and moved north again to his old roost at Sutanati (or Calcutta). More huts were built on that long mud ridge, more forest cleared, and after so many experiments it looked as if the English had at last found somewhere to their liking – neither too remote from the commercial centres of upper Bengal nor too impossible of access for their ocean-going fleets in the Bay.

ii

Poring over rather inadequate maps of the Ganges delta in an effort to follow the peregrinations of their Bengal factors, Sir Josiah Child and his fellow directors in London were taking a somewhat different view of their war. It was at about this time that in Surat John Child was claiming to have secured the capitulation of the Moghul authorities simply by raiding their merchantmen on the Arabian Sea route. Why could not the

Bengal factors make equally short work of the opposition? In letters loaded with sarcasm the hawkish directors lambasted their servants for their 'sheepishness' and 'insensible patience' in not having sacked Hughli when they had the chance.

> We are not without great fear that your own backwardness and hankering after your profitable easy old habitations, as the Israelites did after the onions and garlick of Egypt, may deprive us of the fruit of all our cost . . . You must seriously consider and lay to heart the Company's excessive charge for the honour of our King and Country, and make all possible reprisals you can on the enemy for our reimbursement and the maintenance of our forces, the likeliest place for doing of which effectually, we think, is the surprizal of Dacca itself if you can contrive such a design with such secrecy that the Nabob have no foreknowledge of your purpose.

This was written in September 1687. Far from attacking Dhaka – which was about as practicable as attacking Delhi – the much depleted Bengal 'army' was just emerging from its long sojourn amongst the swamps of Hijili. Needless to say, when news of this gallant defence reached London, it did nothing to mollify the directors. 'We are grieved to see how you trifled away time upon frivilous pretences . . . and engaged our forces in unhealthy places, to the loss of the lives of many of our worthy countrymen, and the irreparable dishonour of our nation, and the ruin of our trade in Bengal.' Even if a satisfactory treaty *had* resulted, it was no thanks to their witless factors but to 'God Almighty's Providence, which hath always graciously superintended the affairs of this Company'. Witness once again, they said, the success of John Child at Surat.

But by the end of 1688 it was beginning to dawn on the directors that John Child's master stroke might have been one of the Almighty's less provident interventions. Their Surat factors were back behind bars and Child was making his escape to Bombay, there to embroil the Company in another desperate struggle and a far from flattering surrender. At least in Bengal their factors had now grounded arms and were supposedly busy fort-building. But why, it was demanded, had they not re-established themselves at Kasimbazar and Hughli and why were they not again pushing their trade for all it was worth?

Great, indeed dazzling, had to be the compensations for serving a Company which so habitually and ungraciously disparaged its long-suffering, often-dying employees. But the curious thing about this particular correspondence is that blame is never directly laid upon the man ultimately responsible for all the shortcomings of the Bengal establishment, Job Charnock. In a letter roundly condemning the whole Bengal council for preferring peace merely as a cover for their 'avarice and faint-heartedness', Charnock emerges unscathed. 'We see no reason to find fault with Mr Charnock's conduct of the war.' Having sung his praises for thirty years it was not in the nature of the Company's directors to admit that they could have been mistaken. Even when things were clearly going badly for their old servant, instead of abusing him they chose to sympathize. 'We are well satisfied of our Agent Mr Charnock's sincerity to our interest, and only wish he were as good a soldier as he is (for aught we see, by long experience of him) a very honest merchant.'

So out of character is this indulgent geniality that one must assume that Charnock's reputation lay in the safe keeping of some very senior figure. We know that he was still in the habit of corresponding privately with Sir Josiah Child; and given the self-made and scruple-free characters of both men, it would be unsurprising to discover that more than information was being pooled. Throughout the 1680s Child dominated the affairs of the Company and was either Governor or Deputy-Governor for each of the four years 1686–90. But he was bitterly opposed by some of his reform-minded directors who, as will be seen, resented both his influence and his tactics. To this dissent at the helm of the Company may be ascribed its erratic course in upbraiding the Bengal factors in one sentence while marvelling at the devotion of their 'Colonel' in the next.

Some such explanation must also account for a quite extraordinary confusion which now arose in the conduct of Bengal affairs. In February 1689 the Court of Directors composed another fulsome address in support of 'good honest Job' (who had again fallen out with one of his senior factors) and strongly urged him to press ahead with the fortification of Sutanati (Calcutta) and the reopening of their other establishments on the Hughli. For, they said, 'we have no manner of doubt of the continuance of our peace in all the Mogull's dominions'. Yet this very peace the self-same Court of Directors had in fact neatly sabotaged. For, during the previous year, they had sent to Bengal another fleet with orders to revive the war by re-evacuating their entire Bengal establishment and proceeding with that oft-commended ploy of attacking Chittagong. Thus, even as the directors wrote of peace and trade on the banks of the

Hughli, their employees had decamped once again and were now priming their guns 300 miles away on the frontier of Burma.

Some years previously it had been Charnock who in an unguarded moment had come up with the idea of Chittagong. He was under the impression that it commanded the riverine approaches to the Nawab's capital of Dhaka, that it was poorly defended, and that it was much coveted by the pirates of Burma's Arakan coast from whom the Moghul had acquired it only twenty years before and who could therefore be counted on to join forces with the Company. All this was, of course, hearsay but it made a big impression in London where Job Charnock's hints so often became Josiah Child's obsessions. Child had his reservations, though.

> There is a material objection which may be made against the design, viz. that it will be a very difficult thing for Captain Heath [of the *Defence*] and the fleet with him to get up the great Ganges as high as Chittegam.

A glance at the map will show just how difficult; Chittagong is not up the Ganges nor up any of its myriad channels but well to the east on a rather humbler stream tumbling from the Lushai Hills. And although a picturesque and bustling port, it was far too remote to be commercially relevant or strategically valuable to a Bengal trading Company.

Blissfully ignorant of these details, and assuming Charnock to be still eking out a perilous existence up some tidal creek on the Hughli, in January 1688 Child and his fellow directors had despatched the *Defence* with several other vessels to scoop them off to Chittagong – and in January 1689 had apparently forgotten all about it.

But all was not lost. The situation would still have been retrievable had the captain of the *Defence* possessed a modicum of good sense or had Charnock retained the authority to overrule him. Unfortunately the directors had precluded both possibilities. According to the historian Sir Henry Yule (whose prose savours of a long acquaintance with the epistolary style of the Company) 'they had never made a worse selection than in the case of the hot-headed, wrong-headed, capricious, and futile, feather-brained skipper' of the *Defence*. This was William Heath and so disappointed were the directors in their Bengal factors that Heath's word was to be final. Charnock therefore found himself superseded. As in Hedges's day he resumed the role of disgruntled critic with some relish.

In September 1688 Heath anchored off Balasore and transferred to a coastal sloop for the journey up the Hughli. Reaching the palm-thatched shacks and godowns of what he was the first to call 'Calcutta', he called a meeting, read the Company's orders and took counsel with Charnock and his companions. They had now been nearly a year upon their ridge and after so many removals and frights they were understandably keen to stay put. Charnock therefore represented his situation as full of promise. They had survived their first monsoon there, trade had been resumed, and even now two of their agents were negotiating at Dhaka and confidently predicting a confirmation of the terms reached at Hijili. 'But he [Heath] slightingly waved the same, saying it would signify nothing, the affair being solely left to his judgement.'

Moreover Heath had his orders. The directors had been unusually specific, insisting that only if the settlement had already been fortified and the peace already ratified was the Chittagong plan to be abandoned. Surveying his surroundings Heath can hardly be blamed for lacking the imagination to visualize the bluff ramparts of Fort William, the graceful estates of Alipur, and the bustle of Chowringhi where now there was only foetid jungle, forlorn tents, and makeshift cabins. As the flood waters of the monsoon evaporated, the steaming swamps and salt lakes behind the ridge contracted, leaving their marine harvest to fester in the sun; the overpowering smell of rotten fish pervaded all and lent credence to the idea that 'Calcutta' was really a corruption of 'Golgotha', the place of skulls, and undoubtedly 'the most unhealthful place on all the river'.

Overruled then, Charnock and his men hastily loaded their stocks, packed their bags, and again sailed off down the Hughli. At Balasore further overtures were received from the Nawab. Shaista Khan had now retired from public life to prepare for a hereafter devoid of quarrelsome Englishmen and his successor seemed genuinely desirous of an accommodation. Indeed he went so far as to propose that if the English were really bent on transferring to Chittagong, he would be greatly obliged if they would transport 3000 of his troops from there to Arakan (on the Burmese coast). In effect he was offering a military alliance against the Arakan pirates, the very people whom Charnock had identified as the Company's natural allies. Somewhat surprisingly Charnock rather favoured this new alignment and replied accordingly.

No doubt it was this enthusiasm for aiding the Nawab against the Arakan pirates which led to the later idea that he was a staunch friend of the Moghul Empire. The confusion is understandable. Even as the

Defence rode at anchor at the mouth of the Chittagong river, it was unclear to the townspeople whether the English had come to uphold the Moghul's authority or to contest it; indeed it was unclear to the English. Charnock had high hopes that, in return for being of service, the new Nawab would duly grant the directors' cherished wish for a defensible factory at Chittagong. Accordingly he insisted on writing to Dhaka and awaiting an answer. But Heath saw all this simply as a cover under which to explore the town's defences. He still pinned his hopes on an alliance with the 'Arakanners' and had already sent two agents to sound them out.

The only thing on which both men were in agreement was that it would be a big mistake to follow orders and storm the town immediately. Not that it was strongly defended. On the contrary, as far as they could establish, it seemed ill-fortified and eminently take-able. But, rather ingeniously, they represented this as being an excellent reason for leaving well alone.

> [For] it is our real opinion that 'twill be impossible to *maintain* the place . . . being the town is of little strength and the people very, very numerous on shore.

On the document that contains this suspect reasoning Job Charnock's always bold signature comes above that of William Heath with the J of the Job slashing like a dagger at the Captain's copperplate. But Heath was still in command and when the town suddenly began to fill with Moghul troops he hastily recalled his men and weighed anchor. Charnock insisted that the troops were just the 'harbinger' or escort of the Nawab's representative come with a response to his letter and to discuss their joint operations. But Heath was unconvinced. He had waited long enough. Now they would go to Arakan to make common cause with its raja and his pirates.

The date was February 1689. On the west coast of India the Sidi's sailors were just scrambling ashore to lay siege to Bombay Castle. And in a cold London office some diligent copyist was just transcribing that Company directive approving of the settlement at Calcutta and rejoicing in the continuance of peace with the Moghul.

Forgotten by his employers and cordially detested by his companions, Heath valiantly sailed into Arakan. Impressive epistles were sent to the Burmese raja, then presents. But the raja was unmoved. He could spare no men for Chittagong and he was quite capable of dealing with any

Moghul invasion on his own. For Heath it was the final straw. In the clipped phrasing of an exasperated skipper he recorded his decision to abort the whole expedition.

> So when found could not persuade those foolish people from the present ruin and destruction that is just upon them, we watered our ships and refreshed our men . . . and sailed directly for this place – Fort St George [i.e. Madras].

iii

So after forty chequered years of trade and four of intermittent war, the Company was out of Bengal on its ear with nothing to show for its labours but a boatload of disgruntled factors. In Charnock's estimation the situation was even worse, for having reneged on his alliance with the new Nawab, they had surely prejudiced any chance of future favours. It was, of course, all the fault of the feather-brained Heath whose conduct he now roundly condemned to the Court of Directors.

> Tripping from port to port without effecting anything, [he] hath not only rendered our nation ridiculous, but hath unhinged all treaties, by which means the trade of Bengal will be very difficult to be ever regained.

But as Charnock and his much travelled companions kicked their heels in Madras, events were rapidly moving towards their ignominious conclusion on the other side of India. In the autumn of 1689 Aurangzeb accepted the submission of the Bombay garrison and graciously restored the Company's trading rights throughout his dominions. It was greatly feared that his humiliating terms might include, as well as the expulsion of John Child, that of Job Charnock. But this proved not to be the case.

Indeed there was now nothing to prevent a return to Bengal. The Nawab was pressing for it; as always his imperial master had need of European silver. So was Madras's President, Elihu Yale, who had no love for the unruly factors from Bengal; 'their number are a great charge to this place, [we] not having any other employment for them than martial discipline which here are weekly practising'. And so were Charnock's men, they 'being,' according to the sarcastic Yale, 'in haste to return to their sweet plenties which sandy Madras could not please them in'.

Thus with the first shipping of 1690 'the Bengal gentlemen' again sailed for Balasore, transferred to sloops at the mouth of the Hughli, and passing Hijili and Ulubari ascended the river so rich in memories. For a third time they moored at Sutanati, looked in vain for the remnants of their previous settlement, and 'the rain falling day and night' recommenced the foundation of Calcutta. Again timbers were felled, reservoirs dug and compounds fenced. Again the Nawab's favours and the Emperor's *farman* were sought. And again the factors fell to quarrelling.

After so many shared experiences one might have expected the old comrades-in- (and out of) arms to have developed a certain loyalty. But that would be reckoning without Charnock whose cantankerousness seems only to have increased with age and become more devious with experience. Now well into his fifties and quite the grand old man in a society where longevity was unheard of, his 'strange disposition' alienated even his closest companions. 'He loved everybody should be at difference,' recalled the usually reliable Sir John Goldsborough, 'further he had another faculty of finding fault with those under him . . . [though] he would say nothing to their faces.'

> And this I believe is most true, that he never wronged Your Honours in the price of your goods, but he rejoiced to find matter to accuse others of so doing, and thought it was enough to write of it home without meddling with them here.

Goldsborough had succeeded Yale at Madras and was therefore also responsible for Bengal. But he had been told to stay well clear of Charnock. For Charnock had now been given an authority 'not formerly given to any Agent in Bengal' which empowered him to appoint and dismiss whoever he chose 'without giving any reason for doing so to any but ourselves [i.e. the directors in London]'. Over the past twenty years the Bengal factors had shown themselves 'not only grossly fraudulent but incurably inclined to faction'. Hence, argued the directors with perverse logic, the need to give Charnock absolute authority.

How he used this authority during the two and a half years which remained to him is open to question. Basing his judgement on the manuscript records, Sir William Hunter sees him as 'a block of rough-hewn British manhood', stoutly defending the undoubted merits of his new settlement against the entreaties of his comfort-loving comrades who pined for the flesh-pots of Hughli. 'Not a beautiful person', continued Hunter, 'for the founders of England's greatness in the East were not such as wear soft raiment and dwell in king's houses.' Uneducated and in old age distinctly eccentric, 'honest Job' is seen as rising above the gibes of his men and the criticisms of Madras, borne aloft on the strength of an over-powering conviction. 'A man who had a great and hard task to do and who did it – did it with small thought of self and with a courage which no danger could daunt nor any difficulties turn aside. It was his lot to found unthanked a capital.'

All of which goes to show the fundamental ambiguity of all historical source material. With access to much the same sources, another nineteenth-century historian describes Charnock's foundation of Calcutta as 'accidental' adding 'there does not seem to be anything great or even remarkable in his character. He had no large or comprehensive views; he was vacillating, timid and cruel'.

There is also some doubt about what, apart from 'continuing there beyond all reason', he actually did for Calcutta. A year after his return his men were still living 'in a wild unsettled condition' with only 'tents, hutts and boats'. Three years later there was still no factory, let alone a fort, and the settlement was still unauthorized by the Nawab. 'Everyone built stragglingly where and how they pleased', reported Goldsborough, 'even on the most properest place for a factory . . . Therefore I thought fit to order the enclosing of a piece of ground with a mud wall whereon to build a factory when we have a *parwanna* [Nawab's permit].'

Already more populous than the 'stragglingly' built settlement was the plot reserved for graves, in one of which lay the mortal remains of Job Charnock. He had died on 10 January 1693 but his very Indian-looking mausoleum, still standing in what later became St John's Churchyard, must have been erected at least a decade later. Domed, three storeys high, and closely resembling other minor tombs of the Moghul period, it must even then have been a prominent and extravagant monument for such a young township. This would seem to argue some early recognition of Charnock's fame as the founder of the future city. Yet curiously his epitaph, neatly engraved on a black slab, makes no mention either of Calcutta or of his connection with the place.

The mausoleum is believed to have been commissioned by Charles Eyre who had married one of Charnock's Anglo-Indian daughters. In 1693 Eyre was appointed Agent for Bengal by Goldsborough, a post which he would hold until 1699 and briefly regain in 1700–1. By any Indian standards, let alone those of Bengal, this constituted a long tenure of office. Charnock had chosen the site, but there is a case to be made for crediting his son-in-law with having secured Calcutta's future.

At first it must have seemed to Eyre that what Charnock had considered the advantages of the place were actually disadvantages. It was true that 'Europe' ships could, with the help of one of the pilots that the Company now maintained, ascend the Hughli river to moor in the Calcutta basin. But the shifting mud banks and the vicious tides continued to make this a dangerous option. Within months of Eyre taking office the *Royal James and Mary* entered the river homeward bound with a cargo of pepper from Sumatra plus some timber from Madras. She was half way up and almost in sight of Calcutta when she 'fell on a sand, . . . immediately over-set and broke her back'. Five men were drowned; apart from what could be salvaged in the way of guns and rigging the ship was a write-off. Thenceforth she served as a marker buoy for the sandbank in question – now 'The James and Mary Sand' – and as a salutary reminder of the river's dangers.

What if anything in the way of Bengal produce awaited the ship had she reached Calcutta the records do not reveal. But just as the new port was proving a little bit too far upriver for safe sailing, so it was proving not quite far enough upriver for expeditious trading. The saltpetre of Patna, the raw silks of Kasimbazar and the muslins of Dhaka had still to be forwarded by smaller river craft, but now, instead of being consigned from Hughli town, they had to pass on down to Calcutta. To the several points at which this river trade was liable to be interrupted by venal officials and adventurous rajas was thus added that of Hughli itself. Most of Calcutta's small complement of troops were permanently engaged escorting cargoes on the river and until Calcutta could attract a commercial infrastructure of money-lenders and commissioning agents, trade there remained something of a white elephant.

To appeal to the trading classes what Calcutta needed was that air of permanence and security which only a sturdy fort and a substantial leasehold could confer. Eyre maintained the pressure on Dhaka for both; but in the event it was thanks to circumstance rather than diplomacy that he got his way. In 1696 a local rebellion broke out in west Bengal. Normally it would have been crushed without comment. But the Nawab was proving exceptionally supine and the rebels managed to interest in their cause some Afghan mercenaries who were roaming northern India throughout the seventeenth and eighteenth centuries. Suddenly the affair assumed major proportions. Hughli fell to the rebels, then Kasimbazar, Malda and the entire west bank of the river. Naturally in this crisis the English proffered their loyal support to the Nawab. Across the river they eyeballed the rebels and using their substantial fleet of river craft they were able to prevent an advance and to relieve the Nawab's isolated garrisons on the west bank. In return it was agreed that on land they might take whatever steps they deemed necessary for their defence. Without too much hesitation Eyre began the construction of 'Fort William'.

By January 1697 four brick bastions were taking shape and cannon were requested from Madras. In May the revolt was suppressed but the building went on. Curtain walls connected the bastions; within, a new store and offices were under construction. Thanks to the disturbances, that commercial infrastructure was also materializing. A local raja had deposited his wealth in the safe keeping of Calcutta and members of the influential Armenian business class took refuge there. It was partly thanks to the representations of one of their number that in 1698 the Nawab granted to the Company the nearest thing to a land-owning grant which the Moghul empire recognized. In return for a payment of 16,000 rupees the Company was given permission to purchase the tax-gathering rights to the three villages amidst which Calcutta was taking shape. At last the Company had a legal right to a few square miles of Bengal plus a fort from which to discourage marauders and a factory within which to conduct its trade.

In the year during which Eyre was out of office that ancient dispute about customs exactions, the one which had so exercised Hedges and which had precipitated the Moghul War, was at last settled in the Company's favour. And when Eyre returned in 1700 it was as head of what was once again a separate Presidency independent of Madras. Of past grievances there remained only the vexed question of a trading *farman* from the Emperor himself. In so far as the terms granted to the English after the submission of Bombay implied a right to continue trading this was not an immediate problem. It would become so after 1707 when Aurangzeb died but then so would other circumstances which the men of Charnock's era had taken for granted. One was the Moghul Empire, now about to succumb to a spectacular slow-motion decline. Another was the Honourable Company itself, now outlawed in England, opposed by new rivals in the East, and about to undergo a very painful reincarnation.

CHAPTER NINE

Renegades and Rivals

PIRATES, INTERLOPERS AND COMPETITORS

A century later, at the impeachment of Warren Hastings, Edmund Burke would describe the rule of the East India Company as 'a government of writing and a government of record'. A standing committee of the Company's directors took charge of correspondence and to their epistolary bombardment of their employees throughout the world they expected a page for page response of frank yet respectful prose. Not for nothing was the largest class of junior factors known as 'Writers'. In this copperplate empire, paperwork was everything. Merchants and accountants by profession, the Company's men lived by the ledger and ruled with the quill.

The resultant records would be a credit to any major state archive and as the historian's source material they are unlikely ever to be exhausted. But it seems that for every researcher who with light and expectant tread enters London's India Office Library and Records, another doyen of scholarship ends his days slumped behind a lectern in mid sentence. There are enough incomplete histories of the Company to justify a health warning.

Undeterred, in 1968 Dr K. N. Chaudhuri immersed himself in a detailed study of the monumental collection of Company Accounts Books. Using a computer and deploying much flow-chart algebra, the professor stuck to his Herculean labour for nearly ten years; even then he declared himself reluctant to relinquish it. The results, published in 1978 (*The Trading World of Asia and the English East India Company*), provide the first comprehensive analysis of the Company's trading fortunes between 1660 and 1760.

To the layman their most surprising feature is the highly erratic growth pattern that emerges from the statistical tables and graphs. Leaping about as on an electro-cardiograph, the lines representing annual import and export totals plunge to the base line, zigzag to new pinnacles of activity, and then plummet once again. The impression is of convulsive fits rather than of solid progress; and of these convulsions the most dramatic is a dizzying climb which occurs between 1660 and 1683. 'Truly phenomenal', observes Chaudhuri; 'imports expanded by £25,430 per year according to the linear model and by 14.4 per cent according to the exponential. The expansion of exports was at a similar rate, though at a slightly lower level.'

Collating quotations of the Company's share values for this period, Sir William Hunter had reached much the same conclusion. £100 of stock purchased under Cromwell's new charter of 1657 had slumped to £70 by 1665 but thereafter appreciated dramatically. By 1677 it was valued at £245 and by 1683 was selling at anything between £360 and £500. Such profits had not been known since the beginning of the century; and such levels of trade would not again be approached until the 1740s.

Any explanation for this sudden growth would have to include a wide range of contributory factors – the Company's favourable treatment by the later Stuarts, the comparative stability in India during the early years of Aurangzeb's long reign, the buoyancy of European markets, the importance of Bengal as a new trading arena, the comparative safety of the sea lanes, and so on. Given the general profitability of Eastern trade, it would be essentially a list of restrictions which for once did not apply. With a free hand and a clear run, the Company could only prosper. But of far greater significance for its future was the suddenness with which this expansion had taken place. Such an impressive turn-round could not pass unnoticed. It prompted unease, envy, and hostility. Was it right, it was asked, that a single company should account for what now amounted to 'above half the trade of the nation'? And was it right that that Company should operate behind the closed doors of a monopoly which excluded even its own servants, never mind outsiders, from a share of its profits?

Profits apart, there was also the question of regulation. Was it constitutional for a consortium of London businessmen to govern overseas territories, construct forts, dispense justice, raise revenues, coin money, and wage war and yet be outside the control of Parliament and answerable only and indirectly (through the royal charter) to the Crown? The Company's cosy relationship with the later Stuarts was fine while it lasted but was bound to be challenged the moment the Company lost the confidence of the City or the Crown the confidence of Parliament. In the event both these crisis would occur almost simultaneously in the late 1680s. They were anticipated, though, both by some within the Company who had serious doubts about its monopoly and by many outside it who were already mounting a direct challenge.

During his brief but pained sojourn in Bengal, Agent William Hedges had been one of the first to recommend the seizure of a fortifiable position at the mouth of the Hughli which might become the Bengal equivalent of Madras or Bombay. A fort provided the necessary base whence to menace with impunity the Moghul's shipping and, just as important, 'it is also the only remedy to prevent the interlopers infesting us'. On 26 September 1683, as Hedges sat drafting his recommendation in the Company's Hughli factory, interlopers – or private traders – were much on his mind. On the river outside his window a certain Captain Alley was even then reclining in a stately barge. A musical quartet played for the Captain's delight and ten stalwart English seamen in a livery of 'blew capps and coats edged with red' rowed him ashore. There, above the landing steps, 'a splendid equipage' waited; it was trimmed with scarlet and lace, attended by eighty servants, and preceded by two flags. Alley was conducting himself 'like an Agent'. Hedges fumed with indignation. But he had to admit that Alley was no fool. 'A gawdy show and great noise adds much to a public person's credit in this country.'

For two decades the Company had been little troubled by interlopers. But once eastern profits had again become the talk of London town, new syndicates formed, new ships sailed, and interlopers reappeared in Indian waters. Alley was one of the first of this new breed. Well financed and protected by powerful interests, he was now on his second if not his third voyage. 'The interlopers must be suppressed in England', insisted Hedges, tis impossible to be done here.' And the Company had of course secured a royal commission for Alley's arrest. But Alley saw to it that he rarely called at any English port where it could be executed. To avoid suspicion he had originally sailed to Cadiz and it was from there and other European ports that he traded to India.

According to the Company's directors, suppressing the interlopers in England was not therefore so simple. Better by far to cut off their trade in India. To this end, valiantly did Hedges endeavour to persuade the Nawab and his governor at Hughli to have nothing to do with Alley. Interlopers, he implied, were little better than pirates, answerable to no one and quite capable of taking by force what they were denied by law. If the Moghul's representatives continued to encourage them, the Company could not be held responsible for the consequences. (Hedges was not to know that European pirates, like interlopers, were also about to reappear in Indian waters, and that equating the two would only confuse the issue.)

But while politely sympathetic to all these arguments, the Nawab did nothing. On the Coromandel Coast Alley had apparently secured some sort of trading permit. From an Indian point of view competition was good. It weakened the English Company's intractable stance over that question of customs duties and it obliged the Company to boost its Indian investment in an effort to outbid its rivals (another reason for that dramatic increase in trade). Without all the overheads of permanent establishments, the interlopers could afford to pay well and bribe handsomely. They were welcome.

In spite of vigorous statements to the contrary, it is clear that they were also welcomed by many of the Company's own factors. No words were too strong, when addressing the Court of Directors, for the 'naughty, huffing' interlopers; but it was a very different story when the same naughty gentlemen came calling round the Company's scattered trading posts with their ships riding high in expectation of cargoes that need never appear in the Company's records and with pocket books open for confidential commissions and private correspondence. Because of the Company's strict monopoly of all trade between England and India it could be extremely difficult to transfer either private funds to India or private cargoes back to England. Yet the temptations to private trade were now so great that the Company had been forced to give its grudging permission in respect of its employees engaging in 'the country trade' (port-to-port in the East). Retired or, more commonly, dismissed servants were also allowed to stay on in the Company's settlements to pursue their own commercial ventures. And as this activity grew, so did the difficulty of distinguishing between legitimate private traders and interlopers. Even some of the Company's men overstepped the mark, like the Reverend John Evans, the 'merchant-parson', who eventually absconded; others merely threatened to do so like Captain Lake who 'if he did not like the Company's employment this voyage, would turn interlopers the next'.

On his own voyage out to India in 1682 Agent Hedges had been hailed in mid Atlantic by the *Crown*, an interloper which had just evaded arrest in England. Her captain was a certain Dorrill and her supercargo (or chief factor) one Thomas Pitt. They too were heading for Bengal and the *Crown* 'sailing best, was almost out of sight next morning'. By the time Hedges reached the Hughli, Pitt and Dorrill were comfortably installed in a Balasore mansion, claiming protection from the Dutch and 'very busy in buying goods'. This was Pitt's third or fourth visit to Bengal and the Company's suspicions that he was hand in glove with their Chief Factor were soon confirmed. Indeed Hedges suspected that every one of the Company's factors had an interest in Pitt's ventures. 'He being a desperate fellow of a haughty, huffying and daring temper' the Company had instructed Hedges to 'secure his person whatever it cost [in bribes] to the government or other natives'. Accordingly Hedges applied to the Nawab during his diplomatic interlude in Dhaka and was duly assured that Pitt and Dorrill would be detained.

In the event, of course, nothing of the sort happened. In Bengal Pitt was a valued customer whose trade was almost as dependable as that of the Company and whose bribes were even more generous. He duly sailed back to England in 1683 with a fortune in the making and another career beckoning. For just as Company servants sometimes took to interloping so interlopers sometimes preferred legitimate employment. Dorrill would become second in command in Bengal under Sir John Goldsborough and Pitt would eventually resurface as the Company's long-serving and influential President at Madras. Ironically he was also the great-grandfather of the prime minister who would one day curtail for good the Company's monopoly.

Whilst lording it in Balasore, Pitt had made a point of 'bespattering' his rivals by putting it about that the East India Company was on its last legs and about to be replaced by a 'new English East India Company' for which he himself was Agent in Bengal. This may have been a ploy to impress the Nawab; but it was also an amazingly faithful, if premature, representation of events. Already the interloping interests in London had found sympathetic allies within the Company who resented the large holdings and the consequent influence accumulated by a group of the directors. Cromwell's charter had ended the monopoly of office; but the creation of a permanent stock and the substantial dividends which it paid had enabled existing investors to keep out new blood and to buy up any stock that came on the market. Very substantial accumulations resulted, a process that was assisted by the Company's growing practice of borrowing at comparatively low rates of interest rather than float new stock.

Thus, though the offices of governor (or chairman) and deputy continued to rotate, they did so amongst an ever dwindling circle of immensely wealthy stock holders.

Perceiving this development as being neither in the nation's nor the Company's interest, Sir Thomas Papillon, MP for Dover and himself a director of the Company since 1663, championed the idea of opening the trade to a wider public. He was opposed by the redoubtable Sir Josiah Child. Child had made his first fortune as victualler to the fleet at Portsmouth. In the 1680s the diarist John Evelyn estimated his wealth at £200,000. Also an MP and director of the Company since 1677, he had once been Papillon's protégé. But while the latter's Parliamentary sympathies disposed him towards a freer system of trade, Child's influence at Court (he had been made a baronet in 1678) and his Tory ideals made him a staunch upholder both of the Company's monopoly of eastern trade and of his own growing monopoly of the Company.

Papillon's first challenge was mounted within the Company when in 1681 he proposed that the joint stock launched under Cromwell's charter of 1657 be wound up and replaced with a new stock to which any might subscribe. Thus the Company's monopoly would be retained by in effect offering to accommodate those who were challenging it. But this move was defeated. An appeal was then made to the Crown in the form of an application by the old Levant Company that the ships of its adventurers might use the sea route by the Cape of Good Hope to reach those parts of the Ottoman Empire (its exclusive trading zone) which bordered on the Red and Arabian Seas. This too was rejected and at about the same time Papillon was removed from the Company's Court of Directors. (It was doubtless in anticipation of one of these challenges succeeding that Pitt confidently announced the foundation of a rival East India Company.)

Having failed in the boardroom and at Court, the opponents of the existing monopoly now turned to the law courts. In 1683 Child, acting on new powers conferred by the King, had seized the ship and cargo of an interloper named Sandys. Some twenty-four other interloping vessels were also seized but it was Sandys's plight which provided the test case. With encouragement from Papillon's lobby, an appeal was made to the King's Bench as the supreme court of common law and a ruling was obtained which obliged Child and the Company to substantiate their action by proving damages against Sandys. Each side engaged the ablest counsel of the day and thus began 'The Great Case of Monopolies between the East India Company, plaintiffs, and Thomas Sandys, defendant'.

Although it was a year before judgement was given, there seems to have been little doubt about whom it would favour. As Lord Chief Justice, the sanguinary Judge Jeffreys could be expected to find for the Crown and the Company; Child was crowing with victory after the first few hearings. But at least the case brought the issues into the public domain. On the one hand there was the sovereign's prerogative to regulate all trade with infidels, a right based on the assumption that an unbeliever was automatically an enemy of the realm. On the other hand there was the merchant's established right to the freedom of the seas plus the nation's legitimate concern for access to a trade now 'the greatest that England ever knew'. Significantly, there also surfaced the interesting question of whether this was not a matter which should really be decided by Parliament. Jeffreys exploded with indignation at this last suggestion and in an extraordinarily partisan judgement compared the interlopers to regicides. He also denounced the very idea of anyone presuming to question a royal prerogative thus inadvertently issuing a challenge to Parliament which, come more propitious times, would be remembered.

Outvoted in the Company and outbribed at Court, Papillon was himself dragged through the courts and obliged to flee to Holland. Sandys was duly fined, and in 1684 some forty-eight interlopers were restrained, amongst them the returning Thomas Pitt. After further litigation Pitt was eventually fined £1000 and retired to Wiltshire. There he bought the rotten borough of Old Sarum and in 1687 sat as a Member of Parliament. So effectually had Child stifled the interlopers that those who failed to restrict their activities to the East now had only two possibilities – to turn Parliamentarian or to turn pirate. Pitt chose the former, John Hand of the *Bristol* chose the latter.

In 1683 Hand sailed from England supposedly for Brazil. Some months later he turned up at Surat, then the Maldive Islands where he fired on the principal town, then Sumatra where he attacked a Dutch vessel. 'Captain, you must consider what you do', cautioned his mate as they boarded yet another disabled ship. But the Captain, 'being a mighty passionate man' devoid of scruple and no lover of small talk, 'kicked him off the quarter deck and several others for the same reason'. It was only poetic justice that, soon after, he accidentally shot himself in the leg and died of the wound. Next year, 1685, his ship was surprised in the Comoro islands off the coast of East Africa by HMS *Phoenix*.

The *Phoenix* had been sent out to carry Sir Josiah Child's crusade against the interlopers to all the havens and high seas east of the Cape. On the face of it, this was a sensible move; for in 1686 more pirates, supposedly belonging to Denmark's new East India company but widely tipped as English interlopers, seized a vessel belonging to Abdul Ghafar, a wealthy Surat merchant. By the Moghul authorities the English Company was held responsible and its trade at Surat stopped. Clearly some policing of the sea lanes was necessary and indeed the *Phoenix* duly caught up with the culprits, ascertained that they were in fact Danes, and so to some extent cleared the air.

But in wilfully confusing interlopers and pirates, and in claiming the right to waylay either wherever they threatened legitimate trade, the Company was setting a dangerous double precedent. Its actions, however legitimate, would come to look just as piratical as those they were supposed to be preventing. Thus in 1687 the captain of an interloping vessel taken in the Red Sea was killed in his cabin 'because he would not surrender up his ship voluntarily'; such strong-arm tactics positively invited retaliation in kind. More ominously, by exercising its right to defend its monopoly, the Company appeared to be accepting some responsibility for suppressing the outrages committed by the likes of John Hand. That, at any rate, was how the Moghul governor of Surat saw the matter. What the Company regarded as its right he soon construed as its obligation and one which he could always enforce by once again holding the Surat factors to ransom. Unwittingly the Company had assumed the responsibility of protecting the Moghul's shipping as well as its own just as the great age of Eastern piracy dawned.

In the short term, protecting the Moghul's merchantmen was scarcely a priority. At Surat and Hughli the first muddled moves in Child's undeclared war against the Moghul empire were just unfolding; it was the Company, not the pirates, who posed the most immediate threat to Indian shipping. In 1688 Alexander Hamilton counted fourteen Surat vessels corralled into Bombay harbour as prizes. In the following year their numbers were swollen by the fleet of provisioning vessels taken by Sir John Child as he fled from Surat. And more prizes were taken, some by Hamilton himself, during the course of the Bombay siege. They scarcely affected the course of the war, let alone beggared the Moghul as Child had predicted. But news of such juicy prize-taking spread far and fast. Arguably it was the ease with which the Company's vessels in the Arabian Sea so quickly overwhelmed the Moghul marine which, more than anything else, alerted the buccaneering fraternities of North America and the West Indies to the possibilities of the India trade.

ii

Dr Chaudhuri's invaluable statistics reveal that the value of the Company's total annual imports, after their dizzy climb to £800,000 in 1684, plummeted to just £80,000 in 1691. Such was the price exacted first by the rivalry of the interlopers and then by the near cessation of trade at Surat and Bengal during the Moghul War (1686–9); Sir Josiah Child had much to answer for. But thereafter the trickle of trade, instead of assuming its earlier volume, languished, falling to a mere dribble of under £30,000 in both 1692 and 1695. The Company's troubles were far from over.

At the time, though, Child and his fellow monopolists could not have been in more buoyant mood. In 1686 James II had issued the Company with a new charter which seemingly inured it to any further challenge from within and empowered it to meet any assault from without. For the charter confirmed all the powers and privileges granted by Charles II, including those of arresting and trying interlopers and of using troops and ships against native princes. It was only seven years since the directors had insisted that they were 'averse to all kinds of war in India'.

> It would [they had explained] be a very great imprudence for us at this distance, (being merchants and engaged in commerce) to contend with those great and mighty princes which might seem to obstruct our trade and ruin us.

Child, already a director, had been a signatory to this caution. Yet five years later, emboldened by the Company's commercial success and impatient alike of the Moghul's exactions and the interlopers' challenge, he had begun to sound like a bullish imperialist.

> If any natives fall upon you [he told the Surat factors], we would have you take the first and best opportunity you can to right us and yourselves without expecting further orders from England, for we are now in such a posture in India that we need not sneak or put up [with] palpable injuries from any nation whatsoever . . .

And now, in 1686, thanks to the new charter, he chose to construe the Company's position as that 'of a sovereign state in India.' Exactly what this meant Child spelled out in uncompromising terms to the new President in Madras.

> That which we promise ourselves in a most espetial manner from our new President and Council is that they will establish such a politie of civil and military power, and create and secure such a large revenue to maintain both at that place [Madras], as may be the foundation of a large, well grounded, sure English dominion in India for all time to come.

Naturally these prophetic words receive a good deal of attention in British imperial histories wherein Child is revealed as an empire-builder with rugged qualities to match his visionary ideals. Perhaps, though, they are also noteworthy as examples of Child's dismal judgement or of his incorrigible bravado. For, within eighteen months of this letter being written, Charnock and Heath had abandoned Bengal, Bombay was under siege as was the Surat factory, and worst of all James II, the Company's champion and benefactor, was a powerless exile in France. The English factors in Bombay, as they pledged their loyalty to William of Orange on the very day that the Moghul siege of the settlement was lifted, must have marvelled how no sooner was one crisis averted than another loomed. Their Dutch rivals were already advising the Moghul authorities that England had succumbed to an invasion from Holland. And in London the Convention Parliament was about to take a long hard look at the whole question of the Company's charter.

Since the failure of Papillon's attempts at reform, criticism of the Company had found expression mainly in anonymous pamphlets. Some of these condemned the India trade as a whole for flooding the home market with imported textiles; others condemned the Company for monopolizing this trade and a clique of its directors for monopolizing the Company. It was said that fourteen shareholders had acquired a third of the entire stock and that one in particular held a seventh of the total. Bestriding the Company's finances as he did its direction, this man was Sir Josiah Child.

Allegations that Child had bought and bribed his way into both the Company's direction and the royal favour are hard to substantiate; but for later critics of the Company, like Lord Macaulay, lack of evidence was no obstacle. 'All who could help or hurt at Court, ministers, mistresses, priests, were kept in good humour by presents of shawls, silks, birds' nest and attar of roses, bulses of diamonds, and bags of guineas.' The Macaulay embroidery may be fanciful but the coat fits. Child's relationships with John Child at Surat and Job Charnock in Bengal invite suspicion while his manipulation of the Company's share values won him recognition as 'the original of stock-jobbing'. In dealings which would have merited prosecution in a later age he floated rumours of shipping losses in order to depress stocks, then bought heavily at the discounted price and sold out when the price had recovered. Domineering, unscrupulous and arrogant, he is sometimes seen as possessing the energy and influence which alone preserved the Company during its years of crisis. Alternatively these same traits may be regarded – as they were by the pamphleteers – as an unbearable provocation and as the root cause of the Company's misfortunes.

The new Parliament was of the latter opinion. And with its Whig sympathies and its distaste for all those on whom the Catholic James had showered his favours, it soon found an unlikely but emotive issue with which to discredit Child and the Company. Compared with the excitements at Bombay and Calcutta, news from the Company's first and half-forgotten settlement at St Helena had rarely troubled the directors' slumbers. So long as the Dutch were kept at bay (preferably the Cape's Table Bay) and so long as St Helena always had enough green vegetables and fresh fruit for scorbutic English crews, the Company had been content to ignore it. Yet for its first inhabitants, originally destined for the Banda island of Run, and for their successors – both Madagascan slaves and English paupers – life in the South Atlantic had been far from congenial.

Originally they had worked their smallholdings for an annual quit rent consisting of a bunch of bananas, a pint of peas, a pound of potatoes and a pound of 'cassava bread'. But in the changed climate of the 1670s the Company had decided against this Cromwellian commonwealth of market gardeners and in favour of a plantation economy in which the erstwhile smallholders became feudal serfs obliged to work the land and supply recruits for the garrison. The change prompted a series of rebellions and a series of ferocious reprisals. In 1683 two apprentices had the tips of their right ears clipped, pot-hooks riveted round their necks, the letter R branded on their foreheads (R for Rogue, P was for Pirate; piratical rogues could end up with both) and were then handed over for a week-long programme of floggings, 'viz. 21 lashes on Friday, 21 on Monday, and on Thursday 6 in town, 6 on top of the hill, 6 at half-way tree, and 6 more on arriving at home'. To merit this calvary the crime had been merely that of breaking and entering.

For the discourtesy of rebellion the punishments were more summary.

In 1684 the Governor turned his guns on a crowd who presumed to ask for the release of one unjustly imprisoned; seventeen protesters were either killed outright or wounded; the rest were rounded up and nineteen condemned to death. When the widow of one was impertinent enough to suggest that her man had been murdered she was given twenty-one lashes, ducked three times at the yard-arm and thrown into prison.

It was a petition from four of this woman's bereaved companions, 'the mournful daughters of St Helena' as they were called, which in 1689 eventually found its way to Westminster and the sympathetic ear of the Convention Parliament. There, without overlong debate, the House of Commons condemned the proceedings, ordered the punishment of the St Helena 'butchers', and – scarcely pausing for breath – set up a committee to enquire into the whole question of the East India trade. Fulfilling Thomas Pitt's expectations of eight years ago, the committee recommended a new Company which was to be established by Parliament rather than by the Crown. The interlopers scented victory at last; a group of them promptly subscribed £180,000. But the House was then dissolved with the matter still unsettled.

Before renewing their challenge the interlopers thus had ample time to summon old friends, like Papillon, and organize themselves afresh. Meeting regularly in the rebuilt hall of the Skinners' Company in Dowgate, the embryonic 'New Company', sometimes called the 'Dowgate Adventurers', was ready for the fray when in 1691 Child, from the 'Old Company's' headquarters in Leadenhall Street (a brickbat's throw from Dowgate), proclaimed victory in his war against the Moghul.

Even by Sir Josiah's own bragging standards, this talk of triumph in India was the grossest of misrepresentations; and it was duly exposed as such when the humiliating terms of Aurangzeb's new *farman* became known. With some reason the Company was now seen as having brought dishonour on the nation; Dowgate rejoiced, Leadenhall Street squirmed, and Parliament was again called on to intervene. Child was unrepentant; for the new House, unlike its predecessor, was more Tory than Whig and so likely to be more amenable. It quickly accepted the idea of a joint stock company under royal charter and resolved that the charter should stay with the Old Company. But there were to be two provisos. The stock was to be considerably increased so that the Dowgate Adventurers could buy into the Company; and no individual holdings were to exceed

£5000, thereby preventing the likes of Child from simply buying up the new stock.

To this not unreasonable compromise Child and his colleagues objected. There could be no question of admitting the Dowgate men, even by the back door; it was to be all or nothing. Nothing, retorted the House, as the bill was dropped and a petition was sent to King William recommending the dissolution of the old Company and the creation of a new one.

Once again Child's incorrigible optimism was undented. 'For the venue', in Sir William Hunter's neat phrasing, 'was now transferred from Parliament, in whose management he was a novice, to the Court, in whose corruption he was a practiced hand.' The King came up with a compromise solution very similar to that already proposed by Parliament. Once again Child rejected it. Then, in March 1693, with the King about to depart for the war in France, Child seized his moment. Bribes totalling £80,000, twenty times the normal level, passed quickly through the Company's books and into ministerial pockets; wilfully, according to Hunter, Child forfeited the existing charter on a technicality, applied for a new one, and before Parliament could reassemble was duly gratified by the well-primed gentlemen of the Privy Council.

In his *History of British India* Hunter illumines the cut and thrust, or more often the feint and posture, of these highly intricate manoeuvres with a masterly commentary. Sadly it was the last chapter he ever wrote. The task of making sense of Child's antics may have over-taxed him. Indeed he was unable to revise this section of what, had it been completed, would surely have been the most authoritative work on the 300 years of British involvement in India. As a result we have no ready-made explanation of why Child should have bullied and bribed to such an extent all for a new charter which was little different from those earlier proposed by the Commons and by King William. Perhaps it was sufficient that he had outsmarted Parliament and that under the new charter he and his cronies retained control.

But not for the first time Child had also overreached himself. Despairing of redress, interlopers were again putting to sea with Thomas Pitt, MP, well to the fore; in 1693 he returned to Bengal and another welcome from the Nawab. Goldsborough, the Company agent at Calcutta, threatened a second Moghul War; the Nawab paid no heed. Meanwhile Child in London vowed to hound the interlopers through the courts. But, when a second Sandys was arraigned, the House of Commons intervened and, with Papillon as chairman, a committee of the whole House declared that the India trade was open to all. Suddenly interlopers like Pitt in Bengal found that they were bona fide traders. The Dowgate Adventurers took new heart.

In 1695 the Commons began an investigation of Child's bribery; in the same year the Scottish Parliament authorized a rival East India company; and in 1697, such was the popular feeling against Child and the monopolists of Leadenhall Street that a mob stormed their premises and had to be dispersed by the militia. All these events were symptomatic of the uncertainty that must arise when a trade opened to all by Parliament was reserved to a single company by the Crown. To resolve this absurdity the Old Company offered a loan to the state of £700,000 in return for Parliamentary confirmation of its exclusive charter. This bid was promptly topped by the Dowgate men with an offer of £2 million. If nothing else, events had established that the licence to trade with the East was a marketable commodity, and that if this licence lay in the gift of Parliament, the state, instead of the King and Court, should benefit. In the wake of an expensive European war, it also followed that the best offer should be accepted. Accordingly, in June 1698, the Commons at last passed a bill for the formation of a new General Society to trade to the East. Such were the expectations of this trade that the £2 million was subscribed within forty-eight hours. Amongst the subscribers the Dowgate men were prominent; so were the King and the Treasury Lords; but far and away the largest subscription was the £315,000 pledged by, of all people, the Old Company.

Child, of course, was hedging his bets. In addition to the substantial leverage thus gained within the General Society (most of whose subscribers formed themselves into a joint stock known as the 'New' or 'English' East India Company), he also secured a three-year stay of execution for the Old Company (now sometimes called the 'London' East India Company as in the days of Elizabeth). Ostensibly this was to allow the Old Company time to wind up its affairs overseas. In reality it gave it a fighting chance to discredit the New Company throughout the East and to prove that without the experience, without the establishments, and without the trading rights won during a century of endeavour, the East India trade would collapse. The scene was set for a final trial of strength to be waged not in London but in the bazaars of Surat, round the ramparts of Madras, up the tidal creeks of the Hughli and in a host of other still further flung outposts.

Although the New Company had secured the all-important charter, like Courteen's Association it entered the Eastern trading world at a great disadvantage. Privileges could be bought, experience could be recruited; nearly all its rapidly appointed agents were drawn from the vast pool of footloose factors who had at one time or another been dismissed by the Old Company. But it lacked factories, let alone forts; it lacked that native network of suppliers, agents and financiers through which all trade in India was conducted; and it lacked trading capital, the original subscription having passed to the Exchequer as the £2 million loan which secured the charter.

By way of offsetting these commercial handicaps, the New Company betook itself to the high ground of diplomatic respectability. Instead of being mere merchants, its agents enjoyed consular status which they employed to advantage in dealing with Moghul governors and which they interpreted as giving them authority over all their fellow subjects, including representatives of the Old Company. Additionally a fully fledged ambassador, the first since Sir Thomas Roe, was dispatched to negotiate with Aurangzeb himself on the New Company's behalf – and at the New Company's expense. Sir William Norris, MP for Liverpool, was the man chosen, and great were the expectations of his embassy. A contemporary rhymester caught the mood of optimism.

> Indians and English both alike shall share
> The Monarch's favour and enjoy his care,
> And Britain's wise ambassador obtain
> Not only leave to trade but also reign.
> Commerce shall spread itself along the coast
> And Norris shall regain what Child has lost.

At Surat and Bombay the New Company's affairs were entrusted to Sir Nicholas Waite, who arrived off Bombay in late 1699. Styling himself 'Consul General and Public Minister' for the whole west coast, he called on the Old Company's President, Sir John Gayer, and peremptorily ordered him to acknowledge his authority and start winding up the affairs of his Company. Gayer was unmoved. He had received no official notification from his own masters and in this, the centennial year of his Company, he was not about to make over its most important possession to a rival outfit headed by a man who was once dismissed from its service (Waite had served as Agent in Bantam). Gayer had been in Bombay six years and had been on the point of retirement. Now he changed his mind. For the next ten years he would remain in India as Waite's implacable rival.

Rebuffed in Bombay, Waite's flotilla sailed on to Surat, which city was to be his headquarters. At Swalley his eye lit upon the Old Company's flag, a St George's cross, fluttering atop their warehouse; before he would even land he demanded it be lowered. He himself flew the flag of King William and it was important, if his authority was to be recognized, that all English establishments should defer to the royal ensign. But the factors of the old Company refused point blank. Like Gayer, they would take orders only from their own Court of Directors. Waite, a peppery character at the best of times, flew into a rage and sent troops ashore to haul it down. Next day it was back, this time on the orders of the Moghul governor.

As Waite soon discovered, the attitude of the Moghul authorities was to prove crucial in the squabble between the two Companies. For suitable payments Waite would quickly obtain trading rights, a factory of his own from which to fly the King's flag, and the grandest reception ever accorded to an Englishman in Surat. But these things did not denote any partiality as between the rival factors. The Moghul officials showed a decided lack of interest in the constitutional rights and wrongs of the situation. They saw it simply as a heaven-sent opportunity to garner double the customary *douceurs* and to settle a grievance which had become as dear to the emperor's heart as it had to the city's traders – namely the upsurge in piracy. Waite's success would depend entirely on the depth of his pocket and the plausibility of his measures to suppress pirates and compensate their victims.

iii

Although a few interlopers had taken up piracy in the days before Child's Moghul War, annual raids on the Indian shipping between Gujarat and the Red Sea began in earnest only after John Child had set the example. The first report of trouble had come in 1689 when the Reverend Ovington heard of three vessels, two English and one Dutch, sheltering in St Augustine's Bay in Madagascar. All were much battered but 'richly laden with store of silks which they had taken in the Red Sea from Asian merchants that traded from Mocha to Surat'. Indeed they were so richly laden that their sails, for want of canvas, had been replaced with silk; in exchange for a few bottles of brandy their crews were prepared to give as much silk as was demanded 'guzzling down the noble wine as if they were both wearied with the possession of the rapine' and anxious only to drown 'all melancholy reflections concerning it'.

Ovington had this news from a ship at St Helena which was transporting slaves from Madagascar to New York. This was undoubtedly the trade route by which word of the rich pickings to be had in the Arabian Sea reached the North American freebooters. By 1690 there were two pirate-cum-slaving bases in Madagascar, one at St Augustine's Bay in the south-west and the other on St Mary's Island off the east coast. From the latter the *Bachelor's Delight* raided Indian shipping in the Red Sea in 1691, each of the crew receiving prize money of £1100 when the vessel returned to Carolina. It may have been this raid which accounted for the plunder of another ship belonging to Abdul Ghafar, the Surat merchant who had lost a cargo to the Danes in 1685. Again the Company's factors in Surat came under suspicion and were confined to their factory pending evidence that the miscreants were not Company employees.

Next year there was a repeat performance and again in 1694. In each case the luckess victim was the same Abdul Ghafar (which was not surprising considering that he was Surat's greatest shipping magnate with a fleet that reportedly exceeded that of the Company); and in each case the English factors came under increasing suspicion. The crunch came in 1695 when the infamous Captain John Avery (alias Henry Every, John Bridgeman, etc.) formed a pirate confederation. As 'The Arch-pirate', 'The King of the Pirates', Avery would be so glamorized by the likes of Daniel Defoe that his origins cannot be clearly discerned. Certain it is, though, that he was an outstanding commander 'daring and good-humoured but insolent, uneasy, and unforgiving to the last degree if at any time imposed upon'. This mixture of *bonhomie* and menace found full expression in a letter, still extant, which he left at the Comoro Islands for any English shipping that called there.

> . . . I have never as yet wronged any English or Dutch, or ever intend whilst I am commander. Wherefore ... make your ancient [flag] up in a ball or bundle and hoist him at the mizzen peak, the mizzen being furled. I shall answer with the same, and never molest you, for my men are hungry, stout and resolute, and should they exceed my desire I cannot help myself. As yet an Englishman's friend,
> Henry Avery.
> At Johanna, 28 February, 1695.

With two American ships, Avery in the *Fancy* sailed north from the Comoro Islands rendezvousing with the Madagascar men as he went. At first the annual Surat-Mocha shipping eluded them; but in September they fell in with the *Fateh Mohammed* carrying treasure valued at £30–40,000. Inevitably she belonged to Abdul Ghafar. Then, off the west coast of India, they finally overhauled the *Gang-i-Sawai*, the pride of the Indian fleet, a gigantic vessel which belonged to the Emperor himself and carried both returning pilgrims and treasure estimated at over 5 million rupees. It was said that the Indian ship made a poor defence, its Captain dressing up some Turki slave girls as soldiers and hiding himself in the hold. Avery's men made no allowances for this considerate behaviour and proceeded to ransack the ship and 'lie with the womenfolk'. Presumably the slave girls were fair game, but to discover the whereabouts of the treasure the pirates soon resorted to torturing the henna-ed pilgrims and 'dishonouring' their veiled companions. Many of the women killed themselves or jumped overboard rather than undergo instant 'marriage'.

For himself Avery is supposed to have secured a Moghul princess. There were certainly high-bred ladies aboard but the only one mentioned in the records as being related to the Emperor was an elderly matron. It seems more probable, then, that 'Mulatto Tom', Avery's son who later carved out a kingdom for himself in Madagascar, was not her offspring but that of one of her attendants. 'All this will raise a black cloud at court', reported the Bombay factors when news of the outrage reached them. They hoped, but can scarcely have believed, that the cloud would 'not produce a severe storm'.

In the event the storm broke first, not at court, but at Surat. On previous occasions the Moghul governor had simply thrown a cordon of troops round the English factory. This served the dual purpose of punishing the factors if guilty and protecting them from their accusers if not. But this time more positive action was called for. Robbery on the high seas was one thing; violating the sanctity of the *haj* another. It was not just a crime but a sacrilege as appalling to the pious old Emperor as to the Muslim mob which now stormed through the city baying for the blood of the English.

Samuel Annesley, the Chief Factor, argued vigorously that a Company dependent on the Moghul's goodwill and his merchants' credit would hardly choose to alienate both by such gratuitous provocation – an argument which would have carried more weight had it not been flatly contradicted by Child's actions in the previous decade. Annesley also offered double compensation to any who could prove that the Company's ships were involved. But this did not mollify the incensed mob. It was known that the pirates were English; they flew the cross of St George and some, evidently ex-employees of the Company, had spoken openly of avenging the siege of Bombay. As the mob paraded a sorry file of dishonoured matrons, maimed patriarchs and wailing relatives past the Governor's house, every Englishman in Surat, Company employee or not, was rounded up and clapped in irons. Three hundred troops took over the English factory and stood guard over the prisoners. 'It is needless to write', Annesley needlessly wrote, 'of the indignities, slavish usages and tyrannical insultings wee hourly bear day and night; and to expatiate on so hateful a subject woud no wayes redress or alleviate our sufferings.'

Their fate now rested with the Emperor whose fury, on hearing of the *Gang-i-Sawai*'s sacking, was wholly predictable. Piracy, sacrilege and *lèse-majesté* had all been compounded in the one action; no punishment was too severe for such treacherous infidels; Bombay and Madras must be attacked immediately, and the English banished for ever. But saner counsels and hefty bribes soon prevailed. Aurangzeb came to appreciate that the English Company might not be wholly to blame; and this being the case, he eventually preferred a scheme whereby they, along with the Dutch and French companies, should henceforth assume the duty of providing an armed escort for the Mocha fleet. This was agreed to by Annesley and his colleagues, although its corollary – that they would accept responsibility for suppressing piracy and for compensating any who suffered by it – was left to further negotiation. After nine months of imprisonment the Surat factors were released and trade resumed.

By then Avery, having divided his spoils at the French island of Bourbon and left some of his men at Madagascar, was living it up in the Bahamas. Other desperadoes had taken over where he left off and, soon after Annesley's release, another of Abdul Ghafar's ships was relieved of its treasure. 'If there be not care taken to suppress the pyrats', wrote Gayer to the directors, the English could expect to have their throats cut and 'your Honours' trade in India will be wholly lost'. Goaded into action by the gravity of this last prediction, the Company in London secured a royal proclamation against piracy and against Avery in particular. Curiously, though, this proclamation was never published in Surat. It seems that the Company's factors baulked at its phrasing, which was tantamount to an admission that the pirates were English, and at its costing of Avery's ill-gotten gains. It was not that they disputed the figure of £130,000, just that any mention of it would be bound to encourage those who were demanding damages.

There was also talk of sending a naval squadron to deal with the pirates. The Government declined on the grounds of expense but then, as it were, put the job out to tender. A syndicate headed by the newly appointed Governor of New York won the contract and duly hired a ship of formidable firepower plus a commander of great experience and unimpeachable character. The former was the well-named *Adventure*; the latter, equally well-named, was Captain Kidd.

Whether William Kidd was really the archetypal cut-throat or just a misunderstood mariner at the mercy of circumstance is not relevant here. Suffice it to note that far from suppressing piracy he was soon engaged in it, most notably in 1697 when he raided several small vessels in the Arabian Sea, and in early 1698 when he took the *Quedah Merchant* with a cargo valued at £30,000. Once again trade at Surat was suspended, the factors placed under house arrest, and heavy compensation demanded. Late in the same year their situation worsened still further with the news that another pilgrim ship as big and nobly patronized as the *Gang-i-Sawai* had been taken, amidst all the usual atrocities, by two of the most notorious Madagascar men.

Of these latter gentlemen one, Captain 'Cutlass' Culliford, was English and the other, Captain Dirk (a proper name in this case) Shivers, Dutch; and it so happened that it was the French who were escorting the convoy which they had attacked. Clearly the scheme for international protection of the Mocha fleet was not working. Aurangzeb, through Surat's Governor, therefore demanded both compensation and a written agreement making the Europeans in future responsible for all acts of piracy. To secure this agreement the English factors were threatened with either expulsion or execution; their native bankers were publicly whipped; trade was at a standstill and the factory again besieged. In vain did Annesley appeal for time and a chance to refer the matter home. He was forced to capitulate and immediately afterwards was dismissed from the Company's service.

iv

Such was the situation when Sir Nicholas Waite arrived off Swalley flying his new flag and proclaiming the New Company. For the factors of the Old Company, the cup of tribulation was running over. Choking on the bitter draught of their new financial and military commitments to the Moghul, they were now confronted with one of the most unprincipled and vindictive mandarins ever to strut upon the Anglo-Indian scene. Waite, with little in the way of commerce to conduct or protect, was a free agent; he was at liberty to make extravagant promises, like undertaking the Moghul's cherished crusade against piracy; and he was at liberty to apply himself to that which he did best of all – discrediting his insolent rivals. The factors of the Old Company were, he told the Moghul authorities, no better than 'theeves and confederates of pyrates'; they must, he told the likes of Abdul Ghafar, be made to pay generous compensation; they might, he hinted to the Moghul governor, decamp to Bombay if not closely guarded. Cash inducements lent weight to his words but still the factors defied his consular authority and responded with lively disparagement of his pretensions.

Throughout 1700 charge and counter-charge whistled back and forth over the rooftops of Surat. Then in November of that year both of the rival factions received an unexpected boost in their firepower when there arrived at the mouth of the Tapti Sir John Gayer, the Old Company's President from Bombay, closely followed by Sir William Norris, the New Company's ambassador to the Moghul.

Norris was not a vindictive man, just an increasingly impatient one. In spite of those brave lines about regaining what Child had lost, he had now been in India more than a year and had yet to secure leave to treat with the Moghul. In part this had been due to an unfortunate decision to launch the embassy from Masulipatnam, the main port of Golconda (Hyderabad) and coincidentally the place where Peter Floris had first raised the Old Company's standard in the Bay of Bengal. Since then Golconda had been brought within the Moghul's domain, while the Old Company had of course downgraded its Masulipatnam operation in favour of Madras. With the latter now under the vigorous rule of the ex-interloper Thomas Pitt and wholly committed to the Old Company, there was a certain logic in the New Company's choosing the former as its Coromandel headquarters.

But it was not a good place whence to track down the Emperor, especially for an ambassador encumbered with a retinue of several hundred servants plus gifts that included twelve brass cannon. There had been a rumour that Aurangzeb was somewhere in the vicinity of Bijapur; but by the time the lengthy formalities of an ambassadorial landing had been completed, the old Emperor's restless campaigning had taken him hundreds of miles to the north and west, much nearer in fact to Surat. Moreover the intervening wastes of the Deccan were still disturbed and practically unknown to Europeans. After nine months of prevarication and expense, Norris had despaired of ever receiving the necessary safe conduct and escort from Masulipatnam, and had taken ship for Surat.

Like Waite, Norris was pointedly shunned by Surat's beleaguered complement of Old Company factors; he took it as a snub to his ambassadorial dignity and so to his royal master. Gayer protested. Word had just reached Surat that in London his Company's fortunes had revived. Under the terms of the bill which set up the General Society, the Old Company was supposed to cease trading within three years, that is by 1701. Now with Sir Josiah Child dead and the directors more conciliatory to Parliament, a stay of execution had been secured. By virtue of its holding in the General Society the Old Company might continue to trade until that £2 million loan was repaid by the Treasury; this meant almost indefinitely. 'Now we are established by Act of Parliament', announced the directors, 'it secures our foundation . . . We can now call our estate our own.' Suddenly matters at Surat took on a very different complexion. The same act also exonerated the Old Company from contributing towards the expenses of the Norris mission, an exemption which seemed to confirm Gayer's contention that he and his men could ignore the ambassador.

Sensing that the tide was about to turn against him, Waite decided to wait no longer. Charging some of the Old Company's factors with calling King William 'a madman and a fool', he demanded that Surat's Governor arrest them for treason. Gayer, as usual, sent a note of protest. But this time the men who delivered it to the New Company's premises were arrested, trussed up with ropes, and charged with forcible entry. Rather incongruously they were also entertained with 'rosted fowles and a piece of beef, boiled, and carrots' plus 'claret, punch, pipes and tobacco'. Next day they were retrussed and dragged through the bazaars to the governor's house, there to be formally charged.

Norris seems to have approved of this action. He was less happy about its sequel but by then he was at last on the road in search of the elusive Emperor. He left Surat at the end of January 1701. A week later Gayer, Lady Gayer, and their companions were all arrested by the Governor at Waite's instigation and confined 'in a little nasty hole where we all lay on the ground'. Later they were given the freedom of the Surat factory but still held as hostages; and so they would remain, thanks to the repeated machinations of the dreadful Waite, for the next nine years.

Sir Nicholas Waite was already assured of a certain notoriety if only because of his recent marriage to his teen-age niece, a union deemed both incestuous and bigamous (there was another Lady Waite in England). But it was his vendetta against the Old Company which most antagonized contemporaries and scandalized posterity. Conveying news of the first arrests to Calcutta, Thomas Pitt hoped that 'our Masters will revenge [them] to the last degree in England and . . . will write it in red letters upon his [Waite's] person'. As for the arrest of Sir John and Lady Gayer 'the like I have not known, heard, nor read of'. For later generations the spectacle of Englishmen, nay baronets, dragging one another through the bazaars and denouncing one another to the natives was just too painful to contemplate. 'In the history of the English in India there is no more shameful episode', writes Annesley's biographer, 'it was race treachery of the worst kind, and its evil fruits remained to be gathered for many dreary years in the tears and maledictions of his [Waite's] countrymen.'

Seen from a Raj perspective it was only right that the Norris embassy, dispatched in the midst of such flagrant betrayals of racial solidarity, should come unstuck. Waite had badly prejudiced its negotiating position by his unauthorized offer to police the seas against pirates, an undertaking which the New Company could not begin to perform and which Norris therefore had to repudiate. But Gayer and his colleagues also did their utmost to frustrate the embassy and even Pitt in Madras seems to have used his influence at Court to assure Norris of a rough ride.

Three months after leaving Surat, Norris was at last ushered into the imperial presence. Preceded by his gifts of cannon, horses, cartloads of cloth and assorted glassware, then by drums, trumpets, bagpipes and flags, the ambassador made the most of his moment of glory. Thereafter there would be little to celebrate. During six months of wearisome and expensive negotiation, the Emperor refused to budge on the piracy issue; unless the New Comnpany would assume responsibility for the suppression of the pirates it could forget about any imperial *farman* for trade and privileges. Norris tried to buy off this stipulation, then to water it down to just convoy duty for the Mocha fleet. All to no avail. Eventually his patience ran out and the embassy withdrew without even a formal leave-taking.

Eleven days later, on 16 November 1701, the Emperor issued an edict for the confinement of all Europeans, the seizure of their goods and the cessation of their trade; the reason given was their failure to protect Indian shipping. Norris himself was detained and released only after another hefty payment. He arrived back in Surat to find that Waite was now as contemptuous of his authority as was Gayer. The embassy had cost a staggering £80,000 and had achieved nothing. It was hardly Norris's fault. Against both Waite and Gayer he vowed to get his revenge back in England; but he died on the homeward voyage, a bitter and broken man.

Meanwhile the Emperor's edict was taking effect. In Surat Gayer came under closer guard, and Waite tasted something of his own medicine. In Bengal the Old Company's factors were comparatively safe behind the walls of Fort William but their rivals of the New Company, scattered through the old trading centres of Patna, Kasimbazar and Hughli, were swiftly rounded up. Bombay was left undisturbed; its Governor, after all, was safely under lock and key in Surat and its trade was negligible. That left just Madras. In January 1702 a Moghul army appeared at San Thomé within sight of Fort St George. 'There are ill designs on foot against this place', surmised the Governor's council. Long immune from the struggles between Aurangzeb and the Company, Madras under the redoubtable Thomas Pitt was about to be drawn into the mainstream of Indian politics; but not before making the most of its independence to champion significant new initiatives in east and south-east Asia.

CHAPTER TEN

Eastern Approaches

MADRAS, SIAM AND CHINA

The port cities of south and south-east Asia were rarely located on the actual sea. For reasons of defence and for the convenience of internal trade and administration they generally lay several miles inland up a tortuous and capricious river system. Having cleared the coastal bar, the approaching seafarer entered a maze of broad silt-laden waterways flanked by sombre mangrove and oppressive jungle. Cormorants watched from the limbs of uprooted trees aground on unseen mud banks; a temple finial gleamed gold amidst the nauseous verdure. Gone were the clean horizons and bracing airs of the ocean. Whether journey's end was to be Calcutta or Canton, Batavia or Bangkok, there was a sameness of setting and a sameness of menace.

Doubtless there were exceptions. Macassar in distant Sulawesi, where the English had retained a toehold in the spice trade until the 1660s, was almost a seaboard city. But then its Bugis population had acquired a reputation as the most aggressive native seafarers in the East; seemingly it was naval prowess alone which made the coasts safe for major settlements. No polity that was vulnerable to seaborne aggression could afford to indulge a taste for esplanades and corniches. Hong Kong and Singapore would have to wait until the Napoleonic Wars had demonstrated that Britannia really did rule the waves. So would Bombay; although already established, the infant settlement would take most of the eighteenth century to emerge from its canopy of coconut palms, bravely front the Arabian Sea, and declare itself the Gateway to India.

In 1700 it was Madras and, of the English settlements, Madras alone that pioneered this new seaside development. Francis Day had built his four-square fort right on the beach and from there the town had spread, north and south along the tideline. Heavy seas often threatened its walls, and for want of a sheltered harbour ocean-going vessels had to lie off the bar, to the considerable discomfort of their disembarking passengers who must brave the breakers in flimsy canoes.

It was 'one of the most incommodious places I ever saw', wrote Captain Alexander Hamilton, the interloper, who seldom had a good word for the Company, its servants or its settlements. One side of the town was pounded by the heaviest surf on the whole Coromandel Coast, the other periodically flooded by a salt-water lagoon which during the rains became a river in urgent search of the sea. There was no natural drinking water within a mile and the soil was so sandy that nothing would grow in it. Additionally Hamilton was most disparaging about Madras's commercial importance. Compared to Bengal or Gujarat, its hinterland boasted neither a good market for English imports nor a manufacturing base from which to draw Indian exports. It was simply an entrepôt 'supplying foreign markets with foreign goods'.

This was a little unfair to The Coast's celebrated weavers and dyers who had been flocking into Madras's so-called 'Black Town' ever since its foundation and who now accounted for a sizeable part of the 80,000 native population. And it was contradicted by Hamilton's previous paragraph in which, with some relish, he had discoursed on the diamond mines of Golconda 'but a week's journey from Fort St George'. It also overlooked the main attraction of the place. For unlike almost anywhere else that an Englishman might seek his fortune in the East, Madras offered reasonable odds on his living long enough to realize it. According to the Reverend Charles Lockyer, who was there for a couple of years at the turn of the century, 'the inhabitants enjoy as perfect a health as they would do in England'; it was 'plainly discovered in their ruddy complexions'; even the summer heat was tolerable, for after a few hours 'the sea breeze coming on, the town seems to be new born'.

With so little fresh water and no sanitation it was potentially as unhealthy as any other Indian – or for that matter, English – town of the period. But thanks to those bracing breezes plus a vigorous administration, the fort area known as 'White Town' looked spruce and felt orderly. The pavements were of brick, well swept, and the central roadways more sand than dirt so less dusty. They formed a grid at the centre of which stood Day's sand-castle fortress, now dwarfed by a stately mansion whose three high-ceilinged storeys reared above the fort's pepper-pot bastions. This was the residence of the Governor and the hub of the settlement. A large airy hall on the top floor doubled as council chamber and stock exchange. Firearms arranged in scallops and florets, 'like those in the armoury of the Tower of London', adorned the walls and from the windows there was a commanding view of the ships in the roadstead. Only one building could claim a greater elevation above the city walls and that was St Mary's, the first Anglican church east of Suez. Lockyer, who had probably preached there, was undoubtedly proud of it, although somewhat at a loss to describe its architecture.

> The church is a large pile of arched building, adorned with curious carved work, a stately altar, organs, a white copper candlestick, very large windows, etc which render it inferior to the churches of London in nothing but bells, there being only one to mind sinners of their devotion.

The neo-classical colonnades and the gracious mansions for which the city would become famous were not yet in evidence. Instead of 'the garden city' it was still a tight-packed town of terraced houses with wooden balconies, flat roofs and castellated parapets. Only the already widespread use of *chunam* gave a hint of things to come. This was a shell-based lime which when polished had a finish like marble. Peeking above its rust-red walls, White Town's *chunam*-ed terraces must have made a brave show in the dancing sunlight. The rows of windows faced the sea. Madras still had its back to the Indian subcontinent and Hamilton was right to the extent that it was less dependent on up-country trade than either Surat or Bengal. Fort St George still looked to the East.

In 1660 this had meant mainly Bantam and Bengal. But Bengal was soon trading and taking orders direct from London while Bantam, so vulnerable to the Dutch in nearby Batavia, had become a place of little consequence and less trade. New markets in the Far East were needed and in 1663 the directors invited Madras to reconsider the benefits of Siamese trade. A ship called the *Hopewell* had chanced to call at Siam and had reported favourably on the prospects. As in the days of Peter Floris, the Dutch were operating most profitably between the Coromandel Coast and the Gulf of Siam; so much so that King Narai, the new Siamese sovereign, was prepared to offer the most generous concessions to any nation which would challenge what amounted to a Dutch monopoly. This report was seconded by the Agent in Bantam. He thought that Cambodia and Bandjarmasin in Borneo were also worth opening and he added the further incentive of a potential trade with both Japan and China whose ships called regularly at all these places.

As usual London's enthusiasm for new ventures was tempered by extreme caution. 'You know that we have resolved to drive a full trade out [to India] and home without dispersing our estate in the settling of new and unnecessary factories', they reminded Madras. But in the case of Ayuthia in Siam there was no need to settle a new factory. The old one, founded by Antheuniss, was still at their disposal and a skeleton staff from the *Hopewell* had already taken up residence there. It was just a question of not removing them; and in this spirit of leaving sleeping dogs to lie, the Siamese trade was resumed. Launched with so little commitment, it would remain supine and was soon festering with mismanagement.

Madras at the time happened to be in the throes of a minor rebellion which was somewhat similar to that led by Kegwin in Bombay. Sir Edward Winter, the ex-Governor and a staunch Royalist, had detected his successor in some loose talk about the monarchy. He therefore arrested him, threw him into prison, and himself resumed the Governorship. One man was killed in the process and the unfortunate prisoner remained behind bars for the three years which it took the Company to sort out the quarrel. This distraction doubtless absorbed much of Fort St George's energy. But it would appear that another reason for Winter's reluctance to forsake Madras was his expectation of a very considerable return from his personal interest in the Siam trade.

Although the Company's hopes of King Narai's patronage were invariably disappointed, its employees were evidently doing rather well out of Siamese trade. Soon after Winter's departure, another unsolicited report on its potential was submitted by one Nicholas Waite, the future scourge of Surat but in the early 1670s also a private speculator in Siam. His glowing, if garbled, address with its offer to subcontract for the entire Siamese trade might well have been the last straw so far as the directors were concerned. But as it happened another Company ship was even then warping up the Menam river past the fort of 'Bencoke' (Bangkok); new factors were taking up residence; another wildly optimistic report was about to be written; and serious consideration was being given to opening factories at Patani and elsewhere on the Siamese/Malay peninsula.

The ubiquitous Captain Hamilton maintained that the attraction of Ayuthia, the Siamese capital, had little to do with Siamese trade and a lot to do with Siamese hospitality. 'The Europeans who trade to Siam accommodate themselves with temporary wives who', the Captain reports with, presumably, inside knowledge, 'generally prove the most obedient, loving and chaste.' They were also wonderfully understanding and raised no objection over their red-faced husbands 'continually carousing in drunkenness with wine and women'. Here was indeed what the Captain calls 'a free country'; and if the Honourable Company's employees chose to live 'in much affluence and luxury' that was their affair. But the new shipload of suitors who sailed up the Menam river in 1675 would have been content just to break bread with a dockside harlot. Of rejection they had had their fill.

ii

Resurrecting the dreams of Jack Saris and the honest Mr Cocks, in 1671 the directors had followed their Siam initiative with a bold new step to make further trial of the Japanese and Chinese markets. As usual the Dutch, whose imports of Oriental silks, porcelain and tea had created an interest in such luxuries in England, furnished the example. They also furnished the opposition. Apart from commercial rivalry, the two countries were about to go to war. As a result, of the several ships directed towards the South China Sea to open a new era of Far East trade, only two, the *Experiment* and the *Return*, plus a small frigate, actually reached the starting line in Bantam.

From there in May 1672 the frigate was dispatched to Tongking, now north Vietnam. A factory was established in the vicinity of Haiphong and, by way of Hanoi, small quantities of Chinese silk were obtained. But it was not trade, not even barter, as understood by European merchants. The King and his officials simply appropriated the Company's silver plus any goods that took their fancy. They then valued them, often at a derisory figure, and supplied silks to that value. Cash figured only in the form of additional exactions.

Meanwhile the *Experiment* and the *Return* had also sailed north from Bantam. They called first at the island of Formosa (Taiwan) in a vain attempt to exchange some of their English cloth for hides. Leather was known to be one of Japan's main imports; but even had they secured a cargo, it would probably not have influenced their reception at Nagasaki. The Japanese had recently expelled the Jesuits, ruthlessly annihilating their converts and repudiating their Portuguese patrons. Information, obligingly provided by the Dutch, that the English were in alliance with

Portugal and that Charles II was married to a Portuguese princess, was enough to damn all hope of trade. Loudly did the English factors declare their own detestation of popery; the Japanese merely pointed to the flag of St George flying at every yard-arm. What was that if not the dreaded cross of Christendom?

By now the Anglo-Dutch war had broken out. From Formosa the *Experiment* had been sent back to Bantam although many of her factors had transferred to her sister ship for the voyage to Japan. The *Return*, alone in waters dominated by the Dutch, was beginning to feel highly vulnerable. Her factors therefore applied for a Japanese assurance that no Dutch ships would be allowed to put to sea for at least two weeks after her departure. Their fears were justified. A few days later the factors of the *Experiment* recognized their old ship bearing down on Nagasaki. She had been captured by the Dutch; 'honest Mr Cocks' would have understood the Englishmen's chargrin precisely. 'God knows what they have done with the ship's company', noted the *Return*'s diarist. In fact they were prisoners in Batavia; and with the Dutch reacting to the new English incursion into their eastern markets with an energy worthy of Jan Pieterson Coen, the *Return* herself was now virtually marooned in the South China Sea.

Assuming the enemy fleet was still lurking somewhere to the east of Malacca, both Bantam and India were out of the question. Formosa and Japan had proved disastrous; and Manila and the Philippines were thought unsafe because of the uncertain attitude of the Spanish. 'It was therefore resolved to make for the port of Macao at which, from the amity between the King [of England] and the Portuguese, it was hoped that at least the ship and the cargo would be safe ...' In this the *Return*'s double complement of factors were not disappointed. But although they eventually off-loaded their Bantam pepper (at an island adjacent to the future Hong Kong), they failed to find a market for their English cloth and were soon deeply distrustful of even their Portuguese allies.

Worse, after more than three years aboard ship, the *Return*'s crew were talking of mutiny 'if kept out any longer'. More in despair than hope, the factors decided to sail for 'Bencoke in the river of Syam'. This then was the vessel which warped up the Menam river in January 1675 loaded with disgruntled factors badly in need of the creature comforts they associated with terra firma.

To ensure a quick turn-round while the easterly winds still blew, the factors speedily arranged to load the *Return* with copper and dispatch her for Surat. Minerals generally sold well in India and there was nothing more galling to the directors in London than news that one of their vessels had missed its sailing. Thus, though the *Experiment* had failed, at least the *Return* would return. But since the *Return* carried no bullion, purchase of the copper meant borrowing heavily from King Narai. It was suggested that disposal of the ship's English cloth would soon liquidate this liability. But it also provided the new swarm of factors both with a good pretext for staying on in Siam and with the trading capital to make the most of their position. While the Company's stock was thus being used to finance private ventures its debt would, if anything, grow.

The King raised no objection to this arrangement since it made the Company's withdrawal from the Siamese market less likely. Neither, for the same reason, did the factors. And perhaps even the Company would have been happy had their trade proved profitable. 'We hope', announced the new factors in typically optimistic vein, 'since we could not carry Syam to Japan, we may have Japan brought to Syam.' In fact nothing of the sort would happen. The Dutch retained their near monopoly on all trade between Siam and Japan; and through private ventures the factors themselves undercut the Company on the trade between Siam and India.

From both India and Bantam several attempts were made to right the Company's financial position in Ayuthia and to purge its factory. But for more than a decade the pattern, set by the *Return*, of Englishmen rapidly succumbing to the easy life and rich pickings of 'a free country' repeated itself. More carrots were dangled before the directors: the Company might have a monopoly of the copper trade; it might have the government of Patani; or it might build a fort and open a free port at nearby Singhora (which, misleadingly anticipating events, is sometimes written as 'Singhapora'). But none of these concessions actually materialized, and among those Company men who found a congenial berth up the Menam river loyalty to their Honourable employers counted for little. All traded on their own account, some resigned the service to become interlopers, others entered Siamese employ.

Of those who remained in the Company's service the American-born Yale brothers proved the shrewdest operators. In the late 1680s Thomas Yale handled their affairs in Siam while Elihu Yale maximized their profits as Governor of Madras. Eventually both attracted the Company's censure and were dismissed for abusing their positions. Elihu was not, however, disgraced and like Thomas Pitt, a close associate in later years, he was able to retain his Indian fortune. Part was donated to his old school, then known as His Majesty's College of Connecticut. In 1718 the grateful trustees renamed it 'Yale College' in his honour.

No such mark of posthumous respectability would attach to two other brothers, George and Samuel White, the Company's and the Yales' main competitors. George White had entered the Company's service only to resign it in favour of private trading, first from Siam and later from London. Before leaving the East he installed his brother Samuel in King Narai's employ. As a naval commander and then as Harbour Master at Mergui on the Indian side of the Siamese/Malay peninsula (and now in Burma) Samuel White built up a commercial empire that was soon contesting the trade of the Bay of Bengal. Using ships built at Mergui and Masulipatnam and sailing under Siamese colours, 'Siamese' White short-circuited the Company's sea-borne trade round the peninsula by consigning goods overland across the Kra Isthmus between Mergui and Ayuthia. This route had been traditionally monopolized by native traders, especially Indians from Golconda (Hyderabad). In 1685 competition between White and the Indians led to a desultory war between Siam and Golconda.

Such hostilities would not have troubled the Company but for the fact that it had factories in Golconda (e.g. Masulipatnam) and that Golconda itself was about to come under Moghul rule. If, as was the Company's wont, one regarded the Siamese flag as purely one of convenience, then White was just an interloper who, the moment his ships began to molest Golconda vessels, became a pirate. Mergui began to appear as another Madagascar; and since White was English, the Honourable Company was sure to be held responsible for him. Indeed, at Masulipatnam the Company's trade and factors were already suffering on his account much as those of Surat had on Avery's account. For the good of the Company's Siam trade, for the protection of its Coromandel settlements, and as part of the general interdict against interloping, White would have to be stopped.

But although the situation on the east side of the Indian peninsula seemed to be a mirror image of that on the west, there were two additional complications in the unlikely persons of Louis XIV of France and Constant Phaulkon (or Constantine Falcon) once of the Greek island of Cephalonia. France had acquired Pondicherry, its first toehold on the Indian coast, only in 1673. *Le Roi Soleil*'s designs on Siam were unexpected and adventurist. But no less unexpected, no less ambitious, and no less decisive was the influence wielded by the plausible Phaulkon.

Like many Ionian islanders the young Phaulkon had chosen a life at sea, somehow entering the Company's service as a cabin boy. Arrived at Bantam he had displayed an aptitude for languages plus an extraordinary resourcefulness which gained the respect of Richard Burnaby, one of the English factors. In 1678 Burnaby had been deputed to Siam in another effort to discipline its wayward factors. Phaulkon went as his interpreter. Under orders from Burnaby and George White he engaged in several trading ventures and then, like Samuel White, was installed in Siamese employ. It was thought that he could there serve English interests and counter Dutch intrigues.

But the plan worked rather too well for its own good. Continuing his meteoric rise through the social firmament the ingenious Greek was soon 'My Lord Falcon', confidant of the King, his leading policy-maker and, as head of the treasury, virtually prime minister of Siam. Meanwhile Burnaby had fallen foul of his employers, George White had returned to England, and the Company was as reluctant as ever to increase its Siamese commitments. Phaulkon was out on his own, a pace-maker who had run the field off their feet. He cast about for support and found it in the French.

For King Narai the overriding concern was still to find a European ally and trading parner to counterbalance the commercial strength of the Dutch. Phaulkon, the obvious man to arrange such an alliance, would probably have preferred to see the English step into this role. But in what was apparently a spontaneous conversion Phaulkon had already been received into the Roman Catholic church by a French Jesuit in Ayuthia; and as his personal influence on Siamese affairs grew so did the expectations of both Rome and Versailles. In 1684 Phaulkon sent emissaries to France, the following year Louis XIV reciprocated with a magnificent embassy to Siam, and in 1686 more Siamese envoys were given a grand reception at Versailles.

Meanwhile the English seemed to be bent on cutting their own throats. In 1683 they had been finally ejected from Bantam after a palace revolution engineered by the Dutch. While the first Siamese mission was in France, another Company deputation, this time from Surat, arrived in Siam and demanded that any Englishmen in Siamese employ, like Samuel White, be discharged; it was also intimated that only an undertaking to buy £30,000 worth of English goods every year would guarantee the continuance of the Ayuthia factory. Such demands showed no appreciation either of Siam's needs or of the Company's good fortune in enjoying 'Lord Falcon's' favour. They were rejected outright.

Whereas *Le Roi Soleil* sent accredited ambassadors and distinguished prelates, the English deputed only boorish merchants and quarrelsome seamen. And when at last James II did accord Phaulkon some recognition of his elevated status, it came through the good offices not of the company but of George White, Phaulkon's erstwhile patron and an arch-interloper. According to one English skipper the Company, in the persons of John Child and Josiah Child, was all for removing Phaulkon and extending its war against the Moghul to include the King of Siam. Phaulkon promptly arrested the skipper in question. But other Company men continued to insist that 'the right treacherous Greek' was devoting his undeniable energies to 'blasting the Hon'ble Company's business'. Meanwhile in the Bay of Bengal Samuel White, the Greek's protégé, was blasting Golconda's shipping.

As usual in a crisis, the Company in London turned to its Stuart patron. James II obligingly issued a proclamation against Englishmen sailing under foreign flags and, acting on this directive, Elihu Yale quickly despatched two ships and forty troopers from Madras. This modest task force under Captain Anthony Weltden was to descend on Mergui and demand the surrender of its English inhabitants, including 'Siamese' White, the Harbour Master, and Richard Burnaby, now the town's Governor. It was also to seize all White's Siamese shipping by way of reparation for the losses suffered by Golconda and the Company.

Arriving off the Mergui archipelago in June 1687 Weltden in the *Curtana* found the English renegades surprisingly co-operative. White was anyway on the point of leaving for England. He had fallen out with Phaulkon, was suspicious of the Greek's overtures to France, and had already taken precautions against prosecution by the Company by forging a pass from the Siamese court. Having first inspired his Siamese colleagues to offer a stout resistance, he allowed one of his (and so Siam's) ships to be taken; then he himself submitted. By July White and Weltden were on excellent terms; as they waited for favourable winds to take them back to Madras they whiled away the hot nights with copious toasts downed to the thunder of gun salutes.

After one such Bacchanalia the sleepless inhabitants of Mergui decided that they had had enough of English treachery. They opened up with the shore batteries, sank one of Weltden's ships, and then rampaged through the town massacring every foreigner they could find. White escaped, but Burnaby was amongst the dead. Weltden, felled by a massive blow, survived thanks only to the cushioning effect of his beaver hat. No casualty figure is available but there were probably more than twenty fatalities.

Considerably shaken, White and Weltden with their two remaining ships withdrew into the Mergui archipelago, thence to Burma and to Aceh. Neither was in a hurry to report to Madras. Weltden's failure would eventually win him severe censure and White could only assume that the massacre would be laid at his door. To escape the Company's clutches he sailed, with Weltden's connivance, first to Pondicherry and then straight back to England and the welcoming arms of brother George and the Dowgate Adventurers.

It was thus in complete ignorance of the tragic turn of events at Mergui that in the summer of 1687 Elihu Yale sent another ship, the *Pearl*, to reinforce the Company's Siam task force. News of Phaulkon's machinations with the French was now shedding a disconcerting light on Anglo-Siamese relations. Originally the Greek had tempted Versailles with the prospect of King Narai's speedy conversion to Catholicism. With a Jesuit confessor ensconced in the royal household the Dutch would need no further reminder of French influence. But when the King showed absolutely no inclination to forsake the Buddhism of his forefathers Phaulkon had cast about for an equally acceptable expedient and had come up with an offer of territory. The French might found their own settlement, an equivalent to Bombay with a French garrison and full sovereignty. He first suggested Singhora, near enough to the Menam to discourage the Dutch but not so near that it would antagonize the native Siamese. Then he changed his mind and suggested Mergui. By now, 1687, a French fleet was on its way out with over 300 troops on board plus the wherewithal to take up residence.

From an English point of view there was only one thing worse than Mergui being a lair of interlopers and that was the prospect of its becoming a French naval base. With Mergui on one side and Pondicherry on the other, the French would be well placed to control the Bay of Bengal. It was therefore to forestall the French by seizing Mergui for the Company that Yale sent the *Pearl* to join Weltden. On board were the one-time Agent from Bantam and one of Yale's senior factors from Madras who were to act as Governor and Port Officer in the new acquisition.

But Weltden had of course slunk away in disgrace; Phaulkon had interpreted his behaviour as hostile and had formally declared war against the English Company; and in Mergui the Siamese were in full control with a Frenchman already installed in White's shoes. Unaware of any of these changes the *Pearl* sailed into port. She was promptly surrounded. Her two very senior factors found themselves compelled to surrender to the Frenchman and were then dragged off in chains to Ayuthia. There they were 'severely confined and used'. The Menam swarmed with French vessels and as well as Mergui, a French garrison had been quartered in the strategic fortress of Bangkok.

It was the end so far as the Company was concerned. Once again its hopes of Siamese trade had brought nothing but heartache. 'Syam,' declared the directors in 1691, 'never did nor will bring the Company two pence advantage, but many thousands of pounds loss.'

In March 1688 the *Pearl*'s factors were released. Eight months later they were followed out of Bangkok and Mergui by the remnants of the French expedition. Its presence had served only to disgrace the mighty Phaulkon and arouse Siamese nationalism. By the end of 1688 Phaulkon had been executed, King Narai was dead, and Siam had put up the shutters to the outside world. Only the Dutch retained their factory and even its importance rapidly declined. For nearly a century and a half the country would continue to nurse the wounds of its first bruising encounter with Europe. This isolationism was no protection against its Burmese neighbour but it did spare the country the traumas of colonialism.

iii

From behind the jaunty walls of Madras's Fort St George, Elihu Yale greatly regretted the loss of the Siamese trade, so much so that in 1691 he and his Council made an unusually public-spirited offer. They would raise, they said, a subscription towards the cost of sending a small fleet to capture Siamese shipping as compensation for the losses suffered. It seems, however, that the Company never took up this offer. Probably, and rightly, it judged that it was not its own losses but those of Yale and his colleagues that were so bothering Fort St George.

Private trade as conducted by Company men and interlopers had undermined the Siamese venture. But such freelancing, whether in Company ships or native vessels, could serve as a useful form of reconnaissance. Compared to the Company's 'out and back' operations the risks were high and the investments small. But there was always the chance of new markets being opened or of new commodities being discovered which, if profitable, the Company could itself take over. Madras was

1. The clove island of Ternate. From Valenijn's *Oud en Niew Oost-Indien* (1724).

2. The Company's factory at Surat as fortified in the eighteenth century. Engraving by M. Rooker.

3. Fort St George (Madras). An engraving after Jan van Ryne (c.1754).

4. Fort William (Calcutta). The factory and fortifications are as redesigned after Siraj-ud-Daula's attack. An engraving after Jan van Ryne (c.1754).

5. Bombay Castle, customs house and wharf
(drawn by John Bellasis between 1821 and 1856).

6. The view from the rear of Bombay Castle across Back Bay towards Malabar Point. An engraving after Jan van Ryne (c.1754).

7. Clive and Mir Jafar after the Battle of Plassey. Francis Hayman, c.1760.

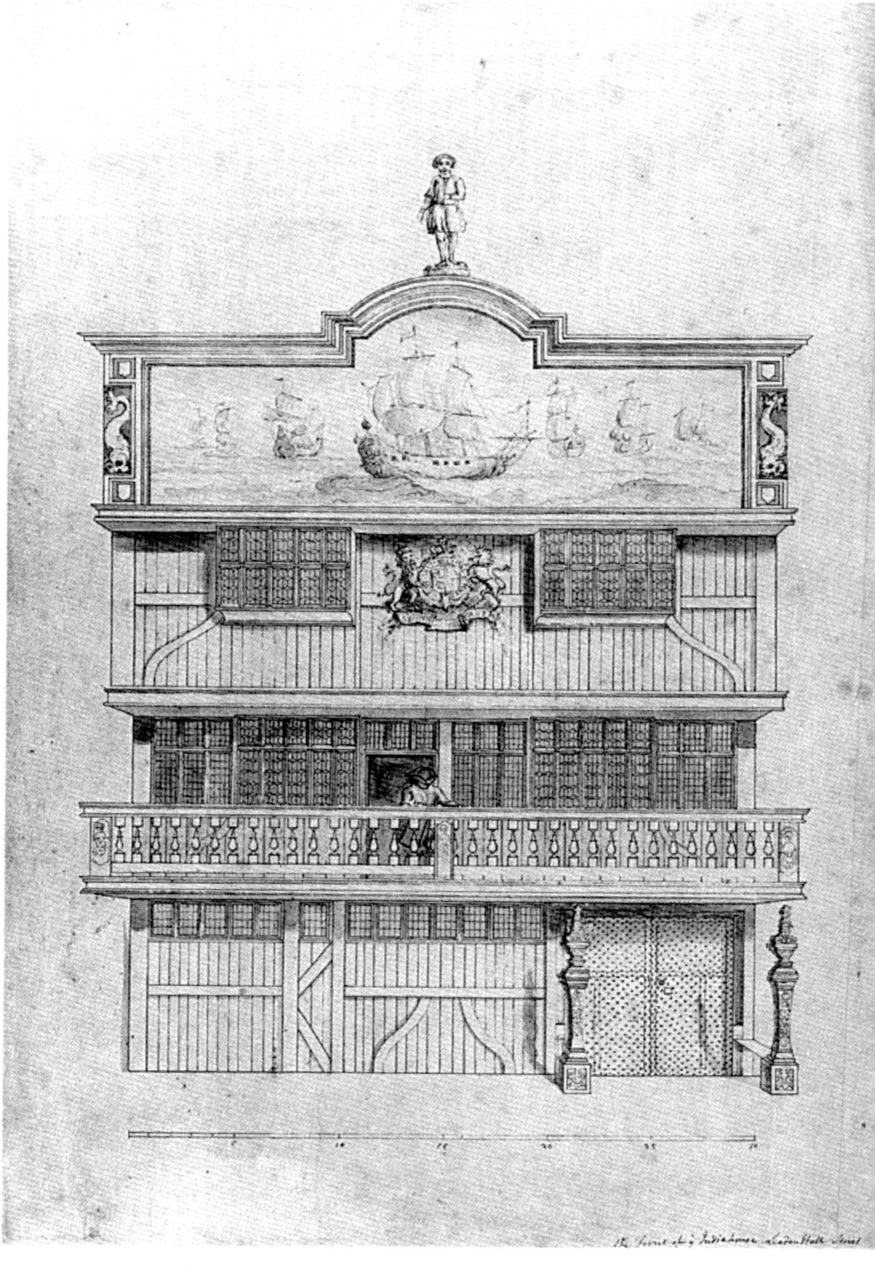

8. The Company's headquarters in Leadenhall Street c.1711.
Drawing by George Vertue.

9. Snug Corner Cove, in Prince William Sound, where ships of the Bengal Fur Company wintered on the North American coast. Engraving by John Webber.

10. The Company's Leadenhall Street headquarters in the late eighteenth century, redeveloped and enlarged in line with the Company's enhanced prestige. Watercolour by James Malton.

11 & 12. Two views of Benares in the 1780s, by Thomas and William Daniels (above) and William Hodges.

particularly well sited for such ventures and, even as Yale and his council rued the loss of Siam, they were already deeply committed to a new and much more exciting field of activity at the mouth of China's Pearl River.

No English ship had attempted to trade at Canton since Weddell's disastrous skirmish there on behalf of Courteen's Association in 1637. It was to be hoped that the Chinese had forgotten that bloody affray and perhaps it was to guard against any repeat performance that Yale sent as chief factor, or supercargo, his ever-dependable brother Thomas. He was less fortunate in his choice of a vessel. It was now 1689, that disastrous year in which Job Charnock and the entire Bengal establishment had been ignominiously withdrawn to Madras. Their ship, the *Defence*, after 'tripping from port to port [Sutanati, Chittagong, Arakan] without effecting anything', was now swinging at anchor in Madras roads; and she was still under the erratic command of Captain Heath. Failing any orders for her disposal, it was this ship and her 'hot-headed, wrong-headed, capricious and futile, feather-brained skipper' that Yale now directed to establish a factory at Canton.

'We are of opinion', wrote Yale to the directors, that it 'will be very advantageous to Your Honours if it could be well procured, that port [Canton] much exceeding Amoy in all sorts of China commodities and is a greater and better government'. Amoy represented the Company's one modest and precarious success from twenty years of sporadic attempts to gain a foothold in China. Following the abortive visit of the *Return* and the *Experiment* in 1672-3, the Company's factors at Bantam had sent further vessels to Taiwan, then as now independent of Peking. For a time its king looked set to make substantial conquests on the mainland, and it was in the wake of these that in 1676 factors first began trading at Amoy on the mainland opposite to Taiwan. Given their ignorance of Chinese commercial practice, the disturbed state of the country and Amoy's isolation, these factors showed remarkable tenacity and in 1681 were expected to find loadings for no less than four ships.

But in the following year the political map again changed. Amoy and then Taiwan fell to the Manchus, Bantam passed to the Dutch, and responsibility for further English endeavours passed to Madras. Although the Amoy trade resumed, it remained a disappointment. The place was too far from the manufacturing centres to be a great market for Chinese silks and as yet the English market for Chinese tea was insignificant. Additionally the exorbitant demands made by a host of local officials tried both the purse and the patience of the English. 'There is no other way to bring them to terms but either to divert trade to Ningpo [in the north] or Canton', reported a gloomy factor in 1689, 'or else to forbear some years whereby the want of our ships may reduce them to a juster usage and commerce.'

Even as he wrote, Captain Heath's *Defence* was dropping anchor in sheltered waters at the mouth of the Pearl River. She was fifteen leagues east of Macao amid a scatter of well-wooded islands which included what is now Hong Kong. Previous attempts to trade at Canton had usually been made through the doubtful offices of the Portuguese at Macao; but Thomas Yale opted for the direct approach. With two other factors and an escort of eight he was rowed to the mainland and then conveyed, the factors in sedan chairs, the escort in wheelbarrows ('much more convenient than our English ones but somewhat more noisy') to Tungkun and thence by boat to the great city.

Describing what was probably the largest port at which Company ships had ever called, Alexander Hamilton would find the people of Canton 'ingenious, industrious, civil, but too numerous'. He reckoned the population at well over a million and there was 'no day in the year but shews 5000 sail of trading junks, besides small boats for other services, lying before the city'. The country was 'as pleasant and profitable as any in the world, the crops abundant'. Chinese meat, however, was to be avoided. It was good, but you needed to know its provenance. Let the Captain explain.

> The abominable sin of sodomy is tolerated here, and all over China, and so is buggery, which they use both with beasts and fowls, in so much that Europeans do not care to eat duck except what they bring up themselves, either from the egg or from small ducklings.

Thomas Yale and his companions were no doubt equally impressed by the metropolis, but they were not there long enough to ascertain such detail. On the day after their arrival they met the *Hoppo*, or Chinese customs officer, and were immediately promised the necessary chop, or permit, for bringing the ship upriver. This was most encouraging. But Yale was reckoning without his skipper. Heath, who seems to have been a capable navigator, always became exceedingly restless and apprehensive when in sight of land. Charnock had come to rue this failing; now it was Yale's turn. For after landing the Canton party, Heath had weighed anchor, taken a long look at the main channel up to Canton and decided against it. He was now somewhere off Macao. Yale and the *Hoppo* spent five days trying to find him.

It was ironical that, when at last an English ship had a chance to go up to Canton, she chose not to take it. But the Captain remained adamant; hence Yale was compelled to conduct the always lengthy negotiations over dues and contracts from Macao. Customs duties in China were usually paid by the Chinese merchants. In their stead the visiting trader paid a charge based on the size of his ship. This involved tedious and expensive measurement and could not even begin until orders had been placed for whatever goods the visitors intended to take away with them. With much bluff and more bribery Yale fought his way through the tangle of red tape and by March 1690 the ship was being loaded.

Meanwhile Captain Heath was waging a battle with the Macao customs over his personal trade and busily refitting for the return voyage. His requirements evidently included a mast, to collect which he took an armed detachment from the ship. The mast was lying ready on the shore but there was something wrong with the Captain's paperwork. He needed, said the Chinese, some additional clearance. Heath would have none of it and proceeded to roll his mast into the water 'when began ye fray'. Blows were exchanged as the mast was lashed to the longboat. The men pulled on the oars and the Chinese kept up a steady bombardment of rocks. 'Fire,' shouted the Captain in panic. The first shots came from the English and one Chinese was killed outright. The English now rowed for open water, cutting loose the precious mast and abandoning the ship's doctor who came rushing down the beach with nine other members of the crew. The doctor 'was miserably cut down in their sight' and then thrown into a hut where, next day, he was reported to be still lying 'on ye ground, chained in his gore most miserably with ye stinking dead corpse [of the Chinese casualty] laid by him and none suffered to come near or dress his wounds'.

Back aboard the *Defence* Yale was beside himself at this latest outrage. 'The Captain . . . having performed what I always feared would be the conclusion of his folly, [had] ruined the public and private trade.' To ride out the storm of protest and resolve the judicial complications of such an incident would take months; it would also eat into the profits. A factor was sent to ransom the doctor and the other prisoners. He reported that the Chinese would not begin to settle the matter for a sum less than three times that already paid in measurement dues. Yale refused and the ship immediately put to sea. Presumably the mast was recovered but of the factor, the doctor, and the rest no more is heard. 'We never had good success in any attempt made of that kind without our own express orders', was the smug comment of the directors. It had been Madras's affair; the Yales must take the blame. In 1692 Elihu was replaced as Governor of Fort St George but he was still in Madras winding up his multifarious affairs six years later.

Whether the voyage had been a failure commercially as well as diplomatically is not revealed. Naturally factors tended to magnify the difficulties with which they had to contend; moreover they were unlikely to reveal the profits of their private trade and were often in no position to gauge those of the Company. Presumably the China trade, especially to Amoy, continued to show a return. It certainly attracted ships and when the New Company commenced operations, Canton was high on its list of priorities. Where the Old Company had stirred up such animosity, it was hoped that the New might find a favourable reception.

Thus in 1699 the New Company's *Macclesfield*, a fast sailing 'galley' of modest size, sailed from London to Macao in under six months. So keen was the *Hoppo* to encourage her trade that the measurement dues, modest enough for a ship of this size, were twice reduced and in September 1700 she moored in Canton's Whampoa harbour. She was probably the first company ship to join the great concourse described by Hamilton although it is significant that she found already there a ship belonging to Abdul Ghafar, the Surat tycoon, and one from Madras.

As supercargo the *Macclesfield* carried Robert Douglas, brother-in-law of Thomas Pitt and one of the Old Company's erstwhile factors in Bengal; he was supported by a Mr Biggs who had been on the *Defence*. Together they had a fund of experience and a better idea of what to expect than any of their predecessors. The Chinese refusal to allow resident factors meant that the factory system as developed in Java and India could not apply. The ship itself was the factory and each vessel must have its resident banker-cum-entrepreneur in the shape of the supercargo. Moreover they must be prepared for long delays, prevarication from the mandarins, and collusion from the merchants. On the other hand, the Chinese usually respected any contract once it had been duly signed and they might even honour penalty clauses. It was all a question of knowing the ropes and at last the English were beginning to feel their way.

Writing to Pitt after the *Macclesfield*'s return to England, Douglas nevertheless portrayed his sojourn at Canton as fraught with severe difficulties. Having made such good speed on the outward voyage he had been detained by the Chinese for nearly a year, thus 'missing the monsoon [winds]' and being obliged to while away six months on an exploratory cruise up the coast. His English goods had been returned to him unsold 'contrary to all justice after they had kept them five or six months'. And the arrival of 'a great ship from Manila' had deprived him of much of the silk he had ordered. 'Notwithstanding all my complaints to the mandarins and all the endeavours I could use, yet I was necessitate to put up [with] all these injuries and a great many more to get in what was due to us.' At Chusan, to which place Douglas had removed in a further effort to sell his English cloth, it was the same story, and after such a catalogue of woe one might assume that the venture was a dismal failure. In reality, as he confided at the end of his letter to Pitt, after all charges had been deducted he was confident of doubling the value of his original stock 'which is more than our Company expected and more than any ship from India or China had done this year'. It was much the most successful venture ever to China, and from the voyage of the *Macclesfield* dates the regular English trade with Canton which would one day become the most profitable in the East India Company's portfolio.

Whereas in India the competition provided by the New Company served merely as an obstruction, in China it stimulated activity. Douglas was the first to sail north past Amoy to Chusan at the mouth of the Yangtse. His object was to reach Ningpo, an important centre for the sale of Nanking silk, and hopefully to find in colder climes a better market for English woollens. Access to Ningpo was refused, but while at Chusan he was joined by Allen Catchpole, another of Job Charnock's disillusioned Bengal factors who had then joined Thomas Pitt as an interloper but was now rejoicing in the role of the New Company's Agent – and, of course, Consul-General – for China and the Far East.

Catchpole remained at Chusan throughout 1701 in which year five New Company ships called at the port. Unlike Sir Nicholas Waite and the other Consuls-General in India he seems to have been a conscientious administrator. But to all the usual impediments to trade with China was added the complication of how and where he was to base himself. The Chinese were adamant that the Consul-General could not reside on Chinese soil. They were highly suspicious of what they took to be some species of English mandarin and in early 1702 they ordered him back to sea. Thereafter he shuttled between Batavia, Bandjarmasin in Borneo where the New Company had also established itself, and back to Chusan. It was a most unsatisfactory arrangement and on Catchpole's strong recommendation his employers at last sanctioned the establishment of a fortified settlement on neutral territory. The place which had caught their Agent's eye was Pulo Condore, an island later infamous as a penal settlement off the coast of south Vietnam. More than 1000 miles from Canton, let alone Chusan, it was nevertheless astride the main sea route up the South China Sea and it was the best that was available. With his council of senior factors, a small garrison and plenty of carpenters, Catchpole went ashore in April 1703.

The island measured twelve miles by four. It boasted a few villages, some useful timber and a couple of anchorages. Catchpole catalogued every one of its vegetable productions and evidently regarded it as some sort of paradise. But it was really no great improvement on all those other islands – Run, Anjediva, Hijili, Mergui – which seem to have dotted the Company's history. Perhaps a few square miles bounded by water exercised some special attraction for an insular race. Catchpole, of course, maintained that it had enormous commercial potential. 'I do faithfully assure your Honours', he told the New Company's directors, 'that I have no fear of vessels in great numbers coming hither with all sorts of goods, so soon as they hear we are settled here and govern as in your Honours other factories.' Thomas Pitt, now Governor at Madras and no friend of the New Company, fully concurred; he reckoned Pulo Condore 'the best design that the English have taken in these parts for many years'.

But from Company historians Pulo Condore would get a bad press. This was the common fate of all inglorious episodes and Pulo Condore was one of the worst. For, just three years after its foundation, Catchpole and nearly all the other Englishmen on the island were massacred. It may be that the Vietnamese were behind this crime; there was talk of some misunderstanding over the terms of the lease and there was a suggestion that the Company's treasure proved too great a temptation. But the perpetrators were in fact the Bugis mercenaries who had been recruited in Borneo as a garrison for the new settlement. Hamilton reports that after three years' service they were due to be relieved and that the English had reneged on this agreement. It took very little to make the Bugis mutiny. Scattered from their home in Macassar by the Dutch they were notorious both as pirates and mercenaries; a similar instance of Bugis soldiery running amok had occurred in Siam in the 1680s.

No attempt was made to reoccupy the island after this débâcle and so it never really got a fair trial. Hamilton thought it 'a bad choice of place for a colony' and Lockyer, the Madras vicar, 'a wrong notion'. The trade of 'a little wild island' could never even defray the cost of its garrison. Witness, wrote Lockyer, Bombay; its Governor (he was referring to Waite) 'has left no stone unturned to promote it, yet I am very well satisfied it is beyond the Company's strength or his art [allowance must be made for sarcasm] to make it a mart of great business; it is improved to the utmost and lies as well for trade as Condore'. Catchpole would probably have settled for this comparison even with the Bombay of 1700.

As it was, his eccentric dream of conducting the China trade from some off-shore, English-run emporium would have to wait. Bandjarmasin in Borneo was briefly projected as just such a base but it too was overrun by Bugis mercenaries in 1707. Six years later the Governor of Benkulen, a place on the west coast of Sumatra which after the loss of Bantam was the Old Company's only outpost in the Indonesian archipelago, was canvassing the merits of his own settlement. He admitted that the idea might seem 'chimericall' and would be 'a work of time'; but it was in fact one of his successors at Benkulen, albeit a century later, who eventually realized Catchpole's dream. His name was Thomas Stamford Raffles, his 'little wild island' Singapore.

iv

Of the few vessels which called at Pulo Condore during its short lifetime one was called the *Union*. This was confusing since the Old Company had just commissioned a ship of the same name. It was also significant. The Company's shipping lists often betrayed its expectations. All those *Speedwells*, *Hopewells*, *Trades Increases*, *Returns* and *Expeditions* represented the hardy perennials. Then there were names suggestive of a particular phase in the Company's trade like the *Clove* and the *Peppercorn*, or the *Surat*, the *Mocha*, and the *Bombay Castle*. Latterly the Siamese venture had produced the *Siam Trader* and even the *Falcon*, while the China trade inspired the *China Merchant* and the *Chusan*. Now, embodying an idea that was becoming increasingly attractive to all concerned in the East India trade, both Companies boasted a *Union*.

That the two Companies should work towards a merger had been a stipulation of the Royal assent to that stay of execution granted to the Old Company in early 1700. Little, however, was immediately done to achieve it. The New Company still placed great store by Norris's embassy to the Moghul and still had high expectations of Waite,

Catchpole and its other Consular Agents. Meanwhile the Old, celebrating its reprieve, was sending out more treasure and ships than for a decade. At the end of 1700 the King renewed his enquiries about the merger talks and both Companies agreed to set up a consultative committee. But again progress was slow, each Company manoeuvring to absorb the other rather than merge with it. The issue dominated the election of 1701 and threatened to dominate the deliberations of the new Parliament.

But outside of Westminster, Leadenhall Street and Dowgate, there was growing resentment against both Companies and their manipulation of the political system. Old arguments that the East India trade was ruining the country's manufacturing capacity resurfaced and resulted in a ban on the wearing of Eastern silk. Henceforth only raw silk was worth importing; it was a bitter blow to the Persian trade which, more even than Bengal or China, relied on silk.

Meanwhile the King was more anxious about events in Europe. A war over the Spanish succession looked inevitable; the French, as in Siam, were already showing a lively interest in Eastern trade; and with the two English Companies so bitterly divided, each would be an easy prey. It would also be difficult, they were told, for the Royal Navy to afford protection twice over. Here was a threat from the throne and the Companies recognized it as such. In April 1702, a week before the declaration of war, both finally accepted the Instrument of Union.

In effect the Instrument set up a third East India Company, 'The United Company of Merchants of England Trading to the East Indies', in which the other two Companies were to have an equal interest. Balancing their stock and assets was an extremely complex undertaking not finally completed until the arbitration known as Godolphin's Award in 1708. And although the United Company began operations immediately, seven years were allowed for the Old and New Companies to continue trading while they wound up their affairs and collected their debts. Thus, for a time, there were three companies in operation, the only difference being that they were no longer competing.

Such at least was the theory; but enforcing the new accommodation amongst sworn enemies on the other side of the world was never going to be easy. On the west coast of India Sir John Gayer was made Governor of Bombay with his old rival Sir Nicholas Waite relegated to the subordinate command of Surat. But Gayer was still a prisoner and Waite determined he should stay so. Instead of informing the Moghul official of the new hierarchy, Waite simply bribed him to keep Gayer under lock and key and assumed the Governorship himself. Bengal tried to get round this problem of precedence by instituting a peculiar system of diarchy in which representatives of the New and Old Companies took it in turns to preside over the United Company. Had the rotation been on, say, a yearly basis it might have worked, but in fact they changed chairs every week. It was a recipe for total confusion.

Only in Madras was the merger achieved without serious friction. Seemingly nothing could shake the firm rule of Governor Pitt. While the Instrument of Union was being drawn up in London Pitt had faced his sternest challenge as Daud Khan, the Moghul Nawab of the Carnatic, closed in on Madras. The Nawab's orders, framed in the aftermath of the Norris embassy, were to stop all trade, seize the town and the Company's assets, and hold its officials. To this end the Moghul army had established its headquarters outside San Thomé, three miles down the beach, and began stopping all supplies to the Fort. Pitt reacted with customary vigour. He put the town on full alert and militias were raised to supplement the two companies of regular troops. But simultaneously he opened negotiations with the Nawab.

The town's fortifications were undoubtedly vulnerable but it had not escaped Pitt's attention that the enemy was without cannon and, as he pointed out to the Nawab, the fort contained 'sufficient for our people for two years, besides the sea open to us'. He could only construe the stopping of provisions as an act of war but to sweeten the Nawab he sent him a crate of oranges from Aceh. A fortnight later he sent more oranges, this time from China, and received a cordial response suggesting an accommodation whereby the Company should make submission to the Emperor and a large donation to his Treasury. Pitt rejected this but sent more oranges. In March 1702, the third month of the siege, came news that in Surat the English had agreed to pay a very substantial indemnity for the piracies of Kidd. In view of this the Nawab was now willing to settle their differences and lift the siege for a not unreasonable 30,000 rupees. Pitt expostulated – and sent yet more oranges, this time from Burma. The Nawab returned them with a hint that they were not appropriate to someone of his station. But Pitt had made his point: Madras was not even short of luxury produce; and the Nawab was now clearly angling for a bribe. In the end 20,000 rupees for the Moghul and 5000 for the Nawab, half payable only after restitution of all seized goods, was enough to end the crisis.

After years spent in the twilight zone of the interloper, Pitt was convinced that every man had his price and every policy its pay-off point. His correspondence repeatedly harps on the need to employ men of both honesty and ability 'but if I was under a necessity to take on a servant that wanted either of 'em, it should be the former. For I could call him to account and oblige him to satisfaction; but fools that want ability can give none.'

> For my particular affairs I employ the cursedest villain that ever was in the world, and see him cheat me before my face, but then he is the most dextrous indefatigable fellow in business that makes me such amends that I can afford to bear with it. 'Tis very true what I formerly wrote you, that the Old Company lost ten times as much by employing fools as they did by knaves . . .

It would be unjust to suggest that Pitt himself was more able than honest but his reputation as the shrewdest merchant of his day certainly applied as much to his personal trade, especially with China, as to that of the Company. And to those same bargaining skills which stood him in such good stead in buying off Nawab Daud Khan he owed his own sensational fortune. Indeed, even as the Moghul army lay about his gates, Pitt was engaged in the most delicate of commercial transactions.

Given the Company's embargo on shipping trade goods to England for any but its own account, the commonest way of remitting home the profits of personal trade was in the form of diamonds. The Company itself encouraged this since diamonds took up none of their precious hold space. And with the main diamond mines located in nearby Golconda, Madras became the Indian Hatton Garden where fortunes from all over the East were converted into gems. Pitt, with more profits than most to invest, dealt heavily in this market and in 1701 received word of a gigantic stone, over 400 carats in weight and undoubtedly 'the finest jewell in the world and worth an immense sum'. He determined to possess it and would invest the major part of his latest Indian fortune in doing so. Henceforth he always refers to it as 'the grand affair', 'my great concern', 'my all'.

Wild rumours would later circulate about the provenance of the 'Pitt Diamond', how it was snatched from the eye socket of a Hindu deity or smuggled from the mines by a slave who hid it in a self-inflicted gash in his thigh. Pitt's deposition, given on oath, is less colourful but quite in character. He was offered 'the great stone' by a dealer with whom he was familiar. It was the size of an egg and of the first water but the asking price of 200,000 pagodas (equivalent to £100,000 at the time) was out of the question and 'too great an amount to be ventured home in one bottom [i.e. ship]'. The dealer halved his price but still Pitt refused. In March 1702, when Daud Khan's siege was at its height, negotiations over the diamond resumed. The price fell to 55,000, then 50,000, pagodas. Pitt would not go above 45,000, then settled at 48,000 (£24,000). Fifteen years later, cut and polished, he would sell it to the Regent of France for £135,000. The feasting and festivities held to mark the retreat of the Moghul army were, not surprisingly, lavish.

No sooner had Daud Khan withdrawn his army and Pitt's son sailed for London with the diamond than news of the union of the Companies began to reach Madras. Governor Pitt had been as dismissive of the New Company's pretensions as any of Leadenhall Street's stalwarts. Against his opposite number on The Coast, the New Company's Agent and Consul-General at Masulipatnam, he had waged a war of words vicious even by the standards of the day. It made no difference that the unfortunate incumbent was in fact his cousin and erstwhile protégé. Or rather it made the man's betrayal still more dastardly and his pretensions still more insufferable. He was, quite simply, 'the haughtiest, proudest, ungratefullest wretch that ever was born'; and Pitt told him so, repeatedly.

On the other hand Governor Pitt, the ex-interloper, cannot but have felt some sympathy for the New Company. Josiah Child had remained his bitter enemy until death (1699) and had strongly opposed his appointment – 'such a roughling and immoral man', according to Child. Had Child not been discredited by 1698, Pitt would never have been appointed to Madras. Additionally, many of the New Company's more respected adventurers, like Douglas and Catchpole, were his friends and associates of old. Indeed it had probably been with the idea that Pitt could be weaned from his new allegiance that his cousin had been sent to Masulipatnam.

But above all, friends and enemies, both in the New Company and the Old, deferred to his talents. No one knew the business better than Pitt and all, except Child, would prefer to have him with them than against them. There was little debate about who should have precedence on The Coast. Thomas Pitt was confirmed as Governor for the United Company, his cousin was relegated and died soon after of 'an appoplecticall fitt'. 'He's dead and there's an end', snorted the Governor not without another swipe at his memory. But towards the New Company's London directors he was far more conciliatory. ''Twas my fate and not my choice', he wrote to them, quoting King William at the Peace of Ryswick, 'that made me your enemy, and since you and my masters are united, it shall be my utmost endeavour to purchase your good opinon and deserve your friendship.'

He was as good as his word. For another seven years, nearly twelve years in all, he continued to preside over the affairs of Madras. 'All matters here are very quiet and I doubt not to keep them so', he reported in 1705 in words almost identical to those once used of Bantam affairs by David Middleton. He saw the Company through the traumas that followed the death of Aurangzeb in 1707 and of the several claimants to the throne he backed the right one in Shah Alam. At his behest new walls were constructed to embrace Madras's Black Town and as a result of his excellent relations with the Moghul's officials further villages were added to the settlement. Future Governors were instructed simply to follow Pitt's example 'which is now so much the easier for the path is well-trodden'. What has been called 'The Golden Age of Madras' was Pitt's creation.

PART THREE

A TERRITORIAL POWER

1710–1760

CHAPTER ELEVEN

The Dark Age

BENGAL AND THE *FARMAN*

Wandering through the City of London sometime in the 1690s the poet-publican Ned Ward spied, atop an otherwise unremarkable Elizabethan building, an enormous and elaborate superstructure. It was both an architectural extension of the façade and a hoarding, for it framed a bright and colourful seascape complete with ships and choppy waves. Fat and fanciful fish, identified as dolphins, flanked the picture and a larger than life cut-out figure, evidently a sailor, stood defiantly hands on hips at its apex. But for its location so far from the river in Leadenhall Street, one might have mistaken the place for a chandler's. Ned Ward's companion knew otherwise. ''Twas the house belonging to the East India Company which', he explained, 'are a corporation of men with long heads and deep purposes.'

For an association of merchants intent simply on driving 'a quiett trade' the Company's long-headed directors had somehow contrived a wonderfully eventful first century quite in keeping with their jaunty hoarding. But as their eighteenth-century equivalents disappeared into the labyrinth of offices and warehouses that now radiated from this unlikely frontage they longed for the obscurity of commerce rather than the celebrity of history. Wars were bad for business and so was dissension. They had long since ceased to notice that garish seascape and when, in 1726, they decided that the existing timbered building was too great a fire risk, they opted for a more sober and anonymous frontage, all grey stone and iron railings. It was high time for the swashbuckling alarms and excursions to make way for profitable trade and peaceful traffic, high time for a few fallow decades, devoid of drama, when nothing much happened except that the warehouses filled, ships sailed, dividends steadied, and fortunes accrued.

By common consent the first forty years of the eighteenth century would be just such a period. Out of the chaos of the 1690s when interlopers, pirates, the rival Company, and the Moghul emperor all conspired to distract the Company from its 'deep purposes', there emerged an era of comparative peace. Secure in the knowledge of its charter, the United Company got down to business. Sir Josiah Child's adventurism had been totally discredited and the Company was now content to exploit the commercial potential of China and Bengal and to consolidate its existing holdings in India.

By 1710 it was regularly sending to the East ten to fifteen ships a year, each of around 300 tons. Five or six commonly made for The Coast and the Bay (Madras and Bengal), two or three for China, two or three for Surat and Bombay, and one each for Mocha (Red Sea), Persia, and perhaps Benkulen (Sumatra) and St Helena. Thirty years later the number of sailings had risen steadily, but not sensationally, to around twenty, each ship being usually of 490 tons. (Over 500 tons and the ship's company had to include a chaplain.) From an annual average of £400,000, imports had risen to £700,000 while London sales remained reasonably constant at about £2 million. Naturally prices and profits fluctuated but there was none of the erratic boom and bust so typical of the previous century. Shareholders came to expect their annual eight per cent dividend and when in 1732 it was proposed to reduce it to six per cent there was such an outcry that the directors had to think again. India stock had become the eighteenth-century equivalent of a gilt-edged security, much sought after by trustees, charities and foreign investors.

All of which, though good news for the Company, is bad news for the annalist. Narrative history needs its thrills and spills and they in turn inspire research. Conversely, a glassy reach of unruffled tideway invites no frantic recourse to the records. Instead the historian, spying white water ahead, unconsciously ups his stroke rate; decades slip past in a paragraph. As a result this period 1710-1750 has come to be regarded as what the Bengal annalist, C. R. Wilson, called 'the dark age of British India'. Wilson endeavoured to illuminate it but his efforts met with little recognition and his three volumes on the *Early Annals of the English in Bengal* were never published in England.

The period was frankly a trifle dull and, worse still, it appeared that that steady march towards eventual dominion in India – often the

English historian's sole reason for following the Company's otherwise tiresome career – had ground to a halt. Instead here was the Company turning its back on a manifest destiny and channelling its energies into such pettifogging irrelevancies as teas and taffetas, *batta* and *dastak* (whatever they were). Happily it was, though, only an aberration. The halt, we are to believe, was merely recuperative; indeed the steady tramp towards dominion was soon to turn into a stampede. India after Aurangzeb was becoming a political vacuum, the French were eager to fill it, and Clive's hour was nigh. After 150 years of 'jarres and brabbles' a new and exciting age was beckoning. If *pour mieux sauter* the Company must perhaps *reculer* for a few decades, not so the historian.

This leap-frogging of more than a generation is responsible for the idea of a second coming for the British in India, the impression being that the Company as a trading corporation slipped into dozy oblivion, buried beneath the weight of its own piece goods, sometime around 1710, only to rise again as a thrusting military enterprise unencumbered by past misdeeds and bursting with patriotic fervour in the 1750s. And certainly a sea change is evident. But this notion of a second coming leaves far too many questions unanswered. How, for instance, did the garrisons, seldom more than 300 strong, which paced the parapets of Forts St George and William suddenly become armies able to contest vast chunks of the subcontinent? Or how did the pirate-plagued marine of Bombay become a formidable navy? When did the 'Consultations' books of the various Presidencies cease to be filled with complaints about last year's consignment of Madeira or what the awful Waite called Bombay's 'unveryhealthfull' climate and come instead to dwell on matters of state and *realpolitik*? It would be interesting to know, too, how and why expatriate communities of comfort-loving merchants came to master their habitual bickering and 'incorrigible sottishness' and to work in concert for the creation of an empire. How was such a role change legitimized; and how come that an association of London businessmen, so naturally cautious, so very distrustful of their overseas agents, and so desperate to avoid political commitments and military overheads, came to countenance such extraordinary developments?

Unfortunately these crucial questions defy either brief or simple answers; there is much to be said for the traditional view that the Company's transformation was simply a necessary gesture of self-defence in the face of French provocation and Indian chaos. But there were also straws in the wind, hints and harbingers of things to come, which suggested a new sort of relationship with the native powers in India and a new sense of solidarity between the Company's three Indian Presidencies. They date back to the days of Governor Pitt in Madras.

Although Pitt had scathingly disparaged the New Company's grand embassy to the Moghul under Sir William Norris – indeed he had done much to undermine it – he was evidently impressed by the idea of reapplying for that long-cherished *farman*. Such a grant, confirming all the Company's commercial and territorial privileges under the imperial seal, would elevate its legal standing to a constitutionality equivalent to that of the various Nawabs and Governors with whom it was habitually embroiled. Such functionaries issued, or more often withheld, their own grants in the form of *kaul*, *sanad*, *parwannah*, and *nishan* but an imperial *farman* would technically trump them all. Although it might not guarantee immunity from local impositions it would certainly legitimize opposition to them.

Pitt appreciated that so long as the implacable Aurangzeb lived, the *farman* was a lost cause. He nevertheless prepared for better times by carefully cultivating connections at the imperial court. Thus in 1707, when the old emperor at last died, there arrived at Fort St George a most encouraging letter from one Ziau-ud-Din whom Pitt knew as The Moghul's Lord High Steward. Evidently the new emperor, Shah Alam, feared that his brother and main rival for the Peacock Throne was heading for Madras. If Governor Pitt could see his way to opposing and perhaps even capturing the traitor, the Emperor might easily be persuaded to grant the *farman*, nay he might go further and grant the Company additional facilities, like a few islands off the Arakan coast or perhaps Pulicat, the erstwhile Dutch factory on the Coromandel Coast.

'I cannot but blush when I think of giving you further trouble,' replied Pitt in suitably unctuous tone. The Arakan islands were of no interest to merchants but there was an island, Divi, just off Masulipatnam which would do very nicely; and instead of Pulicat, would it be possible to substitute San Thomé, the old Portuguese town just down the beach from Fort St George? Of course, the main thing was the *farman* itself. It must be 'generall', that is it must include the Company's privileges in Bengal and Surat as well as Madras. And that reminded him. The Company would appreciate the privilege of establishing a mint at Calcutta for turning its silver imports into coin; and there was still the old problem of unauthorized stoppages of its trade on the river journey up to Patna. The *farman* would also be a good opportunity to stop, once and for all, the liberties habitually taken by the customs officers at Surat. They were the slowest and most rapacious in India and they still insisted on the indignity of a body search 'more becoming slaves rather than merchants'. "Tis your noble and generous mind which has drawn this trouble of our application to you', began Pitt's second letter on the subject. He appreciated that a substantial present must needs be sent to the Emperor along with whoever went to receive the *farman*; indeed such a present was already being assembled. In the meantime he had a few more favours to ask . . .

Back in London the directors marvelled at their Governor's initiative and urged him to stay on at Fort St George to see it through. The present for the Emperor, consisting of elephants, cannon and all the usual cornucopia of clocks, musical boxes, silverware and precious fabrics, was dispatched to Calcutta for forwarding to Delhi; and the Bengal factors were invited to append their own shopping list of favours to that already drawn up by Pitt. But, perhaps piqued by Madras's having made the running and certainly hamstrung by their own indecision (Calcutta still suffered under a rotation Council which changed every week), the Bengal factors failed to respond. Meanwhile, against their better judgement, the Court of Directors had recalled Thomas Pitt following an unseemly row with his advisory council.

In the following year, 1710, Ziau-ud-Din was appointed to the governorship of Hughli whence he renewed his overtures, this time to nearby Calcutta. Simultaneously the Company's rotation government there was at last being wound up and a new President was being installed in Fort William. This was none other than Captain Anthony Weltden, once of the *Curtana*, who had somehow cleared his name of the Mergui disaster and of collusion with 'Siamese' White, and was now deemed just the man to sort out Bengal's always dismal rivalries. Weltden, however, had other ideas. 'His term of governing was very short', recalled Alexander Hamilton, 'but he took as short a way to be enriched by it, harassing the people to fill his coffers'; his legendary reputation for peculation was achieved during a mere seven months in office.

It thus fell to his successor, John Russel, a grandson of Oliver Cromwell, to respond to the new offer of applying for the *farman*. By 1712 the cannon and the candelabra had been dusted off (the elephants had been sold) and the whole present was loaded on boats for the first leg of the journey up-country. From Madras came good wishes, not untinged with jealousy, that Russel might have 'the sole honour of accomplishing what so many able and experienced persons have attempted in vain'. Who, the Madras President asked, would have expected the Act of Union between Scotland and England; after more than a century of fruitless endeavour it had passed in 1707. 'We ought never to despair of succeeding.' But it was hard not to. For from another quarter came news that aborted the whole enterprise: the Emperor Shah Alam was dead.

Throughout 1712, in the sort of blood-letting that accompanied every succession crisis of the later Moghuls, the sons of the deceased Emperor mobilized the might of the empire to contest amongst themselves for the vacant throne. One, lately Nawab of Bengal where he had shown the Company many favours, was forced over a precipice on his elephant; another died in battle; a third briefly gained the throne only to be defeated and strangled before the year was out. The new claimant, Farrukhsiyar, was a son of the late Nawab and news of his unexpected success occasioned great excitement in Calcutta. Again the *farman* seemed a possibility, again the plate and glass of the Company's present was dusted down. For Farrukhsiyar was young, amenable, and an excellent sportsman; he had spent his childhood in Bengal where the Company had appointed itself supplier of toys to the royal nursery, and he was known to many of the Company's servants.

But this being the case, they were also aware of his shortcomings. 'All his most noticeable characteristics', wrote one, 'are connected with his excellence of body.' As a horseman he was unsurpassed but as a statesman he was dull-witted, dilatory and fickle. But for his formidable mother he would never have contested the throne and but for two king-making brothers, the Sayyads, he would never have won it. As Chief Minister (*Wazir*) and Chief of Staff (*Amir-ul-Umara*), the Sayyads now managed the empire while Farrukhsiyar surrounded himself with an assortment of favourites and malcontents who busily intrigued against them. Rival posses roamed the streets of Delhi on the off chance of waylaying a dignitary of the opposing faction; the Emperor took to absenting himself on religious and sporting excursions. Such then was the strife-torn capital and such the factious government to which in 1713 the Company finally determined to send its mission to treat for the cherished *farman*.

News that the English had some forty tons of exotica awaiting dispatch to Delhi naturally delighted a young emperor for whom the pleasures of office entirely obscured the responsibilities. Of course it must be forwarded immediately, and he therefore issued the Company with an interim confirmation of its privileges and ordered passes, armed guards, and free carriage for the entire mission from Patna, where it was assembling, to Delhi.

But this obviated neither the delays nor the expense of mounting such an undertaking. John Surman, the conscientious but unexciting factor who had been delegated to lead the mission, wanted to be sure of a favourable reception in Delhi and to that end protracted negotiations were opened between Khwaja Sarhad, his Armenian interpreter and second in command, and the Khwaja's rather dubious contacts at court. For his part, the Khwaja was profoundly worried about the mission's security across 800 miles of disturbed and bandit-ridden country. As well as a contingent of Company troops and the detachment of imperial foot and horse, further guards were recruited and further sums disbursed to buy off likely adversaries. Then there was the usual complication that any orders from the court in Delhi had to be supported by generous cash inducements before the local authorities would act on them; there was also the question of whether free carriage could be construed as applying to the several tons of piece goods and broadcloth which the mission was proposing to sell in Delhi in order to defray its costs; and there was the purely logistic complication of assembling such a vast caravan. Thus fully a year slipped by in Patna before in April 1715 the cavalcade finally took the high road for Upper India.

Carrying the present and the mission's trade goods 160 bullock carts, each loaded with half a ton, creaked along in single file. Twenty-two more oxen hauled the cannon, also destined for the Emperor, while 1200 porters bent beneath an assortment of loads which included the mission's chintz-lined tents and a selection of richly furnished palanquins. Amidst this concourse, ten hackeries, some fifteen camels and an assortment of horses and ponies jostled for road space. The troops, to a total of 600, patrolled the flanks and guarded front and rear. In all the caravan must have been fully a mile long; when in early May it reached the Ganges at Benares, the mission's diary records four days of 'ferrying over our goods'.

On the third day they were overtaken by what Surman calls 'a prodigious storm of wind and rain'. One imagines the palanquins cartwheeling across the sand dunes, oxen stampeding, and the ferry capsizing as cannon careered across its decks. But all the laconic Surman records is 'some damaging of our goods'. Next day he announces 'We passed the City of Benares.' They had spent four days camped before one of the most famous skylines in the world and had crossed the sacred Ganges at its holiest point. Now they were circumventing the great city of Shiva, the home of Hindu scholarship and the greatest place of pilgrimage in India. It was also an important manufacturing centre. Yet the diary is silent, recording neither admiration nor revulsion, just 'We passed the City of Benares'.

And so, to the historian's intense annoyance, it continued. Two uneventful weeks later they 'arrived on the banks of the Ganges before Allahabad'. They crossed in three days; this time there was not even a storm to raise a ripple of interest. May gave way to June, the hottest month in the north Indian calendar. The dust and discomfort can only have been appalling; they merit not a mention. June 18th found the mission at 'Raj Ghat over against Agra'. All that here separated them from the great white cloud which is the Taj Mahal was the Jumna river, at this time of year a warm and wadable brook. But all that the diary records is that here they 'proclaimed King George'; news had just reached them from Calcutta of the death of Queen Anne and the accession of the first Hanoverian.

Three nights later the camp was entered by robbers. 'We had five men wounded and took two of the rogues.' Another thief was surprised two days later. It was significant that the nearer they approached to the imperial capital the more dangerous was the countryside.

On 6 July 1715, a creditable three months since leaving Patna, the mission made its ceremonial entry into Shahjhanabad (now Old Delhi). With flags, elephants and 200 cavalry, an imperial official conducted them straight to the Red Fort where, after a wait, Farrukhsiyar made an appearance and deigned to accept the first instalment of his present. This was by way of an appetizer consisting of 1001 gold coins, a clock set with precious stones, 'an unicorn's horn' (rhinoceros's?), a gold escritoire, a large lump of ambergris, the inevitable ewer and basin, and a massive globe, more than six feet in diameter, inlaid with gold and silver, and with the place names thoughtfully written in Persian. All went off smoothly and Khan Dauran, the Emperor's favourite courtier and a man strongly recommended by Khwaja Sarhad, hinted at an early and favourable outcome. Surman quickly passed on the good tidings in a letter to Calcutta. 'Considering the great pomp and state of the Kings of Hindustan', he wrote, 'we was very well received.'

A week later Surman was even more confident that 'all will end well'. Governor Pitt's old friend, Ziau-ud-Din, had assured him that they were correct in concentrating on the favourite, Khan Dauran, rather than on the unpopular Sayyad who was *Wazir*. This was precisely what Khwaja Sarhad, the mission's mercurial Armenian, had been saying and for once the much maligned Khwaja was in a tolerable humour. Surman and his three English colleagues – a deputy, a secretary and a doctor – were all in some awe of the Armenian, whose multifarious interests and shady associates often threatened to bring the whole affair into disrepute. But unlike the Englishmen, the Khwaja was not an employee of the Honourable Company; he was on a straight commission – 50,000 rupees if the *farman* was granted. This tended to make him excellent company when things were going well but evasive, secretive and altogether exasperating whenever a reverse was in prospect – and, as soon appeared, a reverse was in prospect most of the time.

The first problem was the Emperor's apparent indifference to the English and their present now that he had both safely installed in his capital. Accordingly, in August His Majesty disappeared on a month-long tour of the neighbouring Punjab, returned only to take to his sick bed, and rose from it only to get married. No sooner was the marriage ceremony over than he took to his bed once again. Needless to say, all public business, including the tedious petition of the English Company, was suspended throughout this period. It was November before Farrukhsiyar felt up to presiding over his interrupted nuptial festivities and at last taking delivery of the mission's present.

This four-month delay severely tested both Surman's patience and the Khwaja's humour. But it did produce an unexpected opening in that William Hamilton, the mission's doctor, was invited to prescribe for the Emperor. Initially Farrukhsiyar's complaint, no doubt the result of sexual excess, manifested itself in two large swellings in the groin. Hamilton successfully treated them and thus, in the patient's words, 'became privy to my nakedness'. This close relationship was renewed when the imperial tumours reappeared. Again Hamilton's ministrations proved effective and the Emperor was uncommonly grateful, showering Hamilton with favours and presents, including an elephant and a set of surgical instruments with shafts of solid gold.

There is, however, no evidence that the Emperor felt indebted to the mission as a whole nor that Hamilton was able to put his privileged position to any use in the matter of the *farman*. On the contrary, when along with the present the English at last submitted their detailed petition, it was simply referred to the clerks of the imperial treasury. More bribes changed hands but the treasury's comments on each of the nineteen articles merely queried precedents or implied that no *farman* was needed. A second petition designed to simplify the request fared no better. It was clear that Khan Dauran, the Emperor's favourite, had failed. After nine wasted months and many thousands of wasted rupees, Surman was advised to reapply through the *Wazir*.

Ignoring this advice, the mission continued to lobby the favourite. Again the *farman* was refused and amidst bitter recriminations against the Khwaja, Surman threatened to withdraw to Bengal. It was now July 1716, a year since the mission had arrived, seven months since the Emperor had been cured, six since the mission had parted with the present – and if anything the *farman* looked more remote than ever. So much for the oft-repeated story that it was thanks to the surgical skills of William Hamilton that the East India Company stole a march on its European rivals in India.

What did suddenly change the situation was a report from distant Surat to the effect that unless the English mission was satisfied, the Moghul governor there had reason to believe that the Company would withdraw its factories in Gujarat and so, in Surman's words, 'that port [Surat] would be ruined'. The threat was genuine enough. The Company's directors were again questioning the value of their Surat establishment which, unlike Calcutta or Madras, was still unfortified and hence vulnerable to every twitch in the protracted death throes of the Moghul Empire. But Surman had also taken a hand, urging the Bombay government to play up this threat. He appreciated that old reciprocity whereby the Moghul economy was nearly as dependent on the Company's bullion exports as the Company was on the Moghul's trade. And he was aware that in the case of Surat, the English presence remained the Moghul's only guarantee of a safe passage for his shipping in the Arabian Sea.

Thus, even as Surman was writing to Calcutta for permission to break off negotiations, Farrukhsiyar was reading the letter from his Surat governor 'which not a little startled him'. Suddenly the mission found that doors hitherto locked could be opened at a touch. They were urged to re-present their petition; the earlier objections of the treasury were quashed; the supposedly hostile *Wazir* eagerly processed the petition, 'our papers no sooner reaching his hands than they received despatch'; and on 20 November orders were issued for the preparation of the *farman*. 'With a little patience and good bribery', wrote Surman, 'our business may be now properly said to have received a good foundation; God grant a happy conclusion to the whole.' It was, he admitted, all thanks to that alarm over English intentions at Surat and, although both patience and bribery still had a big role to play, the *farman* received the imperial signatures on New Year's Eve 1716.

Where Captain Hawkins, Sir Thomas Roe, and Sir William Norris had failed, Surman had succeeded. But it was not in his sober nature to exult. A few years previously the Dutch had come away from Delhi with little more than the sort of assurances with which the imperial treasury had tried to fob off the English. More recently the Portuguese had successfully negotiated a substantial concession only to lose it for want of 'good bribery' in the final stages of ratification. But now the English had cleared every hurdle and were in possession of a lasting title to the most extensive commercial and territorial privileges ever granted to a foreign power. With a long-drawn sigh of relief Surman wrote of his 'inexpressible satisfaction'. There were of course further delays: the Khwaja again alienated his companions by trying to elicit some personal advantage; the Emperor desired that Dr Hamilton remain in his service and was little reassured by the latter's insistence that he must first go to England to replenish his medicines; and many fine points of protocol delayed the final exchange of presents. As a result the mission departed just as the monsoon broke and did not reach Patna till September and Calcutta till December 1717. There Surman finally closed his excruciating diary with a plea that has been little regarded.

> There is no other way of coming to a clear knowledge how this grand affair has suceeded than by a serious scrutiny and perusal of this book from the beginning to the end, for which purpose we heartily and humbly commend it to the Honourable President and Council of Bengal; for since we have acted directly under their influence, to them alone must be imputed the glory. Since the trade of Europeans in these parts [began], there have been sundry attempts of this kind, but the grants obtained have been of very little value though at a much superior expense. May those that we have gained be as lasting as they are great is our earnest wish.

The *farman* would indeed be treasured. But not so Surman's diary. In the early 1750s some pages from the original were 'picked up in a public necessary house [lavatory] which the writers make use of' (J. Long).

ii

News of Surman's success had reached Calcutta in May 1717. The new president, Robert Hedges, (a nephew of Agent William Hedges who had fallen foul of Job Charnock in pre-Calcutta days), promptly declared a public rejoicing. 'Agreed that next Wednesday we make a public dinner for all the Company's servants and a loud noise with our cannon and conclude the day with bonfires and other demonstrations of joy.' But although Surman wished all the credit for Bengal, the original initiative had come from Madras while the conclusive threat had come from Bombay/Surat. All the Presidencies felt equally involved and all received the news with equal satisfaction.

Nowhere were the celebrations more lavish than in Madras where a copy of the imperial *farman* was carried round the city in the Governor's state palanquin accompanied by the Mayor and Aldermen on horseback. A company of foot soldiers escorted them, and all the English merchants plus 'all the English music' followed behind. At each of the city's gates the document was held aloft and a proclamation read out to the effect that here was the imperial *farman* confirming all the Honourable Company's former grants and privileges and adding such extensive new privileges 'with the possession of several lands in many parts of India with such favour as has never before been granted to any European nation'. There followed a grand procession to the 'Tiping Garden' and a magnificent dinner with a 'bonefire' and 'feasting of the soldiers with tubs of punch' – total cost 1022 pagodas. All afternoon a deafening cannonade was in progress as a 151-gun salute from the shore batteries was taken up by the *Marlborough*, the largest ship in port, 'and when he was done, all the Europe ships in the road one after another, and the country ships upon the Europe ships finishing fired all together as fast as they could, the ships being handsomely dressed out with their colours and streamers'. This performance was repeated during dinner with additional salutes for each loyal toast to the Emperor, the King, the Company, etc.

Such extravagant celebrations were partly designed to impress the Moghul's provincial Nawabs; habitual oppressors of the Company, they were to note the extraordinary esteem in which the Emperor now held the English and the important new favours he had granted them. But it was not all bravado. At the time the Company's servants were genuinely excited by the terms of the *farman*; they construed them as giving their Honourable masters a winning advantage over their European rivals and as giving themselves, as private traders, unprecedented opportunities of exploiting the 'country trade'. Subsequently the value of the imperial concession, if anything, appreciated. By 1737 'our dear bought *farman*' had acquired an almost sacrosant character and in 1756 it was by citing the unfulfilled clauses of the *farman* that Robert Clive justified his march to Plassey. A decade later Clive would up the British stakes in India by obtaining the *diwani*, or governorship, of Bengal; but until that day the 1717 *farman* remained 'the Magna Carta of the Company in India'.

And all this in spite of the fact that within a year of Surman's return to Bengal Emperor Farrukhsiyar's brief reign was over. Deposed, imprisoned and blinded by the Sayyad brothers, in 1719 he was finally put out of his misery by strangulation. There followed two years of intrigue and bloodshed remarkable even by the grisly standards of the later Moghul Empire. In an opiate daze one epicene youth was bundled on to the throne only to be replaced within weeks by another consumptive apology-for-an-emperor who in turn coughed his last within a couple of months. Meanwhile anti-Emperors took the field and even the deaths of the string-pulling Sayyad brothers – they were, of course, murdered – failed to restore the imperial dignity. Thereafter all Moghul emperors were but puppets and ciphers. Whereas Aurangzeb and Farrukhsiyar's other illustrious predecessors had never deigned to grant a general *farman*, his wretched successors would never have dared to. The Company's timing had been impeccable.

On the other hand the English could forget about the idea of ever appealing to Delhi for the enforcement of their newly won privileges. In 1739 the Persian, Nadir Shah, occupied the capital and decamped with the Peacock Throne; thereafter the marble halls and sandstone galleries of Moghul might were desecrated by every conquering horde that camped by the Jumna river. After Surman, the next British party to enter Delhi's Red Fort on official business carried guns instead of presents and rather than flatter the incumbent emperor simply kidnapped him. The imperial seal retained its validity as the insignia of sovereignty and legitimacy, but in practice it was more ignored and defied than respected.

Under such circumstances it should come as no surprise that for the next two decades the story of English activities in India, and especially in Bengal, is largely one of abortive endeavours to enforce the terms of the *farman* and of bitter quarrels over their precise meaning. Technically there were in fact three *farman*, one of which was addressed to the Moghul governors and officials in Bengal, another to those of Hyderabad (within which province fell Madras and the Company's other settlements on The Coast), and the third to Ahmadabad (i.e. Gujarat including Surat). Each included a number of directives concerning the privileges to which the Company was entitled; some of these directives appeared in all three *farman*, others dealt with specific local concessions.

In the case of Bengal, the question (which had so exercised Agent Hedges) of commuting the *ad valorem* customs dues in favour of an annual lump sum payment of 3000 rupees (considerably less than the cost of those *farman* celebrations) was conceded. Similarly the grant of the three villages which comprised Calcutta was confirmed. Additionally a further thirty-eight villages, including some like Howrah on the other side of the Hughli river, were to be made available to the Company. There were two currency directives, one of which gave to rupees coined by the Company in Madras parity with those minted by the Bengal government, while the other entitled the Company to use the Bengal mint to turn its bullion into coin. Additionally there were two extra-territorial directives obliging the Bengal administration to apprehend and hand over any stolen goods, thieves, or debtors on whom the Company had a claim. Finally, besides a number of minor provisions, there was an important clause exempting all goods carried under a pass (*dastak*) issued by the Company's chief factors from being stopped, examined, or taxed anywhere within Bengal.

In a later age and another land these terms might have been called capitulations. But if the Moghul had capitulated, his increasingly independent nawabs, diwans and subahdars in the provinces certainly had not. Of all these directives not one was conceded without argument and not a few were never conceded at all.

The thirty-eight villages, for instance, were firmly withheld on orders from the Nawab. In Madras, as will be seen, similar prevarication in respect of villages granted under the *farman* led to open hostilities. But in Bengal the Company had to content itself with trying to arrange for the villages in question to be acquired by its Indian dependants. This was only partially successful and may help to explain why Fort William proved so vulnerable when it came to the great trial of strength in 1756.

If Calcutta could not immediately secure the adjacent villages (or *zamindari*) it could to some extent neutralize them by a strict exercise of its new rights to extra-territorial jurisdiction. A test case arose as early as 1719 when a Hindu who had speculated in Calcutta real estate absconded owing unspecified rents to the Company. He was tracked down in a neighbouring *zamindari* but when the Company's *barquandaz* (described as 'country gunmen' but evidently a rural militia) came in hot pursuit they were attacked and repulsed. The Company thereupon seized hostages from the defiant *zamindar* and he in turn apprehended some of the Company's tenants and plundered one of its agents. 'Such insolent treatment' could not be allowed to go unpunished. With a force of ninety foot and horse Captain Row was immediately ordered to the scene of the trouble. The *zamindar* again followed suit by raising a force of his own; it was put at over a thousand. But, in a series of skirmishes heavy with portent, the untrained, ill-armed levies of the *zamindar* were easily routed. 'We destroyed a great number of their people', reported Row, 'and burnt their villages which has at length obliged them to beg for peace on any terms.' The original debtor was surrendered, the hostages exchanged, and the *zamindar*'s force disbanded. 'We make no doubt', recorded the Calcutta Council, 'that this good effect will be a warning to other *zamindars* not only to refuse protection to any of our tenants, but also to deliver them up to us when demanded . . .'

Of course it was one thing to try strong-arm tactics with a neighbouring landlord, quite another to challenge the Nawab. Disregard of the *farman*'s currency concessions furnished ample provocation from this direction, but as yet the Company always chose to pay up rather than square up. No headway was made on the abolition of the unfavourable exchange rate for rupees minted in Madras. In fact in 1736 the *batta*, or discount, charged on them was neariy doubled. Squeals of protest from Calcutta eventually won a reduction but the disparity remained. Its object was clear enough – to encourage the Company to import the silver used to pay for its Bengal trade investment in the form of bullion rather than coin. And such an arrangement would also have suited the Company had it ever managed to secure that access to the Bengal mint which had been promised in the *farman*. But this too was consistently withheld. A cosy monopoly consisting of the Nawab and his Hindu bankers controlled the mint in an exclusive arrangement which they found both profitable and politic. By occasionally refusing to accept bullion they could quickly bring a European trading company to heel or, more often, to a lucrative accommodation. And should such a company try to hold out by borrowing money for its current investment, it would invariably find that the only loan available was from the same monopoly.

Thus did the Bengal treasury maintain a tight hold on the province's money supply, and all foreigners, not excepting the privileged English, did well to remember it. It was an important check, for in all other aspects the economy of Bengal was becoming increasingly – indeed decisively – dependent on the foreign companies. The English Company's trade in Bengal was already equal to that of all other foreign trading companies together and during the period 1717-27 it more than doubled; from contributing forty per cent of the Honourable Company's total imports, Bengal's share now rose to seventy per cent; and there can be no doubt that these dramatic improvements were all down to the greater security and improved trading terms associated with the *farman*.

But such statistics tell only half the tale. The other half, more difficult to quantify, is the undoubted increase in the volume and value of the 'country trade' conducted by the English. Almost every European in the East, be he ensign or ambassador, prelate or president, engaged in some branch of trade on his own account. The salaries paid its employees by the English Company were still miserly – £200 per annum for a president, £5 per annum for a writer. Even with generous allowances for subsistence and servants it was impossible to live in comfort, let alone make a fortune, without speculating in trade. And this was, of course, even truer of those 'private traders' who were not in the employ of any company. But the term 'private trade' had by this time become misleading. It could denote anything from the modest cargo space allowed by the Company to its factors and ships' captains on voyages to and from Europe to the entire evil-smelling contents of a Hughli barge that would never leave the river, or a part share in a many-decked Surat galleon sailing for the Red Sea.

'Country trade' was slightly more specific in that it denoted any trading activity that began and ended east of the Cape of Good Hope (so excluding St Helena and all European ports). This was the vast trading world, extending from Mocha to Manila, which the Company now accepted as being as legitimate a sphere of activity for its own servants as for those private traders, both European and native, who were outside its employ. All such traders and all such ventures were supposed to be registered in the Company's books and from them it derived a considerable income in the form of customs duties. Additionally, from 1718 a consulage fee of two per cent was levied on all exports from Calcutta.

Nevertheless, it is almost impossible to distinguish private trade or even country trade from that of the Company. An examination of the shipping records for Madras suggests that the number of Company ships calling there was greatly exceeded by the number of ships that did not belong to the Company. Of the latter some are described as Indian,

Armenian or Burmese but this did not preclude their officers being European or their cargoes being all or partly the ventures of European syndicates. Similarly even Company vessels often carried private cargoes since they were commonly leased out pending the favourable season for sailing home. From an examination of the detailed records kept by the Dutch at their Cochin factory, one writer has concluded that the tonnage of 'English country-shipping' more than doubled in the period 1724-42. And this leads him to an interesting conclusion: it was not the Company's 'out and back' trade but 'the steadily increasing participation in the maritime trade of Asia by Europeans in partnership – voluntary and involuntary – with local traders and seamen [which] was the foundation upon which the imperialism of more recent times was built' (H. Furber).

The country trade, then, offered Europeans a lucrative field of speculation that was both legitimate and of some commercial and political significance. Such activity only became reprehensible when someone who engaged in it abused his official position as an employee of, say, the Honourable Company to gain unfair advantage. Typical of such abuses was the use of the Company's money to finance a private investment, or the purchase by Company employees of goods supplied by these same employees as private traders. All those detected in such practices could expect to be dismissed from the Company's service. But there were other areas in which the Company's men enjoyed considerable advantage and where the modalities were far less clear.

For instance, the clause in Farrukhsiyar's *farman* which meant most to the Bengal factors was that endorsing the Company's right to issue *dastak*, or passes. Throughout Bengal, trade was regulated by a system of inland customs dues which applied to virtually everything and which made a considerable contribution to the government's revenue. Confirmation that all goods covered by a *dastak* from the Company should be exempt was therefore a valuable privilege. But the *farman* failed to specify exactly which goods were covered. According to the Nawab and his officials it was only those items, like silk, saltpetre, muslin and broadcloth, which the Company had traditionally imported or exported. According to the Company's men, though, it was any goods they cared to invest in, whether on the Company's behalf or their own and whether for export/import or for internal resale. Further widening of this loophole led to the inclusion of goods belonging to the Company's Indian agents, and there were soon instances of *dastak* coverage being sold to complete outsiders.

This was clearly contrary to the intention of the *farman* and elicited strong protests from the Bengal government. Fines were imposed for the abuse of *dastak* and quite legitimate consignments became liable to summary stoppage and examination. The Company, out of whose funds the fines were invariably paid, made several efforts to discipline its factors; but since those entrusted with enforcement of such orders were also those who stood to gain most by ignoring them, the abuses continued. From this period dates the heavy involvement of the English in the internal trade of Bengal. From Dhaka came complaints that English private trade now exceeded that of the Company, while in Patna it was said that it was more than double that of the Company.

The commodities involved included tobacco, betel, sugar and rice but it was over the river traffic in sea-salt that matters habitually came to a head. Abundantly available in the coastal regions of Bengal and Orissa, salt (sodium chloride) went upriver to Patna where it was eagerly purchased by traders from all over salt-starved upper India. The Company's trade with Patna, on the other hand, was in saltpetre (potassium nitrate) which was extracted in Bihar and shipped downriver. For this purpose the Company annually despatched from Calcutta a large fleet of river boats complete with military escort. What more natural than that for the upriver journey they should load the mostly empty boats with table salt? And what more responsible? Instead of selling guns for gold here was a European trading company buying gunpowder for condiments.

But under the Moghul Empire – as under the British 200 years later – salt duties were an important element in the revenue system. The Nawab took strong objection to the Company using its *dastak* to evade them and rightly guessed that the main culprits were acting in a private capacity. In 1727 government officers seized a huge consignment of salt *en route* to Patna and demanded 10,000 rupees for its release. Hoping to make their point, the Company's men refused and threatened to blockade the Hughli river by sinking any Moghul shipping that tried to pass Calcutta. The Nawab responded with an embargo on all English trade and began arresting the Company's representatives.

The quarrel eventually spread to other areas of contention and was not resolved till 1731 when the English made an ignominious submission. 'To prevent all misdemeanours and encroachments which we have made in our trade', John Stackhouse on behalf of the Company agreed 'not to trade in any goods but what are proper for Europe'. But this undertaking was never ratified by the President and Council in Calcutta.

And although orders were repeatedly issued by the Company against its servants engaging in the salt trade, the practice evidently continued, for in 1734 the escort for the Patna fleet are recorded as having mutinied rather than comply. For the time being the vigilance of the Nawab's government and the vulnerability of the Company's trade meant that abuses could not be allowed to get out of hand. Private trade, both within Bengal and beyond, nevertheless prospered and as the cancer at the heart of the Moghul Empire spread outwards, the private trader found new ways to assuage and circumvent the Nawab's officials.

iii

Over-all the impression must be that in the first half of the eighteenth century the trade of the English grew as much in spite of the *farman* as because of it. But if the Company appeared to acquiesce a little too readily in the Nawab's idea of what Farrukhsiyar had intended, it had its reasons. They came in the shape of a new breed of 'interlopers' – a word which, like 'fire' to the Bantam factors of old, could still panic the Court of Directors in London and set Leadenhall Street ablaze.

> We give you this early caution [wrote the directors to all their Indian presidencies in March 1717] that you do whatever lies in your power to disappoint the interlops expectations of trade either in the sale of goods brought from Europe, or in purchasing goods for Europe, or affording them the least assistance of provisions, necessaries, or other helps, which we think a very reasonable order to give considering this project . . . is of pernicious consequence to the trade of the nation, to His Majesty in the loss of customs, and to this Company who have paid £3,200,000 for the trade thither exclusive of all the subjects of the Crown of Great Britain.

Yet this 'early caution' seems not to have been heeded, for in the same year the directors had occasion to castigate their Madras servants for letting an interloper reprovision at San Thomé and their Bengal servants for selling silks to the same ship. Meanwhile Leadenhall Street was also frantically lobbying Parliament with the result that in 1719 the first of three Acts was passed outlawing British subjects who served under foreign flags. For, as with Samuel White's Siamese interlopers, the newcomers came with the blessing of a sovereign state – in this case the mighty Hapsburg Empire. To the English they were just 'Ostenders' or 'Flemings' but Ostend and Flanders were now, by the Treaty of Utrecht, under

Hapsburg protection and in 1723 it was from Vienna that the new company received its charter. Worse still, the Imperial or Ostend Company had not only formidable patronage but also considerable experience in that many of its backers and most of its supercargoes and skippers had previously served with the English Company. Some, with Jacobite sympathies, had sound political and religious reasons for their defection; most were simply attracted by the more generous allowances in terms of cargo space for private trade which the Ostend Company offered.

The alarm over the appearance of this new rival proved justified. Concentrating on Bengal and China, the Ostenders quickly established themselves as ruthless and highly successful traders. In vain did the English and the Dutch in Bengal disclaim any connection with them and appeal to the Nawab to do the same. 'The answer he made was that he did not care what nation they were so that they did but bring money.' That was in 1720. By 1726 the Ostend Company was able to declare a thirty-three per cent dividend: it now boasted a partly fortified factory at Bankibazar, just fifteen miles upriver from Calcutta, and subordinate establishments at most of the main Bengal trading centres. Silently the Ostend ships glided past the ramparts of Fort William, whence all intercourse with the renegades was strictly forbidden, while their energetic chief, one Alexander Hume, sweetened the Nawab with generous payments.

In the same year there came news from Europe that under pressure from the English and the Dutch the Emperor Charles VI had in fact suspended the Ostenders' charter. But it made little difference in Bengal. Evidently prepared for just such an eventuality, the resourceful Ostenders now claimed that they sailed 'under the King of Poland's pass' and that no one had ever 'called in question His Majesty of Poland's right to send ships with his passport to India'. To the Nawab, Polish, Austrian or Flemish, it was all the same. So long as they kept paying for their trading rights he remained deaf to the insinuations of the custom-free English and cunningly played off the Europeans one against the other.

In a bid to force the issue the English factors once again opted for aggression. With their Dutch allies they commissioned ships to patrol the mouth of the Hughli and others to keep the Ostenders penned up in their basin at Bankibazar. Additionally the contingent of troops annually raised to help escort the saltpetre convoy from Patna was kept under orders. But when a small Ostend vessel was actually taken, the Nawab threatened commercial retaliation and the prize was quickly restored. In

Bengal, as later on the Coromandel coast, so long as Moghul authority lasted, it acted as an effective brake on the rivalries of the European companies. But once it crumbled there would be nothing to stop every European quarrel from spreading to the trading settlements and thence, inevitably, to their hinterland.

In 1730 the tide at last began to turn against the Ostenders. Their trade had slowed and it was intimated that for a hefty payment the Nawab might now disown them and that for an even heftier payment he might overlook one exemplary assault. 325,000 rupees changed hands and the *Saint Therésa*, under Polish colours, was duly corralled into Calcutta. With some reason Hume, the Ostenders' chief, claimed that he had been betrayed. The English factors celebrated their victory as though it were a second Blenheim and quietly wrote off the military expenditure under 'extraordinary charges'. When interlopers were involved even the Court of Directors did not grudge the expense.

Until well into the 1740s the Ostend factory at Bankibazar lingered on. But it never again posed much of a challenge; and neither, for that matter, did the Danish East India Company, which reappeared in Bengal in the 1750s, or the Swedish East India Company – another 'company of convenience' formed by a group of ex-privateers from Madagascar. Much more serious, though, was the growing rivalry of the French. In 1719 the *Compagnie des Indes* was formed to regulate and expand the hitherto uncertain pattern of French endeavour in the East. Although occupied in 1690 it was only now that Chandernagar, the French settlement on the Hughli, began to prosper. In the 1730s under Joseph, Marquis de Dupleix the French trade in Bengal overtook that of the Dutch and was second only to the English. The French had refused to join in the concerted moves against the Ostenders and, as their investment grew, so did their resentment of the privileges and preponderance enjoyed by the English. In 1742 Dupleix was transferred to Pondicherry and the governorship of the French possessions on the Coromandel coast. The English in Bengal heaved a sigh of relief; but Calcutta's reprieve was to prove Madras's downfall.

CHAPTER TWELVE

Outposts of Effrontery

THE LESSER SETTLEMENTS

In managing the affairs of Calcutta, Bombay or Madras, the president/governor was expected to act in consort with his council. This body usually had six to nine members, all senior factors several of whom, as with cabinet ministers, held specific posts like accountant, storekeeper, sea customs collector. In Madras in the early eighteenth century the council met once a week in Fort St George, the consultation beginning at 6 a.m. to avoid the heat and rarely lasting beyond midday. All resolutions, along with any relevant documents and reports, were minuted and entered in a register, 'The Diary and Consultations' books, which invaluable record thus provides a fairly detailed picture of day-to-day concerns.

Here great events, like the granting of the *farman* or the reappearance of the 'interlops', are seen to engage anxious attention; but they are not necessarily given that prominence which history has subsequently accorded them. Sometimes they are quite swamped by matters of distinctly lesser moment; and it is this juxtaposition of affairs of state with domestic trivia – of the Nawab's latest ultimatum with an inventory of the humble effects of some late lamented ensign– which gives the records their considerable charm.

The Company's London directors, whose letters to India were recorded in separate volumes, also made no clear distinction between important policy directives and seemingly petty exhortations. 'Enclosed we send you 2 declarations of war with Spain', begins paragraph 44 of their letter of October 1718. Such startling news comes almost as a reassurance when read in the context of a far longer previous paragraph in which the gentlemen of Leadenhall Street are clearly beside themselves with rage over the drinks bill for the public table at Fort St George. 'This is an extravagancy', they tell President Collet and his Council, 'that every one of you ought to blush at the thought of – to give 9 Pagodas [about 30 rupees] a dozen for Burton ale.' 'If you must have liquors at such prices, pray gratify your pallats at your own, not our, expence.'

Soon after this outburst the public table at which all the Company's officials had once been obliged to dine, but were now simply entitled to dine, was abolished. Instead each received a fixed diet allowance in addition to his salary. The days of collegiate living were gone. From their factories and their forts the English community was venturing forth into the bazaars and the neighbouring countryside. While the President and his colleagues acquired garden estates and airy mansions, the lower orders thronged the punch houses and sampled the local flesh trade. At a Consultation held on 29 April 1717, the President announced that he had 'received very full evidences against Daniel Haines, sentinel, for being guilty of so beastly an action as is not fit to be mentioned in this register'. Given that three months previously one John Boggins, also a sentinel, had been, according to the same register, 'surprised in a sodometical attempt', one wonders about this new abomination. Close confinement on a diet of rice and water, followed by speedy deportation, was the punishment for such unnatural conduct; in this case both men were consigned to penal servitude on the island of St Helena. They were packed aboard the same ship, doubtless happy enough in one another's company.

Although the soldiers of Fort St George were willing to venture forth in search of gratification, they were not yet anxious to invite a military engagement beyond the range of their cannon. In 1701 Thomas Pitt had stood his ground against Daud Khan from within the fort's ramparts. Subsequently he had ordered the fortification of Black Town but as fast as the walls enclosed new ground, further settlements grew up beyond them. Additionally, under the terms of the 1717 *farman*, the English acquired five townships on the outskirts of Madras, one of which, Trivitore (Tiruvottiyur), was a good two hours' march from Fort St George.

Ten years previously these same townships had been made over to Thomas Pitt and then reclaimed by the Nawab on the pretext that the grant was personal to the President; thus when Pitt left, the villages must revert. The Company had protested but had not felt able to risk hostilities. Now, in 1717, the *farman* clearly made over these villages in perpetuity and to the Company rather than to one of its servants. They were duly occupied by the English in September of the same year and, when the Nawab objected, President Collet sat back to await developments, boldly declaring his intention of defending the Company's rights 'to the utmost of our power'.

At the time the Madras garrison consisted of about 360 Europeans, some recruited locally, others sent from England; it was the common belief that the latter had chosen the Company's service in preference to one of His Majesty's prisons. They were divided into three companies, each under an English lieutenant and including both horse and foot. A few of these 'sentinels' had some military experience; most knew no more of warfare than the trained bands of 'peons' and the Portuguese 'topazes' who were recruited in the bazaar and could be summoned from their various trades as a makeshift reserve whenever needed.

On 18 October there arrived at Fort St George a Brahmin intermediary who, 'after a very long harangue wide of his purpose', intimated that the Nawab's troops would reoccupy the five townships unless a substantial cash payment was immediately forthcoming. However, so long and so wide of its purpose was the Brahmin's harangue that before he had unburdened himself of the final ultimatum, news arrived that Trivitore had already been attacked. A force of 1250 had entered the township, torn down the Company's flagstaff, and was apparently determined to stay put.

At the uncongenial hour of 5 p.m. President Collet convened an extraordinary meeting of his Council. The issue was simple. Either they should buy peace and 'sit down tamely with the affront given us of cutting down our flag', or they must 'make a vigorous charge with our forces and endeavour to drive them out'. For once the Madras garrison was up to strength, 'pretty well disciplined and completely officered'. The council had no doubt that it could perform the task in question and that, thanks to the *farman*, they would be acting well within their rights. The final vote was unanimous; at 2 a.m. the following morning Lieutenant Roach with 150 men marched out of the fort. He fell upon Trivitore as dawn broke. The enemy 'presuming we durst not march out of the reach of our cannon' were surprised and dispersed; a second company under Lieutenant Fullerton chased off further marauders; and at nightfall both companies marched back to Fort St George in triumph.

The enemy's losses were put at six horses, a camel, and perhaps a dozen men. The English had sustained no casualties at all thanks, it was said, to the great skill of Lieutenant Roach, who was rewarded with promotion to major, command of all the English forces on The Coast, and a 'gold medal set with diamond sparks (value 300 Pagodas)'. With passing mention, under Extraordinary Charges, of a celebratory feast ('cost 700 Pagodas') the Trivitore affair disappears from the records. And so back to business with news of a property auction in Black Town and of a hefty fine for one Dr Jolly who had disgraced both his nation and his name by 'cruelty in ye treatment of slaves and servants'.

Dr Jolly practised – it is not clear whether his doctorate was in medicine or divinity – at Cuddalore, a port 100 miles south of Madras and near to the French settlement of Pondicherry. It had been acquired by the Company in 1688 and subsequently fortified and renamed Fort St David. Now the second most important English settlement on The Coast, it was more defensible than Madras and a useful vantage point from which to observe and frustrate the energies of the French *Compagnie des Indes*. To Fort St David the English would withdraw after the fall of Madras and from Fort St David Stringer Lawrence and Robert Clive would launch their bid for revenge.

For all its inconsequence, the Trivitore affair had revealed the English as capable of limited military intervention in the increasingly lawless hinterland. As in Bengal, so in Golconda (Hyderabad) the Moghul empire was falling apart at its seams. The Emperor's authority no longer availed the Nawab, or Nizam, in Hyderabad, and in turn the Nizam's authority was no longer paramount in the conduct of his subordinate nawab, and Madras's immediate neighbour, in the Carnatic sub-province. Additionally the Marathas, the scourge of western India, were now extending their raids into both Bengal and the Carnatic. Indeed it was from the Marathas that the English had purchased Cuddalore (Fort St David). Finding themselves uneasily wedged between the devil of political turmoil and the deep blue sea of the Bay of Bengal, the English on The Coast increasingly looked to the likes of Major Roach for their security, and it was a heavy blow when the gallant Major, within weeks of his promotion, succumbed to the temptations of private trade and absconded on a speculative voyage to Manila. As a result of the Trivitore affair the garrison had been increased and new fortifications put in hand, the additional cost being defrayed by a land tax. Echoing the sentiments of Sir Josiah Child, the President explained that since greater security benefited those with substantial land-holdings, it was reasonable that they should pay for it.

Some premonition of the looming chaos may well have guided Collet's predecessor, Edward Harrison, in his plans for the acquisition of

Divi Island. This was a spit of low-lying land just off Masulipatnam, the main port of Hyderabad where Madras still maintained a small satellite factory. The island had originally been requested by Thomas Pitt in his negotiations with Ziau-ud-Din and had finally been granted to the Company in an order from Delhi which accompanied the 1717 *farman*. Susceptible as ever to the charms of off-shore development, the English factors had in the meantime represented Divi as another paradise favoured with abundant timber, excellent water, soil 'fruitful to a wonder', and a capacious harbour. There was no doubt, Harrison reported, 'that the unsufferable usage under the Moor's government upon the mainland will people the island with the most useful persons for the manufactures [of piece goods] and that a handsome revenue may be raised'. By way of preparation for the hand-over, a fifty man garrison had been sent to Masulipatnam and a shallow-draft 'galley' constructed at Madras for shuttling settlers to the new colony.

But Harrison had never actually seen Divi and Collet, his successor, with perhaps a better appreciation of the island's limited potential, was distinctly cool about the whole idea. Moreover, as with the five townships, it was already clear that Farrukhsiyar's generosity did not meet with the Nizam's approval. By 1719 the island had still not been handed over and the Nizam was insisting that since the grant had not actually been included in the *farman* itself but had been the subject of a separate directive, its validity was questionable now that Farrukhsiyar was no more.

In July 1719 Collet and his Council steeled themselves for a long debate on the subject. The Nizam's argument was dismissed for what it was – a ruse to elicit a hefty *douceur*. Already considerable sums had been disbursed to the Hyderabad government and duly condemned by the Court of Directors in London who urged Collet to 'look back into Governor Pitt's time' and emulate his 'husbandry'. This seemed to preclude the possibility of simply buying off the Nizam. Further careful perusal of the Company's orders also suggested that the use of force was not encouraged. Had Collet and his Council felt more enamoured of the project they would undoubtedly have ignored what was simply a routine caution. But Divi was 200 miles up the coast and uncomfortably close to the Nizam's centre of power. Unlike at Trivitore there could be no guarantee of a speedy outcome. On the whole, therefore, and 'under the restrictions we now lie', the Council voted to back down.

Divi was not to be another Bombay nor even another Pulo Run. At this point it disappears not only from the records but also from the maps.

Presumably siltation in the Kistna river delta reclaimed it for the mainland. But like Trivitore, its brief eminence had necessitated a modest increase in the Company's military expenditure. With every furlong of new fortification and with every grant of new territory, putative or real, more sentinels were needed, another ensign was appointed, a new gunnery expert was recruited. By 1720, computing the garrisons of Fort St George, Fort St David and Masulipatnam/Divi, the Madras military establishment had risen to about 800 of whom a third were Europeans. The directors, of course, objected. 'Remember the soldiers are a standing monthly charge which eats deep into the profits of our trade', they had cautioned in 1718. They suspected their servants of being more interested in 'a bare show of grandeur' than in proper 'husbandry'; Governor Pitt would never have countenanced such extravagance.

Nevertheless The Coast's military establishment seems to have remained at about 800 throughout the 1720s and 1730s. In 1742 the acquisition of further townships, plus the threat of a Maratha attack, prompted another increase, especially in the number of Europeans, which brought the total to 1200. Along with the trained bands of Madras and whatever troops could be spared from the Company's ships, this was the military nucleus with which the English faced the troubled times ahead. While Trivitore and Divi had shown the Company not averse to extending its territorial commitments, they had also shown it as anxious as ever to disavow the risk and expense involved. Against a determined challenge, whether Indian or European, the military establishment remained totally inadequate. Survival and eventual triumph in the Carnatic would depend on a new recruitment policy at home, on the raising of a native army, and above all on the availability of Royal regiments and of the Royal Navy.

ii

In deciding against the forcible occupation of Divi Island the Madras Council had taken into consideration the extent and vulnerability of its other territorial commitments. Besides Fort St David (Cuddalore) and Masulipatnam, the president in Madras was heir to the Company's often forgotten and always mismanaged settlements in the Indonesian archipelago. And it was from there in 1719, during the week before the final decision on Divi, that reports began to reach the Madras Council of another of those dismal affrays which had so often punctured the Company's self-assurance in the past.

Known simply – if confusingly – as 'the West Coast', all that now remained of the spice-laden dreams of the Middletons and Jourdain was a place called York Fort, otherwise Benkulen, in south-west Sumatra, plus its several outposts scattered along 300 miles of adjacent but harbour-less shoreline. Following the loss of trading rights at Bantam (Java) in 1683, it was to Sumatra and Benkulen that the English had removed. They had been there ever since. As in the days of James Lancaster, they bought what they could in the way of Sumatran pepper and sold what they could in the way of Indian cottons. The pattern of trade had scarcely changed in more than a century.

Neither, unfortunately, had its volume. To increase and regulate the pepper supply, various schemes were tried including the establishment of plantations for which, as in St Helena, convicts and slaves were imported. But Benkulen remained a trial both to the Company's directors and to its servants. Rarely did the pepper yield even cover the standing costs of the place; the climate was even more poisonous than that of Bombay; and the opportunities for private trade were decidedly limited. It was not a popular destination. Only the disgraced and the truly desperate found their way to 'the West Coast'.

Such a one had been Joseph Collet, the future President of Madras, when he had launched his Eastern career by accepting the governorship of Benkulen in 1712. One may judge of his plight by his need to borrow not only the surety money customarily demanded by the Company of its senior agents, but also the wherewithal to pay for his outfit plus a few hundred pounds 'venture' money with which to launch his private trade. He was in fact a bankrupt who was further beset by the misfortune of having numerous female dependants plus an over-scrupulous conscience. The former expected him to provide for them, the latter insisted that he honour even debts from which the courts had discharged him. Collet was at his wits' end. As a born-again Baptist he could hardly contemplate suicide; but he could contemplate Fort York, regarded by many as an equally certain way of putting an end to things.

Happily for the righteous, Collet's great gamble paid off. Confounding predictions, he invested his trading capital so shrewdly that within three years he had satisfied his creditors. He was also able to relieve his impoverished daughters by sending home sumptuous presents – a slave girl to one, a length of chintz to another, and in time substantial dowries for all. Not without scares he survived Sumatra's malarial plagues for his full four-year term and in so doing outlasted most of those senior to him in the Madras hierarchy. Hence his reward, the premier post in India, the Presidency of Fort St George, to which he succeeded in 1717.

By then he had introduced some important changes on the West Coast which included the construction of Fort Marlborough, a substantial edifice which replaced Fort York and which was still garrisoned a century later when Thomas Raffles took up residence. He had also reorganized the Sumatran pepper trade and predicted a great future for the settlement if only others would follow his example. Time and again Collet had had occasion to complain about the quality of the men sent to serve under him. A Mr Ballard 'drank himself dead a few weeks after his arrival' while Sergeant Eaton, the bearer of impeccable credentials, was arraigned for 'mutiny, piracy and murder' before he had even stepped ashore. Raising moral standards had been even more difficult than raising the pepper yield but by 1715 Collet was already reviewing his labours and seeing that they were good. Another long-awaited recruit had just turned out to be 'a notorious drunkard, a profane swearer and a scandalous defamer'. 'Perhaps formerly he might have met with fit associates in this place', wrote the righteous Collet, 'but I must say that the general reformation of manners here is such as I believe will hardly find credit in England.'

However, intimations that the prospects for Benkulen were not quite as rosy as Collet had suggested began to surface as soon as he left. Trade was again declining and in a letter of 1717 the directors returned to the attack, admonishing their West Coast factors in language that even wayward imbeciles might comprehend. 'We have by every ship pressed you urgently for pepper, showed you the reasons, told you it is the one thing necessary expected of you, urged the charge we are at to obtain it, and allowed all needful disbursements to enable you to get it.' So where was it? In the old days a ship of 600 tons might call at one of the Sumatran pepper ports and come away with a full lading within a matter of weeks. Now, though maintaining a resident staff, a fort, warehouses and plantations, the Company was lucky to get half that much a year. 'Promise upon promise' had been made, 'fine stories' told of new plantations and advantageous arrangements with the native powers. Yet the flow of pepper dwindled and the catalogue of excuses grew. 'Good words will no longer go down with us', they fulminated. A series of minor skirmishes with the local tribes had supposedly disrupted supplies. Did the Benkulen factors not appreciate that just and civil treatment was the only way to guarantee trade and that every instance of oppression 'though it lie for a while festering, will at last break out into a dangerous if not incurable sore'?

These prophetic words were accompanied by paragraph upon paragraph of miscellaneous censure, not all of it unwarranted. The directors were especially scathing about Collet's claimed 'reformation of manners', 'You tell us that all are now diligent, no drunkenness and revelling permitted, all candles are out and all gone to bed before ten at night . . . which is owing to the regular living and good table you keep.' But how then to explain Fort Marlborough's quite astronomical liquor bills which in one month alone came to more than the value of all the pepper exported that year. 'The monstrous month' in question was July 1716, the last of Collet's term, during which the nineteen covenanted servants entitled to the Company's table appeared to have consumed '74 dozen and a half of wine [mostly very expensive Claret], 24 dozen and a half of Burton Ale and pale beer, 2 pipes and 42 gallon of Madeira wine, 6 Flasks of Shiraz [Persian wine], 274 bottles of toddy, 3 Leaguers and 3 Quarters of Batavia arrack, and 164 gallons of Goa [toddy]'.

> It is a wonder to us that any of you live six months, and that there are not more quarrellings and duellings amongst you, if half these liquors were guzzled down . . . We will not have our wine spent but at meals. If you will have it at other times, pay for it yourselves.

Alas, and unknown to the directors in London, their West Coast factors were already 'paying for it'. This revealing letter only survives in the Madras records because it was never forwarded to Benkulen; for by the time it reached Madras, Benkulen was no longer a Company settlement.

Not that Madras was as yet aware of the disaster. In 1718 there had been more evidence of the pepper crisis with one ship being sent away from Benkulen empty and another dispatched home only half laden. There had also been accusations of perfidious treatment of the natives and rumours of a general uprising. But Collet in Madras was more preoccupied with a bitter power struggle among the English in Sumatra which threatened to undo all his good works there. After barely six months in office, his highly commended successor had been implicated in a sensational fraud and sent to England to answer for it. The man deputed to investigate the matter, who evidently had the confidence of the directors but not of Collet, took over the governorship only to be himself arraigned for a series of misdemeanours and sent a prisoner to

Madras. Thomas Cooke, the new inquisitor and one of Collet's subordinates, succeeded.

Benkulen had thus had four governors in two years. It was indicative of the West Coast's plight and, since each renounced his predecessor's commitments, it did nothing for peaceful relations with the local sultans. Besides crimes against the Company, one of the partisan factors stood accused of murdering two Malays, having first removed their fingers joint by joint. Such 'provoking conduct' had apparently resulted in a state of undeclared war, for another factor is accused of incompetence in suppressing a revolt and there is mention of much wanton destruction in the pepper plantations.

But Collet had full confidence in Cooke, his new appointee, and had already congratulated him on having restored order. He was thus happily pursuing the charges against Cooke's predecessor when the first news from the archipelago reached Madras in 1719. It consisted of a slim and soiled package delivered by a Dutch vessel that had happened to call at Moco-Moco, one of Benkulen's remote outstations. The covering letter read as follows.

> To the Governor or Chief of any English Factory or Commander of a Ship.
>
> Sir,
> The occasion of this is to signify the great importance of the accompanying packet, directed to Fort St George, to acquaint the President of the bad state of affairs on the West Coast of Sumatria [*sic*]. Fort Marlborough being quite destroyed accidentally by fire, the Governor [Cooke], his Council and all the Europeans left the place about two months past and embarked on board ship *Masulipatnam*, whom we have not heard of since; so that we are left destitute, standing in need of everything for support, and what is worse, the natives are at war, besides but little gunpowder to defend this factory. Pray expedite the packet that some relief may be sent us. Having no ship or any other vessel, therefore we must all of necessity perish if not succoured in a little time. I salute you with my respects and am, Sir, Your distressed Brother, William Ballett.
>
> Moco-Moco Factory
> June 4 1719

This letter does not appear in the Madras records which are strangely reticent about the whole disaster; presumably President Collet was too embarrassed by his protégé's failure. But by the Bengal Council, never averse to point up its rivals' shortcomings, it was copied in full together with further particulars gleaned from Cooke and his fellow survivors when they eventually reached India by way of Dutch Batavia (Jakarta). From these it appears that the burning of Benkulen was no accident. The place was first cut off by a mass revolt of the natives; in taking to their boats about thirty of the English were either massacred or drowned; the whole settlement was then fired. It was as complete a fiasco as Pulo Condore. Happily Ballett and his 'distressed' colleagues at Moco-Moco were speedily relieved; but it was over two years before the English returned to Benkulen and then only after firm commitments from the sultans and a directive from London that Madras never again interfere in the appointment of governors.

iii

One reason why the Company persisted with loss-making establishments like Benkulen was its reluctance to write off a substantial investment or to relinquish hard-won privileges. Additionally there was every likelihood that, if it withdrew, its rivals – interlopers, Dutch, or French – would quickly move in. And as the danger of European wars engrossing eastern waters became an imminent certainty, such places began to assume a military and logistical importance that overshadowed all else.

The classic case was St Helena. With the Dutch now firmly established at the Cape, and with the French laying claim to the nearby islands of Réunion (Île de Bourbon) and Mauritius (Île de Dauphine or Île de France), St Helena became the English Company's only safe haven, watering place, and larder on the direct route between India and England. The island had no commercial value and, though the directors periodically demanded that it achieve self-sufficiency, it remained a financial burden and an administrative liability. In terms of climate it could only be an improvement on Benkulen but this advantage was offset by a baneful influence not unknown in other Company settlements but here found in an extreme form. 'There seems to have been something about St Helena', explains the island's annalist, 'some sort of spell, which had a disastrous effect upon clergymen.' Almost without exception those sent to minister to the island's spiritual needs contrived to scandalize their congregation and infuriate their superiors; many were clearly mad, most alcoholic.

In other respects there was little to choose between St Helena and Sumatra. Governor Pyke, having ruled the former with a rod of iron for five long years, was deemed just the man to re-establish the Benkulen factory in 1721. His stint on the West Coast again lasted five years and he then returned to St Helena for a further seven years. In shuttling between these two equatorial outposts he was not alone. Hardship ratings as well as the logic of shipping dictated that the only appropriate corrective, short of the gallows, for a St Helenan miscreant was to be exiled to Benkulen and for a Sumatran offender to be exiled to St Helena.

Only Gombroon (Bandar Abbas) on the Persian coast enjoyed a less fashionable reputation. Mocha in the Red Sea had prospered with the increasing demand for coffee but Gombroon, in spite of that share of the customs dues won by Weddell after the siege of Hormuz, remained a place of negligible trade and less enchantment. A sailor's adage of the period had it that 'only an inch of deal stands between Gombroon and Hell'. 'You cannot get excited about Gombroon', wrote James Douglas, the Bombay historian. 'It would be difficult to select a place less known or less calculated to awaken an interest of any kind in the reader.' Point taken.

Excluding the China trade, that leaves just the Company's scattered trading stations on India's west coast. Collected in a haphazard fashion during the previous century and originally adminstered from Surat, these now comprised three settlements, Karwar, Tellicherry, and Anjengo, each controlled from Bombay and each roughly equidistant from the other in a chain that stretched down the coast to its southernmost tip. As with Benkulen, pepper was the mainstay of all three and, as with Benkulen, all were 'run at a loss for the private benefit of their chiefs and factors as country traders' (H. Furber). As the first landfalls on the Indian coast for shipping from England, they were also important communications centres whence news from Europe could be dispatched by runner or coastal craft to Madras, Bombay and Calcutta. It was this prior access to information often of considerable commercial value which made for the popularity of a Malabar posting.

In 1717 by order of the Bombay Council, Anjengo, the most southerly, was entrusted to the Governor's favourite, one William Gyfford, who accompanied by his young and attractive bride duly took up residence in the little seaside fort nestling amongst the palm fronds between Quilon and Trivandrum in what is now the state of Kerala. Elsewhere the English were celebrating the news of Farrukhsiyar's *farman*, but in

Anjengo the Company's 'Magna Carta' was an irrelevance. Moghul rule had never extended to the extreme south and even when, at the turn of the century, Aurangzeb had pushed his authority on the east coast as far down as Madras, on the west coast around Bombay the Marathas had already reclaimed a vast Hindu patrimony. Thus isolated from the ebb and the flow of Moghul-Maratha rivalry, the lush coastline of Kerala was still divided into a patchwork of minor Principalities and trading centres with a political and commercial profile more like that of the south-east Asian archipelago than India.

Anjengo had been acquired in 1693 by arrangement with the local rani, or queen, at nearby Attingal. She is said to have fallen in love with a 'beautiful' young English emissary who, although rejecting the chance of a royal wedding, 'satisfied her so well' that she could scarcely refuse his countrymen anything. As is the way with lovers, she later regretted her generosity and especially the grant of Anjengo. But by 1717 she had passed away and been succeeded, as was customary among the matrilineal Nair caste, by a new queen. At first Gyfford, like his predecessors, was sorely torn between the political temptation of meddling with the peculiarities of Nair sovereignty and the commercial imperative of monopolizing the pepper trade for his personal gain. Two years of intrigue, strife and precious little trade seemed to cure him of the first; and in 1721, 'flushed with the hopes of having peace *and* pepper', he conceived the idea of making amends by leading a grand deputation to the royal court in Attingal.

Bearing gifts in pale imitation of the Surman embassy, he assembled most of the Anjengo establishment, numbering over a hundred, paddled up river and then processed through the coconut groves, flags aloft, to the beat of a drum and the tinkle of 'country music'. 'The details of what followed are imperfectly recorded and much is left to conjecture', writes Colonel John Biddulph (whose own exploits on the wrong side of the Himalayas would, five generations later, also leave much to conjecture). One of rather few Victorian officers to write sympathetically about the Company's 'Dark Age', Biddulph examined the Anjengo affair in some detail and concluded that Gyfford was inveigled into the ambush less by the Nairs' cunning than by his own conceit. Surrounded, disarmed and hopelessly outnumbered, he dashed off a note to those left at Anjengo which ended with a wonderfully absurd 'Take care and don't frighten the women; we are in no great danger'. Minutes later the massacre began. Gyfford himself had his tongue cut out, the tongue was then nailed to his chest, and he then nailed to a log and sent floating down the river. The rest of the deputation were simply dismembered; just twenty horribly mangled survivors made it back to the fort.

There the young Mrs Gyfford and Anjengo's two other Englishwomen were quickly bundled aboard a native longboat. Four weeks later they came ashore in Madras, dishevelled and destitute. Their plight excited great sympathy and even wrung from the Fort St George council a small compensatory allowance. There was, however, some doubt whether Mrs Gyfford would accept charity. Although barely twenty-six years old she had had the presence of mind to come away from Anjengo with the factory records and a useful sum of money which she claimed as belonging to her late husband. She knew better than to let grief get the better of business and she had every intention of extracting more than charity from her husband's employers. For, as will appear, she had been widowed before.

Meanwhile back at Anjengo a long and occasionally heroic siege had ensued. The defendants, down to about thirty-five in number, were marooned on the sand spit where stood their stout but roofless fort. They had access to the sea and received occasional supplies and reinforcements. But it was six months before the relief expedition arrived from Bombay, raised the siege, chastised the Nairs and restored the pepper trade. Such was the cost of condiments, such still the value of the spice trade.

Three hundred miles up the Malabar coast, Tellicherry had requested military assistance from Madras in 1714 and, according to one visitor, was continuously at war with the local Nairs from at least 1703. 'This war and fortifications has taken double the money to maintain them that the Company's investments came to.' The writer was none other than the garrulous Captain Alexander Hamilton whose more than thirty years before the eastern mast had taken him to just about every port between the Cape and Canton. On his last visit to Tellicherry in 1723 the factors were still hard at war with their neighbours.

Karwar, midway between Tellicherry and Bombay, the Captain knew even better. For here, in 1717, he had found himself in the unlikely role of commodore of a fleet of Company warships. How a private trader, renowned for his outspoken criticism of the Company and cordially detested by its factors from Gombroon to Canton, came by the command of its Bombay fleet is something of a mystery. Earlier in the year Hamilton's ship, *en route* from the Persian Gulf, had been assailed by a fleet of Gujarati pirates. Belying his years, the Captain had shown great courage and resourcefulness in disengaging from them and it was presumably news of this action which commended him to the Bombay Council as a doughty commander. He was promptly engaged at eighty rupees a month and sent off with a small squadron to chastise the Raja of Karwar, then besieging the Company's factory.

The expedition was not a great success and within six months Hamilton had resigned his commission and resumed the free and easy life of a private trader. For the trouble at Karwar, as at Tellicherry and Anjengo, he blamed the Company's local chief who 'pretended to be Lord of the Manor', appropriating the profits of the pepper trade to his personal account and antagonizing the Raja with an assortment of contentious claims. Hamilton would have none of it, and was so thoroughly disgusted by the whole affair that his account of the expedition and of its negotiations gives no hint that the author was in fact its commander and chief negotiator.

The disasters at Anjengo and Benkulen, and the near disasters at Karwar and Tellicherry, could be largely ascribed to the inconsistencies of Company policy when left in the hands of ambitious and vindictive men who put personal advantage first. Private trade as conducted by the Company's employees was certainly no crime and not necessarily an evil. It attracted into the Company's service a brand of extraordinarily resourceful and rugged individuals; it relieved the Company of the need to remunerate them properly, and it contributed as much to the growth of British commercial predominance in the East as the Company's own trade. But, particularly in the remoter settlements, it also bred a contempt for the Company's cumbrous and moralizing ways and a devotion to ruthless opportunism. Closer supervision would have helped but was scarcely practical when it could take three to four months to get an approval from Bombay or Madras and at least a year from London. Only war, or some similar danger perceived as common to the whole English community, could effect a closing of ranks, a burying of hatchets.

CHAPTER THIRTEEN

One Man's Pirate

BOMBAY AND THE ANGREYS

In 1737 Lieutenant Clement Downing published a curious narrative called *A History of the Indian Wars*. It was curious because the Company's Indian wars are not usually supposed to have started till after 1737. Downing, however, was referring not to the imminent exploits of Clive and Lawrence but to the confused and protracted hostilities waged by the Bombay Presidency against the Maratha navy during the first half of the eighteenth century. The same struggle forms the main subject matter of Colonel Biddulph's *The Pirates of Malabar*, another curious title in that the Marathas were not from that section of India's western seaboard usually described as the Malabar Coast; nor were they pirates.

Native pirates certainly existed. The Gujarati Sanganians against whom Hamilton had so distinguished himself qualified, as did the Muscat Arabs whose forays reached as far south as the real Malabar. But to describe as pirates all those local rulers on India's west coast who maintained a squadron of fighting ships was a peculiarly English conceit. True the records abound with references to buccaneers with exotic names like 'The Sow Raja', 'The Seedee' and 'The Kempsant'; but on closer inspection these same rogues turn out to be legitimate sovereigns and feudatories going about their usual business of defending a section of the coastline and policing the merchant traffic that used it. 'The Kempsant' was in fact the Khem Sawant Raja of Wadi, the Sidi the Moghuls' naval contractor, and 'The Sow Raja' Satravati Shahu, the legitimate claimant to the Maratha throne. One man's pirate is another man's patriot; in Maratha eyes the worst offenders were undoubtedly those ships which flew the Company's flag.

Pressed to define its legal position, the Company would no doubt have invoked those turbulent times in Surat at the turn of the century when Moghul displeasure over the activities of Captain Kidd and his colleagues had obliged the European companies to accept some responsibility for the suppression of piracy. Thus the Dutch and the French had assumed the job of policing the Red Sea route out of Surat, while the English had taken on 'the southern seas', i.e. the route down the west coast. But this arrangement was intended principally to meet the now declining threat of European piracy, not Indian. The Moghuls had no better claim to the sovereignty of 'the southern seas' than the English; and anyway Moghul sovereignty was now a fiction.

Howsoever, the protracted hostilities between Bombay and its maritime neighbours – in which Downing actually took part – were unquestionably wars. They necessitated the formation of the Bombay Marine, later to become the Indian Navy; they witnessed a greater build-up of Company troops than had yet been necessary anywhere in the East; and they occasioned the first deployment of ships belonging to the King's navy against an Asian enemy. Additionally these wars taught the English much about the shortcomings of their military arrangements and eventually presented them with some of their first martial heroes. If the weakness of the Company's position on land would be first exposed and then rectified in the Carnatic, its weakness at sea would be similarly tested and then rectified in the struggles with the 'Malabar Pirates'. For Bombay it was at times a life-and-death struggle bringing trade to a standstill. But out of it the city emerged from irrelevance as India's premier port and 'the grand storehouse of all the Arabian and Persian commerce'. According to Surgeon Edward Ives the island was, by 1754, 'perhaps the most flourishing of any this day in the universe'.

It was also in these wars that the Anjengo widow Mrs Katherine Gyfford, née Cooke, had learnt to make the most of adversity. By the time of the Anjengo affair she was already a celebrity, twice widowed, once captured. Deservedly to her belongs the distinction of being the first Englishwoman to earn a place in the Company's history.

It had all begun at Karwar in the year 1709 when the *Loyal Bliss*, outward bound for Bengal and carrying the family of Gerrard Cooke, a Fort William gunner, had put in for fresh supplies and water. Twelve days later the *Loyal Bliss* resumed her voyage minus Katherine, the eldest Cooke daughter. 'A most beautiful lady not exceeding thirteen or fourteen years of age', she was also a paragon of virtue for 'to oblige her parents' she had accepted an offer of marriage from John Harvey.

Harvey was chief of the Karwar factory; he was also 'in years' – so probably old enough to be her grandfather – and 'deformed'.

Such sudden and suspect pairings were not uncommon. For bringing to India an English girl who was past puberty there was only one possible reason, to find a husband. In the Company's settlements suitors swarmed round a fresh-faced beauty as thickly as mosquitoes. Had little Miss Cooke been twice as old and half as pretty, she would still have been eagerly courted; but the twelve-day conquest, and of such a senior factor, may be taken as testimony that her charms were indeed exceptional.

Happily they were not long lavished on the repulsive Harvey. Within a couple of years the child-bride was a child-widow and Within a couple of months the child-widow had remarried. This time the lucky suitor was a young factor newly arrived in Karwar called Thomas Chown. Harvey had left an estate large enough to enable the sixteen-year-old to choose a more attractive partner; but as was ever the case, Harvey's personal affairs were hopelessly confused with those of his office. The Company was therefore laying claim to his estate and the Chowns determined to contest the matter. With Katherine already 'heavy with child' (presumably Chown's), they sailed for Bombay in November 1712.

As was usual in waters infested with 'pirates', their ketch, the *Anne*, sailed in convoy with two other vessels. A day out from Karwar the small fleet was attacked by four Maratha 'grabs' (*ghurabs* or square-rigged frigates). Chown was immediately hit in the shoulder by a cannon ball; he bled to death in his wife's arms. The *Anne* and her consorts were then boarded and the twice-widowed Katherine consigned to captivity in the Maratha stronghold of Colaba, about fifty miles down the coast from Bombay. It must have been with some trepidation that she learnt that she was the first European female to be a prisoner of the dreaded Kanhoji Angrey, otherwise 'Connajee' or 'Angria', the man destined to be the scourge of the Company for twenty years and the founder of a naval power that would last for half a century.

Like Sivaji, the founder of Maratha power on land, Kanhoji was a product of his environment. Issuing from the cliff-top forts and secluded valleys of their homeland in the Western Ghats, Sivaji's mounted raiders had exploited the tactical advantages of speed and mobility to probe deep into the Moghul empire, even to Surat. Similar tactics were suggested by the Maratha seaboard. Stretching roughly from Bombay to Goa and known as the Konkan – as opposed to the Malabar Coast further south – this reach of India's interminable coastline is quite unlike any other. Instead of the dunes and sand bars of the Coromandel or the palm-fringed strands of Malabar, here rocky promontories and hidden coves relieve the monotony. Numerous rivers spill down from the ghats to provide sheltered anchorages. Islands screen their estuaries. And wherever cliff or headland commands a narrows, a rock-ramparted stronghold crowns the horizon. Such a place was Colaba, a promontory at low tide, an island at high. Like the coasts of Brittany or Cornwall, that of the Konkan was made for sea rovers.

Kanhoji, though, was no more a pirate than 'The Seedee' or 'The Sow Raja'. By 1712 he had already been appointed *Surkhail*, or Grand Admiral, of the Maratha fleet and Viceroy of the Konkan. These titles the English in Bombay chose, of course, to ignore just as they disdained to apply for Kanhoji's *dastak*, or passes, when sailing through what the Marathas claimed as their territorial waters. Within such a loose organization as the Maratha confederacy the source of authority and legitimacy was often hard to identify; and this was especially true at a time when several claimants to Sivaji's throne were in the field. More to the point, though, Kanhoji's pretensions were not yet backed by great naval might. To the British, mindful of Bombay's last siege, the Sidi as a feudatory of the Moghul appeared the more formidable neighbour.

But Kanhoji Angrey was already building up his navy and reinforcing his strongholds. In 1707 he had made peace with the Sidi, the better to press his claims against the English. In the same year a Company frigate had been attacked and sunk, and in further such raids his fast sailing fleet of rakish 'grabs' assisted by the smaller, many-oared 'gallivats' had invariably worsted the Company's vessels in in-shore waters.

The Maratha admiral also knew better than to push his luck. He was well aware that the taking of two ships, including the *Anne*, the capture of their crews, and above all the plight of the delectable Mrs Chown was provoking Bombay no end. There was talk of a joint Anglo-Portuguese assault on Colaba; it was time to proffer the Maratha equivalent of an olive branch. If 'an Englishman of credit' would come to Colaba, wrote Kanhoji, he was ready to discuss terms.

The Bombay Council hesitated. Knowing him to be 'a man of ill principle', it was out of the question to order one of its servants on such a risky mission. But happily gallantry was not entirely lacking in the Company's ranks. Mindful of poor Mrs Chown, a young Scots lieutenant offered his services. With 30,000 rupees by way of ransom, the volunteer made his way to Colaba, found Kanhoji a man of his word, and duly returned with all the prisoners. According to Downing – who was not there and is no impartial chronicler – Mrs Chown had 'most courageously withstood all Angria's base usage and endured his insults beyond expectation'. By way of illustration Downing mentions that the young widow was discovered in such a state of undress that the Scots lieutenant, well named Mackintosh, 'was obliged to wrap his clothes about her to cover her nakedness'. The whole experience does not, though, seem to have greatly disconcerted Mrs Chown. A few weeks later she duly gave birth to Chown's son. The tide of sympathy persuaded the Bombay Council to grant her an allowance from Harvey's estate; and within a few months she was remarried to the hot-headed young Gyfford. When the latter was posted, not to Karwar of unhappy memory, but to Anjengo, she no doubt heaved a becoming sigh of relief. A new husband, a new home, a new life, she must have thought.

The ransoming of the Colaba prisoners was part of a wider non-aggression pact signed between Kanhoji and the Company in 1713. Under its terms the Marathas agreed not to molest ships belonging to the Company and not to interfere with any shipping in Bombay harbour. In return the Company undertook to see that only ships 'what belong to subjects of the English nation' should fly the Company's colours. Peace of a sort was restored. But it was this latter definition of English shipping which would provide a new bone of contention. Just as in Bengal the Company's servants persistently abused the privileges of the 1717 *farman* by granting custom-free passes (*dastak*) to anyone, English or Indian, who would pay for them, so in Bombay they abused the agreement with Kanhoji by interpreting the term 'English shipping' as denoting not ownership of the vessel but ownership of its cargo. Thus any vessel, whether owned by the Company, a private English trader or an Indian trader, was deemed a Company ship if it carried a consignment belonging to the English or any of those living under their protection.

Needless to say, this was not how Kanhoji understood the matter. In 1716 recriminations flew between the 'pirate' and Bombay over the capture of four Indian vessels which supposedly carried English-owned cargoes. In 1717 the richly laden *Success* belonging to the Company's Indian broker at Surat was taken and another ship, belonging to the Company itself, was relieved of part of its cargo. Again Kanhoji seemed willing to discuss reparations; but Bombay under Charles Boone, its new and vigorous Governor, was not. Boone had made the suppression of 'piracy' his personal crusade; £50,000 a year was being spent on building up the

Bombay Marine; the Company's own fleet of 'grabs' and 'gallivats' was coming off the stocks at Surat and elsewhere; and Bombay itself was being readied for war with the construction of the first city wall. Repeated requests for troops were sent to Madras and Calcutta, and from England as many as 500 recruits arrived in Bombay in a single year.

'Let the bottom [i.e. the vessel] be whose it will', wrote Boone to Kanhoji in protest at the latest prize-taking, 'the money lent on it is worth more than the ship and the goods are English, you well know.' But Kanhoji could not accept this logic. Today the English governor might be chartering only a single ship 'but tomorrow Your Excellency will say that you have a mind to freight fifty or a hundred ships of Surat merchants. If so, what occasion have they to take the pass (*dastak*) that they formerly took of me?' And whence, then, was the Maratha admiral to derive his revenue? But the Bombay Council was unmoved and in 1718 Boone resolved to hit back hard. When one of Kanhoji's 'gallivats' was taken while peacefully going about its business in Bombay harbour, it was the end of the truce. 'From this day forward', wrote the Maratha, 'what God gives, I shall take.' It was no idle threat.

First, though, it was Boone who took the offensive with a raid on the Maratha fleet as it was being laid up for the monsoon in a sheltered inlet behind Gheriah (Vijayadrug), the most impressive of Kanhoji's strongholds. So formidable were the rocky cliffs of Gheriah that an English historian would liken the place to Gibraltar. Not to be outdone, an Indian historian (writing in the first heady days of India's independence) describes Boone's surprise attack as 'Pearl Harbor two centuries before its time'. There was, though, one difference. In spite of a motley armada and some 4000 troops, Boone's raid was a total failure.

Downing, whose claim to have taken part has since been discredited, reports that the considerable firepower of the Company's ships made little impression on the fort, whose rocks were too slippery for a landing and whose walls were too high for the scaling ladders. 'We soon found that the place was impregnable.' A simple boom across the river prevented the Company's fireships, including one hopefully named the *Terrible Bomb*, from reaching the Maratha navy; and when a landing party was sent to deal with this obstacle it first blundered into a swamp and was then raked by fire from the fort. The only mystery was why the Marathas did not take greater advantage of the situation. Downing's explanation, though scarcely consoling, probably contained much truth. 'I question', he wrote, 'whether there were a hundred men in the castle during the siege.' After four days the 'siege' was lifted and the Company's armada returned to Bombay.

Undismayed, Boone used the closed season of the 1718 monsoon to plan a second assault, this time on Khanderi, an island only ten miles down the coast from Bombay itself. Again the fleet was packed with more than enough troops to carry the place, again a landing was effected, and again through sheer incompetence aborted. When Kanhoji himself appeared on the scene at the head of his fleet and threatened Bombay, the Company's ships quickly scuttled back to the protection of the big guns of Bombay castle.

'This ill-success was a great trouble to the President [Boone]' noted Downing. In 1719 no new attack was mounted and there was even talk of peace. But as Kanhoji's confidence had grown, so had Boone's bulldog spirit. 'He now did all in his power to suppress this notorious pyrate', building in addition to more ships 'a great and mighty floating machine'. Called *The Phram*, this contraption seems to have been half raft, half castle, 'pretty flat' with a draft of only six feet, and a single mast and topsail. But what impressed Downing was the thickness of its sides 'made by the nicest composition cannon-proof' and its twelve monstrous guns each of which fired a forty-eight pound cannon-ball. (Twenty-four pounders were the largest guns then favoured by the Bombay Marine.) 'It must of course prove of great service to us against any of those castles which we could approach near enough to cannonade.'

With just such a demonstration in mind, Boone launched a second assault on Gheriah in 1721. As in 1718 the landing parties effected nothing. But great were the expectations of *The Phram*. It was manoeuvred into position, the massive gun carriages were wheeled to the ports, the charges laid and the fuses lit. With an almighty splash the great shells fell into the sea rather less than a stone's throw from the vessel. Someone had miscalculated the angle of fire; either the carriages were too high or the ports too low. *The Phram* was withdrawn for modification.

By the time it was ready for further trials, word had got round the fleet that those armour-plated sides were not much use either; once again insufficient allowance had been made for the elevation of the 'Indian Gibraltar'. If *The Phram* discharged its guns from a distance, its murderous missiles were more of a danger to the waiting landing parties than to the fort, but if it moved into a more effective range the guns of the fort could lob their own shells onto its flat and crowded decks. Both expedients were tried and, amidst heavy casualties, both failed. It was thought that two of Kanhoji's 'grabs' had caught fire as a result of a separate bombardment and with this very doubtful claim to 'victory' the English fleet withdrew.

Meanwhile more merchant shipping was falling into Maratha hands. The trade of beleaguered Bombay was suffering and in a bid to end piracy once and for all the Company's directors in London applied for the assistance of the Royal Navy. With great ceremony a squadron was duly dispatched to the Indian Ocean in 1721, ostensibly to root out those Anglo-American buccaneers still operating out of Madagascar but additionally, and perhaps primarily, to take on Kanhoji Angrey. By now it was painfully obvious that the Company's 'sentinels' made indifferent storm-troopers even when primed with copious liquor and fired by the promise of cash bonuses. Similarly their counting-house masters made dismal admirals. It was time for the professionals to try their hand.

Commodore Matthews in charge of the Royal squadron reached Bombay in 1722 to a welcome soon noted for its acrimony. In a rerun of the quarrels between the Old Company and Ambassador William Norris – the last occasion on which Royal ships had visited India – Matthews claimed precedence by virtue of his commission and was soon planning a series of voyages designed to ensure for himself a handsome share of the Company's profits. He seemed bent on discrediting the Company and, worse still, he completely repudiated the Company's contention that any ship carrying an English consignment was entitled to fly English colours, thus in effect supporting Kanhoji's case. Governor Boone, however, was resolved on one last, all-out offensive. His term of office was drawing to a close; he had just engineered an offensive alliance against the Maratha admiral with the Portuguese; and he desperately needed Matthews's co-operation. Swallowing his pride, he deferred to the Commodore and set about planning the downfall of Colaba.

Unlike previous attacks, that on Colaba was waged from the land, an odd choice given the importance attached to the presence of Matthews's squadron. With a combined strength of 6,500 plus an artillery train, the Anglo-Portuguese forces surrounded Kanhoji's stronghold while the English fleet prevented any relief reaching it from the sea. In spite of the unexpected appearance of a Maratha detachment of horse and foot, the arrangements were more than adequate for the task in hand.

But once again the affair was woefully mismanaged. Without waiting to set up their batteries, and leaving the Portuguese to deal with the Maratha detachment, the English charged the fortress. The gates held, the English ladders were too short, and casualties were heavy. Meanwhile the Portuguese had been routed by the Marathas who now threatened to cut off the English attackers. A chaotic retreat ensued. Had the Marathas followed up their advantage it would have been the worst ever defeat for English arms in India. Matthews's squadron had contributed nothing except 200 marines lent to the land forces; compared to the conduct of the Company's reluctant sentinels, their bravery had been conspicuous.

Immediately after this fourth failure Boone sailed for home while Matthews took his squadron on a trading venture to Surat and Bengal. Ever open to anything that might discredit the Company, in Calcutta the Commodore was approached by a distraught but still pretty widow who was being detained in India pending payment of £9000 from her late husband's estate. Matthews listened to her long and heart-rending story with interest; and convinced that no one who heard it could fail to condemn the Company's ingratitude, he promptly took the young lady under his wing and into his cabin. She was, of course, none other than Mrs Katherine Gyfford, previously Harvey and Chown, née Cooke, lately of Karwar, Colaba, and Anjengo. Together the Commodore and the widow sailed back to Bombay, where old acquaintances were duly scandalized by Mrs Gyfford's new liaison, and then to England. Years of litigation over the tangled affairs of Anjengo followed, their outcome unknown. But evidently Mrs Gyfford returned to India for she died in Madras in 1745.

ii

Following the abortive assault on Colaba, the Portuguese made their peace with Kanhoji thus irrevocably souring their relations with the English. When a Maratha army occupied Portuguese Bassein no help was forthcoming from the Company in adjacent Bombay, and thereafter the Portuguese ceased to be a force to reckon with on the west coast. Much the same could be said of the Sidi; and, although the Dutch and even the French took an occasional swipe at the 'Angrian pirate', it was left to the English to bear the brunt of his attacks. Clearly Kanhoji's strongholds were impervious to anything the Company could throw against them; the most that could be expected of the Bombay Marine was retaliation for individual acts of 'piracy'. Thus in 1723 the sinking of a Company 'grab' and the disabling of another were matched by the capture of a Maratha vessel. This tit for tat produced a curious exchange of letters between Bombay and Colaba in which the 'pirate' showed himself a genial and persuasive correspondent; his offer of terms was rejected but prisoners were swopped and for the next five years both sides did their utmost to avoid hostilities.

The lull ended with Kanhoji's death in 1729. An ensuing contest between his numerous progeny should have played into the Company's hands but whilst one Angrey faction, based at Colaba, did prove more amenable, the other, based at Gheriah, began a new reign of terror. In 1730 two of the Company's latest 'grabs' were engaged, both badly mauled and one captured. Two years later a large Indiaman, the *Ockham*, managed to beat off an attack, but in 1735 the *Derby* put up such a feeble resistance that she was taken intact to Suvarnadrug, another of the Angrey's 'impregnable' bolt-holes. Coming straight from England the *Derby* was laden with ammunition and naval stores plus the treasure that was to have been Bombay's trading capital for the year. Its loss was probably the heaviest the Company ever had to bear from 'Angrian pirates'.

All Company ships were of course armed but, heavily laden, they were easily outmanoeuvred by the native 'gallivats'. To avoid an English broadside the Maratha oarsmen approached from astern, often towing the larger 'grabs' whose prow guns directed their fire at the English rigging. Having thus disabled their prey – and hopefully ensnared its gunners in a tangle of rope and canvas – the Maratha vessels closed in from all sides for the boarding. There was only one way to defeat such tactics and that was by ensuring that other Company ships were always on hand to offer covering fire. Henceforth the system of convoys was more rigorously enforced and during the late 1730s it seemed to be paying off.

Thus in December 1739 the *Harrington*, Captain Robert Jenkins, Bombay bound from China, called in at Tellicherry to pick up her convoy before entering the danger zone of the Konkan. A week later the fleet, now of four ships, was assailed by fifteen 'Angrian' vessels of which six were frigate-size 'grabs'. The engagement lasted two days but so well did the English ships support one another that eventually the enemy 'found to their cost that our metal was too heavy for them'. Captain Jenkins was especially commended. Already something of a celebrity in that the British government was even then engaged in a war with Spain that was named after his ear, he was presented with 300 guineas by the Company's directors and made Commodore of the Marine by the Bombay Council. Sadly he died two years later 'of a fever and a flux', another victim of

Bombay's 'unveryhealthfulness'. The famous ear, originally severed by the Spanish in the West Indies, bottled by its owner, and produced to great effect in the House of Commons in 1738, was buried with him. It was said that he had become more attached to it off than when it was on; he never went anywhere without it.

Lacking such a talisman and such an inspirational commander, the *Princess Augusta* from Benkulen was taken in 1742 and, ignoring smaller losses, the *Restoration*, flagship of the Bombay Marine, in 1749. Both were the work of Tulaji Angrey who had just succeeded his brother Sambhaji in command of the south Konkan. In so far as he had also been disowned by the Peshwa, now the main focus of Maratha loyalty, the Company's insistence on his piratical status for once had some substance. As if to live up to it, Tulaji's fleet harried the western seaboard as never before. Another squadron of the Royal Navy was summoned from Madras to escort the Bombay convoys. Tulaji hung about their flanks picking off stragglers; on one occasion he boldly engaged a flotilla of no less than thirty-six vessels.

Happily, though, and not before time, an end to this galling struggle was in sight. By 1750 events in the Carnatic, including the loss and restitution of Madras and the extraordinary exploits of Clive, had long since upstaged the 'Angrian' wars; and with the Company now transformed into the most effective military and territorial power on the Indian peninsula, it was only a matter of time before arrangements could be made to deal with 'pirates'.

Tulaji, unlike Kanhoji, could expect no support from his Maratha suzerain whose envoys he had sent back with their noses out of joint – literally – plus a message that if the Peshwa wanted to talk he must address himself to what Surgeon Ives delicately describes as 'Tulaji's pr---te p–rts'. Indeed by 1754 Tulaji was actually at war with the Peshwa. An Anglo-Maratha alliance was the natural outcome and accordingly, as soon as peace was restored in the Carnatic, a joint offensive was planned against Suvarnadrug and Gheriah. There could, of course, be no question of storming such 'impregnable' strongholds. Siege tactics were the answer. The English fleet would blockade them from the sea and the Maratha army invest them from the land. Eventually the 'pirates' would be forced to treat.

In command of the Bombay Marine at the time was Commodore William James. Like Jenkins, and in marked contrast to the assorted factors and merchants who had mismanaged Boone's operations, James had been recruited into the Company's service after seeing action in the West Indies. He was a highly experienced and professional sailor and he commanded a frigate, the *Protector*, specially built in England, whose forty-gun firepower and lack of hold space made her a true warship. Additionally the locally built 'grabs', fireships and even 'Phrams' had lately been much improved. For in 1738 the great Parsee shipbuilder, Lowji Wadia, had been persuaded to remove his business from Surat to Bombay. There he set up the first shipyard and provided the Bombay Marine with extensive dry dock and refitting facilities. James may have commanded fewer vessels than many of his predecessors but all were built for war rather than trade, well officered and amply supplied with powder and shot.

Additionally, another Royal squadron was supposedly on its way from Madras. Admiral Watson, the commander, needed the use of the new dockyards to careen his fleet and he was also in search of gainful employment now that hostilities with the French were temporarily suspended. But as the 1755 monsoon approached, Watson made first for the Dutch port of Trinconomalee in Sri Lanka. James despaired of his arrival before the end of the year and resolved to make a start without him. The Marathas also were ready; the target was to be Suvarnadrug.

While the Maratha troops moved into position, James's fleet of only four ships put to flight Tulaji's 'grabs'. Returning to his station outside the harbour, the Commodore then assessed the Maratha positions. It would take his allies weeks, he decided, if not months, to take the place by conventional siege tactics. But the monsoon was imminent and patience had never been one of his virtues; neither had caution. On 2 April 1755, heedless of a danger that would have had two generations of Bombay mariners turning in their graves, he sailed straight into the lions' den.

On the map Suvarnadrug is a mere nick in the Konkan coastline. It was in fact a commodious if shallow inlet, ringed by hills and with a rocky island in its midst. The island was about a quarter of a mile from the shore and on it stood the main fort, some of whose bastions and parapets consisted of natural rock. Three further forts, on which the Marathas were already concentrating their attention, commanded the bay from the surrounding hills. Biddulph, whose description makes the place sound much like Navarone, puts the total of enemy guns at 134. Against them would be ranged the *Protector*'s forty cannon and whatever armaments were carried by the two bomb ketches which accompanied her into the bay.

James was especially anxious about running aground and so spent the first day cannonading the fort from the seaward (western) side. 'Eight hundred shot and shell' were expended at a range of less than one hundred yards and, according to a deserter who came over to the English that night, fearful casualties had resulted. But the same informant advised that there was no chance of causing a breach on that side; the walls there were solid rock eighteen feet thick.

Next day James determined to try his luck on the other, eastern, side – between the main fort and the three lesser forts on the mainland. Soundings taken during the night suggested that at low tide the *Protector* should still have just a foot of water under her keel. Accordingly she stood in at dawn and, sandwiched between the island and the shore, was soon briskly engaged on both sides. 'It would be difficult', writes Biddulph, 'to find a parallel to this instance of a single ship and two bomb ketches successfully engaging four forts at once that far outnumbered them in guns.' As with *The Phram* at Gheriah, there was an additional complication in that only the upper of the *Protector*'s two tiers of guns had the elevation to be brought to bear on the fort's parapets. On the other hand, so closely did the ship approach them that small-arms fire from her rigging drove the defenders from their guns.

At noon a shell set light to a storehouse within the walls. More musket fire from the *Protector*'s sharp-shooters kept the garrison from dousing it and eventually the whole place was engulfed in flames as the main magazines blew up. That evening and well into the night the enemy began to withdraw, coming off in small boats which were quickly intercepted by a frigate left at the mouth of the bay. Early next morning all four forts surrendered. Thus, writes Robert Orme, chronicler of the Company's martial exploits, 'the spirited resolution of Commodore James destroyed the timorous prejudices which had for twenty years [actually thirty] been entertained of the impracticability of reducing any of Angria's fortified harbours'.

Returning to a hero's welcome in Bombay, James accepted *en route* the surrender of another of 'Angria's fortified harbours' while the Maratha land forces continued the good work until the end of the year. By the time the long-awaited squadron from Madras arrived on the scene, it was all over bar the *coup de grâce* – the capture of Gheriah.

Compared to the improbable triumph of Suvarnadrug, the storming of Gheriah would have a faintly ritualistic air. Such were the overwhelming forces at the Company's disposal on this occasion that the outcome can never have been in doubt. It was a set piece in which the attackers agonized more over the division of the spoils than over tactical niceties. With ample time for reconnaissance James had volunteered to make a survey; and after another typically bold foray right into the pirates' nest he had reported favourably on the prospects. In fact he was 'exceedingly surprised' to find Gheriah nothing like as formidable as it had been painted. 'I can assure you it is not to be called high nor, in my opinion, strong' – an opinion amply substantiated by drawings of the place made after its capture. It was big and, like Colaba, impressively sited on the end of a promontory. But there was nothing to prevent warships getting within point-blank range nor to prevent troops from landing nearby and setting up their batteries on a hill that commanded the whole position.

This last consideration was of interest in that, besides the Royal squadron with its two admirals and its six warships mounting some 300 guns, and besides the Company's ten somewhat smaller vessels, and not to mention the Maratha contingents both naval and military, the action was to be graced with the presence of three companies of the King's artillery, 700 men in all, plus a like number of Indian sepoys, all under the command of the then Lieutenant-Colonel Robert Clive.

Clive's presence at Gheriah was incidental and, in the event, not particularly decisive. He and his troops had arrived in Bombay *en route* to some unfinished business with the French in the Deccan. That expedition was cancelled at the last minute as a result of the Anglo-French peace. And so Clive had indented for a slice of the action – and of the spoils – at Gheriah. What these spoils might amount to was uncertain but surely considerable. It was known that the contents of most of Tulaji's prizes, including the treasure-rich *Derby*, had been taken to Gheriah. It was there that he kept his family and his prisoners – mostly English and Dutch; and where a pirate kept such valued possessions, there too would be his treasure.

Before setting out from Bombay, Admiral Watson summoned a meeting of the English commanders to thrash out the question of prize money. A scale was agreed on by which Watson himself would receive a twelfth of the proceeds, his rear-admiral half that, Clive and the captains of the Royal ships rather less, and James and the captains of the Company's ships less still. It would appear that James and his commanders accepted the subordinate role that this arrangement implied. But Clive did not, demanding for himself parity with the rear-admiral. To resolve the argument Watson offered to make good the difference out of his own share. As he would put it to Clive in Bengal at the next division of the spoils, 'money is what I despise, and accumulating riches is what I did not come here for'. But Clive, we are told, then refused to accept the Admiral's money. 'Thus did these two gallant officers endeavour to outvie each other in mutual proofs of disinterestedness and generosity', wrote Ives in a footnote that was doubtless designed to deflect some of the criticism which would dog Clive's every triumph.

Obviously if these arrangements were to be honoured, it was a matter of some consequence that the English and not their Maratha allies should actually take Gheriah. By mid February 1756, when the armada finally arrived on station, they knew that Tulaji was already negotiating with the Maratha commander; they trusted their ally no more than the enemy, and clearly time was running out. When a first formal demand for the surrender of the fort was answered with procrastinating tactics, Watson realized that to be certain of their reward they would have to earn it. He ignored the possibility of a peaceful handover and gave the order for the fleet to move in.

The English entered the harbour in two columns, five great battleships plus the Company's *Protector* forming an inner ring round the fort while the nine assorted 'grabs', sloops and ketches went round the outside to reach the enemy fleet as it lay penned upriver. Naturally the first shot is said to have come from the fort. It was repaid with compound interest as one after another the broadsides were brought to bear. Just over two hours later the entire 'Angrian' fleet was ablaze and the guns of the fort silenced. Briefly they 'briskened their fire' once again; then they fell silent for good.

That night Clive took his men ashore to set up their batteries while the bomb ketches continued to pour their shells into the fort. In the morning the bombardment was taken up both from the land and from the line of battleships. There was no answering fire, the object now being simply to effect a breach or cause such slaughter as would persuade the garrison to surrender. This they did in the course of the afternoon; by six o'clock the English colours were fluttering atop the smoking ruins. Nineteen men of the attacking force had been killed or wounded; of the carnage amongst the defenders there is no record.

Next day the victorious English got down to the serious business – plunder. According to Ives, who was Admiral Watson's personal surgeon, they 'found 250 pieces of cannon, six mortars, an immense quantity of stores and ammunition, one hundred thousand pounds sterling in silver rupees and about thirty thousand more in valuable effects'. It was less than expected but sufficient for several small fortunes, Watson's share being about £10,000 and Clive's about £5,000.

James's was less but, along with other windfalls, enough to enable him to buy a stately farm in then rural Eltham on the outskirts of London. For someone who is said to have started out in life as a Welsh ploughman it was a fabulous reward. The hero of Suvarnadrug retired there in 1759, was awarded a baronetcy, made a director of the Company and eventually its chairman. He died in 1783, supposedly of apoplexy after reading Fox's India Bill which he rightly saw as a parliamentary nail in the Company's coffin. In his memory his wife erected a fanciful replica of the scene of his greatest triumph. Known as Severndroog Castle it still stands on Shooters Hill in south-east London, a castellated curiosity some sixty feet high bearing no conceivable likeness to the original.

CHAPTER FOURTEEN

The Germ of an Army

MADRAS AND DUPLEIX

That nameless Spanish coastguard who, in defence of his country's trading rights in Cuba, sliced off the ear of Captain Robert Jenkins had much to answer for. In an age when even sea dogs wore ample wigs the Captain's loss was of no cosmetic consequence; but the fact that Jenkins ever after cherished the severed organ, regarded it as a talisman, and chose to exhibit it in the House of Commons had far-reaching repercussions. Such was the clamour for retaliation against Spanish high-handedness in the Caribbean that the war, when at last declared by a reluctant ministry, is said to have been the most popular of the century. It was also one of the shortest, for within a few months the Hapsburg emperor had died, opening the issue of the imperial succession and plunging central Europe into conflagration. The War of Jenkins's Ear became subsumed in that of the Austrian Succession and, with Britain already committed against Bourbon Spain, it was unthinkable that Bourbon France would be other than hostile.

The success of the European powers in engrossing the world's trade had had the unfortunate side effect of multiplying and internationalizing their interminable squabbles. If an incident off the coast of Cuba could determine postures in a European war it followed that wherever else the European rivals found themselves in close proximity the same hostile postures would be likely to prevail. Nationalism, let alone religion or ideology, played no great part in these quarrels. Ostensibly they were dynastic or commercial but the issues, often confused in the first place, became hopelessly obscured in the process of export. Local grievances took their place and local conditions determined the scale and duration of any hostilities. The stakes could by mutual consent be kept to a minimum or they could escalate to such heights that in retrospect they dwarfed the often inconclusive results in Europe.

So it was in India. News that Britain and France were officially at war reached the Coromandel Coast in September 1744. By that time the question of the Austrian succession was as dead and buried as Jenkins and his ear. But that scarcely troubled the participants. Two years later Madras would be stormed and captured by the French; and for the next fifteen years the two nations, in the guise of their respective trading companies, would fight a life-and-death struggle for supremacy on The Coast and in the adjacent province of the Carnatic. To strengthen its position, each Company entered into alliances with the native powers, thereby extending both its influence and its territory. Honours would be more or less equally divided but in the end victory and dominion fell to the British; and thanks to the military arrangements necessitated by the war, the British would go on to realize an even greater dominion in Bengal. It is therefore with this war, the War of the (wholly irrelevant) Austrian Succession, that most histories of British India begin; there are even histories of the East India Company which have the same starting point.

The metamorphosis of the Company's Madras establishment from city state to territorial capital, closely followed by the still more dramatic transformation of its Bengal establishment, undoubtedly represents the most important watershed in the Company's history. Bengal at the time accounted for more than fifty per cent of the Company's total trade and Madras for around fifteen per cent. When the call to arms drowned out the commodity wrangling in two such important markets, it was bound to affect the whole posture of the Company.

On the other hand, these stirring events had little bearing on the Arabian Sea trade, based on Bombay, and even less on the important China trade, based on Canton and now entering a period of rapid expansion. In outposts like Benkulen and St Helena the usual grim and inglorious struggle for survival continued regardless. And more significantly, even in Bengal and on The Coast the volume of trade remained high in spite of the political turmoil. The Coast's trading returns would be back to normal within two years of the French occupation of Madras while those of Calcutta would recover from their own 'black hole' in 1756 even more rapidly. In chronicling the political and military adventures of the period it is rather easy to forget that the Company remained a commercial enterprise. 'The combatants aimed at injuring one another's trade, not making conquests', writes Professor Dodwell, editor of the *Cambridge History of India*. Commercial priorities still governed the Company's decision making and it was its financial viability which made expansion possible – though not necessarily desirable.

That said, any student of the Company's fortunes who at last arrives at this watershed period will find little further use for a pocket calculator. With the Company in India fighting for its very existence, the monthly returns of 'The Sea Customer' and 'The Export Warehousekeeper' lose their charm while London's always wordy complaints about the previous year's taffetas seem as irrelevant as Mrs Gyfford's last will and testament. More territory meant more revenue but not necessarily more trade; and for Company diehards that was one good reason for a certain ambivalence about the whole question of territorial expansion.

This shift away from the market place is amply endorsed by all that has been written about the period. Whereas for the first 150 years of the Company's existence the published sources are few and specific, to be eagerly sought and gratefully scrutinized, now the student is suddenly confronted by such a mass of research, analysis, narrative, and polemic as to make his task seem superfluous if not impossible. Sandwiched between the ample volumes of political, military and administrative history stand the classic pontifications of Macaulay and Burke, important French and Indian chronicles, much London-based pamphleteering, and copious biographical writings from which the main protagonists emerge with rich and ready-made personalities. After so long diligently pursuing faceless factors engaged in obscure transactions up forgotten backwaters, it is all rather overwhelming – like emerging from a long night drive through country lanes on to a floodlit freeway. Only a nagging doubt that the freeway may not be heading in quite the desired direction dispels euphoria.

For the fact is that nearly all of this material celebrates the rise of British power in India, a process of consuming interest to several generations of English writers but one in which the Company's prominence becomes increasingly deceptive. For this same process heralded and then hastened the eclipse of the Honourable Company as a private commercial enterprise. Its stock would be quoted for another 130 years but its trading rights would disappear in half that time; its governance would last for over a century but its independence would be gone in just four decades,

How ambivalent the Company was about military adventurism is well illustrated by its reponse to those first tidings of war with France in

1744. During the War of the Spanish Succession, the French and English companies in India had agreed to refrain from hostilities, and it was with the idea of a similar pact that Dupleix, now the Governor of Pondicherry, wrote to Nicholas Morse, his opposite number at Madras. Morse knew that Dupleix's position was weak, that Pondicherry's defences were little better than those of Madras and that there was no French fleet in the offing to boost them. He also knew that a squadron of the Royal Navy was already on its way to bolster his own position. Yet the idea of a pre-emptive strike against Pondicherry seems never to have entered his head. He could not accept Dupleix's offer of a pact because, as he explained, he was not authorized to do so. He was thinking, of course, of the Royal squadron which was sure to take French prizes and over which he had no authority. But neither did he reject the pact. In Bengal the English at Calcutta and the French at their neighbouring base of Chandernagar would observe it; Morse merely prevaricated.

Irritated by this caution Dupleix appealed to the Nawab of the Carnatic who duly reminded both Companies that they held their settlements of the Moghul Emperor on condition that 'they behave themselves peacable and quietly'. In effect the Nawab forbade hostiiities and in the correspondence that followed Morse was obliged to define his position. What happened at sea, claimed the Madras President, was of no legitimate concern to the Nawab but on land he could vouch for the English never being the first to take up arms; their trade was too important, their militia too ineffectual.

By now it was 1745 and the Royal squadron under Commodore Curtis Barnett had arrived in Eastern waters. Instead of making straight for the Coromandel coast, Barnett first cruised off Aceh where he pounced on French shipping richly laden with China goods as it emerged from the Malacca Straits. Four or five vessels belonging to the *Compagnie des Indes* were taken along with a like number of privately owned ships in which the French factors, and especially Dupleix, had a very considerable interest. As with the English of the period so with the French; it is impossible to tell which affront was the more provocative, a tear in the flag or a hole in the pocket. But when, as now, both national honour *and* personal wealth were at stake, a vigorous response could be expected. Dupleix wrote urgently to Mauritius, the *Compagnie*'s main base in the Indian Ocean, for naval support; he again complained to the Nawab of the Carnatic; he protested loudly to Madras; and he began assembling a small expeditionary force in Pondicherry.

News of the last caused consternation in the English settlements. Morse convened his Council in emergency session. It was agreed to hire '200 good peons', or militiamen, from Madras's immediate neighbours and to arm all the city's resident Englishmen with matchlocks; they could take the guns home with them but if they heard a cannon shot during the night they were to 'repair to The Parade before the Main Guard where they would receive the necessary orders from Mr Monson, their Commanding Officer'. Such was Madras's idea of mobilization; never were sabres rattled so diffidently. Fort St David, only ten miles from Pondicherry, was the more obvious target but Morse refrained from sending it reinforcements on the doubtful grounds that that might be just what Dupleix wanted; with Madras deprived of part of its garrison the French might take advantage of a southerly wind and 'surprise us'.

In the event it was all a false alarm. With the English squadron daily expected, Dupleix knew better than to do anything that might invite an attack on Pondicherry; his expedition was intended simply to reinforce a recently acquired factory at Karikal some fifty miles down The Coast. When at last Barnett did arrive at Fort St David, the Madras Council discharged the '200 good peons' and turned its attention to the more agreeable task of provisioning the squadron; meanwhile the squadron concentrated on the even more lucrative task of prize-taking. Trade was not neglected. 'Having at present the prospect of making a very considerable investment this year', the Council's only anxiety was that the usual supply of shipping and treasure from home should reach them safely. This it did in December and not only were there four Company ships but also two further men-of-war and some more recruits for the garrison.

Two months later, in February 1746, news came from Anjengo, that source of so much shipping intelligence, that a French fleet of six warships was now ready to sail from Mauritius. Madras again cast about for mercenaries; in this case '300 Extraordinary Peons' were signed up. But with Barnett still cruising off The Coast there was no panic. At the end of April Barnett died and was succeeded by Edward Peyton, his second in command. Still there was no sign of the French fleet. Peyton then cruised south towards Sri Lanka; there were 'no ships in Pondicherry road' according to a report that was before the Madras Council on 11 June.

The Council was now meeting twice a week, on Mondays and Wednesdays. On Monday the 16th there was further shipping news from Anjengo, this time about a homeward bound Indiaman; then there were some cash advances to Indian buyers to be approved, and an explanation to be sought from a ship's captain lately arrived from Bengal and seven bags short on his manifest of saltpetre. Finally a letter was drafted to Fort St David approving of their design for 'a new arched godown' and promising to send some more field guns 'as opportunity offers'. And so to dinner. No hint of panic, nothing frantic nor even faintly ominous. But at this point, a hundred years after Francis Day had first built his four-square fort on the Madras sands, the Fort St George records fall silent. It would be three years before the 'Diary and Consultations' book was resumed.

Doubtless there were other Council meetings during the few weeks that remained to the English in Madras but either they were too fraught to be minuted or, more likely, the records were destroyed by the French. From other sources, especially the deliberations of the junior Council at Fort St David, we know that within ten days Peyton's squadron had fought an inconclusive action with the French fleet as it passed the Dutch settlement of Negapatnam. Peyton continued south to Sri Lanka for refitting and La Bourdonnais, the French commander, to Pondicherry. The latter's fleet consisted of nine ships, according to the much alarmed factors at Fort St David; many of them were far bigger than the English ships; they off-loaded a vast quantity of treasure and, unreported by Fort St David, they carried some 1200 mainly European troops.

At the end of July the French fleet again put to sea. Again they encountered Peyton off Negapatnam, but this time the English turned tail before a shot was fired. Peyton then continued north, past Fort St David, past Madras, to Pulicat, a Dutch station. Unaware of this development, the English factors at Fort St David watched the French fleet return to Pondicherry.

By now, late August, it was common knowledge 'that their design was against Madras' and 'that not only the Company's expected Shipping but likewise their Settlement were in Eminent [*sic*] danger.' It was Madras's turn desperately to appeal to the Nawab and still more desperately to scan the horizon for a sign of Peyton's fleet. From Fort St David letters were sent 'by three several conveyances' to Negapatnam (Dutch) and Tranquebar (Danish) to summon Peyton 'wherever they heard he was [and] at any expense'. Native catamarans scoured the coastline even down to Sri Lanka; in response to a promised reward of 100 pagodas for the first sighting of the English fleet, some ventured out of sight of land

and into over thirty fathoms. But it was all in vain. Peyton had decided that the fate of the Company's settlements was no concern of his; where was the prize money in it? At the beginning of September he resumed his voyage north to Bengal, safety, and eventual obloquy. Madras stood alone and unprotected.

ii

Writing to Calcutta a year later, the directors in London would place the blame for what followed squarely on the shoulders of Morse and his Council. 'We hope,' they warned, 'that all our Governors who have not the resolution to defend our settlements, as we think was the case at Madras, will resign to such who have.' Ever since a threatened attack by Marathas in 1740 the defence of Madras – and of Calcutta – had figured prominently in the official correspondence. Right liberally had the directors contributed, sanctioning additional fortifications for Madras in 1741, 'an encrease to 600 Europeans' in the garrison in 1742, and the highly rated services of Major Charles Knipe (at the princely salary of £250 per annum) to command the troops and advise on further defences. In 1743 Knipe, an able officer of thirty years' service in the regular army, surveyed the vital west front of Madras. 'Tis no fortification at all', he reported, 'but rather an offensive than defensive wall to your garrison'; but for the support of the numerous Indian homes that had been built against it, 'it could not stand'; 'nor was it more than sufficient for a garden wall when first erected.' The Major proposed a new wall and, in spite of the cost, again the directors assented. So how could the place possibly be described as unprotected?

The answer was simple. Most of these measures had never been realized. Knipe had died less than four months after his arrival and it was over a year before a replacement engineer, one Bombardier Smith, could be borrowed from Bombay. Smith's new design for the west front was still on the drawing board when La Bourdonnais sallied forth from Pondicherry. Meanwhile command of the Madras garrison had devolved by seniority to Lieutenant Peter Eckman, described as 'an ignorant superannuated Swede' whose boast of 'having carried arms above 56 years' must have made him one of the oldest lieutenants ever. Perhaps if he had had those 600 European troops at his command, things would have been different. But in fact there seem never to have been more than 400 on the muster roll and they were not disposed to take much notice of their septuagenarian commander. Of the 400 a quarter were either in hospital, in prison, fictitious, 'deserted', or simply 'men who ought to have been there' (but, presumably were not). The rest are said to have been mainly topazes, 'a black, degenerate, wretched race of the ancient Portuguese', according to a contemporary, 'as proud and bigoted as their ancestors, lazy, idle, and vicious withal, and for the most part as weak and feeble in body as base in mind.'

Others would disagree with this verdict on the topazes, among them young Robert Clive who had arrived in Madras two years previously as a writer (salary £5 per annum), the most junior and menial rank in the Company's commercial hierarchy. He was now, in 1746, twenty-one years old, still homesick for his family and his beloved Manchester ('the centre of all my wishes'), still a writer and not a little impatient of his prospects of wealth and promotion. The popular portrait suggests a broody and hot-tempered youth anxiously awaiting the call to arms and glory; but during the assault on Madras there is no record of posterity's 'heaven-born general' so much as hefting a matchlock.

Not that there was much time for heroics. La Bourdonnais's fleet complete with transports arrived off Madras on 4 September 1746. Some 2000 troops were landed to the south of the city and by the 6th they had worked their way round to the west where they set up batteries and began pounding that suspect western wall. The English replied with a sally by the 'Extraordinary Peons' who were repulsed (and then fled back to their villages) plus a rather ill-directed fire from the fort's bastions. No further sallies were attempted. The garrison had been liberally primed with arrack and rum, alcohol being supposed to put fire in the men's bellies. But in this case, it just put ideas in their heads. They insulted their officers, rampaged through the town, and made it quite clear that against such superior forces nothing would persuade them to venture outside the walls. No doubt the alcohol was also partly responsible for the erratic cannonade. But there was an additional problem. All the gun carriages collapsed under their cannon 'upon the second or third firing'. The efforts of Mrs Morse and the Fort's other ladies, who were valiantly sewing up cloth cartridges, were wasted.

Meanwhile the Black Town, though less affected by the French bombardment, was rapidly emptying. On the first day most of the civilian population decamped; next night 500 'Black soldiers' slipped over the walls, closely followed by the White Town's large contingent of domestics 'insomuch that the gentlemen and ladies could not get servants to kill and dress their victuals or bring them water to drink'. Nor did the continual bombardment enable the gentlemen and ladies to get any sleep, for which after two days 'they were ready to die' according to one of them. Not surprisingly, the ancient Eckman was among the first to withdraw from circulation 'unable to bear the fatigue'; Morse seems to have gone down with chronic melancholia; and Smith, the Bombay bombardier, actually died from exhaustion – or possibly, according to the records, from the discovery that he was 'ill-used by his wife'.

Whether he is to be included in the casualty figure is not clear. By the third day of the bombardment, the English losses stood at six, two of them European. It was not exactly mass carnage but evidently quite unacceptable, for the English now attempted to buy off their opponents. This was standard procedure in Indian warfare; additionally an exchange of pagodas was seen as the only reasonable way for two commercial organizations to compose their differences; with the French *Compagnie*, unlike the English, invariably strapped for cash, it was thought likely to have particular appeal.

La Bourdonnais welcomed the approach. He too had no idea of the whereabouts of Peyton's squadron and was worried lest his own fleet, with its guns now trained on Fort St George, should be surprised in Madras's open roads. But he rejected the English offer. National honour, not to mention the fiery Dupleix, demanded that there must be a victory; Madras must actually surrender and the French must be seen as other than The Coast's underdogs. A reasonable and honourable man, La Bourdonnais had no desire to destroy the place nor indeed to hold on to it. He just wanted the best possible deal for France – and for La Bourdonnais. Under the terms of the final surrender, agreed on 10 September, Madras was to be handed over and then speedily ransomed back by the English Company for 1.1 million pagodas plus another 100,000 for La Bourdonnais himself.

And there, but for the machinations of Dupleix and a change in the weather, matters might have ended. Ten days later the victors made their ceremonial entry. The Company's flag was lowered; a Te Deum was sung in the Catholic church. There was no looting, the ransom terms were agreed, the city was to be evacuated by the French at the beginning of October. But as word of these arrangements reached Dupleix in Pondicherry he evinced a growing mistrust of La Bourdonnais and of the perfidious English – fed, no doubt, by anxiety over his own share in the proceeds of victory – plus an ominous disregard for the conventional status of European trading companies within the Moghul empire.

Insisting that only he and his Council had the authority to negotiate a ransom, he reprimanded La Bourdonnais and advised that anyway Madras could not be returned to the English since he had promised it to the Nawab in return for the latter's neutrality. But either this was a fabrication or else the ploy had miscarried; for in fact the Nawab, after earnest entreaties from the English, was already assembling his troops for an attack on Pondicherry and another on the French in Madras. Far from neutralizing his Moghul overlord, Dupleix's behaviour had provoked the first major trial of strength between European and Indian arms in the peninsula.

Meanwhile La Bourdonnais was proposing a compromise whereby the French should extend their occupation of Madras till January. Dupleix seems to have agreed and, less surprisingly, so did the English who had no choice in the matter and who rightly saw La Bourdonnais's presence as their only guarantee of the ransom being effected. These hopes, though, were dashed by the south-east monsoon which broke with dramatic effect one Sunday night in early October. A cyclone swept on to the harbourless Coast scattering all before it including La Bourdonnais's fleet which was still lying off Madras. Four ships disappeared completely, four more were dismasted. To the English factors at Fort St David, anxiously awaiting their turn as the French squadron's next prey, it was a wondrous example of divine retribution; 'it pleased God to disappoint their views by a gale of wind'. But for their less fortunate colleagues in Madras the gale of wind meant the end of French forbearance. Within a matter of days La Bourdonnais, the guarantor of the ransom arrangement, had gathered up the remnants of his fleet and departed the country.

He left Dupleix's nominee in charge of Madras where the *Compagnie*'s men now addressed themelves to the serious business of mulcting the English metropolis for all it was worth. The ransom arrangements were disavowed; but realizing that an eventual peace in Europe would probably mean the restitution of Madras, the French factors took such measures as would combine instant pickings with an undermining of the city's long-term prosperity. Thus the White Town was ransacked while the Black Town was partially demolished. Wholesale confiscations took place and the Indian merchants and middlemen on whom trade depended were ordered to remove to Pondicherry. Some obeyed; others paid handsomely for the privilege of exemption. Meanwhile the English were given the choice of taking an oath to the French king or being made prisoner. Many, like Robert Clive, simply contrived to escape; either way they were all dispossessed and dispersed.

La Bourdonnais's other legacy to the *Compagnie* was the 1200 troops he had brought to India and who now, marooned there by the destruction of his fleet, were at Dupleix's disposal. Disciplined, well-officered, and equipped with the latest in musketry and field artillery, these troops were soon put to the test. Four days after La Bourdonnais's departure, the Nawab's army approached Madras and, imitating the French a month before, took up positions to the west of the city. Like the English, the French made an early sally; 400 men with a couple of guns issued forth to confront an army said to have been 10,000 strong. It looked like a suicide gesture and contemptuously did the Nawab's cavalry sweep down towards their prey. The French troopers drew aside to clear a field for the guns; the cavalry kept on coming. At unmissable range the first salvo halted the charge without dispersing the horsemen. Confident in the knowledge that no gun could be fired more than once every three minutes, the Nawab's cavalry wheeled aside and reformed to move in for the kill. But long before this manoeuvre could be completed, more men and horses were piling up in front of them. The French boasted a fire rate of twenty rounds a minute and were certainly capable of half that; their infantry were no less adroit with their muskets. In effect every French gun had the firepower of thirty Indian guns and every French trooper could comfortably account for ten ill-armed Moghul mercenaries.

This victory was not enough to end the siege; but when a relieving force sent from Pondicherry arrived on the scene two days later, it was precisely the same story. Again the Nawab's troops were routed by an infinitely smaller French contingent. Quite suddenly the French had set a new pattern for European participation in Indian affairs.

The superiority of European arms came as a revelation comparable with the first discovery of a sea route to the East. While in India ideas of drill, arms, and tactics had scarcely progressed since Akbar, in Europe they had undergone steady refinement and development in a host of campaigns. There was now no comparison. Warfare in India was still a sport; in Europe it had become a science. Officers read Vauban's *Mémoires* and studied the Regulations of the Prussian Infantry. Discipline made *esprit* a corporate responsibility; drill imparted to tactics the irresistible precision of a well-oiled machine. What Robert Orme, the English Company's military historian, and his eighteenth-century contemporaries now recognized as the myth of Moghul superiority in battle had been ruthlessly exposed. Outside the walls of Fort St George 'the French at once broke through the charm of this timorous opinion by defeating a whole army with a single battalion'.

iii

With Madras secure in French possession Dupleix now turned his attention to Fort St David. This was no surprise to its English garrison who, with barely eight miles of scrub and dune between their walls and those of Pondicherry, were wont to consider themselves in a more or less permanent state of siege. Just as the presence of French shipping in Pondicherry roads meant that Fort St David was blockaded, so even innocent foraging could look like an offensive move. Amidst such continual alarms, however, there appear to have been three serious attempts to take the place – in December 1746, March 1747, and June 1748. On all but the last occasion the French found Cuddalore – in effect the Black Town of Fort St David – undefended. Poorly fortified and of considerable extent, it was beyond the means of the English to hold it. But the fort itself, a mile to the north, was a very different proposition. Unlike Madras, it stood on rising ground, was of a regular shape, and had a clear field of fire. For all the disadvantages of proximity to the French capital, it was here that the English had resolved to make their last stand on The Coast.

Already Fort St David had been designated their senior settlement in the peninsula and the hub of what remained of their commercial operations there. Those, like the young Robert Clive, who had made good their escape from Madras and headed for Fort St David, found it on an altogether more warlike footing. Ever since La Bourdonnais's first arrival on the Coast, the Fort's factors had been readying themselves for action by calling in all merchandise, stockpiling provisions and military stores, and recruiting a force of peons which now numbered some 2000. Meanwhile desperate appeals for help, treasure and reinforcements had been sent to London, Bengal, Bombay and even places like Tellicherry and Benkulen. It could only be a matter of time before relief was at hand.

Even so Fort St David's survival seems to have owed as much to Providence, whom its factors invoked with great frequency, as to valour. The failure of the first French assault looks like the result of over-confidence following those resounding routs of the Nawab's forces outside Madras. After a short but hungry night march from Pondicherry, the French troops bivouacked outside the fort and fell to 'dressing their victuals' with true Gallic devotion. The Nawab's hordes had been shadowing their advance and chose this moment to launch a surprise attack. Caught off their guard the French panicked, at which point the English peons issued forth to join in the fray. Clive, who took part, claims that the French 'lost a great many men by the random shot of the Moorish infantry and our peons'. But there was no rout and the French reached Pondicherry in good order.

Having bought off the Nawab with a large cash indemnity, Dupleix should have succeeded at his second attempt. This time the French force was twice as strong and was commanded by the able Monsieur Paradis, the victor of one of those engagements with the Nawab outside Madras. Additionally, the English within the fort were now at their lowest ebb. Twice Company vessels had come within sight of the fort only to put hastily back to sea, without so much as landing their letters, when they heard of the proximity of French shipping. Worse still, it was more than four months since the fall of Madras and there was still no word from Bengal of the men, munitions, treasure and stores which had been repeatedly requested. Nor was there any word of the wretched Peyton and his squadron. 'We endeavour to bear up under the melancholy circumstances', wrote the Fort St David factors but added, not without feeling, that they thought it 'somewhat unkind in our countrymen and fellow servants to have abandoned us.'

Luckily such black sentiments were soon dispelled. On 2 March 1747, after a day-long exchange of artillery fire, the English were forced back behind the walls of the fort. The siege, it seemed, had at last begun in earnest. But the very next day the garrison awoke to a welcome sight for which, of course, only Divine Providence could be responsible. There, riding beyond the Coromandel surf, was the long awaited squadron. Relief must have turned to euphoria when it was learnt that its command had passed from Peyton to Thomas Griffin, a man of considerable resolve if little initiative.

With the tables turned the French quickly returned to Pondicherry lest Griffin should elect to besiege it. In fact Griffin was in no position to take the offensive. His squadron was undermanned and Bengal had been able to spare only 100 European troops. The most he could do was stay put and deter a further attack on Fort St David.

Thus for a year (1747–8) Griffin presided over an uneasy stalemate during which reinforcements trickled in to both Fort St David and Pondicherry. Besides the Bengal troops, the English received nearly 400 topazes, peons and Europeans from Bombay and Tellicherry; there were also a few more recruits from England. There the news of the loss of Madras had prompted the directors to make an impassioned appeal to the Government, as a result of which a new squadron crammed with troops had reportedly sailed from home at the beginning of 1748. But pending its appearance on The Coast the most significant addition to the Fort St David garrison was the arrival there, at about the same time, of Major Stringer Lawrence.

Lawrence's appointment as commander of the Company's forces was a belated response to the death of Major Knipe back in 1743. Like Knipe, he was a veteran of the regular army. He had fought at Fontenoy and Culloden and, though now into his portly and crabbed fifties, he combined military flair with a Churchillian bullishness that endeared him to his troops. While the stalemate lasted, Lawrence concentrated on transforming Fort St David's motley collection of Europeans, topazes and peons into an effective fighting force. The Europeans and topazes became a single battalion, the peons (or now more commonly 'sepoys') were formed into regular companies, and an amply officered command structure was established. It included Robert Clive who, having shown himself to be 'of a martial disposition', had just been commissioned an ensign. Of necessity these new arrangements were perfunctory, but the authority of Lawrence and the charisma of Clive would ensure for them posterity's reverence. According to the former's biographer, 'it was in such humble beginnings that the Anglo-Indian army had its origin'; according to the best of the latter's many biographers this little force 'was the germ of an army that won an empire for England'.

Winning an empire was not, however, the immediate priority. When Griffin and his squadron were at last lured away by a French fleet, Dupleix saw his chance. Again the French troops marched out of Pondicherry under cover of darkness. This time they skirted Fort St David and arrived before Cuddalore which Lawrence, with his augmented garrison, was now holding. Long and low, the walls of Cuddalore positively invited attack and French ladders were soon in position; with surprise on their side, French arms should have triumphed. But somehow word of the plan had already reached the English. Lawrence's men were waiting and the French were thrown back with considerable losses.

Six weeks later Admiral Boscawen's long expected fleet from home anchored off Fort St David. When united with Griffin's squadron Boscawen's fleet formed the largest concourse of European shipping ever seen in the East – thirty-nine vessels including thirteen ships of the line. Additionally he brought munitions, guns, treasure and 1200 troops. Raised by officers of the regular army and formed into twelve companies, these were the first Royal (as opposed to Company) troops to serve in India since that ill-fated garrison sent out by Charles I to occupy Bombay. They were also the first British (as opposed to English) troops, having been largely recruited in Scotland and Ireland. It was forty years since the Act of Union, but only after Culloden and the '45 had Scots begun to play their major role in the affairs of India and of the Company.

Scarcely had the new arrivals found their land legs than they were marching off to the siege of Pondicherry. The tables were turned and it was the British who now took the offensive. With 4000 Europeans (including marines and seamen provided by the fleet) plus 2000 sepoys, the British greatly outnumbered the French. With a force ten times the size of that which had surrendered Madras even Lawrence expected a quick victory. But Dupleix had long been preparing for this eventuality and had greatly improved Pondicherry's defences. Boscawen in over-all command had no experience of siege warfare. And Lawrence was taken prisoner before the siege proper got under way. As a result, the English made a series of disastrous errors, squandered their forces, and inflicted negligible damage. After two months and over 1000 fatalities (mostly due to sickness) the siege was lifted. As with the Company's first trial of strength with a European rival – that with the Dutch in the archipelago more than a hundred years before – the whole affair was as unnecessary as it was ignominious. For in Europe preliminary terms for the Peace of Aix-la-Chapelle had already been agreed in the previous April. They contained a stipulation whereby the hostilities in India were supposed to have already ended.

The Peace of Aix also provided for the exchange of all prisoners (Lawrence had already been freed) and the restitution of Madras. Accordingly, in August 1749 the French garrison hauled down its flag and marched out by the sea gate while the Company's troops marched in by one of the landward gates. They found the fabric of both town and fort 'in extreamly bad condition'. But at least the Indian merchants and middlemen were relieved to see them back; from The Coast's other trading settlements they flocked to the city, trade was resumed, and Black Town again began to expand. It was a sign of the times, and of priorities, that Robert Clive now relinquished his commission and resumed civilian employ as Fort St George's Steward (in charge of purchasing provisions) and as an ambitious private trader. With Lawrence as Acting Governor the Fort's Council resumed its 'Diary and Consultations Book' in November 1749.

The appearance of normality was, however, illusory; both Clive and Lawrence would soon be back in the field. Peace had neither reconciled the two rival Companies, nor dispersed the concentration of troops which each now commanded; nor had it removed the ambitious Dupleix. Indirect hostilities had already broken out before the restitution of Madras. They would continue for six years, their results would far outweigh anything that had been achieved during the previous five years of outright war, and they would be quickly followed by another period of full-blooded confrontation sanctioned by the Seven Years War in Europe. The Peace of Aix had merely concluded the first phase of the struggle.

It would probably be tedious and certainly, given the many published accounts, superfluous to chronicle the military details of this protracted struggle. Similar power games were in progress all over the subcontinent as the fragile confection which was once the mighty Moghul empire crumbled like a crushed papadom. Sometimes large sections would break off more or less intact as was the case with Bengal and Hyderabad. Nominally the Carnatic – the province immediately inland from the French and British settlements – was still subordinate to the Nizam of Hyderabad; but here, at the most friable extremity of the Empire, a combination of Balkanization and Byzantine intrigue had so compounded the confusion that, as the Nizam himself had remarked, every landed *poligar* (feudal chief) considered himself a Nawab and for every so-called Nawabship there were several claimants.

The Carnatic Wars, in which the French and British now became eager participants, mirrored this chaos. In fickle alliances the numerous contenders marched and counter-marched their forces across a rich and champaign land of large horizons and lofty palmyras. Single rocks of Cyclopean size suggested tactical advantage and provided a focus for manoeuvres. The few solitary boulder-strewn hills were invariably fortified – ready-made redoubts for a series of interminable sieges in which besiegers and besieged easily changed places. Like Flanders or Picardy, the Carnatic dictated a diffuse and wearisome species of warfare in which victory contained little promise of peace and defeat was rarely fatal.

Bound over by the European peace, and further constrained by their subordinate status within the old Moghul hierarchy, the French and English Companies could neither oppose one another directly nor make conquests in their own name. Instead they operated by proxy, adopting the causes of rival Nawabs. These dignitaries had a claim on the active support of their European feudatories and thus, in taking the field on their behalf, the French and British could claim to be discharging a legitimate obligation. It was, though, an obligation with strings. For such was now the reputation of European arms that a heavy price could be demanded in return. The territories and revenues which would accrue to the two Companies were acquired not by right of conquest and at the expense of their enemies but by right of cession and at the expense of their allies.

A pattern of sorts was quickly established. Although history usually credits Dupleix with taking the initiative, it was in fact the British who first evinced a taste for mischief. In early 1749, while the peace arrangements were still under negotiation, a force of 1400 British and Indian troops marched south out of Fort St David in support of an adventurer with a doubtful claim to the throne of neighbouring Tanjore (Thanjavur). It seems that Boscawen and Floyer, the Company's new President, had hatched the scheme. The former anticipated restoring the reputation of British arms after the failure to take Pondicherry and the latter welcomed any ploy that would remove from the Company's shoulders the burden of housing and feeding a temporarily redundant army.

There were, though, other considerations of a more traditional and commercial nature. As well as defraying the cost of the expedition, the 'Tanjorine' pretender had undertaken to reward the Company with the grant of Devikottai, a coastal fort fifteen miles south of Fort St David at the mouth of the Coleroon river. Ten years earlier the French had acquired the nearby port of Karikal. It was important for commercial reasons to establish an emporium on the rich Tanjore littoral where, besides the French, both the Dutch (at Negapatnam) and the Danes (at Tranquebar) were already established.

When the first Tanjore expedition failed and a second, commanded by Lawrence and twice as strong, sailed direct for Devikottai, it became clear that this acquisition was the real objective. The 'Tanjorine' in whose name the British were supposedly fighting was simply pensioned off as soon as the fort was taken. In return for a title to the place from the existing Raja of Tanjore, the British agreed to a cessation of hostilities. Mission accomplished. According to Robert Orme, whose usual informant,

Clive, had played a conspicuous part in the attack, Devikottai was not only well situated to tap the local production of 'linnen' but also commanded the mouth of the Coleroon river which, with a bit of dredging, could become the only harbour on the entire Coast 'capable of receiving a ship of over 300 tons burden'. In other words, Devikottai was just another of those obscure anchorages – like Divi, Chittagong, Pulo Condore – in which over-enthusiastic factors detected a second Bombay. Like them, it too failed to live up to expectations, but the whole affair serves to emphasize the continuity of Company thinking. A secure commerce, and not territorial expansion, was still the priority.

It remained so until Dupleix's altogether more imaginative intrigues began to bear fruit. While the British were double-dealing in insignificant Tanjore, the French had found a worthier assignment for their footloose soldiery in promoting the claims to the Nawabship of the Carnatic of the energetic Chanda Sahib ('the only leader capable', in Orme's quaint phrasing, 'of exciting intestine commotions') and those of Chanda Sahib's ally, Muzaffar Jang, to the Nizamate of Hyderabad. Again French arms carried all before them and in July 1749 the confederates duly defeated and killed the incumbent Nawab. Chanda Sahib succeeded. By way of appreciation the French received various territories including Masulipatnam (the port of Hyderabad) and a cluster of villages in the vicinity of Pondicherry. The latter could be seen as a reasonable provision, like the Trivitore grant in the case of Madras, for the future defence and expansion of Pondicherry. But to the British it looked much more sinister. For as a result of the grant, nearby Fort St David was now ringed by French territory and effectually cut off from the inland weaving centres on which its trade depended.

Floyer and his Council responded by seizing San Thomé, the erstwhile Portuguese settlement on the outskirts of Madras, and by having their acquisition confirmed by Mohammed Ali, the son of the Nawab slain by Chanda Sahib and his confederates. Among pretenders to the Nawabship legitimacy was scarcely a relevant consideration given that in both Hyderabad and Delhi the only sanctioning authority was now also up for grabs. But Mohammed Ali had as good a claim as anyone to the Carnatic throne and had shown himself a loyal friend during the late war with France. Henceforth he would be the British candidate. In late 1749 a first trickle of Company troops was put at his disposal. Like his rival, he acknowledged the help by awarding those same villages round Fort St David to the Company. Six months later he added the large district and fort of Poonamallee near Madras, 'the key to all this country' according to the optimistic Madras Council.

But still the British were merely responding to French pressures. It was not until the end of 1750, when the second part of Dupleix's master plan fell into place, that it dawned on them that they were involved in more than a tussle for commercial advantage. First Mohammed Ali, the British candidate for the Nawabship, was roundly defeated; then, two months later in December 1750, the incumbent Nizam of mighty Hyderabad was murdered and Muzaffar Jang, the French contender, took his place. Both the Carnatic and Hyderabad were now ruled by French puppets. Dupleix was heaped with honours and presents, rewarded with further territory said to yield an annual revenue of over 350,000 rupees, and co-opted into the Moghul hierarchy as 'Zafar Jang Bahadur' and the new Nizam's Viceroy for the Carnatic. And all this was only the tip of the iceberg. For with French arms apparently invincible and with the rulers of both the Carnatic and Hyderabad (whose territories stretched west almost to Bombay and north to Bengal) dependent on them, Dupleix was master of half the peninsula.

It would be hard to over-estimate the impact on the Company's men of what the Madras Council called 'this extraordinary revolution'. They now recognized that Dupleix had changed the rules of European involvement in India. For 150 years the Company had been endeavouring to appease the existing political hierarchy; in three years Dupleix had simply usurped it. The English must either follow suit or leave the table.

In the person of Thomas Saunders, who had just succeeded Floyer as President of Madras, they accepted the challenge. In the summer of 1751 all available troops were rushed to Trichy (Trichinopoly, Tiruchirappalli) where Mohammed Ali was making what looked like his last stand; and to relieve the pressure still further by diverting some of the besieging forces, Robert Clive was re-commissioned as a captain and authorized to march on Arcot. 'It is conceived that this officer may be of some service', opined the Fort St David Council. With 800 recruits and three guns Clive left Madras in September 1751 to launch a campaign that would redeem the Company's supremacy; or, in the words of his biographer, that would 'lay the first stone of the foundation of our Indian Empire'.

In the mightily confused struggle that followed, none of the European settlements was directly affected and only Company troops were involved. France and Britain were, after all, at peace. Instead of Madras and Pondicherry, it was Arcot, Chanda Sahib's capital, and Trichy, Mohammed Ali's headquarters, which bore the brunt of the fighting. There were no less than three sieges of Trichy plus countless skirmishes in its vicinity. In all these, as in the few really decisive engagements, European troops again demonstrated their superior firepower. But their numbers were always small. Although some of Boscawen's Royal troops had taken service with the Company, and in spite of an erratic supply of recruits from Bengal, such was the mortality (more from the climate than the fighting) that the Company could rarely deploy over 1000 Europeans; at most engagements there were only a couple of hundred. The same was true of the French, many of whose best troops had marched with Muzaffar Jang to Hyderabad.

In this situation battles were won by opportunism, mobility, surprise, individual acts of bravery, and sheer good luck. A single officer with a taste for improvisation and a reputation for victory could tip the balance. In the Marquis de Bussy the French had just such a man but he was now regulating the affairs of Hyderabad. In Clive and Lawrence the British had two and they were on the spot.

After nine months of fighting their endeavours were rewarded with the surrender of the French at Srirangam and the murder of Chanda Sahib. Peace negotiations were opened but quickly broken off when Dupleix opportunely took delivery of 500 new recruits. The fighting flared up again. It dragged on throughout 1753 with neither party gaining a distinct advantage. More peace negotiations followed in January 1754 with Saunders offering an equal division of the spoils in the Carnatic; but Dupleix declined. By fighting on in the Carnatic, he was drawing the British fire and leaving de Bussy with a free hand in the greater affair of Hyderabad. Only when Dupleix was recalled to France in August 1754 was the way at last clear for a truce and a provisional treaty.

iv

If nothing else the Carnatic war marks the emergence of the European trading companies as territorial powers. As with the grant of Trivitore to Thomas Pitt at the beginning of the century, it was not always clear whether a particular piece of real estate had been made over to one of the Companies in perpetuity or to one of their servants as a life rent, a practice frowned on by both Companies. Dupleix had been in some difficulty on this score. As the Nizam's deputy he was entitled to enjoy the revenues of extensive territories but as a servant of the *Compagnie* he was heavily censured for doing so. It was also true that in the Carnatic several of the estates and townships made over to the French, or their President, were never actually secured. But in Hyderabad it was a different story. There de Bussy and his troops, unopposed by the British, had made themselves indispensable to the Nizam, harrying his Maratha foes from one side of the Deccan to the other and repeatedly shoring up his tottering regime. As a result they had been rewarded with a long slice of coastline and hinterland north of Masulipatnam and known as the Northern Circars. It was now the largest piece of European territory in India.

By contrast the English gains – notably San Thomé and Poonamallee – were modest and mainly designed to constitute a defensive enclave round Madras. They nevertheless had a dramatic effect on Madras's revenue statements. Before the Carnatic Wars the settlements' annual income was about 70,000 pagodas (£30,000), most of it deriving from customs duty on private trade. By 1754 the total had trebled, although 'sea customs' had in fact declined. Instead revenue from dependent territories now made up the bulk. Poonamalee alone contributed 40,000 pagodas (some thirty times what the Trivitore grant yielded) and there was a further figure of 64,000 pagodas from 'countries mortgaged by Nabob [Nawab] Mohammed Ali to the Company towards the discharge of his debt to them'.

Territory was good business – or it could become so as soon as these sums were no longer being swallowed up by the war. To justify his adventurism and its heavy cost to his sceptical employers, Dupleix had gone so far as to declare that the revenues to be derived from the French acquisitions would soon be sufficient to cover the annual investment for French trade; never again need the *Compagnie* send good bullion to India. Although no such claims were made by the English, the thought no doubt crossed their mind. But more to the point, it was plain that with political and territorial control of the main cotton production and finishing centres, the Carnatic trade might be freed from the constant stoppages and impositions which had occasioned a gradual decline in its value ever since the halcyon days of Thomas Pitt.

The motivation for territorial expansion was thus wholly commercial and provoked no great debate amongst the Company's men either in London or the East. Nor was it seen as posing any kind of moral dilemma. Those who imagine that after 150 years of fairly peaceful trade the Company suddenly elected – or was obliged – to embark on a policy of conquest and subjugation completely misunderstand the political situation in India. Imperial conceit would demand a glorious pedigree for 'our Indian Empire' but the plight of India's indigenous peoples in the eighteenth century scarcely affords it.

For in the Carnatic, as in Bengal, the local people – Tamil-speaking Hindus – were already in a state of abject subjugation. No ruler, from the Nawab down to the pettiest *poligar* (feudal chief) seems to have been of Tamil birth. Nor were any of his troops. While the Tamil *ryot* (peasant) took cover amongst the palmyras, the armies, including those of the English and French, which trampled his paddy and commandeered his buffalo were composed of Panjabis, Afghans, Rajputs, Pathans, and Marathas. All were outsiders, adventurers, mercenaries who when not fighting one another were employed in exacting tribute in the guise of revenue. Government was simply a euphemism for oppression under the imperial sanction of Moghul authority.

In acquiring territory accustomed to such rank exploitation it was not obvious to either the French or the British that they thereby incurred some obligation for its better government or that they need propound some justification for their rule. But in so far as their forebears had been a feature on The Coast for a generation or two longer than the Moghul's cohorts, they appeared if anything less foreign and certainly less grasping. In the Company's records Tamil names appear only in relation to agriculture, manufacturing and trade. As growers, weavers, dyers, and merchants, Tamil-speaking Hindus were responsible for the Company's investment and so shared with it a common interest. Given a choice, it could well be, as the Company's men maintained, that the native population preferred the rule of Christian foreigners to that of Muslim foreigners, that of European factors to that of Asian imperialists, and that of a mercantile bourgeoisie to that of a militaristic aristocracy.

But all this was incidental. To the Europeans on The Coast, as to their Asian allies and enemies, territory meant primarily revenue and was worth accumulating so long as the cost was not disproportionate. A similar climate of pragmatic commercialism prevailed in Paris and London. At first the French Company had indulged Dupleix's dreams (in so far as he divulged them) of a puppet Nawab showering trading privileges and revenue possibilities on Pondicherry. But when it became apparent that this could only be achieved – if at all – at the price of a life-and-death struggle with the English Company, and when these fears were swiftly confirmed by Lawrence's victory at Srirangam and the death of Chanda

Sahib, they panicked. A director of the *Compagnie* visited London. He proposed a cessation of hostilities in the Carnatic on terms which the English Company would happily have accepted had they also included the surrender of de Bussy's acquisition of the Northern Circars. They did not; but even so the Leadenhall Street gentlemen might have come round, for in addition the *Compagnie* was proposing another of those non-aggression pacts. In effect this would have made India and the Indian Ocean a zone of peace and neutrality; military expenses could be reduced; trade would be unaffected by another European war. The directors warmed to the prospect.

But at this point the British cabinet stepped in and vetoed the idea. Although the Company might still be free to make peace and war with Indian rulers, in this case its main adversary was a European power. Establishing an ominous precedent, the Government felt entitled to intervene and in fact negotiations were already in progress. In the course of them the French seem to have bowed to the demand that Dupleix be recalled. To the Newcastle ministry this seemed a much better solution than having their hands tied by a non-aggression pact which could only favour the French in that it gave them a free hand in Hyderabad and immunity from the attentions of the usually superior British navy.

This logic, with its implication of continued conflict, the Company was reluctant to accept. Nonetheless, in the words of Professor Dodwell, 'it was forced against its will into participating in the political action of the state'. It was not the first time, nor would it by any means be the last. For its commercial monopoly and its numerous privileges (of establishing settlements, raising taxes, administering justice, employing troops, etc) the Company had always had to pay in concessions as well as cash. Now, in an age of war, its growing dependence on Royal squadrons, regular troops, and political backing meant that the price was climbing steeply.

As if to emphasize the Company's dependent status, another squadron under Admiral Watson together with a further regiment of His Majesty's Foot was readying to sail even as the negotiations dragged on. It got under way in January 1754, somewhat after the French fleet whose reinforcements it was designed to offset. Godeheu, the French commander, therefore reached India first and, knowing of Watson's approach, it was he who swiftly relieved Dupleix of his office and reopened negotiations with Saunders and the Madras Council. Again the Northern Circars of Hyderabad constituted the main stumbling block to an agreement. Godeheu eventually gave way and accepted a situation of territorial parity in the Carnatic in return for relinquishing some of the Circars. But the treaty was purely provisional and no cessions of territory were to take place until London and Paris had approved.

Overtaken by events, this approval was never forthcoming. In the winter of 1755 Watson took his squadron up to Bombay for refitting and then commanded the attack on Gheriah. In this he was joined by Clive on his way back from leave in England and accompanied by more Royal troops. The idea had been that from Bombay Clive would lead an Anglo-Maratha assault on de Bussy's position in Hyderabad; but this was called off partly because of the provisional treaty agreed by Godeheu and Saunders and partly because of Bombay's reluctance to co-operate. After the successful storming of Gheriah in February 1756 both Clive and Watson therefore returned to The Coast, the former as Deputy Governor of Fort St David. They were still there, preparing to meet further French reinforcements which were supposedly on the high seas when, in July, 'a most disagreeable report' reached Madras from quite another quarter. It came from Fort William. Apparently the new Nawab of Bengal had taken it into his head to assault the English factory at Kasimbazar.

> Scarcely were the first transports of our chagrin abated [writes Ives, Watson's personal surgeon] before another dispatch arrived with the news of his having taken Calcutta, and of the dreadful tragedy which happened in the Black-hole prison. This was such a blow as filled us all with inexpressible consternation; and was enough indeed to shake the credit of our East India Company to its very foundations; for hereby they lost their principal settlement in Bengal and a fort which secured to them the most valuable part of their commerce.

Both the Madras Council and Admiral Watson's commanders immediately went into emgergency session. If help were to be sent to Bengal, plans for an attack on the French position in the Northern Circars would have to be abandoned and the whole Coast left at the mercy of the new French reinforcements. Although news of the outbreak of the Seven Years War would not reach India till the end of the year, it was already plain that another Anglo-French trial of strength was in prospect. On the other side of the world fighting had already broken out along the Ohio river, in Nova Scotia, and in the West Indies. The French would strike wherever the British were weakest and, if the expedition were sent to Bengal, that would assuredly mean Madras and the Carnatic.

Nevertheless, Ives was right. The loss of Bengal was tantamount to the destruction of the Company's commercial foundations. With reluctance but great courage, the Madras Council bade good luck and God-speed to Clive, Watson, his squadron, his regiment, and 1000 Madras sepoys.

CHAPTER FIFTEEN

The Famous Two Hundred Days

REVOLUTION IN BENGAL

The events connected with the establishment of the Company's political supremacy in Bengal have been so frequently recounted that, according to Nirad Chaudhuri, the only latitude left to the writer is that of deciding how best to present them. In his *Clive of India* Chaudhuri considered some of the options. An epic style, like that of the *Iliad* or the *Mahabharata*, first suggested itself; but, as he explains, 'that would be too clean a manner for a story interwoven with baseness and squalor'. On the other hand, this baseness and squalor hardly merited a Machiavelli-like analysis when the individual intrigues were 'so inefficient and purposeless'. Chaudhuri, well able to rise to any of these literary challenges, also scouted the idea of telling it all in the disjointed style of a picaresque novel, and was then tempted to extract the more farcical elements for a comic opera. Finally he settled for the safer option of simply 'employing the language of the participants'.

This approach brings out the characters of those involved and the flavour of their endless intrigues. It just about accommodates all the other elements identified by Chaudhuri – the farcical as well as the epic, the adventitious as well as the intended – and it adds one more, a sense of historical awareness. In the midst of momentous changes the participants are revealed as starting to conjecture about the future of the Company in India. At last they see themselves as more than just merchants protecting a valued trade. Empire builders, among whom Clive must be included, would take it for granted that the individual was consciously master of his destiny and well capable of forcing the pace of history. Like revolutionaries, among whom Clive must also be numbered, they made things happen. Perhaps what the story of British expansion in Bengal needs is a Nietzschean gloss.

But, as should by now be obvious, such attitudes of mind were not those to which servants of the Honourable Company had often subscribed. History for them was something that happened around them and to them. It was not something to which they contributed nor into which they expected to enter. They kept journals, ledgers, logs and diaries; occasionally they even penned an account of the geography or commerce of their region. But they did not write histories; they did not see themselves as participants in the historical process.

All this changed with the work of Robert Orme, a contemporary of Clive, whose account of *The Military Transactions of the British Nation in Indostan* was the first history (excluding Downing's modest narrative) composed by a Company servant. Orme was already working on it in the early 1750s, and in 1756 he was a member of the Madras Council which decided to send Clive and Watson to Bengal. He was also Clive's partner in private trade, his attorney, and his confidant. To Clive he looked for first-hand accounts of the engagements and politicking which make up the grist of his tale.

Not without pride, Clive responded with more than a collaborator's zeal; he was not only observing history, he was making it. 'I am possessed of volumes of material for the continuance of your history', he wrote soon after Plassey, 'in which will appear fighting, tricks, chicanery, intrigues, politics, and the Lord knows what; in short there will be a fine field for you to display your genius in.' And then again 'I have many particulars to explain to you relating to the said history which must be published.'

Back in London between the Carnatic campaigns and the attack on Gheriah, Clive had first savoured celebrity. With Orme, who had accompanied him from India, busily chronicling his battles, comparisons had soon been made with the great Comte de Saxe, the recently deceased Marshal of France. The Chairman of the Company presented him with a diamond-studded sword and the directors obtained for him a royal commission as lieutenant-colonel; when he returned to India it was with the promise of succeeding to the Presidency of Madras – yet he was still only in his twenties. To such a disciple of fame news of the fall of Calcutta must have sounded like the muezzin of destiny. Lawrence was too old and too ill to command the land forces of the relief expedition; Colonel Aldercron of the Royal regiment brought out by Watson was too untried and too reluctant to defer to the Madras Council. That left Clive, 'the capablest person in India' according to the faithful Orme. He sailed for Bengal already aware of the bright lights and the sharp focus of history.

It was otherwise for most of his Bengal contemporaries who, like their predecessors, shuffled through their lives, wheeling and dealing, bickering and back-scratching in happy oblivion of posterity's scrutiny. While Clive had been carving his name on the walls of Arcot, Trichy and Gheriah, the Bengal Council had been quietly managing its investment so as to offset the military costs thus incurred. Like the Madras Council ten years earlier, it was well aware that Calcutta's fortifications left much to be desired. 'The fort [Fort William] does not appear to be a place capable of making any long resistance', Boscawen had told the Bengal Council in 1748; 'Pray, Gentlemen, let Calcutta be well secured', advised the highly qualified Mr Robins in what were practically his last words. No less than six proposals had been submitted during the preceding decade; nearly all had been approved but, courtesy of that phenomenal mortality amongst the Company's engineers, none had been carried out.

Thus in 1755 Fort William had still looked 'more like a deserted and ruined Moorish fort than any place in the possession of Europeans'. This was the unwelcome verdict of Captain Jasper Jones, in charge of Bengal's artillery, and it echoed that of Colonel Caroline (*sic*) Scott, the latest expert sent out from London. Scott thought it would require at least 1000 European troops to defend the place 'as it is now fortified, if we may be allowed the expression'. Needless to say, both Scott and Jones submitted new proposals for rectifying the situation; both then died within the year, and so did Scott's successor.

The English capitulation in Madras in 1746 and the successful French defence of Pondicherry in 1748 had convinced the Court of Directors in London that the fortification of Calcutta was both essential and practicable. But it did pose two peculiar problems. For one thing, unlike Fort St George which encompassed Madras's White Town, Fort William was just a fort. The European quarter lay outside it with the flat roofs of its three-storeyed mansions, as well as that of St Ann's Church, completely commanding it. There was less segregation than in Madras, with Indian bazaars within the White Town and the sprawl of Black Town extending outwards on three sides.

In 1742 a ditch had been dug right round the bounds of the settlement in response to a threatened Maratha attack. Significantly the work was instigated and carried out by the native population. But this so-called

Maratha Ditch was never completed and had subsequently filled with rubbish. To replace it with a wall complete with bastions, gates, glacis and garrison would have entailed a commitment in cash, artillery and additional troops which was quite prohibitive. Yet so was the alternative of reinforcing just the fort, since that would entail the destruction of the town's most valuable real estate. The eventual compromise of a palisade halfway between the fort and the ditch merely alarmed the mainly native population outside it without reassuring the mainly European population within it. Some such structure was, however, erected and in 1756 the Maratha Ditch was cleared and a battery commanding the northern approaches to the settlement was under construction.

The second problem concerned the attitude of the Nawab. From his new capital of Murshidabad he was keeping an increasingly wary eye on his European subjects as they plied their trade downriver. It will be recalled that the threat of an incursion by Afghan mercenaries had originally provided the Company with a pretext for building Fort William. The Maratha invasions had found the incumbent Nawab equally amenable. But it was a very different matter when the province was at peace. 'You are merchants', he is reported as saying, 'what need have you of a fortress? Being under my protection you have nothing to fear.' When the French had attempted some defensive works at Chandernagar, the Nawab had immediately condemned them and had threatened dire commercial reprisals until silenced with a bribe. To avoid this complication Colonel Scott had decided to send his plans up to Murshidabad for prior approval. The Company's Agent at nearby Kasimbazar, who was to present them, had sent them back. Either the Nawab would veto them, explained Agent Watts, or else he would demand an exorbitant consideration for his favour and go on making such demands every time a brick was baked.

Of course, what was making the Nawab especially sensitive about any military measures on the part of his European subjects was the extraordinary news that had been reaching Murshidabad from the Carnatic. During the 1740s Nawab Aliverdi Khan had concentrated on meeting the Maratha threat 'with dauntless courage, consummate military skill, and the most unscrupulous treachery' (S. C. Hill). By 1751 he was breathing more easily in respect of the Marathas but was aghast at the effrontery of the Europeans. For it was in this year that the French, having installed their candidate on the throne of the Carnatic, proceeded to do exactly the same thing in Hyderabad. Bengal was the adjacent province to

Hyderabad and it already had a French presence. Truly, observed the Nawab, these Europeans were like a swarm of bees 'of whose honey you might reap the profit, but if you disturbed their hive they would sting you to death'.

Such cautions did not deter Aliverdi Khan from raising that old matter of the English Company's misuse of *dastak*; nor did it stop him from flying into a rage every time the Bengal Council responded with a wave of Farrukhsiyar's *farman*. But news of British victories in the Carnatic and against Angrey on the Konkan only fuelled his fears, fears which he reportedly impressed on his chosen successor, the young and beautiful reprobate known to posterity as Siraj-ud-Daula. After the usual bloodbath Siraj succeeded to the Nawabship in April 1756.

Two months later he dispossessed William Watts and his colleagues of the Company's Kasimbazar establishment and two weeks after that he was master of Calcutta. It all happened so quickly that, in the opinion of those who knew him, the idea for such an attack must have been formed well in advance. It was suggested that he had determined to reduce all the European Companies and that the English, as the most formidable in Bengal, had to be first. Of the three complaints specifically made by Siraj, one concerned the abuse of those privileges contained in the 1717 *farman* and another the erection of those new fortifications. Both were of long standing and both were justified.

The third complaint concerned the sanctuary in Calcutta of a distant and dissident member of the Nawab's family. On the amount of credit to be given to this accusation depends much of the criticism afterwards levelled at President Roger Drake and his Council and much of the dissimulation and impulsiveness credited to Siraj. The facts are quite impossible to establish but in so far as Drake eventually agreed to hand the man over, it would appear that this was by way of a timely pretext.

Assuming, then, that the new Nawab's hostility stemmed from traditional grievances, the English confidently expected a traditional remedy – in other words a financial settlement. When their semi-fortified factory at Kasimbazar was already surrounded by the Nawab's troops, Agent Watts, a man of great experience and ability, had interpreted the offer of a safe-conduct to the Nawab's camp as an encouraging development. The would-be plenipotentiary sallied forth only to find himself bullied and bound as a prisoner. Yet such were still the English expectations of an accommodation that no reprisals were considered and, rather than raise the stakes, the factory was handed over without a shot being fired.

A familiar sense of disbelief, later characterized as rank cowardice, prevailed at Calcutta. When the question of razing all the European houses round the fort was hastily revived, it met with no support. According to Captain Grant, the Adjutant-General, 'so little credit was then given, and even to the very last day, that the Nabob [Nawab] would venture to attack us, or offer to force our lines, that it occasioned a general grumbling and discontent to leave any of the European houses without [i.e. outside the defences]'. Some elementary precautions were taken, like forming a Council of War, recruiting civilians and *Baksaris* (a martial clan from Baksar in Bihar and the Bengal equivalent of peons), and erecting three new batteries; others, like making an inventory of guns and ammunition, were not.

For this oversight Grant blamed his colleague in charge of the artillery, 'a strange unaccountable man' called Witherington. Witherington, had he survived the Black Hole, would certainly have blamed Colonel Minchin, the commanding officer, whose incompetence was immortalized in the acid comment of John Zephaniah Holwell:

> Touching the military capacity of our Commandant, I am a stranger. I can only say that we were unhappy in his keeping it to himself if he had any, as neither I, nor I believe anyone else, was witness to any part of his conduct that spoke or bore the appearance of his being the commanding military officer in the garrison.

But Holwell himself, a Council member and the self-appointed hero of the hour, was not above suspicion. Clive would describe him as 'unfit to preside where integrity as well as capacity is equally necessary'; his colleagues merely winced at the hypocrisy with which 'he wrapped himself in the external practice of religion', psalm-singing all Sunday with his family, while 'for their further example and edification he lived in the closest union with another man's wife'.

Indeed, so universal was the later spirit of recrimination among the Calcutta English that one can only assume that all were guilty of dereliction of duty but that, given the general disbelief about Siraj's intentions, no one chose to make an issue of the matter; 'Such was the levity of the times', recalled Captain Grant, 'that severe measures were not esteemed necessary.'

'The levity of the times' lasted until 13 June 1756 when scouting parties reported that some of the Nawab's troops had been seen at Dum-Dum, nowadays Calcutta's airport. Even then there was still talk of negotiations. But by the 16th the Maratha Ditch was under attack. All British women were taken into Fort William and an assault on the town's northernmost battery was repulsed. It would be the defendants' sole triumph and a minor one at that. The Nawab's troops simply wheeled round to the east and poured across the Ditch where it was undefended.

Report had it that the enemy numbered somewhere between twenty and fifty thousand. Against them the Company was able to deploy just over 200 regulars; with the addition of the militia and volunteers this figure rose to a very precise 515. Had the garrison wasted less time and men attempting to hold more than the fort, had they been amply provided with powder and shot, and had they been ably commanded, the most that could have been expected would have been a brief and bloody moment of glory. It was a contest which even Clive could not have won.

After two days of street fighting a retreat behind the walls of Fort William seemed to offer the only hope. Detachments of Company troops had managed to hold out in their downtown batteries, but were now in danger of being cut off, having failed to halt either the Nawab's cavalry as it careered through the thoroughfares or his myriad levies as they fought and fired their way from house to house. Once these troops were back inside the fort, though, it was obvious that even here resistance could only be short-lived. From the church and surrounding roof-tops the Nawab's sharp-shooters raked the ramparts with their fire. Smoke billowed from the ruins; ever more men pressed round the fort. There was now nothing to prevent Siraj bringing up artillery and very little, given the walls' many excrescences and apertures, to prevent him essaying an immediate onslaught. Only below the fort's west curtain, where stepped landings and piers gave on to the broad expanse of the Hughli river, did safety beckon. There about a dozen ships – Company sloops and privately owned ketches and yachts – swung comfortingly on their moorings.

The last straw came on the sweltering night of 18 June when at an all-night Consultation the 'unaccountable' Captain Witherington finally delivered his inventory of the fort's ammunition. The gunpowder might suffice, he reported, for a maximum of two or three days; but much of it was damp and would first require drying. 'This single circumstance put it out of all doubt but we should be obliged to retreat in that time, having no prospect to effect a capitulation', recalled President Drake. Not only was there no chance of holding out but no chance of a negotiated surrender; evacuation was now the only option. Like old Job Charnock and his not so merry men, the English would again have to abandon their settlement, take to their boats, and drop downriver to an uncertain fate amidst the swamps of the delta.

To the finality of an evacuation there can be, if not much glory, a certain memorable poignancy. What with the women and children – English, Portuguese, Indian, and many shades in between – there were probably about 1000 souls in the Fort at the time. At a push, the ships could have taken them all off. An orderly retreat under fire would have done much for English morale; Drake and his Council would thus have redeemed themselves; and the Black Hole need never have happened.

But tragically at this point all semblance of authority collapsed. At 2 a.m. on 19 June, while the Council were still debating their plans for the withdrawal, a cannon ball hurtled through the consultation chamber. The meeting broke up 'with the utmost clamour, confusion, tumult and perplexity . . . leaving every member to imagine his proposals would be followed and put into execution'.

Next morning this confusion was faithfully mirrored in the scenes on the waterfront. Word had it that the women and children were being evacuated first; but what with the troops guarding them and the husbands and fathers solacing them, rumour soon suggested a general retreat. As the boats filled, men and women, Europeans and Indians began a stampede to the water. Some drowned as boats capsized, others were swept away on the tide. The enemy's shot, passing clean over the fort, threatened to disable the ships which silently, almost guiltily, one by one weighed their anchors and, without hoisting a sail, slid away downstream on the tide. On board were Drake, the President, most of his Council, and most of the military command including Minchin and Grant.

A few days later they moored off Fulta, a Dutch pilot station ten miles upstream from Hijili island. Unlike Charnock, they were left alone with ample time to bemoan their fate, reflect on their conduct and exchange recriminations.

Meanwhile, in Calcutta the unctuous Holwell had assumed command. He promptly condemned the cowardice of his colleagues and vowed to 'hold out the siege'. Many examples of outstanding bravery ensued but this decision was not one of them. Holwell and the remains of the garrison 'held out' for barely twenty-four hours throughout which time he fully expected that either the fleet would return for them or that the *Prince George*, moored upstream, would come to their rescue. (She was in fact aground.) Holwell had been one of the first to recommend evacuation and it was said that he was left behind only because someone had made off with his boat.

The final storming of the fort occurred just before dusk on Sunday 20 June. Holwell says that out of his remaining force of 170, twenty-five fell on that day; but his figures are not reliable, least of all that of 146 for those taken prisoner and consigned for the night to Fort William's detention cell. That this so-called Black Hole was a semi-basement measuring about eighteen feet by fifteen with a raised sleeping area and barred windows on one side seems fairly certain. So is the fact that from suffocation and dehydration many that night died in it. How many can never be known and scarcely matters. What does matter is that John Zephaniah Holwell was one of the twenty-three survivors and that, for all his faults, he was a brilliant publicist. If the sword had failed him, the pen would not. He too sensed a chapter of history in the making that 'must be published', and in highly emotive language he crafted an account of it.

Like that of the Amboina Massacre, Holwell's narrative found a ready audience, so that to people who had never heard of the Hughli, the mention of the Black Hole would yet conjure up a vivid hell. How the prisoners stripped off their clothes, fought for the window space, retched over 'the urinous, volatile effluvia' and finally fell beneath the weight of their comrades became common knowledge. Schoolboys could recite the details – the precious water being passed round in hats, the gaolers leering through the bars, the prisoners sucking the perspiration from their underwear and, it was whispered, even drinking their own urine. And who could fail to be moved by the description of the survivors, 'the ghastlyest forms that were ever seen alive' emerging into a sickly dawn 'from this infernal scene of horror'?

ii

Retrospectively the Black Hole and the wide currency given it by Holwell 'threw a moral halo over the British conquest of India' and gave to Clive's Bengal campaign 'its terrific energy' (Nirad Chaudhuri). Yet at the time it did not feature as prominently as one might expect in the Company's deliberations. 'The amazing catastrophe of Fort William', described by the newspapers of the day as having put 'All London in

Consternation', referred simply to its loss, not to the Black Hole. Undoubtedly events enlightened the general public about the hitherto obscure activities of a remote merchant community and even shed a human and sympathetic light on them. It also alarmed the City's investors who put the loss of Calcutta to the Company at over £2 million.

But the Court of Directors, with damage limitation in mind, showed minimal anxiety. They congratulated themselves on the fact that both Calcutta's warehouses and its treasury had been empty at the time; and by way of censure they contented themselves with dismissing just the incompetent Commandant Minchin. It helped that the news of the disaster had come via Madras and was therefore accompanied by the reassurance that retaliatory moves were already afoot. And it helped even more that a mere seven weeks of high summer elapsed between the bombshell of 'the amazing catastrophe' and the balm of an equally amazing recovery. Thereafter the news of further victories came so fast and fantastic that the fall of Calcutta and even the Black Hole could be seen as blessings in disguise.

The inconvenience of news from their settlements being anything from six to eighteen months out of date had for once worked to the directors' advantage; sailing schedules had delayed the bad tidings while speeding the good. In fact Siraj-ud-Daula had enjoyed the freedom of Calcutta (or 'Ali-nagar' as he had renamed it), and Drake and his men had endured the misery of Fulta, not for seven weeks but seven months. The Madras Council, mindful of its own plight ten years earlier, had indeed rushed reinforcements to its Bengal brethren. They had reached Fulta by the end of July. But this was in response to the first hint of trouble, namely Siraj's move against the Kasimbazar factory. Presuming that a show of strength would be enough to ensure its restitution, this first detachment, commanded by Major Killpatrick, was only 200 strong and quite unequal to the new task of retaking Calcutta.

When Watson and Clive, after a rough and circuitous voyage by way of Sri Lanka and the Burmese coast, finally entered the Hughli, it was mid December and half of Killpatrick's force had already succumbed to the climate. On the other hand, Drake and the Calcutta refugees, though 'crowded together in the most wretched habitations, clad in the meanest apparel, and . . . surrounded by sickness and disease', were in better heart. Survival had been something of a triumph in itself. According to Surgeon Ives, they 'had so long been disciplined in the school of adversity as to make them kiss the rod'.

Perhaps therein lies an explanation for the spirit of reconciliation that had at last surfaced. In time Watts, then Holwell, had both been released, and along with most of the Company's Dhaka establishment, had found their way down to Fulta. Since there was some doubt about the authority of a Fort William Council that could no longer convene in Fort William, they now formed themselves, with Drake, Clive and Watson, into a Select Committee. This *ad hoc* body was to acquire a permanent and influential status; it 'carried out all the Revolutions which gave Bengal to the British . . . and in later years developed into what is now [1905] the Foreign Department' (S. C. Hill).

With Drake and his erstwhile colleagues deriving their authority from the Company's Bengal establishment, Clive and his troops from the Madras Council, and Watson and his squadron from the Crown, the Committee proved a vital forum in which to resolve the always simmering jealousies of a divided command. Clive, with a Royal commission as lieutenant-colonel in addition to his undisputed command of the Madras troops, was eventually able to dominate its deliberations. But its existence can also be seen as evidence of a growing sense of shared purpose amongst the Company's servants in India. Already a young man called Hastings (with the unlikely first name of Warren) was acting as agent and caretaker for the Company's interests in Murshidabad. The future and first governor-general of all the Company's Indian establishments had been making a tour of the rural weaving centres when Siraj had attacked Kasimbazar. Now neither at liberty nor certainly in detention, he was still in Murshidabad, well if precariously placed to act as go-between.

Hastings's news of the Nawab's affairs was not encouraging. Defeat of the English had given Siraj such delusions of grandeur that to the Emperor in Delhi he had announced his success as 'the most glorious achievement in Indostan since the days of Tamerlane'. Such a mighty conqueror could afford to be magnanimous and he had therefore commuted the sentence hanging over the Dutch and French establishments in favour of hefty fines and constant insults; it delighted him to reflect that he had not just conquered the English but had got the other Europeans to pay for it. In October his confidence was further boosted by the defeat of a rival for the Nawabship and confirmation from Delhi of his title. He celebrated the occasion by conducting a public stock-taking of his personal wealth, the grand total coming to 680 million rupees or £85 million. Clearly here was an Indian prince who had no pressing need of further cash. If the British at Fulta were ever to regain Calcutta, it would not be by the time-honoured expedient of dipping into the Company's treasure chests.

Clive and Watson had already written to the Nawab demanding restitution and compensation. When by Christmas 1756 no reply had been received, tents were struck and anchors weighed. While Clive's 1000 Madras sepoys marched upriver, his 800 European troops sailed alongside them in Watson's ships. It was known that Siraj was back in Murshidabad but that his governor of 'Ali-nagar' had taken up position in the fort of Baj-baj which commanded the Hughli just below Calcutta.

Approaching the area Clive and a detachment of his troops were ambushed. Though outnumbered ten to one, they routed the attackers in just half an hour. The fort looked a more formidable proposition and, after a taste of Watson's gunnery, was reserved for a copy-book assault by the cream of the troops on the following day. But this plan was frustrated by an act of notorious indiscipline. While Clive's assault force lay in wait for the dawn, 'one Strahan, a common sailor belonging to the *Kent*', having evidently made too free with the 'grog', was seen to stagger uncertainly forwards, wade the fort's moat, and 'imperceptibly get under the walls'. There, according to Ives, 'he took it into his head to scale a breach that had been made by the cannon of the ships'. Chance thus found him on top of one of the bastions and surrounded by incredulous guards 'at whom he flourished his cutlass, and fired his pistol'. 'Then after having given three loud huzzas, he cried out "The place is mine".'

Responding to this outburst, some of his comrades, who had also 'accidentally' wandered into the same no-man's-land, rushed the breach. They found Strahan bloodied but unbowed and still defending himself with 'incomparable resolution' plus the stub of his broken cutlass. By now the whole place was in an uproar. Sailors, sepoys and troopers poured into the breach; the fort's garrison melted into the night. Thus Baj-baj, the first and, in the event, the only obstacle to the capture of Calcutta, fell to the British by mistake. The only casualty, a Scots captain, also fell by mistake; 'he was unfortunately killed by a musket-bullet from one of our own pieces.'

Watson was hard put to conceal his delight at the mighty Clive being upstaged by one of his common sailors. It would have been a good moment to quote Lancaster's grudging remark when adrift off the Cape – 'these men regard no commission'. Instead Watson appeared to reprimand the miscreant. Strahan was taxed with a flagrant breach of discipline and duly confessed his guilt; it was indeed he who had taken the fort, he said, but he 'hoped there was no harm in it'. Watson pretended to be unmoved. As the offender was led away to a punishment that never materialized he was heard to utter a solemn oath to the effect that, if flogged, he 'would never take another fort by himself as long as he lived, by God'.

Such self-denial proved of no evil consequence when two days later the squadron began pounding Fort William. In less than an hour the Fort's guns fell silent as someone ashore 'hoisted an English pendant on a tree'. The British retook Calcutta as easily as they had lost it, noted the chief of the Dutch factory at Chinsura. The town's inhabitants came out to welcome back their old masters and the only serious altercation was that between Captain Eyre Coote, the Royal officer who actually took possession of the place on behalf of Watson and the Crown, and Colonel Clive who immediately claimed possession for the Company by virtue of his superior rank and the command invested in him by the Madras Council. At one point the quarrel looked like ending in the arrest of Clive or even an exchange of fire.

It was not just a question of to whom belonged the honours. Clive seems to have viewed the situation as an important test of his authority. With the Admiral making common cause with the Bengal civilians, there was a real possibility of a peace being quickly concluded with the Nawab on the basis of the old 1717 *farman* plus compensation, especially for private losses. But Clive had not come to Bengal to restore an unsatisfactory *status quo ante* and enrich the Bengal factors. He was there 'to do great things', as he told his father, not just to retake Calcutta but to leave the Company in Bengal 'in a better and more lasting condition than ever'. The example of the French in Hyderabad, and of the French and then the English in the Carnatic, could be emulated in Bengal. The unpopularity of Siraj, the danger posed by the French at Chandernagar, and – not least – the pecuniary and professional opportunities offered by a Bengal campaign, demanded that the Company take the offensive.

In the end, by a 'pass-the-parcel' compromise, Coote handed Calcutta over to Clive, Clive to Watson, and Watson to Drake and the Bengal Council. Then, evidently as part of the same transaction, the Council, '*persuaded by Colonel Clive* [author's italics], immediately published a declaration of war against the Nabob [Nawab] in the name of the East India Company as did Admiral Watson in that of the King'.

Hostilities commenced immediately with an attack on the Nawab's port of Hughli, which was virtually sacked, plus preparations to engage the army of the Nawab himself, now marching for the second time on Calcutta. Clive drew up plans for a redesigned Fort William and for the demolition of all those grand houses, now sadly ransacked, which commanded it. There was, though, no time to put the Fort on a defensive footing and it was therefore decided to await the enemy in camp just to the north of the settlement.

Meanwhile negotiations of a sort were in progress. In the previous year, with the English at his mercy, Siraj had proposed terms whereby their trading privileges as per the 1717 *farman* would be completely surrendered. This was, of course, totally unacceptable. But similarly the Select Committee now offered terms as extravagantly favourable as Siraj's had been unfavourable. In addition to all the privileges included in the *farman*, many of which had never been conceded by the Nawabs, the Committee also demanded the right to coin its own rupees in Calcutta and to interpret *dastak* in its broadest possible connotation. Siraj ignored these suggestions; but when he next invited overtures, he found that the demands had been increased. It seemed clear that the Committee was determined on a trial of strength.

Nevertheless, the negotiations were still in progress when on 3 February the Nawab's army began to file past Clive's camp and set up its own on and within the eastern bounds of Calcutta. Why Clive did not attack as for two days the columns of horse and foot, elephants, oxen and artillery lumbered past his tent flaps is something of a mystery. Coote guessed there were 40,000 cavalry, 60,000 infantry and thirty cannon. Perhaps Clive simply did not know where to begin. With just 2000 foot, fourteen guns and no cavalry, it was essential to avoid galling and indecisive skirmishes. His preference, born of experience in the Carnatic, was always to strike hard and unexpectedly, often at night and usually against the enemy's greatest concentration.

Such was precisely the intention when twenty-four hours later he did finally take the field. But a late start, plus heavy going across the paddies, meant that it was already daybreak when he reached the Nawab's encampment near Chitpur. Obligingly a dense mist, not uncommon during the winter months, then blanketed his further movements and induced the sort of confusion in which European discipline showed to advantage. Pouring fire to left and right the British passed clean through the camp leaving more than a thousand dead in their wake. They missed, however, the Nawab's headquarters and completely overshot their intended line of retreat. Thus when the sun finally melted the dawn mist, they were still within range of the Nawab's cannon and themselves suffered unacceptable losses – fifty-seven dead – before regaining the safety of the Maratha Ditch.

Clive dismissively called this action 'a tour through the Nawab's camp'. But he also admitted that it was 'the warmest service I was ever yet engaged in'; in retrospect, and not excepting Plassey (his next engagement) it was the nearest thing to a battle that he ever fought in Bengal. Whether he had won it was not immediately clear. After all he had been compelled to retreat under heavy fire and had had to abandon some of his guns. Watson quickly warned the Nawab that it was simply by way of an appetizer; he urged Clive to deliver the full menu without delay. But Clive thought it had served its purpose, and the Nawab put the matter beyond doubt by withdrawing his forces to Murshidabad and hastily agreeing to whatever terms were dictated. These were as proposed before the action.

The Colonel's reluctance to push his military advantage was informed by three considerations. Adding the wounded to the dead, he had lost over 200 men, a tenth of his entire force; he could not afford further such losses. Additionally, having reinstated the Company in Bengal and gained important new commercial rights, like the mint, he knew full well that the directors would not thank him for prolonging hostilities which, however successful, were costly and fatal to trade. A speedy resumption of trade in the Company's most valuable market was more important even than the safety of Calcutta, for on it depended the profitability of the Company and the confidence of its shareholders. 'If I had consulted the interest and reputation of a soldier', Clive told Payne, the Company's chairman, 'the conclusion of this peace might easily have been suspended.' But his ambition now soared beyond soldiering, at which he had never been more than an amateur. To his father he confided his real objective – 'the Governor-Generalship of India . . . if such an appointment should be necessary'. In furtherance of this ambition he needed to impress the Court of Directors with his credentials as a peacemaker, as the man who not only recaptured Calcutta but also restored its trade.

But the third consideration may have been the most decisive. In the same letter he also told Payne that 'the delay of a day or two [in concluding the treaty with Siraj] might have ruined the Company's affairs by a junction of the Nabob [Nawab] with the French'. Throughout their year of troubles with Siraj the British had been anxiously watching their main

European rivals. Refugees from Kasimbazar and Calcutta had found a welcome sanctuary at French Chandernagar whose Councillors had refused to join Siraj on either of his marches against Calcutta. But neither had they joined the British in resisting Siraj. There were renegade Frenchmen in the Nawab's army and French gunpowder had allegedly been used by the Nawab's artillery.

The French maintained that they had scrupulously observed that old non-aggression pact between the two companies in Bengal; but this vague understanding was not such as someone bloodied in the campaigns of the Carnatic was likely to respect. Before leaving Madras Clive had made his intentions quite clear. He would 'relieve the French of Chandernagar' the moment word of a resumption of Anglo-French hostilities in Europe reached India. Rumours of just such an event had begun circulating in late 1756; they were duly confirmed at about the time of the Chitpur engagement when Commodore James, the hero of Suvarnadrug, made an unexpected appearance in the Hughli.

James, whose navigational skills stand comparison with his martial exploits, had conceived the idea of establishing a winter route between the west and east coasts of India, hitherto considered impossible because of the coastal winds, by sailing right round the Indian Ocean. Accordingly he had left Bombay heading south-west till ten degrees below the Equator, then bore east for Sumatra, and finally up the Malay peninsula. After 'a feat unexampled in the navigation of those seas' (C. R. Low) he delivered news of the outbreak in Europe of the Seven Years War. He also brought 500 welcome, if somewhat disorientated, Bombay troops. According to Ives, they 'enabled us immediately to act offensively against the French'.

Although delighted, and perhaps indeed decided, by this unexpected reinforcement, Clive and Watson faced a number of problems. The French were pressing for a renewal of the old neutrality pact and in this they were half-heartedly supported by the Calcutta civil establishment and whole-heartedly by the Nawab. 'If you are determined to besiege the French factories', Siraj warned, 'I shall be necessitated . . . to assist them with my troops.' In effect the situation was precisely the same as that on the Coromandel coast at the beginning of the War of the Austrian Succession. Then the proximity of Barnett's squadron had given Morse occasion to prevaricate over neutrality. Now the presence of Watson's ships made the Bengal Committee prevaricate. The only difference – and it was a big one – was that on The Coast French shipping had been the temptation; in Bengal it was Chandernagar, the principal French settlement.

Watson himself was the second problem. Chandernagar's defences, like those of Gheriah and Baj-baj, cried out for the sort of cannonade which only his ships could deliver. It had to be a naval attack. Yet the Admiral was a real stickler for the niceties of engagement. As commander of a King's fleet in time of war he was obliged to attack. Yet to do so on Bengali soil could be seen as flaunting the authority of the Moghul Empire, infringing the recently concluded treaty with the Nawab (which spoke vaguely of abjuring hostilities), and inviting the very conjunction of the French and the Nawab which Clive hoped to pre-empt.

On the whole then Watson seems to have preferred the idea of a neutrality pact; but here another problem arose. It transpired, although it should have been obvious from the start, that the French in Chandernagar could vouch only for their own neutrality, not that of Pondicherry nor, more crucially, that of de Bussy at Hyderabad. De Bussy was reportedly about to march on Bengal. He was coming to support the Nawab, said the French; against the Nawab, said the English. Either way, he was not going to observe any pact made by the subordinate councillors of Chandernagar. In an agony of indecision, Watson paced the poop of his flagship and invited guidance from the Select Committee. They stalled. A new approach was being made to the Nawab.

If Watson's dilemma was the result of scruple, the same could not be said of Siraj's predicament. Before his treaty with the British had been signed, he had awarded to the French all the concessions contained in it, thus for the first time giving the *Compagnie* a chance of trading on equal terms with the Company. Nothing could have been more provocative. At one fell swoop, the French had acquired all those privileges so painfully negotiated by Surman and so doggedly pursued by his successors. The British naturally assumed that this generosity presaged some secret understanding between Chandernagar and Murshidabad; yet the French, in spite of vigorous lobbying, failed to persuade the Nawab to declare himself. Possibly he was too anxious about de Bussy's intentions. More probably he was worried about the effect on the British. Agent Watts was back at his post in Murshidabad and busily intriguing to bring all possible pressure to bear. Even Watson weighed in with a couple of resounding letters demanding of the luckless Nawab full implementation of the treaty, failing which 'I will kindle such a flame in your country as all the water in the Ganges will not be able to extinguish.'

But the final straw seems to have been the news of quite a different threat – not the first and by no means the last – from the other end of Siraj's domain. Afghan troops, having sacked Delhi, were said to be advancing on Bihar, presumably to extort from Siraj some of that £85 million in his treasury. Although this particular attack never materialized, it seemed real enough at the time. Siraj ordered his own troops to advance to Patna and asked Clive to come to his aid. He was given to understand that the British would happily oblige but for the danger of leaving Calcutta exposed to the French. It was under these circumstances that Siraj wrote, or possibly someone forged, a note of sibylline opacity (and lavish punctuation) which the British chose to interpret as a *carte blanche* to attack Chandernagar.

> You have understanding and generosity [went the note]; if your enemy, with an upright heart, claims your protection, you will give him his life; but then you must be well satisfied of the innocence of his intentions; if not, whatever you think right, that do.

Only one steeped in Oriental intrigue and conversant with the finer points of diplomatic utterance could possibly have seen in this an invitation to make war on the French. Perhaps the whole episode goes to show how adept the Company's servants were becoming in these deep arts. In the course of a few weeks, they had turned Siraj from enemy into accomplice. Having master-minded a policy revolution, why not a palace revolution?

First, though, Chandernagar. In anticipation, Clive had already taken his troops across the Hughli. On 13 March 1757 he attacked and easily overran the suburbs, losing just one man in the process. The French had sensibly elected to make their stand within 'Fort d'Orléans' which bore much the same relationship to Chandernagar as Fort William to Calcutta. There they were safe until Watson began his bombardment on what Ives calls 'the *glorious* morning' of 23 March. Although it lasted for only three hours the engagement deserves that 'glorious' tag as one of the hottest and, as battles go, one of the most exciting ever staged.

Fifty miles from the open sea and twenty above Calcutta, the river is here about a quarter of a mile wide. Watson's plan was to engage the fort's whole waterfront with his three largest ships, the sixty-gun *Tiger*, the seventy-gun *Kent*, and the fifty-gun *Salisbury* drawn up in line astern. There had been grave doubts about whether such large ships could operate so far upriver; and there were further doubts about whether they could dodge the numerous vessels sunk by the French to prevent their closing. By dint of careful reconnaissance, the three warships negotiated these difficulties and amid heavy fire from the fort's guns, including many 32-pounders, they manoeuvred into position. By now the tide, which had facilitated their approach, had turned. The *Tiger* took up position just fifty yards from the north bastion but the *Kent*, which was supposed to engage the middle of the curtain wall, drifted downstream to a position opposite the south bastion, thus elbowing the *Salisbury* out of the action.

'The fire now became general on both sides and was kept up with extraordinary spirit', writes Surgeon Ives who was soon busy attending to the casualties. Broadside and at stone's throw range, the two tiers of the ships' guns could scarcely miss, while from the tops of the rigging the marines poured small-arms fire on to the ramparts. Musket balls that passed over and into the walls of the Governor's house in the centre of the fort were found to have been 'beaten as flat as a half-crown' by the impact. But, unlike Gheriah, Chandernagar boasted European artillery and European gunners. The rigging of the *Kent* was shot away in its entirety and hei hull holed in 138 places; some of the French shells passed clean through one side and out the other; at one point she appeared to be ablaze and half the crew took to the boats only to be shamed into returning. Out of the *Kent*'s total complement of about 200, thirty-seven were killed and seventy-four wounded including all but one of the officers. The ship was a write-off. Although the *Tiger* fared less badly, her casualties were also appalling and 'almost equalled those of the *Kent*'.

'Perhaps you will hear of few instances where two ships have met with greater damage than the *Kent* and the *Tiger* in this engagement', wrote one of the survivors. When the fort finally capitulated it meant the end of French prospects in Bengal; La Bourdonnais's storming of Madras and Boscawen's failure at Pondicherry had been amply avenged; and the British had at last afforded the Nawab awesome and incontrovertible evidence of their martial capabilities. But in the words of the same survivor, 'we have never yet obtained a victory at so dear a rate'.

iii

Clive rated the capture of Chandernagar as 'of more consequence to the Company than the taking of Pondicherry itself'. He was at pains to suggest that without his troops it could never have been effected and, in an effort to associate himself with the final capitulation, he again incurred the wrath of the Admiral. By depriving the French of their most profitable operation and of the base from which both Pondicherry and their Mauritius establishment were provisioned, it undermined the *Compagnie*'s whole position in the East.

It also undermined the Nawab's position. 'I am in hopes this last stroke will fix him', wrote Clive. Such a resounding victory would surely convince the Nawab that a speedy compliance with all the obligations, mostly to do with compensation, incurred in the recent treaty was unavoidable. Certainly the defeat of the French had had a profound psychological impact on the unhappy Siraj. Henceforth fear of British displeasure dictated his every mood and informed his every move. With the absurd idea that Watson's ships might set a course for Murshidabad, another fifty miles inland, he began intercepting the shallow draught barges and *budgeroes* which alone could use this part of the river; he then blocked it in two places. At one of these, about twenty miles below Murshidabad, he stationed a large part of his army. The spot was known as Plassey.

Clive's expectations of the Nawab buckling under to British demands were disappointed, in part because the demands themselves were being continually increased. The terms of the treaty signed after Chitpur, as reinterpreted by Watts and expanded by the Bengal Committee, represented a crushing blow to both Siraj's purse and his authority. To these terms were now added demands for the surrender of the French establishments at Kasimbazar and Dhaka plus the repudiation of a small French contingent under Jean Law, the French agent at Murshidabad. In happier times the duel of intrigue and bribery that was now joined between Law and Watts at the Nawab's court could have played into Siraj's hands. Now it merely played on his nerves, turning a hapless prince into a vacillating and vindictive hostage to circumstance. Law was threatened then fêted, exiled then recalled (in vain), all within a few days; Watts fared little better and, with the idea of forcing a conclusion, even the Nawab's advisers took to fuelling his fears.

At last in May the recurrent rumours of an impending coup by some of Bengal's most senior dignitaries assumed substance. Watts passed word to Clive and Clive willingly invoked the king-making exploits of Dupleix and de Bussy. Along with the Bengal Committee he immediately endorsed this far more effective way of 'fixing' the Nawab.

Evidence for the contention, found in both English and Indian works, that the plot enjoyed popular support and was some kind of Hindu protest against Muslim rule is hard to substantiate. Mir Jafar, the man finally selected as the substitute for Siraj, was a relative by marriage of the previous Nawab and a Muslim. His principal backers were men of differing origins. They included the *diwan* Rai Durlabh who was a Bengali Hindu, the great banking family of the Seths who were Marwari Jains from Rajasthan, and Amin Chand (or 'Omichand') who is said to have been a Sikh (but sounds more like a Jat or a Jain). Unlike the Carnatic, Bengal had been under Muslim rule for several hundred years during which time native Hindus had become well established at all levels of the administration. There had also been many Bengali converts to Islam; it was a more integrated society. Yet the court of Murshidabad was as remote from the Bengali peasantry as that of Arcot from the Tamil peasantry. A self-contained power structure, it reflected the foreign origins of the Moghuls themselves and included, as well as north Indians, Kashmiris, Persians, Arabs and Armenians. Like its counterparts in Hyderabad and Arcot, it ruled by oppression and equated administration with taxation. The army was the only enforcement agency and from the humble *Baksari* to the Pathan janissary or the European gunner, the Nawab's troops were as much mercenaries as those of the Company.

The 'revolution', as Clive rightly called it, cannot be justified on consensual grounds. It was simply a palace coup – an expedient for transferring power that had become so common in late Moghul India as to constitute a normal form of succession. The only support vital to the Murshidabad conspirators was not popular but military, which meant ensuring disaffection in the Nawab's ranks and, even more important in the aftermath of Chandernagar, ensuring British support. Clive provided it on the grounds that he feared that any moment he might be recalled to defend Madras against the French. He needed a quick settlement in Bengal and he saw more chance of it in the highly favourable terms being offered by the solid Mir Jafar than he did in the endless prevarication of the erratic Siraj.

By the end of May, after various subterfuges and a busy exchange of coded letters, the secret treaty with Mir Jafar was ready for signature. There arose a final complication over the share of the spoils to be allotted to Amin Chand, once the Company's chief Indian agent and a man who claimed to have great influence with Siraj. He now demanded an exorbitant five per cent of the Nawab's treasure. It was feared that, if the demand was not met, he would reveal all to Siraj and that, if it was met, the other conspirators would back out in disgust. Under the circumstances Clive had no hesitation in duping the wretched Chand by the rather obvious expedient of preparing two versions of the treaty. One, on red paper, included Chand's share; the other, on white paper and deemed the real treaty, did not.

In the context of a revolution, and compared to some of the intrigues conducted by others (British as well as Indian), this little piece of duplicity would scarcely rate a mention. But eighty years later Thomas Babington Macaulay, like a finicky public health inspector, would pounce on it as incontrovertible evidence of the blackest turpitude in 'the founder of our Indian empire'. Every subsequent biographer has, as a result, felt obliged to dissect the incident and agonize over its significance. The crime appeared all the worse because the fastidious Watson had also drawn attention to it by himself refusing to sign the red treaty, thus obliging someone else – 'we almost blush to write it' crowed Macaulay – to sign it for him. Clive's biographers insist that he was not the forger. The evidence suggests that he would have been, had a colleague's calligraphy not been preferred.

On 13 June, a year to the day since Siraj had begun his attack on Calcutta, 3000 British troops (a third of them Europeans) left Chandernagar heading north for Murshidabad. In spite of the treaty, Clive was still doubtful whether Mir Jafar and the other conspirators would come over to him. His anxieties surfaced publicly on 21 June when a Council of War, attended by all the senior officers, convened at Katwa just south of the Nawab's encampment but on the other side of the river. The question posed was whether to attack 'without assistance and on our own bottom' or whether to wait 'till joined by some country power'. Clive voted to wait; so did more than half the Council. But an hour, or possibly a day, later the Colonel changed his mind. A letter from Mir Jafar egging him on had tipped the balance. On the 22nd the troops crossed the river and on the 23rd they faced the Nawab's army at Plassey (Placis, Palasi).

What followed has been well described as more in the nature of a transaction than a battle. The fighting began with a four-hour exchange of artillery from which the British withdrew behind a ditch. It ceased when a heavy monsoon shower dampened the enemy's powder. In spite of Mir Jafar's assurances, the British forces were still 'fighting on their own bottom' and Clive was again assailed with grave doubts. Having no idea which, if any, sections of the restless horde that nearly surrounded him were commanded by his co-conspirators, he decided to postpone any further action till after dark. No doubt he was hoping for more news from Mir Jafar in the meantime. He had thus retired to his quarters to change into a dry uniform when the really decisive action occurred.

Siraj meanwhile, equally uncertain of who was fighting for whom, had reached much the same conclusion. His most dependable general had been killed in the earlier cannonade and in turning now for advice to men like Mir Jafar he was also testing their loyalties. The results were not encouraging. All counselled a withdrawal to their fortified encampment till after dark. If such was the opinion of those who commanded the bulk of his forces there was no point, however suspect the advice, in attempting to fight on. As a first move, therefore, the forward artillery was withdrawn from the depression it had been occupying.

It was this movement that caught the eye of Major Killpatrick (he who had commanded the first detachment from Madras) while Clive was attending to his wardrobe. In defiance of orders Killpatrick with a small force swept forward to occupy the depression. At last the British were within the sort of range at which their field pieces and musketry could have effect. Clive rode on to the scene breathing fire at Killpatrick but was soon shouting for reinforcements. A massed cavalry charge against the new British position failed to materialize, probably because of Siraj's orders to withdraw. So did a flanking movement which could easily have severed Killpatrick's advance from the rest of the force. Evidently all the troops massed along the British flank were friendly spectators under the command of Mir Jafar and the other conspirators. Vastly encouraged by this realization, Clive's men pressed bravely forward to the kill.

If the Nawab's army numbered 50,000 in all, scarcely 12,000 actually stood by him and took part in the 'battle'. Experience showed that a superiority of four to one was never enough in a straight fight between Moghul mercenaries and well-trained Company troops. There was thus sense as well as treachery in the advice to withdraw; as a result the Nawab's casualties were kept to less than 500. British losses, in what posterity chose to regard as one of the world's decisive battles, came to a grand total of four Europeans and fourteen sepoys, roughly the same as died from a single explosion aboard the *Kent* during the attack on Chandernagar.

Clive entered Murshidabad in triumph six days later and duly handed Mir Jafar to the Nawab's throne. After a brief spell on the run, Siraj was captured and assassinated by Mir Jafar's son on 2 July; it was exactly two hundred days since Clive and Watson had started up-river from Fulta.

The famous Two Hundred Days in which the British had made themselves masters of Bengal included only one decisive battle, Chandernagar, won at appalling cost by Watson and the ships of His Britannic Majesty's navy. In whetting Orme's appetite for his tale of 'fighting, tricks, chicanery, intrigues, politics and the Lord knows what', Clive should have reversed the order of play. Bengal was not won by fighting but by subterfuge. The triumph belonged to Clive but it was a triumph of subversion not conquest. On the face of it Plassey had guaranteed the success of the conspiracy; in reality it was the conspiracy which guaranteed the success of Plassey. The ritual of battle merely legitimized the transfer of power.

iv

Needless to say, there had been no possibility of inviting direction from London as these momentous events unfolded. In July 1757, as Calcutta celebrated the overthrow of Siraj and the imminent division of his spoils, London was trying to digest the Black Hole and diminish the loss of Calcutta. Supremacy in Bengal had been won by the British in Bengal and for the roughly two years that it took to receive a considered response from London it was up to them how they chose to exercise it. Under the new dispensation enormous opportunities existed – for an immensely lucrative trade freed of all restrictions, for territorial and revenue concessions, and for political power. They were rivalled only by unheard of inducements to personal enrichment. The Company had long since acknowledged that private wealth and the public good were by no means exclusive. Witness Thomas Pitt who amassed his second fortune without prejudice to his status as Leadenhall Street's darling. But while Pitt is remembered for his famous diamond, there is something about the way in which Clive and his colleagues now closed ranks to work the Murshidabad treasury which is more suggestive of Kimberley in the diamond days of Cecil Rhodes.

Had the Murshidabad treasure really amounted to the £85 million calculated by Siraj or even the £40 million supposed by Watts, all might have been well. But in fact, as Clive's agents ascertained the moment they reached the capital, it came to only £1.5 million. Against this Mir Jafar's liabilities in the form of compensation and presents promised to the English under the terms of the secret treaty came to over £2.5 million. Less than half of this was due to the Company as indemnity for the loss of Calcutta. The remainder was destined for private individuals – prize money to the army and navy, a handsome consideration for the Select Committee, individual presents for Clive, Watts, Watson etc, and further sums for the Indian conspirators. Clive's share under these different heads totalled £234,000 – and there was more to come.

At a time when a house in Berkeley Square cost £10,000 and ten square miles of rural Shropshire £70,000 – both of which Clive soon acquired – £234,000 was an enviable windfall bound to occasion some criticism. But there was nothing illegal about these transactions. Far from concealing his good fortune, Clive was inclined to boast of it. On the day of his victorious parade through Murshidabad, a place 'as extensive, populous and rich as the city of London' (unlike Calcutta which was merely 'something bigger than Rotherhithe and Deptford'), he claimed to have been bombarded with much better offers and 'might have become too rich for a subject'. Indeed he could not but marvel at his own 'moderation'.

Such moderation, however, was no comfort to Mir Jafar whose financial plight, though critical, was studiously ignored. The Murshidabad treasury was simply emptied and the contents sent downriver to Calcutta on a flotilla of barges. That covered half the total debt; the other half was rescheduled with the banking Seths and then rescheduled again. Each rescheduling occasioned the cession by the new Nawab of further privileges and/or territory. To the thirty-eight villages originally made over to the Company in the 1717 *farman* (but not conceded until the treaty with Siraj) were added, under the secret treaty with Mir Jafar, the twenty-four Parganas, a substantial slice of territory extending downriver from Calcutta to the sea. In 1758 the districts of Burdwan, Nadia and Hughli, all upriver of Calcutta, plus Hijili island and part of Dhaka were also pledged to the Company. And within four years there was a further grant which included distant Chittagong. It was as if the British were consciously acquiring title deeds with a view to redeeming past failures.

The revenues thus made over to the Company were revenues lost to the new Nawab. His efforts to make up the deficit alienated his feudatories; his troops, their pay in arrears, became hopelessly unreliable. Clive's stated policy was to support the Nawab and uphold the offensive and defensive alliance which features in the secret treaty. But the effect of such financial constraints was to reduce Mir Jafar to a liability and turn him against the Company. The Select Committee blamed his 'extremely tyrannical and avaricious and at the same time indolent' character; but similar words had been used of his predecessor and a similar fate would befall his successor. Clive himself would eventually accept that the arrangement was unworkable and would dismantle it during his second administration.

So while Clive and his colleagues amassed vast fortunes, Bengal was destabilized and impoverished by a disastrous experiment in sponsored government. Unfortunately these two features of the post-Plassey situation were related, and therein lies the main indictment of Clive and his Council. Mir Jafar endeavoured to play the role assigned to him with conviction. Twice he honoured Calcutta with a state visit, always a lucrative occasion for the hosts since while the presents from the Nawab went straight into their pockets, those to the Nawab were charged to the Company (including a curious selection of waxworks itemized as '1 Virgin Mary, 12 standing Venuses to pull off behind, 1 lying ditto, 6 kissing figures, 8 ladies under a glass, and 1 Mary and Joseph').

In these, and the more substantial disbursements made at each rescheduling of his debt, Mir Jafar seems to have assumed that by gratifying the Bengal councillors he might expect a more lenient interpretation of his commitments. If so, he was sorely disillusioned. For Clive had so arranged matters that in return for five per cent of all sums made over to the Company and its servants, Rai Durlabh, one of the main conspirators and the man in charge of the Murshidabad treasury, would detach himself from his allegiance to the Nawab and become a focus of British interests and intrigues at Murshidabad. It was he who interpreted the details of the secret treaty to maximum British advantage, ensured that private individuals like Clive benefited, and assisted Clive's agents in acquiring lucrative revenue farming contracts under fictitious Indian names. When in 1758 this betrayal was in the open, Warren Hastings wrote of the inevitable prejudice to British interests and influence. Soon after, Rai Durlabh was given sanctuary in Calcutta and British troops were detailed to escort his family down from Murshidabad. But not before a highly suspicious correspondence had come to light which seemed to implicate Clive's agents and Rai Durlabh in a plot to assassinate the new Nawab. Hastings took the matter seriously; Clive dismissed it, but with a disclaimer that must rankle as much for its hypocrisy as for its prejudice. 'I would leave all trickery to the Hindoos and Mussalmen to whom it is natural, being convinced that the reputation we have in this country is owing . . . to the ingenuity and plain dealing for which we are distinguished.'

In Bihar, the western sector of the Moghul province of Bengal, it was a similar story. Immediately after Plassey, Clive had sent troops to Patna to enforce Mir Jafar's authority and replace the incumbent Governor with the new Nawab's nominee. In the event he changed his mind, confirming in office a man openly contemptuous of Mir Jafar and now firmly attached to the British. Two years later Bihar was invaded by the rebellious Shahzada, the Moghul crown prince, aided and abetted by the neighbouring Nawab of Oudh. With every reason to doubt the loyalty of his Governor, Mir Jafar was obliged to call again on Clive's help. The enemy quietly withdrew on word of Clive's approach, but it was as a result of this action that the Nawab conferred on Clive the infamous *jagir*. It was valued at £30,000 per year for life, so was potentially worth far more than the £234,000 he had already accumulated; and unlike other *jagirs* there was a peculiarly good reason to suppose that he would not incur great expense in collecting it.

A *jagir* was the endowment of land and revenue by which a high official of the Moghul Empire was enabled to support his status and feudal responsibilities. Clive would insist that he had never solicited such a grant and that it was all thanks to the Nawab's 'generosity'. Naturally he, like most of his colleagues, had been accorded grand Moghul epithets. In the courtly language of Murshidabad and Delhi, Clive was variously known as 'Sabut Jang', 'Saif Jang', 'Amir-ul-Mamalik', etc. ('Firm in War', 'Sword of War', 'Grandee of the Empire'). These titles were no more significant than the English habit of sloppy transliteration whereby Siraj-ud-Daula became 'Sir Roger Dowlet'. ('Had he really been a baronet?' asked one of the Company's directors.)

As a military commander rather than a despised merchant, Clive had also attracted titles of rank. In the Carnatic Mohammed Ali had conferred on him the honorary status of *Nawab* and after Plassey he had solicited and received through Mir Jafar the rank of *mansabdar* in the imperial hierarchy. As William Hawkins had discovered 150 years earlier, this rank entitled the holder to a *jagir*. Clive was well aware of it and though having no intention of discharging the obligations of office, like maintaining several thousand horsemen, he nevertheless urged his claim on Mir Jafar.

What did come as a surprise was the location of the *jagir*. He had been refused lands in Bihar as too strategically sensitive; but he was probably unprepared for the grant of the twenty-four Parganas, the very districts so recently ceded to the Company. Herein lay the guarantee of payment plus the near certainty of objection. For it could hardly go unremarked that by accepting this *jagir* Clive became the Company's overlord in the Moghul hierarchy or, in English parlance, its landlord. The Company, as *zamindar* of the twenty-four districts, collected and administered the revenue; but henceforth it must remit the fees for this privilege not to the Nawab but to one of its own employees. If not 'too rich for a subject', the *mansabdar* 'Sabut Jang' had certainly become too grand for a servant. Unsurprisingly he would soon be looking beyond Leadenhall Street for recognition and encouragement.

There were yet other avenues for enrichment. Some, like tax farming, were below a *mansabdar*'s dignity. Others, like preferential trade, were not. After Plassey, in addition to their cash presents, many of the Bengal councillors (including Clive) became recipients of free passes for their internal trade and of concessions for government monopolies like salt. When that old chestnut of *dastak* came up for negotiation, Clive was to the fore in insisting that not only the Company's goods but also those of their servants, their servants' servants, and just about anyone else enjoying (or willing to pay for) British favour should enjoy custom-free movement throughout Bengal. At one fell swoop the Nawab was thus deprived of another source of revenue while the flood gates were thrown open for a bout of unscrupulous profiteering remarkable even by the standards of oppressed Bengal. Four years later Warren Hastings would observe that the entire inland trade had been engrossed by the British or those trading under British colours and British *dastak*.

Theoretically the favours flowing so freely from Murshidabad should have benefited the Company even more than its servants. What Dupleix had promised, Clive had delivered. For at least the next three years, he predicted, there should be no need for the Company to export bullion to Bengal. The purchase of the year's trade investment, as well as the expenses of its establishment, should now all be met from the Nawab's treasury or from the territorial revenues made over to the Company. At the same time the Company's trade should almost double, European competition having been virtually eliminated with the destruction of French Chandernagar and, soon after, the repulse of a Dutch initiative.

But these rosy expectations so confidently proclaimed in the wake of Plassey took account neither of the dangers to Indo-European trade posed by the Seven Years War nor of the enormous military expenses being incurred in India. The Company's Bengal trade did quickly recover to pre-1756 values, but by 1760 it was still showing no signs of exceeding them. On the other hand the military expenses being incurred in Bengal alone must have been ten times those of the pre-1756 period.

All this occasioned harsh words from the Court of Directors in London. Clive wanted a permanent Bengal army of 2000 Europeans and three times as many sepoys (he had already raised his first Bengal regiment). The directors thought that with a friendly Nawab and no European rivals 300 European troops should be ample. They forbade the fortification of any of the outlying factories and were aghast at Clive's ambitious plans for making Fort William impregnable.

> You seem so thoroughly possessed with military ideas [they wrote in 1758] as to forget your employers are merchants and trade their principal object, and were we to accept your several plans for fortifying [Calcutta], half our capital would be buried in stone walls.

The Directors saw Bengal as a place of flourishing trade but surprisingly little profit, a feature which they ascribed to 'the luxurious, expensive and idle manner of life' which prevailed among their employees there. Happily the new turn of events provided the occasion for a thorough reform and with their usual gusto they proceeded to inveigh against every supposed indulgence from the abuse of *dastak*, 'a practice we have ever disclaimed', to the popularity of palanquins. They also took exception to 'the vile manner' in which the Bengal Council recorded its 'Consultations'. 'Basely copied entries frequently erased . . . indexes omitted and other 'unpardonable irregularities' could only denote 'a loose and negligent government'.

This was supposedly borne out by the Council's failure to supply a complete inventory of the plunder taken from Siraj's administration in Calcutta and from the French in Chandernagar. The awards made to the troops out of Mir Jafar's treasury were also censured and the directors were becoming increasingly uneasy at the boom in bills drawn on the Company in London. This was a normal method for employees to remit home their private profits. They lent money to the Company in India against bills redeemable at home, an arrangement that suited both parties. But it could easily get out of hand and, as private incomes rocketed while Company profits languished, the directors stigmatized the whole system as 'cruel and barbarous'. All in all then, the Bengal administration was not only 'amazingly weak' but also operating in a style that was 'highly injurious to our interests'.

Such wholesale censure was nothing new and deserved no more than the usual response of evasion tinged with indifference. Obviously the directors had again been listening to men jealous of the Bengal Council's achievements and desperate to win a share in the new bonanza. But, considering those same achievements, the Bengal councillors had reason to feel genuinely aggrieved; and none more so than Robert Clive. During his four years in Bengal Clive had acquired an unrivalled ascendancy over both the Select Committee and the Council. As Chairman of the former he had neutralized the resentment against his Madras-based authority by a string of dazzling successes. When the Court of Directors decreed a rotation style presidency, similar to the disastrous system introduced after the union of the New and Old Companies, the Council had agreed to flout orders and install Clive as acting President. In due course the directors had applauded this unprecedented exhibition of Council harmony and finally endorsed Clive as 'Governor and President in Bengal'.

Secure, as it seemed, in the confidence of the directors and the esteem of his colleagues, the Colonel and President not only resented criticism but presumed to challenge it. In December 1759, a few weeks before his intended departure from India, Clive wrote to the directors.

> Permit us to say that the diction of your letter is most unworthy [of] yourselves and us in whatever relation considered, either as masters to servants or gentlemen to gentlemen. Mere inadvertencies and casual neglects arising from an unavoidable and most complicated confusion in the state of your affairs has been treated in such language and sentiments as nothing but the most glaring and premeditated frauds could warrant . . .

He went on to accuse the Court of Directors of giving credence to knaves and betraying such favouritism as would 'tend to cool the warmest zeal of your servants here and anywhere else'. Presumably he reasoned that from a 'Grandee of the Empire', a 'Heaven-born General', and the Company's *jagirdar*, such presumption would hardly be dismissed as impertinence. If so, he was wrong. This outburst was a direct challenge to the authority of the Company and it would cost him dear.

It would, perhaps, be going too far to suggest that Clive, having master-minded a revolution in Bengal by subverting the authority of the Nawab, was now bent on a revolution in London and the subversion of the Honourable Company. Now, as later, he would probably have preferred to control the Company rather than remove it. But just as he was the first President openly to criticize its direction, so he was the first to go on record as questioning its existence. In January 1759, with many corrections and rephrasings, he drafted a long and unsolicited letter on Indian affairs and sent it secretly to William Pitt (the Elder), then the dominant figure in the war-time administration, the man who had dubbed his generalship 'heaven-born', and of course the grandson of 'Governor Pitt'.

In this highly revealing letter Clive contended that a glorious future awaited the British in India. If only the Company would 'exert themselves' and 'keep up such a force as will enable them to embrace the first opportunity of further aggrandizing themselves', they might take 'the sovereignty of Bengal upon themselves' (i.e. replace the Nawab). He was confident that the Moghul emperor would accord him imperial recognition since he, Clive, had himself been offered the *diwani*, the second most senior position in the province. This would have given him control of the province's revenue collection and an easy position from which to claim the sovereignty; but he had felt obliged to refuse 'for the present', mainly because the Company would not authorize the troops 'to support properly so considerable an employ'.

> But so large a sovereignty may possibly be an object too extensive for a mercantile company; and it is to be feared that they [i.e. the directors] are not of themselves able, without the nation's assistance, to maintain so wide a dominion. I have therefore presumed, sir, to represent this matter to you [Pitt], and to submit to your consideration, whether the execution of a design that may hereafter be still carried to greater lengths ['perhaps of giving a king to Hindostan,' as he explained to his father], be worthy of the government's taking it in hand.

From Bengal alone he anticipated an annual income of 'upwards of two millions sterling' and he was certain that that, plus the possession of 'the paradise amongst nations', was worthy of 'public attention'. The whole business could be managed without draining the mother country 'as has been too much the case with our possessions in America'. 'A small force from home will be sufficient . . .'

No response to this letter had reached Clive when, partly for health reasons, partly for career reasons, he sailed for home in early 1760. Pitt obviously had other things on his mind – like the Seven Years War. But, as will emerge, 'Clive's letter was the germ of the Parliamentary measures which led step by step to the transfer of the substance of authority from the Company to the Crown' (Sir George Forrest).

PART FOUR

A PARTING OF THE WAYS

1760–1820

CHAPTER SIXTEEN

Looking Eastward to the Sea

SOUTH-EAST ASIA AND THE CHINA TRADE

As a result of Plassey and the emergence of the Company as a major political power in India its priorities were bound to change. If supremacy in Bengal meant that revenue replaced commercial profits as its financial support then administration must replace trade as the profession of its employees. A proliferation of boards, councils and committees began to participate in the direction of its affairs in both London and India. Its Bengal establishment grew prodigiously and increasingly its outward-bound ships carried more in the way of troops and stores, passengers and European luxuries than they did of broadcloth. Ledgers became tax rolls, warehouses arsenals. Men who had once been proud to call themselves 'servants of the Company' now preferred to be seen as 'serving in the Company' – as if it were no different from serving in the Navy or the Treasury. The Company was perceived as a branch of government; and, ere long, it became a branch of government. Only lawyers called it 'The United Company of Merchants of England trading to The East Indies'. To others it was the 'East India Company' or, more significantly, just 'The India Company'.

Naturally this transformation could not be achieved without strains and contradictions. The anomaly – some said scandal – of a private enterprise presuming to govern vast territories, wage wars, collect taxes, and grossly enrich its employees/public servants pitched the affairs of the Company into the public and parliamentary domains. So long as its establishment had comprised just a fleet of ships, a few ports, a London office, and a sheaf of trading concessions, only those with a financial interest in its affairs bothered to interfere. But an empire was something else. It needed regulation and, in time, regulation meant nationalization. By the politician the Company's commercial monopoly and its overseas trading concessions came to be regarded merely as assets waiting to be stripped. But its territories, its subject peoples, its diplomatic commitments and its military establishment – these properly fell within the purview of the state. On them, therefore, the attentions of government and politicians focused. And since the Company's patrimony would be not just nationalized but 'imperialized', on these same features generation after generation of British historians would also focus in a brave attempt to elucidate the origins of the 'British Raj'.

This extraordinary interest in the aftermath of Plassey, though important for the history of India and for the history of the British Empire, again distorts the history of the Company. It was only in India, and indeed until the 1780s only in Bengal and adjacent areas of Hyderabad, that the Company found itself administering extensive territories and treading on the toes of the home government. Elsewhere trade remained as much a priority as ever and, in one sector, even more so. It is ironical that while Westminster was busy clipping the Company's wings, on the other side of the world a new generation of commercial endeavours was hatching. And while in Calcutta feathers flew in the squalid cockfighting, further to the east the Company was again sailing seas and coming home to roost in the lands where Lancaster and the Middletons, Floris and Saris had first opened its account.

What may be regarded as the Company's commercial swan song was inspired by three considerations new to Company thinking; none either originated in Bengal, owed anything to Clive, or was particularly relevant to the rhetoric of Westminster. They were, first, the naval and strategic priorities dictated by a succession of wars with all the Company's major competitors in the East – France, Spain and eventually Holland. Second the Company's growing dependence on, and concern for, its trade with China. And finally a major shift in the thrust of private or 'country' trade.

All these elements surface during the course of the Seven Years War. Commonly represented as affecting the Company only in so far as it saw the culmination of that Anglo-French struggle for supremacy in the Carnatic, the Seven Years War was 'the first world war' and in fact had repercussions for the Company way beyond India. Eventually it would create some interesting possibilities in the Philippines; initially it prompted an unhappy experience in Burma.

Coinciding precisely with Clive's triumphal progress in Bengal, and yet utterly devoid of either glory or consequence, the Burmese or 'Negrais Affair' is readily consigned to oblivion. As with other things Burmese, the facts are obscure and the locations unfamiliar. Quite reasonably one could dismiss the whole business as just another example of that disastrous British obsession with off-shore properties – Pulo Run, Pulo Condore, and now the island of Negrais. Alternatively – and this was the view taken by Alexander Dalrymple, a man of whom more will be heard – Negrais was the first uncertain step towards the re-establishment of the Company's trade in south-east Asia. It should be bracketed not with Pulo Run but with Singapore, not with Pulo Condore but with Hong Kong.

From the Company's settlements at Masulipatnam, Madras and Calcutta, English private traders had been calling at the ports of southern Burma ever since the mid-seventeenth century. Syriam, their usual destination, was the main outlet for the Mon kingdom of Pegu which also controlled the wide Irrawaddy delta. Here rubies and lac (a resinous red dye) were sometimes available although the main attraction was Burmese teak, the finest shipbuilding material in the East. For repairing Indiamen the timber was freighted to Bombay and Calcutta while the smaller vessels operated by country traders were usually repaired and indeed built in Syriam itself. By the 1730s the volume of this business had justified the appointment of an English 'Resident' who although not a Company servant handled both Company and private business. His few European companions included a representative of the French *Compagnie des Indes* whose ships' timbers were also repaired with Burmese teak. But there seems to have been no great hostility between the two and when in 1743 Syriam was twice sacked as a result of renewed fighting between the Mons and the up-country Burmans, both men withdrew to their parent establishments at Madras and Pondicherry.

With southern Burma in turmoil and with the European trading companies locked into their own war over Jenkins's ear and the Austrian Succession, no further attempts were made to reopen a Burmese establishment until 1750. In that year Mon representatives appeared in Pondicherry with a proposal which Dupleix, having just handed Chanda Sahib on to the throne of the Carnatic, was happy to consider. The Mons wanted military assistance against their Burman rivals. There was the possibility of opening another grand field for French ambition. More to the point, Dupleix welcomed the proposal as a means of securing a safe haven on the opposite side of the Bay of Bengal.

The absence of harbours on the Coromandel Coast has already been stressed. With the arrival of those squadrons under Barnett (then Peyton), La Bourdonnais, and Boscawen and with the consequent inauguration of the Bay of Bengal as a theatre for naval warfare, this deficiency became critical. Every monsoon the fleets must desert their station or risk the sort of losses suffered by La Bourdonnais after the capture of Madras. Similarly every time ships needed refitting they must leave the coastal settlements to the tender mercies of the enemy and make for Dutch Trinconomalee (Sri Lanka), Mauritius or Bombay.

Under the impression that they might have found a solution, Boscawen and Lawrence had just wrenched the port of Devikottai from the Raja of Tanjore. But Devikottai proved as useless for ships of deep draught as every other inlet on The Coast. Word, therefore, that Dupleix had sent a French envoy to Pegu to negotiate for a Burmese harbour threw Madras into consternation. President Saunders wrote immediately to London and, without waiting for an answer, prepared to forestall the competition by occupying the island of Negrais.

At the south-western extremity of Burmese territory and therefore the nearest point to Madras, Negrais had been recommended by one of the numerous Englishmen engaged in private trade between The Coast and Burma. Curiously neither he nor Saunders seems to have been aware that the Company actually had a claim on the place. Sixty years previously it was to Negrais that Captain Weltden had repaired after he and Samuel White had been attacked at Mergui. Weltden had allegedly hoisted the English flag on the island and had left an inscription, beaten in tin, recording his claim. It was a pity that this memorial was not rediscovered. The memory of the Mergui massacre might have alerted the Negrais settlers to the possibility of a repeat performance.

Negrais had been chosen by Saunders on the grounds that it had potential for 'a capacious harbour for shipping being well secured against all sorts of winds'. What he did not realize, but what the thirty-odd pioneers quickly discovered, was that it was not secured against all sorts of tides. After a few weeks of being flooded out every time a high sea and a spring tide coincided, the disgruntled and fever-ridden settlers sailed away to the mainland and the comparative comfort of Syriam.

In the meantime the Court of Directors in London had received Saunders's letter and approved his anxiety about a French naval base in the Bay. In 1752 they wrote endorsing the Negrais settlement and in 1753, on learning that Dupleix's envoy was in high favour at Pegu,

Saunders made a second attempt to establish a settlement. This time it was on a much larger scale. Four ships were to convey the new pioneers across the Bay and two covenanted servants, one from the St Helena Council, the other from Benkulen, were to take command. The appointments were made by the directors in London who no doubt recalled the disastrous jealousies aroused when such matters were left to Madras. But it is indicative of the unpopularity of the enterprise that the Benkulen man opted out, preferring even Sumatra's pestilential climate to waterlogged Negrais. Shipwrights and labourers had to be impressed into service; the guard of thirty-odd Europeans and seventy peons mutinied soon after arrival.

To the problems of fever and flood was added that of famine. It was hoped that the settlers would soon be either self-sufficient or able to obtain rice from the mainland. But the Burmese refused any trade and, though the island abounded in game, it was also a paradise for tigers. The settlers lived off turtles; the tigers lived off settlers. Hunt, the man from St Helena, died of dysentery, the work of fortification ground to a standstill, and the Mon authorities steadfastly refused to countenance the new settlement.

Nevertheless the disconsolate settlers, now commanded by Henry Brooke, a writer from Madras, stayed put. By 1754 the Mon-Burman war was going badly for the Mons. Disappointed in their French allies, there seemed to be a real prospect of the Mons granting, in return for military aid, not only Negrais but also the adjacent mainland port of Bassein plus extensive privileges in Syriam. The British contingent in Syriam played along with their Mon hosts; but to Saunders in Madras and to Brooke at Negrais it was now evident that they were backing a loser. When Burman troops occupied Bassein and much of the intervening Delta, Brooke therefore switched allegiance. Missions were exchanged between Negrais and Alungpaya, the Burman sovereign, who was then encamped beside the mighty Shwe Dagôn pagoda at a place which he renamed Yangon (Rangoon). The Company moved its Syriam establishment to the new capital and by 1756 both Company and private ships were calling there for repairs.

While the storm clouds gathered in Bengal, Burma seemingly basked in sunshine. At last the British had backed a winner and, within a month of Siraj-ud-Daula's capture off Fort William, Alungpaya had taken Syriam, the French had been expelled, their agent roasted alive, and the British were constructing a fort at Bassein which, with a fine sense of

Highland symmetry, they called Fort Augustus. Amazingly for a sovereign who considered himself more than a match for the Moghul, Alungpaya had even committed his favourable sentiments to writing by opening a correspondence with George II, or rather 'The King of England, Madras, Bengal, Fort St David and Devikottai'. In a letter which took the form of a tray of gold covered with Burmese characters there was barely room to do more than recite the titles of the writer. But the 'King of Burma, Thailand and Cambodia', 'the Lord of the Mines of Rubies, Gold, Silver, Copper, Iron and Amber', the Lord, too, of 'the White Elephant, the Spotted Elephant and the Red Elephant' not to mention 'the Vital Golden Lance', many golden palaces, sundry other kingdoms, etc, in short 'the Descendant of the Nation of the Sun' did positively transfer the desired site at Bassein and looked forward to 'a constant union and amity with His Majesty of England, Madras, Bengal [etc] and his Royal Family and subjects'.

Perhaps if this letter had received the gracious response it undoubtedly deserved, lives could have been saved. It did indeed reach George II but no answer whatsoever did either he or the Company send; the last that is heard of the priceless missive is an unseemly wrangle about whether the tray had originally been encrusted with rubies and, if so, what had happened to them. By opening a correspondence with a mere earthling the lord of all those elephants had chanced his solar dignity. It was not something he did lightly. In the following year he put his seal to a treaty of friendship with the Company but thereafter, as the months slipped by without so much as an acknowledgement from the Hanoverian, he began to take an exceedingly dim view of British protestations of amity.

There were, though, other sources of friction. British ships putting into Rangoon for repairs and cargoes had fallen foul of Alungpaya's officials and had even joined the Mons in several abortive attempts to storm the place. The Bassein/Negrais settlers were not held responsible for these outrages but, under the terms of the new treaty, Alungpaya did expect them to supply him with the guns and powder which had so often been promised. Yet, excepting the odd presentation cannon and a few barrels of powder, of arms – as of answer – came there none. Worse still, it appeared that the Company was now keen to wash its hands of both Alungpaya and his country. In Madras Saunders had been replaced by the more sceptical Pigot, in Negrais Brooke had been relieved by a man who succumbed to the climate almost immediately, and in London, with rumours rife of Siraj's advance on Calcutta, the directors had espoused a retrenchment which included withdrawal from Negrais. News of Plassey failed to change the corporate mind. 'Schemes of this kind,' they wrote in 1758, 'must be deferred till more tranquil times.' It was, after all, year two of the Seven Years War.

But it was also year six of the Negrais establishment which, against all the odds, now boasted some substantial buildings, plentiful stocks of teak and a modest population. A partial evacuation was effected in April 1759 but there remained a small guard under Ensign Hope and a considerable civilian population. In view of frequent French visits to the Bay of Bengal it seemed prudent to maintain a presence. Later in the same year Captain Southby came ashore from the *Victoria* as Hope's replacement. His arrival coincided with that of an East Indiaman in search of provisions plus three small Burmese vessels accompanying the local Governor. October was one of Negrais's better months. While the *Victoria* unloaded and the Indiaman took on water, Hope and Southby entertained the Governor ashore with two days of feasting and compliments. Of Portuguese extraction, he seemed to appreciate the hospitality and to enjoy the company.

His hosts were thus totally off guard when at the farewell reception the Governor's Burmese escort suddenly bolted all the doors and drew their daggers. Hope and Southby were cut to pieces immediately. Of the other European officers and guards only one escaped and only two were taken prisoner. The rest were butchered along with countless Indians. If the figure of sixty men and four women is correct for those taken off by the boats, the carnage must have been at least three times that of Plassey. The settlement was then looted and burnt to the ground. A week later Captain Alves of the *Victoria*, while remaining on station to warn off other British shipping, went ashore for a last look. The corpses were now rotting, the tigers gorged, the fires out. Alves, then on the threshold of a long and intriguing career as a private trader, was profoundly disturbed. It was 'one of the most shocking sights I ever beheld'.

ii

What, if anything, lay behind the Negrais Massacre is unknown. Alungpaya would deny all responsibility and, nine months later, Alves would travel unmolested right up to Mandalay to secure the release of the prisoners. One can only bracket the mindless carnage with all those other tropical affrays in which the degree of premeditation is as unfathomable as the degree of provocation.

Happily no such uncertainty surrounded British thinking. The object of Company policy over Negrais had been to prevent the French from gaining a naval base in Burma and so supremacy in the Bay of Bengal. In the event Alungpaya had done the job for them. His sack of Syriam in 1757, which had resulted in the extinction of the French interest, coincided almost exactly with Watson's bombardment of Chandernagar. Taken together, these two reverses meant that henceforth the French could operate in Indian waters only at a severe disadvantage.

It also meant that for the British Negrais became superfluous. Significantly the first, partial evacuation of the settlement had been carried out from Calcutta and it was from there that Hope, Southby and Alves all hailed. The Burmese adventure had been Madras's initiative and Madras could no longer support it. Alungpaya had been disappointed in his expectation of military assistance, and the Negrais settlers had been left to fend for themselves, because Madras had neither the men nor the matchlocks to spare. Indeed when in 1758 the orders for withdrawal arrived from London, Fort St George was itself under siege. The Seven Years War had at last been joined in India.

In this war, as in that of the Austrian Succession, military manoeuvres in India would be restricted to the Carnatic, although with a related campaign in Hyderabad. And as in the old war so in the new, the French opened proceedings by attacking Forts St David (Cuddalore) and St George (Madras) while the British closed them, three years later, with a grand assault on Pondicherry. This helpful resemblance, though, is superficial; for the important point is that in every instance the outcome was different. This time Fort St David was attacked first and taken, Fort St George held out, Pondicherry did not. The result was therefore decisive. French ambitions in India collapsed. It was the end of a chapter, not the beginning.

The outcome owed much to the availability of supplies, troops and above all funds from Calcutta. If Madras's troops had saved Bengal in 1756–7, Bengal's rupees saved Madras in 1758–60. It was not just a question of repaying a favour. Had the French made good their second bid for hegemony in the Carnatic, Bengal itself would have been threatened. Clive was well aware of this and in not returning to Madras after the recapture of Calcutta – as he had promised and as Madras desperately urged – he took a terrible risk. It paid off thanks to the heroics of the squadron under Admiral Pocock, Watson's successor. Not for the first time, Clive's reputation was saved by the Royal Navy.

More even than in the earlier war, seapower proved crucial. Three naval battles, each more decisive than the last, offset the French superiority in land forces and dictated the course of the struggle ashore. As in the Americas so in India; it was courtesy of the King's navy that Britain emerged from the Seven Years War with a global empire. Any narrative, therefore, that presumes to disentangle the Company's history from that of the British Navy, or indeed of British India, may be excused from treating the final phase of the Anglo-French struggle in any detail.

Briefly then, the French took the field first. In September 1757 the first reinforcements to reach India since the outbreak of war had been landed at Pondicherry. Because of the imminent monsoon, the fleet which brought them immediately scurried back to Mauritius. Without a fleet, the French held their offensive. In February Pocock's fleet arrived on The Coast from Bengal and in April a second French fleet under the Comte d'Ache made its way up to Pondicherry. Pocock managed to intercept and just about came off best in a very untidy encounter. He failed, though, to disable the French vessels which duly landed a second regiment, a train of artillery, and the Comte de Lally as Commander-in-Chief and President of all the French settlements.

With d'Ache remaining on The Coast to distract Pocock, de Lally immediately took the offensive. His now formidable army crossed the dunes to Fort St David, quickly drove the garrison from straggling Cuddalore, and began the laborious ritual of constructing breaching batteries to pound the Fort. The British held out for less than a month. It was a great disappointment considering the supposed strength of the place and, true to form, the directors blamed their servants; 'the whole siege was one scene of disorder, confusion, mismanagement, and total inattention to every branch'.

Such bluster carries little conviction. Hopelessly outnumbered and outgunned, and quickly deserted by most of their native troops, the Fort St David councillors had little chance. They had counted on Pocock coming to their rescue but adverse winds prevented his approach. With four batteries trained on their walls and with insufficient troops to mount a foray, they wisely capitulated. De Lally razed the place, then took Devikottai, and finally staged a triumphal march through Pondicherry. Apart from some insignificant garrisons at places like Trichy and Arcot, all that now hindered a continuation of his triumphal progress north to Hyderabad, de Bussy and Bengal was Fort St George.

De Lally favoured an immediate advance and had this been possible,

Madras might well have fallen. But no siege could be effective with Pocock's squadron still in the offing. De Lally therefore ordered d'Ache to engage it. D'Ache refused, probably because he preferred to cruise in search of the year's fleet of Indiamen. This meant a four-month delay until the October monsoon would oblige Pocock to desert his station. De Lally passed the time with an attack on the still independent 'Tanjoreens', a traditional expedient for raising funds; Madras readied itself for action.

Thus far the British had not been wholly passive observers of French progress. Trichy had seen yet more manoeuvres as a French force invested the fort and was then drawn off by a largely sepoy army under Captain John Caillaud of the Company. Meanwhile Fort St George itself was being ringed with the whole Vaubanesque vocabulary of ravelins and lunettes, glacis and bastions. The vulnerable west front was said now to be 'pretty well secured' (Ives) with more angles and faces than the much-cut Pitt diamond. Partly overgrown and partly over-built, they are yet visible in today's Fort St George, the most impressive relic of the Company (as opposed to the Raj) in India. But as well as an acute shortage of troops thanks to Clive's absence in Bengal, Madras was hamstrung by an incompetent commander in the bumbling person of Colonel John Aldercron of the 39th. This was the regiment brought to Madras by Watson in 1756, the first Royal regiment to serve in India. Its artillery had been siphoned off to Bengal by Clive and for the next three years the efforts of the Madras Council 'were directed to getting the use of Aldercron's troops without Aldercron' (Biddulph). They succeeded when in 1758, as the entire regiment was recalled to England, half its members signed up in the Company's forces. At about the same time the first detachments of a new regiment, His Majesty's 64th under the able Colonel Draper, landed at Madras. With Stringer Lawrence still at the head of the Company's troops and Draper leading the royal troops, Madras awaited de Lally's army of 6000 with a garrison of 4000, ten times that of 1746.

Meanwhile Pocock had at last cornered the reluctant d'Ache. Off Negapatnam – where else? – the British won a victory which, if not exactly resounding, confirmed d'Ache's anxieties. Taking this engagement with the previous one, he had suffered 900 dead and wounded to Pocock's 300 while his ships, though still afloat, stood badly in need of repairs. Nothing would now stop him, not even a Council of War, from withdrawing to Mauritius. He limped away in September. In so far as

Pocock was also obliged to withdraw ahead of the monsoon, it did not materially affect the balance of power.

But it did mean that de Lally, unlike La Bourdonnais, had to reach Madras overland. It was not Lawrence's intention to contest this advance but with seventy miles between the French capital and the English, it was obvious that their supply line would be vulnerable. Accordingly a small British force was left to hold Chingleput, a strategic fort twenty miles south of Madras. De Lally debated whether to take it but decided that he could afford neither the men nor the time. The monsoon was slowing his progress and, even without fighting, it was 12 December 1758 before he finally entered Madras's Black Town.

The siege now began in earnest – but with a British offensive. Learning that the French troops had discovered Black Town's main distillery, Draper deemed the moment ripe for action. Six hundred men with a couple of guns charged out of one of the fort's gates and, having terrorized the township with a militarily pointless but psychologically useful manoeuvre, charged back through another. They lost both their guns and sustained heavy losses; but so did the French.

In the event this puzzling action proved to be the only serious engagement of the entire siege. De Lally's batteries opened fire in January but the new defences stood up well to the heavy bombardment. Even when a breach was made, so properly contrived and so hotly defended were those ravelins and lunettes that no escalade was deemed possible. Siege warfare, like the art of fortification, depended heavily on convention. Each side knew what to expect of the other and, as the shot and shell whistled overhead, each was busy underground digging mines and counter-mines. Certain actions were, however, taboo. In the midst of hostilities de Lally had occasion to complain to Pigot, the Fort St George President, that someone had presumed to fire on his headquarters. It was, of course, a terrible mistake. Pigot had been under the impression that de Lally had based himself in the Capuchin church. Obviously he was wrong. 'If you will do the honour to inform me at which pagoda [place of worship] you fix your headquarters, all due respect will be paid them.' After all, 'in war mutual civilities and mutual severities may be expected'.

De Lally, a stickler for the civilities if not the severities, had convinced himself that under the rules of engagement the British ought to have handed over Chingleput. In fact they had reinforced it. By February Caillaud (a Company officer in spite of his name) and the sepoys from Trichy had joined the Chingleput garrison and had advanced almost to

San Thomé on the outskirts of Madras. A determined French assault failed to dislodge them; equally Caillaud was incapable of breaking through the French cordon. But once again the besiegers were beginning to feel like the besieged.

This impression was reinforced by news from further afield. Although Clive still declined to desert Bengal's rich political and commercial pickings, he had at last dispatched a considerable force by sea to the Northern Circars. These were the coastal districts of Hyderabad north of Masulipatnam which had been ceded to de Bussy by the Nizam. The expedition, under Colonel Francis Forde, was intended as a diversionary tactic to prevent French troops being moved down to the Carnatic.

In the event Forde quickly exceeded these modest expectations. De Lally had obligingly recalled de Bussy to assist in operations against Madras. The ablest of French generals thus became a disenchanted and obstructive subordinate while his conquests were squandered by the less experienced Marquis de Conflans. In early December, as de Lally came in sight of Madras, a pitched battle was being fought near Rajahmundry in which the British and their local ally won a decisive victory. Three months later Forde would take Masulipatnam and sign a treaty with the Nizam for the expulsion of all French troops and the cession of the Northern Circars to the Company.

For the hard-pressed garrison of Fort St George still more cheering news arrived from Anjengo in late January. Pocock, who had been in Bombay, had met up with the fleet of Indiamen conveying the rest of Draper's regiment from England and was now rounding Sri Lanka. Within a week the first vessel arrived off Madras with ammunition and treasure; and on the evening of 6 February six more ships were 'descried in the north-east standing towards the road'. They anchored off the fort that night. Next day the garrison woke to the sight of de Lally's entire army decamping towards the west.

'Joy and curiosity carried out everyone to view and contemplate the works from which they had received so much molestation for . . . 42 days,' writes Orme. With that remorseless concern for detail that distinguishes his work, Orme claims that the fort had fired 26,554 rounds from its cannon and 7,502 shells from its mortars. 1,990 hand grenades had been heaved from the battlements, 200,000 cartridges fired from the muskets. His casualty count gives 934 as the dead and wounded amongst the British but 'the loss of men sustained by the French army is no where acquired'. 'Thus ended this siege, without doubt the most strenuous and regular that had ever been carried on in India.' Orme, who had devoted seventy strenuous and regular pages to it, heaved a sigh of satisfaction. 'We have detailed it, in the hopes that it may remain an example and incitement.'

Although the tide had turned, the British were slow to take advantage. Before moving against Pondicherry they needed more troops – the new arrivals barely offset those lost during the siege – and undisputed command of the sea. In September d'Ache and his fleet reappeared on The Coast. Pocock, for the third and last time, moved to attack. The result was much as before only more so. D'Ache limped into Pondicherry and two weeks later sailed back to Mauritius never to visit The Coast again. In the following month Eyre Coote, Clive's second in command at Plassey, arrived with a new battalion from home.

With de Lally's unpopularity and Pondicherry's insolvency provoking open mutiny amongst the French troops, Coote moved rapidly to the kill. In January 1760 he routed the enemy at the battle of Wandiwash, half way to Pondicherry, and by May had reduced all the outlying French garrisons and had begun the blockade of Pondicherry. In desperation de Lally looked for allies among the native powers. His best hope, a formidable army under the adventurer Hyder Ali from Mysore, abandoned him in August. In the same month Coote also received reinforcements but of a more reliable nature. Among the new batch of recruits sent from home was 'part of a Highland regiment supplied by the government'. Evidently excited by these first Highlanders ever to serve in India, Orme was moved to record the event in a sentence of such puzzling obscurity that only unedited quotation can do it justice.

> These mighty aids [the Highlanders] witnessed in this quarter of the globe, as equal efforts, wheresoever necessary, in every other, the superior energy of that mind, who possessing equally the confidence of his sovereign and the nation, conducted the arduous and extensive war in which they were engaged against their great and only rival.

The Highlanders had little opportunity to exercise 'the superior energy of mind' because Pondicherry, unlike Madras, was to succumb more to starvation than bombardment. The blockade depended heavily on the British fleet which made only the briefest of monsoon excursions to Trinconomalee and was back off the city by December. There, like La Bourdonnais before Madras, it was overtaken by a cyclone; several ships were sunk, many more dismasted. De Lally hailed the event as his deliverance and, had d'Ache reappeared, the blockade must have collapsed. But d'Ache was still in Mauritius and, as Pocock's scattered men-of-war returned to their station, French hopes evaporated. On 16 January 1761 the emaciated garrison finally surrendered. Not a cat, not a rat, not a crow had survived the ravenous attentions of the besieged. They marched out from a ghost town and the British engineers moved in to destroy its fortifications once and for all. Although peace in Europe would eventually restore both Pondicherry and Chandernagar to their rightful owners, they would never again constitute a threat to British supremacy.

iii

Begun with a pre-emptive snip in Burma, the process of clearing France's exuberant growth in Indian waters had continued with a lop in Bengal and a veritable felling programme in the Circars and the Carnatic. It ended with a cosmetic flourish when Mahé, the only French establishment on the Malabar Coast, was overwhelmed by an expedition from neighbouring Tellicherry.

But the British were not to have it all their own way. Britannia, in the words of the song written by Thomas Arne a few years earlier and now lustily sung by every Tilbury tar, 'ruled the waves' but only around India; elsewhere Britons were all too easily 'made slaves'. In 1760 Benkulen and its satellite trading posts on Sumatra's west coast were 'shamelessly' surrendered to a French flotilla; and in the same year the Company's men were driven from their unhappy home at Gombroon in the Persian Gulf.

Even the trade with China was at risk to French warships lurking in the Straits of Malacca. Taken along with the withdrawal from Burma, the temporary loss of Benkulen highlighted the Company's weakness east of India. Henceforth the protection of the immensely valuable China trade would become something of an obsession occasioning a significant reawakening of interest in almost every shoreline in south-east Asia. Many and often bizarre would be the solutions propounded. But few were quite as improbable and sensational as the first, a major offensive against the Philippines in 1762. It was launched, like so many of the later eastern initiatives, from Madras.

The Philippines still belonged to Spain, her consolation prize for losing out to Portugal in the spice race, and Spain had thus far stood neutral in the Seven Years War. But when, in 1761, after the breakdown of

Anglo-French peace talks, the Bourbons renewed their Family Compact, Whitehall detected a hostile alliance and formally declared war on Madrid. Indeed, plans for an offensive had been hatched well ahead of the actual declaration and predictably they were directed at Madrid's colonial empire. In a two-pronged attack Pocock, lately returned to England from his tussles with d'Ache, was to storm Havana while on the other side of the world Draper, who had left Madras immediately after the siege, was to lead an assault on Manila.

The Philippines expedition seems to have been the brainchild of Lord Anson, now First Lord of the Admiralty. Twenty years previously, in the War of Jenkins's Ear, Anson had rounded Cape Horn, attacked Spanish possessions in Peru, and then crossing the Pacific had taken a Spanish galleon laden with Mexican silver off the coast of Luzon (the Philippines). One or two such galleons reached Manila every year giving the mother country an access to the trade of China, India, and the archipelago which, though small by comparison with the turnover of the English Company, was nevertheless immensely profitable. Anson's idea was to close this Spanish trapdoor into 'the eastern treasure house' by occupying Manila.

To that extent the whole scheme was a product of Whitehall's global strategy and not of the Company's ambitions – a distinction that becomes increasingly relevant in the late eighteenth century. The first that the directors heard of it was when Anson divulged the plan to Sulivan, the Company's chairman, in December 1761. The declaration of war came a week later and just seven weeks after that Draper and the British contingent sailed from Plymouth. If the idea was to take Manila by surprise, the effect was also to take the Company by surprise. The Philippines undoubtedly lay within the area covered by the Company's trading monopoly and since the Company had come to rely on the British government for military assistance in India, the government argued that it had a right to reciprocal assistance for any national schemes within that monopoly area. Thus Draper was not only to find ships and troops from among the Royal forces in India but also to enlist Company troops, artillery and transports.

Time did not permit of an exploration of this novel argument but, by way of sugaring the pill, it was emphasized that Manila, once taken, would be handed over to the Company. The capture of Pondicherry, like the recapture of Calcutta, had occasioned an unseemly row between Royal and Company officers. It was important to reassure the Company on this score and, lest Manila should be handed back to Spain at the end of the war, there was also mention of a second base, ideally on the southern island of Mindanao, as an alternative settlement.

The directors, though, remained distinctly cool. As will appear, they had reason to believe that they already had an option on a settlement in the vicinity of the Philippines. But informed that their co-operation would be an 'acceptable testimony of their due sense of the King's most gracious attention to their interests' during the struggle with de Lally, they could hardly refuse. They did voice serious doubts, particularly about depleting either their forces or their shipping in India; and they also made it clear that, whatever the commercial compensations Manila might or might not afford, they expected their assistance to be paid for.

These reservations were shared by President Pigot and Colonel Lawrence when Draper reached Madras in July 1762. Although such worries were genuine enough, a further concern that weighed heavily with the Madras Council was the likely effect of the expedition on Madras's private trade with Manila. As with Burma so with the Philippines; English trade in a variety of guises had been reaching Manila ever since the middle of the seventeenth century. By Governor Pitt's time one or two private vessels had been sailing for the Philippines every year with Indian piece goods and returning to Madras with Mexican silver. This invaluable source of silver must dry up if the Spanish were ousted from Manila. It was not obvious that the indigenous produce of the Philippines would ever sustain a like trade, nor that whatever security a British Manila might afford to the China trade would offset this loss.

Even now, as Draper frantically assembled his armada in Madras, most of the local councillors, his erstwhile comrades-in-arms from the days of the siege, were more concerned for a vessel that had just left for Manila. On board her was £70,000 worth of their private trade and, according to Draper, 'they were afraid that the venture would suffer by the loss of Manila and took any method in their power to discourage the attempt'.

Faced with what he chose to construe as wilful sabotage, Draper was able to obtain from the Company only three small transports, 600 sepoys, and 300 European troops most of whom were deserters from the ranks of de Lally's army. 'Such banditti had never been seen since the time of Spartacus', he observed. The Company did, however, provide him with a sufficient complement of civilians to form a Manila council and take over the administration and commerce of the place. They included Henry Brooke, lately of Negrais, presumably because of his experience of pioneering. Draper preferred to rely on the officers of his own (Royal) regiment, which seems now to have included some of those recently tamed Highlanders. They would be the backbone of the expedition and when he sailed from Madras at the end of July, he was still quietly optimistic. 'Tho' we cannot do all we wish,' he wrote by way of valedictory, 'we are determined to do all we can and try we will.'

Six months later he was back, *en route* to England, with news of a wholly satisfactory outcome. Word of the war having been slow to reach the extremities of the Hispanic world, the fleet had sailed into Manila Bay unopposed. Unopposed the British troops had been landed at Ermita, just a mile from the fort (and today the heart of Manila's nightlife), and against only token resistance the first battery had been set up. A week later the first breach was successfully stormed. British and Indian losses had been 'trifling' – barely thirty fatalities – and under the terms of surrender the Spanish were to pay an indemnity of £1 million. In addition, one of the Acapulco galleons, a gigantic vessel of some 2000 tons, had been taken. And finally Manila had reluctantly been handed over to the Company. 'In short', announced the jubilant Draper, 'it is a lucky business.'

Unfortunately the luck ran out with Draper's early departure. The Company would hold Manila and claim sovereignty over the Philippines for only eighteen months. But that was long enough for some of the troops to mutiny, long enough for the Governor to fall out with his own council, with the military and the navy, and long enough for a Spanish-Filipino resistance so to harry the British that they scarcely dared venture outside the fort. It was with a sense of relief that in April 1764 the place was finally handed back to Spain in accordance with the terms of the Treaty of Paris. All along the Company had been developing its own ideas about how best to support the China trade and re-establish its interests in the south-east Asian archipelago. They did not include the occupation of Manila and it was entirely appropriate that the man who eventually stepped in, when the Company's governor had resigned in disgust, to hand back Manila was also the moving spirit behind these other initiatives. His name was Alexander Dalrymple.

iv

Dalrymple, from a distinguished Edinburgh family, had like Clive joined the Madras establishment as a writer in 1753. Headstrong in youth as he would become cantankerous in age, he devoted his early energies not to acquiring instant wealth or military acclaim but to studying maritime journals. In the siege of Madras he acquitted himself with distinction; but not without a streak of perversity he ignored the Company's self-evident destiny in India and became obsessed with reviving its long-forgotten ambitions further east. Specifically he lit upon the idea, so doggedly pursued in the previous century by Saris, Adams, Cocks and Catchpole, of finding or founding a haven where the Company could establish direct trading links with the Chinese Empire.

In so far as Company ships in ever increasing numbers had now been trading profitably at Canton for fifty years, this idea might have seemed redundant. In fact it was the greatly augmented value of the China trade which made it so attractive. Because the Company was becoming so financially dependent on its China trade some new expedient for securing it both from Chinese exactions and European interference had become an imperative.

The origins in the previous century of a trade that promised well for the export of English woollens and the import of Chinese silks have already been mentioned. So have the unsuccessful attempts to push this trade at Taiwan, Amoy, Chusan and Pulo Condore as a result of which European trade with the Celestial Empire had since 1703 been confined to the Pearl River. Portuguese Macao, at the mouth, provided a holding area whence the Canton authorities were notified of new arrivals. When contracts for the sale and purchase of cargo had been agreed with the Canton merchants, the ship was measured by the *Hoppo* (customs officer), taxed accordingly, and allowed to proceed upriver to Whampoa, the main port. Meanwhile, a few miles further upstream, the foreigners had set up a temporary home and office in their allotted factory on the Canton waterfront.

These factories had no resident staff, the supercargoes and their subordinates coming and going with each year's shipping. It was thus impossible to manipulate the market or to explore its commercial origins. Competition between the various European companies was ferocious if fair; and for all its faults, the system was well regulated. But it was heavily weighted in favour of the Chinese and, when Europe's demand for Chinese produce suddenly began to soar, this weighting gave to the seller an irresistible leverage.

Responsible for this phenomenal expansion in demand was the Englishman's newly acquired thirst for tea. Tea, of the most expensive green variety, had first been imported as a medicine and *digestif* in the 1660s.

Samuel Pepys approved of it and by 1685 the directors were requesting further supplies 'to make presents therein to our great friends at Court'. By the 1690s small quantities were reaching London each year through Madras's private trade with Canton and through the Dutch at Batavia. The price fell from 50 shillings a pound to around 16 shillings, but it was still mostly green tea for novelty consumption by the *beau-monde*.

The first quantum leap in demand came in the 1720s and has been linked to a like expansion in the import of sugar from the West Indies. By concentrating on the cheaper bohea tea, prices fell to around 7 shillings a pound and tea entered mass reckoning as an agreeable way of imbibing sugar. The 200,000 pounds sold by the Company in 1720 was up to an average of over one million pounds a year by the end of the decade; and, with occasional lapses, it continued to rise. In 1760 it was just under three million and by 1770 nine million. Meanwhile the price of bohea had fallen to 3 shillings a pound and instead of an average of five Company ships a year visiting Canton, the usual total was now over fifteen. Imports of Chinese porcelain complemented the vogue, providing the merchant with the necessary ballast, or kintledge, for his vessel and the consumer with the socially desirable crocks in which to brew and drink his beverage.

But these figures tell only half the story. The number of Company vessels calling at Canton was matched by a growing number of privately owned vessels operating out of Madras, Calcutta and Bombay; and, in a new twist to the interloping theme, the quantity of tea imported by the Company was matched by a like quantity imported into Europe by rival trading companies and then smuggled across the Channel.

In effect tea revolutionized the Company's trade in the eighteenth century in the same way that cottons had in the seventeenth. As a result, by 1770 it was the single most important item in the Company's portfolio and the value of the China trade had come to rival that of all its Indian settlements combined. In India, of course, the Company now to some extent dictated its terms of trade; but even as it assumed political power in India, the balance of its commerce swung decisively towards China where it enjoyed no more security and leverage than it had in Surat under the Moghul governors.

Chinese exactions increased in proportion to the growth of trade. In the 1720s the Co-Hong, a cartel of the leading Canton merchants operating a price-fixing monopoly, made its first appearance. The Company responded by ending the competitive tendering of its supercargoes and organizing them into a united council. But failing concerted action with all the other European trading companies, the Hong merchants continued to enjoy the advantage. Also in the 1720s an *ad valorem* tax of ten per cent on all imports and exports was levied and to the measurement dues was added a fixed charge of 1950 taels (about £650). It should be said that these impositions scarcely equalled those being levied on imports of China tea by the home government; by 1750, these exceeded 100 per cent of the cost price (and hence all that smuggling). But it was one thing to enrich the British treasury, a service to which the directors were wont to point with pride, and quite another to subsidize a foreign power – a power, moreover, which consistently treated merchants with utter disdain, depriving them of their firearms and confining them to what the French scholar Louis Dermigny nicely calls *un lazaret commercial*.

Often and loudly did the foreigners protest, but since they were permitted to seek redress only from those local mandarins who stood to gain most by the exactions, it was to no avail. The alternative, of course, was to hold back their ships or, better still, to threaten to send them and their trade elsewhere. Both these ploys were tried in the 1750s as part of a bold new initiative in which the name of one James Flint is prominent.

The choice of Flint as the man to bid defiance to the Celestial Emperor was eccentric, to say the least. As a small boy, probably an orphan, he had been shipped out to Macao with the idea that a language impenetrable to any adult European might be learnt by one of tender years. That was in 1736. In 1739 he was in Bombay and Madras whence he was sent back to China to continue his 'endeavours to make myself acquainted with the Mandareen'. Somehow or other he was apprenticed to Chinese merchants with whom he travelled inland, becoming the first Englishman to master not only Mandarin but also the language of Fukien (Fujian). He lived and dressed as a Chinese and must by now have completely forgotten the land of his birth. But his loyalty to the Company, who occasionally relieved his penury, remained strong and in 1746 he reappeared as official linguist to all the Canton supercargoes on an allowance of 90 taels (£30) per ship. This would have made a respectable salary and Flint, or sometimes the more sinicized 'Flink', was obviously considered a great asset.

Smarting under the treatment received at Canton, in 1755 the directors ordered one of their ships to attempt to open trade at Ningpo (near the modern Shanghai); and by way of preparing the ground, they sent on ahead their senior supercargo accompanied by Flint as interpreter.

The Ningpo mandarins were taken by surprise but 'received us very graciously, not at all like the *Hoppo* of Canton', reported Flint. Pending reference to higher authorities the ship was allowed to trade on most reasonable terms as were the two vessels sent in the following year. In 1757 Flint returned to Ningpo expecting to take up residence prior to opening a factory. Unfortunately the Canton authorities had other ideas. Their complaints to the emperor had resulted in a decree forbidding European trade anywhere but in the Pearl River.

Nothing if not desperate, the Company resolved on a final throw, sending Flint back to Ningpo in 1759 with a long list of complaints which, if he was refused admission, he was to deliver in Peking itself. No Englishman had yet got within a thousand miles of the Forbidden City. Even official embassies laden with largesse, led by aristocratic scions, and accompanied by well-armed guards, would, come their day, find it hard going. Flint, a solitary pigtailed Englishman with no official credentials and the most presumptuous of communications, had no hope; he would be lucky to get away with his life.

And so it proved; but not before the unlikely emissary had seemingly pulled off the coup of the decade. Sailing in a small snow, a two-masted vessel of about 100 tons, he was duly turned away from Ningpo where such was now the panic among the heavily censured authorities that they would not even allow him to purchase supplies. He managed, however, to drop off a copy of his petition and then, shadowed by war junks, continued north along the coast. 10 July found the optimistically named *Success* entering the Tientsin (Tianjin) river. Here he was forbidden to sail any further by a local mandarin who turned out to be a man he had once met in Canton. As this man's guest he was permitted to proceed to Tientsin, twenty miles up-river and only 100 from the Forbidden City.

The mandarin now concocted an elaborate story whereby Flint, supposedly 'drove ashore by stress of weather', might be exonerated for his act of trespass. But Flint would have none of it. 'I told him that it could not be so, for if they would not make a proper representation to the Emperor, I would go as far as the foot of the Great Wall, and he [the mandarin] must take care of himself for I should acquaint them of my having been here.'

This was bold talk from a mere 'linguist' but it had its effect. The mandarin proposed a new scheme whereby they should distribute copies of the English petition to so many officials that 'they for fear of each other will not think to keep it from the Emperor'. It might, though, mean ostracism for the mandarin who therefore requested a hefty recompense. Realizing that the Canton officials 'would now be quite up and there would be no bearing them hereafter', Flint agreed and the plan went ahead.

It worked brilliantly. The petition reached the ear of the Emperor, the Canton *Hoppo* was immediately recalled, and by September two top-level commissioners, accompanied by Flint, were heading for Canton to investigate. Their findings were sympathetic. Punishment was promised to the offending mandarins and redress to the aggrieved Europeans. But no concessions were made for trading rights anywhere but Canton, and the commissioners showed an unhealthy curiosity about the identity of the man who had helped Flint to draft the original petition. Evidently the presumption of addressing an appeal direct to the Emperor was considered every bit as much a crime as the infringements it detailed.

When the commissioners departed, Flint was summoned to appear before the Canton viceroy. Fearing for his fate, all the Company's supercargoes went with him. At the palace they were surrounded by soldiers, deprived of their swords, hustled into the august presence, and thrown down when they refused to perform the kowtow. Flint was sentenced to three years' detention at Macao after which he was to be exiled from China forever; the unfortunate Chinese who had helped him to draft the original petition was strangled. And needless to say, most of the exactions against which it complained continued in force and were in fact embodied in a new imperial decree.

In London the directors would protest vigorously, sending their own emissary, a certain Captain Skottowe (who was to be known as 'Mr' Skottowe and represented as the brother of His Majesty's Under-Secretary of State) to complain to the Viceroy and secure Flint's release. He failed. The luckless Flint served out his sentence and trade remained at the mercy of the Canton *Hoppo*. The supercargoes did eventually obtain permission to reside in their Canton factories throughout the year and in the 1770s the Co-Hong was partially abolished. But though tea sales topped new heights, no further attempt to take grievances to Peking was launched until the missions of Cathcart in 1788 and of Lord Macartney in 1793.

V

While Flint and Skottowe tried the direct approach, Alexander Dalrymple had seized upon the stalemate at Canton to explore alternative arrangements for circumventing the Co-Hong's monopoly. As something of an authority on the maritime history of the Company in eastern waters, young Dalrymple numbered among his many nautical acquaintances a Captain William Wilson of the Indiaman *Pitt*. In September 1758 the *Pitt* had arrived at Madras just in time to land Draper and his regiment to man the walls against de Lally but too late to continue its voyage to Canton, winds in the South China Sea being unfavourable after the end of September.

Commodore James had recently brought the news of the outbreak of the Seven Years War from Bombay to Bengal by sailing south of the Equator and entering the Bay of Bengal from the east. Wilson wondered whether a similar plan, a wide arc through the Indonesian archipelago and into the Pacific, would enable him to outflank the adverse winds of the South China Sea. He consulted Dalrymple, who although as yet no sailor, dug out the terse but revealing log of John Saris. Saris had made his epic voyage from Bantam to Hirado during the winter months, albeit 145 years previously, by sailing first for the Moluccas then north across the Pacific to a landfall at Okinawa. Clearly it was possible, and with the blessing of President Pigot, Wilson had ventured forth having bought a snow to lead the way in uncharted waters.

This latter vessel was in fact the *Success* which, on arrival at Canton, was taken over by the Company's supercargoes for Flint's voyage to Tientsin. Indeed in the following year it was in company with Wilson in the *Pitt* that Flint sailed out of the Pearl River heading for Ningpo. Wilson, on the other hand, was about to repeat his discovery of what was called the Eastern Passage by returning to Madras the same way. Leading through the Moluccas, past the tip of New Guinea, and east of the Philippines, this route was a long way round. But it meant that Canton could be reached at all seasons of the year, and that the China trade was no longer at the mercy of whoever happened to have a fleet in the Malacca or Sunda Straits. It also meant that British shipping had again a legitimate reason for claiming free navigation in the Dutch archipelago plus a less legitimate one for again coveting its island trade.

Meanwhile Madras had been besieged and relieved, and with no word as yet from Canton about the *Pitt*, Dalrymple had himself set off in search of the Eastern Passage. Such, at any rate, was the object of his voyage as detailed to the directors by President Pigot. It was soon, however, apparent that the 'secret service' on which Dalrymple was engaged involved more than just navigation. It was in fact the first of a series of voyages designed not just to secure the China trade but, if possible, to relocate it. Imbued with the ideas of Saris and his generation, Dalrymple was convinced that the China trade would be less vulnerable and more profitable if conducted from a *Hoppo*-less off-shore entrepôt served by the junks that sailed each year from all the China ports. And from his studies of the charts and histories of the region he thought he knew just the place. It had to be outside the Spanish possessions in the Philippines and the Dutch in the Indies – and ideally in between the two; and it had to be astride the main routes from China to the Spice Islands. In effect there was only one such place, the archipelago of the Sulu Sea between Borneo and Mindanao.

In this connexion it is significant that as Dalrymple sailed from Madras he was accompanied by Draper who was on his way home, via Canton, after the Madras siege. As a result of this voyage Draper became aware of the unsatisfactory state of affairs at Canton and interested in the idea of gaining a foothold in the Philippines. And it was almost certainly as a result of conversations with Dalrymple that the instructions for the Manila Expedition would include that mention of a permanent settlement in Mindanao.

But by then Dalrymple had forestalled it. In 1759, aboard the schooner *Cuddalore*, the antiquarian-turned-sailor explored to the north of Luzon. Returning to Macao in time to witness Flint's disgrace, he next year ranged along the opposite shore of the South China Sea surveying the coast of Hainan island and calling at Tourane (Da Nang) in Annam. By the end of the year he was back at Canton offering the *Cuddalore*'s services as scout, and his own as pilot, to a fleet of Indiamen embarking on the Eastern Passage. It was rumoured that the French fleet which had earlier surprised Benkulen was lurking in the Malacca Straits.

With the idea of at last sizing up Sulu, he conducted his convoy down the west coast of the Philippines to Mindanao where, in spite of the *Cuddalore*'s crew taking continuous soundings, one of the ships ran aground. Undeterred by her loss, the five remaining vessels gingerly felt their way through the maze of reef-ringed islands as far as Jolo, the largest and the home of the Sultan of Sulu. Delighted with his Promised Land, Dalrymple had time only for a quick survey and a provisional trading agreement with the Sultan. He then led his convoy through the Macassar Straits and out into the Indian Ocean between Sumbawa and Flores.

Dalrymple accompanied them no further and, after surveying this extremity of the Indonesian archipelago, returned to the Sulu Sea. He spent most of 1761 there and in the Philippines where his surveys included Manila Bay (although there is no evidence that they were available to the next year's expedition). By early 1762 he was back in Madras after a three-year absence.

Nothing if not wildly enthusiastic, Dalrymple now lobbied for a permanent settlement within the Sultan of Sulu's watery domain. This was something which, like the Negrais plan, the Madras Council felt obliged to refer to London; but in the meantime they sent Dalrymple back to Sulu to open trade with the Sultan and select a site for the settlement. Accompanied this time by the young James Rennel, later Surveyor-General of Bengal, Dalrymple explored the coast of north Borneo (Sabah), over which the Sultan of Sulu claimed sovereignty, and eventually lit upon the island of Balambangan in the strait of Balabac between Borneo and Palawan (now in the Philippines). The Sultan officially ceded it in September 1762, just as Draper was landing his troops on what is now Manila's corniche. In January 1763 Dalrymple went ashore to take formal possession.

Balambangan thus became the Company's first non-Indian acquisition since Negrais and, save for Pulo Condore, the first ever in the South China Sea. In many ways its situation resembled that of another still uncharted island, Singapore. Each commanded one of the few points of entry into the South China Sea, each stood at the junction of two distinct trading zones, the one operated by Chinese junks and the other by Bugis and Malay *prahus*, and each consequently was a haunt of pirates. In one sense Balambangan appeared the more promising, being considerably nearer to both the Chinese seaboard and the eastern archipelago with its spices. Anticipating Singapore, Dalrymple envisaged his island being colonized by Chinese living under British protection, and like Singapore he urged that, at least to begin with, it should be a free port, its trade open to all free of duty. He even anticipated its becoming a centre to which the trade of Japan, Korea, New Holland (Australia), and the south Pacific would be drawn.

It was not, of course, to be. No forest of masts would ever clog Balambangan's beckoning harbour, no colonial skyline ever usurp its dense canopy. The place is today indistinguishable from all the other coral and coconut paradises which dot the Sulu Sea. But if the cloak of obscurity was never to be lifted, it was not for want of special pleading, perseverance, even pugnacity on the part of its promoter. For most of the next decade Dalrymple would be poised to embark at a moment's notice for his beloved Balambangan. The Company's directors, although dilatory and divided in what was proving to be their most turbulent decade ever, did eventually sanction the scheme. And the Government, whose approval for snatching what Dalrymple called 'so rich a jewel' from under the noses of the Dutch and Spanish was deemed necessary, did eventually endorse it. But by then, 1770, Dalrymple had put himself out of the running as a founding father.

No doubt temperament had a lot to do with it. He had insisted on dictating his own terms of employment, including a handsome remuneration for life and absolute command of the whole project; and when these terms had been rejected, he had preferred to retaliate rather than compromise. He was an obstinate man. If Balambangan might have been as successful as the Singapore of Stamford Raffles, its method of government would have been more like the Sarawak of the autocratic Raja Brooke. On his last visit, an unchronicled and roundabout tour *en route* to London in 1763–4, there had been rumours that he was about to go it alone. Word had reached Madras that he had shipped 2000 Chinese from Manila to Balambangan, had recruited 120 soldiers, and was stockpiling ammunition and even artillery. This intriguing report may have been purely malicious but, in the later negotiations in London, Dalrymple made it clear that he expected to make the island his home and to stay there for life 'laying the foundation of a great and permanent extension of the Company's commerce'.

By 1772, when at long last the Balambangan settlement did go ahead, Dalrymple was somewhat inured to disappointment. Although strongly recommended by the Royal Society as the ideal man to lead the 1768 scientific expedition to the south Pacific, he had been passed over in favour of the Admiralty's candidate, one Captain James Cook. He would never again visit the East. But as the Company's and eventually the Admiralty's first Hydrographer, as the editor and author of innumerable works on the history, commerce and navigation of practically all the real (and some imaginary) landfalls east of India, and as an indefatigable promoter of trade throughout the Pacific basin, he would sail vicariously through an endless tropical archipelago for the rest of his long and contentious life.

Deprived of his guidance, he was probably unsurprised that the Balambangan settlement proved a short-lived and abject fiasco. The man chosen to take his place, one of Benkulen's ever venal factors, plumbed new depths of embezzlement and was soon driven back to sea by the outraged Suluans. His proceedings, according to the Court of Directors, 'exhibited a scene of irregularity, duplicity, and presumption not to be equalled upon the records of the Company' – which, if true, was saying something.

More notable were the exploits of Captain Thomas Forrest, one of Balambangan's pioneers, who in furtherance of Dalrymple's plan to attract not only the trade of China but also that of the eastern archipelago, set off from Balambangan for the Spice Islands in 1774. To avoid arousing Dutch suspicions, Forrest emulated David Middleton's example at Ceram by sailing in a native *prahu*, renamed the *Tartar*, with just two English companions. Cramped quarters were no novelty to the eighteenth-century seaman but in the ten-ton *Tartar* there can scarcely have been room to sling the hammocks. Nevertheless, in this unlikely craft, Forrest and his men pushed further east than any of his Company predecessors. In Geelvinks Bay on the north coast of New Guinea (Irian Jaya) he found one of the few nutmeg forests outside of the Banda Islands and Dutch control; further west he explored the Gilolo Passage between New Guinea and the Moluccas; then on to Mindanao, where the Sultan gave him the pick of the off-shore domains as a possible British base, to Borneo where the Balambangan settlers had removed after losing their island, and so to the Malay peninsula where at Kedah the sixteen-month, 4000-mile odyssey ended when his companions refused to serve any longer. One sympathizes with them on learning that, when sold, the *Tartar* fetched £9 7s 6d.

Forrest published an account of this voyage and of a subsequent exploration of the Mergui Archipelago. A version of the latter was also put out by Dalrymple whose copious publications testify to the remarkable upsurge of commercial exploration after the Seven Years War. Included are voyages to many of the Indonesian islands and still further afield to the Chagos and the Cocos (both in the Indian Ocean), the Marianas (in the Pacific) and Timor. Forrest figures prominently in these itineraries, as does Walter Alves who had witnessed the destruction of Negrais in 1759. Five years later Alves apparently explored the north coast of Mindanao as captain of the *London* and in 1765 he was among 'the islands on the Coast of China'. On 12 February, in what seems to have been one of the earliest mentions of the place, he hauled to the north of the island he called 'Heong Kong'. 'The tide being done, [I] anchored in six fathoms, mud, distant from Heong Kong about a mile, Lantao peak bearing west 8 degrees south.' For some reason Dalrymple took exception to this. In a footnote he insisted that 'what he [Alves] calls Heong Kong is Fanchin-chow'. Not for the first time, Dalrymple's protest fell on deaf ears.

A few months later the *London* was 'pirated' and Alves killed off the coast of Borneo where further attempts were being made to open trade at Bandjarmasin (the New Company had briefly operated from there at the turn of the century). Pasir on the east coast of Borneo was another favoured spot. These, and similar initiatives in Bali and at the eastern extremity of Java, were mounted from Benkulen which, following its capitulation to the French, had been reoccupied. But the reoccupation was supposed to be only temporary. The Sumatran councillors were under orders either to make Benkulen pay by developing a profitable sideline in the exchange of Bengal opium for contraband spices, or else to remove somewhere where they could. Various incentives were offered to assist in these developments, and during the late 1760s Benkulen witnessed scenes of unprecedented activity as a variety of Company and private vessels plied between its harbourless coast and such ports further east as were not under Dutch surveillance.

The Dutch of course protested and hastily bore down on any local potentate willing to indulge the British. Somewhat lamely the Company responded by insisting on its right to free navigation throughout the archipelago. But navigation was no guarantee of trade and this did not solve the problem of Benkulen. In the 1770s an alternative solution was suggested involving removal to Aceh or one of the ports on the Malay peninsula. Significantly, the new initiative was prompted by precisely the arguments advanced in favour of Balambangan.

vi

But Benkulen's customary deficit was as nothing compared to the anxieties created by the booming China trade. Adumbrated by Dalrymple in a succession of publications, these anxieties centred not only on its vulnerability – to Chinese restrictions and exactions and to European competition and interruption – but even more critically on problems of its finance.

English woollens had met with no greater demand in Canton than they had in India. It was hoped that by opening trade with the colder northern provinces either through Ningpo or through an off-shore development like Balambangan such a demand would be created; in the meantime Chinese tea was purchased almost entirely by the export of silver. As in the seventeenth century, English cloth weavers objected to this neglect of their product and they were supported by homespun economists ever eager to bemoan the drain of specie. Even the Company was uneasy. For at the very moment when Clive was reporting that the revenues in Bengal should obviate the need to export treasure for the India trade, treasure for the China trade was draining its resources as never before.

There was of course a simple solution – redirect the Indian surplus to finance the China deficit. But without the Company's bullion shipments, Bengal was soon chronically short of specie. India's only surplus was in kind, not cash, and although some Indian cottons and saltpetre could be sold at Canton, it was not until Canton relaxed its strict prohibition on the import of Bengal opium that this simple solution was possible.

Meanwhile Dalrymple had outlined an alternative as part of his master plan for Balambangan. He observed that China's overseas trade traditionally hinged on the import of primary produce from south-east Asia and the archipelago. As well as pepper and spices it comprehended a pungent cornucopia of everything from tin ore to gold dust and animal skins, from sea-slugs to birds' nests and sharks' fins. Tearing a leaf this time not out of Saris's journal but out of that of Peter Floris, he also observed the archipelago's demand for Indian cottons and opium. The solution then was a three-way exchange – Indian produce for that of south-east Asia, south-east Asian produce for that of China.

Dalrymple expressed himself with clarity and cogency but in reality he was not so much formulating a new policy as rationalizing an existing state of affairs. Ever resourceful, the 'country' or 'private' trader had already moved in on the south-east Asian market.

No aspect of the Company's history so successfully evades analysis as private trade. By the eighteenth century the Honourable Company's monopoly was enforced only over the 'out and back' carrying trade between Europe and the East. Within the East all trade, be it the river traffic of Bengal, the coastal traffic of the Malabar and Coromandel ports, or the oceanic intercourse between India, Arabia, Persia and China, was a legitimate field for private speculation. The life-blood of the Company's major settlements, it engrossed the energies of all their inhabitants, be they European or Indian, civil or military, Company's servants or 'free merchants'.

It was this combination of a profusion of participants with an incredible diffusion of markets which made the trade so impossible to regulate – and which makes it so difficult to analyse. But it seems clear that whereas at the beginning of the century the long-distance trade was mainly between the Arabian Sea ports, by the 1760s it had swung decisively to the other side of India. As noticed, it was private trade that preceded the Company's links with Burma, the Philippines and the archipelago. And the same was true of the Malay peninsula which had thus far been left entirely to the private trader.

'Private' shipping could be anything from a ten-ton prahu like the *Tartar* to a 500-ton Indiaman. It might be owned or chartered. The owners or charterers, who might or might not be responsible for its cargo, could be an informal partnership, an established syndicate, or a society with monopolistic tendencies not unlike those of the Honourable Company. The Benkulen factors, in their private capacity, operated as a 'General Concern'; in Bombay, Madras and Calcutta the first 'Agency Houses' were taking shape.

One such was the firm of Jourdain, Sulivan and de Souza which in 1770 became 'The Madras Association'. Based at Fort St George, it had built up a thriving trade with the Malay peninsula and Aceh by selling Indian cottons to the Malay and Bugis traders and buying from them produce suitable for the China trade. It had agents in Aceh (Sumatra) and Kedah (Malaya) who handled not only their own company's trade but also that of other private traders from Bengal or elsewhere. In effect the firm was operating a local monopoly in these ports and as such its operations came to the attention of the Court of Directors in London. In 1772, on their orders, Madras dispatched an agent to the Sultan of Aceh with a view to planting a settlement and developing this trade for the Company's benefit. The overture was rebuffed and a similar mission to both Kedah and the Rhio (Riau) islands, a mere twenty miles from modern Singapore, also failed.

Kedah and Rhio had been suggested by Captain Francis Light, one of the Madras Association's employees who had originally come out to the East as an officer in the Royal Navy. As well as the commercial value of a base in the vicinity of the Malacca Strait, Light could clearly see its strategic importance as a half-way house for the China trade. Thus when Rhio dropped out of the reckoning, he was quick to come forward with alternative sites including the island of Penang. Meanwhile Forrest, who had also once served under Admiral Pocock, drew attention to the other strategic need, that for a safe haven during the monsoon in the Bay of Bengal. He rightly observed that nothing had been done about this since the Negrais disaster, and the validity of his concern was painfully highlighted when in 1782 a French fleet again entered the Bay. After a succession of typically indecisive battles, the British fleet returned to Bombay to refit. Briefly the French had the run of the Bay and 'nearly succeeded in blockading Calcutta' (D. G. E. Hall).

As a result of this scare, further attempts were made to establish a Company presence in both Aceh and Rhio. The Dutch quickly pre-empted Rhio while Aceh guarded its independence as jealously as it had in the days of James Lancaster. Its Sultan, another Ala-uddin, nevertheless valued his European friends. When Forrest called there in accordance with instructions from Calcutta to make one last bid for a Company settlement, the Sultan conferred on him the Order of the Golden Sword and graciously accepted a copy of Voltaire's works. It is not recorded whether Forrest knew that Lancaster's crew had sung a psalm for the Sultan; but as if to repeat the courtesy, Forrest also presented Ala-uddin with a musical token, in this case a rendering of a traditional Malay verse 'to the *Correnti Vivace* of the 3rd Sonata of Corelli'.

With Rhio and Aceh out of the running, that left Penang. Light was still on good terms with the Kedah Sultan who owned it and in 1786 the Sultan ceded the island to the Company. Light took possession, renaming it Prince of Wales Island. Thus, a whole generation of false starts and missed opportunities since Negrais, the Company again had a foothold in mainland south-east Asia.

Penang would prove ideal neither as a commercial emporium for the produce of the archipelago, nor as a half-way house on the route to China, nor even as a naval base in the Bay of Bengal. But it would slowly acquire the security and permanence which had eluded Negrais and Balambangan. From Penang political and commercial opportunities would tempt the Company to intervene on the Malay peninsula and to exploit the weakness of the Dutch in the archipelago. And on Prince of Wales Island Thomas Stamford Raffles would take up his first overseas post. All that stood between Penang and Singapore was just over 300 miles of dazzling coastline and just over thirty years of burgeoning trade, plus the global repercussions of the Napoleonic Wars.

CHAPTER SEVENTEEN

The Transfer of Power

LONDON AND BENGAL

Turning again from the tinkling East to the ever grinding importunity of India, it is as if the East India Company were now in fact two companies, one maritime, the other continental; one commercial, the other territorial; one East, the other India. This dualism could conceivably be traced back to the Company's origins and the rival establishments at Bantam and Surat; or indeed forward to the Victorian juxtaposition of, on the one hand, a free trade or 'informal' empire of the seas with, on the other, that colossal landed dominion that was 'our Indian empire'.

Tempting as it is, such theorizing would, though, be as misplaced as the commoner fallacy of concentrating on one of these strands to the neglect of the other. For it is only in the late eighteenth century that anything like parity between them emerges. Thanks as much to the ever expanding China trade as to political developments in Bengal, then indeed the Company seemed to be straddling two horses. Inevitably questions began to be asked; should it continue purely as a mercantile association and follow the suggestions eagerly proffered by the likes of Dalrymple for opening up China, the Pacific, and even Australia and north-west America? Or should it abjure such speculative markets and embrace what seemed the surer prospect of trade and revenue on the Indian subcontinent?

Logically Clive had surely been right when in that letter to Pitt (Chatham) of 1759 he had urged the idea that 'so large a sovereignty' as was available in Bengal was 'too extensive for a mercantile company' and required 'the nation's assistance'. Like a building contractor whose excavations had unexpectedly unearthed some fabulous city, it was appropriate that the Company should be relieved of responsibility for its 'find' by those who understood how to manage such things. Let it instead concentrate on that for which it was constituted – 'trading to the East Indies' – and let the business of sovereignty and government be left to sovereign governments.

But in fact, and for reasons that will be examined, precisely the opposite would occur. If, as an independent mercantile association, the Company was ill equipped for 'so large a sovereignty' as India, the solution that transpired was that it should be restrained and reformed until eventually it ceased to be either independent or mercantile and became instead a manageable and responsible administrative service. It was like designating the building contractor as a preservation society, dressing the brickies up as curators and expecting the digger-drivers to switch to trowels. The whole idea was crazy; unsurprisingly its implementation would prove slow, painful, and fraught with misery both for the Company and the people of Bengal.

> Whoever considers the nature of our territorial acquisitions in the East Indies and the constitution of the several Courts of Proprietors and Directors [of the Company] by which they are governed, will, if he is a wise man, see, and if he is an honest man, confess, that nothing can be more absurd and preposterous than the present system.

Thus wrote John Robinson, Secretary to the Treasury and the British government's leading authority on Indian affairs in the 1770s. Yet 'absurd and preposterous' as it was, Robinson was adamant 'that the Government should *not* take the management of these acquisitions into its own hands'. He gave five reasons. He could not see how the Bengal acquisitions could be 'properly' transferred, that is, without infringing the Company's chartered rights; he was against severing the commerce of Bengal from its administration because it was only through trade that the Bengal revenue could find its way to Britain; and he was 'violently against' any arrangement which would make the British government and the British exchequer responsible for Indian commitments.

This last concern was undoubtedly prompted by current experience of the American colonies. Indeed another of Robinson's reasons for not wanting the Government to take on direct responsibility for India was that it already had one colonial revolt on its hands without inviting another. Had the whole Indian debate not coincided precisely with the loss of Britain's first overseas empire in America it might well have taken a very different path. It would certainly have been conducted with less caution and less passion. But what was happening in North America dictated what must not happen in India. Hence, while ducking direct involvement by the Government, Robinson insisted that the independence of the Company and the 'democratic' nature of its shareholders must be suppressed.

Finally he suggested that, since there were bound to be 'errors' in the management of such distant acquisitions, it was convenient that the Company's directors should remain the scapegoats rather than the King's ministers. In fact, given that these same ministers could scarcely command respect and authority at home, he thought that Leadenhall Street, once reformed, would be in a much better position to run Bengal than would Whitehall.

Robinson was writing in the context of Lord North's ailing administration; but he could just as well have been referring to any of its weak predecessors or its immediate successors. This was an age of ministries rather than governments, each representing a coalition of factions rather than parties, and each serving self-interest rather than principle. In England notions of public service were scarcely more developed than in India. Office, however transitory, was seen more as a reward than a responsibility and incumbents agonized more over the dispensing of its perquisites than over the mastering of its paperwork. Direct state administration of Bengal promised to be no more disinterested and distinctly less consistent than Company administration. Indeed the great fear, voiced by both Government and Company, was that a state takeover would confer such a reservoir of desirable patronage on the King and his ministers as to enable them to buy off all opposition and thus subvert the constitution and possibly subordinate domestic priorities to the exigencies of Indian policy.

Looked at in retrospect, then, one might conclude that the Company was 'set up'. If the prospects for corruption, exploitation, mismanagement and censure made Bengal too hot to handle for the Government, it was obvious that an association of self-confessed fortune-seekers would be virtually incinerated. Echoing Burke, imperial historians would invariably shudder and blush over the enormities perpetrated by the Company's servants in the aftermath of Plassey. Misappropriation was commonplace; so were extortion and outright oppression. But it is noteworthy that at the time, and well into the 1780s, Burke himself remained silent. He wholly approved of the Company's rule, vigorously supported it during the debates on the 1773 Regulating Act, and let fly with his first salvoes of indignation only when the worst abuses had been curbed and the main culprits replaced. Thus Warren Hastings, his chosen target, is now generally regarded not as the dragon who laid low the Bengali economy but as the St George who by ending the most draconian ravages laid the foundations of a more equitable empire.

Faced with the bonanza that was Bengal, it was inevitable that riot should precede rule and that flagrant grounds for state intervention would result. But what is surprising is that state intervention was initially so casual and counter-productive as to suggest collusion; and that eventually the Company in India was so successful in conducting its own reform that, by the time state intervention was formalized, the Company's administration was well on the way to becoming a model of its kind and indeed the envy of Whitehall.

The troubles may be said to have started with the return from Bengal in 1760 of a sick but vengeful Clive determined to employ fame and fortune in acquiring in England the eminence he had recently enjoyed in Bengal. At first he stood aloof from Company politics just as in Calcutta he had considered himself above the squabbles of the Bengal Council. But he had not forgotten the directors' carping criticism of his administration; nor had the directors, although probably ignorant of his secret correspondence with Pitt, forgotten that scathing response, signed by Clive, in which the Bengal councillors accused them of listening to knaves and dwelling on 'mere inadvertencies and casual neglects'. For such unheard-of defiance all the other signatories were now dismissed. But many, like Clive, were already heading home with fortunes made and grievances festering. It was they who would make the running while Clive waited in the wings, convalescing and accumulating influence including an Irish peerage, a seat in the Commons, and a modest parliamentary following.

With good reason to fear an inquisition into the source of their instant wealth, the returnees – soon known as the 'Bengal Club' and then the 'Bengal Squad' – were fortunate to find in Leadenhall Street a Company which behind its sober new frontage was already in some disarray. Entering the labyrinth now commonly known as 'India House', the Bengal Squad therefore made straight for the source of this disturbance by wheeling right for the double doors and doubtful acoustics of the General Court Room. Here, in the largest of the building's public rooms, the twenty-four directors (previously 'committees') seated in line behind the bar confronted their shareholders, now known as 'proprietors', who packed the opposing tiers of benches.

Since the formation of the United Company (following the amalgamation of the New and Old Companies) the General Court, or Court of Proprietors, met quarterly, its function being to rubber-stamp policy decisions, approve the dividend, and elect the directors from a previously agreed list. Anyone with more than £500 of Company stock was currently entitled to vote and, although many of the proprietors represented particular 'interests', or syndicates (concerned with shipping, finance, etc), the directors could expect to control them thanks to their monopoly of patronage. In other words they 'managed' the General Court just as the government of the day 'managed' Parliament – by the judicious distribution of perquisites and offices. But in 1758 this cosy equilibrium had broken down with a split amongst the directors, an appeal from the disappointed minority to the proprietors, and a hotly contested election.

The victor was the formidable if unexciting Lawrence Sulivan, a one-time Bombay councillor described by H. H. Dodwell as 'a man without an idea in advance of the low level of his time'. This is true only in so far as Sulivan, by resisting Clive and betraying no sympathy with the idea of a Crown dominion in India, would find few champions amongst the historians of British India. On the other hand his integrity was unimpeachable, which in the 'low level of his time' is more than can be said for most. He understood the Company's business thoroughly, respected its traditions, and for the next twenty years would aggressively champion its traditional role as an independent mercantile enterprise.

Of the gold-digging Bengal servants he ever disapproved and the 1758 controversy had in fact arisen over who should succeed Clive as President Governor in Bengal. Its bitterness was a clear indication of the enormous value that now attached to Indian patronage. In Bengal, and to a lesser extent in the Carnatic, the Company was seen to have in its gift a dazzling new array of appointments by means of which aspirants, whether civilian or military and regardless of age, experience or ability, could expect to acquire such wealth as would sustain the comforts of opulence and the fruits of influence for several generations to come. Calcutta had become a veritable Klondike; the stampede was on. In Burke's emotive phrasing of twenty years later, 'animated with all the avarice of age, and all the impetuosity of youth, they roll in [to Bengal] one after another; wave upon wave; and there is nothing before the eyes of the natives but an endless, hopeless, prospect of new flights of birds of prey and passage, with appetites continually renewing for a food that is continually wasting . . .'

Such rampant profiteering was taking its toll of the Company as well as India. Already the directors, who met round a handsome horseshoe table in a chamber adjacent to the General Court Room, had shown their disapproval of the vast presents being dispensed by the Nawab and of the misuse of *dastak*, both of which diverted specie from the Bengal treasury into English pockets. They had also protested against the deluge of bills of exchange reaching London whereby their servants remitted home this same specie, in effect lending money to the Company in India against repayment, with interest, in London. With the Bengal land revenues foreseen by Clive proving hard to collect and being readily absorbed by military costs, this source of Indian finance helped to pay for the Company's commercial purchases in India without the need to export silver. But silver was needed more than ever for the China trade, and whatever saving was being made in respect of Bengal was offset by the need to meet those bills of exchange in London. Thus the Company was experiencing severe and worsening financial embarrassment at the very moment when its erstwhile servants of the Bengal Squad were to be seen purchasing estates and influence – and, worse still, mobilizing their wealth to undermine the direction of the Company.

The first clash came in 1763 when, supported by the Bengal Squad, the parliamentary Opposition questioned the Government's and Sulivan's handling of the Indian arrangements contained in the Treaty of Paris which ended the Seven Years War. Clive, who was only too aware that his infamous *jagir*, far and away the most valuable asset acquired by any individual, was also the most vulnerable, had thus far held his fire. But he did join in this protest and, when it was duly defeated, he issued a direct challenge by serving notice that he would raise the matter in Leadenhall Street and would contest the forthcoming election of directors in the Court of Proprietors.

Once again Sulivan would triumph. But the important feature of the 1763 election is that Clive and his colleagues introduced tactics which, familiar enough to any city tycoon today, were unprecedented in the Company's history and would have won the grudging regard even of that arch 'manager', Sir Josiah Child. Indeed, in what many have seen as a personal vendetta between Clive and Sulivan there are frequent echoes of that earlier tussle betwen Child and Papillon. But whereas Child had confined himself to manipulating stock and bribing shareholders, Clive and his supporters hit on the idea of actually creating shareholders. This was done by forming an elaborate consortium of brokers, jobbers and banking houses to buy up and then split large shareholdings into £500 lots which were then distributed to their followers for the duration of the contest. In this way something like 100 new votes were created within the General Court of Proprietors.

Initially funded by wealth acquired in the Company's service, this system of 'splitting' was, in the words of Dame Lucy Sutherland, its tenacious analyst, 'to prove a veritable Frankenstein's monster to its creators'. For it 'called into action a number of forces in no way directly concerned with the welfare of the Company', notable among which were His Majesty's Government and then the Opposition. To offset Clive's 'splitting' tactics Sulivan called to his aid the Ministry of the day. Public funds were thus deployed to match Bengal fortunes and more stock was split. The parliamentary Opposition responded in kind by 'splitting' further holdings on behalf of Clive. His tally rose to 220 newly created votes while Sulivan's rose to 163, most of which were provided by the Government's influence. The General Court's debate over the terms of the Treaty of Paris, which rivalled that in Parliament and attracted enormous public interest, went in favour of Clive's party; but in the even better attended elections for the Directorate, Clive and his nominees were routed. Two weeks later Sulivan took his expected revenge by ordering that the payment of Clive's *jagir* be stopped pending investigation.

To Clive the £23,000 a year was everything. It was unprecedented recognition for unprecedented services; in the Moghul hierarchy it placed him where he ever yearned to be, above the Company and its wretched sermonizing; and it guaranteed his political prospects in England. 'My future power,' he wrote, 'my future grandeur, all depend upon the receipt of the Jaghire money.' To regain it became an obsession, first dictating an appeal to his old friends in the parliamentary Opposition and, when this failed, an appeal to the new Ministry of Lord Grenville. Grenville also advised that no redress would be likely at Westminster; but, in return for the support of Clive's parliamentary following, he agreed to pressurize the Company. When this too failed, another trial of strength in the General Court of Proprietors was inevitable. Much the same frantic lobbying and 'splitting' preceded it. The difference was that this time the Ministry was on the side of Clive and his colleagues and the Opposition was for Sulivan and the majority in the Court of Directors. It would still have been a close-fought contest had there not arrived from India in early 1764 news so dismal that it spelt doom to Sulivan and glorious vindication to Clive.

ii

While the Company in London was entering its stormiest decade, something equally disruptive and ominous had been brewing in Bengal. There Clive had been briefly succeeded by Holwell, the unctuous 'hero' of the Black Hole, and then by Henry Vansittart, a young star from Madras. Vansittart enjoyed the support of both Clive and Sulivan. It boded well for firm leadership and, as if to display it, Vansittart's first move had been to implement a scheme, hatched by Holwell, for replacing the Nawab.

Mir Jafar, though lulled by Clive's promises that the English never deserted an ally, had always refrained from open defiance. He had simply failed to play the quite impossible role assigned to him. Clive and the Bengal Council had assured him that they would not interfere with his administration so long as he discharged his financial and military obligations. But such were their expectations of his generosity, such the demands of their trade, the expense of their troops, and the burden of compensation due to the Company, that the Nawab's treasury was permanently empty and his troops permanently mutinous. However anxious to please, there was no way that he could discharge such obligations.

Caillaud, who had succeeded as Commander-in-Chief in Bengal, bitterly protested at his failure to offer wholehearted resistance to the invasions of Bihar by the Moghul Shahzada (Crown Prince). Going further, Holwell concluded that the moment was ripe for the British to by-pass the Nawab altogether and negotiate direct with the Shahzada with a view to the Company itself assuming the Nawabship. But Vansittart, mindful of the arrangement made with Mohammed Ali in the Carnatic and deferring to Clive's legacy of non-interference in the Moghul hierarchy, preferred to strengthen the Nawab's authority. Wrongly, as it appears, he found fault with the man rather than the system. To buttress the Nawab's rule and end his vacillation he proposed installing his son-in-law, the more able and energetic Mir Kasim, as regent. Mir Jafar objected and in October 1760, with his palace ringed by Company troops, he resigned. Mir Kasim was installed in his place. To safeguard revenue expectations three more districts, Midnapur, Burdwan and Chittagong, were ceded to the Company. The old Nawab retired with his sixty wives and accumulated trappings to a pension in Calcutta; the new Nawab graciously showered Vansittart, Holwell and the rest of the Select Committee with handsome rewards for services rendered. Once again Christmas had come early in Bengal.

'A man of understanding, of uncommon talent, and great application and perseverance, joined to a thriftiness . . . most essentially necessary to restore an impoverished state.' Such was the verdict on the new Nawab voiced by Warren Hastings who now joined Vansittart's Council. Hastings had reservations about Mir Kasim's military qualities but had admitted that such natural timidity effectually safeguarded the Company against any resistance. Or, at least, it would have done but for extraordinary provocation. In the event 'a spirit superior to that of a worm when trodden upon' must have bridled at 'the many daily affronts which he was exposed to'.

If Mir Jafar had been so ineffectual that he could only be a puppet, Mir Kasim was so adroit that he resented the puppeteer's every tug and would not rest until the strings were snipped. Agreeable to expectations he duly reformed his finances, reorganized and rearmed his troops, and stamped his authority on the province. Perhaps a Clive would have been able to manage him. But Vansittart was not Clive and his 'revolution', unlike Clive's, never enjoyed the Bengal Council's full support. Thus the 'daily affronts' came above all from the disaffected councillors. They went out of their way to discredit Mir Kasim, they toasted 'Mir Jafar for ever', they accused the Select Committee of having arranged the revolution for the personal advantage of its members, and they reopened the question of negotiating with the Shahzada (now Emperor as Shah Alam II) for the Company's elevation to the Nawabship. In Bihar, where Company troops continued to be deployed, a permanent state of insubordination followed on the dismissal of Clive's protégé, the Governor Ram Narayan. Successive commanders-in-chief openly insulted the Nawab. So did William Ellis, the chief of the Patna factory who, anticipating events, actually sent troops against the royal palace on the suspicion that it might contain some Company deserters.

Worst of all, though, was the furore over internal trade. Enough has already been said on the subject of *dastak*; and anyway, by now the legality or otherwise of private British trade enjoying customs exemption within Bengal was irrelevant. It was simply common practice. The booming internal trade, which had once made a useful contribution to the Murshidabad exchequer, now passed through the province duty-free under British colours. Indeed by selling *dastak* to Indian merchants, the Company's servants had effectually transferred this revenue to their own pockets. Naturally, as a good businessman, Mir Kasim resented this situation. But attempts to collect even the little that might still be due on *dastak*-less shipments proved disastrous. A bona fide consignment would have to be defended against the Nawab's officials; they in turn had to ambush their legitimate prey. From both sides the complaints rained down on Calcutta. Trade, not to mention revenue collection, was being conducted at the point of a gun. Hastings, who travelled up to the Nawab's new capital of Monghyr in 1762, was appalled at what he saw. Native agents were terrorizing the countryside with the approval of their British principals, who in turn were openly defying the agents of the supposedly sovereign Nawab. The only solution was a redefinition of the whole status of private trade.

Acting on this suggestion the well-intentioned Vansittart negotiated an arrangement with the Nawab whereby all inland trade conducted by the Company's servants would again pay duty but at a rate far below the normal. The concession occasioned an uproar within the Bengal Council. Vansittart's position had just been greatly undermined by London's dismissal of several of his supporters. (They were the men who, with Clive, had put their names to that letter of defiance back in 1759.) The Council was now overwhelmingly hostile and, though under no illusions as to the disastrous effect on relations with Mir Kasim, it unhesitatingly repudiated the agreement.

It was this news of dissension within the Bengal Council in early 1763 which, reaching London a year later, confounded Sulivan's prospects as he entered the ring for a second trial of strength with Clive and his supporters. The directors drafted a letter to Calcutta dismissing four of the rebellious councillors and naming a Bombay man to succeed Vansittart whose term of office was coming to an end. Clive and his following saw this as further evidence of Sulivan's victimizing the Bengal establishment; from friends of the dismissed councillors they drew additional support and votes. But before the letter could actually be sent, more news from India revealed an even worse situation.

Mir Kasim, it seemed, had responded to the Council's repudiation of the new terms for inland trade by abolishing all customs duties, thus neatly negating the advantages of *dastak*. Overruling Vansittart, the Bengal Council condemned this move as provocative and outside the Nawab's powers. Hastings realized that it might be the former but could not possibly be the latter. He urged calm and compromise; but it was too late. Anticipating hostilities the Nawab seized a shipment of arms; a deputation from Calcutta was detained in his capital; and when Ellis, the Company's hot-headed chief in Bihar, stormed Patna he was quickly overpowered and captured by the Nawab's troops. In June 1763 war was formally declared. Five thousand troops were sent north towards Monghyr while in a rewind of the 1760 revolution, Mir Kasim was declared unfit to rule and Mir Jafar reinstated amidst the usual handout of five-figure gratuities. Needless to say, high on the restored Nawab's agenda was the reinstatement of the Company's *dastak* – or rather the reimposition of normal dues. Vansittart and Hastings were in despair. Powerless to control the Council or to halt the collapse of their plans, both men indicated that they would resign as soon as the war was over.

But if Vansittart felt powerless, how much more so Sulivan and his fellow directors in embattled Leadenhall Street? With Clive increasingly confident of getting his revenge, with the most stalwart amongst the proprietors expressing deep anxiety over affairs in India, and with the Ministry openly critical, Sulivan's position was fragile. Add to this a war in India which promised to be – and indeed was – the longest and bloodiest ever fought by the Company in Bengal, plus the dangers implicit in its being conducted by a deeply divided and rebellious Council, and the wonder must be that his defeat was not more decisive.

This time everything hinged on who should succeed Vansittart. With that, on average, twelve-month sea-lag between an Indian crisis and the receipt of news of it in London, the directors were somewhat in the position of astronomers monitoring galactic developments which, for all their immediacy, were in fact occurring in some previous era. There was no point agonizing over instructions which, if not irrelevant at the time they were issued, would certainly be of no more than historical interest by the time they reached India. All they could do was to lay down general principles – which their servants would inevitably read as so much sermonizing – and send out men whom they trusted. Patronage, as well as being their most prized asset at home, was also their most effective means of influencing policy abroad.

Before the depth of the Bengal crisis had become apparent, Sulivan and his fellow directors had committed themselves to John Spencer, a Bombay man like Sulivan himself, as President in Calcutta. After the now usual 'splitting', an attempt to reverse this appointment in the General Court failed; but by then, 'as if by inspiration', an anonymous shareholder leapt to his feet and proposed the name of Clive. The Court roared its approval. Who better for such a crisis than My Lord Plassey himself? In a speech so carefully phrased that it rather undermined the supposed spontaneity of the proposal, Clive rose to explain that, though indifferent to office, he recognized the obligations of duty. He would consider the matter; naturally his acceptance would depend on the directors being as supportive as the shareholders.

It seemed a reasonable stipulation. But as transpired in two subsequent votes, it actually meant the removal of Sulivan from the Directorate and the reinstatement of Clive's right to his beloved *jagir* money. Both demands were met, but only after tumultuous debate and by the narrowest of margins. With a fine sense of irony the session which approved the payment of the *jagir* also approved a motion forbidding the acceptance of any presents without the consent of the directors. A month later, in June 1764, Clive sailed for India for the third and last time. Besides rescuing the Company from the political complications that had arisen from his first Bengal 'settlement', he was expected to suppress those abuses – like extortionate present-taking, privileged private trade, and open defiance of authority – in which he had himself set the example.

As was usual with a June sailing, the voyage proved a long one, indeed nearly as long as his sojourn in Bengal. Stormbound in Brazil he happily wrote of how he would think himself 'deserving of everlasting infamy' if with a single battalion he failed to force the surrender of Rio de Janeiro inside twenty-four hours. It was October and almost to the day, but on the other side of the world, a real battle of greater consequence than any Clive had fought was deciding the fate of northern India and establishing that lasting British supremacy with which he himself is so often credited.

Pushing up from Calcutta Major John Adams had already inflicted four successive defeats on Mir Kasim's troops. Two at least were desperate affairs more hotly contested than Plassey; 'the campaign was one of the most successful ever fought by the English in India and was more responsible than Plassey for establishing them as the real masters of Bengal' (Sir Penderel Moon). For what the enemy lacked, compared with Siraj-ud-Daula, in numbers they more than made up for by having been trained by Europeans and armed by the Company itself. Yet such is the unease with which imperial historians have viewed this 'shameful decade' that both Adams and his battles have been consigned to obscurity. Not so, of course, Mir Kasim's 'atrocities'. To stay the advance he threatened the lives of his British captives. The advance continued; the prisoners were massacred. They included three Bengal councillors, the fiery Ellis amongst them.

By the end of 1763 Adams had reached Bengal's easternmost border in Bihar and Mir Kasim had escaped across it into the neighbouring province of Oudh (roughly today's Uttar Pradesh). There he was soon conspiring with the Oudh Nawab, Shuja-ud-Daula, and their mutual overlord, Shah Alam II, for a combined invasion of Bengal. Meanwhile Adams had died, mainly from exhaustion, and his troops had become restive. Four hundred miles from the fleshpots of Calcutta, desperately short of supplies, and deeply resentful of the non-payment of prize money due on the reinstallation of Mir Jafar, some deserted and others remained in a semi-mutinous state which neither part-payment nor courts martial subdued. In April 1764 Mir Kasim and his new confederates re-entered Bihar. In some confusion the British troops withdrew to Patna.

Only the sternest measures restored order. Major Hector Munro, dispatched from Bombay to replace Adams, had twenty-five mutineers blown from guns and one of the sepoy battalions ignominiously 'broken'. He then advanced on the confederates' army encamped at Baksar on the Oudh-Bihar border. It was the subsequent battle of Baksar, far and away the mightiest engagement yet fought by the Company in India, which coincided with Clive's stopover in Brazil and which proved so decisive. At least 2000 of the enemy perished and Munro lost nearly half as many. But as usual the British forces emerged victorious and had thus, at one fell swoop, disposed of the three main scions of Moghul power in Upper India. Mir Kasim disappeared into an impoverished obscurity, Shah Alam realigned himself with the British, and Shah Shuja fled west hotly pursued by the victors. The whole Ganges valley lay at the Company's mercy; Shah Shuja eventually surrendered; henceforth Company troops became the power-brokers throughout Oudh as well as Bihar; there was even talk of an advance on Delhi.

As if by way of a postscript, five months later, and just over a year after being handed to the throne for a second time, Mir Jafar died. The installation of his half-witted son, Najm-ud-Daula, provided the perfect excuse for reducing the Nawab to little more than a Company cipher. Henceforth his ministers were chosen by the Bengal Council which also regulated his relations with the Emperor. The Council made some further attempt to reform the operation of inland trade; but as soon as it became known that Clive himself was on his way, reforms were put in abeyance and the councillors contented themselves with securing the maximum personal advantage from what was the fourth change of Nawab in eight years.

Clive expressed indignation at such changes having been made in advance of his imminent arrival. But the importance he attached to Baksar and to the demotion of the Nawab is well shown by an excited and somewhat contradictory letter which he immediately addressed to Thomas Rous, the man who had replaced Sulivan as Chairman. Clive had expected to find a situation similar to that of 1756 with the Company's very existence in Bengal under threat. Instead he found it stronger and more flourishing than ever. Indeed 'that critical conjuncture which I have long foreseen' had arrived. 'The whole Moghul Empire is in our hands . . . we must indeed become the Nabobs [Nawabs] ourselves in fact, if not in name . . . we must go forward, to retract is impossible. As usual he wanted more troops and more guns. For 'if riches and stability are the objects of the Company this is the method, the only method, we now have for attaining and securing them'.

Yet, selecting further extracts from the same letter, a precisely opposite construction can be placed upon it. 'I mean absolutely to bound our possessions, assistance and conquests to Bengal, never shall the going to Delhi be a plan adopted . . . by me.' His priority would be to reform the administration, cleanse what he called 'the Augean stable', and stamp out 'rapacity and luxury' regardless of how unpopular it might make him. 'I am determined to return to England without having acquired one farthing addition to my fortune.'

The letter was written from Madras where, during a brief stopover, Clive first caught up with events in India. It was accompanied by another letter, written in code and addressed to John Walsh, his agent in London, which gave instructions for 'whatever money I may have in public funds or anywhere else and *as much as can be borrowed in my name*' to be invested in Company stock. The transaction was to be carried out 'without loss of a minute' and in complete secrecy. What he had in mind is unclear. His biographers like to think that he was simply acquiring the wherewithal to create more votes amongst the Company's shareholders, his critics that he wished to ensure for himself a further share of Bengal's revenues (which he was about to claim *in toto* for the Company). Either way there can be no question that the transaction was prompted by the news that he gathered at Madras and that he used this news for personal advantage.

It throws grave doubt over the much-acclaimed disinterest that supposedly informed his second term of government in Bengal. And, more significantly, it started a period of intense speculation in Company stock as an exciting financial investment. This new development was to have consequences every bit as dire as his earlier innovation of using Company stock to fabricate votes. Indeed there was a direct relationship between the two. With enough support among shareholders, and enough stock to influence the market, there would be a grave temptation to force the Company into paying dividends which its finances could not justify.

Reaching Calcutta in May 1765 Clive immediately set about reimposing his considerable authority and cleansing 'the Augean stable'. By way of a broom he employed the Select Committee, staffed by four of his followers and to which the directors had given supremacy over the large and unruly Bengal Council. Anticipating that their new Governor might face a crisis like that he had found at Fulta in 1756, the directors had envisaged the Committee acting as a war cabinet. Clive, while stressing the critical nature of the times as a justification for invoking this powerful weapon, in fact used it as a Star Chamber. Individual councillors were summoned to appear before it and explain their gains; some resigned or were suspended; all were obliged to sign a covenant against accepting future presents.

Such ferocious tactics would go down well with posterity; but they also provoked the hostility of the councillors, many of whom had powerful friends amongst the Bengal Squad, Clive's natural allies in London. 'The brotherhood of exploitation, the freemasonry of graft, had been violated', explains Professor Spear, one of Clive's more recent biographers. The victims 'sharpened their mental knives of revenge on the grindstone of hate while dipping their quills of complaint in the ink of defamation'. Clive himself used even richer language, likening Calcutta to a Gomorrah of corruption, 'rapacious and luxurious beyond conception' and confessing himself unable to restrain 'the tribute of a few tears to the departed and lost fame of the British nation'. It was not that he condemned presents outright. How could he when, as John Johnstone, the most outspoken of the disgraced councillors reminded him, 'the approved example of the President, Lord Clive himself' had been their guide? What he objected to was that presents had been showered on men 'of inferior pretensions and even in inferior stations'. As he reminded Johnstone, his own *jagir* had been 'a reward for real services rendered to the Nabob at a very dangerous crisis'. He could see no parallel with the untried youths and incompetents who had enjoyed the munificence of subsequent nawabs.

A similar ambiguity underlies Clive's other reforms. His solution to the problem arising from the misuse of *dastak* (customs exemption) was to make the commodities of inland trade a Company monopoly administered by, and paying dividends to, the senior Bengal servants. He reasoned that they could not survive on their Company salaries and must be given some compensation for surrendering such a lucrative activity as private trade. In fact the scheme antagonized both the directors, who were totally opposed to any interference in inland trade, the junior Company servants, who were excluded from it, the native traders, who suffered as much as ever, and the native consumers, who found the price of essentials rising rapidly. Only the lucky subscribers benefited. For no risk and no effort they received about £200,000 per annum, Clive's share being over £21,000.

The Nawab, of course, received nothing. Clive would insist that all possible respect be paid to his office but in reality his government was now just the Company in Bengal's letterhead. If Clive and his successors had to manage without presents it was as much thanks to Murshidabad's empty coffers and the fact that the Nawab was now a pensioner of the Company as to any Company covenants against the practice. Under the terms of an agreement reached with Mir Kasim's erstwhile allies – Shah Alam II and Shuja-ud-Daula – Oudh had been returned to the latter on condition of the payment of an indemnity to the Company and on condition of the cession of two large districts to Shah Alam. The Emperor in turn, having first been perilously seated on a throne constructed from a suitably draped armchair perched on top of Clive's dining table, had ceremoniously conferred on the Company the *diwani* of Bengal, an event which has been variously hailed as 'the great act of the constitutional entrance of the Company into the body politic of India' (Edmund Burke), 'the formal beginning of the British Raj' (V. T. Harlow), and 'the first British experiment in "indirect rule"' (H. H. Dodwell).

Originally an office distinct from that of nawab and equally influential, the *diwani* entailed the management of a province's revenue and the remission of part of it to the imperial treasury. In the past Bengal's Nawabs had usually secured the appointment of their own *diwans* and had thus suborned the independence of the office. But since Moghul government amounted to little more than revenue management, it followed that a decree resurrecting this office and awarding it to the Company virtually extinguished the pretensions of Murshidabad. It is true that under Clive's so-called Dual System, the assessment and collection of the revenue would be left to the existing network of venal officials and grasping tax farmers. But before reaching the Nawab's treasury, the flow of rupees would now be diverted to the Company who became responsible both for maximizing and distributing the receipts. These, like the sums that were supposed to have accrued under the terms of his treaty with Mir Jafar, Clive grossly overestimated. After the deduction of all costs and expenses he foresaw an annual surplus of nearly £2 million, enough to meet the cost of trade purchases, the expenses of all the Company's other settlements, and still leave substantial profits. It was sweet music to the ears of the directors, sweeter still to those of anyone who had had the foresight to invest their all – and whatever could be borrowed in their name besides – in Company stock.

iii

News of Clive's intention to assume the *diwani* reached London in April 1766. There it had two important repercussions. First the Company's stock, a normally unexciting performer on the financial markets, suddenly began to climb. It added eight points, about five per cent, in a single day and it went on climbing, nearly doubling in value over the next eight months. Clive's friends, acting on those secret instructions from Madras, bought heavily; but as word of his optimistic calculations of the Bengal surplus leaked out, outside investors also leapt on the bandwagon. On the Amsterdam and Paris markets the bubble went on growing and as the wilder speculators moved in, the greater became the pressure to keep the bubble from bursting.

An obvious way of preventing such a catastrophe was by boosting confidence still further with a hefty increase in the annual dividend. If Clive was right about that £2 million annual surplus, the Company could well afford such a gesture; even if it could not, Clive's innovation of 'splitting' stock to create votes could be used to force it to co-operate. Accordingly, in September 1766, the General Court of Proprietors moved for an increase from six to ten per cent. The directors, still dominated by Clive's allies, did not support the motion; but neither did they organize the necessary 'splitting' to defeat it, thus in effect allowing it to pass. As a result, stock values continued to climb.

While the City of London was thus in turmoil, across town in Westminster the *diwani* was having equally alarming results. In June 1766

Lord Chatham (the elder Pitt) formed his last precarious ministry. Echoing the words first used by Clive in his letter of 1759 (suggesting that 'so large a sovereignty' could and should be exploited by the nation) Chatham saw the *diwani* revenues as what he called 'a kind of gift from heaven' sent to offset the debt accrued during the Seven Years War and so secure 'the redemption of a nation'. Playing on that old resentment against the Company's monopoly, on the growing unease about its management of its Indian territories, and on the jealousies being aroused by the *nouveau riche* 'Nabobs' of the Bengal Squad, the Ministry scented a popular cause.

But how to wrest this providential windfall from the Company posed serious problems. Chatham seems to have favoured a direct assault in Parliament on the Company's right to hold territory. The threat of such a heavy-handed approach had a salutary effect on Leadenhall Street but it failed to win the support of his divided Ministry. If chartered rights were to be infringed, it was a near certainty that other chartered bodies, amongst them the City of London itself, would protest. And if the office as well as the income of the *diwani* was to be claimed by the state, all sorts of constitutional problems would arise, not least that of George III becoming a feudatory of the Moghul.

On the whole, therefore, the Ministry preferred the softer approach of negotiating with the various interests within the Company. As Chatham slipped towards a dithering senility, negotiations were handled by the more amenable Earl of Shelburne; but with both the Ministry and the parliamentary Opposition as faction-ridden as the Company, these proved complex and protracted. In unlikely alliance with a section of the speculative investors and a group of disgruntled 'Nabobs' who had fallen foul of Clive (and which included Johnstone's extensive kin), Lawrence Sulivan staged a gradual recovery. Clive's supporters, in return for not opposing the Ministry's demands, eventually secured an extension for a further ten years of the *jagir*, Johnstone was reinstated, and the Company's chartered rights were confirmed, albeit on a temporary basis. In return, the Ministry secured as much as it had ever hoped for, namely a guaranteed annual payment from the Company of £400,000 per year. Additionally and almost incidentally it had secured the passage of two bills, one designed to prevent 'splitting', the other to prevent the Company from raising its dividend (which had now gone up to twelve and a half per cent) without Government sanction. Neither of these measures proved particularly effective but they established a highly significant precedent for parliamentary interference in the internal affairs of the Company.

Less obvious but equally ominous was the continued process of infiltration whereby, on the one hand, ministerial influence saturated the Court of Directors while, on the other, Indian wealth buoyed up the Court of Proprietors. As yet the final battle lines were far from clear. Sulivan was still in the wilderness; Clive, who returned from India in 1767, still dominated the Directorate. But, because the compromise just reached was to last only two years, the Ministry, with an eye to the next round of negotiations, continued to pursue connections within the Court of Directors. It was thus, for instance, as a Government ally, that Commodore Sir William James, the hero of Suvarnadrug, was elected a director in 1768.

Meanwhile, with every returning Indiaman, there came new recruits for the Bengal Squad and new money for voting shares in the Court of Proprietors. As the Bengal Nabobs squeezed up to make room for their colleagues, adjacent benches filled with Madras Nabobs, equally affluent and equally anxious to protect the sources of their affluence. Such was their combined voting strength that Burke would one day observe that instead of the directors appointing their servants, the servants were now appointing their directors. 'The seat of supreme power is in Calcutta [as opposed to Leadenhall Street]', he declared, failing to add that it was also in Whitehall. Henceforth it was virtually impossible to secure election as a director without the support either of the Ministry or of a large section of the Nabobs. And inevitably such support imposed reciprocal obligations once the candidate was safely installed round the horseshoe table.

In the event the renewed negotiations in 1769 did little more than prolong the 1767 compromise for a further five years. The Company was to continue to pay the state £400,000 per year; additionally it accepted a stipulation, of some future significance, to boost its export of English manufactures. But more pressing matters were again postponed. One consisted of a proposed trade-off whereby the still unsettled expenses incurred by the Company during the Manila expedition should be offset by a reduction in the excessive duties charged by the Treasury on tea imports from China. Another sought statutory backing to enforce the Court of Directors' control over their Indian servants. Both proposals came from the Company. The first, had it been acted on, could well have averted the financial crises that were about to engulf Leadenhall Street;

and the second must have ameliorated the political scandals that were again looming in India. But both were rejected by a supine Ministry.

There followed in the Court of Proprietors 'one of the most fiercely contested elections of the century' (Sutherland) from which Sulivan was at last returned to the Court of Directors. The price was high. To secure this result Sulivan, Vansittart, and their allies had mobilized and 'split' stock on an unprecedented scale. Because of the recent legislation, this stock was still in their names when, a month later, news from India sent stock values plummeting. Triumphant in April, Sulivan was practically bankrupt in May. So was Vansittart whose only hope of redeeming his fortune lay in a return to India. Such an opportunity arose almost immediately; sadly he took it, never to be heard of again.

The news which had prompted the financial panic came not, for once, from Bengal, but from Madras and Mauritius. The former appeared to be under threat from a rampaging Hyder Ali who had just usurped the throne of Mysore and, under the sort of local British provocation which Leadenhall Street was so anxious to curtail, had turned on the Company. Meanwhile Mauritius, a place of sinister repute ever since the days of La Bourdonnais, appeared to be hosting another build-up of France's Indian Ocean navy. Time would show that as yet neither of these scares need have been taken so seriously. But this was no consolation to the impoverished and chastened Sulivan who, under Ministerial pressure, at last came to terms with Clive. Nor was the all-clear sounded soon enough to prevent the dispatch of three Supervisors, two of them Clive's nominees, one (Vansittart) Sulivan's, with extensive powers to purge the Company's ranks, reorganize its revenue administration, and conduct its external relations in a less provocative manner.

The Supervisors sailed on the frigate *Aurora* in October 1769. In spite of past failures dating back to the unfortunate experiences of Sir William Hedges at the hands of Job Charnock, Leadenhall Street retained a touching faith in such plenipotentiary commissions and great were the expectations of the new Supervisors. They carried instructions to tackle the debts accumulated by Mohammed Ali which lay at the root of all Madras's problems, they had the authority to revise the now evident failings of Clive's Dual System, and they combined the sympathies and acumen necessary to confront the great natural catastrophe that was about to overtake Bengal. Making good speed, the *Aurora* called at the Cape just before Christmas. Thereafter she was never sighted again. Besides the Supervisors, her complement included two Scots whose very different claims to celebrity seemed to offer contrasting explanations for the mystery. Thus hopes for the *Aurora* hinged on Midshipman Robert Pitcairn who had already given his name to one desert island. Probability, though, pointed to Purser William Falconer who was also a poet, his best-known composition being a vivid three-part elegy ominously entitled *The Shipwreck*.

Back in London 1770 and 1771 passed in comparative harmony as first news of the Supervisors' transactions was awaited. Lord North's administration succeeded that of Chatham-Grafton; Sulivan was removed from the Directorate and then returned to it; a bust of Clive wrapped in a toga was erected in the main hall of 'India House'. When the loss of the *Aurora* became an accepted fact the directors did what was probably the next best thing and appointed Warren Hastings, then in Madras, to the governorship of Bengal. Hastings was encouraged 'to stand forth' as *diwan* by jettisoning Clive's 'hands-off' Dual System and directly involving the Company in supervising the assessment and collection of the revenue. This was a big step towards transforming the Company into an administrative service and it was taken on the Company's own initiative. Simultaneously Sulivan in London drafted two proposals designed to strengthen the Company's authority over its servants in India. Both required statutory power and, as before, both were frustrated by a combination of indifference on the part of the Ministry and opposition from the Bengal Squad. But at least they showed that within the Company there existed an influential element who appreciated that reform was not incompatible with resistance to state intervention. Indeed, though it required a degree of state endorsement, reform was seen by Sulivan as the best defence against state intervention.

Public opinion, such as it was in the eighteenth century, failed to appreciate these niceties. Dimly aware that the British nation had somehow acquired by proxy a remote but exotic slice of south Asia, it was becoming all too familiar with the catalogue of misdemeanours and oppressions that were evidently jeopardizing this exciting development. Grisly tales of peculation and skulduggery flowed from the pens, 'dipped in the ink of infamy', of Alexander Dow, born in Benkulen but who had served in the Bengal army, and of William Bolts, one of Johnstone's less reputable partners. Both men had fallen foul of Clive. At him they therefore directed their jibes, thus neatly deflecting any attack on the Nabobs as a whole. Consequently, when Sulivan attempted to obtain parliamentary sanction for his reforms, the debate degenerated into a slanging match between Clive and the cohorts loyal to Johnstone. With the kettle publicly blackening the pots and the pots publicly blackening the kettle, it was hardly surprising that a motion to set up a Select Committee for investigating 'the most atrocious abuses that ever stained the name of civil government' received general applause.

To this Select Committee of the House, a Secret Committee was added before the end of 1772. The first was to review past abuses; the second was to pave the way for immediate legislation. For yet another crisis in the Company's affairs had blown up, this time in the shape of imminent bankruptcy. The economic fall-out threatened to engulf the nation. Parliament was sitting in emergency session. Any chance of the Company being allowed to set its own house in order had passed for good.

The new crisis stemmed from financial irresponsibility at home highlighted and exacerbated by a major disaster in India. For more than a year rumours of one of the ghastliest famines ever to afflict Bengal had been fuelling the flames of indignation against the Company and its extortionate servants. The calamity, begun with the failure of the 1769 monsoon, raged throughout 1770. No official report was ever published but a century later Sir William Hunter compiled a well-authenticated summary from the official records.

> All through the stifling summer of 1770 the people went on dying. The husbandmen sold their cattle; they sold their implements of agriculture; they devoured their seed-grain; they sold their sons and daughters, till at length no buyer of children could be found; they ate the leaves of the trees and the grass of the field; and in June 1770 the [British] Resident at the Darbar [of Murshidabad] affirmed that the living were feeding on the dead. Day and night a torrent of famished and disease-ridden wretches poured into the great cities . . . The streets were blocked up with promiscuous heaps of the dying and dead.

Estimates of the mortality varied between a third and a half of the entire population of Lower Bengal. The resultant decline in the province's prosperity was identified by Hunter as 'the key to the history of Bengal during the succeeding forty years'.

Although the Company's servants could hardly be blamed for a natural disaster, the revenue assessment was in fact increased by ten per cent during the height of the famine and there were several accusations of

British collusion in the inevitable hoarding and profiteering. No relief measures of any significance were undertaken and Clive's decision to make the inland trade a monopoly of the Company's servants appeared, probably unfairly, to have exacerbated matters. Worse was the contrasting opulence of the Nabobs which now appeared in a positively obscene light. All this was fuel for the Select Committee but it was the famine's effect on the Company's finances which precipitated the real crisis.

Ever since Clive had assumed the *diwani* the Company had been living on credit. Military and administrative expenses had continued to escalate, the revenue surplus had never approached the £2 million per annum envisaged, and those repeatedly increased dividends plus the £400,000 per annum to the state had compounded the problem. A doubling in the value of the Company's Indian trade had to some extent disguised the situation but, to finance this investment, heavy debts had been incurred in India and more bills of exchange had been made available to returning Nabobs. These also served to delay an appreciation of the financial effects of the famine. In fact it had cut deep into the revenue receipts and dramatically reversed the trade expansion. The scale of the problem became apparent in the summer of 1772 when, amid a general credit crisis, the Company found itself liable for over £1.5 million in bills of exchange alone. Even its considerable stocks of tea, written down in value as a result of the glut of cheaper contraband tea, could not meet such liabilities.

After agonized debate the directors decided to suspend dividend payments and apply to the Government for a £1 million loan. Stock values immediately plummeted and the Government, sensing another South Sea Bubble about to burst, summoned Parliament. If it was a case of saving the nation's credit, it was also understood that, in return for the necessary loan, the Company would have to pay dearly in terms of its independence. With this in mind the Secret Committee was soon hammering out the necessary legislative proposals. Meanwhile the Court of Directors, under enormous Ministerial pressure but in the teeth of bitter opposition from the Court of Proprietors, had come forward with its own suggestions. The final bill, which became Lord North's Regulating Act of 1773, was thus a compromise between these two sets of proposals.

As was to be expected with a piece of panic legislation, it would prove far from satisfactory, compounding the Company's difficulties rather than solving them. It was, however, the first big step in state intervention. 'Here began the participation of government in the administration of India' (Dame Lucy Sutherland). It also established a political precedent and a procedural system for further encroachment, while its soon apparent failings made such encroachment both inevitable and imminent.

iv

To be fair, the 1773 Regulating Act was never intended as more than a temporary expedient. Renewal or amendment after five years was envisaged; the Company's charter itself was anyway due for renewal in 1780. George III, an interested and active party, declared that it laid 'the foundation for a constant inspection from Parliament into the affairs of the Company which must require a succession of regulations every year'. But recurrent parliamentary interference was not what Lord North had in mind. His idea was to supervise and reform the Company by less direct methods. Thus two provisions, one raising the stock qualification for voting in the Court of Proprietors to £1000 and the other changing the annual election of all the directors to an annual election of only a quarter of them, were designed not only to ensure a greater continuity in the direction and less 'splitting' among the shareholders but thereby to make the exercise of ministerial support and management that much easier.

Additionally the bill provided for Government access to all correspondence with India which dealt with revenue, political or military subjects. Revenue matters were studied by the Treasury and there in particular this provision resulted in a growing understanding of the complex issues raised by Indian administration. (John Robinson, author of the 1778 analysis already quoted, was a Treasury Secretary.) But as yet it does not seem to have resulted in much active participation by government in the day-to-day running of the Company. For this the Government relied on the Act's most important provision: the creation of a governing Council in Calcutta, its five members nominated by Parliament and including three representing the Government's interests who could – and, invariably and implacably, would – outvote the two Company members. The Council was headed by Warren Hastings, the incumbent Governor who now became the first Governor-General with an ill-defined supervisory authority over the Bombay and Madras Presidencies and Benkulen. Finally the Act set up a Supreme Court of Justice in Calcutta with, again, an ill-defined jurisdiction over the Company's servants. It was supposedly designed to satisfy Sulivan's repeated requests for some means of disciplining them; but, since the judges were nominated by the Crown, the Court proved more inclined to challenge the Company's authority than to support it.

The final legislation consisted of three bills, one authorizing the loan, the second that was the Regulating Act itself, and a third, easily ignored in the excitement over state intervention and apparently of very marginal significance, which allowed the Company to claim back all customs duty paid on tea that was subsequently re-exported to the American colonies. Again this measure was presumably in response to Sulivan's earlier pleas for some easing of the excessive duties charged on the Company's tea trade. More than half the tea being drunk in England was now in fact being imported into Europe by the Company's Continental competitors and then smuggled duty-free across the Channel and the North Sea. Simultaneously large stocks of duty-paid tea were accumulating unsold in the Company's warehouses. Under the new dispensation these stocks were to be 'dumped' on the American market where, before the year was out, the colonists duly dumped them in Boston's harbour. The incident was to have serious repercussions.

But of more relevance to the Company's history may be the relationship, as yet only dimly perceived, between the financial difficulties which precipitated each dose of state intervention and the fiscal handicaps under which the Company conducted its tea trade. A detailed examination of this relationship badly needs to be undertaken. Although it was still understood that the state should not interfere in the Company's purely commercial activities, it can be no coincidence that concessions in the duty on tea accompanied every draught of the state pathogen and would go a long way towards sugaring its final death-dealing dose.

Tea apart, the Regulating Act, according to Professor Roberts's neat summary, had thus 'neither given the state a definite control over the Company, nor the Directors a definite control over their servants, nor the Governor-General a definite control over his Council, nor the Calcutta Presidency a definite control over Madras and Bombay'. Such imprecision, the product of poor drafting as well as muddled thinking, told more in India than in London. No sooner had the three councillors from London taken their seats in Calcutta's council chamber than ferocious disagreements arose on every single issue. Hastings and Barwell, the two Company men, found their past policies condemned and reversed, their agents removed, and their integrity impugned. The personal clash between Hastings and Philip Francis, ablest of the newcomers, was destined to last three decades and to occasion one duel, much brilliant polemic, the most sensational trial of the century, and a vast literature. They will be considered elsewhere. Here it is sufficient to note that as early as 1776 the Government accepted the need to remove Hastings and Barwell and duly deployed its influence in the Court of Directors to secure a vote for their recall.

But now the limitations of the new settlement as it affected London became apparent. Amid tumultuous scenes and after a twelve-hour debate attended by the leaders of the Government, the Opposition, and the Lords, the Court of Proprietors rejected the proposal. Hastings, who had already restored some order to Bengal's finances and reformed the revenue administration, was held up as a symbol of integrity and of the Company's independence, while the triumphant majority in the Court of Proprietors came to see themselves as a bastion of Company tradition against state interference. This was certainly an over-simplification. Consisting on the one hand of the Bengal Squad including the Johnstone clan plus part of the parliamentary Opposition and, on the other, of the reform-minded Sulivan-Hastings group, the victors represented an improbable coalition which required as much 'management' as the Ministerial majority in the Court of Directors. But success did generate a certain sense of purpose. Evidently the heavily drugged corpus of the Company, if sufficiently provoked, could yet administer a hefty kick. Henceforth this grouping represented the spirit of defiance.

(The only Bengal interest which it did not embrace was that of Clive. After weathering a final attack on his administration and his *jagir* from the Select Committee, a sick and embittered Clive had committed suicide in 1774; but not before renewing his vendetta with Sulivan and poisoning the minds of Francis and the new Councillors against Hastings.)

Frustrated by the Court of Proprietors, Lord North threatened to refer Hastings's dismissal to Parliament, whereupon Lauchlin MacLean, Hastings's agent in London, proffered his master's resignation. This was possibly the result of a misunderstanding, possibly an ingenious ploy hatched by MacLean, one of several plausible and intriguing – in both senses – adventurers operating on the speculative margins of the Company. Either way, the news deflated the crisis and 1777 passed in expectation of Hastings's early return. In April 1778 it emerged that he had not resigned, had never intended to resign, and was now, thanks to the death of one of the Councillors, in a stronger position than before. News of another death, that of his assumed successor as Governor–General, further confirmed his renascence, while at home Sulivan, his patron, secured enough votes to get himself reinstalled, for at least the fourth time, in the Court of Directors.

All this was bad news for North's Government. It was, though, as nothing compared to the American tidings of Burgoyne's surrender at Saratoga and of the French entry into the war. Briefly the probable loss of Britain's transatlantic empire eclipsed all else, paralysing the administration and shattering the confidence of its leader. When the Court of Proprietors again lashed out, this time to reject the proposals drawn up by Robinson to amend the Regulating Act, North merely limped off to seek Sulivan's backing, thus signalling the near collapse of Ministerial control over the Directorate. Sulivan's price was a renewed commitment to Hastings's Governor-Generalship and a strengthening of the Governor-General's authority over his Council and over the subsidiary presidencies. In the press of American business, the Regulating Act was simply renewed annually until, in 1781, it was superseded by another temporizing measure which addressed neither the crisis in Government-Company relations nor that in the Calcutta Council chamber. 'A paltry performance' was Sulivan's verdict.

The year 1781 ended with the surrender at Yorktown; it was followed, three months later, by the resignation of the North Government. In a crisis atmosphere of recrimination and disillusionment, plus a growing demand for reform of the domestic administration, four coalition ministries succeeded one another in two years. This instability in government gave to a Parliament no longer stifled by 'management' the chance to make itself heard. It did so by turning, as if by way of consolation for the loss of the American colonies, increasingly towards India; and at last the train of events, set in motion back in the 1760s, moved rapidly towards a conclusion.

As in the run-up to the Regulating Act, two parliamentary committees took the lead. The first, a Select Committee staffed mainly by opponents of the North administration, was supposedly investigating complaints against the Supreme Court set up in Calcutta under the Regulating Act. But fired by the high-minded rhetoric of Edmund Burke and fuelled by the revelations and animosities of Philip Francis, it, like its predecessor, was soon engaged in an impassioned and wide-ranging attack on the Company's misgovernment, on its servants' transgressions, and in particular on the character and conduct of Warren Hastings. Meanwhile a

Secret Committee had been necessitated by another Indian crisis – Hyder Ali was again rampaging through the Carnatic – and another looming financial crisis. Organized by North's Government and staffed by his Indian specialists including Robinson and the highly ambitious Henry Dundas, the Secret Committee also extended its deliberations way beyond its ostensible remit (the causes of the Carnatic war) and became in effect a policy-making body.

Between them these two committees issued eighteen lengthy reports whose cumulative effect was to convince even the Court of Proprietors that some radical change was unavoidable. While the sensational and impassioned revelations of Burke's Select Committee 'made some sweeping reforms inevitable', it was the more dogged and pragmatic deliberations of Dundas's Secret Committee which 'laid down the nature of those reforms' (L. Sutherland). In this eighteenth-century transfer of power in India, the high-minded Burke, albeit by rhetoric rather than example, played the Gandhi role and the affable Dundas the Nehru.

First in the field, Dundas moved again for the recall of Hastings. Parliament approved the motion and the Court of Directors seconded it; but again the Court of Proprietors rejected it, twice. Without the proprietors' approval the directors were powerless to act. Six months later Dundas responded by introducing his own bill for a root-and-branch reform. It included the right of the Crown to appoint and recall the Governor-General and since it also greatly strengthened the position of the Governor-General *vis-à-vis* his Council and the subsidiary Governors of Madras and Bombay, it in effect by-passed the authority of Leadenhall Street. But a change of government meant that Dundas was now in opposition and his bill, awarding such important powers to the Crown, never stood a chance in a House profoundly suspicious of royal patronage. Its proponent and many of its provisions were, however, incorporated in Pitt's final solution.

Next, though, it was the turn of the Select Committee in the person of Charles James Fox, who had just formed an unpopular minority government in coalition with the discredited North. Fox's India Bill, actually two bills, is now thought to have been inspired and partly drafted by Burke himself whose profound horror of the Company and all its servants it vividly reflected. Yet, compared to Dundas's bill, it concentrated more on arrangements in London than in India, proposing, instead of a surgical by-pass of India House, a veritable heart transplant. If, as Burke was wont to declaim, the Company had really broken every treaty it had ever made and sold every title it had ever dispensed, then it had forfeited its sacred charter, not to mention its assets, and must be cast out. In its place the bill allowed for seven Commissioners, nominated by Parliament, to replace the Court of Directors at the helm of Indian affairs plus another nine Assistant Commissioners to manage the Company's trade and fix its dividend. 'It will be a vigorous and a hazardous measure', Fox had predicted. He made it all the more so by nominating to those seven all-powerful Commissionerships seven all-loyal Foxites.

This was too much for the Company which alerted every other chartered body in the country to such an 'unconstitutional and unprecedented' seizure. It was also too much for the Opposition, who foresaw that an administration with the patronage of India in its gift might be able to hold the reins of government indefinitely; too much, too, for old Sir William James who died of a fit of apoplexy brought on by what he must have regarded as depredations more piratical than Angrey's; and too much for George III whose detestation of both the Ministry and its bill led him to advise the peers of the realm that any Lord who voted for it was 'not only not his friend but his enemy'. Thus, though the bill passed in the Commons, it was defeated in the Lords and the Government was promptly dismissed.

Enter the twenty-five-year-old William Pitt (the Younger). As the great-grandson of Thomas Pitt, interloper and Governor of Madras, and as the scion of a family which owed its prominence to an Indian fortune acquired before such things became reprehensible, Pitt was in a happily ambiguous position. More to the point, the alarm caused by Fox's bill meant that almost any alternative now stood a fair chance of favourable consideration even by the likes of Sulivan in Leadenhall Street. Indeed, Pitt had already secured the support of the most knowledgeable and able of the India managers, especially Dundas and Robinson. He narrowly failed to win over Sulivan but could nevertheless claim that his India bill had the support in principle of the majority of the directors. A majority in the House of Commons as yet eluded him. His first India Bill was defeated in January 1784 and it was not until the following July, after Pitt had won the general election handsomely, that the India Act was finally passed.

Pitt's India Act combined elements of both Dundas's and Fox's bills. Like the former it made the Governor-General in India a royal appointment while his authority over his Council and over the subsidiary Presidencies was somewhat enhanced. But like the latter it set up in

London a body of Commissioners, six in number and known as the Board of Control, who would henceforth 'superintend, direct and controul [*sic*]' the government of the Company's possessions. An objection was raised to the word 'direct' but it was not removed. The Board was to work through the Company, 'directing' the directors by an elaborate system of scrutiny and consultation which soon left Leadenhall Street with no greater powers of initiation and revision than any other branch of the civil service.

The members of the Board included a Secretary of State and the Chancellor of the Exchequer, both government appointments, but to avoid the obvious criticism it was emphasized that all Indian patronage was to remain with the Company. The Company was also to continue to manage its purely commercial activities without government interference. If respected, these were important concessions and went a long way towards reconciling Leadenhall Street to an Act which, in the words of the late Professor Roberts, 'converted the Company into a quasi-state department' and rendered its final abolition in 1858 merely 'a formal and explicit recognition of facts already existing'.

One other concession is also of relevance. After the failure of Pitt's first bill but immediately before the passage of the second, a so-called Commutation Act had been passed. This imposed a tax on windows by way of making good the loss of government revenue resulting from a dramatic reduction in the duties charged on tea; they were slashed from a variable rate of between 79 per cent and 127 per cent to just 12½ per cent. It is not possible that the Company was unaware of the effect this concession would have on the most lucrative branch of its trade. In return for surrendering administrative independence in India the Company was rewarded with the most important commercial opportunity in its history. What was lost in terms of Indian revenue was to be made up on the China trade.

CHAPTER EIGHTEEN

Too Loyal, Too Faithful

HASTINGS'S INDIA

Concluding a history of the East India Company poses the sort of problems faced by the biographer of a long-lived celebrity. After a suitably paced narrative covering the subject's active life, the question arises of how to present the empty decades of disengagement and retirement when, with failing faculties and supported gait, the public *persona* fades into the obscurity of an irrelevant old age. One solution is to fill this blank by anticipating the later progress of the ideas and institutions spawned by the subject. But in the case of the Company this would mean charting the history of the British Empire in the East, a daunting task which has not been neglected by others.

Alternatively the declining years can be simply condensed into a short and serene graveside epilogue. Again, though, the Company does not lend itself to this treatment. To reach the graveside means leaping six decades and alighting amid the far from serene scenes of the 'Indian Mutiny'. For these the Company and its erstwhile overlord, the Moghul Emperor, would be made scapegoats; the latter was exiled, the former dissolved. Both institutions were by then, however, long moribund as anything other than constitutional conveniences. The Company no more resembled 'the Grandest Society of Merchants in the Universe' than did Bahadur Shah, 'the little old man of Delhi', his illustrious predecessors on the Peacock Throne.

Even after its final dissolution in 1858 the Company, though divested of its fictive powers, would obstinately refuse to die. With its operational expenses pared down to a few hundred pounds per annum, and with no fixed abode after the demolition of India House in 1862, it wandered, doddery and destitute as an Indian *sannyasi*, from one temporary address to another. Not till 1873 was it finally wound up and not till 1884, exactly a century after Pitt's India Act, was the last cheque to be drawn on the East India Stock Dividend Account honoured by the Bank of England.

It is, then, difficult to fix a precise date for the demise of the Company. If by demise is meant its supersession by the state, any number of dates could be suggested ranging from the infiltration of the Directorate in the 1760s to the 1773 Regulating Act, the 1784 India Act, the 1813 Charter Act (which finally claimed for the Crown the sovereignty of all the Company's possessions), or the 1858 dissolution.

A similar calendar, beginning with Plassey or Baksar and ending with the reforms of Cornwallis and Shore, could be constructed for the transformation of the Company from commercial enterprise into administrative service. But here an added complication arises in that while the state was successfully challenging the Company's political independence and while reforms were transforming it into a more effective branch of government, its commercial privileges were being upheld. When they too were eventually challenged it was on quite different grounds and accorded with yet another calendar. It was not until 1813 that the Company's trade with India was thrown open to competitors and not until 1833 that the same happened with the China trade.

This suggests, though, a possible line of retreat. The Company's exclusive trading rights had always been its most prized possession. The essence of Queen Elizabeth's founding charter, its privileged monopoly of eastern trade, had been confirmed in every subsequent charter and without it the Company ceased to be a recognizable society of merchants. On the other hand, so long as it possessed all or part of that monopoly, so long as Company ships loaded pepper at Benkulen and tea at Canton, so long as the directors erupted over the slightest deviation in the quality of a Dhaka muslin, and so long as their servants saw in every desert island another off-shore entrepôt, talk of the Company's demise was premature. Nor in these days of growing political responsibilities was trade a purely marginal activity. 'For financial reasons', writes Louis Dermigny, 'control of India necessitated control of the tea trade.' Arguably and ironically it would be the Company's sensational commercial success in China as a result of the 1784 Commutation Act that made possible the creation of British India.

First, though, something remains to be said of the extent to which this Indian dominion was the product of Company, as opposed to

Government, policy. After Pitt's India Act the direction of Indian affairs would rest with the Government's new Board of Control which, under the forceful Dundas, would soon infringe the few discretionary powers supposedly left to Leadenhall Street. But before this, during the twilight years of debate and defiance which intervened between the Acts of North and Pitt, the Company in India had weathered its stormiest decade to emerge with a profile almost unrecognizable from that of 1770. Then Clive had just left Bengal after his final brief administration. He had been succeeded, after a couple of years and a couple of governors, by Warren Hastings who as Governor of Bengal and then, under the Regulating Act, as Governor-General, controlled the Company's destinies in India for thirteen years. Subsequent governors-general would owe their appointments more to Whitehall than India House and would almost invariably be chosen from outside the Company. Hastings was therefore the only governor-general of any stature to emerge from the Company's ranks. The first governor-general, he was also the last of the Company's proconsuls; and, arguably, he was the greatest.

No other governor-general or viceroy would last anything like as long as Hastings and no other would approach his profound understanding of India or his affection for its peoples. 'The Great Moghul', as Hastings was called in Calcutta's first newspaper, stood alone, a sad and self-righteous Caesar, embattled but unbowed, solicitous but ruthless, fastidious but careless, lofty yet devious – a man, in short, crying out to be misunderstood. Contemporaries duly obliged; so has posterity. For acting in what he believed to be the best interests of his employers he was impeached by Parliament. Though he was honourably acquitted, the next generation arraigned him for failings that were moderate by contemporary standards and for sympathies which now seem wonderfully enlightened. When eventually the Raj did claim him for its own it was on the basis of those policies which were not of his choosing. And even today his reputation rests on the two seemingly irreconcilable assertions that he was both the architect of British India and the one ruler of British India to whom the creation of such an entity was anathema.

None of this is altogether surprising if some allowance is made for the simple fact that Hastings was no more prescient than other mortals. If he had a model for Bengal it was inspired not by dreams of British empire but by what he took to be the traditions of Moghul empire. Outlining his proposed reforms to the Chairman of the Company he stressed that they included 'not one which the original constitution of the Mogul Empire hath not before established . . . and rendered familiar to the people'. He would 'found the authority of the British government in Bengal on its [Bengal's] ancient laws'. India was, had been, 'a great nation'; its people were 'not in a savage state' and they had little to gain from the imposition of 'a superior wisdom from outside'. India should be administered by Indians and in accordance with Indian custom although, in Bengal at least, a British supremacy consisting of the Governor and Council in Calcutta should replace that of the Moghul Nawab and his court in Murshidabad.

In thus disclaiming any idea of direct British rule, Hastings stood shoulder to shoulder with Vansittart, Clive, and just about every other servant of the Company. But unlike Clive and Vansittart, Hastings had little influence or support outside the Company. He was a complete Company man with all that that implies in the way of personal ambition, resourcefulness, impatience of London's control, and an adventurer's eye for opportunity. His impeachment he would rightly see as 'less my trial than that of the East India Company and [thinking presumably of his accusers] of the British nation'. But by then, old and embittered, he too was a political irrelevance, just like the Company.

This identity between the servant and his honourable masters had been marked throughout his career. Entering the Company as a £5 per annum writer in 1750, he had known a Bengal which was still under the able Nawab Aliverdi Khan and a Calcutta which was just one of the province's several beleaguered European trading posts. When, six years later, Siraj-ud-Daula stormed Calcutta, Hastings had typically been checking piece goods on the 'factory' floor of one of the Company's outlying *aurungs* (depots). He thus escaped the débacle of the evacuation and the Black Hole and, though briefly arrested, managed to operate as an informant at the Nawab's capital. Later, after Clive and Watson had wreaked their revenge, he continued his unspectacular rise through the Company's civilian ranks. As one of Henry Vansittart's councillors he became closely identified with the ill-fated policy of installing Mir Kasim as a more effective alternative to Clive's Mir Jafar and of curtailing the damage caused by the abuse of *dastak*. From such schemes he also profited and when he resigned, for the first time, in 1765 he had amassed £30,000. By the standards of the day this was an unremarkable fortune which justified neither his critics' talk of rapacity nor his supporters' claims of incorruptibility.

Reinstatement came in 1769 as a reward for his impressive defence of the Company delivered before the first of Parliament's Select Committees of Enquiry. With the support of that Company diehard, Lawrence Sulivan, henceforth his indefatigable ally in Leadenhall Street, Hastings was sent to Madras as Second-in-Council. There he invested in the Madras Association which had succeeded to Jourdain, Sulivan and de Souza's virtual monopoly of the trade with Aceh. Officially he was also Export Warehousekeeper and in this role he busied himself with reforming the system of ordering and collecting the annual investment in piece goods. Once again he was knee deep in cottons when disaster struck. This time it was the loss of the *Aurora* and of the three-man commission which sailed in her. Experience, ability and authority all told in the appointment of Hastings to the governorship of Bengal where he was to 'stand forth as diwan', to effect 'the complete reformation' that had been expected from the ill-fated Commissioners, and to end Bengal's crippling drain on the Company's finances. Interpreting these vague instructions as a *carte blanche* Hastings arrived in Bengal in 1772 determined to return the government to its 'first principles'.

These 'first principles', though supposedly derived from Moghul precedent, have a familiar ring. The Nawab's residual administration, overlaid by a proliferation of Company agents and revenue officials, meant that Bengal was being hopelessly over-governed and over-mulcted. Whether to encourage what would now be called a free market economy or whether to reduce the amount of revenue lost in the process of collection, a retraction of both the Nawab's and the Company's agents plus a degree of centralization was vital. Accordingly the Nawab's deputies in Bengal and Bihar were dismissed and sent for trial; his system of civil and criminal courts was taken over and reformed with special emphasis being placed on the study and codification of Hindu and Muslim law; and his Treasury, now administered by a board of Company servants, was removed from Murshidabad to closer supervision in Calcutta. In a re-enactment of the arrangement reached with Mir Kasim, all inland customs posts were also withdrawn and all *dastak* abolished in favour of a small flat rate duty. This last supposedly ended the privileged position of Company servants and free merchants *vis-à-vis* other European and Indian merchants. Certain items, though, notably salt and opium, were made a Company monopoly which, while affording the Company a new source of revenue, also gave to those to whom such monopolies were farmed ample opportunities of enrichment.

Similar opportunities continued to be exploited in the revenue collection which was also thrown open to competitive tendering. Unlike Clive, Hastings did not rant about 'Augean stables' and in fact he consistently resisted pressures from home to organize an inquisition into past malpractices. Servants of a merchant company were, he felt, 'not exempted from the frailties and wants of humanity' and were entitled to something more in the way of remuneration than their still measly salaries. Where possible salaries were increased by setting aside a small percentage of the Company's net receipts to be divided among the relevant functionaries. Where this was not possible, particularly amongst the lower ranks of Company servants, there was a tacit understanding that as of old a man might look to his own interests.

Nevertheless Hastings's flurry of legal reforms and commercial prohibitions did serve to curtail and contain the worst forms of extortion. If the flood of complaints scarcely abated this was in part due to the fact that there now existed channels for their expression and prospects of their redress. Given the right regulatory framework, the most rapacious of servants could be held in check and the most oppressed of peasants could take heart. Ideally Hastings would have liked to recall to Calcutta all those Englishmen who, under the guise of revenue supervisors and free merchants, were currently operating their own lucrative little cartels in the provinces. He would replace them with Indian supervisors who alone stood some chance of understanding the conflicting rights of the innumerable functionaries engaged in assessing, recording, collecting and enforcing the revenue. The directors also favoured such a recall, yet such were their individual commitments in support of their various protégés in Bengal that all Hastings was able to achieve was a clipping of the supervisors' wings by the establishment of provincial revenue boards. That and a change of name. Henceforth the district supervisor became the district collector, or rather the District Collector.

Part administrator, part magistrate, part tax man, and part development officer, the District Collector was destined to join those many-armed gods in the Hindu pantheon and to become a feature of the Indian landscape. For those with a starry-eyed regard for the Indian Civil Service, British India begins with the D.C., and Hastings was therefore 'wrong' to interfere with such an office.

> He was fighting against the genius of the country [writes Philip Woodruff]. The way India wants to be governed, the way she feels

to be naturally right, is not by centralized rules but by personal decisions, on the platform beneath the pipal tree in the village, on the threshing floor of polished mud, on the balks between the rice fields.

Hastings might have gone along with this. His centralizing measures were designed to rein in government, not to extend it, and his objection was not to the collector as such but to his necessarily being of British birth. But even supposing Hastings lacked the I.C.S. man's insight into India's preferred method of government (he would surely have despised the paternalism that it implied) it must be doubtful whether he would have accorded a high priority to rural consensus when, in the aftermath of the 1770 famine, the threshing floor was choked with weeds and the rice fields rapidly reverting to jungle. The plight of the country moved Hastings and his collectors alike. From this period dates the first firm evidence of British administrators – or rather, Company servants – evincing a genuine concern for the lot of the peasant. It was somewhat ironical that at Hastings's impeachment, Burke would seize this high moral ground to discomfit the accused and disparage his whole administration.

Hastings appeared to go even further with the novel suggestion that any government of India should enjoy the approbation of the people, a notion which furnished the later Raj with another good reason for co-opting him as a founding father. But at the time his priority was simply to restore Bengal to prosperity, thereby winning that approbation and at the same time boosting the Company's much reduced revenue receipts. What was good for Bengal must also be good for the Company, he argued. But events proved him wrong and while the Company's receipts did improve, the incomes of the Bengali peasantry did not. Like everyone else, Hastings had over-estimated the province's wealth and so over-assessed the possible revenue. That Bengal had the potential for immense wealth he made no doubt; and he opined that whoever commanded it might one day acquire the dominion of all India – 'an event which I may not mention without adding', he added, 'that it is what I never wish to see'.

Yet – and in this lies his real claim as architect of British India – Hastings did, reluctantly though with undeniable satisfaction, preside over events that did more to further such a dominion than even Clive's adventures.

ii

Responding to the voluminous documentation generated by Parliament's attempts to recall and impeach him, historians of British India have usually dwelt at length on Hastings's supposed crimes. Happily these transgressions need scarcely detain a student of the Company. A mischievous little campaign against the Afghan Rohillas, a blatant piece of extortion in respect of Benares, some broken pledges and ferocious vendettas, a hint of bribery, a judicial murder – even if proved these transgressions were neither exceptionally heinous nor, spread over thirteen years, cumulatively damning. More and worse had been perpetrated in Bengal during each of the preceding decades.

Similarly the remorseless opposition with which Hastings had to contend – from his Council, from the Courts, from the other Presidencies and from London – was nothing new. His frustration, heightened by a naturally imperious temperament and voiced with martyred eloquence, has won him a deal of sympathy. And in so far as his opponents, most notably Philip Francis and the other Councillors wished on him by the Regulating Act, enjoyed Parliamentary sanction, his authority was distinctly more vulnerable than had been that of, say, Clive. On the other hand the knowledge that Sulivan and an influential section of opinion in India House were sympathetic to his plight encouraged a volubility of complaint and defiance not heard since William Hedges had chafed at the opposition of the cantankerous Charnock. That Presidents/Governors were still invariably opposed and often outvoted by their Councils is well illustrated by contemporary events at Madras. There, like Hastings, one governor fought a duel while another was deposed by his Council. The latter was Pigot, governor of Madras during the Seven Years War, and now back with an unpopular mandate that led not only to his deposition but to his arrest and death. Hastings, who had managed to reverse his own Council's attempt at superseding him, showed no sympathy for the unfortunate Pigot and in fact supported his opponents.

Much, of course, depends on one's perspective. From the standpoint of nineteenth-century British India the idea of a governor-general being defied by anyone was quite monstrous. So was that of a governor-general stooping to personal vengeance against an Indian courtier (Nand Kumar), or emptying a duelling pistol into one of his Councillors (Philip Francis), or buying off the husband of his prospective bride (Marian Imhoff who became Mrs Hastings in 1777). But from the Company's eighteenth-century standpoint such conduct was not at all unusual.

Conversely the tramp of British troops across the length and breadth of the Indian subcontinent and the capture of supposedly impregnable strongholds a thousand miles from Bengal, though unremarkable to anyone acquainted with Wellesley's campaigns in the early 1800s, made a profound impression in the 1780s when only Hastings dared to anticipate, and dread, a British India that stretched from Calcutta to Bombay and Madras.

It goes without saying that Hastings, a good Company civilian, disowned the idea of military conquest. When in 1772 the Emperor Shah Alam II accepted overtures from the resurgent Marathas to help him recover his patrimony, and when he then proposed to transfer to them the two districts (Allahabad and Kora) granted him by Clive and garrisoned for him ever since by the Company, Hastings saw merely a good opportunity to disengage from 'a remote connection' and reduce Bengal's deficit. Accordingly he stopped the Company's payments of 2.6 million rupees per year (made to the Emperor by way of tribute for the *diwani*), and restored the two districts to the Nawab of Oudh for 5 million rupees. 'Shocking, horrible and outrageous' would be Burke's verdict on this 'breach of faith' with the Moghul. Hastings contended that the Emperor had broken faith first by entering into an alliance with the Marathas.

A year later, though, he cheerfully invited an even remoter connection by undertaking to support the Nawab of Oudh in a dubious campaign against the latter's Rohilla neighbours on the upper Ganges. This eventually entailed deploying British troops, albeit as mercenaries, within 100 miles of Delhi itself. Hastings evidently regretted his commitment and did his best to wriggle out of it. But when the Nawab was insistent, he complied.

This time a breach of faith had clearly been avoided; instead Burke would accuse him of naked aggression and the genocide of an innocent and Arcadian people (i.e. the warlike Rohillas). It was another gross overstatement, and Hastings could fairly claim that in both cases he was loyally standing by the Nawab of Oudh and loyally trying to rescue Bengal's finances. He set great store by securing Oudh as part of a 'ring fence' designed to keep out the Marathas and any other restless warlords capable of threatening Bengal's tranquillity. In that the Nawab of Oudh, like his opposite number in the Carnatic, was always billed for the loan of British troops, Hastings in effect transferred to the Nawab the crippling military expenses of the Bengal establishment. Neatly summarized by Dr

K. M. Panikkar, the idea of the ring fence was simply 'the defence of your neighbour's territories, of course at his expense, in order to protect your own territories'. Thus, in the early years of his administration, and before his responsibilities were extended by the Regulating Act to include Madras and Bombay, Hastings may be seen as pursuing a policy of retrenchment in external affairs that matched that of retraction in internal affairs.

It is nevertheless evident that, in the words of Messrs Thompson and Garret, he 'sat loose to principles as we use the word today'; 'his place is not with the proconsuls of our orderly period, but with such men as Akbar'. Constraints he knew aplenty but, in a man answerable only to his eighteenth-century conscience, they did not include an obsession with consistency nor great delicacy in the respect of human consequences. Decision, improvisation, and the chess-player's cool orchestration of a crowded board are the qualities on which rest his reputation as 'the greatest of all British statesmen'. 'Amid such a coil and swirl of possibilities' as awaited and all but engulfed him, they would be sorely tested. Seldom can a ruler so averse to war and so avowedly indifferent to conquest have been engaged on so many different fronts.

iii

South, across the wide and rolling spaces of central and peninsular India, the demise of Moghul power had opened up rich and extensive possibilities for a new generation of power brokers. Excluding de Bussy and his now aborted exploits in Hyderabad, these aspirants had not so far included a European power. The British presence, though formidable enough in upper India, elsewhere remained marginal, extending no further than the coastal plain of the Carnatic, the islets that constituted Bombay, and those invariably beleaguered trading posts on the Malabar shoreline. No Company troops had yet tramped up either the Eastern Ghats on to the uplands of Mysore nor the craggier Western Ghats into Maharashtra. Here, and across the vast intervening plateaux, the power struggle raged between that ex-Moghul feudatory, the Nizam of Hyderabad, his upstart neighbour, Hyder Ali of Mysore, and the ubiquitous, hydra-headed Maratha confederacy.

From Gujarat to Orissa, the patchwork of Maratha territories now spanned the subcontinent and straggled north almost to Delhi. But rapid expansion had entailed many reverses including rout at the hands of Afghan invaders in 1761 and a growing tendency towards political fragmentation. The great Maratha commanders were carving out their own regional power bases – the Gaikwars of Baroda in the west, the Scindias of Gwalior in the north, the Bhonslas of Berar in the east, and the Holkars of Indore in the middle. Meanwhile a series of succession crises weakened the authority which still supposedly attached to their nominal overlords, the Peshwas of Poona in the south. Although formidable when united, the Marathas were increasingly engaged in scheming and skirmishing among themselves.

Such dissent had not gone unnoticed in Bombay and Surat, the only British enclaves in Maratha territory. Surat, wrested from its long nominal Moghul Governors by the British in 1759, remained a place of commercial importance but of no political pretensions. It was otherwise with Bombay. Long the poor relations among the Company's servants in India, the inmates of Bombay Castle had watched their colleagues in Forts William and St George accumulating territory and fortunes at the expense of their Indian neighbours. They had also noted how effective was European firepower against India's unwieldly armies, how marketable this advantage could be, and how lucrative the princely liaisons that might result. Having finally disposed of the maritime threat from the Angreys in the 1750s, Bombay began to cast covetous glances towards its continental hinterland.

The first move was obvious. In 1739 the Marathas had evicted the Portuguese from their old base at Bassein and from the adjacent island of Salsette. Although nowadays unrecognizable as part of an archipelago (its current attractions include Juhu Beach, the Bombay film studios, and the international airport), Salsette was then the last stepping-stone between the Company's island properties and the mainland. For the security of Bombay's harbour and the free passage of its inland trade, some control over Salsette was highly desirable. Arguably these few square miles of marsh and mangrove should have been handed over to Charles II (and thence to the Company) as part of Catherine of Braganza's Indian dowry; the directors in Leadenhall Street seemed to think so and in 1772, when Warren Hastings took up the reins of government in Bengal, they again urged Bombay to look to its landward security. Accordingly the cession of Bassein and Salsette figured prominently in the then current negotiations between the Bombay Council and a disaffected scion of the Poona Peshwas. These negotiations stalled; but they were sufficient to prompt the Portuguese in Goa to consider a pre-emptive strike to reclaim their old patrimony, news of which in turn furnished the British in Bombay with just the pretext they needed. Thana, the main fort on Salsette, was accordingly stormed and taken in late 1774.

Such a blatant move by one of the now subordinate Presidencies was clearly contrary to the intentions of the 1773 Regulating Act in that it posed a direct challenge to the superintending powers entrusted to the new Governor-General and his Council. The action was therefore roundly condemned by Calcutta. But it was soon equally clear that over this, as over every other issue, Hastings and his new Council were bitterly divided. While the faction led by Philip Francis condemned the capture of Salsette, Hastings secretly applauded it; and later London would positively endorse it.

Confused but by no means discouraged, the Bombay authorities cheerfully proceeded to explore these differences by embarking on an infinitely more ambitious policy of aggrandizement. Less than two months after the capture of Thana an army of 2500 men was sailing for Surat to join Raghunath Rao (Raghoba), the leading claimant to the Peshwa-ship, and march with him on Poona. Bombay argued that Raghoba was the legitimate heir and that only by supporting him could they be sure of having the conquest of Salsette ratified. If the campaign was successful, Bassein and several of Bombay's off-shore islands were also to be awarded to the Company plus the revenues of two undefined districts on the mainland. It was an offer, in short, that was too good to refuse; it was also an opportunity too good to jeopardize by a reference to Calcutta.

When word of this undertaking leaked out, Calcutta reacted predictably. 'We totally condemn the measure', wrote Hastings and his Council in a rare display of unanimity. The treaty of Surat with Raghoba was invalid, the war itself 'impolitic, dangerous, unauthorized and unjust'. And both were 'expressly contrary to the late Act of Parliament'.

> You have imposed on yourselves the charge of conquering the whole Maratha empire for a man who appears incapable of affording you an effectual assistance in it; the plan which you have formed, instead of aiming at a decisive conquest, portends an infinite scene of troubles without an adequate force, without money or certain resources to extricate yourselves from him; nor have you the plea either of injury sustained from the party which you have made your enemy, or of any prior obligation to defend the man whose cause you have espoused.

There was truth in all this. Raghoba was bankrupt, his other allies – including the mighty Scindia – failed to materialize, and his own forces waited only an occasion to desert. By engaging in a Maratha power struggle, Bombay had invited retaliation against the British and their allies elsewhere in India and had subverted Hastings's policy of containment and retrenchment. Nevertheless, it is hard to avoid the suspicion that Calcutta's criticisms might have been blunted had news of the war been preceded by the reasoned arguments retrospectively marshalled by Bombay, or had it been overtaken by the rather impressive reports that were soon coming from the battle front. For contrary to Calcutta's expectations, the Bombay forces under Colonel Keating were making steady progress, albeit in an unlikely quarter.

Raghoba's troops were tied down near Ahmadabad in Gujarat and it was between there and Baroda, a very long way indeed from Poona, that Keating scored two initial successes and then narrowly defeated the entire Poona army at the battle of Arras (Adas). Excluding those skirmishes with Sivaji's troops during the defence of Surat a century earlier, this was the first time British troops had engaged the Marathas. Both sides suffered heavy casualties, the British loss, including eleven out of the fifteen British officers, being reckoned 'greater than was ever known in India' – a record destined to be quickly broken. But the Marathas, the most awesome military force in the whole subcontinent, had been forced to retreat and Keating was confident that, if funds could be found to hold Raghoba's army together during the monsoon, they would reach Poona during the ensuing campaign.

It was not to be. As Keating swept through Broach and on to his monsoon quarters at Dabhoi, Calcutta damned the whole enterprise and ordered a cessation of hostilities, unconditional withdrawal, and direct negotiations with Poona. Bombay protested at great length – but in vain. 'We sincerely lament', they told Keating, 'that these gentlemen [a disparaging reference to the Governor-General and Council] have so unluckily taken upon themselves to interfere at this juncture.' Nevertheless, they had no choice but to order his withdrawal to Surat. Later in the year an emissary from Calcutta arrived in Poona to negotiate.

At this point proceedings, already a trifle confusing, took a sharp turn towards the labyrinthine. Calcutta was evidently once again divided with Hastings, though furious at Bombay's defiance, equally furious at Philip Francis's unwillingness to sacrifice the advantage gained by Keating's victories. This dissent, however, was as nothing compared to that which reigned at Poona where, with Raghoba's rival for the Peshwa-ship as yet a babe-in-arms, the regency junta combined mutual suspicion with consummate prevarication. Events faithfully mirrored the confusion. In February 1776, with the idea of breaking the deadlock at Poona, Calcutta countermanded its previous countermanding order and bade Bombay resume its 'invalid' treaty with Raghoba and march again. But these orders reached Bombay just as news came from Poona of the conclusion of the new treaty (of Purandhar) by which the Company undertook to disown Raghoba. Whereupon Bombay showed its contempt of Calcutta's emissary by offering Raghoba asylum; Hastings did not like the new treaty either and recalled his unfortunate emissary; and London set a third cat among the pigeons with a dispatch wholeheartedly approving the original treaty (of Surat) by which Bombay had first pledged its support to Raghoba.

Next year, 1777, word that a French representative had been welcomed in Poona added a further complication. M. de St Lubin, who claimed to be an accredited envoy seeking an alliance between the Marathas and the French crown, had apparently imported sufficient firearms and uniforms (though he had forgotten the buttons) to equip a force of 15,000. There was talk of a secret agreement having already been made, of further troops being sent from France, and of the Marathas having made over one of their ports as a French base. No one was quite sure that St Lubin was not a brilliant impostor; equally no one could be sure that, even if he was, a France on the brink of war with Britain would not readily endorse any alliance he might arrange. St Lubin had evidently studied de Bussy's *Mémoires*. If, like de Bussy at Hyderabad or Dupleix at Arcot, he could insinuate into Poona a body of French troops buttoned or unbuttoned, then 'we can expect nothing', predicted the Bombay Council, 'but a repetition of the scene of wars and intrigues formerly acted on the coast of Coromandel, which will certainly be fatal to the influence of the English on this coast, and may end in our total subversion'.

Hastings shared this anxiety; and the timely disaffection of a member of the Poona regency council duly supplied the justification for interference. Raghoba's cause was resurrected, Bombay was vindicated, and Poona was once again to be invaded. Thanks to the death of one of Philip Francis's supporters, Hastings was now able to outvote the dissident faction in his Council. Francis condemned the new policy with his usual string of adjectives – it was 'illegal, unjust, impolitic'. Hastings ignored him. Perhaps it was indeed somewhat contradictory to be invoking the Purandhar Treaty, by which the British had disowned Raghoba, as a basis for now supporting him; but, with Hastings as with most of his contemporaries, exigency outweighed principle. The Purandhar Treaty had never been implemented (by either party) and the French threat must be snuffed out. Accordingly Bombay was authorized to prepare to storm the Western Ghats while a supporting contingent of the Bengal army was ordered to march from Oudh.

The idea of marching six battalions complete with artillery and the inevitable horde of camp-followers clean across the subcontinent was nothing if not bold. No such feat had ever before been contemplated by the British and even private travellers seldom strayed into the jungles of central India. The march provided tangible proof that the Company's hitherto isolated settlements now acknowledged a common purpose and formed a single political unit. It presumed a right of passage through what had previously been regarded as inviolable sovereignties. And it foreshadowed an attitude of mind that would regard the whole of India as one political entity.

It was also exceedingly timely. For without waiting for these reinforcements, the Bombay army had crossed to the mainland, begun crawling up the Ghats, and fallen an easy prey to a combined Maratha force headed by the redoubtable Scindia. Although incompetently commanded and pathetically inadequate for the task in hand, the real problem for the Bombay force had been logistical. Baggage trains that could lumber across the plains at ten miles a day could scarcely manage two miles a day on the steep gradients and amongst the deep defiles of the Ghats. The expedition had practically ground to a standstill before it sighted the Maratha troops. It then abandoned its guns and turned tail before a shot had been fired only to find that in retreat it was just as slow and even more vulnerable. Harassed and then surrounded by the Maratha horse, it had finally chosen to capitulate rather than fight.

The resulting Wargaum (Wadgaon) Convention, signed on the spot in January 1779, was admitted even by its crestfallen British signatories to be 'humiliating in the highest degree'. Raghoba was to be surrendered, the advancing Bengal force was to be sent back, even Salsette was to be given up. There was implicit mention of British guilt, and two British hostages were handed over by way of guarantee for its implementation. Not since Bombay's other capitulation nearly a century earlier to Aurangzeb had an Indian power forced such humiliating terms on the

Company. Hastings was profoundly mortified. This time he repudiated the agreement openly and, though it meant all-out war against the whole Maratha confederacy plus an abrupt end to his financial retrenching, he determined 'to efface the infamy which our national character has sustained'.

Happily the Bengal contingent under Colonel Thomas Goddard, after protracted negotiations with the Bhonslas in what is now Madhya Pradesh, had crossed the watershed and was entering Maharashtra. On receiving news of the Wargaum fiasco Goddard, instead of turning back, forced the pace still harder and at last saluted the Indian Ocean at Surat having covered the final 300 miles in nineteen days. The march 'through regions unknown in England and untraced on our maps' was a personal triumph both for Hastings, who had authorized it against fierce opposition from his Council, and for Goddard who was now promoted to general and appointed Commander-in-Chief.

Thus removed from the ambit of Bombay's faint-hearted counsels, Goddard attempted to dictate new terms to Poona. The negotiations dragged on throughout 1779 to no purpose. Both sides used the lull for a diplomatic offensive, with the Marathas pursuing a triple alliance with the Nizam and Hyder Ali – of which more later – while the British explored Maratha dissensions. By January 1780 the Gaikwar of Baroda had come over and Goddard moved north into Gujarat. Retracing Keating's footsteps he took Dabhoi, rolled back the Poona forces and successfully stormed Ahmadabad.

Meanwhile Hastings had dispatched a second Bengal detachment under Captain William Popham to make common cause with one of Scindia's disaffected neighbours in the country south of Agra. This modest diversionary tactic had the most unexpected results. With no guns and only 2000 men, nearly all sepoys, Popham invaded Scindia's territory, took the fort of Lahar, and then moved presumptuously against Gwalior, the capital. A new front had been opened. Hastings urgently ordered more troops to reinforce Popham. It was over this order that Philip Francis broke his recent compact with the Governor-General not to interfere with the conduct of the war. Hastings accused him of bad faith; Francis issued his challenge. Thus it was that just before dawn on 17 August, in the midst of one of the Company's most critical wars – and to the intense surprise of a small crowd of curious Indian villagers – the Governor-General and his leading councillor stood back to back, took fourteen paces, and emptied their pistols in one another's direction.

Francis fell. Although only wounded he accepted defeat and soon after sailed from Calcutta to seek revenge in England.

A week later the news from Popham at Gwalior should have made Hastings's cup of joy overflow. Gwalior, a classic table-top fortress elevated several hundred feet above the surrounding plain, and with its scarps of sheer rock crowned by battlements, was probably the strongest natural fortress in all India. It appeared impregnable; yet such was its strategic importance astride the main roads leading south from Delhi and Agra that no government claiming dominion over both the north and the peninsula had ever been able to ignore it. Hastings acknowledged that it was 'the key to Hindustan'; but having no territorial ambition, he seems never to have entertained designs on it. News, therefore, that Popham and his men, without artillery but evidently with plenty of rope, had somehow scaled its cliffs, surprised its garrison, and were now in proud possession of the place caused a sensation. Comparisons were drawn with Wolfe at Quebec; Hastings likened its psychological impact to Plassey. Now at last the Marathas would surely listen to peace overtures.

They did no such thing; and any euphoria that Hastings allowed himself was extremely short-lived. For, within a month, Popham's triumph, indeed the whole Maratha war, was overshadowed by a disaster of the first magnitude. Madras, hitherto unaffected by the war and in fact able to supply Bombay with troops, had contrived its own Wargaum – only rather worse. Its entire army had been virtually annihilated.

iv

Since the end of the Seven Years War Madras had ceased to loom large in the Company's thinking. Compared to Bengal, its political and commercial consequence had declined while its strategic importance was only really relevant at a time of war with France. Then proximity to Pondicherry and command of the sea lanes in the Bay of Bengal could be crucial to Calcutta's security. Otherwise it was something of a liability, dependent on Bengal for provisions but somewhat careless of Bengal's ever delicate relations with its neighbours. Although happy to remind Calcutta that it was the Madras army and the Madras government in the person of Robert Clive who had made Bengal what it was, 'the gentlemen of the Coast', instead of king-making and government, had remained true to their vocation – namely, making money.

Private trade with Aceh, Manila and Canton played its part but a new and surer source of wealth had been discovered nearer home in the ever obliging person of Mohammed Ali. Now known as the Nawab Walajah, Mohammed Ali continued to rule the Carnatic without, like Mir Jafar and Mir Kasim, incurring the Company's displeasure. This he managed by cheerfully accepting his role as a British puppet, gratefully incurring the considerable cost of maintaining Company troops, and happily dividing his entourage, which included eight European doctors, between no fewer than twenty sumptuous Madras residences. Of course, it was expensive and his indebtedness to the Company, heavy enough after the French wars, grew ever heavier. Here was a Nawab from whom six-figure 'presents' were not to be expected.

On the other hand, here was a Nawab whose rule was underwritten by the Company and whose financial embarrassment had a certain attraction to the investor. Loans to the Nawab were gilt-edged; it was like buying government stock except that the rates of interest (twenty to twenty-five per cent) were infinitely higher. So 'the gentlemen of The Coast' invested secretly but heavily, and the Nawab borrowed discreetly but excessively. Each benefited. The revenues of the Carnatic found their way into English pockets without all the hassle and recrimination that went with Bengal-style peculation; and the Nawab, with his political masters also his financial dependants, enjoyed an improbable degree of security and even indulgence.

To what extent the Nawab actually influenced policy must remain a matter of conjecture. Intrigue and rumour successfully concealed the full extent of both his financial and political connections. But his creditors certainly included more than one president of Madras plus a succession of councillors, while his political agents were active not only in the courts of India but also in that of St James. In 1770, much to the fury of the directors whose then plight made them especially sensitive to any government moves behind their backs, the Nawab received and greatly impressed Sir John Lindsay who, as well as commanding a visiting squadron of the Royal Navy, was accredited as a royal plenipotentiary to investigate the Nawab's grievances against the Company.

Soon after, the Nawab secured Madras's support for an unprovoked invasion and annexation of neighbouring Tanjore; its revenues were deemed a necessary security for yet more loans. In 1775 Pigot was reappointed to Madras specifically to rectify this abuse of power and oversee the restoration of Tanjore to its rightful Raja. But the Nawab and his creditors (the so-called 'Arcot Interest') were not to be deprived of their gains so easily. Pigot was arrested by a majority of his own councillors and promptly died in captivity; some said it was from hard usage, others from 'exposing himself to the sun while gardening'. The facts remain obscure in spite of subsequent convictions; but there can be no doubting the Nawab's complicity. (This tangled affair is also notable for the brief reappearance of Henry Brooke, once of Negrais and Manila, who was one of the leading conspirators, and of Alexander Dalrymple, who had returned to Madras to lend support to Pigot, his erstwhile patron in the Balambangan project. Suspended from the Council at the time of Pigot's arrest, Dalrymple returned to London with another noble cause to publicize.)

Unlike Tanjore, the Nawab's other neighbours – Hyder Ali in Mysore and the Nizam in Hyderabad – posed more of a threat than a temptation. As the Nawab had impressed on Lindsay, the ideal guarantee of his own security and that of his Madras allies-cum-creditors would have been a counterbalancing alliance with the Marathas against Mysore and Hyderabad. But the problem here was Bombay whose difficulties with the Marathas commended a rather similar counterbalancing alliance but with Hyder Ali and the Nizam. In short, the diplomatic requirements of Madras and those of Bombay were directly opposed. Thus when Hyder Ali successfully overran the coastal principalities of what is now Kerala, Bombay applauded while Madras winced.

Similarly with the Nizam. To Hastings it was self-evident that while the Company was engaged in a life-and-death struggle with the Marathas, its alliance with the Nizam must at all costs be maintained. Yet Madras seemed to be going out of its way to antagonize Hyderabad, first by detaching (and then leasing to Mohammed Ali as a further security for loans) a chunk of the Northern Circars and then by interfering with the financial terms of the existing alliance. A possible explanation may be that, from past experience, Madras was far more concerned about the recently declared war (of American Independence) with France than it was about that with the Marathas. As soon as news of France's entry into the war reached India, the Madras army had marched once again against Pondicherry and quickly reduced it (1778). The justification for interfering in Hyderabad was the presence there of a corps of French mercenaries. And similarly it was to eliminate the French outpost of Mahé that in 1779 an expedition from Madras infuriated Hyder Ali by barging into Kerala, which he now claimed as being under his protection.

Suddenly the danger of that unthinkable triple alliance between the

Marathas, Hyder Ali, and the Nizam looked a distinct possibility. Should the French also choose this moment to unleash one of their troop-carrying armadas into Indian waters, the Company must be done for. To Hastings, as to posterity, it beggared understanding that the subsidiary presidencies could have behaved so blindly, so selfishly, and so incompetently in this hour of crisis. What was the use of the Governor-General's supervisory powers if they could be so blatantly flaunted?

Luckily, though, the French would arrive on the scene a year too late; and luckily Hastings, by repudiating Madras's negotiations with the Nizam, was able to limit the damage done in Hyderabad. That left Mysore as the only power disposed to threaten Madras and so deflect Hastings from the war with the Marathas. It was well known that Hyder Ali held Mohammed Ali in profound contempt and regarded the Madras Council as perfidy incarnate. It was also well known that he was concerting his plans with the French and that his own army included both artillery and officers of French origin, including de Lally's son. In the first Mysore War of 1767–9 he had easily out-marched the British forces and had successfully surprised Madras itself. (This was the action which precipitated the collapse of the Company's stock in London and the dispatch of the three Commissioners in the ill-fated *Aurora*.) Undoubtedly Hyder Ali was the ablest commander of his day; and in his son, Tipu, he had a no less daring and charismatic lieutenant.

Nevertheless the Madras Councillors refused to take the Mysore threat seriously. Mohammed Ali warned them of Hyder's intentions and so did their own agents. Yet as late as April 1780 the outgoing President of Fort St George was able to assure his countrymen that 'there is the greatest prospect that this part of India will remain quiet'. Pondicherry had been taken, a Royal squadron under Sir Edward Hughes had arrived on The Coast, and a King's regiment, the 73rd Highlanders, had just been disembarked at Madras. It would be madness for Hyder Ali to invade. Panic-mongers might urge a concentration of the Company's forces, the requisitioning of stores and transport, the strengthening of outlying garrisons; but as Captain Munro of the Highlanders put it, 'advice at this time was deemed an insult to judgement'.

Three months later, with the new President also pooh-poohing the idea of war, Hyder struck. In the space of a month he overran the entire Carnatic save for a few obstinate forts. The Nawab's capital of Arcot was heavily invested and Hyder's dreaded cavalry galloped past the paralysed British forces and entered the suburbs of Madras, 'surrounding many of the English gentlemen in their country houses, who narrowly escaped being taken'. The air blackened with smuts as the enemy scorched the earth in a wide arc round the city.

With the idea of relieving Arcot, the Madras army of some 4000 men under Sir Hector Munro eventually moved inland. At Conjeeveram (Kanchipuram) they halted to await the arrival of Colonel Baillie with a further 3000 men from the Northern Circars. By 6 September Baillie was within ten miles of the main army; but Tipu was opposing his progress, so Munro sent a detachment of 1000 to his aid. This combined force, now representing half Munro's troops, was surrounded by Hyder's entire army during the night of the 9th near a village called Polilur. Next day it was systematically destroyed in a savage encounter 'such as cannot be paralleled since the English had possessions in India'. Sixty out of eighty-six British officers plus about 2000 British and Indian troops perished; about 1000 more were taken prisoner and eventually led away to Hyder's capital of Srirangapatnam; there more died and still more would have preferred death, such were the privations they suffered.

Polilur stands apart from other battles in the Company's history. The carnage is explained by the fact that there was no possibility of retreat but what rankled even more was the shame of knowing that it could so easily have been avoided. Munro could actually hear the battle going on. But so unreliable were his spies and informants, so hopeless his maps, and so cumbersome his forces that he failed to appreciate the gravity of the situation, could not locate the battlefield, and anyway was too encumbered to reach it. To make matters worse, his precipitate retreat to Madras involved further heavy casualties and resulted in the jettisoning of all his baggage and most of his guns. It is not an exaggeration to say that Polilur meant the virtual annihilation of the Madras army.

From Mysore's point of view it was, of course, a glorious victory and in Tipu's summer palace a series of magnificent murals was painted to commemorate the event. There they were duly noted by General Baird when nineteen years later he led the final assault on Srirangapatnam that ended the Mysore Wars; he recognized them because he was one of those who had been wounded at Polilur and then incarcerated at Srirangapatnam for four years.

British historians have naturally tended to play down the significance of such a total defeat but, taken along with Wargaum, it may be seen as evidence that India's native armies were no longer easy prey. Many of the Mysore troops had been trained by British officers in the service of

Mohammed Ali or by French officers under Chanda Sahib and the Nizam; the words of command were given in English; native cavalry, instead of making fruitless charges against the British guns, were now cleverly deployed to outflank them. At Wargaum, the British forces had been under a joint command that included General John Carnac who had fought in the war against Mir Kasim. Sir Hector Munro, the dupe of Polilur, was also Sir Hector Munro, the victor of Baksar; and his successor in Madras, Sir Eyre Coote, had been the man responsible for goading Clive into action at Plassey and for hounding the French in the Carnatic during the Seven Years War. Nor were their troops in any way inferior. In Madras the proportion of King's regiments, mostly Highlanders, to Company regiments was higher than ever. The fact was that reputations easily won in previous decades were now proving hard to sustain against the new generation of opponents. Even Goddard, the hero of the hour in Bombay, only narrowly avoided his own Wargaum when, at the end of the year, he too was bundled back down the Western Ghats after another abortive march on Poona.

News of Polilur reached Hastings in Calcutta a month after Gwalior and the duel with Francis. Although Bengal's finances and its military resources were already at breaking point, he recognized that only 'the most instant, powerful, and hazardous exertions' could possibly save Madras and so prevent the French from snatching this golden opportunity to re-establish themselves in the peninsula. Requisitioning ships and stopping all investment in trade goods, he despatched by sea Coote, the most inspirational commander in India, along with 4000 troops and 1.5 million rupees. At the same time Colonel Thomas Pearse, his second in the recent duel with Francis and a close friend, was ordered to emulate Goddard's feat and march overland from Bengal to Madras with a force of 5000. Meanwhile the Maratha war would have to take second place. Goddard was ordered to explore the possibility of an armistice with Poona while Hastings doubled his efforts to ensure the neutrality of the Bhonslas on Bengal's border. Soon after, he began to put out feelers to a Scindia much impressed by the loss of Gwalior and subsequent reverses.

'Bullocks, money, and faithful spies are the sinews of war in this country', wrote Captain Innes Munro who seems to have fought in every engagement of the Second Mysore War and later published an account of it that makes happy reading compared to Orme's wordy narrative of the earlier Carnatic wars. A dearth of all three had been responsible for Polilur plus, perhaps, the lack of a cipher which had resulted in Sir

Hector Munro (no immediate relation) and Colonel Baillie corresponding, as and when they could locate one another, in Gaelic. Coote brought money, and his enormous reputation improved the chances of securing reliable intelligence. But the problem of bullocks would remain unsolved in this Mysore war and the next. It was not till Arthur Wellesley, later Duke of Wellington, assembled the largest cattle drove in history – over a quarter of a million bullocks – that the problem looked to be solved and the British at last advanced to that triumph of Baird's at Srirangapatnam.

Frequently immobilized by this lack of transport and never able to move far from the coastal shipping which was their only alternative means of supply, Coote's forces lumbered back and forth between Madras and Pondicherry for three years in a dreary repetition of previous Carnatic campaigns. In August 1781 the gallant Pearse, after a nine-month march 'little short of that made by the ten thousand under Xenophon', reached Madras. It was another dramatic pointer to the integration of the subcontinent. But in spite of this and later reinforcements, and in spite of several modest victories, the British proved incapable of pressing home their advantage against the mobile Mysoreans. Arcot fell, and most of the remaining forts were abandoned because of the difficulty of provisioning them.

Meanwhile, as in previous Carnatic wars, everything depended on the balance of power at sea. When Holland entered the war (of American Independence) as a French ally in 1781, Admiral Hughes duly battered into surrender the Dutch bases of Negapatnam and then Trinconomalee in Sri Lanka. A few months later the latter was recaptured by a large French squadron under Admiral Suffren who then in a long series of seldom decisive but always devastating engagements gradually got the better of Hughes. Coote's sea-borne supplies were consequently interrupted and his manoeuvres further curtailed. An added distraction was that Suffren had landed 2000 French troops who promptly occupied Cuddalore and sat tight to await reinforcement. In the Madras roads a fleet of supply vessels was dashed to pieces by the inevitable typhoon; to the Presidency's catalogue of problems was added that of famine.

In 1782, with Hughes obliged to retire to Bombay for refitting, Suffren briefly enjoyed complete supremacy on The Coast, raiding the Company's settlements in the Circars and capturing supply vessels as far north as the mouth of the Hughli. Madras itself looked doomed until December brought better news; Hyder Ali had died – according to

Colonel Love, 'of a carbuncle in the district now called North Arcot' or, as the Madras Council reported, 'of the violent discharge of a boil upon his back'.

Hastings was convinced that the tide was finally turning. In spite of destructive and unauthorized meddling by both Bombay and Madras, his diplomatic overtures to the Marathas were having effect. Any threat to Bengal had been removed by neutralizing subsidies to the Bhonslas while in the north Scindia had been converted from enemy number one to peacemaker and go-between in negotiations with Poona. The great confederacy was thus split and the resultant treaty of Salbai, worked out in 1782 though not ratified till later, came to be regarded by Hastings as one of his crowning achievements.

'We want nothing from the Marathas except an alliance against Hyder', he had written; and that, plus the retention of Salsette and a pledge from Poona not to admit the French, was all he got. Gwalior and Ahmadabad were surrendered; so were lesser acquisitions round Bombay like Bassein and Broach; no indemnity was involved. For four years of crippling expense and less than glorious campaigning, the compensation was minimal. In the crude terms used to evaluate advantage by Clive's generation, Salbai looked like a climbdown and, by the next generation, like a stopgap. More recently its terms have been described as 'humiliating' (P. Nightingale).

But to Hastings it appeared otherwise; (and likewise to Luard in the *Cambridge History of India*; 'its importance cannot be over-estimated . . . [as] the turning point in the history of the English in India'). Allies like the Gaikwar had been rewarded, pledges in respect of Gwalior had been honoured, Scindia's attachment to the British secured. Calcutta had substantiated its right to conduct the external affairs of the other settlements and to deal honourably and on terms of equality with India's major power-broker. In the past local commanders and governors had too often sacrificed the Company's broader interests for immediate financial or territorial gain. Such had been the cause of both the Maratha and Mysore wars, and it had to stop. Hastings rejected as impracticable the idea that the Company should forgo its political responsibilities and revert to a trading body, and as undesirable the idea that it must inevitably aspire to an all-Indian supremacy. Instead it should aim to exert, from behind its ring fence of subordinate states, a stabilizing and responsible influence as one among several of the subcontinent's powers.

The keystones of Salbai were therefore a provision whereby both signatories undertook to oblige their allies to observe the peace indefinitely and, following from that, a provision whereby the Marathas were to force Hyder Ali, their erstwhile ally, to withdraw from the Carnatic and likewise observe the peace thereafter. Here was the basis for a comprehensive and lasting settlement. It did indeed justify Hastings's boast of 'preserving India to Great Britain' and should have been the Company's noblest bequest to its successors in Whitehall. But Hastings was reckoning without his still obdurate colleagues on The Coast. If the treaty of Salbai foreshadowed a future in which the British were to play their part as an integrated and responsible polity, the treaty of Mangalore, which would end the Mysore War, resurrected the bad old days when it was each Presidency for itself and devil take the consequences.

To the glad tidings of Hyder's timely death in December 1782 had been added news of a highly successful incursion into Mysore territory by part of the Bombay army, now freed from its Maratha commitments and operating against the common enemy from the Malabar Coast. As with the Marathas at Gwalior, Mysore had thus been taken in the rear and Tipu was immediately obliged to withdraw troops from the Carnatic and hasten home to meet the new threat. This should have provided Madras with an opportunity to strike back. But so obsessed was the Madras Council with the French presence and so dismal were the relations between its civil and military authorities that no advantage was taken of the situation.

In a dazzling little campaign Tipu's battle-hardened troops made short work of the Bombay army, leaving only the heavily invested port of Mangalore in British hands. Then Suffren put in a new appearance on the other side of the peninsula. Three thousand more French troops were landed at Cuddalore; worse still, their commanding officer turned out to be none other than the great de Bussy. Hughes and his squadron doggedly returned to the fray; Suffren for once scored a convincing victory. That left the Madras forces minus the redoubtable Coote, who had died earlier in the year, besieging a numerically superior force in Cuddalore with a resurgent Tipu in their rear and the all-powerful Suffren blockading the coast. Seldom can news of a European peace, which reached Madras in June, have been so welcome. It remained only to settle accounts with Tipu.

Hastings urged that any negotiations with Tipu must be conducted from a position of strength and must fit within the context of Salbai.

Madras, invoking London's orders for an early settlement, ignored him. It dispatched its own emissaries to Mangalore – which place had just surrendered to the Mysore army – and they, under conditions bordering on duress, concluded a peace, in March 1784, which restored all conquered territory. Thus, like Salbai, Mangalore brought no territorial accessions and in this respect Hastings should have welcomed it. But it also took no account of the general settlement envisaged by Salbai and contained neither compensation for British losses nor safeguards for the return of all the British prisoners.

Tipu was clearly delighted with these terms and would have no compunction in renewing hostilities with both the Marathas and the Company. Conversely, the Company's officers, who for four years had been chasing his shadow or languishing in his prisons, saw them as an abject betrayal. So did Hastings. It was not for such a peace-at-any-price with rascally Mysore that he had squared the Marathas and impoverished Bengal. Either Mangalore must be repudiated, he argued, or failing that its terms must be altered. In fact the treaty was ratified. As of old, Hastings was again at the mercy of a hostile Council and a dangerous new rival.

Lord George Macartney, President of Madras since 1781, although lacking the wit and venom of Philip Francis, more than made up for them with an unsullied reputation and dazzling connections. Unduly conscious of these credentials but knowing nothing whatsoever of India or the Company's business, he was typical of the coming generation of proconsuls and, of course, the very antithesis of Hastings. The quarrel had begun with his meddling in the Maratha negotiations and then with the conduct of the Mysore war and, in particular, over the authority vested in Eyre Coote. Macartney had complained that Coote rode roughshod over the Madras establishment and treated him personally as no more than his 'bullock-agent'. Coote had responded by accusing him of sabotaging the war effort and had urged Hastings to suspend him.

Nor did Coote's death defuse the situation. General Stuart, his successor, proved even more contemptuous of civilians and was duly removed by Macartney for 'premeditated, wilful, repeated, and systematic disobedience'. The 'removal' was precisely that. Stuart, who had equipped himself with a cork leg to replace one shot away by Hyder Ali, had to be carried bodily from his quarters and in the same manner bundled on board a ship for London 'with 59 packages'. The incident had serious repercussions. Stuart held his commission from the King, not the Company. Macartney had clearly overstepped his authority in dismissing him, and all the other King's officers promptly declined orders in protest. Although a full-scale mutiny was narrowly avoided, Stuart continued to demand satisfaction of Macartney and eventually exacted it with a flesh wound inflicted on the duelling ground.

Macartney's drastic action may have been prompted by panic. Stuart had been one of the leading lights in the earlier conspiracy against Lord Pigot and could conceivably try it again. Macartney certainly detected the same conjunction of a disgruntled military and an incensed Nawab (Mohammed Ali) who was as usual eagerly encouraged by his sinister coterie of creditors. Indeed it was Macartney's highly provocative treatment of the Nawab which constituted his bone of bitterest contention with Hastings. For the duration of the war Hastings himself had proposed that the Nawab must sign a large part of his revenues over to the Company. This did not go down well with the Nawab's creditors and it is just possible that they won Hastings round to their way of thinking. (They commanded an influential following in both Westminster and Leadenhall Street; Hastings sorely needed any support he could get; even Pitt and Dundas would eventually find it expedient to capitulate to the 'Arcot Interest'.) Whatever the reason, Hastings soon found Macartney's treatment of such an old ally as Mohammed Ali unnecessarily harsh and tantamount to a usurpation of his rights. When Macartney refused to back off, Hastings again recommended his suspension and was again frustrated by his Council. Clearly Macartney's influential connections were no secret in Bengal; neither was the fact that Hastings's recall was being demanded by Parliament; and neither were Macartney's expectations of himself being appointed the new Governor-General.

The Mangalore treaty, which also completely ignored Mohammed Ali's rights, was the final straw. 'You act criminally towards your country', Hastings had told Macartney in a résumé of the latter's transgressions. Yet again he moved for suspension and yet again the Council refused to oblige. Worse still, even Leadenhall Street seemed to be taking Macartney's side. With Parliament, the Court of Directors, his own Council, and the subordinate Presidencies all ranged against the Governor-General, with age catching up on him and with ill-health, or arrogance, upsetting his judgement, it was time to go. A sizeable fortune, estimated at £175,000 and culled from a variety of sources both legitimate and suspect, awaited him at home – or at least it should have done had it not been for his habitual 'generosity, carelessness, and extravagance'. Mrs Hastings, his beloved Marian, was already in England; and he had promised to follow her within the year. He waited only for news of his successor – or at any rate confirmation that it would not be Macartney.

And yet there was still just a chance that he might stay. Fox's India Bill, which would have dissolved the Company and which Hastings had characterized as 'impudence and profligacy unequalled', had been defeated. Now young Pitt's star was in the ascendant and it was just possible that the great-grandson of Governor Pitt would reassert the Company's rights and at long last give to its Governor-General the full and undisputed authority necessary to conduct its Indian affairs. In the event, of course, Pitt's India Bill did no such thing. On learning its terms, Hastings threw in the towel. To John Scot, his agent in London and an ex-officer of the Company, he wrote that 'an Act more injurious to his [Scot's] fellow-servants, to my character and authority, to the Company . . . and to the national honour could not have been devised . . .' It was an 'unequivocal demonstration that my resignation of the service is expected'. He immediately obliged, sailing from Calcutta in February 1785.

There remains just his impeachment in the House of Lords – more theatre than politics, it was both a personal tragedy and a public farce which ran for nine years longer than it should have –plus the rather more intriguing question of why Hastings took so long to relinquish office. If there was ever a moment when the Company in India might have withheld its allegiance to the Directorate it must surely have been in 1784–5. Political extinction in the shape of Dundas's, Fox's, and finally Pitt's bills stared it in the face. The defiant example of the American colonies was fresh to the mind and indeed largely responsible for focusing so much parliamentary attention on India. Moreover, in Hastings India had a Governor-General who, provoked beyond reason, just might have fancied his chances. Cornwallis, who would succeed him two years later, conceded that he was 'beloved by the people' and even Macaulay, his fiercest critic, would credit him with 'a popularity such as . . . no other governor has been able to attain'. His ability was also unquestioned. The loyalty of the Nawabs of Oudh and the Carnatic was founded on his personal friendship. The Nizam and Scindia were firmly attached to the British interest. Only Tipu remained to give trouble and Tipu could have been tamed with a renegotiated Mangalore.

But whether a unilateral declaration of independence was ever seriously entertained we shall never know. History is constructed from what men did and what they wrote. What they thought and said in private – especially if of a treasonable nature – is seldom apparent. One can only conjecture.

It seems clear enough, though, that Hastings was not the only one who felt bitter. In letters quoted in Professor Furber's biography of Dundas, George Smith, a member of the Bengal Council, refers to a 'furore of petitioning' against Pitt's bill in both Calcutta and Madras. Disaffection was rife among the King's officers who resented Macartney's conduct towards Stuart, among the Company's officers who resented the increasing numbers and privileges of the King's officers, and among the Company's civilians who took exception to the censures included in Pitt's bill and to its provisions against profiteering. But Smith's advice to Dundas was to make no concessions. It was concessions that had encouraged the American colonists to fight. Better just to stand firm until 'chimerical ideas of Independence . . . droop and drop, for our [i.e. Indian] condition is very different indeed from that of the Irish and Americans'.

And what of Hastings? 'He might have attempted, and successfully, a dismemberment of this country from the British Empire'; but, as Smith added, he was too loyal, too faithful to the Honourable Company. 'I owe to my ever honourable employers the service of my life', Hastings wrote. 'My conscience . . . prompts me to declare that no man ever served them with a zeal superior to my own, or perhaps equal to it.'

CHAPTER NINETEEN

Tea Trade Versus Free Trade

THE FAR EAST AND THE PACIFIC

Spanning the period of the transfer of power in London, Hastings's Governor-Generalship may be seen both as a culmination of the Company's rule and as the inauguration of the Raj. It was like the end pillar of India House's new classical colonnade which, depending on your viewpoint, could be seen as terminating the building's somewhat chaotic side elevation or as beginning its grandiose frontal façade. Although drawing heavily on past precedents, both Indian and British, Hastings seems to have been more than conscious of the changing British role in India; and to this change he made another vital contribution.

It was something to do with his perception of India. Although most eighteenth-century Englishmen in India affected oriental customs to the extent of smoking a hookah and taking lower or half-caste women to bed, they viewed the subcontinent with an understandable detachment, albeit tinged with avarice and anxiety. The social whirl of Calcutta and the civic pride of Madras are reminiscent of the starched table-linen and frantic gaiety of a cruise liner. Outside, in the dusty *mofussil* and further 'upcountry', India's political disarray surged around them. They followed its progress for the opportunities it offered. But looking ever to the revenue receipts, the trade investment, and above all their own perquisites, they felt no sense of identity with their Indian surroundings, let alone with the subcontinent as a whole.

It was different with Hastings. Perhaps because he was there so long, perhaps because he had mastered Urdu and Bengali, or perhaps just because he liked the place, Hastings saw beyond the immediate and often sordid political and commercial realities to an Indian totality that was both geographical and historical. Admiration for this vast and noble entity fired his curiosity. Like many who have followed him, he longed to comprehend India's profusion and diversity, to fathom its antiquity, and to explore its extent.

Thanks to Hastings's patronage, in the face of the usual obstruction from his Council, Charles Wilkins, the first Englishman to master Sanskrit, published a translation of the *Bhagavad-gita*, the devotional core of the *Mahabharata*. Hastings wrote his celebrated introduction to it during those last anxious months in India. The *Gita*, he declared, evinced 'a sublimity of conception, reasoning and diction almost unequalled' and a theology to which even a dedicated Christian could not take exception. This and other masterpieces from an age predating civilization in Europe would, he predicted, 'survive when the British dominion in India shall have long ceased to exist and when the sources which it once yielded of wealth and power are lost to remembrance'. In encouraging Hindu scholarship (and in founding a Muslim college in Calcutta) Hastings declared his policy to be that of 'reconciling the people of England to the natives of Hindustan'. Such notions had no precedent among the Company's servants. Hastings may be credited with having established the idea of a lasting and responsible British participation in India's history and of having made India a respectable subject for statecraft and dominion.

Also under his patronage Sir William Jones founded the Asiatic Society of Bengal which quickly became the great clearing-house for oriental scholarship. Jones, a Supreme Court judge and polymathic genius who shunned British society in favour of his Brahmin tutors, defined the Society's field of enquiry as all-embracing. It was to investigate India's geography, history, grammar, rhetoric, agriculture, industry, science, music, architecture, poetry, medicine, plus 'whatever is rare in the stupendous fabric of nature'. 'If now it be asked what are the intended objects of our enquiries within these spacious limits, we answer Man and Nature, whatever is performed by the one or produced by the other.'

Such enlightened sentiments accorded exactly with Hastings's own and are echoed in the wide-ranging briefs drawn up by him for his two most important initiatives outside India. Both were prompted by fortuitous circumstance; and both had specific commercial and political objectives. But by endowing them with a wider significance Hastings persuaded himself that they were not purely speculative. They were to serve the cause of science and scholarship and they were to promote the idea of British Bengal as an established and honourable Asian polity. The first of these intitiatives also anticipated by nearly a century British

India's obsession with its Himalayan and central Asian frontier; and the second revived the dreams of Saris, Floris, Catchpole, and latterly Dalrymple for an entrepôt through which the China trade could if necessary be rerouted away from Cantonese mandarins.

In the 1770s Tibet, Bengal's northern neighbour, fairly merited its invariable epithets of 'unknown' and 'inaccessible'. No Briton had yet so much as penetrated the Himalayas. But as 'Button' or 'Botton', Bhutan had occasionally scored a mention in the Company's records and was often confused with Tibet itself. This was understandable. Tibet exercised a somewhat vague and fluctuating authority over many of the Himalayan states and it was thus on behalf of Bhutan that a Tibetan mission made its unexpected appearance in Calcutta in 1774. The Bhutanese had recently been worsted by four companies of sepoys sent to repel one of their habitual incursions into northern Bengal; their own territory was now threatened by way of reprisal; so the Grand Lama of Tashilunpo in Tibet was writing to Calcutta to plead negotiations and save the wayward Bhutanese.

Hastings responded enthusiastically. Tibet, known to be uncommonly cold, might be the long-sought market for English woollens. Additionally, its trade with India, which traditionally passed through Nepal, had recently been interrupted. And still more to the point, Lhasa was known to be somehow subject to Peking and might therefore represent a back door into the Chinese Empire. Could this be a channel for re-presenting the grievances of the Canton factors? The commercial possibilities were enormous. But George Bogle, the Scot who was immediately dispatched to explore them, was also to investigate the manners, morals, customs, politics, etc of the Tibetans – and not simply for what Sir Clement Markham calls rather snidely 'the personal satisfaction of Warren Hastings'.

Bogle, a Company servant, is described as 'a gentleman of distinguished ability and remarkable equanimity of temper'. The 'distinguished ability' would be somewhat wasted on the Tibetans for although his overtures were welcomed by the Tashi (or Panchen) Lama, only the authorities in Lhasa could conclude an agreement and they, jealous of the Tashi Lama and much under Chinese influence, refused Bogle permission to approach the capital. But that 'remarkable equanimity of temper' stood him in excellent stead. Neither the prevarication of the Bhutanese nor the gradients of the eastern Himalayas could ruffle the beaming Bogle; the Tashi Lama became a close and revered friend; and Bogle's six months in Tibet he reckoned the happiest of his life. Like many subsequent travellers he was completely seduced by the Tibetans. 'Farewell, ye honest and simple people,' he wrote on his departure; 'may ye long enjoy that happiness which is denied to more polished nations, and while they are engaged in the endless pursuit of avarice and ambition, defended by your barren mountains, may ye continue to live in peace and contentment, and know no wants but those of nature.' These were odd sentiments for an ambitious servant of a decidedly avaricious Company, odder still for a man supposedly engineering the commercial and political penetration of the country.

Making the most of his contacts, Bogle had compiled a dossier on Tibet's export trade in such exotica as gold dust, musk, and shawl wool, and he foresaw great possibilities for Indian exports. Henceforth the encouragement of trans-Himalayan trade would be regarded as a British responsibility; more important, its interruption would be seen as a blow to British interests. Bogle hoped that in time the British would be able to participate in it directly and in this connection he expected much from the representations which the Tashi Lama promised to make during his forthcoming visit to Peking. Unfortunately the Lama died in Peking and Bogle himself died a few months later. Two follow-up missions from Bengal failed to gain access to Tibet, although trade with Bhutan was put on a regular footing. Then in 1782 word arrived from Tashilunpo that the Lama's new incarnation had been discovered. Metempsychosis had its advantages. Naturally Hastings must congratulate his old friend who now, as an eighteen-month-old baby, was embarking on his seventh term of office. Accordingly Captain Samuel Turner, a cousin of Hastings, was sent back to Tibet with a brief almost identical to Bogle's.

Turner's mission also returned empty-handed. Again the Lama, in spite of his lack of years, made a deep impression; again Lhasa refused to have anything to do with the British; and again hopes rested on Tashilunpo pleading the British case in Peking. Nothing came of this, partly because Hastings was about to leave India. The Tibetan initiative, though encouraged by the directors, had been very much his own project; when he left, all official contact with Tibet ceased. It would be seventy years before the British endeavoured to make good their ignorance about Tibet and nearly twice as long before they had regained the ground lost in the meantime. 'Under Warren Hastings, British influence had penetrated further into the Himalayan areas, into Bhutan, Sikkim, and Tibet, than it was to again until the opening years of the twentieth century . . .' (A. K. Jasbir Singh). On the other hand the intriguing detail and the romantic image conveyed by Bogle's and Turner's published narratives proved irresistible to a long succession of freelance travellers. Hastings would have been gratified to think that he had brought the Himalayas and the lands beyond within the realms of geographical enquiry.

No such consolation would be afforded by his other venture outside India for the simple reason that the long coastal strip of mainland south-east Asia which is today Vietnam posed less of a challenge to geography. From the Hirado factory in Japan, Adams and 'the honest Mr Cocks' had attempted to establish trade links with Vietnam in the early seventeenth century. Later in the century the Company had opened its own factory in north Tongking (north Vietnam) and, soon after its closure in 1697, Catchpole and his colleagues of the New Company had established themselves briefly and disastrously at Pulo Condore (off the south Vietnamese coast).

Thereafter it had been the French who had been making the running. Dupleix had sent a representative to explore the possibilities for French trade and so had the *Compagnie des Indes* from Paris. The idea that France might compensate itself for losses in India by establishing a naval and commercial bridgehead in mainland south-east Asia was frequently canvassed; and as the China trade figured ever more prominently in the finances of the English Company, so did the strategic potential of a French base astride this trade route. News that the Nguyen dynasty of Annam (roughly southern Vietnam with Hué as its capital) was being hard pressed by a revolt among its own subjects eventually provided the perfect pretext. To aid the beleaguered Nguyen, in 1777 Jean-Baptiste Chevalier of the French factory at Chandernagar in Bengal dispatched an expedition to the Annamite port of Tourane (Da Nang). 'In this kind of business', observed Chevalier, 'it is he who arrives first who has all the advantages.'

Hastings would come to appreciate this sentiment. At the time he was unaware of the French move. But happily for his cause, those unsung heroes of British enterprise, the country traders, had never given up on the Vietnamese market just as they had never given up on the Indonesian archipelago. Vietnam was the speciality of a Calcutta agency house then trading as Messrs Crofts and Kellican; and it so happened that as the French expedition put into Tourane's capacious harbour, Crofts and Kellican's ship *Rumbold* was already there, affording to the Nguyen the very support and sanctuary which the French had hoped to provide. He who arrived first already had all the advantages. Six months later, with the French having abandoned their mission and with the Nguyen forced to evacuate the Tourane area, the *Rumbold* returned to base in Calcutta. Besides a tidy profit on its Indian exports, its cargo included two prominent and resplendent Nguyen mandarins.

Presented with such a diplomatic windfall, Hastings again responded quickly. The mandarins had originally asked to be landed in the Mekong delta where the Nguyen were regrouping. Bad weather had prevented the *Rumbold* from making the necessary landfall but the mandarins were still keen to return and would undoubtedly accept a French passage if their English hosts hesitated to oblige. With France about to enter the American War of Independence, and with the mysterious St Lubin already intriguing with the Marathas at Poona, it was not the moment to invite French rivalry for the Far East trade. Hastings therefore treated the mandarins like royalty. Of course he would return them to Vietnam, but not without adequate protection in the shape of a naval escort – the *Amazon* and a smaller vessel named the *Jenny* – an accredited agent of the Company – Mr Charles Chapman – plus a second Company agent, a surgeon, presents, Indian exports, and assorted interpreters. Besides landing his charges, Chapman was to seek a commercial treaty with their overlord, endeavour to establish a British agency in the country and, of course, compile a thorough dossier on all matters political, commercial, social and geographical that came to his attention. The mission – for such it now was – sailed from the Hughli in April 1778.

In spite of the ministrations of Surgeon Totty, one of the mandarins died in the Straits of Malacca. His colleague, called by Chapman 'Ong-tom-being', thereupon seemed to weaken in his resolution and when Chapman at last made contact with Nguyen supporters near Saigon, he positively refused to be put ashore. This threatened the entire enterprise. If Chapman was to avoid anywhere that the 'Mandarine' suspected of being in hostile hands, 'I was at once excluded from the whole country'. 'Unwilling, however, or indeed,' as the pleasantly candid Chapman put it, 'rather ashamed to leave Cochin China [i.e. Vietnam] almost as totally uninformed as when I sailed from Bengal, I resolved at all events to prosecute my voyage as far as the Bay of Turon [Tourane].'

Contact was made *en route* with the dreaded Tayson rebels. As Ong-tom-being cowered in the depths of the *Amazon*, Chapman went ashore for an audience and found the enemy surprisingly friendly although diplomatically somewhat naive. They seemed to imagine that any agreement with the Company must entail a military alliance whereby they would soon be enabled to make themselves masters of all south-east Asia. On the whole Chapman preferred the idea of first sounding out the Tongking authorities. The Trinh rulers of Tongking were at least legitimate sovereigns and had recently taken advantage of the Nguyen's eclipse to establish themselves in the old capital of Hué. An invitation from the Trinh viceroy in Hué was therefore readily accepted. Leaving the *Amazon* at Tourane, Chapman transferred to the shallow-draught *Jenny* to enter the Perfume River and then to a local galley for the journey up to imperial Hué.

Of the city's famed and hyacinth-choked waterfront Chapman says little, although he noted with satisfaction the presence there of a large fleet of China junks and was as delighted by the genial old Viceroy as Bogle had been by the Tashi Lama. Less pleasing was his reception by the city's military governor who turned out to be 'a monster disgustful and horrible to behold' and a pedantic eunuch to boot. He held court in a darkened shrine 'like a clothes press' that barely contained more flesh than Chapman had ever encountered. 'Great flaps hung down from his cheeks like the dewlaps of an ox, and his little twinkling eyes were scarcely to be discerned for the fat folds which formed deep recesses round them.'

This 'devil incarnate' Chapman would hold responsible for what followed. During August, while negotiations with the Viceroy proceeded and the *Jenny*'s cargo was sold off, all went well. But in September the *Amazon* approached the mouth of the river to land its dying captain. His funeral in October coincided with mounting complaints against the British plus the departure of Ong-tom-being, the surviving Nguyen mandarin, for sanctuary ashore. An obvious omen, this move also proved a godsend. For it was Ong-tom-being, sincerely grateful for all the hospitality he had received, who in early November tipped off Chapman that he and his vessel were about to be seized.

A precipitate retreat downriver to the *Jenny* went without hitch. But there adverse winds and a heavy swell precluded a dash for the open sea. Forced to temporize, Chapman tried to negotiate. The Trinh authorities responded with two armed galleys which, contrary to Chapman's orders, were fired on, then taken and scuttled; so, as a result, was any chance of an accommodation. Downstream batteries were soon being erected to command the exit; upstream more galleys and fireships were said to be preparing. Against them the *Jenny* boasted 'eight old and very bad two pounders for which we had scarce any shot, two swivels, some wall pieces and twelve muskets'; her complement, including one English sailor, amounted to thirty.

As she edged towards the wall of breakers at the mouth of the river, the *Jenny* made an easy target for the shore batteries. Most of her rigging was shot away and the one English sailor was killed. When a boat bringing reinforcements from the *Amazon* went down in the surf, Chapman hoisted the white flag. His narrative suggests that he just wanted to parley. More credibly the Vietnamese took it as a token of surrender and ceased firing. Their mistake was not to board the vessel immediately. For as darkness came on, the wind suddenly changed and the captain, having little to lose, decided to make a run for it. 'I must confess for my own part', wrote Chapman, 'I expected nothing better than to be wrecked amongst the breakers.' But, without a single grounding – and without, for once, so much as an acknowledgement to Divine Providence – the *Jenny* and her crew bobbed through to safety.

Three months later, back in Calcutta, the resilient Chapman seems either to have conveniently forgotten this Hué experience or else to have determined on making his report a work of fiction. For Vietnam he now portrayed as a merchant's paradise. The coastline consisted of a succession of magnificent natural harbours, the rivers provided an ideal means of inland transport, the climate was a joy, and the people as a whole 'courteous, affable, [and] inoffensive'; as for the ladies, 'the active sex', they welcomed 'temporary connections with strangers' and were esteemed for their fidelity. Moreover, 'no country in the East, and perhaps none in the world, produces richer or a greater variety of articles proper for carrying on an advantageous commerce'. There was silk, cotton, spices, timber, and ivory. There was also gold (the *Rumbold* and now the *Jenny* had both sold their Indian exports for bullion). And there was a substantial and direct trade with Japan, as of old, and with China, as evidenced by all those junks in the Perfume River.

In short it would be madness not to form a settlement. The plight of the Nguyen offered a legitimate and unrepeatable pretext. 'For this and every other purpose' fifty European soldiers plus a couple of hundred sepoys and a few artillery would suffice. The reward would be out of all proportion to the expense. And if the Company did not act, the French would.

It all had a rather familiar ring. By now the Company's records bulged with similar reports on a host of unhappy landfalls – Hirado, Pulo Condore, Divi, Devikottai, Negrais, and latterly Balambangan. Indeed it could well have been written by the indefatigable Dalrymple who, before plumping for Balambangan, had himself inspected the Vietnamese coast. Dalrymple's ideas had been very much in Hastings's mind when the Chapman mission was first launched and in his report Chapman duly reproduced the same arguments. To get round the restrictions and exactions imposed on trade at Canton, and to open trade with other Chinese ports, the only solution was to acquire a foothold somewhere in the South China Sea to which the produce of China could be brought by Chinese junks. Even the fiasco of Balambangan had not weakened the argument. Quite the contrary. With every year the China trade became more vital to the Company and with every year the Canton restrictions became more vexatious. A base at, for instance, Tourane would solve the problem once and for all.

ii

Yet Chapman's mission, like those of Bogle and Turner, would never be followed up. With the outbreak of hostilities with France, then Mysore, and then Holland, Hastings had his hands full in India. Not even fifty Europeans could be spared for Vietnam. Besides, the capture of Pondicherry and the presence of Hughes's squadron seemed to reduce the chances of a French move into south-east Asia; and meanwhile the likes of Thomas Forrest and Francis Light were urging that if there was to be a new British base east of India, the Malay peninsula offered greater strategic advantages than Vietnam. After the restoration of peace and the departure of Hastings, Light duly accepted the Sultan of Kedah's offer of Penang.

But Penang would not be the end of the long quest for an Eastern base. Although it did have some advantages, it scarcely addressed the problems of the China trade. Ideally there were four requirements for any new settlement. It must possess the potential for a naval base in terms of deep water, shelter, timber, and provisions. It must be strategically placed to protect and supply shipping *en route* to and from Canton. It must be within easy reach of China's junk trade as an alternative to Canton. And it must be able to provide or attract those commodities (sharks' fins, birds' nests, etc from the archipelago) which were most suitable for sale in China. Penang answered only the first and to some extent the second It was on the wrong side of the Malay peninsula for the junks; and although it was well placed for furnishing Malay tin, it was too far north to attract the exotic produce, so valued by the Chinese, of the archipelago.

Providing cargoes suitable for the China market was absolutely vital. From this commercial point of view either Balambangan or Tourane would have been far preferable to Penang; and with the phenomenal growth in the tea trade after the 1784 Commutation Act, the commercial point of view was paramount. Already in the 1770s the China trade, mainly in tea, outstripped that of India. But during the decade after 1784 the Company's tea imports more than trebled in volume. And so it would continue. There consequently arose what would now be called a trade gap of quite phenomenal proportions. Protecting the China trade was as nothing compared to the problem of financing it.

Ideally, of course, the revenues of India should have paid for the tea of China. But such were the mounting military and administrative costs of the Company's Indian establishments that revenue surpluses became a rarity. Instead of Indian revenues financing the China trade, it would soon be a case of the China trade financing the Company's Indian establishments. On the other hand India did still generate a lot of surplus produce and manufactures, and it did still provide its British residents with sizeable personal fortunes. Both could be mobilized to purchase tea. The system of bills of exchange by which Company servants were repaid in England for fortunes invested with the Company in India has already been noticed. But the issue of such bills in India was strictly limited, the Company much preferring to issue them on Canton. Thus there arose the problem of how first to transfer or transform an Indian fortune into a Chinese one.

An obvious answer was to invest in Indian goods that could be resold in Canton. Unfortunately the Celestial Empire prided itself on being self-sufficient and was therefore notoriously indifferent to foreign imports. There were a few exceptions, like the culinary exotica of the archipelago, the mechanical curios of Europe, and some magical and medicinal items of extraordinary rarity; but cotton piece goods were not amongst them. Towards the turn of the century, however, a shortfall in Chinese agriculture did open the way for considerable imports of raw cotton, mainly from Bombay. This India–China trade, like all that within Asia, was open to the private or 'country' trader and spawned a number of Bombay 'agency houses' with representatives in Canton/Macao.

Similar activity in Calcutta centred round the purchase, from the Company monopoly recently established by Hastings, of locally grown opium which was then exported to the Far East. In spite of Peking's prohibition of the drug, some opium was already being shipped direct to

China; but it would be another generation before this trade came into its own. In the meantime the country trader and the agency house looked to south-east Asia and the archipelago to buy their opium and furnish in exchange the sharks' fins, sea slugs, birds' nests and spices that appealed to the Chinese.

This roundabout trade, occasioned by the problem of financing the Company's tea imports, was undoubtedly the making of the agency houses. Partnerships like Crofts and Kellican in Calcutta, Jourdain, Sulivan and de Souza in Madras, and Scot, Tate and Adamson, the big cotton shippers in Bombay, absorbed and replaced individual private traders. In addition to their own ships, usually locally built for a specific trade, they freighted cargo on the Company's ships within the East and even bought up the privilege tonnage allowed by the Company to its captains and officers for their own private trade to and from Europe. It has been estimated that in the 1780s nearly three-quarters of all British and Indian goods reaching Canton were being dispatched by country traders.

Still the insatiable home demand for tea far outstripped the supply of acceptable produce reaching Canton courtesy of the agency houses. The consequent shortfall, estimated at about one-third of the total in the 1780s, was made up, as had once been the case with the Indian trade, by bullion shipments. But most bullion, whether garnered by way of Spain in London or by way of Manila in India, originated in Spanish America; and when, for instance, Spain entered the War of American Independence, this supply dried up. As a source of finance it was neither dependable nor desirable. Hence the importance attached to the existence of gold deposits in both Tibet and Vietnam and hence Chapman's emphasis on the fact that the Vietnamese paid for Indian imports with specie.

Another obvious and, as ever, ideal solution would have been to discover or create a demand in China for British manufactures. As yet the Chinese showed even less interest in English woollens and Wedgwood than the Indians. Except for clockwork curios and a certain amount of tin and lead, any British goods that reached Canton were invariably sold at a loss. This situation was about to be reviewed and a determined effort made to redress it. But the Company was not optimistic about the outcome and in the meantime the search for commodities that would command a certain sale in China went on. Having scoured the ports of mainland Asia and the archipelago, the more adventurous private traders were about to turn their attention to the Pacific and beyond.

The impetus for such an ambitious and improbable development was provided by the discoveries of James Cook and seconded by the ever passionate advocacy of Cook's one-time rival for Pacific laurels, Alexander Dalrymple. Now the Company's hydrographer, Dalrymple was not content simply to collect and publish navigational charts. As befitted a student of the Company's first voyages, he was as excited by commercial prospects as by geographical discoveries and had come to regard the Pacific as a trading basin with as much potential as the Indian Ocean. Hence his obsession with the existence of a Southern Continent other than Australia; and hence his reports on, and encouragement of, the Alaskan fur trade.

About the latter, Cook was his main source of information. On his Third Voyage (1776–80), which was directed towards the discovery of the Pacific entrance into the supposed North-West Passage, Cook had sailed up the north-west coast of America and through the Bering Strait before conceding defeat. Thereafter he had withdrawn to the Sandwich Islands (Hawaii) only to be clubbed to death. But an account of this voyage was subsequently compiled by James King who gave it as his opinion that small expeditions to anywhere north of the Nootka Sound on what is now Vancouver Island could prove highly profitable. For what made this remote littoral 'a new gold coast' (W. Irvine) was its superabundance of small furry otters. Described as 'the ermine of Asia' the sea otter's pelt was literally worth its weight in silver and was much prized by, above all, the Chinese.

King's account of Cook's last voyage appeared in 1784. Evidently James Strange, a Company servant heading for an appointment in Madras, bought a copy just before he left London. Certainly by the time his ship called at Bombay he had reached the bit about the sea otters and formed a plan which he communicated to David Scot of Scot, Tate and Adamson. Scot, later a director of the Company and one of Dundas's allies in urging a more adventurous commercial policy, jumped at the idea. Two ships, now suitably named the *Captain Cook* and the *Experiment*, were placed at Strange's disposal. Manned entirely by Europeans and provisioned for years rather than months, they sailed out of Bombay harbour amid strict secrecy in December 1785.

Meanwhile a copy of the book must also have reached Calcutta. For there, unknown to Strange or Scot, something called 'The Bengal Fur Society' had sprung into existence and begun canvassing support for a similar voyage into the unknown. Just three months after the departure of the Strange expedition, two equally well-equipped vessels sailed out of the Hughli. They were commanded by John Meares, a naval lieutenant made redundant by the peace of 1783; and in this case there was less secrecy for they had been renamed the *Nootka* and the *Sea Otter*.

Neither of these expeditions was mounted by the Honourable Company itself. In fact to smoothe their reception at Canton and Macao both had elected to sail under Portuguese colours. But both also proclaimed themselves as voyages of discovery in the hope that the Company would look favourably on their promoters' disinterested zeal. Meares claimed that his scheme had the support of the Governor-General and that Sir John Macpherson, the new incumbent, had actually subscribed towards it. The Scot-Strange venture was authorized by the Bombay council who also gave Strange leave of absence from his Madras posting plus the services of a few Company soldiers. On the other hand no time was wasted seeking approval from London and no secret surrounded the identity of the promoters – private agency houses – nor their real objectives – 'a new channel of . . . commercial intercourse between America and China' (Strange), 'to supply the Chinese market with furs and ginseng' (Meares).

But this begged all sorts of questions. Private traders operated under licence from the Company and the Company's charter granted it a monopoly of all trade east of the Cape of Good Hope. It did not, however, clearly specify where this trading zone ended. There must, though, have been doubts about whether it was supposed to cover the entire Pacific Ocean as well as the Indian, and large parts of America as well as Asia. If it did not cover these areas, the authorities in India had no right to be authorizing voyages there; and if it did, the question arose as to whether the delegated rights of private traders to engage in the country trade of Asia extended also to America. All in all, and as events soon confirmed, a reference to London would have been a sensible precaution.

Seemingly unconcerned about such niceties, both expeditions took about six months to reach America. Strange worked north from Vancouver Island, 'discovering' Queen Charlotte Sound, which he took possession of in the name of the King rather than the Company (another apparent contradiction), and of course buying sea otters. In the autumn he reached Prince William Sound on the south coast of Alaska and there ran into Meares. To Strange the discovery that, in spite of all the secrecy, he was not to have the fur trade all to himself came as a crushing revelation. Although only 600 pelts had been collected, he determined to sail straight for Canton. Possibly he wanted to be sure of getting there ahead of Meares's *Sea Otter* and the slump in prices which must result from a sudden over-supply; more probably he just wanted out from a trade which he could not now claim as exclusively his. The pelts sold well and he would later urge the Company itself to assume responsibility for future trade with America and to establish a permanent settlement on Vancouver Island. But his patron, Scot, had returned to England and neither Bombay nor Strange took any further active part in trans-Pacific commerce.

Meanwhile Meares in the *Nootka* had elected to spend the winter in Alaska. Cold-shouldered by the Russians at what is now Anchorage, he signed trading agreements with some of the local Inuit and built a large cabin in a place ill-named Snug Corner Cove. The ice closed in round the ship. The dark Arctic winter prompted fond thoughts of Calcutta. To an intensity of cold for which the expedition was ill prepared was added the scurge of scurvy. Out of thirty-one men who went ashore in December only ten survived to witness the May thaw; and with the thaw came another unwelcome visitation.

Given his plight, one might have expected Meares to have been overjoyed at the news of a vessel with a red ensign ploughing through the ice-floes towards Snug Corner Cove. But it immediately transpired that Captain George Dixon of the *Queen Charlotte* was only eight months out of London. In other words he and his consort vessel had reached Alaska via Cape Horn, not the Cape of Good Hope; and although he had taken the precaution of obtaining the Honourable Company's permission, he actually represented the 'King George Sound Company', an enterprise also inspired by Cook's voyage but specifically authorized by the British government to open north Pacific trade, all of which made Meares an interloper. Having given a bond not to trespass any further on the new Company's preserve, Meares headed west for Canton, whither Dixon soon followed him. Between them they had nearly 3000 pelts.

Evidently the prices obtained from the Chinese lived up to expectations, for further capital and encouragement were immediately forthcoming. Nothing more is heard of 'The Bengal Fur Company' but, in association with an up-and-coming Canton agency house then trading as Cox and Beale (and later Magniac and Co and eventually Jardine, Matheson and Co), Meares himself returned to north-west America in 1788 and more ships were sent in 1789. By then the King George Sound Company had also entered into a partnership with Cox and Beale which gave the former an easier entrée to the Canton market and enabled

Meares to continue in business. It has been calculated that in all some thirty-five British ships engaged in the trans-Pacific fur trade during the decade 1785–94.

Undoubtedly it would have been more but for increasing competition from American vessels and but for the so-called Nootka crisis of 1789 when three of Meares's ships were taken by a Spanish squadron. The Spaniards, who regarded the whole American west coast as their exclusive preserve, claimed to be simply dealing with an unauthorized and bellicose incursion. But the Pitt government, egged on by Meares's often exaggerated account of his establishment on Vancouver Island, took a very different view. A Royal squadron had just been ordered to effect a permanent settlement there collecting *en route* men and stores from New South Wales. Now the whole fleet was ordered to sea. War was avoided, but only just and only after much diplomatic brinkmanship in London and Madrid.

iii

The willingness shown by the British government, and particularly by Dundas at the Board of Control, to lend active support to commercial expansion in the East introduced a new element into the Company's situation. Here surely was one of the bonuses of Pitt's India Act. Having shouldered responsibility for the government and security of the Company's territories, it was natural that the Board of Control, i.e. the British government, should now vigorously espouse the trade on which their prosperity depended. And so it did. But that was not good news for the Company. For Dundas, on the advice of David Scot, late of Bombay, had understandably inferred that the most dynamic and elastic sector in the Company's commerce was that operated not by the Company but by the country traders. Hence the support for Meares and his colleagues. And hence the launch, in spite of the Company's opposition, of a simultaneous but much more ambitious attempt to tackle the problems of trade at Canton.

This took the form of the Macartney Mission to Peking of 1793, described as the most elaborate and expensive diplomatic initiative ever undertaken by a British government. Led by someone as jealous of his own dignity as Hastings's old rival at Madras, and combining the paraphernalia of a trade fair with the pretensions of an academic symposium plus the pomp of a state occasion, the mission was bound to scale new budgetary heights. But the stakes were also high. Had Macartney, as envisaged, ended China's diplomatic isolation, installed a British ambassador in Peking, opened the country to British imports, secured a British enclave on Chinese territory, won access to China's northern ports, and obtained a relaxation of the trading restrictions at Canton – not to mention reopening trade with Japan, renewing contacts with the Philippines, and founding sundry settlements in the archipelago – it would indeed have been money sensationally well spent.

In the event the Mission proved no more successful, and made itself no less ridiculous, than those previous interventions by the Court of St James led by Roe, Norris, and Lindsay. But as always, the government's embarrassment was mitigated by the comforting thought that it was the Company which was to be saddled with the bill, in this case £80,000.

The Company had warned right from the start that such a mission might prove counter-productive. It therefore played a reluctant and minimal part in the affair and benefited from it not at all. In spite of a voluminous and often colourful documentation, the Mission scarcely merits attention in a history of the Company. Yet there surfaced in the long correspondence that preceded it a number of considerations that are highly relevant.

They included a recitation of the notorious handicaps to which all foreign trade at Canton was subject. The trading companies were still obliged to withdraw their entire establishments to Macao during the slack summer months; they were forbidden to bring any guns or any women up to Canton; there were strict rules about the conduct and domicile of ships' crews while there; and there were heavy penalties for any merchants who strayed outside the waterfront ghetto where the foreign companies had their factories. To some extent the Company's representatives, or supercargoes, had become resigned to these restrictions. After 1784 their tea purchases quickly came to exceed those of all the other foreign companies combined. Together with their long experience of Chinese methods, it gave them a certain status and leverage.

But it was very different for the country traders and the private agency houses, many of whom were only now establishing themselves in Canton. With no legal status, they either sheltered beneath whatever grudging protection the Company's Select Committee of Supercargoes might afford them or, like Meares, they opted for Portuguese or some other bogus European accreditation. Either way the arrangement was not calculated to make them other than profoundly resentful of the so-called Select Committee.

Additionally all foreigners fretted at the capricious nature of the various fiscal impositions levied on their trade and at the Co-Hong system whereby a small cartel of Chinese merchants was alone licensed to trade with them. The Co-Hong system invited price fixing; it also concentrated the risk element so that while some Hong merchants accumulated massive fortunes, others ran up equally massive debts. Given rates of interest comparable with those offered by Mohammed Ali in Madras, foreigners – and in particular British country traders – were not averse to becoming their creditors. But whereas the Nawab's debts were secured by an alliance with the Company and a powerful parliamentary interest, those of the Hongists were virtually unsecured. As a result, when in the 1770s a succession of Hongists defaulted, the creditors had had no redress other than to appeal to the British government. The Company was eventually persuaded to intercede on their behalf and secured a settlement that amounted to about twenty-five per cent of the sums claimed. But it is significant that the idea of an embassy to Peking first surfaced as a result of this appeal to London by the country traders.

It resurfaced in 1784 as a result of the *Lady Hughes* affair which highlighted another ancient grievance, that of Chinese jurisdictional claims over the foreign community. While firing a salute, the *Lady Hughes*'s gunner, an old and absent-minded tar, let off a round of shot which killed two Chinese in a passing sampan. The gunner then went into hiding; but, when the Chinese secured the person of the ship's supercargo by way of hostage, the luckless culprit was found, handed over and, without so much as a hearing, judicially strangled. That a British sailor guilty of nothing worse than absent-mindedness should be subject to China's summary ideas of justice provoked an outcry even in London. Calls for an appeal direct to the Emperor were renewed and, though opposed by the Court of Directors, won a favourable hearing from the Board of Control. For the *Lady Hughes* was a private ship; indeed it seems probable that had she been a Company ship, Chinese justice might, as on previous occasions, have proved more lenient. Once again the vulnerability of the private or country traders was represented to Dundas in vivid terms, and within a matter of months he decided to act. As a suitable person to confront the Emperor of China his choice initially fell on Lieutenant-Colonel the Honourable Charles Cathcart.

The long delay between this decision in 1786 to send an embassy and its eventual arrival in China in 1793 is accounted for by Cathcart's death *en route* in 1788 and by the subsequent difficulty of deciding on a successor. By the time Macartney was appointed nothing much had changed in Anglo-Chinese relations; but it so happened that the interval coincided with a major assault on the Company's commercial privileges that changed the emphasis of the mission and that was soon to prove fatal for the Company.

A two-pronged affair, the first prod in this assault had come with a renewal of those charges by British manufacturers that the Company was ignoring the national interest. Instead of importing textiles from India, it should, they argued, be exporting finished textiles from Lancashire and importing only the raw materials. The Company's response was that India's raw materials could not compete with those of, say, America and that Lancashire textiles could not compare with those of India. But this argument was losing its force. The quality of machine-made textiles was improving dramatically while the cost of shipping in raw cotton was being grossly inflated by the Company's powerful shipping interest.

This latter argument was taken up by the other prong of the attack, namely the private traders. Men like David Scot of Bombay had demonstrated that hold space on outward-bound Indiamen, if let at reasonable rates, could be put to profitable use by the private trader – in Scot's case by shipping raw cotton from India to Canton. Back in London, Scot now urged that this co-operation between the Company and the private trader be extended. To handle the much increased tea imports, Indiamen were being built with a displacement of 1200 or more tons. Hold space was available not just between India and China but also on the earlier leg from London to India. Only the Company's still jealously guarded monopoly of all British trade between Europe and the East prevented the private trader from taking up this hold space and filling it with British exports, argued Scot.

The Company replied that, although it was at last making steady progress with the export of woollens to China, the demand for British manufactures in India was limited to the British communities. That was because the Company's freight charges were ridiculously high, retorted the traders; that was because the Company in India was now more interested in revenue than trade, retorted the manufacturers. Dundas sympathized with both; and they were surely right. The Company was no longer primarily a commercial concern; its directors and shareholders were no longer obsessed with dividends (patronage was far more valuable); and its organization no longer fitted it for exploring commercial sidelines. But Dundas could also understand the Company's anxiety to prevent an invasion of India by commercial interests outside its control. Who was to prevent an arms salesman, for instance, from peddling his wares round Tipu's capital of Srirangapatnam?

'Regulated monopoly' was the answer according to Dundas and, in the 1793 renewal of the Company's charter, clauses were incorporated which guaranteed 3000 tons of cargo at cheap freight rates between London and the East for the use of private traders. Like North's earlier Regulating Act, 'regulated monopoly' satisfied none of the parties concerned and served only to encourage further demands. But it was as a result of all the lobbying by British manufacturers that the Macartney embassy partook of the character of a trade fair, encumbering itself with samples of just about everything that Britain could produce in the hope that they would appeal to the Chinese. And it was as a result of the pressure from private traders that great emphasis was laid on the desirability of Macartney securing a British commercial enclave on Chinese territory whence they could trade with the Chinese on equal terms with the Company.

iv

The Macartney Mission's catalogue of failures did not end with the Emperor's indifference to the requests of what he called 'the tribute bearing envoy from England' nor with his mandarins' disdain for the achievements of British science and industry. Macartney had also been entrusted with the task of renewing commercial contacts with Japan, realizing Dalrymple's dream for a British settlement somewhere between the Dutch Archipelago and the Spanish Philippines, and reviving Hastings's contacts with Vietnam. He had actually called at Tourane (Da Nang) on the way out. But Annam was still in political turmoil and Macartney decided that a commercial establishment there would be of advantage only if his China mission failed. He therefore postponed negotiations till he could call again on his return.

This visit, like those to Japan, the Philippines, and the archipelago, never took place. For when his crestfallen Lordship returned to Canton from Peking it was to be greeted with the news that war with France had broken out again. The Paris of the Jacobins posed an even more alarming threat than the Versailles of the Bourbons; within a matter of months Holland would capitulate to the Revolutionaries and be fighting beside them as the Batavian Republic. It was no time for a diplomat and an aristocrat to go cruising in the archipelago.

Macartney did, however, glean some unexpected and valuable intelligence about Dutch strength in the archipelago. This came courtesy of two small 'cruisers' which reached Macao while he was in China. Although the ships belonged to the Company's Bombay Marine, the service which had borne the brunt of the war with the Angreys, it transpired that they actually hailed from the opposite direction, in fact from a Pacific paradise of whose bearings even the now venerable Dalrymple might have been uncertain.

The 'Pelew Islands', now Palau, lie about 500 miles east of the Philippines and rather more than that north of New Guinea. Although of no known commercial value, it transpired that the Company had, rather surprisingly, acquired one of these islands. On it, according to the captains of the two cruisers, there now stood a proud edifice known as Fort Abercromby (after the then Governor of Bombay). And from it the two ships had managed to conduct a reconnaissance of the Dutch position in the eastern archipelago. No less intriguingly, they reported that the man responsible for this unlikely achievement was still there, having resigned the Company's service and opted for a life of ease among the 'Pelewese'.

This legendary figure was Captain John McCluer who had previously been engaged in making surveys of the coasts of Persia and western India. Dalrymple, as the Company's Hydrographer, had thought highly of his work and may well have stimulated his interest in more distant shores. Certainly he was a natural choice for the Pelew expedition which, on instructions from London, had been dispatched by the Bombay government in 1790. Officially the mission was supposed to be conveying to the King of Pelew the belated thanks of the Company for having assisted the crew of a ship wrecked on the Islands some seven years earlier. Several survivors from that wreck were now sailing back to Pelew with McCluer; but not alas Prince Lee Boo, the King's son, who had come away with them and had even reached London, only to die there of smallpox.

It soon became apparent, however, that there was more to the mission than a courtesy call. After leaving Benkulen the ships closely inspected the southern coast of Java and then explored so many 'islands and places to the eastward' that it was five months before they made the Pelews. There the old Pelew hands had, as one of them put it, 'the unspeakable pleasure of once more being embraced by the benevolent [King] Abba Thulle'; meanwhile his thoroughly delightful subjects overwhelmed the newcomers with their gentle favours. To the Grenadiers' March played on fife and drum, McCluer trudged ashore over the coral sands to present an assortment of hardware and piece goods plus some brahminee cattle. A scene enacted so many times during the Company's history can seldom have been so rapturously received. The crowd was 'struck with amazement', the King 'perfectly at a loss for utterance or how to express his gratitude to the English *rupacks* as he styled the Hon Company'. In return, McCluer was invested with 'the Order of the Bone' and an island was ceded as 'Englishmen's land'.

As Fort Abercromby took shape, the troops joined the King in several canoe-borne assaults on the neighbouring atolls while McCluer sailed off to continue his probing of the archipelago. Clearly the Company had deduced that however jealous the Dutch might be of British incursions from Benkulen and Penang, they were totally unprepared for any Pacific-based initiative. While making a survey of New Guinea, McCluer innocently called on the Dutch Governor of the Moluccas in Ambon (Amboina). McCluer's were 'the first English ships that had visited that island for a century', observed the hospitable Governor. Actually it was nearer two centuries; and had he had a better grasp of history, the Governor would have realized that it was not a good omen. Only five years would elapse before the British were back – and back with a vengeance.

Concluding the New Guinea survey McCluer's party coasted along the northern shores of New Holland (Australia) and visited Dutch Timor where they were again 'most hospitably received'. Then they worked their way back to Benkulen for supplies, and finally returned to the Pelews by way of the Sulu Sea. It was now 1793, three years since they had left Bombay, and the reconnaissance was complete. But like many a Company servant before him, McCluer was reluctant to relinquish his island paradise. Very properly he therefore resigned his command, made over all his surveys and papers, and bade God-speed to the two cruisers as they sailed for Macao and a meeting with the Macartney Mission. 'It is nothing but the zeal for my country that prompts me to follow this resolution', explained McCluer, adding only slightly more plausibly, 'I hope to succeed in the plan I have formed, which may benefit my country and the world in general, by enlightening the minds of the noble islanders'.

Quite what this plan was is not clear, although suspicions would be aroused. After fifteen months alone in the Pelews, McCluer again took to the ocean, now in a six-oared longboat. He failed to reach Ternate in the north Moluccas, where he was presumably bent on more reconnaissance, but eventually fetched up in Macao. For the entire voyage of some

1600 miles he and his Pelewese crew had subsisted on coconuts and water. Not surprisingly McCluer was far from well. But evidently he had not tired of his islands for in Macao he sold the longboat for something more substantial and then sailed back.

In the following year, 1795, he turned up in Benkulen. This time he was accompanied by a large party of mainly female Pelewese, some of whom he put aboard a vessel bound for Bombay while with the rest he sailed for Calcutta. He was never heard of again. The assumption was that 'his craft foundered in the Bay of Bengal' (C. R. Low). 'Should I fail in the attempt [to "enlighten" the Pelewese?],' he had declared when bidding farewell to his original companions, 'it is only the loss of an individual who attempted to do good to his fellow-creatures.' As for the Pelewese damsels sent to Bombay, they 'being without friends,' according to Low, 'were for many years maintained by Lieutenant Snook' who had been part of the original expedition. To his 'singular charity and forgetfulness of self' the ladies owed their eventual return to the islands by way of Macao in 1798.

The year 1798 was also the fourth year of what, with Napoleon landing in Egypt, could now be called the Napoleonic Wars. As usual hostilities in the East had opened with the capture of the French settlements in India – now something of a formality; for Pondicherry it was the fourth surrender in as many decades. In the Indian Ocean the main threat still emanated from the French base in Mauritius; but before this could be attacked Holland, or rather the 'Batavian Republic', declared for its fellow republic in France, thus making all the Dutch possessions in the East potential French bases. As during the previous War of American Independence, this threat to British trade in the East could best be met by indulging in the long-cherished opportunity of gobbling up the Dutch settlements.

In dire financial straits exacerbated by a virtual cessation of trade during the previous war, the once glorious V.O.C. (Dutch East India Company) was on its last legs. Its possessions were poorly defended, its servants divided in their loyalties; for apart from the uncertainty engendered by the first moves towards its dissolution, there had been an appeal from William of Orange, the exiled Stadholder, that the V.O.C. surrender to the British rather than co-operate with the French. In quick succession, therefore, the Royal Navy assisted by the Bombay Marine secured Table Bay and the Cape, Trinconomalee and Sri Lanka, all the Dutch possessions in India, and the strategically vital port of Malacca commanding the Straits of that name. Thence, acting on the information supplied by McCluer and giving a wide berth to the main concentration of Dutch forces on Java, Admiral Peter Rainier sailed for the Eastern Archipelago.

By the end of February 1796, his squadron was off Ambon and, according to Professor C. Northcote Parkinson, 'ready to avenge the massacre which took place there in 1623'. But Fort Victoria, where so very long ago Gabriel Towerson and his colleagues had spent their last gruesome days, lay too close to the shore to offer any kind of resistance; the whole town surrendered after just two days. 'Having thus cornered the bulk of the world's supply of cloves', Rainier headed for Banda and the nutmegs. Here the Dutch governor quietly capitulated in accordance with the Stadholder's instructions and on the understanding that his salary would continue to be paid. The 85,000 pounds of nutmeg, 20,000 of mace, and 66,000 rix-dollars, when added to the cloves and spoils of Ambon, more than paid for the expedition and provided Rainier and his officers with the best prize pay-out of the war. Of McCluer's targets there remained only Timor, which was taken in the following year, and then, something of an afterthought, Ternate, now the main depot for the clove crop of the north Moluccas. Here the Dutch fortifications proved a greater challenge and it was not until 1801 that Captain Hayes, also a Bombay marine surveyor who had extended McCluer's surveys right down to Tasmania, successfully stormed Fort Orange.

So after 170 years the Company was back in the spice business. Unfortunately the trade now counted for little in the global economy. An intriguing French adventurer, once a missionary in Vietnam, latterly an administrator in Mauritius, who went by the gloriously apt name of Pierre Poivre, had already spirited away seedlings of the clove and nutmeg. They were now yielding good crops in Madagascar and Réunion whence their seedlings would in turn be carried to Zanzibar. The Honourable Company installed its own Governor in Ambon and also exported seedlings which led to further spice plantations at Benkulen and Penang. Meanwhile the ubiquitous British country traders were encouraged to uplift the produce of the Moluccas and carry it to Canton where it made a useful contribution to the Anglo-Chinese balance of payments.

This happy state of affairs lasted only five years. By the Peace of Amiens in 1802 all the Dutch possessions in the East Indies – though not Sri Lanka or the Cape which became Crown colonies – were returned to

Holland. Reluctantly Governor Farquhar, whose authorization of the attack on Ternate had just been condemned as 'a splendid but most injudicious conquest', hauled down the flag in Ambon and sailed west. But only as far as the Sulu Sea. Here, keeping a wary eye on the notorious Sulu pirates as he threaded the scatter of islands between the Philippines and Borneo, Farquhar quietly slipped over the coral bar and into the azure waters of Balambangan harbour. Strange cattle, the progeny of those abandoned by the 1773 settlement, scavenged along the shoreline; exuberant vegetation festooned the old palisades. Thanks to the always assertive policies of Richard Wellesley, the current Governor-General of India (who was also Lord Mornington and the brother of Arthur Wellesley), Dalrymple's dream was to live again.

If anything Robert Farquhar was even more sanguine about Balambangan's prospects than Dalrymple. With seedlings brought from Ambon, spice groves were planted. Chinese settlers were shipped in. Dalrymple's treaties with the Sultan of Sulu and with the neighbouring chiefs of Borneo were re-examined and his concessions reclaimed. As a free port at the fulcrum of the Eastern trade routes, Balambangan was projected as the most lucrative entrepôt in global trade and 'the foundation of one of the richest empires of the Eastern world'. And so it might have been. But a gloriously arbitrary destiny seems to preside over human geography. Less than a year later Farquhar was transferred to Penang and in 1805, with his initiative countermanded by the Court of Directors, Wellesley ordered the withdrawal of the settlement. Once again Balambangan disappeared off the map.

V

Farquhar's extravagant claims for Balambangan echoed not only those of Dalrymple but also those advanced by Francis Light for his foundation at Pulo Penang. Renamed Prince of Wales Island with the British settlement known as Georgetown and its inevitable stronghold as Fort Cornwallis, Penang's future nevertheless hung in the balance for nearly twenty years. For to doubts about whether it would ever be other than a financial millstone like Benkulen were added serious political complications with the Sultan of Kedah. The Sultan's understanding of the terms under which he had ceded Penang in 1786 included a commitment by the Company to assist him against his enemies, and in particular against the King of Siam who claimed tributary rights over Kedah. Light agreed and argued the case vigorously. But the Company, with nothing but dismal memories of Siam and its sovereigns, positively refused to give any such commitment, thus rendering the whole cession of dubious legality.

Meanwhile, thanks to a waiving of all customs duties, the place did prosper, although not sensationally so. Trade between Bengal and the Malay states tended to concentrate in Georgetown and, like all the Company's settlements, it steadily attracted a lively population; by 1804 it numbered some 12,000. To feed them, an adjacent chunk of the Malay peninsula had been purchased by the Company in 1800 and renamed Province Wellesley. But what did greatly enhance the island's prospects were the naval hostilities with France. Penang, with its sheltered harbour between the island and Province Wellesley, became a useful base at which to station warships on convoy duty with the China fleet and and an excellent marshalling port for operations further east. Rainier sailed from here to requisition the Moluccas in 1795 and two years later Penang became the assembly point for a massive task force designated for Manila. Unlike Draper's invasion during the Seven Years War, this one never sailed; the fourth and final war with Tipu Sultan of Mysore required the presence of the troops in India. But among those who got as far as Penang was Colonel Arthur Wellesley, the later Duke of Wellington. He took the occasion to pen a lengthy report on the place which, while criticizing its military defences, made no doubt that it was 'of infinite advantage to the Company' and 'a most desirable place to retain'.

As Governor-General, his brother Richard concurred and, when French naval activity in the Bay of Bengal again pointed up the need for a monsoon haven that was nearer than Bombay, even the Admiralty smiled on Penang. In 1805, in return for a commitment from the Navy to convert Penang into a base and dockyard, the Company agreed to upgrade its establishment there and to improve its fortification. Thus did the infant settlement achieve overnight a precocious status as the Company's fourth Presidency with a civil establishment on a par with that of Bombay or Madras. And thus did it acquire the services as Assistant Secretary in this top-heavy administration of one Tom Raffles, lately a clerk in India House.

Penang's elevation, however premature, was not of course the bold new thrust that historians of British India have sometimes assumed. South-east Asia had been home for the Company's first Presidency and for much of its 200 years either Bantam, Batavia, or Benkulen had enjoyed a similar status under a governor or lieutenant-governor. On the other hand it had been comparatively rare for a Company servant to end up in south-east Asia with absolutely no experience of India and, as in Raffles's case, no apparent ambitions to join one of the Indian establishments. Small, energetic, and of obscure origins, Raffles directed his considerable ability and his near-suicidal ambition towards less trammelled pastures. Fame he craved more than fortune; Napoleon intrigued him more than Hastings.

As early as 1808 Raffles became convinced that Penang would never realize the role envisaged for it nor serve his own purposes as a springboard to glory. As a commercial entrepôt it was too far from Burma's teak forests, and as a strategic base on the China route it could never compare with the old Portuguese, Dutch and now British strongpoint at Malacca. Yet Malacca, which should have been handed back to the Dutch in 1802 but was still in British hands when war broke out again in 1804, was being systematically dismantled. The Company's reasoning was that one day it would indeed be handed back and, since it was so strategically placed not only on the China route but also at the gateway to the archipelago, the best policy was to render it down. Hence its population and its trade were being encouraged to relocate in Penang.

Raffles thought this madness. With the help of William Farquhar, a Malay specialist and the British representative at Malacca (and no relation apparently to Robert Farquhar, recently of the Moluccas), he made a detailed study of the archipelago's internal trade, noticing in particular the crucial role of those Bugis traders from Sulawesi (Celebes) and Borneo. The result was a masterly analysis of a little understood subject which demonstrated that Penang's future, far from depending on the destruction of Malacca, actually hinged on Malacca remaining a going concern and remaining in British hands. Unbeknown to Farquhar he then forwarded his thoughts to Lord Minto, the new Governor-General. Minto reversed the Government's policy over Malacca and duly noted the name of Thomas Raffles.

Two years later Ambon, Banda and the rest of the Spice Islands were again captured by the Navy. On a hint that he might be in the running for the Governorship of Ambon, Raffles hastened to Calcutta. Minto had to disappoint him; but in the broadest of hints the Governor-General directed his roving gaze towards Java, the seat of Dutch empire in the East. An expedition against Batavia, the capital, had been planned in 1801 but aborted in order to concentrate on expelling Napoleon from Egypt. Now Egypt was safe, even Mauritius was about to capitulate, and only Java remained as a possible base for Franco-Dutch operations in the

East. Minto's mere mention of the place was 'enough to encourage me', wrote Raffles, 'and from this moment all my views, all my plans, and all my mind were devoted to create such an interest towards Java as should lead to its annexation to our Eastern Empire'.

The actual invasion took place in 1811. Raffles had prepared the ground, chosen the invasion route, and thoroughly mastered the political situation. He was rewarded with the governorship of what he now called 'this other India'. Populous, rich in produce and history, and the greatest commercial asset in the archipelago, Java was 'the Bengal of the East Indies'. Its possession by the Company afforded quite simply 'the most splendid prospect which any administration has beheld since our first acquisition of India itself'.

All of which was true. But it rather overlooked the fact that neither the Court of Directors nor the Board of Control had the slightest interest in annexing Java. The idea was simply to pre-empt its use by the French and, if absolutely necessary, to retain the place until a European peace permitted its return to a friendly Holland. In undertaking a complete reorganization of the country's fiscal, agrarian and commercial structure, Raffles often disobeyed orders and wilfully ignored the inevitable. Had his reforms even produced a surplus – which they did not – there is no evidence to suggest that either the Company or the Crown, to each of whom he appealed in turn, would have changed its mind about retention.

The inevitable came courtesy of Arthur Wellesley's triumph at Waterloo. Java and Malacca were handed back and Raffles's hopes were dashed. By way of consolation he was appointed Lieutenant-Governor of Benkulen, the Sumatra factory which had evidently changed little since Collet's day. It was, declared Raffles, 'the most wretched place I ever beheld'. But 'they say that I am a spirit that will never allow the East to be quiet', he wrote, 'and that this second Elba in which I am placed is not secure enough'. So it proved.

First he tried to extend the Company's territories in Sumatra with, among others, a claim to the island's southernmost tip which would have given command of the Sunda Straits (between Sumatra and Java). When this move was disowned, he turned again to the Malacca Straits. Although the Dutch had been allowed to resume Malacca itself, it was not intended that they should use it to preclude British shipping from the archipelago nor to interfere with the vital China trade. Yet so predatory was Raffles's conduct that the Dutch were speedily provoked into taking exactly the sort of action which could be so construed. As one by one the islands and harbours of the Straits were persuaded to sign exclusive treaties with the Dutch, Raffles's arguments for a British countermove gained weight. To match the Dutch at treaty-making William Farquhar was sent to the west coast of Borneo and among the islands at the entrance to the Straits. 'Mynheer' had beaten him to both. There remained only Raffles's most drastic solution – to seize, occupy, and promote a new British settlement, then argue about the rights of the matter later.

In the long search for an eastern entrepôt it is as if the Company had all along been steadily narrowing its focus. From places as far apart as Pulo Condore, Tourane, Balambangan and Penang, the search had become concentrated on the Malacca Strait. Now, as Raffles and Farquhar sailed down it with the orders, troops, and bricks necessary for the final solution, the focus narrowed still further to the island clusters at the very tip of the Malay peninsula.

According to reports reaching Penang, the Rhio group had just been snapped up by the Dutch. They also held the Lingga archipelago while the Carimons, though favoured by Farquhar, were quickly rejected by Raffles. That left in effect only one place, an island hard against the shore of Johore, covered like all the rest with dense jungle, inhabited by a few Malay fishermen, and of no current commercial consequence whatsoever. It was called Singhapura. On 28 January 1819 Raffles's little fleet anchored at the mouth of the Singapore river. Next day he went ashore with Farquhar and one sepoy. The local chief welcomed them into his rattan house and served them with rambutans and other fruit. When, in return for a substantial allowance, he agreed to authorize a British factory, the troops were immediately disembarked. But the arrangement was subject to the approval of the ruler of Johore and, as Raffles fully appreciated, that depended on who actually was the rightful ruler of Johore. Since the Dutch supported the *de facto* ruler, Raffles hunted out his elder brother. Though cordially disliked by the British party, he was immediately acknowledged as Sultan. On the following day he presided with Raffles at a ceremonial signing complete with red carpet laid across the sand, guard of honour, and numerous artillery salutes.

The military nature of the occupation was important. The Dutch were to understand that any attempt to evict the British would be met with force. Raffles gambled on their opting for a diplomatic offensive which, however effective, would give his settlement the few months necessary to establish its utility. So it did. Within a matter of weeks over 2000 Malays and Chinese had decamped from Malacca to set up shop in Singapore. By the summer, when news of the acquisition reached London, the population already exceeded 5000 and included representatives of several of the main agency houses. Whatever the rights and wrongs of Raffles's conduct, and whatever the legality of the cession, there could be no going back. 'Our object is not territory but trade,' wrote Raffles, 'a great commercial emporium and fulcrum whence we may extend our influence politically as circumstances may hereafter require . . . One free port in these seas must eventually destroy the spell of Dutch monopoly; and what Malta is in the West, that may Singapore become in the East . . .'

The vision, the energy, and the effrontery, which made Singapore the success which Balambangan and Penang had never been, were Raffles's. But it is not at all certain that the idea was his. Farquhar had certainly suggested Singapore; so had Captain Ross, the chief surveyor with the expedition. Raffles had supposedly adopted it as a result of his studies into Malay history. He declared Singhapura 'classical ground' since it had been a place of some consequence in the fourteenth-century Srivijayan empire; a historical pedigree lent dignity and substance to his creation.

The name is so impressively Sanskrit (Singha-Pura – Lion-City) that the wonder is that every passing Indophil had not noted the place. Yet the first mention of it seems to have been not by an etymologist or an empire builder but by the meticulous commander of the Company's Seventh Voyage, Peter Floris, on his return from Patani to Masulipatnam. A century later that ever outspoken apostle of private trade, Captain Alexander Hamilton, he who fell foul of John Child, briefly commanded the Bombay Marine at Karwar, and had strong objections to eating Cantonese duck, also noticed it.

> In anno 1703 I called at Johore on my way to China [writes the Captain] and he [the prince of Johore] treated me very kindly and made me a present of the island of Singapore; but I told him that it could be of no use to a private person, though a proper place for a Company to settle a colony on, lying in the centre of trade . . .'

CHAPTER TWENTY

Epilogue

In an exhaustive study of *Trade in the Eastern Seas* around the year 1800 Professor C. N. Parkinson neatly summarizes the peculiar changes which had overtaken the Company. Since it was still officially 'The United Company of Merchants of England trading to the East Indies', 'there would be nothing manifestly reckless', writes Parkinson, 'in concluding that India House sheltered a body of English merchants trading with India'.

> Nevertheless, such a conclusion would be wrong: the men within were not merchants, and they were not trading with India. One might add, a little unkindly, that they were not always united, and that they were not all Englishmen.

Indeed they were not. With India itself awash with Campbells, MacLeods, MacPhersons and Mackenzies, and with both Malacca and the Moluccas under Farquhar rule, it was as if Hastings and Raffles were the only Englishmen around. What Lord Rosebery called 'the Scoticisation of India' was being directly attributed to Henry Dundas, soon to be ennobled as Viscount Melville of Melville and Baron Dunira of Dunira in the County of Perth. So much for the theory that the Board of Control left the Company's patronage intact.

> How was the East India Company controlled [continues Parkinson]? By the Government. What was its object? To collect taxes [i.e. revenue]. How was its object attained? By means of a large standing army. What were its employees? Soldiers, mostly; the rest, Civil Servants. Where did it trade to? China. What did it

export from England? Courage. And what did it import from China? Tea.

For 'courage' one might substitute 'men and guns'. Otherwise the summary may stand. For as of 1813 all that remained of the Company as a self-governing commercial enterprise was its partial monopoly of the China trade.

In 1800 Dundas had proposed that ships built in India and operated by country traders should be admitted to the London–India trade. This looked more like a direct attack on the Company's monopoly than an extension of the 1793 concession (allowing some cargo space to country traders in Indiamen operating this sector). Led by the Company's shipping interest – an immensely powerful group of ships' captains and agents who had acquired hereditary rights in the construction, supply and command of the Company's fleet – the directors had successfully stalled. But in 1813 the Company's charter again came up for renewal and this time the monopoly of the London–India trade was finally broken.

The challenge came not from the country traders but from that other prong of the free trade lobby, Britain's manufacturing industries. Giving the Company's monopoly a stern drubbing in the process, Adam Smith's *The Wealth of Nations* had first urged the logic of free trade back in the 1770s. But it was not until the turn of the century that British manufacturers, and in particular the cotton kings of Lancashire, were sufficiently confident of their products' quality and price structure to adopt the cause of deregulation. Until then their attacks on the Company had focused on restricting the quantity and quality of Indian piece goods entering Britain and so posing an 'unfair' competition for the domestic product. Now, thanks to greater mechanization and better supply arrangements for raw cotton, the Manchester Chamber of Commerce welcomed competition as eagerly as the country traders.

Throughout the new industrial heartlands of England and Scotland petitions were drawn up and Members of Parliament were lobbied. Since the Company was signally failing to sell British manufactured goods in the largest markets known to man, it was only common sense to let others try. Other ports, went the argument, must be free to compete for the trade with London and other shippers free to compete with the Company. British jobs depended on it; and so, more decisively, did votes. Once the movement had gathered momentum there was no stopping it. However eloquent the Company's defence of its loyal Indian artisans, there was no political mileage in protecting Bengali weavers from being overwhelmed by a continuous roll of mass-produced, duty-free prints. Against the need for full employment in Manchester, Midnapur stood not a chance. After all, what was the use of subject territories if they did not afford a market for the imperial manufacturer? Especially when their only other promised return, revenue, was being so readily absorbed in maintenance costs.

The Company's directors, bitterly divided amongst themselves and in the process of negotiating a new £2.5 million loan from the Government, were in no position to resist. Nor could they have resisted. Whereas once they were answerable only to the General Court of Proprietors, now they were subject to the control and direction of an elected government whose political priorities were paramount. After 213 years that cherished monopoly of Eastern trade, so resented by the interlopers and so hotly defended by the Company's servants, must finally end. But two exceptions of great importance were made. By mutual consent China, now far and away the largest market, and tea, now far and away the most profitable commodity, were reserved to the Company. Although this residual commerce was destined to stay with the Company for only twenty years, the part it played in transforming Indian revenues into British wealth was a crucial factor in the development of empire.

'India does entirely depend upon the profits of the China trade , declared the Company's auditor in 1830. By then it was not simply a question of individuals remitting home their savings and of the Company recovering the wherewithal to meet its home charges (i.e. dividends, salaries, the purchase of military stores, etc). For now duties on tea – which had steadily increased almost to their pre-Commutation Act levels – were providing the British Exchequer with over £3 million per year, almost one-tenth of its total revenue receipts from the whole of England. At £30 million a year, tea imports represented the largest single item in the country's trading account.

The Company had faced no greater commercial challenge than the China market and it was therefore fitting that in its dotage it should enjoy the tea trade to the full. More to the point, it was generally felt that the xenophobic nature of the Chinese and the delicate character of commercial dealings in Canton argued against the admission of new competitors. It was hard enough to exercise an effective control over the existing country traders. In spite of its dependence on them, twice during the 1780s the Company had tried to remove these often unruly colleagues from their Canton factory only to find them reappearing under foreign colours. Thus Meares's associate, Daniel Beale, resurfaced as Consul for the King of Prussia while his partner, Henry Cox, returned under Swedish colours. Like the interlopers of old, country traders were none too particular about national loyalties. Instead of Anglo-Ostenders, Canton now swarmed with Anglo-Poles, Anglo-Portuguese, Anglo-Genoese, and even Anglo-Sardinians. Joining this cosmopolitan set in 1827 James Matheson, successor to the Cox and Beale partnership, boasted Danish nationality.

It was also hard to avoid the impression that the Company was actually handling the China trade rather effectively. The export to Canton of raw Indian cotton was about to decline, but that of English products, especially woollens, steadily increased while that of Indian opium had grown so dramatically that it had redressed that adverse trade balance at Canton. In 1804 the value of British and Indian exports to China for the first time exceeded the value of its imports from China. At last the flow of bullion could be reversed and, as this favourable trade surplus grew, so did the flow of silver back to British India, there to be employed in the purchase of British manufactures.

Where an existing monopoly was proving so beneficial, and where the consequences of its abolition could so materially affect the nation's prosperity, deregulation was not an issue. Like the Lancashire cotton kings, the Government only invoked free-trade principles when confident of not losing by them.

It was the same with Raffles in Singapore. Singapore's remarkable growth is rightly attributed to Raffles's insistence that it be constituted a free port, open to all nations and charging no duties. As such it became the model for Britain's 'Free Trade (or Informal) Empire' of the mid-nineteenth century. It was, of course, ironical that this design originated with a servant of the Honourable Company; and it was also fortuitous. For until then Raffles had shown no sympathy with free trade. In Java he had actually championed what he called 'the extension of our liberal and national principles of monopoly' in relation to the spice trade, to the opium trade, and to the import of Indian cottons. Similarly at Benkulen in agriculturally backward Sumatra, he promoted colonization and a plantation economy in which the Company would remain as the purchasing agency. It was not *The Wealth of Nations* but the ideas of Dalrymple and the example of Penang, where for the first decade or so no duties had been charged, which inspired Singapore's free-port status.

James Matheson, already a country trader at the age of twenty-two, passed Singapore just four months after Raffles's first landing. William Farquhar had been left in charge of the infant settlement and although there were as yet no British merchants in residence 'this is a disadvantage which,' opined Matheson, 'as there are no duties or port charges, will soon vanish'. He saw a great future for the place under Farquhar's 'mild sway' and dazzling prospects for anyone with a small capital to invest, Singapore 'being within four miles of the direct tract to China'.

As Matheson would soon appreciate, so long as the Company retained its monopoly of the China trade, this proximity constituted a double advantage. Or in other words, Singapore prospered courtesy of the Company's remaining monopoly. For while the Company alone was entitled to ship European products direct to Canton and Chinese products direct to London, Singapore was treated as an Indian port from which direct trade with London was now permitted thanks to the 1813 charter concessions. Coupled with the long-established rights of the country traders in the port-to-port trade of the East, this presented a neat way of by-passing the China monopoly by using Singapore as a place of trans-shipment. Thus English manufactures, for instance, could now be legally shipped to Singapore by private traders, and there legally trans-shipped for forwarding to Canton as part of the country trade. The same worked in reverse, especially in respect of Chinese silks, although not for tea which remained a commodity monopoly of the Company. Trans-shipment soon became a mere formality of documentation and thus by 1830 non-Company shipping had already captured a sizeable slice of the China trade.

But all this was as nothing compared to the inroads made by the country, or now 'free', traders thanks to the opium boom. Dr Michael Greenberg, whose researches into Jardine Matheson's archives vividly illustrate the importance of opium, quotes from a contemporary work by James Phipps which describes the opium trade as 'probably the largest commerce of the time in any single commodity'. From small shipments by tortuous supply routes in the eighteenth century, the export of Indian opium direct to China was by the 1820s showing profits high enough both to stifle any moral scruples felt by the British and to negate the prohibitions frequently invoked by the Chinese. In British India one-seventh of total revenue now derived from the Company's continued monopoly over the manufacture and sale of Indian opium. And given that by 1828 the receipts from opium sales alone were sufficient to pay for the entire tea investment, at home that one-tenth of English revenues that derived from the duty on tea imports was also indirectly provided by opium.

Although the Company managed all opium production in India, it played no part in the shipping or sale of a drug regarded by the Chinese authorities as contraband. To have done so would have been to jeopardize its trading rights at Canton and so its tea purchases. Instead the opium crop was sold to agency houses in India who then forwarded it for resale in China. On the other hand it was no secret that the Company's tea purchases depended on opium sales. Occasionally the Company's supercargoes used the argument that opium sales might be reduced if the Chinese would purchase more British manufactures. They did so but it had no measurable effect on the flood of opium. By the late 1820s when James Matheson and William Jardine, previously a surgeon on the Company's ships, took over the agency house that had once been Cox and Beale, opium represented almost their entire import business. And it was the same with most of the other Canton agency houses.

Once arrived in Chinese waters, opium was traditionally smuggled ashore from ships moored in Whampoa and further down the Canton river. The smuggling was conducted by Chinese using small craft and disbursing large bribes to Canton's conniving mandarins. Imperial attempts to suppress the smugglers merely dispersed the trade. Instead of off-loading in the river, firms like Jardine Matheson moored surplus shipping among the off-shore islands that now constitute Hong Kong territory. These hulks became floating depots, adequately armed to repel war junks and supplied by fast sailing clippers shuttling back and forth to Calcutta and Singapore. Smaller clippers ran the ineffectual blockade of imperial junks to distribute the drug further up the coast.

In 1830 William Jardine, now recognized as *Taipan* of the country traders, criticized both the Company's monopoly and the Canton Co-Hong in the name of free trade; but it is hard to see how his main business, opium, was to benefit from an end to such monopolies. In fact the agency houses became distinctly ambivalent about the whole question of the Company, many seeing it as a useful front providing direct access to Canton and to the Chinese merchant community with whom they did business. When, finally and decisively, the demand for an end to the Company's China monopoly was, as in 1813, taken up by the manufacturing interests at home, Jardine Matheson began to think again. It was now suggested that any such change must be accompanied by guaranteed access to China's internal commerce or, failing that, by securing a permanent off-shore base to offset the loss of the Company's protection in Canton. Jardine suggested Taiwan, Matheson the nearer island of Lintin.

When in 1833 another renewal of the Company's charter saw the manufacturing petitioners once again triumphant over the Company's residual monopoly, this demand for an extra-territorial entrepôt on China's doorstep was taken up with greater urgency. Ten years and an Opium War later, it was conceded in the shape of Hong Kong island. Like Singapore, Hong Kong fulfilled many of the requirements envisaged for places like Balambangan and Pulo Condore. It was also an obvious response to the demise of the Company's unique position in Canton.

A maritime empire based on free trade was an improbable legacy from a mercantilist and monopolistic entity like the Honourable Company. But perhaps no more so than the vast continental empire based on military supremacy that was the Raj. With a few exceptions, like Sir Josiah Child and Lord Clive, the Company's servants had seldom craved political supremacy. Some form of informal commercial dominion had ever been closer to their ideals. Had James Lancaster or Jack Saris, Governor Methwold or Governor Pitt, been vouchsafed a glimpse of the future, they would scarcely have found the Raj enviable or comprehensible; but in off-shore metropolises like Penang, Singapore and Hong Kong they must have rejoiced.

Bibliography

GENERAL

Auber, P., *Rise and Progress of British Power in India*, 2 vols, 1837.
Bruce, J., *Annals of the East India Company*, 3 vols, 1810.
Dodwell, H. H. (ed.), *Cambridge History of India*, Vol. 5, 1929.
Gardner, B., *The East India Company*, 1971.
Hall, D. G. E., *History of South-East Asia*, 1955.
Hunter, W. W., *History of British India*, 2 vols, 1899–1900.
Kaye, J. W., *The Administration of the East India Company*, 1853.
Kincaid, D., *British Social Life in India 1608–1937*, 1938.
Love, H. D., *Vestiges of Old Madras 1640–1800*, 4 vols, 1913.
Low, C. R., *History of the Indian Navy*, 1877.
Moon, P., *The British Conquest and Dominion of India*, 1989.
Morse, H. B., *Chronicles of the East India Company Trading to China 1635–1834*, 4 vols, 1926.
Mottram, R. H., *Traders' Dream; The Romance of the East India Company*, 1939.
Muherjee, R., *The Rise and Fall of the East India Company*, 1974.
Roberts, P. E., *History of British India under Company and Crown*, 1934.
Spear, T. G. P., *History of India*, 1965.
Spear, T. G. P., *The Nabobs*, 1932.
Tate, D. J. M., *The Making of Modern South-East Asia*, vol. 1, 1971.
Wheeler, T., *Madras*, 1861.
Wilbur, M. E., *The East India Company and the British Empire in the Far East*, 1970.
Willson, B., *Ledger and Sword*, 2 vols, 1903.
Yule, H., and Burnell, A. C. (ed.), *Hobson-Jobson*, 1903.

The Honourable Company

PART ONE

Best, T., *Voyage to the East Indies*, ed. W. Foster, 1934.

Burman, J., *Bay of Storms*, Cape Town, 1976.

Chaudhuri, K. N., *The English East India Company 1600–40*, 1965.

Cocks, R., *Diary*, 2 vols, 1883.

Danvers, F. C., *The Portuguese in India*, 1894.

Downton, N., *Voyage to the East Indies*, ed. W. Foster, 1939.

East India Company, *The Journals of Capt. W. Keeling and Master T. Bonner, 1615–17*, ed. Strachan and Penrose, Minneapolis, 1971.

East India Company, *Relations of Golconda in the Early Seventeenth Century*, ed. W. H. Moreland, 1934.

East India Company, *The Dawn of British Trade to the East Indies . . ., 1599–1603*, ed. Steven and Birdwood, 1886.

East India Company, *Original Correspondence of and Minutes of Court of Committees of*, ed. N. Sainsbury, 1862–92.

East India Company, *Letters Received from its Servants in the East*, ed. Danvers and Foster, 6 vols, 1896–1902.

East India Company, *Register of Letters etc. of the Governor and Company of Merchants of London trading into the East Indies, 1600–1619*, ed. Birdwood and Foster, 1892.

East India Company, *The English Factories in India, 1618–1669*, ed. W. Foster, 13 vols, 1906–27.

East India Company, *A True Relation of the Unjust, Cruel, and Barbarous Proceedings against the English at Amboyna*, 1624.

East India Company, *The Embassy of Sir Thomas Roe* etc., ed. W. Foster, 1926.

East India Company, *Selected Seventeenth Century Works*, 1968.

Floris, P., *Voyage*, ed. W. H. Moreland, 1934.

Foster, W., *John Company*, 1926.

Foster, W., *England's Quest of Eastern Trade*, 1933.

Hanna, W. A., *Indonesian Banda*, no date.

Hawkins, J. R. and W., *Voyages*, ed. C. R. Markham, 1878.

Jourdain, J., *Journal of 1608–17*, ed. W. Foster, 1905.

Khan, S. A., *The East India Trade in the 17th Century*, 1923.

Lancaster, J., *Voyages to Brazil and the East Indies 1591–1603*, ed. W. Foster, 1943.

Lancaster, J., *Voyages to the East Indies*, ed. C. R. Markham, 1877.

Middleton, H., *The Voyage to Bantam and the Maluco Islands*, ed. B. Corney, 1855.

Middleton, H., *Voyage to the Moluccas*, ed. W. Foster, 1943.

Paske-Smyth, M., *A Glimpse of the English House, etc. at Hirado 1613–23*, Kobe, 1927.

Prestage, E. (ed.), *Chapters in Anglo-Portuguese Relations*, 1935.

P.R.O., *Calendar of State Papers, Colonial Series, East Indies, China and Japan, 1513–1621*, ed. W. N. Sainsbury, 2 vols, 1862–70.

Purchas, S., *His Pilgrimes*, Vols 2–5, 1625.

Purnell, C. J., *The Log Book of William Adams*, 1916.

Rawlinson, H. C., *British Beginnings in Western India*, 1920.

Saris, J., *Voyage to Japan*, ed. E. Satow, 1900.

Williamson, J. A., *The Age of Drake*, 1938.

PART TWO

Anderson, J., *English Intercourse with Siam in the Seventeenth Century*, 1890.

Anderson, P., *The English in Western India*, 1856.

Auber, P., *China . . .*, 1834.

Barlow, E., *Journal, etc.*, ed. B. Lubbock, 2 vols, 1924.

Bowrey, T., *A Geographical Account of Countries round the Bay of Bengal 1669–79*, 1905.

Burnell, J., *Bombay in the Days of Queen Anne*, 1933.

Chatterton, E. K., *The Old East Indiamen*, 1933.

Chaudhuri, K. N., *The Trading World of Asia and the English East India Company 1660–1760*, 1978.

Chaudhuri, K. N., *Trade and Civilisation in the Indian Ocean*, 1985.

Child, J. ('Philopatris'), *A New Discourse on Trade*, 1693.

Collis, M., *Siamese White*, 1936.

Cotton, E., *The East Indiamen*, 1949.

Dalton, C. N., *The Real Captain Kidd*, 1911.

Dalton, C. N., *Life of Thomas Pitt*, 1915.

Das, H., *The Norris Embassy to Aurangzeb 1699–1702*, 1959.

Douglas, J., *Bombay and Western India*, 1893.

East India Company, *The English Factories in India 1618–1669*, ed. W. Foster, 13 vols, 1906–27.

East India Company, *The English Factories in India 1670–1677*, ed. C. Fawcett, 2 vols, 1936.

Edwardes. S. M., *The Rise of Bombay*, Bombay, 1902.

Fawcett, C., *The First Century of British Justice in India*, 1934.

Fryer, J., *A New Account of the East Indies and Persia . . . 1672–1681*, 2 vols, 1909–15.

Gosse, P., *St Helena 1502–1938*, 1938.

Gosse, P., *The History of Piracy*, 1930.

Hall, D. G. E., *Mergui to Singapore* in Journal of Siam Society, 41, No. 1, July 1953.

Hamilton, A., *A New Account of the East Indies*, 1710.

Hedges, W., *Diary 1681–1689*, ed. R. Barlow and H. Yule, 4 vols, 1887.

Hill, S. C., *Notes on Piracy in Eastern Waters*, Bombay, 1923.

Hutchinson, E. W., *Adventurers in Siam in the Seventeenth Century*, 1940.

Johnson, C., *A General History of the Robberies and Murders of the Most Notorious Pyrates*, 1726.

Lockyer, C., *An Account of Trade in India*, 1711.

Master, S., *Diaries*, 1911.

Mundy, P., *Travels etc*, 4 vols, 1907–25.

Ovington, J., *A Voyage to Surat in the Year 1689*, 1696.

Pitts, J., *et al.*, *The Red Sea and Adjacent Countries at the close of the seventeenth century*, ed. W. Foster, 1949.

Pringle, E. H., *Jolly Roger, the Story of the Great Age of Piracy*, 1953.

Pritchard, E. H., *Anglo-Chinese Relations during the 17th and 18th Centuries*, Urbana, 1930.

Rawlinson, H. G., *British Beginnings in Western India*, 1920.

Siam, *Records of Relations between Siam and Foreign Countries in 17th Century*, 6 vols, Bangkok, 1915.

Strachey, R. and O., *Keigwin's Rebellion 1683–4*, 1916.

Sutton, J., *The Lords of the East, The East India Company and its Ships*, 1981.

Wheeler, T., *Madras*, 1861.

Wright, A., *Annesley of Surat*, 1918.

PART THREE

Bence-Jones, M., *Clive of India*, 1974.

Bhattacharya, S., *The East India Company and the Economy of Bengal 1704–1740*, 1953.

Biddulph, J., *Pirates of Malabar*, 1917.

Biddulph, J., *Stringer Lawrence*, 1901.

Chaudhuri, N. C., *Clive of India*, 1975.

Dodwell, H. H., *Dupleix and Clive*, 1920.

Dodwell, H. H., *Nabobs of Madras*, 1926.
Dodwell, H. H., *Private Letter Books of Joseph Collett*, 1933.
Douglas, J., *Bombay and Western India*, 1893.
Downing, C., *A History of the Indian Wars 1715–1723*, 1924.
Duff, J. C. G., *A History of the Mahrattas*, ed. S. M. Edwardes, 3 vols, 1921.
East India Company, Fort St David, *Diary and Consultations Books 1745–6*, 1935.
East India Company, Fort St George, *Diary and Consultations Books 1717–1720*, 1930.
East India Company, Fort St George, *Dispatches from England 1717–1721*, 1917.
Edwardes, M., *Plassey*, 1963.
Edwards, S. M., *The Rise of Bombay*, Bombay, 1902.
Forrest, G. W., *Life of Lord Clive*, 1918.
Forrest, G. W. (ed.), *Selections from Letters, etc., in the Bombay Secretariat*, Home Series Vols 1–2, 1887.
Foster, W., *The East India House, Its History and Associations*, 1924.
Furber, H., *Bombay Presidency in the mid 18th Century*, Bombay, 1965.
Gill, C., *Merchants and Mariners of the 18th Century*, 1961.
Gosse, P., *St Helena 1502–1938*, 1938.
Hamilton, A., *A New Account of the East Indies*, 1710.
Hill, S. C., *Bengal in 1756–1757*, 3 vols, 1905.
Hill, S. C., *Notes on Piracy in Eastern Waters*, Bombay, 1923.
Ives, E., *A Voyage from England to India in 1754*, 1773.
Long, J., *Selections from the Unpublished Records of the Government of Bengal 1746–1767*, Calcutta, 1869.
Majed Khan, A., *The Transition in Bengal 1756–1775*, 1969.
Malgonkar, M., *Kanhoji Angrey, Maratha Admiral*, 1989.
Marshall, P. J., *Bengal; The British Bridgehead* in *The New Cambridge History of India*, 1987.
Marshall, P. J., *East Indian Fortunes*, 1976.
Marshall, P. J., *Problems of Empire: Britain and India 1757–1813*, 1968.
Mason, P., *A Matter of Honour*, 1974.
Orme, R., *A History of the Military Transactions of the British Nation in Indostan*, 1803.
Spear, T. G. P., *Master of Bengal: Clive and his India*, 1975.
Stewart, C., *History of Bengal*, 1813.
Sutherland, L., *The East India Company in 18th-Century Politics*, 1952.
Wheeler, E. T., *Early Records of British India*, 1878.

Wilson, C. R., *Early Annals of the English in Bengal*, 3 vols, Calcutta, 1895–1917.

Wilson, C. R., *Old Fort William in Bengal*, 1906.

PART FOUR

Auber, P., *China*, 1834.

Bassett, D. K., *British Trade and Policy in Indonesia and Malaysia in the late 18th Century*, 1971.

Bastin, J. S., *The British in West Sumatra*, 1965.

Bastin, J. S., *The Native Policies of Raffles*, 1957.

Chaudhuri, N. C., *Clive of India*, 1975.

Collis, M., *Raffles*, 1966.

Cushner, N., *Documents Illustrating the British Conquest of Manila 1762–1763*, 1971.

Dalrymple, A., *Oriental Repertory*, 1793–1808.

Dalrymple, A., *Journal of the Cuddalore*, 1771.

Davies, C. C., *Warren Hastings and Oudh*, 1939.

Davis, R., *The Rise of the British Shipping Industry in the 17th and 18th Centuries*, 1962.

Dermigny, L., *La Chine et L'Occident; Le Commerce à Canton au XVIIIe Siècle*, 4 vols, Paris, 1964.

Dodwell, H. H., *Dupleix and Clive*, 1920.

Embree, A. T., *Charles Grant and British Rule in India*, 1962.

Feiling, K., *Warren Hastings*, 1954.

Forbes, J., *Oriental Memoirs*, 1834.

Forrest, G. W., *Life of Lord Clive*, 1918.

Forrest, G. W. (ed.), *Selection from Letters, etc., in the Bombay Secretariat*, Maratha Series, 1885.

Forrest, G. W. (ed.), *Selections from the State Papers of the Governors-General; Warren Hastings*, 1910.

Fry, H. T., *Alexander Dalrymple and the Expansion of British Trade*, 1970.

Furber, H., *Henry Dundas, First Viscount Melville*, 1931.

Furber, H., *John Company at Work*, 1970.

Gleig, G. R., *Memoirs of Warren Hastings*, 1841.

Gough, B. M., *India Based Expeditions of Trade and Discovery in the Northern Pacific in the late 18th Century* in *Journal of the Royal Geographical Society*, Vol. 155, Pt 2, July 1989.

Greenberg, M., *British Trade and the Opening of China 1800–1842*, 1951.
Hall, D. G. E., *Early English Intercourse with Burma*, 1968.
Hall, D. G. E., *From Mergui to Singapore 1668–1819* in *Journal of the Siam Society*, Vol. 41, No. 1, July 1953.
Harlow, V. T., *Founding of the Second British Empire*, 2 vols, 1952.
Hunter, W. W., *Annals of Rural Bengal*, 1897.
Hunter, W. W., *Bengal Manuscript Records*, 1894.
Ives, E., *A Voyage from England to India in 1754*, 1773.
Jasbir Singh, A. K., *Himalayan Triangle*, 1988.
Keate, G., *An Account of the Pelew Islands, etc.*, 1788.
Keay, J., *India Discovered*, 1981.
Lamb, A., *The Mandarin Road to Hué*, 1970.
Marshall, P. J., *East Indian Fortunes*, 1976.
Marshall, P. J., *The Personal Fortune of Warren Hastings* in *Economic History Review*, Vol. XVII, 2, 1964.
Marshall, P. J., *Problems of Empire: Britain and India 1757–1813*, 1968.
Marshall, P. J., *The Impeachment of Warren Hastings*, 1965.
Meares, J., *Voyages from China, etc*, 1790.
Mills, L. A., *British Malaya 1824–1867* in *Journal of the Malayan Branch of the Royal Asiatic Society*, Vol. 3, Pt 2, Nov. 1925.
Monckton-Jones, M. E., *Warren Hastings in Bengal 1772–1774*, 1914.
Munro, I., *A Narrative of the Military Operations on the Coromandel Coast, etc*, 1789.
Nightingale, P., *Trade and Empire in Western India, 1784–1806*, 1970.
Orme, R., *A History of the Military Transactions of the British Nation in Indostan*, 1803.
Pannikar, K. M., *The Evolution of British Policy towards the Indian States*, Delhi, 1986.
Parkinson, C. N., *Trade in Eastern Seas 1793–1813*, 1937.
Parkinson, C. N., *War in Eastern Seas 1793–1813*, 1954.
Philips, C. H,. *The East India Company*, 1961.
Philips, C. H., *Correspondence of David Scot*, 1951
Pritchard, E. H., *Anglo-Chinese Relations during the 17th and 18th Centuries*, Urbana, 1930.
Pritchard, E. H., *The Crucial Period of Anglo-Chinese Relations 1750–1800*, Washington, 1936.
Spear, T. G. P., *Master of Bengal: Clive and his India*, 1975.
Sutherland, L., *The East India Company in 18th-Century Politics*, 1952.
Thompson, E., and Garret, G. T., *Rise and Fulfilment of British Rule in India*, 193

Woodruff, P., *The Men Who Ruled India*, Vol. I *The Founders*, 1953.
Wright, H. R. C., *East Indian Economic Problems in the Age of Cornwallis and Raffles*, 1961.
Wurzburg, C. E., *Raffles of the Eastern Isles*, 1954.

Index